Lecture Notes in Artificial Intelligence   4635

Edited by J. G. Carbonell and J. Siekmann

Subseries of Lecture Notes in Computer Science

Boicho Kokinov   Daniel C. Richardson
Thomas R. Roth-Berghofer   Laure Vieu (Eds.)

Modeling
and Using Context

6th International and Interdisciplinary Conference
CONTEXT 2007
Roskilde, Denmark, August 20-24, 2007
Proceedings

 Springer

Series Editors

Jaime G. Carbonell, Carnegie Mellon University, Pittsburgh, PA, USA
Jörg Siekmann, University of Saarland, Saarbrücken, Germany

Volume Editors

Boicho Kokinov
New Bulgarian University, Department of Cognitive Science and Psychology
21, Montevideo Str., Sofia 1635, Bulgaria
E-mail: bkokinov@nbu.bg

Daniel C. Richardson
University of California, 273 Social Sciences 2
Santa Cruz, CA 95064, USA
E-mail: dcr@ucsc.edu

Thomas R. Roth-Berghofer
Deutsches Forschungszentrum für Künstliche Intelligenz DFKI GmbH
Trippstadter Straße 122, 67663 Kaiserslautern, Germany
E-mail: thomas.roth-berghofer@dfki.de

Laure Vieu
Institut de Recherche en Informatique de Toulouse, CNRS, France
and Laboratorio di Ontologia Applicata, ISTC, CNR
Via alla Cascata, 56/C, 38100 Trento, Italy
E-mail: vieu@irit.fr

Library of Congress Control Number: 2007932620

CR Subject Classification (1998): I.2, F.4.1, J.3, J.4

LNCS Sublibrary: SL 7 – Artificial Intelligence

ISSN   0302-9743
ISBN-10   3-540-74254-9 Springer Berlin Heidelberg New York
ISBN-13   978-3-540-74254-8 Springer Berlin Heidelberg New York

Springer is a part of Springer Science+Business Media

springer.com

© Springer-Verlag Berlin Heidelberg 2007
Printed in Germany

Typesetting: Camera-ready by author, data conversion by Scientific Publishing Services, Chennai, India
Printed on acid-free paper   SPIN: 12108701   06/3180   5 4 3 2 1 0

Preface

Context affects a wide range of activities in humans and animals as well as in artificial agents and other systems. The importance of context is widely acknowledged, and "context" has become an area of study in its own right, as evidenced by numerous workshops, symposia, seminars, and conferences on this area. CONTEXT, the oldest conference series focusing on context, is unique in its emphasis on interdisciplinary research. Previous CONTEXT conferences have been held in Rio de Janeiro, Brazil (CONTEXT'97), Trento, Italy (CONTEXT'99, LNCS 1688), Dundee, UK (CONTEXT 2001, LNCS 2116), Palo Alto, USA (CONTEXT 2003, LNCS 2680), and Paris, France (CONTEXT 2005, LNCS 3554). Each of these brought together researchers and practitioners from a large range of fields to discuss and report on context-related research and projects.

The CONTEXT 2007 conference was held at Roskilde University, Denmark. The first two days were devoted to workshops on specific areas of interest to the context community and, in parallel, the doctoral consortium. The remaining three days featured invited talks, presentations, and posters on both theoretical and applied context research.

This volume contains the papers presented at CONTEXT 2007, the Sixth International and Interdisciplinary Conference on Modeling and Using Context. There were 121 submissions to the conference. The committee decided to accept 42 papers on the basis of a thorough and highly selective review process. We believe that the papers of this volume represent a snapshot of current work and contribute to both theoretical and applied aspects of research.

Gärdenfors, Hans Kamp, and David Kirsh for their contribution to the success of this conference. Particular thanks go to the Program Committee and additional reviewers for their efforts and hard work in the reviewing and selection process. We thank the Organization Chair, Henning Christiansen, and his team for the professional preparation and organization of the conference.

We are also grateful for the work of the Workshop Chair, Stefan Schulz, as well as the chairs of the seven workshops and their various committee members for preparations for the workshops. We very much appreciate the work of Paolo Bouquet who put together the Doctoral Consortium. We thank all the authors who submitted to the conference to make this program possible and gratefully acknowledge the generous support of the sponsors of CONTEXT 2007. We thank the Steering Committee for their guidance throughout the preparation of the conference.

This volume was prepared using the Easy Chair system, and we would like to express our gratitude to its author, Andrei Voronkov. We also thank Springer for the continuing support in publishing this series of conference proceedings.

August 2007

Boicho Kokinov
Daniel C. Richardson
Thomas R. Roth-Berghofer
Laure Vieu

Conference Organization

General Chair

Boicho Kokinov, New Bulgarian University, Bulgaria.

Program Chairs

Daniel C. Richardson, University of California, Santa Cruz, USA
Thomas R. Roth-Berghofer, DFKI GmbH and TU Kaiserslautern, Germany
Laure Vieu, IRIT-CNRS, France, and ISTC-CNR, Italy

Workshop Chair

Stefan Schulz, The e-Spirit Company GmbH, Dortmund, Germany

Doctoral Consortium Chair

Paolo Bouquet, University of Trento, Italy

Steering Committee Chair

Chiara Ghidini, ITC-irst, Italy

Organization Chair

Henning Christiansen, Roskilde University, Denmark

Conference Sponsors

Nokia Research Center, Finland
The Danish Research Council for the Humanities
Apple, Denmark (primary exhibitor)
The Programming, Logic and Intelligent Systems Research Group & Department
of Communication, Business and Information Technologies, Roskilde University,
Denmark

Program Committee

Agnar Aamodt, Norwegian University of Science and Technology, Norway
Varol Akman, Bilkent University, Turkey
Elena Andonova, New Bulgarian University, Bulgaria
Nicholas Asher, IRIT, France, and University of Texas, USA
John Barnden, University of Birmingham, UK
John Bell, University of London, UK
Carlos Bento, University of Coimbra, Portugal
Patrick Blackburn, LORIA, France
Patrick Brézillon, University of Paris 6, France
Cristiano Castelfranchi, CNR, Italy
Keith Cheverst, Lancaster University, UK
Kenny Coventry, Northumbria University, UK
Anind Dey, Carnegie Mellon University, Pittsburgh, USA
Christo Dichev, Winston-Salem University, USA
Bruce Edmonds, Manchester Institute of Technology, UK
Babak Esfandiari, Carleton University, Ottawa, Canada
Tim Fernando, Trinity College, Dublin, Ireland
Bruno Galantucci, Haskins Lab, USA
Jonathan Ginzburg, King's College London, UK
Avelino Gonzalez, University of Central Florida, USA
Maurice Grinberg, New Bulgarian University, Bulgaria
Pascal Hitzler, University of Karlsruhe, Germany
Jerry Hobbs, University of Southern California, ISI, USA
Eric Horvitz, Microsoft, USA
Anthony Jameson, DFKI GmbH, Saarbrücken, Germany
Theo Kanter, Ericsson Research, Sweden
Mohamed Khedr, Arab Academy for Science and Technology, Egypt
Kepa Korta, University of the Basque Country, Spain
Alex Lascarides, University of Edinburgh, UK
Ramon López de Mántaras, IIIACSIC, Spain
Ana G. Maguitman, Indiana University, USA
Heiko Maus, DFKI GmbH, Kaiserslautern, Germany
Markus Nick, Institute for Experimental Software Engineering IESE, Germany
Rolf Nossum, Agder University College, Norway
Dana Pavel, Nokia, USA
Enrico Rukzio, Lancaster University, UK
David Schlangen, University of Potsdam, Germany
Luciano Serafini, ITC-irst, Italy
Eldar Shafir, Princeton University, USA
Barry Smyth, University College Dublin, Ireland
John Sowa, VivoMind Intelligence Inc., USA
Alice ter Meulen, University of Groningen, The Netherlands
Rich Thomason, University of Michigan, USA
Roy Turner, University of Maine, USA

Carla Umbach, University of Osnabrück, Germany
Johan van Benthem, University of Amsterdam, The Netherlands
Kristof van Laerhoven, Lancaster University, UK
Chris Welty, IBM Research, USA
David C. Wilson, University of North Carolina, Charlotte, USA

Steering Committee

Varol Akman, Bilkent University, Turkey
Massimo Benerecetti, University of Naples, Italy
Paolo Bouquet, University of Trento, Italy
Patrick Brézillon, University of Paris 6, France
Anind Dey, Carnegie Mellon University, USA
Fausto Giunchiglia, University of Trento, Italy
Boicho Kokinov, New Bulgarian University, Bulgaria
David B. Leake, Indiana University, USA
Luciano Serafini, ITC-irst, Italy
Rich Thomason, University of Michigan, USA
Roy Turner, University of Maine, USA
Roger A. Young, University of Dundee, UK

Organizing Committee

Troels Andreasen, Roskilde University, Denmark
John Gallagher, Roskilde University, Denmark
Mads Rosendahl, Roskilde University, Denmark
Jørgen Villadsen, Technical University of Denmark (Publicity)
Rie Lynge, Roskilde University, Denmark (Secretary, logistics)
Agnete Nebsager, Roskilde University, Denmark (Secretary, budget)

Additional Reviewers

Rodrigo Agerri	Claudio Baccigalupo	John Bell
Stephan Bloehdorn	Henning Christiansen	Kenny Coventry
Padraig Cunningham	Cornelia Endriss	François Gagnon
Penka Hristova	Evgeniya Hristova	Neil Hurley
Tahar Kechaid	Anders Kofod-Petersen	Markus Krötzsch
Andreas Lorenz	Dermot Lynott	Martin Memmel
George Metaxas	Ronan O'Coallaigh	John Patterson
Francisco Pereira	Georgi Petkov	Michele Piunti
Guilin Qi	Robert Ross	Sebastian Rudolph
Sven Schwarz	Eldar Shafir	Michael Sintek
Alan Smeaton	Jostein Trondal	Dirk Trossen
Yimin Wang	Andreas Zimmermann	

Table of Contents

Default Inferences in Metaphor Interpretation

Rodrigo Agerri, John Barnden, Mark Lee, and Alan Wallington

School of Computer Science, University of Birmingham
B15 2TT, Birmingham, UK
{R.Agerri,J.A.Barnden,M.G.Lee,A.M.Wallington}@cs.bham.ac.uk

Abstract. In this paper we provide a formalization of a set of default rules that we claim are required for the transfer of information such as causation, event rate and duration in the interpretation of metaphor. Such rules are domain-independent and are identified as invariant adjuncts to any conceptual metaphor. Furthermore, we show the role that these invariant mappings play in a semantic framework for metaphor interpretation.

1 Introduction

It is generally accepted that much of everyday language shows evidence of metaphor [1]. We assume the general view that metaphor understanding involves some notion of events, properties, relations, etc. that are transferred from a source domain into a target domain. In this view, a metaphorical utterance conveys information about the target domain. We are particularly interested in the metaphorical utterances that we call *map-transcending*. Consider the following example:

(1) "McEnroe starved Connors to death."

We do not address in this paper the issue of when an utterance is to be considered metaphorical. Instead, we aim to offer an explanation of how a metaphorical utterance such as (1) can be interpreted. If we infer, using our knowledge about McEnroe and Connors, that (1) is used to describe a tennis match, it can be understood as an example of the conceptual metaphors (or, in our terminology, 'metaphorical views') DEFEAT AS DEATH and NECESSITIES AS FOOD. However, these metaphorical views would not contain any relationship that maps the specific *manner* of dying that constitutes *being starved to death* (we say that "starving" is a map-transcending entity as it goes beyond known mappings). Yet one could argue that the *manner* of Connors's death is a crucial part of the informational contribution of (1).

A possible solution would be to create a new view-specific mapping that goes from the form of killing involved in *starving to death* to some process in sport, but such enrichment of mappings would be needed for many other verbs or verbal phrases that refer to other *ways* in which death is brought about, each requiring a specific specific mapping when occurring in a metaphorical utterance. Thus, finding adequate mappings could become an endless and computational intensive process. Moreover, there are even cases in which we may not find a plausible mapping. Consider the following description of the progress of a love affair:

B. Kokinov et al. (Eds.): CONTEXT 2007, LNAI 4635, pp. 1–14, 2007.

(2) "We're spinning our wheels."

It is not very clear what could be a target correspondent for 'wheels'; the unavailability of a correspondent would therefore prevent the source to target transfer of information needed for the interpretation of the metaphorical utterance. Thus, an account of metaphor ought to explain what extra information map-transcending entities provide. Furthermore, how the transfer of information occurs should be account for in a viable computational manner.

ATT-Meta [2] is an AI System and approach to metaphor interpretation that, apart from providing functionalities such as uncertainty and conflict handling [3], introduces two features central to the interpretation of metaphorical utterances such as (1) and (2): Instead of attempting the creation of new mappings to extend an existing metaphorical view, ATT-Meta employs query-driven reasoning within the terms of the source domain using various sources of information including *world* and *linguistic knowledge*. The reasoning connects unmapped ideas used by utterances, such as wheels and starving, to other source-domain ideas for which a mapping is already known. These known mappings may be constituents of a particular metaphorical view, but previous work [4,5] has shown evidence that there metaphorical aspects (such as relations and properties between events) that, subject to being called, invariantly map from source to target (we call these mappings View-Neutral Mapping Adjuncts or VNMAs). These allow many mapping effects, which would otherwise have to be duplicated across all view-specific mappings, to be factored out into separate mappings.

In our approach, source domain reasoning takes place in a special, protected computational context that we call the "pretence context". We use the term 'reality' to refer to the space outside the pretence where propositions are about reality as the understander sees it. The nature of source domain reasoning in metaphor interpretation has not previously been adequately investigated, although a few authors have addressed it to a limited extent [6,7,8,9].

Currently ATT-Meta implements the VNMAs by including them in view-specific rules, but we plan to make the system more modular and its view-specific mappings more economical by implementing VNMAs as separate default rules. The first step towards that goal is to provide a formalization of these mappings and to clarify their role in metaphor interpretation. In order to do so, we embed them in a semantic framework for metaphor interpretation inspired by Segmented Discourse Representation Theory [10] tailored to capture the main aspects of the ATT-Meta approach. In this sense, it is not an aim of this paper to propose an SDRT-based account of metaphor but instead adapt its semantic representation structures to represent the ATT-Meta view on metaphor understanding. Other authors seem to have merely assumed the existence of a special type of invariant mappings similar to the VNMAs [1] but they do not address the issue explicitly, aside from the early work of Carbonell [6].

The next section briefly describes the ATT-Meta approach focusing on source domain inferencing and VNMAs. Section 3 describes a number of VNMAs that are used to interpret various metaphorical utterances. In section 4 we discuss the main components to be included in a semantic account of metaphor. We then propose to adapt the SDRT formal framework to our purposes of providing a semantic account of metaphor interpretation based on the ATT-Meta approach. Section 5 shows how VNMAs can explain examples discussed by other authors in a uniform and systematic manner. Section 6 presents some conclusions and discussion on further work.

2 Within-Pretence Inference and Invariant Mappings

Let us go back to example (1):

(1) "McEnroe starved Connors to death."

Assuming a commonsensical view of the world and if (1) is being used metaphorically to describe the result of a tennis match, a plausible target interpretation would be that McEnroe defeated Connors by performing some actions to deprive him of his usual playing style. In the ATT-Meta approach, within-pretence inferencing produces a proposition to which we may apply a mapping to transfer that information. An important feature of the pretence space is that it takes the meaning of source domain utterances as *literal*. Thus, and assuming a commonsensical view of the world, a within-pretence meaning would be that McEnroe *starved* Connors to death in a biological sense. The inferencing within the pretence can then conclude that McEnroe *caused* Connors's death by *depriving* or disabling him. Leaving some details aside, the partial logical form (in the pretence) of the metaphorical utterance (1) may be represented as follows (without taking into account temporal issues):

(i) $\exists x, y, e(McEnroe(x) \wedge Connors(y) \wedge starve - to - death(e, x, y))$

This says that there is an event e of x starving y to death (we use the notion of event á la Hobbs [11] to describe situations, processes, states, etc.). It may be suggested that if we were trying to map the partial expression (i), its correspondent proposition in the target could be expressed by this formula:

(ii) $\exists x, y, e(McEnroe(x) \wedge Connors(y) \wedge defeat(e, x, y))$

According to this, the event of x defeating y in the reality would correspond to the event of x starving y to death in the pretence. However, by saying "McEnroe starved Connors to death" instead of simply "McEnroe killed Connors" the speaker is not merely intending to convey that McEnroe defeated Connors, but rather something related to the manner in which Connors was defeated. Following this, *starving* may be decomposed into the cause e_1 and its effect, namely, "being deprived of food":

(iii) $\exists x, y, z, e_1, e_2, e_3(McEnroe(x) \wedge Connors(y) \wedge food(z) \wedge starve(e_1, x, y) \wedge$
    $death(e_2, y) \wedge deprived(e_3, y, z) \wedge cause(e_1, e_3))$

Note that by factoring out "starving to death" in this way we not only distinguish the cause from the effect but doing so allows us to establish a relation between "death" in the pretence to "defeat" in reality using the known mapping in DEFEAT AS DEATH (and possibly "starving" to "McEnroe's playing" although we will not press this issue here).

Now, by means of lexical information regarding "starving", it can be inferred that McEnroe deprived Connors of a necessity (see, e.g., Wordnet), namely, of the food required for his normal functioning (the NECESSITIES AS FOOD metaphorical view would provide mappings to transfer food to the type of shots that Connors *needs* to play his normal game). In other words, Connors is defeated by the particular means of depriving him of a necessity (food) which means that being deprived causes Connors's defeat. This fits well with the interpretation of (1) where McEnroe's playing deprived Connors of his usual game. Moreover, linguistic knowledge also provides the fact that starving someone to death is a gradual, slow process. The result of within-pretence inferencing may be represented as follows:

(iv) $\exists x, y, z, e_1, e_2, e_3 (McEnroe(x) \wedge Connors(y) \wedge food(z) \wedge starve(e_1, x, y) \wedge$
$death(e_2, y) \wedge deprived(e_3, y, z) \wedge cause(e_1, e_3) \wedge cause(e_3, e_2) \wedge rate(e_1, slow))$

'Slow' refers to a commonsensical concept in the pretence related to the progress rate of *starving*. Now, the existing mapping DEFEAT AS DEATH can be applied to derive, outside the pretence, that McEnroe defeated Connors, but no correspondences are available to account for the fact that McEnroe *caused* the defeat of Connors by depriving him of his normal play. Furthermore, the same problem arises when trying to map the slow progress *rate* of a process like starving.

In the ATT-Meta approach to metaphor interpretation, the mappings of *caused* and *rate* discussed above are accomplished by a type of default mappings that we specify as VNMAs (the Causation and Rate VNMAs, respectively; see [12] for an informal but detailed description of a number of VNMAs). VNMAs account for the mapping of aspects of the source domain that do not belong to a specific metaphorical view but that often carry an important informational contribution (or even the main one) of the metaphorical utterance. These source domain aspects can be captured as relationships and properties (causation, rate, etc.) between two events or entities that, subject to being called, identically transfer from the pretence to the reality.

Summarizing, the following processes, amongst others, are involved in the understanding of map-transcending utterances: 1) Construction of within-pretence domain meaning of the utterance. 2) Placing of it in the pretence context. 3) Source-domain reasoning within the pretence cocoon, using the direct meaning constructed in 1) with world and linguistic knowledge about the source domain. 4) Transfers by application of specific mappings in metaphorical views and often invariant mappings specified as VNMAs. The remaining of the paper focuses on the characterization and formalization of VNMAs from a semantic point of view.

3 Description of VNMAs

By using VNMAs and within-pretence inferencing, we do not need to extend the mappings in the metaphorical view to include information about "depriving of a necessity", "food" or "causing Connors's death". VNMAs transfer those properties or relations between mappees that are *view-neutral*. Moreover, VNMAs are *parasitic* on the metaphorical views in the sense that they depend on some mappings to be established for the VNMAs to be triggered. That is why VNMAs are merely "adjuncts". VNMAs can also be seen as pragmatic principles that guide the understanding of metaphor by transferring aspects of the source domain that remain invariant.

In example (1), there are two VNMAs involved in the transfer of the causation and the "slowness", namely, the Causation and Rate VNMAs which are described below. Additionally, we also discuss two more VNMAs related to the temporal order of events and the value-judgement that agents assign to events (others are described in [4,5,12]).

3.1 Causation/Ability

The idea is that there are relationships and properties (causation, (dis)enablement, etc.) between two events or entities that identically transfer from the pretence to the reality. We use the $\mapsto$ symbol to express that this mapping is a default.

Causation/Ability VNMA: "Causation, prevention, helping, ability, (dis)enablement and easiness/difficulty relationships or properties of events between events or other entities in the pretence, map to those relationships between their mappees (if they have any) in the reality." The invariant mapping involved in the interpretation of (1) could be represented as follows:

$$\textbf{Causation:} \forall e_1, e_2 (cause(e_1, e_2)_{pret} \mapsto cause(e_1, e_2)_{rlt})$$

As an additional note, the specific mapping of each event or state variable does not depend on the VNMA but on the metaphorical view in play. For example, if we consider the contemporary situation in which McEnroe and Connors are tennis pundits on TV, we may need a metaphorical view such as ARGUMENT AS WAR to interpret the utterance "McEnroe starved Connors to death". In other words, VNMAs do not themselves establish the mappees between the pretence and the reality.

3.2 Rate

Rate: "Qualitative rate of progress of an event in the source domain maps identically to qualitative rate of progress of its mappee. E.g., if an event progresses slowly (in the context of the everyday commonsensical world), then its mappee progresses slowly (in the target context)".

Consider the following utterance:

(3) My car gulps gasoline.

Briefly, the metaphorical view involved is MACHINES AS CREATURES, that maps biological activity to mechanical activity. The within-pretence reasoning may be performed along the following lines: It can be inferred in the pretence that gasoline helps the car to be alive, therefore, it helps the car to be biologically active. The Causation/Ability VNMA (which deals with helping) combined with the above metaphorical view provide the target domain contribution that gasoline helps the car to run. Given that we can assume that an act of gulping is normally moderately fast the use of the Rate VNMA allows us to conclude that the car's use of gasoline is moderately fast. The logical form of this VNMA is could be expressed as follows:

$$\textbf{Rate:} \forall e, r (rate(e, r)_{pret} \mapsto rate(e, r)_{rlt})$$

If the rate an event e in the pretence is r, then the rate maps to the mappee event in the reality, that is, it also has rate r; r refers to the qualitative rate of progress or duration of an specific event e.

3.3 Time-Order

Time-Order: "The time order of events in a source domain is the same as that of their mappee events, if any".

Time-order is quite useful for map-transcending examples such as

(4) McEnroe stopped hustling Connors.

We might infer in the pretence that McEnroe was once hustling Connors which would be transferred by the Time-Order VNMA. For the formalization of this VNMA, we say that if event e_1 precedes event e_2 in the pretence, then the mappee events in the reality exhibit the same ordering.

$$\text{Time-Order: } \forall e_1, e_2 (precede(e_1, e_2)_{pret} \mapsto precede(e_1, e_2)_{rlt})$$

3.4 Value-Judgement

Value-Judgement: "Level of goodness, importance or other types of value assigned by the understander to states of affairs in the source domain map identically to levels of goodness, etc., of their mappee states of affairs, if any."

(5) That is a gem of an idea.

We could argue that a metaphorical view IDEAS AS OBJECTS is used to interpret this example. However, this view does not provide correspondences for mapping the fact that we see 'gems' as valuable or precious. Instead of trying to find correspondents to map different types of objects to different types of ideas we assume that it is possible to infer in the pretence that gems are valuable and this value judgement about objects that are gems is transfer by the Value-Judgement VNMA. This mapping is expressed by the following formula:

$$\text{Value-Judgement: } \forall e, v(value(e, v)_{pret} \mapsto value(e, v)_{rlt})$$

4 A Semantic Framework for Metaphor Interpretation

Embedding the VNMAs in a semantic framework for metaphor interpretation is useful as a first step towards their implementation as default rules in the ATT-Meta system, but it is also interesting in its own right to show the contribution that the ATT-Meta approach can make towards a semantics of metaphor.

4.1 A Contextual and Query-Driven Approach

In the somewhat simplified discussion on the within-pretence reasoning and mappings necessary to interpret metaphorical utterances such as (1), we have not paid too much attention two main issues. Firstly, the actual source domain reasoning performed by the ATT-Meta system is *query-driven*.

Although in previous sections we used various sources of contextual information to license certain within-pretence inferences, we have only considered isolated metaphorical utterances, and metaphor understanding has been pictured as a process of forward reasoning from the direct meaning of utterances (in the pretence) and then the application of various metaphorical mappings to the result of source domain reasoning to arrive at the informational contributions in the target. Moreover, other possible inferences that could be drawn were ignored without specifying any principles or criteria whereby the reasoning could be guided towards the particular informational contributions discussed. The notion of discourse-query-directed reasoning provides such guidance. When analyzing previous examples, we assume that the surrounding discourse context supplies queries that guide source domain reasoning in broadly the reverse order to that in which we described them in section 2 (see [13] for a detailed description of query-directed reasoning in ATT-Meta). Other authors such as Hobbs [7] and Asher and Lascarides [14] also acknowledge the importance of context-derived reasoning queries in the interpretation of metaphorical utterances.

We are not claiming that query-directed reasoning may be the only type of reasoning involved in the processing of metaphor, but it seems to be particularly important in the processing of connected discourse. Although the ATT-Meta system at present works with single-sentence utterances (albeit with the aid of discourse-query-directed reasoning), an aim for future versions is to extend it to the processing of *discourse*, and the semantic framework will need to allow for this.

Secondly, we have been using various sources of contextual knowledge that interact in the processing of the utterance: a) View-specific mappings provided by the relevant metaphorical views (DEFEAT AS DEATH and NECESSITIES AS FOOD); b) Linguistic and contextual information necessary for reasoning in the pretence; c) Relations and properties between events such as *causation* and *rate* that are inferred in the pretence; d) VNMAs that transfer within-pretence event relations and properties to reality. In our view, a suitable semantic approach to metaphor should include at least these five components.

4.2   VNMAs in a Semantic Framework

Metaphor is a highly contextual phenomenon, and one of the most interesting semantic approaches that model context are dynamic semantics such as Discourse Representation Theory [15] which views meaning as a *relation* between the contexts that compose a discourse. Furthermore, we are interested in representing relations between events such as causation and temporal order in the pretence context.

There are two prominent computationally-oriented semantic approaches [16,10] that take into account contextual and linguistic information to stress the importance of relations between semantic representations of events in discourse interpretation. Specifically, we adapt the semantic representation procedure of Segmented Discourse Representation Theory or SDRT [10] to build pretence contexts as Segmented Discourse Representation Structures (SDRSs) consisting of the result of source domain reasoning. The conclusion of within-pretence inference can in turn be mapped to reality by using various view-specific mappings and VNMAs. In other words, we can see the pretence SDRS as the input for what the ATT-Meta system does when interpreting metaphor – it will reason with it, producing an output of inferred reality facts which we may also represent by means of an SDRS. The result of reasoning in the pretence context to interpret (1) would now looks as follows:

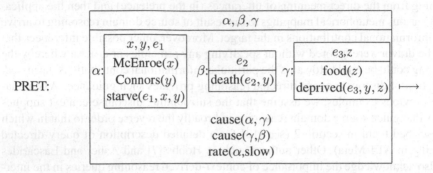

where α and β are labels for DRSs representing events, PRET for a pretence space and $\longmapsto$ mappings (VNMAs and central mappings) needed in the interpretation of the metaphorical utterance. Importantly, the VNMAs would pick upon aspects such as causation and rate from pretence to transfer them to reality producing an output which could also be represented as a SDRS:

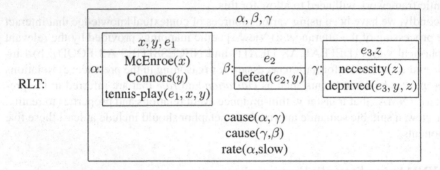

Note that this formal representation integrates the systematicity of mapping invariantly certain aspects of metaphorical utterances by formulating them as relations and properties of events that can be represented as relations and properties of DRSs. For this purpose we will need to modify the construction rules of SDRSs to be able to infer properties and relations involving individuals ($x, y, \ldots$) and not only DRSs' labels such as α and β. In addition to this, we need to capture the interaction of the various sources of information used (linguistic knowledge, world knowledge, etc.) to infer causation and rate in the pretence. Thus, we partially adopt SDRT formal framework to represent ATT-Meta's within-pretence reasoning, event relations, event properties and VNMAs with the purpose of developing a semantic account of metaphor interpretation.

4.3   Context and Knowledge

Within-pretence reasoning partially relies on inferences provided by the discourse context and linguistic and world knowledge. In the ATT-Meta system, world knowledge roughly corresponds to source domain knowledge. On the one hand, we have been using our commonsensical knowledge about McEnroe and Connors to interpret example (1) as metaphorically describing a tennis match. On the other hand, linguistic knowledge is used to *pretend* that the direct meaning of the metaphorical utterance is true, which allows us to derive *causation* and *rate*. Thus, we assume that the understander possesses some world knowledge that provides information about "starving someone to death":

- If e_3 where y is deprived and e_1 where x starves y are connected, then by default, e_1 *causes* e_3.
- If e_2 where y dies and e_3 where y is deprived are connected, then by default, e_3 *causes* e_2.
- If e_1 where x starves y, then by default, the rate of progress of e_1 is *slow*.

Furthermore, common sense about causation tells us that "if e_1 causes e_3 then e_3 does not occur before e_1". Following this, the knowledge needed to interpret example (3) needs to include the that the drinking rate is fast:

If e where x gulps, then by default, x in e drinks moderately fast.

Asher and Lascarides use a non-monotonic logic (Commonsense Entailment) which is designed to handle reasoning with conflicting knowledge resources. SDRT specifies where in the preceding discourse structure the proposition introduced by the current sentence can attach with a discourse relation. In order to do that, it is necessary to provide a set of rules for the understander to infer which discourse relation should be used to do attachment. We adopt a similar notation to represent discourse update (see [10] for details on the discourse update function) so that defeasible knowledge about causation, rate, temporal order, etc., allows the inference of event relations and properties in the pretence.

Let us suppose that in a context (pretence) *pret* [1] we want to attach some event denoted by β to α, such that $\langle pret, \alpha, \beta \rangle$. This update function can be read as "the representation *pret* of a text so far is to be updated with the representation β of an event via a discourse relation with α" [10]. Let $\leadsto$ represent a defeasible connective as a conditional, and let $ev(\alpha)$ stand for "the event described in α"; although $ev(\alpha)$ is quite similar to the notion of main eventuality me defined by Asher and Lascarides [10], we do not commit to other assumptions of their theory.

Thus, some of the source domain knowledge about causation in (1) discussed above could now be represented as follows:

$$\langle pret, \alpha, \beta \rangle dies(connors, ev(\beta)) \wedge starves(mcenroe, connors, ev(\alpha))$$
$$\leadsto cause(ev(\alpha), ev(\beta))$$

We can then infer in the pretence a *causation* relation between α and β if the event represented in α normally causes β:

Causation: $\langle pret, \alpha, \beta \rangle \wedge (cause(ev(\alpha), ev(\beta)) \leadsto causation(\alpha, \beta)$

---

[1] See Lee and Barnden [17] for cases in which more than one pretence is involved in the interpretation of metaphor.

Note that 'cause' refers to the epistemic notion of one event causing another, whereas 'causation' refers to an inferred semantic relation between segments of discourse or, in other words, between semantic representation of events by means of DRSs. In order to include properties (and not only relations) in this framework, we assume a conceptualist point of view and consider that properties such as rate or value-judgement denote *concepts* (fast, slow, good, bad) which may correspond to the absolute rate in a commonsensical view of the world. Its representation in our semantic framework could be defined by adding an extra clause to the definition of DRS-formulae:

- If P is a property symbol and α and r are an episode label and a property label respectively, then $P(\alpha, r)$ is an DRS-formula (see [10] for the complete definitions of DRS-formulae and SDRS construction).

Thus, a rule encoding contextual knowledge to infer rate in the pretence would look as follows (note that when considering event properties we only need to consider one DRS α in our rules, even though a discourse usually consists of one or more DRSs):

$$\langle pret, \alpha \rangle gulps(car, gasoline, ev(\alpha)) \rightsquigarrow fast(ev(\alpha))$$

Supported by this rule we can then infer an event property in the pretence for its subsequent transfer to reality via the Rate VNMA (when the Rate VNMA is instantiated):

Rate: $\langle pret, \alpha \rangle (fast(ev(\alpha)) \rightsquigarrow rate(\alpha, fast)$

4.4   VNMAs Revisited

Section 3 described several VNMAs and showed their contribution to the analysis of four different metaphors. VNMAs are considered to be default mapping rules that transfer relations and properties from pretence contexts to reality. Furthermore, we claim that VNMAs are adjunct to central mappings provided by the metaphorical view(s) (DEFEAT AS DEATH, IDEAS AS OBJECTS) used in the utterance context.

We use the VNMAs introduced in section 3 and the above points about within-pretence inferencing and contextual knowledge to offer SDRT-based semantic representations for an analysis of examples (3) and (4) based on the ATT-Meta approach to metaphor. We leave out any details not directly relevant to the discussion on VNMAs.

We claimed in section 3 that the transfer to reality of the within-pretence information relative to how fast the car drinks/uses gasoline (derived from linguistic knowledge about "gulp") was performed via a Rate VNMA. The following (partial) picture of a discourse captures this:

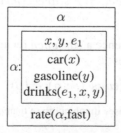

'Fast' refers to a commonsensical concept in the pretence related to the rate of "gulp-ing". From here, the Rate VNMA would transfer $rate(\alpha, fast)$ to reality. We do not represent the correspondent representation for the sake of brevity. Note that we are only considering the aspects directly involved in the use of Rate VNMA, and as such we do not include the discourse in which an utterance such as (3) may occur. It should be stressed that the context-driven character of the ATT-Meta approach accounts for the transfer of a feature such as *rate* in a discourse context in which the consumption of gasoline is being considered. Thus, features other than rate could be important in other uses of 'gulp' (e.g., such as the fact that gulping usually refers to a noisy way of drinking).

We follow the same process with respect to example (4) involving time-order:

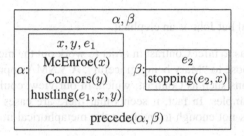

Summarizing, the semantic framework outlined in this section consists of:

- DRSs and SDRSs consisting of events, individuals, states, etc. They can be thought of as situations or as representation structures as in dynamic semantics. A context consists of one or more DRSs, DRSs relations and properties.
- Event relations and properties such as *causation, rate, time-order, value-judgement*, etc inferred in the pretence for the systematic transfer of certain type of information conveyed by metaphorical utterances. The transfer of this type of information via VNMAs is a contribution of the ATT-Meta approach to metaphor interpretation [4,5].

5 Comparison to Other Approaches

Following the ATT-Meta claim that often convey crucial information via VNMAs, some examples of metaphor proposed by other authors. Consider the following utterance:

(6) Sam is a pebble.

Asher and Lascarides [14] claim that it is not possible to calculate the meaning of an utterance such as (6) on the basis of the domain information about pebbles, but that it is possible to process it if it is discourse related to other utterance, e.g., as in "John is a rock but Sam is a pebble" (we could infer a *Contrast* rhetorical relation, which would help us to work out the metaphorical meaning of (6)). However, by using VN-MAs and within-pretence reasoning an addressee of (6) may reach an interpretation without necessarily needing a Contrast rhetorical relation to guide the reasoning. In our case, linguistic knowledge and within-pretence reasoning about 'pebbles' establish that they are small, and a very frequent association of unimportant entities with "small size" allows the defeasible inference that something is low, inferior, limited in worth (see Wordnet or any other lexical database). Using the Value-Judgment VNMA ("Levels of goodness, importance, etc., assigned by the understander in the source domain map identically to levels of goodness, etc."), we can convey the meaning that Sam is limited in worth (worthless). Like Asher and Lascarides, Hobbs also claims that inferring discourse structure is crucial to understand certain metaphorical utterances [16]:

(7) John is an elephant.

Which Hobbs argues can only be interpreted if we add extra information so that it now reads:

(8) Mary is graceful but John is an elephant.

Which now allows us to infer Contrast in order to work out the meaning of "John being an elephant" as oppose to "Mary being graceful". A VNMA approach is not so reliant on rhetorical relations such as Contrast, which, in our view, could be an advantage to analyze certain examples. In fact, it seems that there are cases in which inferring a discourse relation is not enough to interpret the metaphorical utterance. Consider the following utterance:

(9) Mary is a fox and John is an elephant.

In this case, we can infer a Coordination relation to account for the conjunction of the two segments [18]. However, it seems that inferring Coordination would not be enough to guide the interpretation of (9) towards some attributes of Mary (e.g., being cunning, small, etc.) and John (big, having good memory, etc.). In our approach, and subject to the appropriate contextual query to be provided by the discourse, size-related features might be transferred by a Physical Size VNMA; in an appropriate context (9) could also be used to convey that John has a good memory and that Mary is cunning. In this case, forgetfulness could be seen a tendency to perform a mental act of a certain type and non-forgetfulness could be handled by a Negation VNMA, Mental states VNMA and a Event-Shape VNMA (for tendencies).

Studying the interaction, if any, between VNMAs and discourse relations may allow us to naturally extend the study of metaphor to discourse. However, this issue exceeds the purposes of this paper. In any case, it seems that information relative to events rate, duration, value-judgement, etc., cannot be captured solely by means of rhetorical relations.

With respect to the context-driven character of the ATT-Meta approach, a further issue could be raised, namely, why consider principles such as VNMAs at all? It could just be that the types of features transferred by VNMAs happen to be commonly transferred things, and any feature could be transferred in a view-neutral way, if context asks for it. However, there is in fact evidence that not all types of features can be view-neutrally transferred. Suppose that there are two long, thin pencils, on red and the other yellow. Following the contrast-based examples discussed above, it would be very odd if someone utters

(10) Peter's pencil is yellow, but Mike's is a tomato.

The use of 'tomato' to describe a pencil only would seem to appropriate if the pencil were quite short and bulbous, which would mean that it will very difficult to transfer the colour without also mapping the shape. We face similar problems when trying to analyze utterances such as

(11) Peter has dark hair but Mike is an elephant.

just because the latter had grey hair. In this sense, we are a taking a conservative approach, only proposing that a particular type of feature is view-neutrally transferred if we have evidence.

6 Concluding Remarks

This paper investigates the formalization and semantic representation of the ATT-Meta approach to metaphor interpretation. The ATT-Meta approach is backed up by a powerful implementation that performs sophisticated reasoning to interpret metaphorical utterances. We have focused on description and formalization of several VNMAs, mappings for the systematic transference of invariant aspects from source to target. We have shown how a dynamic semantic approach can be adapted for these purposes to offer an unified semantic representation of ATT-Meta's view of metaphor interpretation.

Map-transcending entities pose a problem for several analogy-based approaches to metaphor interpretation, both from a computational and a theoretical point of view. With respect to the computational approaches, theories of metaphor interpretation based on analogy [19,20] usually require a conceptual similarity between the source and the target domains. Map-transcending entities need to be mapped by extending on the fly the metaphorical views with new correspondences. We have argued that this strategy is both computationally expensive and in some cases, plainly impossible.

Formal semantic approaches [10] do not account for metaphorical utterances including map-transcending entities. Other works [6,7,8,9] have addressed source domain reasoning to a limited extent, but its role in metaphor interpretation has not previously been adequately investigated. Moreover, map-transcending entities pose a problem for analogy-based approaches to metaphor interpretation [19], which usually require a conceptual similarity between the source and the target domains.

References

1. Lakoff, G., Johnson, M.: Metaphors We Live By. University of Chicago Press, Chicago (1980)
2. Barnden, J., Lee, M.: An artificial intelligence approach to metaphor understanding. Theoria et Historia Scientarum 6, 399–412 (2002)
3. Barnden, J.: Uncertainty and conflict handling in the att-meta context-based system for metaphorical reasoning. In: Akman, V., Bouquet, P., Thomason, R.H., Young, R.A. (eds.) CONTEXT 2001. LNCS (LNAI), vol. 2116, pp. 15–29. Springer, Heidelberg (2001)

4. Barnden, J., Glasbey, S., Lee, M., Wallington, A.: Domain-transcending mappings in a system for metaphorical reasoning. In: Conference Companion to the 10th Conference of the European Chapter of the Association for Computational Linguistics (EACL 2003), pp. 57–61 (2003)
5. Wallington, A., Barnden, J., Glasbey, S., Lee, M.: Metaphorical reasoning with an economical set of mappings. Delta 22 (2006)
6. Carbonell, J.: Metaphor: An inescapable phenomenon in natural-language comprehension. In: Lehnert, W., Ringle, M. (eds.) Strategies for Natural Language Processing, pp. 415–434. Lawrence Erlbaum, Hillsdale (1982)
7. Hobbs, J.: Literature and Cognition. CSLI, Lecture Notes, Stanford (1990)
8. Martin, J.: A computational model of metaphor interpretation. Academic Press, New York (1990)
9. Narayanan, S.: KARMA: Knowledge-based action representations for metaphor and aspect. PhD thesis, Computer Science Division, EECS Department, University of California, Berkeley (1997)
10. Asher, N., Lascarides, A.: Logics of Conversation. Cambridge University Press, Cambridge (2003)
11. Hobbs, J.: Ontological promiscuity. In: Annual Meeting of the ACL, Chicago, pp. 61–69 (1985)
12. Wallington, A., Barnden, J.: Similarity as a basis for metaphor: Invariant transfer and the role of VNMAs. Technical Report CSRP-06-02, School of Computer Science, Univ. of Birmingham (2006)
13. Barnden, J., Lee, M.: Understanding open-ended usages of familiar conceptual metaphors: An approach and artificial intelligence system. Technical report, Technical Report CSRP-01-05, School of Computer Science, Univ. of Birmingham (2001)
14. Asher, N., Lascarides, A.: The semantics and pragmatics of metaphor. In: Bouillon, P., Busa, F. (eds.) The Language of Word Meaning, pp. 262–289. Cambridge University Press, Cambridge (2001)
15. Kamp, H., Reyle, U.: From Discourse to Logic: Introduction to Modeltheoretic semantics of natural language, formal language and Discourse Representation Theory. Kluwer Academic Publishers, Dordrecht (1993)
16. Hobbs, J.: An approach to the structure of discourse. In: Everett, D. (ed.) Discourse: Linguistic, Computational and Philosophical Perspectives (1996)
17. Lee, M., Barnden, J.: Reasoning about mixed metaphors with an implemented ai system. Metaphor and Symbol 16, 29–42 (2001)
18. Gomez-Txurruka, I.: The natural language conjunction 'and'. Linguistics and Philosophy 26, 255–285 (2003)
19. Falkenhainer, B., Forbus, K., Gentner, D.: The structure-mapping engine: algorithm and examples. Artificial Intelligence 41, 1–63 (1989)
20. Holyoak, K., Thagard, P.: Analogical mapping by constraint satisfaction. Cognitive Science 13, 295–355 (1989)

MDD Approach for the Development of Context-Aware Applications

Dhouha Ayed, Didier Delanote, and Yolande Berbers

Department of Computer Science, K.U. Leuven
B-3001 Leuven, Belgium

Abstract. Context-aware systems offer entirely new opportunities for application developers and for end users by gathering context information and adapting systems behavior accordingly. Several context models have been defined and various context-aware middleware has been developed in order to simplify the development of context-aware applications. Unfortunately, the development of an application by using these middleware products introduces several technical details in the application. These technical details are specific to a given middleware and reduce the possibility of reusing the application on other middleware. In this paper, we propose an MDD (Model Driven Development) approach that makes it possible to design context-aware applications independently of the platform. This approach is based on several phases that approach step by step the context platform and allow designers to automatically map their models to several platforms through the definition of automatic and modular transformations. To be able to apply this approach we define a new UML profile for context-aware applications, that we use to explore our approach.

1 Introduction

Model Driven Development (MDD) is an approach to developing software that proposes using machine-readable models at various levels of abstraction as its main artifacts. The key idea is to automatically transform highly abstract models into more concrete models from which an implementation can be generated in a straightforward way. The MDD approach is supported by the MDA (Model Driven Architecture) initiative of the OMG (Object Management Group), which introduced the notion of PIM (Platform Independent Model) and PSM (Platform Specific Model). A PIM is a model of a system that contains no technical details while a PSM is a representation of the same system containing all technical details that are needed to realize it on a concrete technology platform. The mapping between PIM and PSM is realized using an automatic transformation. This way, PSMs can be generated for different technology platforms. Platform specific knowledge is moved to the transformations, effectively separating those concerns from the main application.

Context-aware applications can collect context information and quickly adapt their behavior to context changes. Context is any information that can be used

B. Kokinov et al. (Eds.): CONTEXT 2007, LNAI 4635, pp. 15–28, 2007.

to characterize the situation of entities that are considered relevant to the interaction between a user and an application, including the user and the application
themselves. Context is typically the location, preference and state of people and
computational and physical objects.

Design and development of context-aware applications is particularly complex.
First, Context acquisition is not an easy process. Context information, which can
be acquired from heterogeneous and distributed sources (sensors, files, applications), may be dynamic and may require an additional interpretation in order to
be meaningful for an application. Second, the adaptation process can be based
on different types of mechanisms depending on the required dynamism and may
be related to the semantics of the application. Consequently, context-aware applications need specific development mechanisms.

Several middleware products have been defined to ease the development of
context-aware applications, but no solution has been specifically proposed to
design context-aware applications. The applications that are developed with the
existing middleware are not portable. They include several technical details that
are specific to a given technology and their reuse on a different technology platform requires redevelopment. This problem can be avoided by concentrating
efforts on application design, modeling the application independently from the
platform, and automatically generating the code for several platforms.

In this paper, we propose an MDD approach that makes it possible to model
context-aware applications independently from the platform. In order to be able
to apply this approach, we propose a UML profile that allows designers to model
the contexts that impact an application and the variability of the application
according to this context. The application is modeled independently from the
complex and heterogeneous mechanisms that are required to acquire context information and to perform adaptations. These mechanisms are approached step
by step for more model extensibility and reusability in several platforms. The
defined platform independent models (PIMs) can be automatically mapped to
several platforms through the definition of automatic transformations. The transformations we use have a more general sense of separation of concerns than just
pure technical concerns by separating non-functional concerns from the functional application concerns.

The paper is organized as follows. Section 2 gives an overview of the phases
of our MDD approach. This approach is detailed phase by phase in Sections 3
to 7. Section 8 discusses related work. The paper concludes in Section 9.

2   Phases of an MDD Approach for the Development of Context-Aware Applications

An MDD-based project includes several preparation activities that structure
and plan the work. These preparation activities enable knowledge reuse, which
is one of the main benefits of the MDD. We propose six phases in order to follow
an MDD methodology for the development of a context-aware application (see
Figure 1). These phases are described as follows.

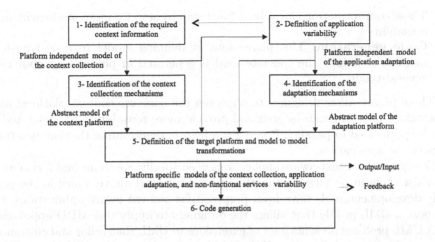

Fig. 1. MDD Phases for the Development of Context-aware Applications

1. **Identification of the required context information:** This phase aims at modeling context information that can have an impact on the application. Several context elements have to be specified during this phase, such as the context types, the required context quality, and the specification of the collection process. These specifications must be made independently from the platform that will be used to collect context information.

2. **Definition of the application variability:** This phase aims at specifying how the application can adapt to the context. It consists in defining structure, behavior or parameters of the application that will vary according to context. The result of this phase is a model of how the structure, the behavior or the parameters of the application need to be changed, specified independently from the platform that will be used to perform the adaptation activities.

3. **Identification of the context collection mechanisms:** This phase aims at defining an abstract model of the platform that will be used to collect context information. It consists in specifying the mechanisms required for the collection of context elements that were specified in the first phase. The defined abstract platform model allows designers to determine the concrete context platform that will be used.

4. **Identification of the adaptation mechanisms:** This phase aims at defining an abstract model of the platform that will be used to perform the adaptations. It consists in specifying the required mechanisms that will make the adaptations that were specified in the second phase.

5. **Definition of the target platform and model to model transformations:** Once context collection mechanisms and adaptation mechanisms are identified, the designer can specify the concrete target platform and use model transformations to automatically generate more concrete models.

These transformations must be defined step by step for more modularity and reusability.

6. **Code generation:** This phase aims at defining model to code transformations that take the concrete models generated in phase 5 as input and generate code.

These phases allow designers to approach the concrete context platform and adaptation platform step by step and provide more reusability. Phases 1 and 2 can be performed in parallel. Phase 2 can help in determining the contexts that impact the application.

Designers of context-aware applications need specific solutions and formalisms to assist them in performing the phases we mentioned above. Since in the past only development tools have been proposed for context-aware applications, we propose a UML profile that allows the designers to apply this MDD approach.

A UML profile represents a set of extensions of UML that tailor and customize it to specific areas or domains. UML provides several extension mechanisms, such as stereotypes, tagged values and constraints. This way, a UML profile allows the existing and large UML practitioner community to embrace our approach without giving up their existing modeling environment and process. It also allows the context-aware applications designed by this profile to be integrated with existing UML-based software without special difficulties.

In the following sections we detail the various phases we mentioned above and for each phase we describe the UML profile elements that play a role in this phase.

3   Identification of the Required Context Information

Not all applications are sensitive to the same types of contexts. Consequently, the first step that a designer has to perform is to identify the types of context information that can impact the application, and to specify the requirements of the application in terms of their collection process. The specification of the collection process consists in defining how each type of context information must be collected i.e. to specify if the collection has to be performed synchronously or asynchronously, the frequency, and the quality attributes of the collection. The result of this phase is a platform-independent model of the context collection process. Figure 2 presents the elements of the context-aware profile we propose that allow a designer to specify such a model. These elements are defined in the *StaticContextIdentification* package. They extend the UML class diagram. The stereotypes are defined as classes stereotyped with $<< stereotype >>$. UML metaclasses are defined as classes stereotyped with $<< metaclass >>$. Tagged values are defined as attributes for the defined stereotypes. The elements of the *staticContextIdentification* package are as follows:

– The $<< Context >>$ stereotype describes the context type, such as the location zone of the user, network bandwidth, and user preferences. It permits to determine the context sources that will be used to collect this information once the context-aware middleware has been chosen.

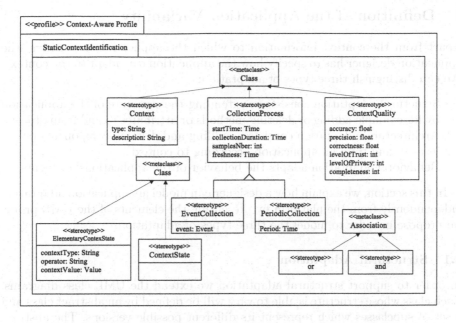

Fig. 2. Extensions of the UML class diagram to model the context

- The << *CollectionProcess* >> stereotype represents the elements necessary to collect the context, such as the starting time of collection, collection duration (e.g. three hours), number of samples (e.g. 100), and freshness which specifies how recent the context data must be. This stereotype is abstract, and it is used only to define the common tags of two types of context collections: event-based collection (defined by the << *EventCollection* >> stereotype) and periodic collection (defined by the << *PeriodicCollection* >> stereotype). The *event* tag indicates the condition that must be satisfied by the context before a new context value is returned. The *period* tag indicates the rate at which context data should be collected.
- The << *ContextQuality* >> stereotype represents the quality attributes that must be satisfied by the context such as the accuracy, the precision, the correctness, and the levelOfTrust.
- The << *ContextState* >> stereotype makes it possible to specify the relevant context states that have an impact on a given application in order to be filtered. The base tags of an << *ElementaryContextState* >> stereotype represent the context type, an operator, and a particular value of the context. The binary conjunction and disjunction relationships between elementary context states and context states is specified by means of associations with the << *And* >> and << *Or* >> stereotypes, respectively.

All the context elements mentioned above are important for the collection of context information and the identification of the context states that are relevant to the adaptation process of a given application.

4 Definition of the Application Variability

Apart from the context information to which the application is sensitive, the application designer has to specify how the application can adapt to the context. We can distinguish three types of adaptation:

- Structural adaptation consists in extending the structure of the application by for example adding or deleting methods or attributes to and from objects.
- Architectural adaptation consists in adding and deleting components or objects to and from an application according to context.
- Behavioral adaptation adapts the behavior of the applications' elements.

In this section, we explain how a designer can model an application adaptation independently from the platform by presenting the elements of the UML profile we propose in order to model the three types of adaptation.

4.1 Structural Adaptation

In order to support structural adaptation we extend the UML class diagrams. Each class whose structure is able to vary will be defined by an abstract class and a set of subclasses which represent its different possible versions. The abstract class will be defined with the stereotype $<< VariableStructure >>$ and each subclass will be defined with the stereotype $<< version >>$. An object can be instantiated from one of the subclasses according to the context. The tag *contextStateIds* is applied to the classes stereotyped with $<< version >>$ in order to specify in which context states a given subclass version is used to instantiate an object. This *contextStateIds* represents a set of identifiers of relevant context states that have already been specified by the designer (see Section 3).

When several context states associated with different subclasses are satisfied, a new subclass that represents a disjunction of the attributes and the operations of these subclasses is generated during the model transformation in order to be used in the instantiation process.

4.2 Architectural Adaptation

In order to support architectural adaptation we extend the UML class diagram with the $<< Optional >>$ stereotype. This stereotype specifies the optionality of an object. To specify in which context states an optional object has to be instantiated in an application, we associate a tag *contextStateIds* to the class stereotyped with $<< Optional >>$. This *contextStateIds* tag represents a set of identifiers of context states that have already been specified by the designer (see Section 3).

4.3 Behavioral Adaptation

Since behavioral adaptation impacts the dynamic aspect of an application and the UML sequence diagram models this dynamic aspect, we propose to extend

the UML sequence diagram. For this purpose, we introduce two stereotypes
<< *VariableSequence* >> and << *SequenceVariant* >>.

<< *VariableSequence* >> is associated with interactions which are variable
according to the context. For a given context, only one interaction variant defined
by this stereotype will be present in the derived sequence diagram. The different
variants of one variable interaction are defined by a << *SequenceVariant* >>
stereotype. This stereotype is tagged by the *contextStateIds* tag in order to
indicate the context states in which each interaction variant will be executed
(see Section 3).

4.4   The Adaptation Profile Structure

Figure 3 presents the adaptation aspects of the context-aware profile we propose. The extensions proposed for class diagrams are defined in the *StaticAdap-
tationAspect* package and the extensions proposed for the sequence diagrams are
gathered in the *DynamicAdaptationAspect* package.

Each of the << *VariableStructure* >> and << *Optional* >> stereotypes
are applied to the Class metaclass. The << *Version* >> stereotype inherits
from the << *VariableStructure* >> stereotype, which means each version is
a variable structure. The << *OptionalLine* >> stereotype is applied to the
Lifeline metaclass and the << *VariableSequence* >> stereotype is applied to
the Interaction metaclass. The << *SequenceVariant* >> stereotype inherits
from the << *VariableSequence* >> stereotype, which means each sequence
variant is a variable sequence.

All the profile elements we described in this section allow designers to create
a PIM adaptation model in the second phase.

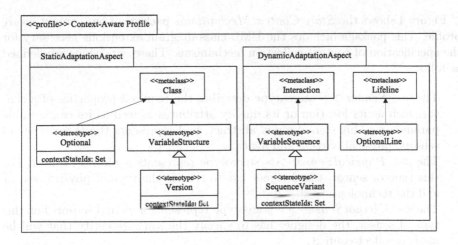

Fig. 3. UML extensions for adaptation modeling

The goal of the first and the second phases is to model the required context and the adaptation of the application independently from the platform. The goal of the third and fourth phases is to step by step approach the platforms that will be used to collect context and to perform adaptations by defining the mechanisms they require. We describe phase three in Section 5 and phase four in Section 6.

5   Context Collection Mechanism Requirements

The goal of the first phase is to model the required context independently from the platform. The role of this third phase is to approach the platform that will be used to collect context by defining an abstract model of this platform (see Figure 1).

During this phase, designers identify the mechanisms and the technologies required for the collection of the contexts that were specified in the first phase and specify the types of sensors that are necessary for that purpose.

Sensors can be classified in three types:

- Physical sensors: represent hardware sensors capable of capturing physical data, such as photodiodes to capture light, microphones to capture audio, and biosensors to measure skin resistance or blood pressure.
- Virtual sensors: these sensors collect context data from software applications. For example, it is possible to determine the activity of a person by browsing his electronic calendar.
- Logical sensors: these sensors use several context sources, and combine physical and virtual sensors with additional information in order to derive higher level context. They can interpret and reason about context information.

Figure 4 shows the *StaticContextMechanisms* package of our context-aware profile. This package includes the UML class diagram extensions necessary for the specification of context collection mechanisms. These extensions are defined as follows:

- The << *Sensor* >> stereotype describes the required properties of a sensor, such as its location or its quality attributes as well as its configurable parameters. This stereotype is abstract, and represents the three types of sensors: physical, virtual and logical.
- The << *PhysicalSensor* >> stereotype represents a physical sensor. For this type of sensor, the designer has to specify the type of physical sensor and the technology used.
- The << *VirtualSensor* >> stereotype represents a virtual sensor. For this type of sensor, the designer has to specify the software entity that will be used to collect context.
- The << *LogicalSensor* >> stereotype represents a logical sensor. For this type of sensor, the designer has to specify the software entity that will reason about the collected context information, but he has also to specify which

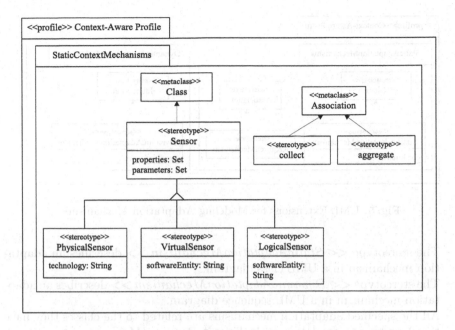

Fig. 4. UML Class Diagram Extensions for Modeling Context Collection Mechanisms

context sensors will be used by this logical sensor in order to aggregate context information. The relationship between a logical sensor and another sensor that collects coarse context information is specified by an association with the $<< aggregate >>$ stereotype.

– All sensors are related to the context types they collect by an association with the $<< collect >>$ stereotype.

6 Adaptation Mechanism Requirements

The goal of the second phase is to model the adaptation of the application independently from the platform. The role of this fourth phase is to approach the platform that will be used to perform adaptations by defining an abstract model of this platform. During this phase, designers identify the mechanisms that are required to adapt the application as specified in the second phase.

Among the existing adaptation mechanisms we can mention reflection, aspect oriented programming, contracts, and the component-based paradigm.

In this phase, the designer specifies for each class stereotyped with $<< VariableStructure >>$ or $<< Optional >>$ and for each interaction stereotyped with $<< VariableSequence >>$ the various mechanisms that can be used to achieve the adaptation. These mechanisms can be specified by using the following profile elements (see Figure 5):

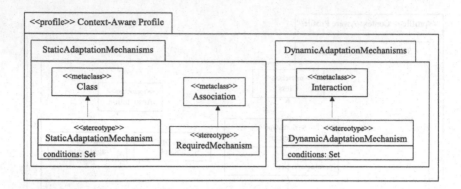

Fig. 5. UML Extensions for Modeling Adaptation Mechanisms

- The stereotype $<< StaticAdaptationMechanism >>$ describes an adaptation mechanism in a UML class diagram.
- The stereotype $<< DynamicAdaptationMechanism >>$ describes an adaptation mechanism in a UML sequence diagram.
- All the specified adaptation mechanisms are related to the classes they have to adapt by an association with the $<< RequiredMechanism >>$ stereotype.

Since it is possible to associate several possible adaptation mechanisms with only one variation point, the stereotypes $<< StaticAdaptationMechanism >>$ and $<< DynamicAdaptationMechanism >>$ have a *conditions* tagged value that allows the designer to specify in which conditions a mechanism can be used.

The third and fourth phases approach the platforms that will be used to collect context and to perform adaptation without specifying technologies that are specific to a given platform. This intermediate step between the definition of the PIM and the definition of the concrete platforms allows a designer to identify efficiently the various platforms that are possible to use. Moreover, the defined abstract platforms permit the definition of intermediate transformations (from the PIM to these abstract platforms) that can be reused for several PSM transformations.

7   Definition of the Target Platform and Model to Model Transformations

The goal of this phase is to identify the target platform and to transform the platform independent models defined in phases 1 and 2 to more concrete models according to the mechanism requirements specified in phases 3 and 4.

Model transformations can provide a more general sense of separation of concerns than just pure technical concerns by separating non-functional concerns, such as distribution, security, and transactions from the functional application concerns. In this case, it is not practically attainable to implement all the concerns in one single big transformation. Besides splitting up transformations according to technical concerns (a separate transformation for each PSM), we should also decompose transformations according to non-functional concerns. Ideally, each transformation should address only one non-functional concern so that it becomes easy to implement and to reuse. As a result, we get a chain of transformations that need to be applied subsequently to weave all non-functional concerns into the application model.

In this phase, the designer first has to define the abstract transformations that transform the models without introducing technical details. Then he has to define more and more concrete transformations that generate concrete platform-specific models. Consequently he will first define the non-functional transformations. Then he will identify the target platform. Finally, he will specify the technical transformations. In the following, we describe each of these steps.

7.1   Non-functional Transformations

In this step, the designer has to identify the non-functional services required by the application that must be provided by the underlying middleware, such as distribution, security, remote data access, deployment, etc.

In the case of context-aware applications, these services are also required to be adaptive. Our goal is to automatically generate the variability models of these non-functional services so designers are relieved from specifying this variability. For this purpose, transformations of the application variability that was specified in the second phase (see Section 4) have to be defined. These transformations generate variability models of non-functional services that are still platform-independent.

As a proof of concept, in [1] we elaborated a non-functional transformation. In this report, we designed a platform independent model of application adaptation for a concrete example, and transformed this into an application variability model.

7.2   Definition of the Target Platform

Once context collection mechanisms (see phase 3), adaptation mechanisms (see phase 4), and required non-functional services are identified, the designer can study the existing context and adaptation platforms and choose the one that best satisfies the requirements in terms of these mechanisms

7.3   Technical Transformations

In this step, the designer specifies the PIM to PSM transformations that will transform the abstract models defined throughout the phases of the MDD approach into concrete models that are specific to the chosen context platform and adaptation platform respectively. The generated variability models of the non-functional services also need to be transformed according to the services provided by the chosen underlying middleware.

We elaborated a technical transformation for a concrete adaptation platform in [1]. The application variability model acquired through a non-functional transformation, was transformed into a service variability model using a technical transformation.

8 Related Work

Several context models have been defined, such as the key-value pairs [2], the object-oriented model [3], the sentient object model [4], and the models based on ontologies [5]. The aim of these models was to provide a high level abstraction of context information in order to store, manage, and process the context, but no solution has been proposed in order to model context-aware applications and their adaptation according to this context.

The majority of existing work has proposed solutions to simplify the complicated development of context-aware applications without tackling the problem of their modeling or defining a complete process to model and develop them. These existing solutions consist in middleware and frameworks that enable context collection and that can even provide adaptation mechanisms.

The most consistent attempts at developing reusable solutions for context acquisition, interpretation, and rapid prototyping of context-aware applications is context Toolkit [6], SOCAM [7], CoBrA [8], CASS [9], and CORTEX [10].

Among middleware solutions that allow developers to implement adaptation mechanisms we can mention CARISMA [11], K-Components [12], ReMMoc [13], CORTEX [10], and RAM [14].

The advantage of the existing context-aware middleware consists in enabling the separation of context management and processing from the development of applications. They play a significant role in simplifying the development of context-aware applications by implementing the mechanisms that collect and interpret the context as well as the mechanisms that adapt the application to the context, but introduce several technical details in the developed applications and reduce their portability.

[15] proposes a UMLbased solution to design context-aware web services. [16] is another modeling approach that includes an extension to the ORM (Object-Role Modeling) by context information. This approach allows developers to program with context at a high level without the need to consider issues related to context collection. These works are focused on context modeling and do not support adaptation aspects.

The MDD approach we propose in this paper defines a complete process that covers all the production phases of context-aware applications. This approach specifies how to model the applications independently from the platform and how to automatically generate its code by using step by step transformations.

9   Conclusion

Design and development of context-aware applications is particularly complex. They require the identification of the context information that has an impact on the application and the specification of the various behaviors of the application according to this context information.

In this paper, we propose an MDD approach that enables the concentration of efforts on applications design and their modeling independently from the platform. This platform independence hides the complexity and the heterogeneity of the context-aware and adaptive mechanisms.

The MDD approach we propose defines phases that cover preparation activities that structure and plan the work. These phases make it possible to first model the contexts that impact an application and the variability of the application according this context in an abstract manner, and then to approach step by step the mechanisms required to acquire context information and perform adaptations. The step by step approach followed by these phases provides a model extensibility and reusability in several platforms.

The MDD approach we propose defines a methodology to model a context collection process and the variability of an application structure, as well as its behavior and its architecture, independently from the platform. The defined platform independent models can be automatically mapped to several platforms through the definition of automatic transformations. The transformations we use have a more general sense of separation of concerns than just pure technical concerns by separating non-functional concerns from the functional application concerns. In addition to platform specific models they are able to generate the adaptation models of the required non-functional services.

In order to be able to apply this approach, we propose a UML profile that allows designers to model context-aware applications. This profile allows the existing UML practitioner community to embrace our approach without giving up their existing modeling environment and process. It also allows the context-aware applications designed by this profile to be integrated with existing UML-based software.

To evaluate the approach we proposed, we made an implementation of the UML profile, non-functional and technical transformations as presented in this paper. More details concerning implementation and evaluation can be found in [1]. This report also describes an example of a context-aware adaptive application, developed with the MDD approach we propose.

In further phases we intend to extend the context-aware UML profile we propose to support ontologies, in order to introduce more intelligence in the modeled context-aware applications by deducing new adaptation rules. We also want to define how to check the consistency of the adaptation rules during the design of applications.

References

1. Ayed, D., Delanote, D., Berbers, Y.: MDD Approach and Evaluation of Development of Context-Aware Applications. Technical Report CW495, Dept. of Computer Science, Katholieke Universiteit Leuven, Belgium (May 2007)
2. Schilit, B., Theimer, M., Welch, B.: Customising mobile applications. In: Proceedings of USENIX Symposium on Mobile and Location-Independent Computing, pp. 129–138 (August 1993)
3. Henricksen, K., Indulska, J., Rakotonirainy, A.: Modeling context information in pervasive computing systems. In: Pervasive 2002, Switzerland, pp. 167–180 (2002)
4. Harter, A., Hopper, A., Steggles, P., Ward, A.: The anatomy of a context-aware application. In: Mobile Computing and Networking, pp. 59–68 (1999)
5. Preuveneers, D., Berbers, Y.: Semantic and syntactic modeling of component-based services for context-aware pervasive systems using owl-s. In: Managing Context Information in Mobile and Pervasive Environments, pp. 30–39 (2005)
6. Dey, A., Abowd, G., Salber, D.: A Conceptual Framework and Toolkit for Supporting the Rapid Prototyping of Context-aware Applications. Human-computer Interaction 16(2-4), 97–166 (2001) (special issue on context-aware computing)
7. Gu, T., Pung, H.K., Zhang, D.Q.: A Middleware for Building Context-aware Mobile Services. In: IEEE Vehicular Technology Conference (VTC), Milan, Italy (2004)
8. Chen, H.: An Intelligent Broker Architecture for Pervasive Context-Aware Systems. PhD thesis, University of Maryland, Baltimore County (2004)
9. Fahy, P., Clarke, S.: A Middleware for Mobile Context-aware Applications. In: Workshop on Context Awareness, MobiSys (2004)
10. Sorensen, C.F., Wu, M., Sivaharan, T., Blair, G.S., Okanda, P., Friday, A., Duran-Limon, H.A.: Context-aware Middleware for Applications in Mobile Ad Hoc Environments. In: Middleware for Pervasive and Ad-hoc Computing, pp. 107–110 (2004)
11. Capra, L., Emmerich, W., Mascolo, C.: CARISMA: Context-Aware Reflective mIddleware System for Mobile Applications. IEEE Transactions on Software Engineering 29(10), 929–945 (2003)
12. Dowling, J., Cahill, V.: The K-Component Architecture Meta-model for Self-Adaptive Software. In: Reflection 2001 (2001)
13. Grace, P., Blair, G.S., Samuel, S.: Remmoc: A reflective middleware to support mobile client interoperability. In: International Symposium on Distributed Objects and Applications (DOA), Catania, Sicily, Italy (November 2003)
14. David, P., Ledoux, T.: An Infrastructure for Adaptable Middleware. In: Meersman, R., Tari, Z., et al. (eds.) CoopIS 2002, DOA 2002, and ODBASE 2002. LNCS, vol. 2519, Springer, Heidelberg (2002)
15. Sheng, Q.Z., Benatallah, B.: ContextUML: A UML-Based Modeling Language for Model-Driven Development of Context-Aware Web Services. In: The 4th International Conference on Mobile Business (ICMB'05) (2005)
16. Hendricksen, K., I.J., Rakotonirainy, A.: Generating context management infrastructure from high-level context models. In: Chen, M.-S., Chrysanthis, P.K., Sloman, M., Zaslavsky, A. (eds.) MDM 2003. LNCS, vol. 2574, Springer, Heidelberg (2003)

Of Situations and Their Neighbors

Evolution and Similarity in Ontology-Based Approaches to Situation Awareness

Norbert Baumgartner[1], Werner Retschitzegger[2], Wieland Schwinger[2], Gabriele Kotsis[2], and Christoph Schwietering[3]

[1] team Communication Technology Management GmbH,
Goethegasse 3/3, 1010 Vienna, Austria
norbert.baumgartner@te-am.net
[2] Johannes Kepler University Linz,
Altenberger Str. 69, 4040 Linz, Austria
{werner.retschitzegger,wieland.schwinger,gabriele.kotsis}@jku.at
[3] ASFINAG Traffic Telematics Ltd.,
Klingerstr. 10, 1230 Vienna, Austria
christoph.schwietering@asfinag.at

Abstract. Ontology-based approaches to situation awareness have gained increasing popularity in recent years. However, most current approaches face two inherent problems. First, they lack sufficient support for assessing evolutions of situations, which is crucial for informing (human) agents about emerging instances of interesting situation types. Second, they are confronted with the problem of recognizing situations that are just similar to a situation type an agent is interested in. Our approach contributed in this paper is based on conceptual neighborhoods of relations which we generalize to conceptual neighborhoods of situations. These conceptual neighborhoods turn out to be the basis for addressing both problems, the assessment of evolving as well as similar situations. The applicability of our approach is demonstrated by an in-depth case study in the domain of road traffic management.

1 Introduction

A profound basis for decision making of (human) agents in highly-dynamic, heterogeneous environments—like operators in the field of road traffic management—has to provide a perception of the available information that is tailored to the decision maker's context. *Situation awareness* (SAW) aims at providing such a perception based on *situations*, which describe a state of affairs adhering to a partial view of the world. Our conceptualization of situations, which is motivated by Situation Theory [1], involves physical *objects*, their intrinsic *attributes*, and their *relations* to other objects, which altogether may potentially contribute to *relevant* situations, i.e. the ones an agent is interested in. These relevant situations are defined by abstract *situation types* that should be instantiated during situation assessment. In recent years, *ontologies*, i.e. their interpretation coined by Gruber [2],

B. Kokinov et al. (Eds.): CONTEXT 2007, LNAI 4635, pp. 29–42, 2007.

have been regarded to be suitable for providing the vocabulary for describing situations and their involved concepts (e.g. [3]).

Endsley [4] points out that SAW also involves the estimation of the future of recognized situations, meaning that also the *evolution* of situations has to be assessed. Consequently, agents should be informed of an emerging relevant situation, in order to take pro-active action. A further problem is to inform agents about situations that are just *similar* to the relevant situation types (e.g. sensors still just capture a very limited image of the real world). Unfortunately, ontology-based SAW approaches face the problem inherent to the mainly symbolic representation of situations. This leaves the questions how to determine that a situation is on its way to turn into a relevant situation or that a situation is similar to a situation type? At first sight, both problems, assessing evolving and similar situations, are unrelated. In the scope of this paper, we contribute an approach based on conceptual neighborhoods of relations, which, generalized to conceptual neighborhoods of situations, turn out to be the basis for addressing both problems. Our approach is established as a case study in the road traffic management domain, which is, as indicated above, a prominent candidate for applying SAW systems. Road traffic operators have to control road traffic based on the assessed traffic situations using, for example, speed controls or warning messages. In order to elaborate a realistic setting, we collaborate with ASFINAG Traffic Telematics Ltd., a subsidiary of Austria's highways agency, regarding the interesting types of traffic situations and the actions taken by a traffic operator upon their occurrence.

The paper is structured as follows. First, we introduce an ontology for road traffic SAW and a formalism to specify situation types in Sect. 2. Next, we elaborate our approach in Sect. 3 and subsequently, in Sect. 4, apply it in the scope of a case study involving various traffic situation types and their occurrences in a complex scenario. Finally, we provide an overview of related work in Sect. 5 and conclude the paper in Sect. 6, in which we critically discuss our contribution and indicate further prospects of our work.

2   Road Traffic Situation Awareness

In order to explain our approach elaborated in Sect. 3 by means of illustrative examples, we introduce an ontology for road traffic SAW and, thereupon, a formalized description of an interesting but simple situation type in this section. The ontology and the according formalism to describe situations and situation types are also the basis for our case study in Sect. 4.

2.1   An Ontology for Road Traffic Situation Awareness

The ontology depicted in Fig. 1 is based on our previous work which focused on spatio-temporal extensions to a simple, OWL[1]-DL-based ontology for road

---

[1] Web Ontology Language, cf. http://www.w3.org/TR/owl-features

traffic SAW [5]. Whereas the road traffic concepts are extended, the SAW concepts, which are the core of the ontology, are simplified in the scope of this paper. In short, the classes WrongWayDriver, BlackIce, etc. are traffic-relevant entities and are combined in the package roadTraffic. The SAW concepts on top of these traffic-relevant entities have various origins. The basic components, essentially the classes Object, Situation, and Attribute are motivated by the top-level concepts we have identified in our survey of domain-independent ontologies for SAW [6]. The class Object subsumes all traffic-relevant entities and is associated with all subclasses of Attribute, like, for example, Lifespan and Location. Relations, which are deduced from attributes, relate objects and are subject to the largest simplification of the original SAW ontology [5]. In contrast to a class taxonomy, we use derivatives of the object property isRelatedWith for relating objects, assuming that properties of these relations are modeled outside of OWL-DL. Instances of the class Situation are constituted of objects as well as the relations that contribute to the situation. Situations have, like relations, an implicit time interval of validity. Evolutions of situations are represented as sequences using the object property hasNextState.

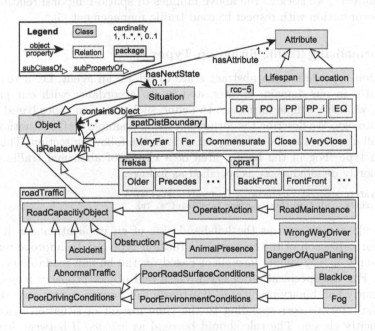

Fig. 1. An ontology for road traffic SAW

The depicted derivatives of the object property isRelatedWith are primitive relations which provide the concepts for defining situation types or more complex relations [7]. The different relations are again organized into packages. We call each package a *family of relations* because all contained relations model a specific *aspect* of the relationships between two objects. The currently incorporated families, which are based on well-known calculi from the field of qualitative spatio-temporal reasoning, originate from our previous work [5] and have been chosen for this paper because they provide the minimal spatio-temporal aspects for defining the traffic situation types introduced in the following sections.

The family (1) rcc-5 [8] models the mereo(topo)logical relationships between the spatial regions occupied by two objects (e.g. DR means 'discrete from'). (2) spatDistBoundary [9] models a simple interpretation of qualitative distance between two objects based on the minimal distance between their boundaries on the road network. (3) freksa [10] models temporal relationships between time intervals, i.e. the lifespans of two objects. (4) opra$_1$ [11] models the aspect orientation in an intrinsic way without a reference point. Two objects are regarded to be oriented points with respect to the road network (e.g. BackFront indicates one object being in front of another object travelling in the same direction on the same road).

Note that one may also define more complex families of relations, like, for example, the level of obstruction between two traffic objects. In the rest of this paper, however, we stick to the above families of spatio-temporal relations and their interpretation with respect to road traffic management [5].

2.2 Formalizing Traffic Situation Types

A situation type defines an abstract state of affairs an agent, i.e. a road traffic operator in our domain, is interested in. In accordance with our previous work [5], we use a simple formalism to define such situation types based on the above ontology. We describe the formalism using a simple traffic situation type, which will also serve as the running example in the following section. The traffic situation type 'Fog in the border area of a chunk of abnormal traffic (traffic jam)', shortly denoted as S_0, is specified as follows:

```
roadTraffic:AbnormalTraffic(?a) ∧ roadTraffic:Fog(?b) ∧
rcc-5:PO(?a, ?b) ∧ spatDistBoundary:VeryClose(?a, ?b)
```

This rule can be seen as the left-hand side of an implication, i.e. it represents a formalization of the trigger for situation type S_0. To improve readability, we apply a very simple formalism based on the human-readable syntax of SWRL[2]. For the specification of OWL class and object property membership we use unary and binary predicates. For reasons of brevity, we suppose that the valid time intervals corresponding to the time instant of situation assessment are implicitly chosen. The rule should be read as follows. If between instances of the classes roadTraffic:AbnormalTraffic and roadTraffic:Fog the relations rcc-5:PO (partly overlapping) as well as spatDistBoundary:VeryClose hold, an instance of S_0, i.e. an instance of a subclass of Situation, is created.

Although such rules allow us to recognize instances of situation types, they are restricted to exact matches of the *most critical* instant in the evolution of a situation. Our approach to counter this restriction is introduced in the next section.

---

[2] Semantic Web Rule Language, cf. http://www.w3.org/Submission/SWRL

3 Assessing Evolving and Similar Situations

Whereas a situation type is a template for a *state of affairs*, the evolution of a situation or a situation type may be seen as a *course of events* [1]. Let us consider the *possible* courses of events between two arbitrary situations. With our current knowledge based on the formalization of situation types, we just know that there are—even if regarding just the contributing relations—possibly infinite variations between these two situations. That is, we have no a priori knowledge about the evolution of situations and we, consequently, can not determine for a situation, whether it may evolve into or it is similar to an instance of a most-critical situation type. Our approach to handle both problems is elaborated in the following subsections, in which we describe the notion of *conceptual neighborhoods* of relations and situations, and, thereon, provide a method to model evolutions of situations using *landmark situation types*.

3.1 Conceptual Neighborhoods of Situations

We elaborate our approach based on two assumptions. First, two relations are, according to Freksa [10], '*conceptual neighbors*, if a direct transition from one relation to the other can occur upon an arbitrarily small change in the referenced domain'. We assume that for each family of relations, a directed graph specifying the *conceptual neighborhood* is given. This conceptual neighborhood graph (CNG) is defined by a set of vertices, the relations, and a set of edges, the direct neighborhoods of the relations in the corresponding family. This leads us to the second assumption—a relation between two objects evolves in the form of *smooth transitions* with respect to the CNG of its corresponding family. Fig. 2 shows an exemplary CNG for rcc-5. For example, if between two objects the relation DR (discrete from) holds, it can only evolve to EQ (equals) by traversing over PO (partly overlapping).

In fact, these two assumptions are very common in the field of qualitative spatial and temporal reasoning, because they restrict the complexity of reasoning calculi. However, we suggest that the assumptions can be interpreted as requirements for general families of relations that are modeled in a SAW application. For example, the level of obstruction between two traffic objects also adheres to our premises.

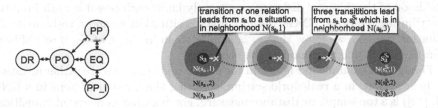

Fig. 2. The CNG of rcc-5   **Fig. 3.** The evolution of s_a into $s_a^{S_0}$

The generalization from one relation to all relations that contribute to a situation is straight-forward and has already been investigated with respect to relation-based similarities between spatial scenes (e.g. [12]). We generalize this work to relation-based similarities between situations and apply it to define the possible situations on the way from one situation to another. What follows is the direct *neighborhood of a situation*—the *set of situations* containing the same objects and the relations that are reachable by a single transition of one relation that contributes to the situation. The neighborhood of a situation type is defined analogously by the substitution of concrete object instances with unified variables. In the following, we denote an arbitrary situation a being an instance of a situation type S_i as $s_a^{S_i}$. We omit S_i if s_a is an anonymous situation, i.e. it is just an instance of the most general situation type Situation. Moreover, we designate the conceptual neighborhood of a situation, which is reachable by a transition of n relations, as $N(s_a^{S_i}, n)$.

Let us demonstrate the concept using the exemplary situation type S_0, 'Fog in the border area of a chunk of abnormal traffic', which we have defined in the previous section. Assume we got the following formalization of a concrete, anonymous situation s_a that involves the two objects obj1 and obj2:

```
roadTraffic:AbnormalTraffic(obj1) ∧ roadTraffic:Fog(obj2) ∧
rcc-5:DR(obj1, obj2) ∧ spatDistBoundary:Commensurate(obj1, obj2)
```

We want to determine whether s_a may evolve into an instance of S_0. Based on the CNGs of the families rcc-5 and spatDistBoundary, we know that s_a is, at minimum, three transitions away from being an instance of S_0 (DR→PO, Commensurate→Close→VeryClose). Hence, $s_a^{S_0} \in N(s_a, 3)$. Fig. 3 depicts an exemplary evolution of s_a into $s_a^{S_0}$ across anonymous situations in its neighborhoods visualized by means of concentric circles around each evolution. The different sizes of the circles indicate that the number of reachable situations in a neighborhood differs (e.g. in rcc-5, we got one possible transition from DR in contrast to four transitions from PO; cf. Fig. 2). Note that the neighborhoods need not necessarily be symmetric as it may be assumed from Fig. 3, i.e. a CNG with asymmetric neighborhoods of relations may lead to cases in which an instance of S_0 is in the neighborhood of s_a, but not the other way round.

If we investigate the example in detail, we find an approach to tackle both our problems. First, we are now in a position to determine the *minimal distance* between two situations or situation types regarding the number of necessary transitions of their contributing relations. Note that we do not talk about the likelihood of the minimal distance—we simply know each possible path from the contributing relations' CNGs. Second, given a situation s_a and a to-be-matched situation type S_0, we know that s_a is similar to an instance of S_0, if one of both is in the direct neighborhood of the other one.

Though the example in Fig. 3 and the elaborated approach are rather intuitive, we believe that, in a real-world setting, counting the number of hops in a CNG (cf. [12]) is a too simplistic distance measure. For example, concurrent transitions may occur, or the relevance of transitions may vary across families or situations. Nevertheless, the elaboration of such a distance measure is beyond the scope of this paper. Rather, we assume that a function $D : (s_a, s_b) \to [0..1]$, which maps a pair of situations or situation types to the interval between 0 and 1, is given. D corresponds to the normalized, minimal distance between both situations or situation types. Regarding the application of our approach to the scenario in the following section, we will provide a simple heuristic for D.

While we are now in a position to assess for any situation, whether it may evolve into or it is similar to a most-critical situation, a situation may still have many evolutions from which just a few are relevant for an agent. Hence, we want to provide further means for modelling the *relevant* courses of events.

3.2   Landmark Situation Types

Landmarks are used in various domains for highlighting significant entities of interest (e.g. robot navigation [13]). We follow these examples and introduce *landmark situation types* in order to delineate the relevant states of affairs in a course of events. Moreover, we separate these landmark situation types into three categories. The situation types discussed and explicitly modeled up to now, which represent the most-critical types of situations agents are interested in, are further on called *climax* situation types. In addition, there may be various *trigger* situation types before a climax situation type, i.e. situations that are likely to evolve into a climax situation. After a climax situation type, we add various *clearance* situation types. Although their formalization equals climax situation types, trigger and clearance situation types match, unlike climax situation types, situations in a fuzzy way—they mark the beginning and the end of a matching *phase*. That is, once a trigger situation type is instantiated, the evolutions of the situation towards the climax situation stay instances of the trigger situation type. The other way round, with the first deviation of a climax situation towards a clearance situation type, all evolutions of the situation are instances of the clearance situation type. Accordingly, we call the evolutions before and after a climax situation type the *trigger phase* and *clearance phase*.

Fig. 4 shows such an exemplary course of events based on our climax situation type S_0 which we have extended by the trigger situation type S_0T_0 and the clearance situation type S_0C_0. Once we have assessed a situation $s_a^{S_0T_0}$, the situation's successive states towards the climax belong to the trigger phase. In the given example, s_a evolves to an instance of the climax situation type by two transitions, i.e. $s_a^{S_0} \in N(s_a^{S_0T_0}, 2)$. The climax situation is valid as long as it matches, whereby the first deviation causes an instantiation of S_0C_0 which marks the beginning of the clearance phase. If the clearance situation type finally matches, the course of events ends.

The clearance situation type S_0C_0 indicates a further problem when dealing with evolving situations—one may define a landmark situation type that consists of a different number of objects than the subsequent landmark situation type. In case we are dealing with a trigger situation, the distance to the following landmark situation can just be determined with respect to the remaining relations. In fact, a trigger situation may, in case the remaining relations already match, spontaneously evolve into a climax situation without further relation transitions—

S_0T_0: roadTraffic:AbnormalTraffic(?a) ∧
    roadTraffic:Fog(?b) ∧
    rcc-5:DR(?a, ?b) ∧
    spatDistBoundary:Close(?a, ?b)
S_0C_0: roadTraffic:Fog(?b)

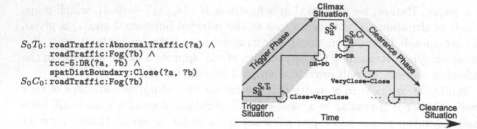

Fig. 4. An exemplary course of events based on landmark situation types

the object just 'pops up' at the adequate position. Such circumstances may be smoothed, for example, by the provision of distance measures for the co-occurrence of subclasses of Object in our ontology. Furthermore, following the course of events, the trivial *default* clearance situation types are determined by the drop out of *any* or *every* object that contributes to a climax situation type. The first case, i.e. the drop out of any object, may be overridden by a specific clearance situation type like, for example, S_0C_0. This clearance situation type means that the chunk of AbnormalTraffic determines the length of the clearance phase; if it drops out, and just the Fog remains, the course of events ends.

The final approach to assess evolving and similar situations shapes up as follows. At every time instant of situation assessment, we search for evolutions of previously assessed landmark situations. If an evolution finally matches the last clearance situation type, the situation ends. In addition, when trying to match a climax situation type without prior evolution, we follow our approach to assess situations similar to situation types, i.e. a situation also matches if it is in the near neighborhood of the climax situation type.

4   A Case Study in Road Traffic Management

We demonstrate our approach to assess evolving and similar situations by means of a case study which is made up of a formalization of exemplary traffic situation types and their assessment in a concrete scenario.

The exemplary traffic situation types shown in Table 1 are motivated by typical tasks of a road traffic operator and will be the basis for showing different aspects of the assessment of evolving and similar situations in the subsequent scenario. Apart from the formalization introduced in Sect. 2, the informal descriptions of the four climax situation types and their corresponding trigger or clearance situation types indicate exemplary workflows of traffic operators that are triggered by the occurrence of such situations in a real-world setting. In case a trigger or clearance situation type is missing, there is no interesting evolution of the corresponding situation from a traffic operator's point of view.

The scenario presented below serves as a test bed for our approach and consists of five states of affairs at consecutive, but not contiguous time instants (t_0 to t_4). Table 2 lists the four states of affairs with their corresponding results of

Table 1. A description and formalization of the four relevant courses of events

$S_i[T_i\|C_i]$	Description – Formalization
$S_1 T_0$	An OperatorAction (for reasons of brevity, we omit the name of the package roadTraffic), i.e. a capacity-restricting action taken by the road operator occurs. Examples are roadworks or blocked lanes. OperatorAction(?a)
S_1	An OperatorAction causes AbnormalTraffic. The restricted capacity causes abnormal traffic, i.e. a traffic jam. The main workflow of this type of situation is the mitigation of the abnormal traffic by stopping the corresponding operator action. OperatorAction(?a) ∧ AbnormalTraffic(?b) ∧ rcc-5:PO(?a, ?b) ∧ freksa:Older(?a, ?b) ∧ opra1:BackFront(?a, ?b)
$S_1 C_0$	The AbnormalTraffic disperses. After the dispersion, a traffic operator may consider the resumption of a previously cancelled operation action. Note that this situation type overrides the default clearance situation type, i.e. the AbnormalTraffic determines the extent of the situation. OperatorAction(?a)
S_2	PoorDrivingConditions cause an Accident. Typical workflows triggered by this climax situation type would be the alarm of local authorities and the publication of special warnings to road drivers. Note that we have not defined a trigger for this climax situation type, since there are no specific actions in case of poor driving conditions without an accident. PoorDrivingConditions(?a) ∧ Accident(?b) ∧ (rcc-5:PO(?a, ?b) ∨ rcc-5:PP(?b, ?a)) ∧ freksa:Older(?a, ?b) ∧ spatDistBoundary:VeryClose(?a, ?b)
$S_2 C_0$	The area of PoorDrivingConditions moves away from the Accident. PoorDrivingConditions(?a) ∧ Accident(?b) ∧ rcc-5:DR(?a, ?b) ∧ spatDistBoundary:Commensurate(?a, ?b)
$S_3 T_0$	AbnormalTraffic potentially grows together with AbnormalTraffic. AbnormalTraffic(?a) ∧ AbnormalTraffic(?b) ∧ rcc-5:DR(?a, ?b) ∧ spatDistBoundary:Close(?a, ?b)
S_3	AbnormalTraffic grows together with AbnormalTraffic. Two chunks of abnormal traffic that grow together should be treated as a single object. Hence, the single, more critical traffic jam would result in a different control strategy. AbnormalTraffic(?a) ∧ AbnormalTraffic(?b) ∧ rcc-5:DR(?a, ?b) ∧ spatDistBoundary:VeryClose(?a, b?)
$S_3 C_0$	Grown-together chunks of AbnormalTraffic split. AbnormalTraffic(?a) ∧ AbnormalTraffic(?b) ∧ rcc-5:DR(?a, ?b) ∧ spatDistBoundary:Commensurate(?a, ?b)
$S_4 T_0$	A WrongWayDriver heads toward a chunk of AbnormalTraffic. WrongWayDriver(?a) ∧ TrafficJam(?b) ∧ rcc-5:DR(?a, ?b) ∧ opra1:FrontFront(?a, ?b) ∧ spatDistBoundary:Commensurate(?a, ?b)
S_4	A WrongWayDriver rushes into AbnormalTraffic. An instance of this situation type would be very critical, because it would imply an accident at an already congested part of the road network. Again, such a situation would trigger the alarm of local authorities. WrongWayDriver(?a) ∧ AbnormalTraffic(?b) ∧ rcc-5:PO(?a, ?b) ∧ opra1:FrontFront(?a, b?) ∧ spatDistBoundary:VeryClose(?a, ?b)

situation assessment. For each state of affairs, a simple graphic depicts the valid objects, which are, for reasons of brevity, located on the same carriageway of the same highway. Note that the driving direction is from the right to the left and there are several junctions at which one may leave or enter the highway. The object classes are represented by classic traffic signs and different shadings. The spatial extent of all objects is indicated by the boxes surrounding them.

Below each state of affairs, Table 2 provides the assessed situations followed by a description of the aspects covered by the example. The first column *Id*, which contains the identifier for a situation, is followed by the instantiated situation type and the column *Concrete Match*—the formalization of the assessed situation. The last three columns provide three distance measures based on our function *D*. For this scenario, *D* is the average distance of all relations that contribute to a situation. The distance per relation, i.e. the number of transitions from one relation to another, is normalized by the length of the longest non-cyclic path between any pair of relations in the corresponding CNG (e.g. DR to PO takes one hop, the length of the longest path in rcc-5 is 2, thus, the normalized distance is 1 / 2 = 0.5). D is not defined for situations with different objects. $D_{\leftarrow}$ and $D_{\rightarrow}$ indicate the distance from the previous and to the next landmark situation type in a course of events; both are just determined for trigger or clearance phases, whereas $D_{\sim}$, the distance from a climax situation type, just applies to climax situations.

Summing up the core of our case study, we have demonstrated our approach by applying it to a scenario involving all the previously defined, relevant traffic

Table 2. The scenario and the corresponding results of situation assessment

t_i		Scenario			
	Id	$S_i[T_i|C_i]$	Concrete Match	$D_{\leftarrow}$	$D_{\rightarrow}$ $D_{\sim}$

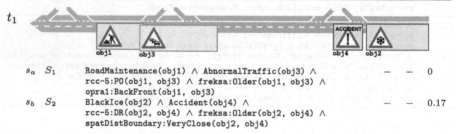

t_0

	s_a	$S_1 T_0$	RoadMaintenance(obj1)	0	n.d. —

This state of affairs is an example for an assessed *trigger* situation with a *missing object* (the AbnormalTraffic). The triggered course of events is brought to the operator's attention, although we can not determine the minimal distance to the climax situation. Contrarily, the area of BlackIce is consciously *not* instantiated, because we have not defined a corresponding trigger situation type for S_2.

t_1

	s_a	S_1	RoadMaintenance(obj1) ∧ AbnormalTraffic(obj3) ∧ rcc-5:PO(obj1, obj3) ∧ freksa:Older(obj1, obj3) ∧ opra1:BackFront(obj1, obj3)	— —	0
	s_b	S_2	BlackIce(obj2) ∧ Accident(obj4) ∧ rcc-5:DR(obj2, obj4) ∧ freksa:Older(obj2, obj4) ∧ spatDistBoundary:VeryClose(obj2, obj4)	— —	0.17

Whereas s_a has *evolved* to its *climax*, an Accident has been reported near an increasing area of BlackIce. Although the actual situation is just *similar* to the corresponding climax situation type, it matches with some deviation. The situation causes the traffic operator to dispatch a warning to motorists advising them to drive with extreme caution.

t_2

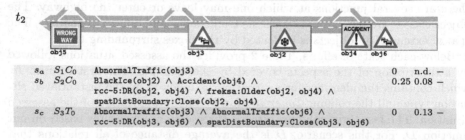

	s_a	$S_1 C_0$	AbnormalTraffic(obj3)	0	n.d. —
	s_b	$S_2 C_0$	BlackIce(obj2) ∧ Accident(obj4) ∧ rcc-5:DR(obj2, obj4) ∧ freksa:Older(obj2, obj4) ∧ spatDistBoundary:Close(obj2, obj4)	0.25	0.08 —
	s_c	$S_3 T_0$	AbnormalTraffic(obj3) ∧ AbnormalTraffic(obj6) ∧ rcc-5:DR(obj3, obj6) ∧ spatDistBoundary:Close(obj3, obj6)	0	0.13 —

Table 2. (*continued*)

t_i		Scenario				
	Id	$S_i[T_i|C_i]$	Concrete Match	$D_\leftarrow$	$D_\rightarrow$	$D_\sim$
	s_d	S_4T_0	WrongWayDriver(obj5) $\wedge$ AbnormalTraffic(obj3) $\wedge$ rcc-5:DR(obj5, obj3) $\wedge$ opra1:FrontFront(obj5, obj3) $\wedge$ spatDistBoundary:Commensurate(obj5, obj3)	0	0.33	–

The operator has reacted and cancelled the RoadMaintenance. Thus, s_a is in its *clearance* phase which will eventually end when the chunk of AbnormalTraffic *disperses*. At the same time, the area of BlackIce has moved and, because of winter maintenance, shrunk. Therefore, s_b has evolved—in this case due to the *transition* of its contributing *relations*—to a state of affairs shortly before final *clearance*. Moreover, the Accident has caused AbnormalTraffic, which seems to be growing together with the existing chunk of AbnormalTraffic. In addition, a WrongWayDriver suddenly emerges. The operator informs police of the detected WrongWayDriver and the imminent large chunk of AbnormalTraffic (s_c, s_d). Both situations *may evolve* to their climax by a *transition* of their contributing *relations*, what is reflected by the available distance measures.

t_3

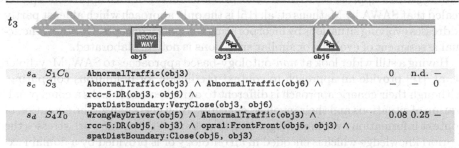

	s_a	S_1C_0	AbnormalTraffic(obj3)	0	n.d.	–
	s_c	S_3	AbnormalTraffic(obj3) $\wedge$ AbnormalTraffic(obj6) $\wedge$ rcc-5:DR(obj3, obj6) $\wedge$ spatDistBoundary:VeryClose(obj3, obj6)	–	–	0
	s_d	S_4T_0	WrongWayDriver(obj5) $\wedge$ AbnormalTraffic(obj3) $\wedge$ rcc-5:DR(obj5, obj3) $\wedge$ opra1:FrontFront(obj5, obj3) $\wedge$ spatDistBoundary:Close(obj5, obj3)	0.08	0.25	–

Thanks to the previously notified fire department, the Accident and, hence, situation s_b have been finally cleared. Whereas s_c has evolved to its *climax* by a *transition of relations*, s_d is not yet there. Note that especially s_d reveals the shortcomings of the simple distance function—although just two possibly concurrent transitions are left, the distance measure to the climax situation is rather high.

t_4

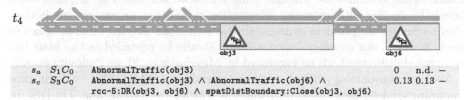

	s_a	S_1C_0	AbnormalTraffic(obj3)	0	n.d.	–
	s_c	S_3C_0	AbnormalTraffic(obj3) $\wedge$ AbnormalTraffic(obj6) $\wedge$ rcc-5:DR(obj3, obj6) $\wedge$ spatDistBoundary:Close(obj3, obj6)	0.13	0.13	–

Finally, the WrongWayDriver has vanished, what causes s_d to disappear as a result of the *trivial clearance* situation types. Moreover, in anticipation of the WrongWayDriver rushing into the already large chunk of AbnormalTraffic, the operator has diverted road traffic away from the highway what resulted in the diminution of AbnormalTraffic. In fact, situation s_c is in its clearance phase, because of the transition of the contributing relations.

situation types. Although the scenario as a whole will scarcely happen in this compact form in real-life, the single situations are typical for road traffic management. During situation assessment, both our goals, i.e. the notification of operators of emerging and similar climax situations, have been demonstrated by corresponding examples. Moreover, various distinguishable aspects of evolution have been illustrated. In short, we have dealt with courses of events involving missing objects as well as evolutions based on transitions of relations.

5   Related Work

Searching for the notion *situation* in related work from different research communities, one discovers that, although many of them—intentionally or not—share some common grounding, the actual conceptualization is payed varying attention. For example, whereas the information fusion community has identified situations as the key to informed decision making [3] more than a decade ago, explicit representations of situations have not such a long tradition in approaches to SAW for ubiquitous computing (e.g. [14]).

Starting with closely related work, it is first of all interesting to note that there are currently, to the best of our knowledge, no specialized, formal ontologies for the area of SAW in road traffic management. Thus, we increase the scope of related work beyond the road traffic management domain and examine domain-independent *ontology-based* approaches to SAW. Our previous survey of such approaches [6] revealed that SAWA by Matheus et. al. [15] is the only approach which at least partly addresses evolving situations by incorporating temporal concepts. However, the actual assessment of evolving or similar situations is not yet elaborated.

Having a still wider look at *non*-ontology-based approaches to SAW, Mayrhofer et. al. [16] provide an approach to context prediction for ubiquitous computing. Although their generic approach is different to ours, because it lacks a conceptualization of situations and their involved concepts, they also analyze the evolution of context information over time. Regarding this characteristic, our work stresses the a priori knowledge which is encoded in an ontology or is provided by a domain expert in contrast to the probabilistic approach followed by Mayrhofer et. al. Widely related is also the work by Padovitz et. al. (e.g. [17]). Again with respect to ubiquitous computing, they propose context spaces, a generic, multi-dimensional approach to model situations. Though being similar to Mayrhofer et. al., their work focuses on dealing with imprecise information rather than on context prediction, what resembles our problem to assess similar situations. Having different goals in mind, however, our ontology-based solution should be regarded as the *basis* for, e.g., probabilistic methods as suggested by Mayrhofer et. al. or Padovitz et. al.

Another non-ontology-based work we examine is BABY-SIT—a logic programming environment based on *Situation Theory* by Akman and Tin [18]. In their work, they give an overview of systems akin to BABY-SIT and make ontological commitments that are closely related to our conceptualization of situations. Although they do not mention the assessment of similar situations, they use methods alike forward chaining in order to model and infer evolutions of situations. On the one hand, this approach is, like ours, based on the a priori knowledge about situation types. On the other hand, we further lift this a priori knowledge from situation types to the constructs available for defining them, i.e. the conceptual neighborhoods of relations. This leads to an implicit definition of evolution which results in simpler specifications of situation types. Similarly related is McCarthy's *Situation Calculus* and its derivative by Reiter [19] which focus on planning actions and inferring their effects. Although we may clearly face these problems if, for example, we want to plan the actions of a traffic operator in order to avoid climax situations, it is currently beyond the scope of our work—we just deal with the perception of situations and their possible evolution without any *explicit* actions.

Only recently, similarity measures for instances of ontology concepts, which is the final and farthest related work, have been proposed (e.g. [20]). In short, our approach substantiates parts of these domain-independent similarity measures with respect to SAW by the provision of conceptual neighbors of situations.

6 Discussion and Future Work

In this paper, we have proposed a method to assess evolving and similar situations in ontology-based approaches to SAW. Subsequently, our approach, which is mainly based on conceptual neighborhoods of relations that contribute to situations, has been demonstrated in form of a case study in the road traffic management domain. The case study involved an ontology for road traffic SAW, a formalization of relevant situation types, and the application of our approach to assess these situation types in a complex, real-world scenario. Although our approach performs as expected, we want to point out that we just regard it as a novel basis for traditional approaches to SAW. The bottom line is that one should incorporate the a priori knowledge encoded in ontologies or available from domain experts in situation assessment processes.

In the course of our work, we have also identified some open issues. The most prominent one is the distance function D which should be more sophisticated in order to obtain a more realistic behaviour. For example, it should provide distances for the co-occurrence of objects or should enable weights indicating the contribution of a family of relations to a situation type. A further issue is the current focus on evolutions of relations. A complete approach should also consider evolutions of intrinsic attributes for situation assessment. Another matter are interdependencies between families of relations (e.g. externally connected objects imply zero distance between their boundaries) which may result in inconsistent, not reachable neighborhoods that could further restrict the search space. The final issue is the incorporation of scheduled or forecast information which would raise the evidence that a situation actually evolves into a subsequent landmark situation. Thus, statements about the probability of a concrete evolution would be possible.

Regarding future prospects of our work, we are currently developing a software framework for SAW which is based on the approach proposed in this paper. In the near future, we are going to deploy a prototypical implementation of this framework for the road traffic domain in order to support traffic operators achieving SAW in complex road traffic management scenarios.

References

1. Barwise, J., Perry, J.: Situations and Attitudes. MIT Press, Cambridge (1983)
2. Gruber, T.R.: A translation approach to portable ontology specification. Knowledge Acquisition 5(2), 199–220 (1993)

3. Llinas, J., Bowman, C., Rogova, G., Steinberg, A.: Revisiting the JDL data fusion model II. In: Proc. of the 7th Int. Conf. on Information Fusion, Stockholm, Sweden, pp. 1218–1230 (2004)
4. Endsley, M.: Theoretical Underpinnings of Situation Awareness: A Critical Review. In: Situation Awareness Analysis and Measurement, pp. 3–33. Lawrence Erlbaum Associates, New Jersey (2000)
5. Baumgartner, N., Retschitzegger, W., Schwinger, W.: Lost in time, space, and meaning—an ontology-based approach to road traffic situation awareness. In: Proc. of the 3rd Workshop on Context Awareness for Proactive Systems, Guildford (2007)
6. Baumgartner, N., Retschitzegger, W.: A survey of upper ontologies for situation awareness. In: Proc. of the 4th IASTED Int. Conf. on Knowledge Sharing and Collaborative Engineering, St. Thomas, USVI, pp. 1–9 (2006)
7. Baumgartner, N., Retschitzegger, W.: Towards a situation awareness framework based on primitive relations. In: Proc. of the IEEE Conf. on Information, Decision, and Control, Adelaide, Australia, pp. 291–295. IEEE Computer Society Press, Los Alamitos (2007)
8. Cohn, A.G., Bennett, B., Gooday, J.M., Gotts, N.: RCC: A calculus for region based qualitative spatial reasoning. GeoInformatica 1, 275–316 (1997)
9. Clementini, E., Felice, P.D., Hernandez, D.: Qualitative representation of positional information. Artificial Intelligence 95, 317–356 (1997)
10. Freksa, C.: Temporal reasoning based on semi-intervals. Artificial Intelligence 54(1), 199–227 (1992)
11. Moratz, R., Dylla, F., Frommberger, L.: A relative orientation algebra with adjustable granularity. In: Proc. of the Workshop on Agents in Real-Time and Dynamic Environments (2005)
12. Bruns, H.T., Egenhofer, M.J.: Similarity of spatial scenes. In: Proc. of the Conf. on Spatial Data Handling, Delft, The Netherlands, pp. 31–42 (1996)
13. DeSouza, G.N., Kak, A.C.: Vision for mobile robot navigation: A survey. IEEE Trans. Pattern Anal. Mach. Intell. 24(2), 237–267 (2002)
14. Dey, A.K., Abowd, G.D.: Cybreminder: A context-aware system for supporting reminders. In: Thomas, P., Gellersen, H.-W. (eds.) HUC 2000. LNCS, vol. 1927, pp. 172–186. Springer, Heidelberg (2000)
15. Matheus, C.J., Kokar, M.M., Baclawski, K.: A core ontology for situation awareness. In: Proc. of the 6th Int. Conf. on Information Fusion, Cairns, Australia, pp. 545–552 (2003)
16. Mayrhofer, R., Radi, H., Ferscha, A.: Recognizing and predicting context by learning from user behavior. Radiomatics: Journal of Communication Engineering 1(1), 30–42 (2004)
17. Padovitz, A., Loke, S.W., Zaslavsky, A.B., Burg, B., Bartolini, C.: An approach to data fusion for context awareness. In: Dey, A.K., Kokinov, B., Leake, D.B., Turner, R. (eds.) CONTEXT 2005. LNCS (LNAI), vol. 3554, pp. 353–367. Springer, Heidelberg (2005)
18. Tin, E., Akman, V.: Situated nonmonotonic temporal reasoning with BABY-SIT. AI Commun. 10(2), 93–109 (1997)
19. Reiter, R.: Knowledge in Action: Logical Foundations for Specifying and Implementing Dynamical Systems. MIT Press, Cambridge (2001)
20. Albertoni, R., Martino, M.D.: Semantic similarity of ontology instances tailored on the application context. In: Proc. of the 5th Int. Conf. on Ontologies, DataBases, and Applications of Semantics, Montpellier, France, pp. 1020–1038 (2006)

Conceptual Analysis of Interdisciplinary Scientific Work

Pieter J. Beers[1] and Pieter W.G. Bots[1,2]

[1] Delft University of Technology, The Netherlands
p.j.beers@tudelft.nl
[2] Cemagref, Groupement Montpellier, France
pieter.bots@cemagref.fr

Abstract. The main advantage to interdisciplinary professional practice is that it can produce novel product designs and problem solutions. However, it requires knowledge sharing and integration to leverage this potential. This paper reports on a study with a method of conceptual analysis to elicit, analyse and compare conceptual models used by individual researchers, with the ultimate aim to facilitate researchers in sharing and integrating their conceptual notions. We build on an earlier study by extending an existing conceptual model with conceptual notions from two additional researchers from an interdisciplinary research project. The results of the present study suggest that the time costs of adding more information to the existing model diminish with each addition to the existing model, and that the method of conceptual analysis can validly represent researchers' conceptual notions. Furthermore, our results offer some indication that conceptual analysis can reduce transaction costs related to grounding.

Keywords: Conceptual analysis, interdisciplinary research, knowledge sharing, knowledge integration.

1 Introduction

The main advantage to interdisciplinary professional practice is that it can bring together multiple disciplinary and domain perspectives to produce novel product designs and problem solutions [1]. It requires knowledge sharing and integration to leverage this potential. Researchers and practitioners from different disciplines have therefore sought to facilitate such knowledge sharing and integration. In the social sciences, researchers have stressed the importance of knowledge being implicit, 'sticky', and difficult to formalise [2]. In this view, learning occurs through what is called "the legitimate peripheral participation of individuals in groups" [3], and knowledge is seen as situated and socially constructed [4]. In the information sciences, researchers have emphasised the potential of systems that make codified knowledge ubiquitously accessible as information with well-defined semantics [5]. In this view, people learn from each other by exchanging information, and knowledge takes the form of explicit, externally available information [6].

Although these views seem to present a choice [7], we believe that the characteristics of interdisciplinary scientific practice call for an attempt at synthesis.

B. Kokinov et al. (Eds.): CONTEXT 2007, LNAI 4635, pp. 43–55, 2007.

First, scientific practice is a social endeavour and the resulting theories and paradigms have been shown to be social constructs [8], the meaning of which is negotiated [9]. Second, in science there are explicit rewards on knowledge sharing. For instance, scientists are increasingly judged by their yearly number of publications and their citation indices [10]. In fact, *not* sharing knowledge is frowned upon, and knowledge externalisation is explicitly rewarded [11]. Third, scientific knowledge is particularly formalised in comparison with other fields of profession [12]. Science uses definitions, theories, conceptual models and even formal models to capture knowledge, and the scientific method involves formal validity criteria, such as replicability of experiments and reproducibility of results [13].

Knowledge in scientific practice thus is socially constructed meaning, but also characterised by a high degree of explicitness (on account of rewards for sharing), and a high degree of formalisation (on account of generally accepted methodological principles). The method of conceptual analysis we put forward in this paper should therefore combines elements from both the social sciences perspective and the information sciences perspective. It focuses on the conceptual models underlying scientific work. It aims to uncover the concepts that are necessary to describe a researcher's disciplinary knowledge and how these concepts are related (cf. [14, 15]). This produces a highly explicit account of a researcher's knowledge that allows him/her to reflect on it and compare it with / relate it to the knowledge of other researchers, thus affording knowledge sharing and integration.

The method we propose, in particular the construction of an overarching conceptual model that it involves, may give the impression that we believe that disciplinary differences can be resolved by unification of knowledge in a single 'true' model of reality. This is not the point we want to make. The conceptual analysis should be seen as a hermeneutic activity in the spirit of Gadamer (see e.g. [16]), and the models it produces as a trigger for researchers to partake in such an activity and as a means to facilitate them in gaining an understanding of the languages other researchers use.

In a previous paper [17], we reported on an exploratory study in which we performed a first test of our method in the context of a multidisciplinary research project. In that study, the method was found to be effective in eliciting concepts, also those used implicitly. In addition, interview data revealed certain strategies and mechanisms by which researchers adopt new concepts and choose terms. However, the analysis costs were very high, while the benefits remained uncertain. In this paper we report on a follow-up study within the same research project, involving conceptual analysis of the work of two additional researchers. The aims of this follow-up study were (1) to extend the initial conceptual model derived in the previous study, (2) to fine-tune our procedure so as to make it less labour- and time-intensive, while preserving its validity, and (3) to reflect on the viability of the method.

We have structured our report as follows. We start by arguing why we believe that conceptual analysis has good potential to support interdisciplinary knowledge construction. We then describe our method in a formal way as well as on a more practical level. Next, we describe some selected results, permitting ourselves a few illustrative examples while focusing on those observations that reveal certain problems that seem inherent to the method. In the final section, we summarise our findings and draw some tentative conclusions.

2   Facilitating Interdisciplinary Knowledge Construction

We realise that when writing about conceptual analysis, our own concepts must be clear. We define a '*multi*disciplinary research project' as a project in which at least two researchers a and b, with knowledge and skills particular to different disciplines A and B, participate with the objective of producing *new* scientific knowledge k. Assuming that a and b are individually capable of producing new knowledge K_A and K_B, their project becomes *inter*disciplinary only when k is such that $k \notin K_A \cup K_B$, that is, that k could not have been produced within disciplines A or B alone.

New, interdisciplinary knowledge k comes about by induction from empirical observation when researchers a and b work on some empirical phenomenon that they cannot fully explain using concepts from A or B. It requires that both a and b (1) can meaningfully relate k to their respective disciplinary knowledge, (2) have sufficient understanding and awareness of each other's knowledge to be able to accept that k is related to both disciplines, and (3) agree that their understandings of k are similar enough for their current purposes of collaboration (cf. [18]). In other words, they need to negotiate some *common ground* as to the meaning of k and its relation to their respective disciplines.

Such 'grounding' processes have high transaction costs, that is, they require much time and effort from researchers, resources that can be allocated more efficiently to mono-disciplinary research. Empirical studies of interdisciplinary research [19, 20] show that the incentive structures in the present institutional context impede interdisciplinarity. While these structures remain, we should try to lower the transaction costs of 'grounding'. We believe that conceptual analysis may help to achieve this.

Conceptual analysis of domains A and B produces a set of definitions that affords researchers a and b more explicit knowledge about their own disciplinary knowledge and about how the concepts in A and B do (and do not) relate to each other. It enables them to exchange knowledge without the need for a "globally shared theory" [21]. To achieve common ground, a and b must each discover what they have in common (i.e., A∩B) and extend their 'language' to A+C and B+C where C consists of the concepts needed to better understand the empirical phenomenon they investigate. We expect that conceptual analysis will lower

- the cost of discovering A∩B because the results of a conceptual analysis of A and B are explicit and can be re-used when other researchers from A and B engage in interdisciplinary research
- the cost of negotiating the concepts in C because the process of conceptual analysis provides focus and rigour to the grounding process, which leads to a concise and unambiguous set C that is easier to relate to the concepts in A and B, especially when these also have been rendered concise and unambiguous
- the cost of mutual misunderstandings due to homonyms and synonyms in the discourses of a and b [22], which, when undetected at first, may pose much difficulty later [23].

Our aim is to offer researchers in interdisciplinary teams explicit information about the relation between their and others' knowledge by enabling meaningful conceptual comparisons while avoiding labour-intensive group negotiations. Our first study [17] showed that conceptual analysis is a valid means to this end, but also suggested that our method would be too time-consuming to be adequate. In the follow-up study we therefore wished to address these questions in particular:

1. Do the marginal costs of conceptual analysis diminish for every additional researcher included in the analysis?
2. Does the structure of scientific articles permit selective reading without loss of validity of the conceptual analysis?

3 Methodology

To be able to precisely describe our methodology for this follow-up study, we first define our method of conceptual analysis. We will then outline the empirical context and the more specific methods we used in our data collection and analysis.

3.1 Conceptual Analysis

A conceptual model is defined as a 3-tuple $M = (C, R, Q)$ where C is a set of concept types, R a set of relation types between these concept types, and Q the set of question types that can be answered using M. The analysts aim to conceptually model the knowledge that is generated and/or used by the participants $P = (p_1, ..., p_n)$. To that end they peruse the scientific articles produced by each person p_i and codify the knowledge it contains in n separate conceptual models. Ideally, for each of these models $M_i = (C_i, R_i, Q_i)$,

- C_i contains all concept types used (explicitly or implicitly) by researcher p_i
- R_i contains all relation types between these concept types (i.e., of the type $r \subset C_i^j$ for some $j \geq 2$) used (explicitly or explicitly) by researcher p_i
- Q_i contains the questions that researcher p_i seeks to answer, expressed (insofar as possible) in terms of elements of C_i and R_i

The analysts also construct a conceptual model $M = (C, R, Q)$ that can be conceived of as the 'master model', because for all i, $C_i \subseteq C$ and $R_i \subseteq R$. The sets in M will necessarily be larger than the union of their respective subsets in the models M_i because the 'master model' should answer questions that are typically not posed by the individual researchers, so the analysts will have to define additional relation types (notably to represent incompatibility) and possibly additional concept types as well (for example, to explicitly represent the researchers and their disciplinary perspective).

The analysis process involves a series of operations performed by analysts:

1. Select the set of researchers P
2. For each $p_i \in P$, select a set A_{pi} of scientific articles (co-)authored by p_i and relevant to the interdisciplinary research project under study
3. Initialise the 'master model' M. Note that this need not imply that $M = (\emptyset, \emptyset, \emptyset)$, because C, R and Q will at the onset contain the generic concepts, relations and questions that are used by analysts (notably the methodological concepts, such as 'researcher', 'concept', and 'relation')

4. Initialise the conceptual model for each researcher, which here does imply that $M_i = (\emptyset, \emptyset, \emptyset)$ for $i = 1..n$

Then iterate over the following five steps:

5. Select and peruse a scientific article $a \in A_{pi}$, searching for potential concepts
6. For each potential concept, determine whether there is a corresponding $c \in C_i$. If not, determine whether there is a corresponding $c \in C$. If not, add c to C. Add c to C_i
7. Peruse article a in search for relations involving c
8. For each relation, determine whether there is a corresponding $r \in R_i$. If not, determine whether there is a corresponding $r \in R$. If not, add r to R. Add r to R_i
9. Periodically check whether M_i is coherent. If it is not, see if an explanation can be found (implicit concepts and relations? poor line of argument?)
10. Peruse article a in search for research questions q. If needed, rephrase q in terms of C and R. Determine whether there is a corresponding $q \in Q_i$. If not, determine whether there is a corresponding $q \in Q$. If not, add q to Q. Add q to Q_i

The main challenge for the analysts is to define the elements of C and R. The analysts must not only develop an adequate understanding of the concepts and relations used (explicitly or implicitly) by the researchers involved, but also resolve the problem of homonyms and synonyms, choosing words to define the elements of C and R in such a way that

-   the elements of C and R allow valid representation of *all* concepts and relations used by the researchers involved (completeness);
-   the definitions can be understood not only by the analysts, but also by the researchers p_i and permit them to validate 'their' model M_i (comprehensibility); and
-   C and R do not contain more elements than necessary to achieve the previous two goals (parsimony).

3.2 Empirical Context

Project. Our research is part of the Next Generation Infrastructures program (NGI, see http://www.nginfra.nl), an international, multi-university, interdisciplinary research effort that comprises projects in fields ranging from applied mathematics to philosophy of technology, and from information sciences to spatial planning. The NGI program focuses on infrastructures for energy supply, transport, telecommunications, and water: large-scale socio-technical systems of high and increasing societal and economic importance.

Participants. The four junior researchers P1, ..., P4 that took part in our research all work on the Understanding Complex Networks theme of the NGI project. P1 investigates innovative methods for research, learning and intervention based on multi-actor simulation and gaming, P2 explores industrial ecology and agent-based simulation of infrastructure development, P3 studies the use of distributed energy generation with micro-combined-heat-and-power generators as an alternative to classic, centralised electricity generation in power plants, with the aim to increase energy efficiency, and P4 uses game-theoretical insights to mathematically analyse tolling strategies to alleviate traffic congestion.

Articles used in the analysis. We asked the participants for their recent writings pertaining to their NGI project. This yielded three conference papers for P1, four conference papers and a book chapter in preparation for P2, seven conference papers for P3, and six conference papers and an unsubmitted manuscript for P4. These writings of the participants served as data for our analysis.

Models. In our first study [17], we used the writings of P1 and P2 to construct 'their' conceptual models M_1 and M_2, and the encompassing master model M. In the follow-up study we report in this paper, we constructed the conceptual models M_3 and M_4 and updated the master model M.

3.3 Practical Methods

The previous section covers operations 1 through 4 of our method of conceptual analysis. To perform operations 5 through 9 we qualitatively analysed the participants' writings using open coding (cf. [24, 25]). Rather than coding excerpts directly as concepts, relations or questions, we first classified them according to a small set of content type categories [17]:

1. Real-world Notions: Statements that refer to abstract and / or concrete aspects of what the researcher considers as the real world
2. Model-world Notions: Statements that refer to formal or informal representations of such real-world notions
3. Techniques: Statements about a modelling technique used by the researcher
4. Model: Statements about the model used and / or developed by the researcher
5. Real-world Questions and Aims: Research questions and aims pertaining to the real-world
6. Model-world Questions and Aims: Research questions and aims pertaining to scientific theory
7. Case: Statements about a research case or research client.

The excerpt categories were then analysed in search for concepts c, relations between concepts r, and / or research questions / aims q. The meaning inferred from the excerpts pertaining to a new element was recorded in one or more short phrases. Together, the summaries of all excerpts thus define the elements C_i, R_i and Q_i.

To test the validity of these summaries, the first author conducted a semi-structured interview with each participant. The analyst informed the participant in general terms about the approach that had been taken for the content analysis, paying special attention to the categories that were used to structure the data. During the interview, the analyst read aloud the category summaries for the participant's research. Three questions were repeatedly asked throughout the interview:

1. Is there anything in the summary that is unclear to you?
2. To what extent does the summary match your research:

   a. Does the summary contain elements that are not part of your research? And if so, which?

   b. Does your research contain elements that are not part of the summary? And if
     so, which?
   c. Does the summary contain errors? And if so, which?
3. Do you have any further comments on the summaries?

The first question aimed to get any problems in understanding out of the way. The
second question focused on whether the summaries (a) contained misinterpretations,
(b) were complete, and/or (c) contained errors. The third question was aimed at
improving the summaries.

3.4 Differences in Procedure Between the Studies

In the original study, all articles were read and categorised in their entirety, and each
category was analysed for the presence of new concepts. On the one hand, this
procedure is very reliable in the sense that the chances of missing conceptual
information are very low, and therefore it yielded valid results. However, it also
required reading and analysing redundant material, and the associated time costs were
high. In the present study, we did not categorise all writings, nor did we analyse all
categories. Instead, we used a strategy of selective reading: we only categorised an
excerpt if it did not contain redundant material, and we only analysed excerpts in the
real-world notions and model-world notions categories, because we expected the
other categories not to contain additional concepts. These alterations were expected to
result in less time costs, but also to incur a risk of lower validity.

4 Results

The study reported is a small-scale test of our method of conceptual analysis. We
carried out all the steps necessary to complete the analysis for researchers P3 and P4,
and added this new data to the results obtained for P1 and P2. Reading the papers and
summarising the data cost about one week, which amounts to one third of the time in
the first study, for the same number of researchers. A detailed presentation and
discussion of the resulting models M_3, M_4 and the extended master model **M** are
beyond the scope of this paper. Instead, we wish to give the reader an idea of the type
of results the analysis yields, and we present some aspects of the validity of the
procedure

4.1 Extending the Master Model

The most important difference between the present study and the previous one is that
the initial model **M** was not empty, but instead already contained the concepts from
the first analysis [17]. If indeed model convergence takes place, then concepts
identified in the previous study should be usable in the present analysis. To show that
this was the case we use a subset of the previous analysis, which contains definitions
of a number of concepts regarding systems (see Table 1).

    The analysis showed that, in total, about 35% of the concepts in M_3 and M_4 were
already present in **M**. Using systems-related concepts as an example, P3 uses the
concepts "system" "subsystem," "system state," "system change," "technical system,"

"social system" and "socio-technical system" in his work. In the specific case at hand, all those similar concepts already present in **M** can be used to fill M_3. Of the concepts in table 1, P4 only used "system", so **M** was less useful for describing P4's convictions related to systems. Nevertheless, the data show that concepts from earlier, related conceptual analysis efforts can be used to partially fill conceptual models of additional researchers. Thus, one is spared the effort of starting from scratch with every new topic that an additional researcher brings in.

Table 1. Excerpt from the Original Master Model

Concept	Definition
System	A bounded, coherent part of reality consisting of elements within an external environment
System environment	The part of reality outside the system that can influence the system
Subsystem	S1 is a subsystem of S0 when the system elements of S1 are a subset of the system elements of S0 and they are structured the same way
System structure	The system elements and the (type of) relations that exist between them
System state	The system at some moment in time
System change	The difference between the state of system S at some moment in time t1 and the state of S at some previous moment in time t0
Artefact	Some thing that is the product of human action, dividable into physical artefacts and social artefacts
Natural system	A system that does not contain any artefacts
Technical system	A system that contains at least one physical artefact
Social system	A system that contains at least one social artefact
Socio-technical system	System consisting of at least one technical system and one social system that are mutually influencing each other, i.e., their respective system boundaries have common elements

The analysis of the writings of P3 enabled us to elaborate on the notion socio-technical systems, by introducing the notions of institutional domain and economic domain as aspects of the notion of social system. This means that an existing model **M** can be used as a source of conceptual definitions to begin describing the convictions of an additional researcher. Also, the model M_3 could next be used to extend and improve upon **M**. For instance, from M_3 additional concepts about systems were added to **M**. To name a few:

- "system level" – a subsystem that relates hierarchically to other subsystems;
- "system heterogeneity" – the extent to which a system consists of parts that are mutually different;
- "system organisation" – the way the various subsystems relate to each other; and
- "hierarchy" – example of system organisation in which decisions taken in one subsystem (higher level) can impose rules on another subsystem (lower level).

The analysis also yielded two homonyms that were present both in **M** and in M_3, but had different meanings. One example was "emergence", as the following dialogue between analyst (A) and participant (P3) shows:

A: "Emergence means that system behaviour can not be directly deduced from the behaviour of the different parts of the system."

P3: "That concept of emergent behaviour is not so clear in different stories. . . . . Some say that emergence is nothing more than a question of adding things; that is just deductivist, reductionist, . . . others bring in a lot of higher stuff, and in between those there are lots of other variants. . . . . You might say that the market price comes about through emergent behaviour of the economy, but it still follows logically from what everybody's doing. So it follows directly from local behaviour."

From the interview data it appears that the participant's conception differs from the definition offered by the analyst, in that the participant assumes that the total behaviour of a system can be understood from the behaviour of the system's parts, whereas according to the definition in **M** it can not. For **M**, this means that the present definition of emergence had to be altered, and another had to be added, so both "versions" of emergence could be expressed with concepts in **M**.

In sum, concepts from **M** could be used to initialise the participants' models M_3 and M_4. Furthermore, the analysis of P3 and P4 could be used to enrich **M**. In some cases the analysis explicated conceptual tensions between participants, for instance, when one word appeared in both **M** and a participant's model, while still referring to different concepts in each of the models, tensions that the analyst then resolved by adding more fine-grained definitions with terms that resolved the homonyms.

4.2 Issues of Validity

Neither participant P3 nor P4 found any part of our summary of their writings unclear. Furthermore, neither summary contained elements that the participants thought did not belong there. Both participants made many additions throughout the interviews. However, these additions did put validity at issue, because either they could not have been drawn from the data, or they did not pertain to conceptual notions, for instance when a participant added information about results. This finding suggests that it indeed is sufficient to analyse only those excerpts coded real-world notions and model-world notions. In some cases, however, the participants did make corrections to the summaries proposed by the analyst.

The interview data contained several statements that are important with regard to the validity of our approach. First, there were two examples in the interview data in which a participant expressed ambiguity regarding a certain concept. In both cases, the concepts were important to the paper in which they were mentioned, but not essential to the participant's work. The first example is the relation between "complexity" and "interactivity":

P3: "[Interactivity] also changes the complexity of a system. Or perhaps it is more of an enabler for complexity. I'm not sure whether it then would be an aspect of complexity."

A: "So it is an aspect and not an enabler?"

P3: "If I'd have to choose then I'd say yes. But maybe you could just as well make a case for an enabling role. . . . It hasn't yet been necessary for me to make such choices."

From the interview data it appears that the participant's model-world notions have not fully matured, whereas related concepts are already present in his writings.

The second example was a case in which the information in the papers actually differed from the participant's convictions. At first it appeared that the analyst had misinterpreted the participant's work with regard to the meaning of the concept of multi-level decision-making. In the case of multi-level decision-making, decisions are made at two levels that are hierarchically related to each other. The decisions made on one system level influence the decisions made on another level. The analyst's interpretation was that the higher level constrained the decision space of the lower level, and thus that the influence was unidirectional. However, in the interview it became clear that in the participant's conception, the constraints on the decision spaces were mutual, and therefore not the criterion by which the different decision-making levels were distinguished. The actual difference is in power and authority:

P3: "The higher level has more power, more authority. That's why you define it as the higher level. . . . . The thing that matters is the power to decide about certain parameter-settings."
A: "That very precise difference [between constraints and authority to make decisions]. Did I gloss over that while reading your paper?"
P3: "You didn't miss that. . . . In a number of publications . . . I have formulated it in this way, as it has been written down in these papers. But I didn't look in the more fundamental work to find . . . what the formal characteristics of a multi-level decision-making exercise are."
A: "So my interpretation would be justified on the basis of what I have read?"
P3: "Yes."

Another phenomenon affecting validity was the occurrence of interpretational differences between analyst and participant. In some cases, it was clear that there was a conceptual difference in understanding between analyst and participant, which could not be explained by the data. One such case was the concept of "full information":

A: "[In your research,] different actors have different information, so nobody has full information."
P4: "No, in the deterministic models everybody is assumed to have full information, while in the stochastic models . . . there is some random component which they don't know. . . . The travellers always have less information than the road authority." . . . .
A: "So full information then really means that they have all information they need for their decision."
P4: "Yes."

From the interview data, the analyst appears to assume that "full information" means access to all information available to all actors in a system, whereas the participant uses it in the sense that an actor has access to all information it needs in order to make a decision. The difference is that there is information in the system that some actors do not need. Imagine the case where an actor has all the information it needs to make a decision, but not all information available within the model. Initially, the analyst would have concluded that the actor did not have full information, whereas the participant would have concluded that it did.

In sum, the interview data yielded two ways in which validity might be negatively influenced by the procedure. First, participants included concepts in their papers while not having made final decisions regarding their meaning. It may thus be the case that in the data one conceptual conviction may be present, whereas the participant him/herself holds a different, or an additional conviction. Second, the interview data revealed cases where the analyst's interpretation of the data differed from the participant's intended meanings. These cases could only be identified with use of the interviews, and could not be derived from the data alone.

5 Conclusion and Discussion

Interdisciplinary scientific practice requires scholars with different disciplinary backgrounds to share and integrate their knowledge. To that end it is important that they have a correct understanding of each others' contributions. In this paper we have introduced a method for conceptual analysis, built on the assumption that eliciting the participants' conceptual models $M_1, \ldots, M_n$ and constructing a master model M can enhance this process. The master model M is expected to reduce transaction costs of grounding by making it easier to identify the concepts that are shared between researchers, and identifying which are potentially different. In this paper, we addressed two questions regarding the effects, validity and viability of the method.

1. Do the marginal costs of conceptual analysis diminish for every additional researcher included in the analysis?

   With regard to the goal of reducing transaction costs due to grounding, the results lend some credence to the conclusion that conceptual analysis provides such reduction. This conclusion can be drawn from the fact that we used the master model M to initialise the participants' models M_3 and M_4, which enabled identification of differences and similarities between all models. In other words, comparison of a new conceptual model M_i with the master model M can give insight in differences and similarities between the new model M_i and *all* models that are represented in M. Without the use of M this would have had to be done via comparisons of M_i with all other models M_j.

2. Does the structure of scientific articles permit selective reading without loss of validity of the conceptual analysis?

   Our results indicated that it indeed is sufficient to analyse only those excerpts coded Real-world Notions and Model-world Notions. Although the participants did add information to the analysis, such additions did invalidate the method, because either they could not have been drawn from the data, or they did not pertain to conceptual notions. It seems that our strategy of selective reading did not lead to an under-representation of conceptual content. However, the interview data did yield two ways in which validity might be negatively influenced by the procedure. Participants included concepts in their papers while not having made final decisions regarding their meaning, and there were cases where the analyst's interpretation of the data differed from the participant's intended meanings. These cases could only be identified with use of the interviews, and could not be derived from the data alone.

Thus, the results show that even when the procedure is made less rigorous and time-consuming, it can still produce valid conceptual models from researchers' writings. However, it has also become clear that doing interviews should not only be included for validation purposes, but also to allow for corrections on the analysis. The interview data have indicated that unwarranted differences in interpretation may occur if no interviews are conducted. Therefore they must be included in the procedure, which will have the unfortunate side-effect of making it more time-consuming.

In sum, the present study has indicated that conceptual analysis can be used to validly identify a researcher's conceptual notions. Furthermore, the results suggest that only a small part of the total amount of data is actually needed in the analysis. This results in a reduction in time costs compared to our first study of conceptual analysis. However, the results also indicated that validatory interviews should be used to check, and in case of problems, modify the analysis. Although conceptual analysis initially takes some effort, this effort appears to diminish with every new researcher who's work is added to the analysis. This appeared to be due to convergence of the master model **M**: concepts that already exist in **M** can be used for initialising conceptual models of additional researchers. This latter result also indicates that conceptual analysis can reduce transaction costs related to grounding.

References

1. Lomi, A., Larsen, E.R., Ginsberg, A.: Adaptive learning in organizations: A system-dynamics-based exploration. Journal of Management 23, 561–582 (1997)
2. Von Hippel, E.: 'Sticky Information' and the locus of problem solving: Implications for innovation. Management Science 40, 429–439 (1994)
3. Wenger, E.: Communities of practice: Learning, meaning and identity. Cambridge University Press, Cambridge (1998)
4. Brown, J.S., Collins, A., Duguid, P.: Situated cognition and the culture of learning. Educational Researcher 18, 32–42 (1989)
5. Staab, S., Studer, R., Schnurr, H.-P., Sure, Y.: Knowledge processes and ontologies. IEEE Intelligent Systems 16, 26–34 (2001)
6. Davenport, T., De Long, D., Beers, M.: Successful knowledge management projects. Sloan Management Review 39, 43–57 (1998)
7. Swan, J., Newell, S., Scarbrough, H., Hislop, D.: Knowledge management and innovation: Networks and networking. Journal of Knowledge Management 3, 262–275 (1999)
8. Latour, B.: Science in action: How to follow scientists and engineers through society. Harvard University Press, Cambridge (1987)
9. Wenger, E.: Communities of practice and social learning systems. Organization 7, 246–255 (2000)
10. Hasan, H., Gould, E.: Support for the sense-making activity of managers. Decision Support Systems 31, 71–86 (2001)
11. Scardamalia, M., Bereiter, C.: Computer support for knowledge-building communities. Journal of the Learning Sciences 3, 265–283 (1994)
12. Fuchs, S.: The professional quest for truth: A social theory of science and knowledge. State Univerity of New York, Albany (1992)
13. Ehrenberg, A.S.C., Lindsay, R.M.: The design of replicated studies. The American Statistician 47, 217–228 (1993)

14. Guarino, N.: Formal ontology, conceptual analysis and knowledge representation. International Journal of Human-Computer Studies 43, 625–640 (1995)
15. Jackson, F.: From metaphysics to ethics: A defence of conceptual analysis. Clarendon Press, Oxford (1998)
16. Kinsella, E.A.: Hermeneutics and critical hermeneutics: Exploring possibilities within the art of interpretation. Forum Qualitative Sozialforschung / Forum: Qualitative Social Research 7, Art. 19 (2006)
17. Beers, P.J., Bots, P.W.G.: Eliciting conceptual models to support interdisciplinary research. In: Sprague, R.H. (ed.) 40th Hawaii International Conference on System Sciences, Computer Society Press, Los Alamitos (2007)
18. Clark, H.H., Schaefer, E.F.: Contributing to discourse. Cognitive Science 13, 259–294 (1989)
19. Leroy, P.: Sciences environnementales et interdisciplinarité: une réflexion partant des débats aux Pays-Bas. Natures Sciences Sociétés 12, 274–284 (2004)
20. Tress, B., Tress, G., Fry, G.: Researchers' experiences, positive and negative, in integrated landscape projects. Environmental Management 36, 792–807 (2005)
21. Gruber, T.R.: Toward principles for the design of ontologies used for knowledge sharing. International Journal of Human-Computer Studies 43, 907–928 (1995)
22. Van Someren, M.W., Reimann, P., Boshuizen, H.P.A., De Jong, T. (eds.): Learning with multiple representations. Elsevier, Oxford (1998)
23. Beers, P.J., Boshuizen, H.P.A., Kirschner, P.A., Gijselaers, W.: Common ground, complex problems and decision making. Group Decision and Negotiation 15, 529–556 (2006)
24. Marton, F.: Phenomenography - A research approach to investigating different understandings of reality. Journal of Thought: An interdisciplinary quarterly 21, 28–49 (1986)
25. Strauss, A.L.: Qualitative analysis for social scientists. Cambridge University Press, Cambridge (1987)

Towards a Methodology for Context Sensitive Systems Development

Tarek Ben Mena[1,2], Narjès Bellamine-Ben Saoud[1], Mohamed Ben Ahmed[1], and Bernard Pavard[2]

[1] RIADI-GDL / ENSI University of Manouba, Tunisia
[2] IC3-IRIT University Paul Sabatier Toulouse, France
tarek.benmena@riadi.rnu.tn, narjes.bellamine@ensi.rnu.tn,
mohamed.benahmed@riadi.rnu.tn, pavard@irit.fr

Abstract. The aim of this paper is to present a methodology for context sensitive systems development. Based on a generic definition of context, the proposed methodology allows modeling of contexts for a specific system with different abstraction level. This methodology can be integrated in the classical engineering process. The application of this methodology for the development of an agent based simulator for social complex systems allows us to define a context model for social and cooperative multiagent systems.

1 Introduction

The context concept plays a crucial role in various disciplines such as the pragmatic ones, the semantics of natural language, linguistics, cognitive psychology, and the artificial intelligence (AI).

In AI, the context is used in several various sectors. It was only towards the end of the Eighties and the beginning of the Nineties that the context became a largely discussed issue. Giunchiglia [1] and McCarthy [2] started to work on a formal theory of context. The goal was to explain the properties of the context and the contextual reasoning in a systematic way. Since, the context was employed in various types of knowledge representations and reasoning applications and more and more context sensitive systems were developed. In this case, several questions are highlighted: at which phases of engineering process should we introduce contexts for this kind of systems? What must be taken into account? What to put in these contexts? and how to model context?

As knowledge engineering which is interested in knowledge structuring and reasoning on it and since the context is a set of knowledge (in broader sense), we can think about context engineering which is interested in context structuring and reasoning according context. Whereas, Roque et al. [3] define context engineering as a framework to organize ideas about previous development experience. Our attempt is to present generally a context engineering definition and especially a methodology for contextual systems design.

In this article, in section 2, we present some context definitions and design methodologies founded in literature. In section 3, we propose a definition of the

B. Kokinov et al. (Eds.): CONTEXT 2007, LNAI 4635, pp. 56–68, 2007.

context notion, and then a methodology of context identification and construction while developing context sensitive systems. In section 4, we present a case study of applying our methodology on an agent based simulator development in order to support organizing emergency rescue plans for a large-scale accident.

2   Background

2.1   What Is a Context? A Generic Definition

As soon as the context has been more or less considered in many AI related fields, and in different ways, we notice that defining context univocally is a hard issue. Although, Giunchiglia and Bouquet [4] tempted to give a unified definition, it becomes too general especially by defining context like an infinite set of "things". The importance of the context notion for modeling human activities (reasoning, perception, language comprehension, etc.) is an established fact as well in social sciences as in computing. The traditional approaches of AI highlighted the theoretical difficulties associated to formalization of this concept. Indeed, within framework of representational AI theories, context can be identified with difficulty by a finite list of factors [5], [2]. These difficulties will be reflected on the proposition of a generic context definition. In fact, in cognitive sciences, [6] presents the context like a manner of structuring knowledge and its use in problems resolution tasks. In Logic, McCarthy [2] states that each time we fix an axiom, a criticism can say that the axiom is not true only in a certain context where this context supposes capture all what is not explicit in the axiom. For [7] the context at the moment t is the office plurality of the situations between t_0 and t for the realization of a task by the user. In multiagent systems, Bucur [8] defined the context like a pair made up of finality, and a set of contextual informations called contextual attributes.

According to definitions presented above, we notice that context definitions and characteristics vary according to the framework of context use, the nature of the future use of context and of the future developed system. Nevertheless, there are recurring key questions i.e. "invariants" characteristics in the definitions such as the context relates always to an entity, is used to solve a problem, depends on the scope of use (domain) and time, and also that context is evolutionary by regarding it as a dynamic process in a dynamic environment and not as a set of states [9].

2.2   Context and Design Methodologies

In literature, we notice the absence of clear approach allowing identification and building of the adequate context to take into account during the context sensitive systems development. There are few attempts to associate context to engineering process. The majority of the proposals for methodologies found in literature [10], [11], [12], [13] present methodologies of software engineering which are interested specifically in context-aware systems development. Taking context into account is hidden in engineering process. Some integrate it into the requirements analysis level, others into conceptual one. We do not find in these methodologies clear stages to follow from the beginning of a development process to its end taking context into account. We can then say these methodologies do not take into account context identification with the classical engineering process. [14] proposed an approach based upon the use of multi-context systems for a general method of defining architectures for logic-based agents which can be directly executed. [3] presented context engineering for the information systems development as taking context into account in the engineering process not in developed system. It is a framework to organize ideas about previous development experience. [15] presented a similar idea for systems development methodology enactment.

For us, 'context engineering' is a branch of software engineering which treats design, development and manufacture of systems sensitive to context, at the same time hardware and software. Context engineering allows the construction of content-based systems with dynamic reasoning and contexts integration in knowledge representation and reasoning.

3 Discussion and Propositions

3.1 From a Generic Context Definition ...

According released "invariants" characteristics, we suggest defining context as an abstract notion. Firstly, we state that defining and studying context depend closely on the domain, and application nature. For example, in an agent based simulator development, where agents are sensitive to context, defining context depends on a study of the multiagent systems(MAS) domain and of which developer want to simulate. Often, the context is always confused with domain. Domain represents the possible world where is located a study, a development process, a work, an analysis, etc.

Secondly, we can say that the context is at the same time an abstract and a relative notion because it has meaning only related to its object (e.g. a sentence, an agent, a user, etc.) that we call the entity of context. In fact, context is always related to an entity; for example the context of a sentence, the context of an agent, of a task or also the context of the user. Moreover, context cannot exist without the entity to which it is attached. Thus, we cannot speak about context in an absolute way. This entity belongs to a domain and its type is fixed by the domain nature. An entity can be a proposal, a sentence, a concept, an object, an agent, a task, a process, the user, a system, a device, etc.

Thirdly, it is notable that the context, in context sensitive system development and particularly in reasoning and decision making, is used to facilitate comprehension, to remove ambiguities, to clear up a situation, to improve a decision-making, to make a choice, to optimize a treatment, to simplify a resolution, etc. We can then say that the context helps to solve a problem. Since the problem to be solved depends on the world in which we are located i.e. domain.

Consequently, on the basis of these three statements, we can say that Context at a high level of abstraction depends on a triplet $< Domain, Entity, Problem >$.

In other words, within a specific given domain, an entity has (or is subject to) a problem, requires a context to solve it. For example, in linguistics (Domain) as soon as a sentence (Entity) causes ambiguities (Problem), we require a Context for its comprehension. Also, in multiagent systems (Domain), an agent (Entity) which needs to make a decision (Problem) requires a Context to reason and decide. In context-aware systems (Domain) a device (Entity) requires a context to adapt its treatment (Problem).

These three concepts are closely inter-related and the definition of each of them depends on the definition of both others. Indeed, an entity belongs to a domain and the problem can be explicitly defined only in one domain [16]. Domain is characterized by a set of elements (entities), relations between them such as functions, operations, rules and constraints on the elements. It represents also the problem resolution world. For example, domain of linguistics is the set of symbols, words, sentences, languages, semantic rules, grammatical rules, spelling, etc. To summarize, an entity is an element of the set of elements constituting a specific domain. Moreover, a problem is always connected to an entity in a domain and can be solved only with the elements of that domain (rules, constraints, axioms, etc.).

We point out that the context is relative to an entity. So, it is necessary to define the context content of each entity by determining its characteristics, the characteristics of the other entities and those of the relations by taking into account some of the following dimensions: physical, cognitive, linguistic, social, cultural and emotional.

- Physical dimension considers what refers to the physical environment in which the entity is and refers to the external state of other entities.
- Cognitive dimension is taken into account only in the case of cognitive entities. It represents knowledge, objectives, goals, attitudes, intentions, beliefs, competences, etc.
- Social or relational dimension considers what is in relation with organization or in interaction with the entity, considers also roles played by these entities.
- Cultural dimension is the set of implicit knowledge and beliefs shared by the various entities.
- Emotional dimension: is related to the internal entity state.
- Linguistic dimension: considers the semantic contents in the event of messages exchange between entities.

These six kinds of dimensions are a summary of all kinds we found in literature, mainly in [17], [18], [19]. According to the target of the system to be developed, several or all these dimensions can be considered.

3.2 . . . to a Contextual Systems Engineering Process

We notice that the context definition presented in the preceding section is at the same time generic and abstract. It is defined in an abstracted conceptual level and thus it can be used and applied only by the means of an approach making it possible to get from the conceptual abstracted level to a concrete operational one.

Thus, on the basis of the context definition (see section 3.1), we present hereafter a methodology allowing to identify and build context according to the system to be developed and mainly requirements specifications. This process of context building belongs to engineering process and must be done in parallel with it. We consider that engineering process is composed of a requirements analysis, a global design, a detailed design, and a realization stage. The context building process can so be divided to 3 phases: conceptualization which defines the conceptual model of context, contextualization which defines the contextual model and to finish operationnalisation. Each one of these phases will be detailed in the following sections. Figure 1 shows the parallelism between the engineering process and the context identification process and shows also possible connections between them. This context identification process is an extension of the traditional engineering process. Our aim is to introduce context in the system engineering process. The conceptualization of the context model should be integrated in the system global design. The contextualization process which defines the contents of the context, will be made on the same level as the detailed design. We notice even an analogy in the level of abstraction. Indeed, in one hand, global design (high abstraction level) handles modules, packages and meta-models. Analogically we find the same thing in conceptualization as the conceptual model. In the other hand, In detailed design and contextualization (low abstraction level), we find respectively classes attributes and context contents.

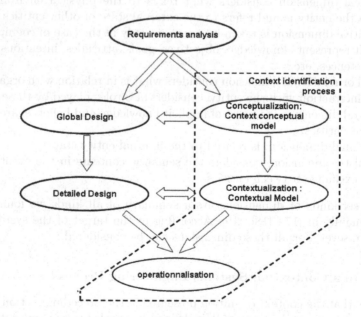

Fig. 1. Context identification process in engineering process

In this global process, we start by a common stage: the requirements analysis which is an informal study of system functions without technical analysis. It is a stage that allows understanding and defining problems to be solved by locating it in a precise domain which is closely related to the final requirements or aims.

Conceptualization: In this phase, we consider as entry informal functionalities study of context sensitive application to develop. We set as hypothesis that the conceptualization can be done in a non ambiguous way only in a specific domain [16]. In the first stage, a functional analysis will allow designer to identify the domain where the system will be developed, for example agent based simulation, context-aware systems, Human Machine Interaction systems. This domain can be decomposed into sub domains and analyzing them allows the identification of intervening elements in the development process. During the stage of domain identification, designers identify firstly the set of entities composing the domain and the relations between them and classify entities by types. We point out that an entity must be atomic and the level of granularity depends on the designer. From this selection of entities, it is necessary to define those which will be context sensitive. In the second stage, this study allows also identifying sub problems to solve those related to requirements. It's worth noting that analysis and problem identification can never be complete nor exhaustive. The third stage of this phase consists of a mapping between entity set $\{e_1, e_2, ..., e_n\}$, and problems set $\{p_1, p_2, ..., p_m\}$. In this mapping, we assign to each entity, the problems that it must solve and assign to each problem the entities which are dependent on (entity which must solve it and entities related to it by relations)(Fig. 2). We mention that it is also possible to make this mapping between the set of entities types and set of sub problems. The model represented by these entities and relations between them represent the context conceptual model. This conceptual model represents the context meta-models. Therefore, the context model of an entity is an instantiation of this meta-model. To each type of entity taken context into account will be associated a specific context conceptual model.

Contextualization

Definition 1. *The context c_i of an entity e_i for the resolution of problem p_k is defined as the set of entities e_j $(j \neq i)$ related to p_k and in relation with e_i and set of relations $R_{i,j}$ between e_j and e_j.*

In this phase, starting from the conceptual model and based on the definition 1 (see Fig. 2), we define the possible contexts related to each entity for each problem. The next stage is contexts contents structuring with a semi-formal knowledge representation.

The following stage is the structuring of contexts themselves by the construction of relations and hierarchies between various contexts relating to the same entity and by the construction of relations and hierarchies between various contexts relating to the various entities. This association will allow determining shared contexts (common part to various contexts of the various entities).

To finish, it is necessary to define two reasoning types, the first related to the extraction of context i.e., in the case of the autonomous entities, they should be

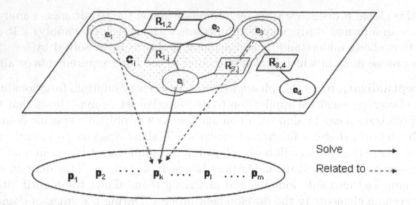

Fig. 2. Context of an entity for a problem resolution

able to identify their own context by themselves and the second reasoning is for the action relating to the problem solving according to the context: what we call contextual reasoning. In this last stage, it is also necessary for supplementing reasoning to define operations on contexts as update, fusion, intersection and difference. Thus, we obtain what we call contextual model.

Operationalisation: This phase focuses on the contextual model transcription in a formal and operational language of knowledge representation. This work must be undertaken by the knowledge engineer. It should be noted that this process is iterative ; many loops are necessary to build operational contexts adapted to the system and requirements. let us notice to finish that this process of context identification is bottom-up, i.e. one starts with entities to represent knowledge on which they are dependent, to lead to a formal representation. But a top-down construction is also possible, which consists in choosing an operational model of representation, according to the aim of context use, then with instantiation of this model with the entities of domain.

4   Case Study: Agent Based Virtual Environment of Accident Emergency Rescue

4.1   Overview of the Case Study

In this case study, we intend to develop an agent based simulator in order to support organizing emergency rescue plans of a large-scale accident. A catastrophic situation can be defined as a situation where there is brutal inadequacy between needs for help and available resources. The purpose of rescue plans is to manage the rescue process in catastrophic situation and accidents at large scale. All rescuers collaborate to minimize losses by evacuating the most victims and reducing delays.

In this study, decision-making is far from being an easy task especially in the case of social complex systems operating under many constraints and utilizing several human resources, several technical features which collaborate and cooperate according to evolutionary social networks and via various communication networks.

In fact, these social agents must reason dynamically according to the system evolution and adapt their behavior to the current situation. In this case, decision is not only one choice among several alternatives, but it depends on experience of the decision maker and his capacity to recognize the situation where he is involved. Social agents must thus take into account context while reasoning. Analysis of real rescue activities has been conducted in collaboration with medical experts and based on French rescue plans ORSEC, Red Plan, White Plan [20] in order to understand the collaborative process. Based on the emergency analysis, a first agent-based model and simulator was constructed [21].

4.2 Application of Context Identification Methodology

We already said that the context identification process is done in parallel with the traditional engineering software process. In the case of multiagent systems (MAS) development process, the stage named global design (Figure 1) represents a stage of agentification where agents and their roles are identified.

Phase 1: Conceptualization. Firstly, in conceptualization phase, we start by defining the three components of the context: domain, problems and entities. In this case, one should not confuse the application domain which is the multiagent systems with the use application domain which is the agent based simulation of the emergency rescues. The identification of use application domain will be taken into account in the agentification phase and the identification of the application domain will be taken into account in the conceptual model. In fact, agent based simulator of emergency rescue is a multiagent system. We are interested at the beginning to a high level analysis (multiagent domain). Conceptualization of MAS domain will enable us to identify entities types. However, conceptualizing rescue emergency domain enable us to identify entities which are instantiation of entities types founded in a higher level. Indeed rescuers (human actors) will be represented by agents (entity types).

Domain identification: It is difficult to define an entire multiagent system domain in some lines; we summarize the main concepts related to this domain. Multi-agents systems domain is composed of elements such as environment, objects, relations between objects, agents characteristics: knowledge, beliefs, intentions, desires, roles, goals, capacities, perception, reasoning, etc.

From a particular point of view, by taking again multiagent definitions according to [22] and [23] we can generalize the modeling of such system according to the three following concepts: Agent, Object and Relation.

We notice that objects encapsulate part of knowledge on the world (environment) in which they evolve. The environment is largely described by the objects. We can say that the environment is constructed only by the objects that belong to it. From a conceptual view, the agent has knowledge relating to various objects which constitute the environment. The characteristics of these objects can be implicitly propagated in the environment and then we consider them as environment characteristics. We can then simplify the problem by assigning to the agent the knowledge related to the environment.

In suggested agent definitions, the agent must be able to perceive and act on environment, to communicate and interact with the other agents, to obey to a standard of organization [24], [25], [26], [22], [23]. Thus, we can consider multiagent system as relations between agents themselves and objects constituting the environment. Indeed, we will distinguish:

- Simple n-ary relations between two objects or a set of objects O* for example an object is above another: Relation = R (O*, O*)
- Action of an agent on another one or on object is a relation between Actant and the entity which undergoes action A, O. This relation has the capacity to change the entity state having it undergoes: Action = R (A, A, O)
- Perception of the environment (objects and other agents which surround the observer) is a relation between agent and percept object which surrounds it (objects O*, agents A* perceived and relations between them R (A*, O*) and R (O*, O*)): Perception = R (A, O*, A*, R (A*, O*), R (O*, O*))
- Interaction is a relation of information exchange (communication and collaboration) between agent and one or more agents A*: Interaction = R (A, A*)
- Organization is a relation of hierarchy between several agents A* to carry out their common objective: Organization = R (A*, A*)

This domain analysis allows us to define a context meta-model for multiagent systems. In fact, entities which are sensitive to context are agents. An agent context must contain the other objects and agents, relation between them and information about environment (see Fig. 3) are represented with UML[1] notation.

Problem identification: The problem to be solved depends on the application domain. In this case, problem is an agent decision-making in front of evolutionary and non deterministic situations. The problems in this application domain are multiple. We briefly present them here. We can quote the global one which is rescuing the maximum of victims in a minimum of time by taking into account various constraints and specific ones: to move away a victim because fire can approach, to refuse an order to satisfy an extreme emergency, etc. All these problems can be solved in the most optimal possible way only in one given context relative to the solver entity.

Entity identification: After this application domain analysis, it is obvious that the central entity of this domain is the agent which represents the principal Actant in this case. Indeed, the tasks of resolutions of the identified problems will be assigned to various agents. The global problem resolution will be the common objective of the agent society and sub-problems resolution will be individual objectives and goals of agents. The resolution of a problem by an agent represents

---

[1] Unified Modeling Language.

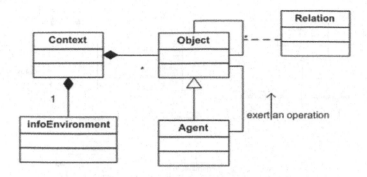

Fig. 3. Meta-model of context for multiagent systems

the Role affected to it and which will be carried out in an instantaneous situation. The agent must be able to reason dynamically in front of an evolutionary environment and thus must be context-aware.

Phase 2: Contextualization

Contextual Model: In preceding phase we defined the conceptual model which is composed of agents, objects and 5 kinds of relations: simple relation, perception, action, interaction and organization. We get now to structuring context contents according to entities and relations defined during the first phase. We point out that the entity is the agent and that context is related to agent we must then describe the system from entity point of view. An agent is characterized by its autonomy. However, an agent will have a subjective vision of context: its goal is to collect information (what requires a certain capacity of recognition of context) related to its problem, in order to fix a resolution space; it will define the context like a set of conditions and surrounding influences which make the situation single and make it possible to understand it [27]. Considering an agent A, we propose that the context must contain information on:

- Agent A itself: its knowledge, believes, internal state, roles, goals, competences, (cognitive, cultural, emotional dimensions)
- Environment perceived by A (physical dimension)
- particularly perceived objects (physique dimension) : static and dynamic characteristics
- Other agents : identifier, position, goals, competences (cognitive, social, cultural dimensions),
- Nature of known relations between objects including agents from the agent A point of view: perception, action, interaction, communication organization (social and linguistic dimensions).

Agent Building and Using Context: We describe in the following section, the process of context identification by an agent A face with a situation. A plays several roles characterized by a set C of competences $Cp = \{cp_j\}$:

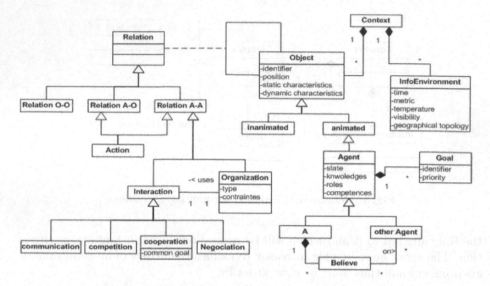

Fig. 4. Context model for cooperative MAS from Agent A point of view (UML notation)

(1) *Information collection:* perception of environment, other objects and agents. In this stage A constructs in his mind (knowledge) a cognitive representation (in the form of graph having as nodes agents and objects connected by relations) based on instance of agents (rescuers, doctors, firemen, etc.), objects (obstacle, dangerous zones, fire, etc.) and relation (communication, action, etc.). Thus, this social representation is an instance of conceptual model (general context). From this perception and its goals list, A

    (a) identifies a set of perceived problems P, associates to each a priority degree and sorts them in decreasing priority order $P = \{pi/i \in N\}$ where i is the priority.

    (b) Scans this sorted list problem, seeking the first problem p_k which it can solve item with a competence cp_j from Cp.

    (c) If there $i > k$ i.e. problem priority greater than p_k, A informs the most suited agent able to solve p_i. The choice of suited agent is done from its cognitive representation especially from knowledge on agent's competences.

(2) *Context identification:* reasoning to define context from acquired knowledge and from new collected knowledge. In this stage A will parse its cognitive representation and identify the suited context for selected problems. This context identification is based on context definition presented in Definition 1 where entities are agents and objects. For an agent its context for selected problem is agents and objects with their characteristics and environment information related to selected problem.

(3) *Context categorization:* comparison of recognized context and with existing contexts in a contexts base to benefit from the experiment. In this stage A

will compare identified context to old ones for executing suited behavior to solve p_k. In the case of no profitable comparison, agent executes behaviors associated to its set of competence Cp.

(4) *Learning:* addition of the new context in the base of contexts. In this stage agent will learn from its experience and add this context to context base.

5   Conclusion and Future Work

In this article, we presented a methodology allowing design of context sensitive systems. We started from a generic context definition presented as a triplet $< domain, entity, problem >$ to propose an integration, in the traditional engineering process, of complementary stages which are done in parallel with the old ones and which allow to focus on context. Thus, these stages of conceptualization, contextualization and operationnalisation allow defining and modeling contexts to be taken into account during the development of the system. We tried to apply this process on a case of study in the Domain of Multiagent Systems for the development of a simulator of social cooperation. The application of the stages enabled us, initially, to define a meta-model of context for the multiagent systems, and then to refine it in the second stage. For the contextual reasoning we limited ourselves to present a process allowing agent to identify the adequate context for the resolution of a problem. The third phase of the process still requires an improvement to choose the best means of system operationnalisation. We also think of applying this methodology to other types of application in other fields such as linguistics for the computational linguistics or also for interactive systems.

References

1. Giunchiglia, F.: Contextual reasoning. In: proceedings of the IJCAI'93 Workshop on Using Knowledge in its Context LAFORIA, pp. 39–48 (1993)
2. McCarthy, J.: Notes on Formalizing Context. In: Proceedings of the 13th International Joint Conference on Artificial Intelligence, Chambery, France, pp. 555–560 (1993)
3. Roque, L., Almeida, A., Figueredo, A.D.: Context Engineering: An IS Development Approach (2003)
4. Giunchiglia, F., Bouquet, P.: Introduction to Contextual Reasoning An Artificial Intelligence Perspective. In: Kokinov. B (eds.) Perspectives on Cognitive Science, vol. 3, pp. 138–159 (1996)
5. Guha, R.V.: Contexts: A Formalization and Some Applications. Unpublished doctoral dissertation, Stanford University (1991)
6. Sperber, D., Wilson, D.: Relevance: Communication and Cognition. Basil Blackwell, Oxford (1986)
7. Gaëtan, R.: Systèmes interactifs sensibles au contexte. Unpublished doctoral dissertation, Polytechnic National Institute of Grenoble ENSIMAG, France (2001)
8. Bucur, O., Beaune, P., Boissier, O.: Representing Context in an Agent Architecture for Context-Based Decision Making. In: Serafini L., Bouquet P. (eds.) Proceedings of the CRR'05 Workshop on Context Representation and Reasoning (2005)

9. Brézillon, P.: Représentation de pratiques dans le formalisme des graphes con-textuels. In: Bastien, J.M.C. (ed.) Actes des Deuxèmes Journées d'étude en Psychologie Ergonomique (2003)
10. Anliker, U., Junker, H., Lukowicz, P., Troster, G.: Design methodology for context-aware wearable sensor systems. In: Gellersen, H.-W., Want, R., Schmidt, A. (eds.) PERVASIVE 2005. LNCS, vol. 3468, pp. 220–236. Springer, Heidelberg (2005)
11. Bolchini, C., Schreiber, F.A., Tanca, L.: A context-Aware Methodology for Very Small Data Base Design. Sigmod 33(1), 71–76 (2004)
12. De Virgilio, R., Torlone, R.: A General Methodology for Context-Aware Data Access. In: MobiDE'05, Baltimore, Maryland, pp. 9–15 (2005)
13. Ozturk, P.: Towards a knowledge-Level Model of context and context use in Diagnostic Problems. In: Applied intelligence 10, pp. 123–137. Kluwer Academic Publishers, Boston (1999)
14. Parsons, S., Jennings, N.R., Sabater, J.: Agent specification using multi-context systems (2002)
15. Rowlands, B.H.: The user as social actor: a focus on systems Development methodology Encatement, SAC'06, Dijon, France, pp. 1540–1545 (2006)
16. Furst, F.: L'ingénierie ontologique, Technical Report, Computing Research institute of Nantes, France, No 02-07 (2002)
17. Kaenampornpan, M., O'Neill, E., Kostakos, V., Warr, A.: classifying context classifications, an activity theory perspective. In: 2nd UK-UbiNet Workshop, University of Cambridge (2004)
18. Dey, A.k., Abowd G. D.: Towards a Better understanding of context and context-Awarness. In: At the CHI 2000 Workshop on the What, Who, Where, When, Why, How of context-Awareness (2000)
19. El Jed, M., Pallamin, N., Pavard, B.: Towards rich context virtual worlds. In: proceedings of the International workshop on Context: Cooperative Systems and Context (Context 2005) Paris, France (2005)
20. Ecollan, P.: Le plan blanc, Unpublished doctoral dissertation, Faculty of Medicine Pitié-Salpêtrière, Paris, France (1989)
21. Bellamine-Ben Saoud, N., Ben Mena, T., Dugdale, J., Pavard, B.: Assessing large scale emergency rescue plans: an agent based approach. The International Journal of Intelligent Control and Systems 11(4), 260–271 (2007)
22. Ferber, J.: Les Systèmes Multi-Agents, vers une intelligence collective. InterEditions (1995)
23. Demazeau, Y.: From interactions to collective behaviour in agent-based systems. In: Proceeding of the 1st European Conference on Cognitive Science, Saint Malo, France, pp. 117–132 (1995)
24. Russell, S.J.: Rationality and intelligence. Artificial Intelligence 94, 57–77 (1997)
25. Wooldridge, M., Jennings, N.R.: Agent theories, architectures, and languages. Intelligent Agents, pp. 1–22 (1995)
26. Shoham, Y.: Agent-oriented programming. Artificial Intelligence 60, 51–92 (1993)
27. Brézillon, P.: Context in Artificial Intelligence: I. A Survey of the literature. The Knowledge Engineering Review 14(1), 1–34 (1999)

Meaning, Contexts and Justification

Claudia Bianchi[1] and Nicla Vassallo[2]

[1] University Vita-Salute San Raffaele, Faculty of Philosophy, Palazzo Borromeo, I-20031
Cesano Maderno (MI), Italy
`claudia2.bianchi@hsr.it`
[2] University of Genova, Department of Philosophy, via Balbi 4, I-16126 Genova, Italy
`nicla@nous.unige.it`

Abstract. Contextualism in philosophy of language and in epistemology are two distinct but closely entangled projects. The epistemological thesis is grounded in a semantic claim concerning the context-sensitivity of the predicate "know": we gain insight into epistemological problems by investigating our linguistic intuitions concerning knowledge attribution sentences. Our aim here is to evaluate the plausibility of a project that takes the opposite starting point: the general idea is to establish the semantic contextualist thesis on the epistemological one. According to semantic contextualism, virtually no sentences of a natural language express complete propositions – meaning underdetermines truth conditions. In our paper, instead of assuming the traditional view of meaning in terms of truth conditions, we suggest that a theory of meaning as justification may shed new light on the contextualist approach. We thus show how the notion of justification can be contextualized, arguing that our attempt provides an interesting and quite straightforward way of contextualizing meaning.

1 Introduction

Epistemological contextualism and semantic contextualism are two distinct but closely entangled projects in contemporary philosophy. According to epistemological contextualism, our knowledge attributions are context-sensitive.[1] That is, the truth-conditions of knowledge ascribing sentences – sentences of the form of

(1) S knows that *p* -

vary depending on the context in which they are uttered: the predicate "know" is context-dependent. According to the classic view in epistemology, knowledge is justified true belief. Invariantism claims that there is *one and only one* epistemic standard for knowledge. On the contrary, contextualism admits the legitimacy of *several* epistemic standards that vary with the context of use of (1); it is right to claim – for the same cognitive subject S and the same proposition *p* – that (1) is true in one context, and false in another.

---

[1] Cf. DeRose (1992), (1996), (1999), (2002), and (2004); Cohen (1999); Hawthorne (2004); Stanley (2004).

B. Kokinov et al. (Eds.): CONTEXT 2007, LNAI 4635, pp. 69–81, 2007.
© Springer-Verlag Berlin Heidelberg 2007

The epistemological contextualist thesis is grounded in a semantic claim about the context-sensitivity of the predicate "know": we can gain insight into epistemological problems[2] by investigating our linguistic intuitions concerning knowledge attribution sentences. Broadly speaking, the semantic thesis grounding epistemological contextualism is that a sentence of the form (1) does not express a complete proposition. Different utterances of (1) can, in different contexts of utterance, express different propositions. The proposition expressed by a knowledge attribution is determined in part by the context of use: we must add in information about the context in order to determine the proposition expressed by (1). If we fill in the gaps by appealing to low epistemic standards, (1) might be evaluated as expressing a true proposition; if, in a different context, we fill in the gaps by appealing to high epistemic standards, (1) might be evaluated as expressing a false proposition.

Many scholars have tried to spell out the semantic contextualist thesis on which epistemological contextualism is grounded.[3] Their goal is to examine various kinds of linguistic context dependence, and to assess their relevance to epistemological contextualism: ellipsis, ambiguity, indexicality, context-sensitivity of scalar predicates and dependence on standards of precision.

Our general aim in this paper is to evaluate the plausibility of a project that takes the opposite starting point, i.e. that of establishing the semantic contextualist thesis on the epistemological one. Our paper is structured as follows. In section 2 a standard version of semantic contextualism is presented. According to contextualism in philosophy of language, the truth conditions of any sentence are not fixed by the semantics of the sentence: different utterances of the same sentence can, in different contexts, express different propositions. In section 3 a theory of meaning is sketched according to which the meaning of an assertion is its justification: our account is based on Wittgenstein's view of language and Dummett's theory of meaning as justification. In section 4, following Annis (1978), we show how the notion of justification can be contextualized. S may be justified in uttering p in context C_1, but not justified in uttering p in context C_2: justification depends on a specific issue-context, which determines the appropriate objector-group. In section 5 and in the conclusion, we argue that if Annis' attempt is sound, it could provide an interesting and quite straightforward way of contextualizing meaning.

2   Semantic Contextualism

As Kent Bach rightly points out, epistemological contextualism is a semantic thesis about a given expression, or a family of expressions – namely about "know" and knowledge-ascribing sentences. According to Bach, this sort of contextualism is not to be confused with contextualism in philosophy of language. Here the term is used for a radical thesis concerning virtually *all sentences*: no sentences express complete propositions – meaning underdetermines truth-conditions.[4]

---

[2] Especially skepticism: see DeRose (1995) and Williams (1999).
[3] Cf. Schiffer (1996), Stalnaker (2004), Stanley (2004), Partee (2004), Bianchi & Vassallo (2005), and DeRose (2005).
[4] Bach (2005), p. 54n.

2.1 The Standard View

First of all, let us briefly characterize the traditional image of language.[5] According to the Standard View in semantics, the expressions of a natural language have stable meanings fixed by language conventions, and truth conditions determined once and for all. More particularly: a) every expression has a conventional meaning - a meaning determined by the form of the expression; b) the meaning of a sentence is identified with the truth conditions of the sentence; c) the meaning of a complex expression is a function of the meanings of its parts.

2.2 Semantic Underdetermination

According to the Standard View, if we abstract from ellipsis, ambiguity and indexicality strictly understood[6], it is possible to attribute truth conditions to a sentence independently of its context, that is in virtue of its meaning alone. Over the past thirty years, however, linguists and philosophers have begun to underline the phenomenon of *semantic underdetermination*, that is the fact that the encoded meaning of the linguistic expressions employed by a speaker underdetermines the proposition explicitly expressed by the utterance. According to contextualism[7], most sentences of a natural language do not express complete propositions, and hence do not have fixed truth-conditions – even when unambiguous and devoid of indexicals. Every utterance expresses a proposition only when completed and enriched with pragmatic constituents that do not correspond to any syntactic element of the sentence (neither an explicit constituent, as in cases of syntactic ellipsis, nor a hidden indexical present at the level of the logical form of the sentence) and yet are part of the semantic interpretation of the utterance.

2.3 Wittgenstein, Searle and Travis

Contextualism is a view suggested by the later Wittgenstein. The motto "meaning is use"[8] is one of the most notorious and controversial of Wittgensteinian theses. Ordinary language philosophy[9] and, as a result, contemporary contextualism are based on interpretations of this very thesis: to understand a word is to know how to use it.

---

[5] Held by philosophers and logicians like Gottlob Frege, Bertrand Russell, the earlier Ludwig Wittgenstein, Alfred Tarski and Willard Quine, and nowadays by model-theoretic semanticists.

[6] That is concerning only a small number of expressions such as true indexicals and demonstratives.

[7] The individuation of a single "contextualist paradigm" is far from obvious; it is nonetheless possible to identify a general research program, common to several authors, in the works, initially, of John Searle and Charles Travis, and more recently of Kent Bach, Robyn Carston, François Recanati, Dan Sperber and Deirdre Wilson. The labels are different: "pragmatic view" (Travis (1997)), "contextualism" or "truth-conditional pragmatics (Recanati (1993) and Carston (2002)), "inferential communicative model" (Sperber & Wilson (1986/1995)).

[8] Cf. Wittgenstein (1953) § 43: "For a large class of cases - though not for *all* - in which we employ the word 'meaning' it can be defined thus: the meaning of a word is its use in the language".

[9] The later Wittgenstein, Friedrich Waismann, John Austin, Paul Grice, Peter Strawson.

Most contextualists ascribe to Wittgenstein the view that semantic underdetermination is *essential* to natural language. John Searle and Charles Travis explicitly take their thought experiments and their methodology from Austin and Wittgenstein.[10] For rather innocent sentences like

        (2) The cat is on the mat,
        (3) Bill cut the grass,
        (4) There is milk in the refrigerator,
        (5) Tom opened the door,
        (6) Bob opened his eyes,
        (7) The surgeon opened the wound,
        (8) Sally opened the can.[11]

Searle and Travis set up anomalous or strange contexts: the cat and the mat are traveling in interstellar space, Bill is cutting grass like a cake, Tom is opening the door with a knife, the refrigerator is filled wall-to-wall with milk, prepared to trap the unwary opener in a deluge. These examples are meant to show that every sentence has a literal meaning only against a background of contextual assumptions fixing its truth conditions: the background states, for example, that gravitation is, or is not, effective, or the way people "normally" cut things, and grass in particular, or open doors, eyes, or wounds. What is more, this background is not unique, constant or fixed once and for all: it may change with different occasions of use. Consequently, Searle and Travis argue, following Wittgenstein, that the semantic properties of an expression depend on the context of use of the expression: the conventional meaning of a sentence, if taken independently of any context whatsoever, underdetermines its truth conditions. In examples (5) – (8), the conventional meaning of *open* does not change, but its interpretation is different in each sentence: so, for example, we could ask ourselves if (5) would be true, if Tom opened the door with a can opener, or a scalpel. What satisfies the application conditions of *open* is different in each case: the stable, conventional meaning of the predicate seems to determine a different contribution to the truth conditions of each sentence. Following Searle and Travis, contextualism criticizes the thesis - essential to the Standard View - according to which there are stable meanings conventionally associated with linguistic expressions, and sets of truth conditions conventionally associated with sentences.

3 Meaning as Justification

We have said that contextualism is a view many scholars ascribe to the later Wittgenstein and to his motto "meaning is use": to understand a word is to know how to use it in a variety of different contexts. This very idea was fundamental for Logical Positivism's thesis "the meaning of a sentence is its verification condition"[12]; it can be traced to Sellars and his inferential theory of meaning, and, more recently, to

---

[10] Cf. Wittgenstein (1953) and Austin (1961). See Searle (1979), (1980) and (1992), and Travis (1975), (1981), (1985), (1989), (1996), (1997) and (2000).
[11] Searle (1983), p. 147.
[12] Cf. Carnap (1928) and Ayer (1936).

Brandom.[13] In this paper we will focus exclusively on Michael Dummett's interpretation of Wittgenstein's slogan.

3.1 "Meaning Is Use": Wittgenstein and Dummett

According to Dummett,[14] Wittgenstein is suggesting a conception of meaning as justification: as Wittgenstein writes, "it is what is regarded as the justification of an assertion that constitutes the sense of the assertion".[15] Following Wittgenstein, Dummett claims that justification completely exhausts meaning – in other words, the meaning of an assertion is given by its justification or its assertion conditions: "We no longer explain the sense of a statement by stipulating its truth-value in terms of the truth-values of its constituents, but by stipulating when it may be asserted in terms of the conditions under which its constituents may be asserted".[16] In this perspective, semantics and epistemology are entangled: knowing the meaning of a sentence amounts to knowing the justification one must offer for it. In this way, we end up with an *epistemic* account of meaning. Dummett gives a general account of meaning, arguing for a rejection of classical logic, and opposing the traditional view of meaning in terms of truth conditions. This paper will not scrutinize the details of Dummett's or Wittgenstein's proposals[17]; nevertheless it may be useful to understand which theory of justification is compatible with their views.

3.2 Foundationalism

In contemporary epistemology we find four main theories of justification: foundationalism, coherentism, reliabilism, and proper functionalism. Foundationalism is the more traditional theory of justification.[18] Its central idea is that beliefs are divided into basic ones and derived ones. The former need no inferential justification, but have an immediate one. The latter are founded on the former and derive their justification from them through deductive and inductive inferences. Basic beliefs are useful to stop the regress of justification, and in fact, according to foundationalism, regress must stop in immediately justified beliefs.

Wittgenstein may be interpreted as holding a foundationalist conception of justification – that distinguishes between basic propositions and inferentially justified propositions: "If you do know that *here is one hand*, we'll grant you all the rest. When one says that such and such a proposition can't be proved, of course that does not mean that it can't be derived from other propositions; any proposition can be derived from other ones. But they may be no more certain than it is itself".[19] Furthermore, Wittgenstein embraces the foundationalist answer to regress: regress must stop in

---

[13] Cf. Sellars (1963); Brandom (1994) and (2000).
[14] Cf. Dummett (1976), (1978), and (1979).
[15] Wittgenstein (1969a, I, 40).
[16] Dummett (1978), pp. 17-18.
[17] For a more detailed analysis about both Dummett's theory and our criticisms of meaning as truth conditions, see Vassallo & Bianchi forthcoming.
[18] It has been maintained by Aristotle, Descartes and Locke – to mention a few outstanding philosophers.
[19] Wittgenstein (1969b, 1).

immediately justified beliefs.[20] As a matter of fact, he writes: "Giving grounds, however, justifying the evidence, comes to an end; - but the end is not certain propositions' striking us immediately as true, i.e. it is not a kind of *seeing* on our part; it is our *acting*, which lies at the bottom of the language-game";[21] and "I KNOW that this is my foot. I could not accept any experience as proof to the contrary.- That may be an exclamation; but what *follows* from it? At least that I shall act with a certainty that knows no doubt, in accordance with my belief".[22]

As we have said, Dummett's inspiration is Wittgenstein. It is utterly reasonable to claim that both authors hold a foundationalist view about justification and distinguish between basic beliefs – justified by observation and experience - and inferentially justified beliefs.

4 Contextualizing Justification

Epistemology has long been dominated by invariantism, the thesis claiming that there is *one and only one* epistemic standard. The contextualist thesis is quite recent.[23] It admits the legitimacy of several epistemic standards that vary with context of use of

(1) S knows that *p*

or

(9) S is justified in believing that *p*.

So, according to this thesis, it might be right to claim – for the same cognitive subject S – that (1) is true in one context, and is false in another context; the same holds for (9).

The locus classicus of contextualism about justification is David Annis' article "A Contextualist Theory of Epistemic Justification".[24] The model of justification proposed by Annis is that of a person's being able to meet certain objections: the key point is the ability of the cognitive subject to reply to objections couched in terms of precise epistemic aims, that is achieving true beliefs and avoiding false beliefs. Concerning a proposition *p*, the epistemic claims of a cognitive subject S may be objected to in two different ways: (A) S is not in a position to know that *p* is true; (B) *p* is false. Because we do not want to have conditions so strong that S cannot satisfy them, not every objection is possible or, at least, S is not required to answer every objection. Objections must be "based on the current evidence available", and "must be a manifestation of a real doubt where the doubt is occasioned by a real life situation".[25]

---

[20] Cf. Wittgenstein (1969b, 192). But cf. Wittgenstein (1969b, 253) suggesting a different interpretation.
[21] Wittgenstein (1969b, 204).
[22] Wittgenstein (1969b, 360).
[23] See footnote 1.
[24] Annis (1978) is a seminal work. There are of course other works that maintain that the notion of justification can be contextualized: see for example Williams (1991) and (1999).
[25] It may be said that S "is not required to respond to an objection if *in general* it would be assigned a low probability by the people questioning S". Cf. Annis (1978, p. 207).

The main question is: is S justified in believing that *p* is true? According to Annis, this question is always relative to an *issue-context* or to a conversational context. Let us suppose that we are going to decide if House – an ordinary person in an ordinary context – is justified in believing that

(10) Polio is caused by a virus.[26]

We ask House: "Why do you believe it?" We are satisfied if he answers that he has read it in a newspaper and that newspapers are generally reliable, because we apply a rather relaxed epistemic standard – we are in an ordinary context. Of course the same answer is not accepted if the context changes. Let us suppose that the context is an examination for the M.D. degree. We do not judge House to be justified at all in his belief if he appeals to his having read the newspaper, because in this new context we apply a rather elevated epistemic standard. So, with regard to an issue-context a person can be justified in believing a proposition *p*, and with regard to another issue-context the very same person may not be justified at all in believing the very same proposition. It is evident that the issue-context "determines the level of understanding and knowledge that S must exhibit, and it determines an appropriate objector-group".[27] So, while in an ordinary context, the appropriate objector-group is constituted by ordinary people, in the context of the examination for the M.D. degree it is constituted by qualified medical examiners.

For a better understanding, let us consider another example. Here is Cameron – an ordinary person in an ordinary context (let's say, a party). She is in perfect psychophysical condition and would like to drink a glass of red wine. She grabs a glass of red wine and says:

(11) This wine is red.

Is she justified in believing (11)? The issue-context is an ordinary situation, and it is neither a physics examination, where Cameron would be requested to have a good knowledge of light transmission, nor a cognitive science examination, where Cameron would be requested to have a good knowledge of color perception. The room is an ordinary context where the objector-group is constituted by ordinary people with good perceptual abilities, and cognition of standard perceptive conditions and of causes of perceptual errors. In such a familiar context, objections are not usually raised: Cameron's belief is considered immediately justified and, as such, is to be regarded as contextually basic. But suppose that Chase, who knows that the room is illuminated by a red light, raises the following objection: "The wine might appear red just because of the red light ". If Cameron does not find a way to reply, her belief is to be regarded as unjustified. However, she might answer: "Yes, I know about the red light, but the waiter guaranteed me that the wine is red also under a normal light". Her belief would be justified in virtue of this answer and, therefore, the justification for (11) would be derived. Given a certain issue-context, if the appropriate objector-group asks S for reasons for her belief, this belief is not a basic one in that context, because it will be derived from reasons and, therefore, from beliefs that are meant to

---

[26] This is, of course, an adaptation of Annis' example: cf. Annis (1978, p. 208).
[27] Annis (1978, p. 208).

support it. In the above ordinary context Cameron's belief is obviously derived, because the basic belief is:

(12) Waiters are generally reliable.[28]

The regress problem seems solved, without the necessity to postulate basic beliefs given forever and so without the possibility of referring to them as the myth of the given: according to contextualism, contextually basic beliefs vary with issue-context.[29]

According to DeRose, contextualism may be seen as compatible with foundationalism. He writes: "If you're a foundationalist, then if you're also a contextualist, you may well come to think of the issue of which beliefs are properly basic (i.e., the issue of which beliefs are justified to a degree sufficient for knowledge independent of any support they receive from other beliefs), and/or the issue of how strongly supported a belief in the superstructure must be in order to count as knowledge or as a justified belief, to be matters that vary according to features of conversational context".[30]

5 Contextualizing Meaning

Let us assume that the contextualist account of justification given above is acceptable. What is more, at least according to DeRose, the account is compatible with foundationalism – the theory of justification Dummett is inclined to accept. The notion of justification can be contextualized; it follows that the notion of meaning – if you accept a theory of meaning as justification - can be contextualized.

Let's go back to Searle and Travis' examples:

> (2) The cat is on the mat,
> (3) Bill cut the grass,
> (4) There is milk in the refrigerator,
> (5) Tom opened the door.

As we have said, these examples are meant to show that every sentence has a literal meaning only against a background of contextual assumptions fixing its truth

---

[28] Of course, in a context where waiters' reliability is in question, the belief expressed by (12) will not be basic anymore.

[29] Williams proposes a similar solution with his notion of *methodological necessity*: "Not entertaining radical doubts about the age of the Earth or the reliability of documentary evidence is a precondition of doing history *at all*. There are many things that, as historians, we might be dubious about, but not these. *Disciplinary* constraints fix ranges of admissible questions. But what is and is not appropriate in the way of justification may also be strongly influenced by what specific objection has been entered to a given claim or belief. So to disciplinary we must add *dialectical* constraints: constraints reflecting the current state of a particular argument or problem-situation": Williams (1991, p. 117).

[30] DeRose (1999, p. 190). Henderson (1994) also claims that contextualism can make use of foundationalism. We must point out, however, that Annis (1978) interprets contextualism as an *alternative* to foundationalism. He considers contextualism superior to foundationalism because the former is able to face the regress problem in a satisfactory way, since it does not postulate beliefs given forever, and is therefore not subject to objections raised against the latter. Cf. also Williams (1991) and (1999).

conditions, and that this background is not unique, constant, fixed once and for all. Now, if we accept an account of meaning as justification along Dummett's lines, we must say that the meaning of (2), for instance, is given by the justification the speaker has to assert (2): knowing the meaning of (2) amounts to knowing the justification one must offer for it. In a foundationalist account, (2) can be a basic proposition or a derived one. If (2) is a basic proposition, it will be justified by observation and experience; if (2) is a derived proposition, its justification will be derived from basic propositions through deductive and inductive inferences.

Moreover, if Annis' proposal is sound, we can contextualize the notion of justification: it is right to claim – for the same cognitive subject S – that (2) is justified in one context, and unjustified in another context. When asking whether S is justified in believing or asserting (2), we must consider this relative to some specific issue-context, which determines the level of understanding and knowledge required; this in turn determines the appropriate objector-group.

Suppose that Foreman – an ordinary person in an ordinary context – asserts (2): is he justified in his assertion? The issue-context is an ordinary situation and ordinary people constitute the objector-group. In such a familiar context, objections are not usually raised: Foreman's belief is considered immediately justified and, as such, is to be regarded as contextually basic. But suppose that Chase, knowing that House has been fooling around with their new Graviton, raises the following objection: "What if the Graviton is on, and gravitation is no longer effective? How do you know that the cat is on the mat? Maybe there is no gravitational field relative to which the cat is above the mat and they are both floating freely". If Foreman does not find a way to reply, his utterance of (2) is to be regarded as unjustified. However he might answer: "Yes, I know about the Graviton, but I've checked: it is switched off". His belief would be justified in virtue of this answer and, therefore, the justification for (2) would be derived. Given the new issue-context, if the appropriate objector-group asks Foreman reasons for his belief, this belief is not a basic one in that context, because it will be derived from reasons and, therefore, from beliefs that are meant to support it.

Or, let us suppose that we are going to decide whether House – who is having breakfast with Cameron – is justified in believing that

(4) There is milk in the refrigerator.

We ask House: "Why do you believe it?" We are satisfied if he answers that he has just checked, and there was something that looked like a perfectly normal bottle of milk, because we apply a rather relaxed epistemic standard – we are in an ordinary context. The same answer is not accepted if the context changes. Let us suppose that some patient, fed up with House's bad temper, has been trying in various ways to kill him – sabotaging his motorbike, sawing his cane, substituting his pain-killers, poisoning his food. If Cameron raises the following objection. "What if the crazy patient replaced the milk with some poison?", we will no longer judge House justified in uttering (4). In this new context we apply a rather elevated epistemic standard: in order to attribute justification to House, it is necessary that he be able to rule out the possibility raised by Cameron. Of course House is not required to answer *every* objection. But in the crazy patient case, the objection is based on the current evidence available, and is a manifestation of a real doubt, occasioned by a real life situation.

6 Concluding Remarks

Semantic contextualists claim that virtually no sentences of a natural language express complete propositions. The encoded meaning of the linguistic expressions underdetermines the proposition explicitly expressed by the utterance: meaning underdetermines truth conditions. This form of underdetermination threatens the Standard View for at least two reasons. According to contextualism: i) the meaning of *any* sentence underdetermines its truth conditions - underdetermination becomes a *general property* of meaning; ii) the contextual factors that could become relevant for determining the truth conditions of a sentence cannot be specified in advance, and are not codified in the conventional meaning of the sentence. In this paper, we suggest that a theory of meaning as justification provides an interesting and straightforward way of contextualizing meaning – via the contextualization of justification.

In closing, we would like to underline a final point: in many ways Annis' issue-context may be assimilated to Searle's background. The issue context is the specific issue that is being raised, relative to a certain proposition *p*: it establishes the level of understanding and knowledge that S must exhibit, determining, in other words, the kind of objections S is required to answer. Annis claims that "social information – the beliefs, information and theories of others – plays an important part in justification".[31] In a similar vein, Searle underlines the point that "as members of our culture we bring to bear on the literal utterance and understanding of a sentence a whole background of information about how nature works and how our culture works".[32] However, he goes much further, claiming that not all the elements of the background have propositional content: needless to say, Searle's notion of background owes its non representational nature to Wittgenstein's forms of life. A sentence like (2) expresses a proposition only with regard to certain assumptions, practices, goals and ways of doing things. Assumptions, practices and goals *cannot* be made fully explicit, otherwise we incur an infinite regress. First, assumptions are indefinite in number and content: "we would never know when to stop in spelling out the background"; secondly, each specification of an assumption tends to bring in other assumptions; third, each specification we add needs an interpretation; as Wittgenstein famously put it, "in the course of our argument we give one interpretation after another; as if each one contented us at least for a moment, until we thought of yet another standing behind it".[33]

References

1. Annis, D.B.: A Contextualist Theory of Epistemic Justification. American Philosophical Quarterly 15, 213–229 (1978). In: Moser P.K. (ed.) Empirical Knowledge. Readings in Contemporary Epistemology. Rowman & Littlefield, Lanham, Maryland, pp. 205–217 (1996)

---

[31] Annis (1978), p. 209.

[32] Searle (1980), pp. 226-227.

[33] Wittgenstein (1953) § 201; cf. Searle (1980), pp. 228: "The conditions which make representation possible need not themselves all be representations".

We would like to thank three anonymous referees for their useful suggestions.

2. Austin, J.L.: Other Minds. In: Philosophical Papers, pp. 44–84. Oxford University Press, Oxford (1961)
3. Bach, K.: The Semantics-Pragmatics Distinction: What It Is and Why It Matters. In: Turner, K. (ed.) The Semantics-Pragmatics Interface from Different Points of View, pp. 65–84. Elsevier, Oxford (1996)
4. Bach, K.: You don't say? Synthese 128, 15–44 (2001)
5. Bach, K.: The Emperor's New 'Knows'. In: Preyer, G., Peter, G. (eds.) Contextualism in Philosophy. Knowledge, Meaning, and Truth, pp. 51–89. Clarendon Press, Oxford (2005)
6. Bianchi, C.: Context of Utterance and Intended Context. In: Akman, V., Bouquet, P., Thomason, R.H., Young, R.A. (eds.) CONTEXT 2001. LNCS (LNAI), vol. 2116, pp. 73–86. Springer, Heidelberg (2001)
7. Bianchi, C.: How to Refer: Objective Context vs. Intentional Context. In: Blackburn, P., Ghidini, C., Turner, R.M., Giunchiglia, F. (eds.) CONTEXT 2003. LNCS, vol. 2680, pp. 54–65. Springer, Heidelberg (2003)
8. Bianchi, C.: How to Be a Contextualist. Facta Philosophica 7, 261–272 (2005)
9. Bianchi, C.: Nobody loves me: Quantification and Context. Philosophical Studies 130, 377–397 (2006)
10. Bianchi, C. (ed.): The Semantics/Pragmatics Distinction. CSLI, Stanford (2004)
11. Bianchi, C., Vassallo, N.: Epistemological contextualism: a semantic perspective. In: Dey, A.K., Kokinov, B., Leake, D.B., Turner, R. (eds.) CONTEXT 2005. LNCS (LNAI), vol. 3554, pp. 41–54. Springer, Heidelberg (2005)
12. Brandom, R.B.: Making it Explicit. In: Reasoning, Representing & Discursive Commitment, Harvard University Press, Cambridge (1994)
13. Brandom, R.B.: Articulating Reasons. In: An Introduction to Inferentialism, Harvard University Press, Cambridge, Mass (2000)
14. Brower, B.W.: Contextualism, Epistemological. In: Routledge Encyclopedia of Philosophy. Routledge, London, pp. 646–650 (1998)
15. Carnap, R.: Scheinprobleme in der Philosophie. Berlin (1928). English translation: Pseudoproblems in Philosophy. University of California Press, Berkeley (1967)
16. Carston, R.: Thoughts and utterances: the pragmatics of explicit communication. Blackwell, Malden (MA) (2002)
17. Cohen, S.: Knowledge, Context, and Social Standards. Synthese 73, 3–26 (1987)
18. Cohen, S.: How to be a Fallibilist. Philosophical Perspectives 2, 91–123 (1988)
19. Cohen, S.: Contextualist Solutions to Epistemological Problems: Scepticism, Gettier, and the Lottery. Australasian Journal of Philosophy 76, 289–306 (1998)
20. Cohen, S.: Contextualism, Skepticism, and the Structure of Reasons. In: Philosophical Perspectives, Epistemology, vol. 13, pp. 57–98. Blackwell, Oxford (1999)
21. DeRose, K.: Contextualism and Knowledge Attributions. Philosophy and Phenomenological Research LII, 913–929 (1992)
22. DeRose, K.: Solving the Skeptical Problem. The Philosophical Review 104, 1–52 (1995)
23. DeRose, K.: Relevant Alternatives and the Content of Knowledge Attributions. Philosophy and Phenomenological Research LVI (1996)
24. DeRose, K.: Contextualism: An Explanation and Defence. In: Greco, J., Sosa, E. (eds.) Epistemology, pp. 187–205. Blackwell, Oxford (1999)
25. DeRose, K.: Assertion, Knowledge, and Context. Philosophical Review 111, 167–203 (2002)
26. DeRose, K.: Single Scoreboard Semantics. Philosophical Studies 119, 1–21 (2004)
27. DeRose, K.: The Ordinary Language Basis for Contextualism and the New Invariantism. Philosophical Quarterly 55, 172–198 (2005)

28. Dummett, M.: What is a Theory of Meaning (II)? In: Evans, G., McDowell, J. (eds.) Truth and Meaning. Essays in Semantics, Clarendon Press, Oxford (1976)
29. Dummett, M.: Truth and Other Enigmas. Duckworth, London (1978)
30. Dummett, M.: What does the Appeal to Use do for the Theory of Meaning. In: Margalit A (ed): Meaning and Use. Reidel, Dordrecht (1979)
31. Gettier, E.L.: Is Justified True Belief Knowledge? Analysis 23, 121–123 (1963)
32. Hale, B., Wright, C. (eds.): A Companion to the Philosophy of Language. Blackwell, Oxford (1997)
33. Hawthorne, J.: Knowledge and Lotteries. Oxford University Press, Oxford (2004)
34. Ludlow, P.: Contextualism and the New Linguistic Turn in Epistemology. In: Preyer, G., Peter, G. (eds.) Contextualism in Philosophy. Knowledge, Meaning, and Truth, pp. 11–50. Clarendon Press, Oxford (2005)
35. Morawetz, T.: Wittgenstein and Knowledge. University of Massachusetts Press, Amherst, Mass. (1978)
36. Moser, P.K.: Empirical Knowledge. In: Moser P.K. (ed.) Empirical Knowledge. Readings in Contemporary Epistemology. Rowman & Littlefield, Lanham, Maryland, pp. 1–34 (1996)
37. Partee, B.: Comments on Jason Stanley's On the linguistic basis for contextualism. Philosophical Studies 119, 147–159 (2004)
38. Recanati, F.: Direct Reference: From Language to Thought. Blackwell, Oxford (1993)
39. Recanati, F.: The Alleged Priority of Literal Interpretation. Cognitive Science 19, 207–232 (1995)
40. Recanati, F.: What is said. Synthese 128, 75–91 (2001)
41. Recanati, F.: Literal Meaning. Cambridge University Press, Cambridge (2004)
42. Schiffer, S.: Contextualist Solutions to Scepticism. Proceedings of the Aristotelian Society XCVI, 317–333 (1996)
43. Searle, J.: Expression and Meaning. Cambridge University Press, Cambridge (1979)
44. Searle, J.: The Background of Meaning. In: Searle, J., Kiefer, F., Bierwisch, M. (eds.) Speech Act Theory and Pragmatics, pp. 221–232. D. Reidel Publishing Company, Dordrechtz (1980)
45. Searle, J.: Intentionality. In: An Essay on the Philosophy of Language, Cambridge University Press, Cambridge (1983)
46. Searle, J.: The Rediscovery of the Mind. MIT Press, Cambridge (Mass.) (1992)
47. Sellars, W.F.: Science, Perception and Reality. Routledge, London (1963)
48. Sellars, W.F.: Epistemic Principles. In: Castaneda, H.-N. (ed.) Action, Knowledge, and Reality, pp. 332–348. Bobbs-Merrill, Indianapolis (1975)
49. Shiner, R.: Wittgenstein and the Foundations of Knowledge. Proceedings of the Aristotelian Society 78, 102–124 (1977)
50. Sperber, D., Wilson, D.: Relevance. In: Communication and Cognition, Blackwell, Oxford (1986/1995)
51. Stalnaker, R.: Comments on From contextualism to contrastivism. Philosophical Studies 119, 105–117 (2004)
52. Stanley, J.: On the linguistic basis for contextualism. Philosophical Studies 119, 119–146 (2004)
53. Travis, Ch.: Saying and Understanding. Blackwell, Oxford (1975)
54. Travis, Ch.: The True and the False: the Domain of Pragmatics. Benjamins, Amsterdam (1981)
55. Travis, Ch.: On What Is Strictly Speaking True. Canadian Journal of Philosophy 15, 187–229 (1985)

56. Travis, Ch.: Meaning's Role in Truth: Mind 105, 451–466 (1996)
57. Travis, Ch.: The Uses of Sense. In: Wittgenstein's Philosophy of Language, Clarendon Press, Oxford (1989)
58. Travis, Ch.: Pragmatics. In: Hale, B., Wright, C. (eds.) A Companion to the Philosophy of Language, pp. 87–107. Blackwell, Oxford (1997)
59. Travis, Ch.: Unshadowed Thought. In: Representation in Thought and Language, Harvard University Press, Cambridge (Mass.) (2000)
60. Vassallo, N.: Contexts and Philosophical Problems of Knowledge. In: Akman, V., Bouquet, P., Thomason, R.H., Young, R.A. (eds.) CONTEXT 2001. LNCS (LNAI), vol. 2116, pp. 353–366. Springer, Heidelberg (2001)
61. Vassallo, N., Bianchi, C.: Grounding semantic contextualism on epistemological contextualism (2007) (forthcoming)
62. Williams, M.: Unnatural Doubts. In: Epistemological Realism and the Basis of Scepticism, Blackwell, Oxford (1991)
63. Williams, M.: Skepticism. In: Greco, J., Sosa, E. (eds.) Epistemology, pp. 35–69. Blackwell, Oxford (1999)
64. Wittgenstein, L.: Philosophische Untersuchungen (English translation by G. E. M. Anscombe: Philosophical Investigations). Basil Blackwell, Oxford (1953)
65. Wittgenstein, L.: Philosophische Grammatik (English translation by A. Kenny: Philosophical Grammar). Basil Blackwell, Oxford (1969a)
66. Wittgenstein, L.: Uber Gewissheit (English translation by G. E. M. Anscombe, D. Paul: On Certainty). Basil Blackwell, Oxford (1969b)

Local Context Selection for Aligning Sentences in Parallel Corpora

Ergun Biçici

Koç University
Rumeli Feneri Yolu 34450
Sariyer Istanbul, Turkey
ebicici@ku.edu.tr

Abstract. This paper presents a novel language-independent context-based sentence alignment technique given parallel corpora. We can view the problem of aligning sentences as finding translations of sentences chosen from different sources. Unlike current approaches which rely on pre-defined features and models, our algorithm employs features derived from the distributional properties of sentences and does not use any language dependent knowledge. We make use of the context of sentences and introduce the notion of Zipfian word vectors which effectively models the distributional properties of a given sentence. We accept the context to be the frame in which the reasoning about sentence alignment is done. We examine alternatives for local context models and demonstrate that our context based sentence alignment algorithm performs better than prominent sentence alignment techniques. Our system dynamically selects the local context for a pair of set of sentences which maximizes the correlation. We evaluate the performance of our system based on two different measures: sentence alignment accuracy and sentence alignment coverage. We compare the performance of our system with commonly used sentence alignment systems and show that our system performs 1.1951 to 1.5404 times better in reducing the error rate in alignment accuracy and coverage.

1 Introduction

Sentence alignment is the task of mapping the sentences of two given parallel corpora which are known to be translations of each other to find the translations of corresponding sentences. Sentence alignment has two main burdens: solving the problems incurred by a previous erroneous sentence splitting step and aligning parallel sentences which can later be used for machine translation tasks. The mappings need not necessarily be 1-to-1, monotonic, or continuous. Sentence alignment is an important preprocessing step that effects the quality of parallel text.

A simple approach to the problem of sentence alignment would look at the lengths of each sentence taken from parallel corpora and see if they are likely to be translations of each other. In fact, it was shown that paragraph lengths for the English-German parallel corpus from the economic reports of Union Bank of Switzerland (UBS) are highly correlated with a correlation value of 0.991 [6]. A more complex approach would look at the neighboring sentence lengths as well. Our approach is based on this knowledge

B. Kokinov et al. (Eds.): CONTEXT 2007, LNAI 4635, pp. 82–93, 2007.

of context for given sentences from each corpus and the knowledge of distributional features of words, which we name Zipfian word vectors, for alignment purposes. A Zipfian word vector is an order-free representation of a given sentence in a corpus, in which the length and the number of words in each entry of the vector are determined based on the quantization of the frequencies of all words in the corpus.

In this paper, we examine alternatives for local context models and present a system which dynamically selects the local context for a given sentence pair which maximizes the correlation for the pair in the given parallel corpora. The resulting learning methodology is language-independent; it handle non-monotonic and noisy alignments; it does not require any stemming, dictionaries, or anchors; and it extends the type of alignments available up to 6-way. Sentence alignments of given parallel corpora are determined by looking at the local context of a given sentence which consists of surrounding sentences. Therefore, we investigate the selection of context in relation to the performance increase in the sentence alignment task.

The problem of sentence alignment is a central problem in machine translation and similar in essence to many other problems that involve the identification of mappings. It is a subset of the problem of *sequence comparison*, which deals with difficult comparisons that arise when the correspondence of items in the sequences are not known in advance [9]. We used a publicly available and easily accessible dataset [5] for our experiments, so that our results can be easily replicated by others.

We observe that valuable information can be inferred from the context of given sentences and their distributional properties for alignment purposes. The following sections are organized as follows. In the next section, we review related work and present its limitations. In Sect. 3, we give some notation about sentence alignment, define Zipfian word vectors, present our feature representation, and discuss context in sentence alignment. We also present the properties of local context in sentence alignment and our sentence alignment algorithm in this section. In Sect. 5, we present the results of our experiments and the last section concludes.

2   Related Work

Brown *et. al.* [2] provide a statistical technique for sentence alignment using the number of word tokens in each sentence in addition to anchor points. The dataset they used (Canadian Hansards corpora [1]) contains comments that serve as anchor points. They define a bead as groupings of English and French sentences that have close lengths and an alignment as a sequence of beads. Gale and Church [6] observe that sentence lengths of source and target sentences are correlated. They limit their alignments to 1-1, 1-0, 0-1, 2-1, 1-2, and 2-2 types of mappings, where the numbers represent the number of sentences that map to each other. The reason for their choice in using sentence lengths in terms of characters rather than in terms of word tokens as was chosen by Brown *et. al.* [2] is that since there are more characters there is less uncertainty.

Both Brown *et. al.* and Gale and Church [6] assume that the corpus is divided into chunks and they ignore word identities. Chen [4] describes an algorithm that constructs a simple statistical word-to-word translation model on the fly during sentence

---

[1] Available from Linguistic Data Consortium at http://www.ldc.upenn.edu/

alignment. The alignment of a corpus (S, T) is the alignment $\mathbf{m}$ that maximizes $P(T, \mathbf{m} \mid S)$, where P denotes the probability. Chen found that 100 sentence pairs are sufficient to train the model to a state where it can align correctly. Moore's [10] sentence alignment model combines sentence-length-based and word-correspondence-based approaches, achieving high accuracy at a modest computational cost. Moore uses a modified version of the IBM Translation Model 1 [3]:

$$P(T \mid S) = \frac{\epsilon}{(l+1)^m} \prod_{j=1}^{m} \sum_{i=0}^{l} \mathrm{tr}(t_j|s_i),$$

where $\mathrm{tr}(t_j|s_i)$ corresponds to the translation probability of the word $t_j \in T = \{t_1, \ldots, t_m\}$ given $s_i \in S = \{s_1, \ldots, s_l\}$ and ϵ is some small fixed number. Instead of $P(T|S)$, Moore makes use of $P(S, T)$.

Context and its selection is very important in many areas of natural language processing. Most of the work on context focuses on finding an optimal context size which gives good performance globally on the test cases. Yet this optimal value is sensitive to the type of ambiguity [16]. The dynamic nature of the context is noticed for the word sense disambiguation task by Yarowsky and Florian [17] and they further claimed that the context sizes for nouns, verbs, and adjectives should be in the 150, 60-80, and 5 word vicinity of a given word respectively. Wang [15] gives a nice example of word senses' context dependence in Fig 1. As we increase the size of the context, the sense of the Chineese word varies between think and read. Ristad [12] makes use of a greedy heuristic to extend a given context for the purpose of finding models of language with fewer parameters and lower entropy. In this work, we accept the context to be the frame in which the reasoning about sentence alignment is done. We examine alternatives for local context configurations and demonstrate that our context based sentence alignment algorithm performs better than prominent sentence alignment techniques.

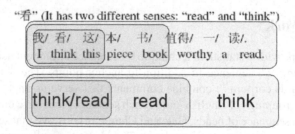

Fig. 1. Word sense dependence on context

Previous work on sentence alignment assume that the order of sentences in each corpus is preserved; as the beads on a string preserve the order, their models assume that the mapping function $\mathbf{m}$ is monotonic. Sentence alignment literature makes extensive use of simplifying assumptions (e.g. the existence of anchors, dictionaries, or stemming), biased success criterion (e.g. selecting only 1-1 type alignments or removing badly aligned sentences from consideration), and the use of datasets that cannot be qualitatively judged and compared to other results. In this paper, we overcome these limitations by removing simplifying assumptions about the dataset and generalizing the problem space by generalizing our representation of the data. Our goal is not to seek the best performance in only 1-1 type alignments since machine translation tasks cannot be reduced to 1-1 type alignments. We also introduce a new measure of success, sentence alignment coverage, which also considers the number of sentences involved in the alignment. We use the Multext-East [2] corpus, which provides us access to large amounts of manually sentence-split and sentence-aligned parallel corpora and a good dataset for the evaluation of performance. As this dataset contains alignments for 9 different language pairs, it suits well for demonstrating our system's language independence.

3 Sentence Alignment

3.1 Problem Formulation

A *parallel corpus* is a tuple $(\mathcal{S}, \mathcal{T})$, where $\mathcal{S}$ denotes the source language corpus and $\mathcal{T}$ denotes the target language corpus such that $\mathcal{T}$ is the translation of $\mathcal{S}$. Since the translation could have been done out of order or lossy, the task of *sentence alignment* is to find a mapping function, $\mathbf{m} : \mathcal{S} \to \mathcal{T}$, such that a set of sentences $T \in \mathcal{T}$ where $T = \mathbf{m}(S)$ is the translation of a set of sentences $S \in \mathcal{S}$. Then, under the mapping $\mathbf{m}$, we can use T whenever we use S.

We assume that $\mathcal{S} = \{s_1, \ldots, s_{|\mathcal{S}|}\}$ and $\mathcal{T} = \{t_1, \ldots, t_{|\mathcal{T}|}\}\}$, where $|corpus|$ refers to the number of sentences in corpus and s_i and t_i correspond to the ith sentences in $\mathcal{S}$ and in $\mathcal{T}$ respectively. The sentences in $\mathcal{S}$ and $\mathcal{T}$ form an ordered set where an *ordered set* is an n-tuple, denoted by $\{a_1, a_2, \ldots, a_n\}_\leqslant$, such that there exists a total order, $\leqslant$, defined on the elements of the set. We also assume that a set of sentences $S \in \mathcal{S}$ where $S = \{s_i, s_{i+1}, \ldots, s_j\}$ is chosen such that $\forall k, i \leq k \leq j,\ s_k \leqslant_\mathcal{S} s_{k+1}$. The same argument applies for a set of sentences selected from $\mathcal{T}$. Therefore, it is also meaningful to order two sets of sentences S_1 and S_2 selected from a given corpus $\mathcal{S}$ with the following semantics: Let start_{S_1} and start_{S_2} be the starting sentences of S_1 and S_2 correspondingly, then, $S_1 \leqslant_\mathcal{S} S_2 \Leftrightarrow \text{start}_{S_1} \leqslant_\mathcal{S} \text{start}_{S_2}$. A mapping $\mathbf{m} : \mathcal{S}_{\leqslant_\mathcal{S}} \to \mathcal{T}_{\leqslant_\mathcal{T}}$, is *monotone* or *order-preserving*, if for $S_1, S_2 \in \mathcal{S}$, $S_1 \leqslant_\mathcal{S} S_2$ implies $\mathbf{m}(S_1) \leqslant_\mathcal{T} \mathbf{m}(S_2)$, where $\mathbf{m}(S_1), \mathbf{m}(S_2) \in \mathcal{T}$.

The usual evaluation metric used is the percentage of correct alignments found in a given set of alignments, which we name as sentence alignment accuracy. This measure does not differentiate between an alignment that involves only one sentence as in 1-0 or 0-1 type alignments and an alignment that involves multiple sentences as in 1-5. Therefore, we define sentence alignment coverage as follows:

Definition 1 (Sentence Alignment Coverage). *Sentence alignment coverage is the percentage of sentences that are correctly aligned in a given parallel corpus.*

Thus, for sentence alignment coverage, an alignment of type 1-5 is three times more valuable than an alignment of type 1-1.

---

[2] Also available at http://nl.ijs.si/ME/V3/

3.2   Zipfian Word Vectors

It is believed that distribution of words in large corpora follow what is called Zipf's Law, where "a few words occur frequently while many occur rarely" [18]. We assume that distributions similar to Zipfian are ubiquitous in all parallel corpora. Based on this assumption, we create Zipfian word vectors by making use of the distributions of words in a given corpus.

Definition 2. *Zipfian Word Vector Given a set of sentences, S, chosen from a given corpus, $\mathcal{S}$, where* maxFreq *represents the frequency of the word with the maximum frequency in S, and a binning threshold, b, the Zipfian word vector representation of S is defined as a vector V of size* $\frac{\log(\text{maxFreq})}{\log(b)}$*, where $V[i]$ holds the number of words in S that have a frequency of* $\lfloor \frac{\log(\text{freq}(w))}{\log(b)} \rfloor = i$ *for word $w \in S$.*

Thus, each bin contains the number of words with similar frequencies in the given corpus. We assume that ZWV(S) is a function that returns the Zipfian word vector of a given set of sentences S. Thus, for a single sentence as in:

$S =$ " big brother is watching you ", the caption beneath it ran.,

the Zipfian word vector becomes:

$$\text{ZWV(S)} = [14, 1, 3, 0, 1, 3, 2, 0, 1, 1, 2],$$

where the sentence length in the number of tokens is added to the beginning of the Zipfian word vector as well. Note that Zipfian word vectors contain information about anything that is recognized as a token after tokenization.

The TCat concept [8] used for text classification is similar in its use of Zipfian distribution of words. While TCat is based on three levels of frequency (high, medium, and low frequency levels) we vary the length of the Zipfian word vector to increase the accuracy in the learning performance and adapt to the problem. Also, in TCat, each level of frequency behaves as a binary classifier, differentiating between positive and negative examples whereas each bin in our model behaves as a quantization of features to be used in learning.

3.3   Feature Representation

We assume that $\mathcal{S} = \{S_1, \ldots, S_i, \ldots, S_N\}$ and $\mathcal{T} = \{T_1, \ldots, T_i, \ldots, T_N\}$ where N is the total number of alignments and S_i and T_i correspond to the set of sentences involved in the ith alignment. For each set of sentences, S_i or T_i, that become a candidate for alignment within the sentence alignment algorithm, we create what we call the *Zipfian word matrix*. The Zipfian word matrix of a given set of sentences, S_i, is essentially the matrix we get when we concatenate the Zipfian word vectors surrounding S_i based on S_i's local context, which contains at most $2 \times w + 1$ rows for a given window size of w. Then the decision whether T_i is the translation of S_i is based on the two dimensional (2D) weight decaying Pearson correlation coefficient of their corresponding Zipfian word matrices.

Weight decaying is applied to the sentences that are far from S_i, which is the sentence according to which the context is calculated. Exponential decaying is applied with decaying constant set to 0.7. The use of weight decaying for 2D Pearson correlation coefficient does not improve statistically significantly, but it increases the accuracy and decreases the variance; hence giving us a more robust value.

3.4 Context in Sentence Alignment

The sentence alignment algorithm we have developed is context-based in the sense that features belonging to the sentences that come before and after the current sentence are also considered. We represent the local context of a given set of sentences as a pair, the number of sentences to consider before and after the given set of sentences. The sentences in a given corpus vary in content and size, therefore setting the local context to a specific value might not be effective. A sample scenario of sentence alignment is depicted in Fig. 2 where the sets of source and target sentences that are being compared are drawn in ellipses. The local context for the given source and target set of sentences in the figure can be represented as $(2, 4)$ and $(3, 3)$ respectively. Although the local context shows variance, for two sets of sentences to be judged as translations of each other, the total length for the source and target sets of sentences' local contexts should be the same. This is because the comparison is based on the value of the 2D weight decaying correlation coefficient score, which is retrieved by using the local contexts of each pair of set of sentences compared.

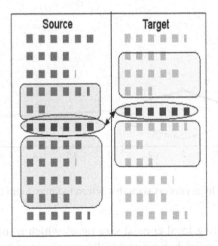

Fig. 2. Example Sentence Alignment Scenario

Let S be the set of sentences from the source corpus and let its local context be represented as (b_s, a_s) representing the number of sentences that come before and after S. Similarly, the local context for the corresponding set of sentences T in the target corpus can be represented as $(b_t, b_s + a_s - b_t)$. For a given context window size limit,

w, there can be w^3 such local context selections for the pair S and T. We call this the *full local context search*.

Given a set of local context configurations, $\mathcal{C}$, how are we going to make better decisions? There are three alternatives that we consider:

- Accept the *maximum* score attained from among $\mathcal{C}$ alternatives for the quality of the alignment and store the corresponding local contexts for observing what kind of local context configurations results in the highest scores.
- Accept the *average* score attained from among $\mathcal{C}$ alternatives for the quality of the alignment.
- Accept the *average of the top k* scores attained from among $\mathcal{C}$ alternatives for the quality of the alignment. We chose k to be 5 for our experiments. Evaluating according to the average of the best k results is a technique which is successfully used in discriminating the semantics among different word pairs [14,1].

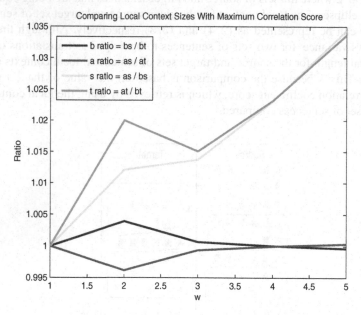

Fig. 3. Comparing local context sizes that return the maximum correlation score

Fig. 3 plots the resulting local context size ratios which result in the highest score after full local context search when we accept the maximum score to be the score for the given pair. These results were collected when w is set to 4 for the Lithuanian-English dataset using the full local context search. The actual average context sizes are listed in Table 1. One interesting observation from the results is that a_s and a_t are increasingly larger than b_s and b_t as we increase w. This is in line with the intuition that the sentences that come before have a larger weight in determining the context. Another observation is that the corresponding local contexts for S and T get closer as we increase w. We can see that on the average their sizes are the same with ± 0.001 difference in their ratio. The

Table 1. The ratio of exactly the same sized local contexts and average context sizes with full local context search for the Lithuanian-English pair

	$w=1$	$w=2$	$w=3$	$w=4$	$w=5$
Same Context Size Ratio	1	0.6950	0.6306	0.6302	0.6300
b_s	1	1.4256	1.8029	2.0422	2.2414
b_t	1	1.4200	1.8017	2.0422	2.2422
a_s	1	1.4429	1.8277	2.0895	2.3186
a_t	1	1.4484	1.8289	2.0895	2.3178
Static Context Accuracy	0.9082	0.9184	0.9184	0.92177	0.9116
Static Context Coverage	0.8892	0.8990	0.8990	0.9023	0.8909

first row of Table 1 shows that the ratio of exactly the same sized local contexts flattens to 63% as w is increased. So in nearly two thirds of the local context configurations, the local context sizes for S and T are exactly the same as well.

Based on these observations, considering only those local contexts that are symmetric (i.e. $b_s = b_t$ and $a_s = a_t$) appears to be a feasible approach. For a given context window size limit, w, there can be w^2 such local context selections for the pair S and T. We call this the *symmetric local context search*. The resulting local context sizes for each language pair with the maximum score selection when w is chosen to be 4 is given in Table 2.

Table 2. Local symmetric context sizes per language - English pairs

Dataset	b	a	Increase
Bulgarian	1.9564	1.9936	1.9%
Czech	1.9610	1.9961	1.8%
Estonian	1.9563	2.0129	2.9%
Hungarian	1.9723	1.9964	1.2%
Lithuanian	1.9720	2.0246	2.7%
Latvian	1.9667	2.0043	1.9%
Romanian	1.9275	1.9688	2.1%
Serbo-Croatian	1.9424	1.9755	1.7%
Slovene	1.9486	1.9765	1.4%

The other option in context size selection is to set it to a static value for all comparisons. The last two rows in Table 1 show the accuracy and coverage performances when w is chosen globally for the whole dataset. Based on these results, we select w to be 4 in our experiments in which the context is static.

3.5 Sentence Alignment Algorithm

Our sentence alignment algorithm makes use of dynamic programming formulation with up to 6-way alignments with extensions to handle non-monotonic alignments. The algorithm is essentially a modified version of the Needleman-Wunsch sequence alignment algorithm [11] with gap penalty set to -0.5. Further discussion on dynamic programming methodology to solve sentence alignment problems can be found in [6] or in [4]. We use the assumption that the alignments are found close to the diagonal of the dynamic programming table to further speed up the alignment process. Another property of our system is its ability to model up to 6-way alignments.

Another benefit in using sequence alignment methodology is our ability to model not only constant gap costs in the alignments but also affine as well as convex gap costs (a good description for affine and convex gap costs is in [7]). However, as the dataset does not provide enough contiguous gaps, we have not tested this capability; yet it is likely that affine and convex gap costs model the gap costs in sentence alignment better.

4 Experiments

We used the George Orwell's 1984 corpus's first chapter from Multext-East [5], which contains manually sentence split and aligned translations for English, Bulgarian, Czech, Estonian, Hungarian, Romanian, Slovene, Latvian, Lithuanian, and Serbo-Croatian. In all of our experiments, the target language pair is chosen to be English. We compared the results of our system with that of hunalign [13] and Moore's system [10]. Without an input dictionary, hunalign makes use of the Gale and Church [6] algorithm which is based on sentence lengths, and builds a dictionary dynamically based on this alignment.

Our first couple of experiments are based on choosing appropriate parameters. We chose to use the Lithuanian-English pair since its alignment types are more complex compared to the other datasets (6 different alignment types: 2-2, 2-1, 1-1, 1-3, 1-2, 1-6 with 1, 7, 274, 1, 10, 1 counts respectively). To reduce the complexity of calculations to a manageable value, the value of b is chosen to be 10.

Our results show that when we use static context and set the window size, w to 4, the algorithm makes 1 mistake out of every 23.16 sentence alignments and out of every 18.72 sentences. If we used the symmetric local context search with local context chosen as the maximum scoring one for the alignment, these numbers change to 22.22 and 17.88 respectively. When we use the average scoring for the symmetric local contexts, then these numbers become 24.40 and 19.64 respectively and become 23.97 and 19.10 respectively when we use the average of top 5 scores. These results were taken after observing 118, 123, 112, and 114 mistakes for the static, maximum, average, and average top 5 local context configuration schemes on the number of alignments and 299, 313, 285, and 293 mistakes for for the static, maximum, average, and average top 5 local context configuration schemes on the number of sentences. hunalign makes 1 mistake out of every 18.59 sentence alignments and out of every 13.26 sentences. Moore's algorithm makes 1 mistake out of every 16.27 sentence alignments and out of every 12.75 sentences. These results were taken after observing 147 mistakes for hunalign and 168 mistakes for Moore's algorithm on the number of alignments and 422 mistakes for hunalign and 439 mistakes for Moore's algorithm on the number of sentences. The total number of alignments is 2733 and sentences is 5596 in all of our data set.

4.1 Results on Sentence Alignment Accuracy

In terms of sentence alignment accuracy, our context based sentence alignment algorithm with static, maximum, average, and average top 5 local context configuration

Table 3. Sentence alignment accuracy per English - language alignments

Language	Sentence Alignment Accuracy					
	hunalign	Moore	static	maximum	average	average top 5
Bulgarian	**96.74 / 3.26**	96.09 / 3.91	96.09 / 3.91	95.77 / 4.23	**96.74 / 3.26**	96.74 / 3.26
Czech	96.14 / 3.86	95.82 / 4.18	**96.78 / 3.22**	**96.78 / 3.22**	**96.78 / 3.22**	96.78 / 3.22
Estonian	**99.68 / 0.32**	98.39 / 1.61	98.39 / 1.61	99.04 / 0.96	98.39 / 1.61	99.04 / 0.96
Hungarian	87.86 / 12.14	88.96 / 11.04	92.98 / 7.02	91.30 / 8.70	**93.98 / 6.02**	91.64 / 8.36
Latvian	95.71 / 4.29	92.74 / 7.26	96.70 / 3.30	96.70 / 3.30	96.70 / 3.30	**97.03 / 2.97**
Lithuanian	88.44 / 11.56	82.31 / 17.69	92.18 / 7.82	**92.52 / 7.48**	91.84 / 8.16	**92.52 / 7.48**
Romanian	89.86 / 10.14	**95.27 / 4.73**	91.22 / 8.78	90.54 / 9.46	91.22 / 8.78	92.23 / 7.77
Serbo-Croatian	**98.70 / 1.30**	97.08 / 2.92	97.73 / 2.27	98.05 / 1.95	97.73 / 2.27	97.73 / 2.27
Slovene	97.70 / 2.30	97.04 / 2.96	98.68 / 1.32	98.36 / 1.64	**99.34 / 0.64**	98.36 / 1.64

schemes reduce the error rate of hunalign by 1.2458, 1.1951, 1.3125, and 1.2895 times
and of Moore by 1.4237, 1.3659, 1.5000, and 1.4737 times respectively. The results
represent the comparison in terms of the total number of errors made over all English-
language alignments. The details can be seen in Table 3.

4.2   Results on Sentence Alignment Coverage

In terms of sentence alignment coverage, our context based sentence alignment algorithm with static, maximum, average, and average top 5 local context configuration
schemes reduce the error rate of hunalign by 1.4114, 1.3482, 1.4807, and 1.4403 times
and of Moore by 1.4682, 1.4026, 1.5404, and 1.4983 times respectively. The results
represent the comparison in terms of the total number of errors made over all English-
language alignments. The details can be seen in Table 4.

Table 4. Sentence alignment coverage per English - language alignments

Language	Sentence Alignment Coverage					
	hunalign	Moore	static	maximum	average	average top 5
Bulgarian	95.34 / 4.66	94.86 / 5.14	95.18 / 4.82	94.86 / 5.14	**95.99 / 4.01**	95.99 / 4.01
Czech	94.92 / 5.08	95.24 / 4.76	**96.35 / 3.65**	**96.35 / 3.65**	**96.35 / 3.65**	96.35 / 3.65
Estonian	**99.52 / 0.48**	98.08 / 1.92	98.08 / 1.92	98.88 / 1.12	98.08 / 1.92	98.88 / 1.12
Hungarian	84.30 / 15.70	85.90 / 14.10	91.51 / 8.49	89.10 / 10.90	**92.63 / 7.37**	89.42 / 10.58
Latvian	92.65 / 7.35	90.26 / 9.74	95.37 / 4.63	95.37 / 4.63	95.37 / 4.63	**95.69 / 4.31**
Lithuanian	84.85 / 15.15	79.15 / 20.85	90.23 / 9.77	**90.72 / 9.28**	89.90 / 10.10	**90.72 / 9.28**
Romanian	86.79 / 13.21	**93.64 / 6.36**	89.72 / 10.28	89.07 / 10.93	89.72 / 10.28	90.86 / 9.14
Serbo-Croatian	**97.75 / 2.25**	96.46 / 3.54	97.27 / 2.73	97.59 / 2.41	97.27 / 2.73	97.27 / 2.73
Slovene	95.81 / 4.19	95.64 / 4.36	98.06 / 1.94	97.58 / 2.42	**98.71 / 1.29**	97.58 / 2.42

5   Conclusion

We have developed a novel language-independent context-based sentence alignment
technique given parallel corpora. We can view the problem of aligning sentences as

finding translations of sentences chosen from different sources. Unlike current approaches which rely on pre-defined features and models, our algorithm employs features derived from the distributional properties of sentences and does not use any language dependent knowledge. The resulting sentence alignment methodology is language-independent; it can handle non-monotonicity and noise in the alignments, it does not require any stemming, or anchors, and it extends the type of alignments available up to 6-way.

The main advantage of Moore's and Chen's methods are their employment of the word translation probabilities and their updates when necessary. It is a custom to feed previous alignment results back into the aligner to further improve on the results. This process is generally referred to as bootstrapping and there may be multiple passes needed until convergence. We can easily improve our model by making use of word translation models and bootstrapping.

We provide formalizations for sentence alignment task and the context for sentence alignment. We introduce the notion of Zipfian word vectors which effectively presents an order-free representation of the distributional properties of a given sentence. We define two dimensional weight decaying correlation scores for calculating the similarities between sentences.

We accept the context to be the frame in which the reasoning about sentence alignment is done. We examine alternatives for local context models and developed a system which dynamically selects the local context for a pair of set of sentences which maximizes the correlation. We can also further improve our model by using a pre-specified dictionary, by dynamically building a dictionary, by using stemming, by using a larger corpus to estimate frequencies and generating Zipfian word vectors based on them, by using larger window sizes to select the local context size from, or by using bootstrapping which makes use of the previously learned alignments in previous steps.

We evaluate the performance of our system based on two different measures: sentence alignment accuracy and sentence alignment coverage. We compare the performance of our system with commonly used sentence alignment systems and show that our system performs 1.1951 to 1.5404 times better in reducing the error rate in alignment accuracy and coverage. The addition of word translation probabilities and models of word order to our system might give us a better solution to the sentence alignment problem.

Acknowledgments

The research reported here was supported in part by the Scientific and Technological Research Council of Turkey (TUBITAK). The author would like to thank Deniz Yuret for helpful discussions and for guidance and support during the term of this research.

References

1. Bicici, E., Yuret, D.: Clustering word pairs to answer analogy questions. In: Proceedings of the Fifteenth Turkish Symposium on Artificial Intelligence and Neural Networks (TAINN '06), pp. 277–284, Akyaka, Mugla (June 2006)

2. Brown, P.F., Lai, J.C., Mercer, R.L.: Aligning sentences in parallel corpora. In: Proceedings of the 29th annual meeting on Association for Computational Linguistics, pp. 169–176, Association for Computational Linguistics, Morristown (1991)
3. Brown, P.F., Della Pietra, S.A., Della Pietra, V.J., Mercer, R.L.: The mathematics of statistical machine translation: Parameter estimation. Computational Linguistics 19(2), 263–311 (1993)
4. Chen, S.F.: Aligning sentences in bilingual corpora using lexical information. In: Proceedings of the 31st annual meeting on Association for Computational Linguistics, pp. 9–16, Morristown, Association for Computational Linguistics (1993)
5. Erjavec, T.: MULTEXT-East Version 3: Multilingual Morphosyntactic Specifications, Lexicons and Corpora. In: Fourth International Conference on Language Resources and Evaluation, LREC'04, pp. 1535–1538. Paris (2004), ELRA. http://nl.ijs.si/et/Bib/LREC04/
6. Gale, W.A., Church, K.W.: A program for aligning sentences in bilingual corpora. Computational Linguistics 19(1), 75–102 (1993)
7. Gusfield, D.: Algorithms on Strings, Trees, and Sequences. Cambridge University Press, Cambridge (1997)
8. Joachims, T.: Learning to Classify Text using Support Vector Machines. Kluwer Academic Publishers, Boston (2002)
9. Kruskal, J.B.: An overview of sequence comparison. In: Sankoff, D., Kruskal, J.B. (eds.) Time Warps, String Edits, and Macromolecules: The Theory and Practice of Sequence Comparison, pp. 1–44. Addison-Wesley, London (1983)
10. Moore, R.C.: Fast and accurate sentence alignment of bilingual corpora. In: Richardson, S.D. (ed.) AMTA 2002. LNCS (LNAI), vol. 2499, pp. 135–144. Springer, Heidelberg (2002)
11. Needleman, S.B., Wunsch, C.D.: A general method applicable to the search for similarity in the amino acid sequences of two proteins. J. Mol. Biol. 48, 443–453 (1970)
12. Ristad, E.S., Thomas, R.G.: New techniques for context modeling. In: ACL, pp. 220–227 (1995)
13. Steinberger, R., Pouliquen, B., Widiger, A., Ignat, C., Erjavec, T., Tufis, D., Varga, D.: The JRC-acquis: A multilingual aligned parallel corpus with 20+ languages, pp. 2142–2147 (2006), Comment: hunalign is available at http://mokk.bme.hu/resources/hunalign
14. Turney, P.: Measuring semantic similarity by latent relational analysis. In: Proceedings of the Nineteenth International Joint Conference on Artificial Intelligence (IJCAI-05), pp. 1136–1141 (August 2005)
15. Wang, X.: Robust utilization of context in word sense disambiguation. In: Dey, A.K., Kokinov, B., Leake, D.B., Turner, R. (eds.) CONTEXT 2005. LNCS (LNAI), vol. 3554, pp. 529–541. Springer, Heidelberg (2005)
16. Yarowsky, D.: Decision lists for lexical ambiguity resolution. In: Hayes-Roth, B., Korf, R. (eds.) Proceedings of the Twelfth National Conference on Artificial Intelligence, Menlo Park. American Association for Artificial Intelligence, AAAI Press, Stanford (1994)
17. Yarowsky, D., Florian, R.: Evaluating sense disambiguation across diverse parameter spaces. Natural Language Engineering 8(4), 293–310 (2002)
18. Zipf, G.K.: The meaning-frequency relationship of words. The Journal of General Psychology 33, 251–256 (1945)

Context in Use for Analyzing Conversation Structures on the Web Tied to the Notion of Situatedness

Nik Nailah Binti Abdullah and Shinichi Honiden

Honiden Laboratory, Intelligent Research Systems Division, National Institute of Informatics,
2-1-2 Hitotsubashi, Chiyoda-Ku, Tokyo 101-8430, Japan
{bintiabd,honiden}@nii.ac.jp

Abstract. Current trend in scientific collaboration focuses on developing effective communication Web media. One of its objectives is to provide informal communication opportunities for collaborating scientists. This paper focuses on analyzing conversation structures of actual collaboration scenarios on the Web. The conversations analyzed model context using *hierarchy of learning* and *communication* tied to *situated cognition* to help understand how *users induce communication protocols* on the Web. The paper focuses on the analysis of the conversation structures that uses context to identify what could possibly *make up a context* and to help understand how *contexts are punctuated*.

Keywords: learning and communication, situated cognition, activity theory, web collaboration, human computer interaction.

1 Introduction

The main focus of the work was concerned with how people *learn to induce communication protocols*. Fundamentally, the work was based on actual communication protocol problems that brought the scientists working together during the Haughton-Mars Project (i.e, HMP) [9] into breakdown situations described in [5]. It was referring to several significant events where *contexts* made an impact for the understanding of how communication and learning is taking place in respect to using *'located' tools* [1].

We focused on several issues; (i) how does human learning and communications mutually influence one another in a situated *context engaged in an activity*? (e.g., using tools for conducting survey or reading and e-mailing procedures)? (ii) After some time, people handle the *context of communications* as if they were *repeatable*. If we are to commit to this notion of repeatable, then we must ask ourselves, how are they in the beginning able to recognize/conduct a *context* as being *context A*? Hence, knowing with what and with whom to communicate (and applying a particular communication protocol) in their situated context.

(i) and (ii) are motivations of the study in *using and modeling context* to understand how *people induce communication protocols* on the *Web*.

B. Kokinov et al. (Eds.): CONTEXT 2007, LNAI 4635, pp. 94–107, 2007.

Our approach to investigate those issues is to first focus on how people learn and communicate in breakdown situations. Since the goal of the work is to build an assistive technology that can help the discrepancies between user and tool in breakdown situations [2]; therefore much understanding is needed to understand how people overcome breakdown situations.

A similar scenario was chosen for investigation; an actual ongoing European Learning GRID Infrastructure (i.e., EleGI)[1] project [1]. The project involved 24 partners coming from different universities and research laboratories working together on a joint project however geographically distributed. All communication exchanges among the collaborators were facilitated by three Web media, (i) BuddySpace instant messaging [7]; (ii) FlashMeeting[2] videoconferencing [7]; and (iii) general e-mail system such as Microsoft Outlook or Mozilla Thunderbird.

We use a natural observation approach where we try as much as possible to capture daily communications to understand the patterns of regularities emerging in *different contexts* of *communications*. This falls under the social cognitive theoretical approach (SCT). The SCT considers the role of personal factors (e.g., beliefs, attitudes, expectations, memory) in addition to the environmental and behavioral aspects of learning [13]. About 50,000 communication exchanges among 6 EleGI members were recorded during the period of 8 months. These recorded conversations were pre-processed using CONSTEPS (i.e., conversion steps) [1] and about 5, 000 formulized messages obtained using *activity states framework* [1], [3]. These converted conversations are referred to as 'conversation structures' throughout the paper. Theoretical analysis was performed on these conversation structures. This paper focuses on how *context* is used for *analyzing conversations structures* in order to understand *how learning and communication in relationship to perception and memory is taking place*. The most important point is that the instant messaging facilitates all the communication exchanges. Thus, it is also about what 'context' may be in the domain of scientific communications on the Web. The paper is organized as the following; (i) a brief introduction to the theoretical foundations and activity states framework; (iii) the collaboration scenarios; (iv) analyses of the conversation structures in relationship to context; and finally (v) discussions and summary.

2 Background Work and Theoretical Foundations

The conversations are analyzed using activity states framework [1],[2],[3]. The activity states framework integrates cognition theories as its foundation[3]. The theories are (i) hierarchy of learning and communication [4]; (ii) situated cognition [6] and (iii) activity theory [11]. The framework aimed at providing explanations on how people comprehend texts and formulate intentions (i.e., actions) situated in the context of their communication. This is performed through the conceptual *modeling* of the *understanding* of *learning and communication* in respect to using located tool(s) in an environment- tying these occurrences to *contexts*. There are three main notions used

---

[1] www.elegi.org
[2] http://flashmeeting.open.ac.uk/research.html
[3] The arguments for using these cognition theories as point of views to analyzing communications on the Web are detailed in [1].

in the activity states, which are (i) object; (ii) subject; and (iii) in-between process. The *object* and *subject* are formulated specifically as: (i) how people conceive what they "read", (ii) comprehending what they read together with what they perceive and (iii) actions are formulated by interaction (speaking or interacting with tools). Object can be defined as 'the perceiving' act of the speaker at that moment (e.g., looking at a bowl). The bowl is the current focus of the speaker. The bowl is an object. A subject is defined as the referential process of the speaker in respect to what she is 'perceiving' (e.g., what I am conceiving when I am looking at the bowl). The in-between processes concern with the occurrences taking place between the *object* and *subject* by relating it to (i), (ii), and (iii). The object and subject notion was based on our own experiments[4] and was validated with the work in activity theory by [11]. The analysis in section 5.1 is being conducted in such a way.

In this paper, we only discuss about the theories on hierarchy on learning and communication [4] and situated cognition [6].

2.1 Bateson's Hierarchy of Learning and Communication: Using Context

In [4], the word 'learning' refers to *changes of some kind*. These *changes*, from *purely habitual responses*, to *highly complex of learning* can be *assumed as learning*. This is the essence of Bateson's work on the ordering of learning level; learning 0, I, II, and III and where *contexts* play a *crucial role* in determining the *changes* in the learning hierarchy. What [4], refer to as 'context' includes the subject's behavior as well as the external events [1], pg. 147. We focus on how contexts are used in each hierarchy from learning 0 to II in the remaining subsections.

2.1.1 Learning Zero

In learning zero, Bateson observes that this is the case in which an organism shows *minimal change* in its *response* to a *repeated item* of sensory input. Phenomena, which approach this degree of simplicity, occur in various contexts. Zero learning is most often applied when there is a *simple receipt* of information from an *external event*, in such a way that a similar event at a later (and appropriate) time will convey the same information. Taking the example from [4], we have "I 'learn' from the factory whistle that it is 12.00 o'clock".

From here, Bateson postulated that the *external event system* contains details (e.g., signals) which might tell the organism: *(i)* from what set of alternatives it should choose its next move; and *(ii)* which member of that set it should choose. The overall notion is that all learning (other than zero learning) is in some degree stochastic (i.e., contains components of trial and error). It follows that an ordering of the processes of learning can be built upon a hierarchic classification of the types of error, which are to be corrected in the various learning processes [4]. Therefore, *zero learning* is the *label* for the *immediate base* of all those *acts* (simple and complex), which are *not subject* to correction by *trial* and *error*.

2.1.2 Learning I

Following the analogy provided by the "laws" of motion (i.e., the "rules" for describing motion) [4] looks for the class of phenomena that are appropriately

---

[4] The experiment details can be referred to (Binti Abdullah, 2006).

described as *changes* in *zero learning* (as "motion" describes change of position). These are the cases in which an entity gives at *time 2* a *different response* from what it gave at *time 1*. This is when context play a significant role. These contexts themselves gives clues to the relationships between *contexts of contexts* that make up from learning 0 to learning I. Readers must remember that this ordering that we are discussing are in an induction nature. Normally, in psychological laboratories, stimulus is somehow assumed to be the "same" at time 1 and time 2. If we assume this "sameness", then we must also delimit the "context", which must (theoretically) be the same at both times. Once we assume that the context is not the same at time 1 and time 2, and then the whole system is not a simple deterministic procedure. It then refers to *differentiating* or correctly put "discrimination" of learning. This discrimination process is in some ways a part of the process to classify the *repeatable context*. Bateson spelled this out in the form of a hierarchy of logical types as follows: (i) Stimulus is an elementary signal, internal or external. (ii) *Context of stimulus* is a meta-message that classifies the elementary signal. (iii) *Context of context of stimulus* is a meta-metamessage that classifies the metamessage and so on.

From here, Bateson later introduced the term "context marker". It is used to describe that an organism *responds* to the "same" *stimulus differently* in *differing context*. Thus, Bateson proposed that one must therefore ask about the source of the organism's information. From what percept does he know *that context A is different from context B*? According to [4], in many instances, there may be no specific signal or label, which will classify and differentiate the two contexts. It is rather hard to pinpoint what exactly allows the organism to *classify the different contexts*. Thus, Learning I is change in specificity of response by correction of errors of choice within a set of alternatives.

2.1.3 Learning II

Now we consider the third level of learning: learning II. Some of the other common notions for this type of learning are: (i) deutero-learning; (ii) set learning; (iii) learning to learn; (iv) transfer learning. Learning II is change in the process of Learning I. An example is a corrective change in the set of alternatives from which a choice is made. The phenomena of learning II can all be included under the rubric of changes in the manner in which the stream of action and experience is segmented or *punctuated into contexts,* together with *changes* in the use of *context markers* [4].

Those phenomena classified under the learning I include a set of *differently structured contexts*. Learning II is now more focused not just on the transaction of a person with his/her environment. It considers the communication between two persons. There are contexts of Learning I, which are likely to lend their shape to processes of Learning II. In such a system, involving two or more persons, there are streams of events that are commonly punctuated into contexts of learning by tacit agreement between the persons regarding the nature of their relationship-or by *context markers* and *tacit agreement* that these *context markers* shall "mean" *the same* for both parties.

2.2 Situated Cognition

We now move on to situated cognition. Situated cognition defines that every human thought and action is freshly adapted to the environment as perceived and conceived by the action in the moment. When we say that every human thought and action is adapted, then our question is: what are the details? This is when we attempt to understand the idea of 'context', what makes up a context; and what are the details that are being actively re-organized during the act of perceiving and articulating speech? Details may be: the signals, or a particular dominant detail that catches a moment of focus and plays a role in the formation on how thought and actions are situated.

"Situated" means that people are not just located in an environment as a social-physical setting. According to [6], the context/environment for the people is categorical through perception and conception. That is the context/environment for a person is a mental construction. Then we must consider what the mechanisms are that enable people to construct "actively" the context they are situated in. Because thoughts and action are adapted to a context/environment, the conceptualization process requires the notion of learning. And context changes all the time.

Hence, a person's thought and action is situated considers that the human memory as "actively doing something all the time" or "actively contextualizing what I am doing". The key idea of relating these theories together is that to understand learning and communication, we must understand memory (how the act of re-sequencing and re-enacting takes place when a person 'perceives' similar context and respond similarly in these contexts). That is to understand how a person differentiates these contexts 'perceives' and recognizes a context that is different; through remembering, responds appropriately.

3 What Is Context in Our Work

There are several different views on the meaning in context. According to [11], from a traditional linguistics point of view, context is seen as a collection of information that helps to interpret language. However it is being regarded as being a given, peripheral, and static. From a socially recent point of view, a language phenomena is regarded as being embedded with the context, where context is simultaneously social, cultural, and cognitive [12].

We take a very general stance of what context is in our work. Context is being referred to 'as a conception' of what a person is doing, and hence the *context* of her action. It is always social. That is to say *the construction* of a context is taking place in parallel to how a person is conceiving and that the *context/environment* for the people is *categorical* through *perception* and *conception* [6].

4 Natural Observations of EleGI Collaboration Scenarios

We shall describe the natural settings of the EleGI collaboration scenarios. The collaborators normally use an e-mail system (on a daily basis) to exchange opinions, and BuddySpace to chat daily with one another. For meetings, they use FlashMeeting video conferencing. In this section, we show only the *BuddySpace* user interface. Specifically, we have analyzed the recorded chats between Pete, the project coordinator and Mathew[5], one of the EleGI executives, from 19/04/2004 until 28/09/2004. Commonly, an EleGI collaborator multi-tasks her job; she may switch her attention from task A to B, vice versa or simultaneously on different communication channels (instant messenger, e-mails, sending images). The selection of communication channels depends on what kind of tasks she has to complete and in turn depends on what kind of functions the tool provides. We refer to these occurrences as *web activities*. The collaborators are constantly adapting their communication channels to deliver a certain task or achieve a certain goal. They are always in an "activity", always adapting their thoughts and actions mediated by these tools. In this paper we focus on the excerpted chat contents between the project coordinator and project executive where they both exhibit breakdown situations. These chats taking place on the BuddySpace.

Fig.1. illustrates the *BuddySpace* user interface. It is the main view of *BuddySpace*. Since the users come from different institutions, e.g., "Eisenstadt, Marc [9 OU/KMI]" represents that the user Eisenstadt is from the Open University (OU), Knowledge Media Institute (KMI). The number 9 denotes the institution in the EleGI project.

How do we relate these activities to the hierarchy of learning and communication, and situated cognition introduced above? Consider this scenario. A collaborator, Jenny is engaged in an activity of drafting the first EleGI article. The *object of focus* of Jenny is her *article* (to be specific 'focused on' the subject 'tools'). The *instant messaging* is a *mediator* for Jenny to achieve her goal (i.e., sending the drafts to her colleague, receiving inputs from them and improving the paper from collective view points[6]). The *subject* in this example is *Jenny*. Whenever Jenny receives a response through the instant messaging from her colleagues, there are certain 'stimulus/signals' that

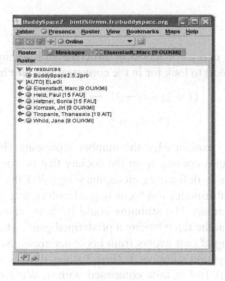

Fig. 1. The main view of the user interface

---

[5] These are not the actual names of the collaborators.
[6] These occurrences are referred to activity theory [10], but the activity theory is not discussed in this paper. Details may referred to [1],[10].

becomes the moment of her focus. It could be the text itself or it could be from the interaction with the tools itself. She may learn that whenever in that situated context it is easier to edit papers together using FlashMeeting tool instead of BuddySpace. How does Jenny know exactly that this is the context where she should be using the e-mail instead of chat system to send this file to collaborator A? How *does Jenny induce the communication protocols* in *different context*?

5   Observing Conversation Structures Using Context and Understanding Context

This section will introduce readers to the basic framework used in modeling context, which is shown in Fig. 2.

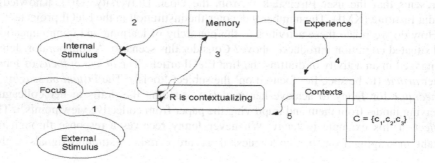

Fig. 2. Communication modeling

Refer to Fig. 2. In every conversation structures we attempt to identify certain parameters (i.e., variables) to look for in the conversations. We have the following.

$$(1 \lor 2) \land (1 \rightarrow 2) \ \rightarrow 3 \tag{Eq}1$$

$$(3 \circ 4) \rightarrow 5 \tag{Eq}2$$

(Eq) 1 and (Eq) 2 is to explain what the number represents. (Eq) 1 states that there could be either a stimulus coming from the society that is external, *1* or an internal stimulus *2*. A stimulus is defined as elementary signal(s) that is either external or internal [4]. An external stimulus has focus (e.g., detail(s)) that may on the other hand trigger an internal stimulus. The stimulus could be both, responding to someone's previous behavior and at the same having a predefined goal[7]. The stimulus here is also coupled to remembering of past events from his experiences. Now, this disjunction is then mapped as a compound stimulus *3*. (Eq) 2 states that the altered processes that had taken place in (Eq) 1; *3* is now composed with *4*. We visualize that that there exist processes that *discriminate* and *generalize* contexts to select the next actions

---

[7] The stimulus coming from the environment and/or internal has some role in the communication response.

denoted by a class C *context* = $\{c_1,c_2,c_3\}$. We give an example: c_1 = decision making; c_2 = debugging tool problem; c_3 = online tutorial. Now, at *5*, a response is given back into the society. As a result, this processes occurring as a whole, during the contextualization. Readers should keep in mind that this model only serves as a guideline to provide us with an idea on what to look for in the conversations analyzed. It is referring to the hierarchy of learning and communication for modeling stimulus-response and what experiences/memory may be according to situated cognition.

5.1 Conversation Structures Analyses

We have described the simple abstract modeling used to model how the 'contextualizing' process might be taking place during the act of perceiving and responding (modeled simply as stimulus-response) in Section 5, Fig. 2. In this section hereafter, we focus at showing how *with the modeling of contexts* help us to identify *punctuation of events* and allowing us to understand the *relationship* between perceiving and action. We will focus on discussing the *re-sequencing/reshuffling* of conversation structures in respect to *memory* and *perception taking place actively in a context*. We select several situations to understand what could possible mark 'contexts' and what construe contexts. First, we describe actual situations that took place. Pete (i.e., the project manager) was new to the BuddySpace environment, and Mathew (i.e., project executive) went online to give him a tutorial. While Pete was exploring the tool function following Mathew's online tutorial, he notices that one of the features did not conform to his colleague's explanation. This is the point where they were both 'thrown' into different situations. Both Pete and Mathew ended up *learning something new* from these situations. We show the excerpted chat logs below.

Event 1. Excerpted from BuddySpace, Dated: 09/03/2004. Total chat time: 44 minutes
Mathew: so you can see when I'm about to reply..
Pete: hum ...
Pete: By the way, how is it that you are not "on line" in the Roster
Mathew: really?
Mathew: oops... I don't know..
Mathew: now YOU showed up as offline ('red')
Mathew: are you still there?
Mathew: (and am I now 'green' in the Roster?)
Pete: I am
Mathew: interesting...
Mathew: I can only reach you now by pressing the little 'eyeball' icon at the top ('show all users') which shows me the 'offline' users too... we will fix this
Pete: and i am neither green nor red, but grey, from the start
Mathew: ah, your OWN icon is different:
Mathew: (because you can be logged in multiple times with different 'resources')
Pete: I do not understand: I thought my status was global !

Mathew: it is: but there is no 'TRUE' view of your own presence!! That is because we allow multiple presence states: I can be in 'Do Not Disturb' mode for my KMi colleagues, but 'Online' for EleGI

Mathew: So we show 'grey' for yourself!

Mathew: (Because you KNOW your own state anyway!!)

Pete: Ok, I get aware of this new dimension

Pete: Thanks a lot for this lesson n°1!

The pre-processed dialogues above are shown in Table 1 below.

Table 1. Conversations structures excerpted from BuddySpace, Dated: 09/03/2004

N	Person M	Person P
1	Confirm m,p (**see**)(p)(**when**)(**abt-re**)(m)	
2		Ack p,m (hum)
3		Inform-ref p,m (**by the way**)
4		Query-ref p, m (**how-is-it**)(m)(¬online)(rooster)
5	Inform-if m,p (really)	
6	Confirm m,p (¬**know**)<4>(**this**)	
7	Inform m,p (**offline**)(p)(shwn)(rooster)(m)	
8	Query-if m, p (online)(p)(**bspace**)(**now**)	
9	Inform-if m,p (is)(shwn)(p)(rooster)(m)(**green**)	
10		Confirm p,m (i)(am)
11	Inform-ref m,p (**interesting**) <10>	
12	Inform m,p (**can-only**)(m)(**reach**)(p)(**prsing**)(**icn**)(**eyebl**)	
13	Inform-ref m,p (icn)(**is-at**)(**tp**)	
14	Inform-ref m,p (**whc**)(**shwn**)(m)(**usr**)(**all**)	
15	Confirm m,p (whc)(shwn(m)(usr)(offline)	
16	Inform m,p x (**will-fx**)(**us**)(this) <x15>	
17		Inform-ref p,m (**and**)(**neither**)(p)(icn)(green)(**nor**)(p)(icn)(**red**)
18		Confirm p,m (**but**)(icn)(**grey**)
19		Inform-ref p,m <18> (**from-the**)(**start**)
20	Disconfirm m,p x(**own**)(icn)(p)(**different**)	
21	Inform m,p (**can**)(p)(**lg-in**)(**mltp**)(**time**)(**mltp**)(**rsc**)	
22		Confirm p,m (←**udst**)(p)(**this**)
23		Query-ref p,m (**thgt**)(**st**)(p)(**glb**)

Table 1. (*continued*)

24	Confirm m,p (**it-is**)(st)(p)(glb)	
25	Inform m,p (←**exists**)(p)(own)(**tr**)(**vw**)	
26	Inform-ref m,p (**allow**)(users)(mltp)(**states**)	
27	Inform m,p (**can-be**)(m)(**dnd**)(**kmi**)(**clg**)	
28	Inform m,p (can-be)(m)(online)(**elegi**)	
29	Inform-ref m,p (shw)(us)(own)(vw)(grey)	
30	Confirm m,p (knw)(p)(own)(states)	
31		Ack p,m ok
32		Confirm p,m (**aware**)(p)(**new**)(**dim**)

Refer to Table 1. The conversations have been pre-processed using CONSTEPS [1]. The message format follows partly the Fipa-Acl [8] format which is in this order: message number (e.g., 1), communicative act (e.g. confirm), sender (e.g. m), receiver (e.g. p), and content 'see'; 'p'; 'when'; 'abt-re'; and 'm'. Row 1, column 1 denoted by N is representing message number. We refer to each word in the content as *primitives*. Row 1, column 2 represents M's (i.e., Mathew) conversation structures and row 1, column 3 represents P's (i.e., Pete) conversation structures. Our observation is carried out in this order. (i) Uses the communication modeling shown in Fig.2, Section 5 to identify the variables (i.e., external/internal stimulus, focus). (iii) Classify the streams of events into 'contexts'.

From here onwards, we refer to specific conversation structures in the table to its message number *N*: person *M/P*. The primitives labeled in *bold*; such as 'see' at 1:M is a *new primitive*. When '**see**' is associated to 'p', then 'p' is considered *old* because it has appeared more than once (in previous dialogs). Now, whenever these old primitives are being associated to new primitives, we tag this old primitive and associate it to the new primitive. It signifies that the old primitive may be the *focus/attention* during that course of conversation. On the other hand, the new primitives are those that are 'evoked/produced' from associating the *focus* to memory/experience. This observation of the re-sequencing of primitives and its communicative act enable us to mark the *beginning*, and *ending* of a context (punctuation of contexts). Hence, it aids us in classifying contexts of conversations. Let us discuss the flow of the conversation structures. The start of the event where the first initial breakdown situation occurred was at 2:P. At 4:P, P query-ref (i.e., query in reference) to M with content 'how is it' 'm' 'not-online' 'rooster' with xa as a composition for the query. At this point from P's response, M attempt to debug the problem and it is shown from 5:M till 16:M, with a short response at 10:P on P's status for validation. The message Confirm p,m 'I am' is p confirming of his status in reference to message 8 denoted by <8>. M could not in the end seek a reason why his status was shown as offline to P; but he had found an alternative on how to allow them to still send messages to one another while M was exploring the BuddySpace features. Now this is taking place from 11:M till 16:M. However during these communications, M has brought P into another 'context' where the 'icon' color is not of 'P's understanding'. Hence, the second breakdown situation has occurred at 17: P.

However in the end they both converged to a common ground again. We represent the conversations in Table 2 as conversation blocks to explain the analyses in detail based on Fig. 2. Refer to Fig. 3. Each of the contents (e.g., see, m, p) is represented as Xn (e.g., x6, x7). We will concentrate on M's conversation structures during the first breakdown situation and discuss only message 5 till 9; and 11 till 16. Observe that there are several particular primitives that have re-appeared during these messages; $x2$ 'P', $x8$ 'M', $x9$ 'online', $x10$ 'rooster' and $x12$ 'show-on'. These primitives appeared initially at message 4. We *focus* on the *new primitives* that have been associated either to the left-hand side (i.e., LHS) or to the right hand side (i.e., RHS). This is denoted by the arrows that point either to the left or right. For example, at message 5, <4> denotes message 4 that has been associated to a new primitive, x11 'really' to the RHS.

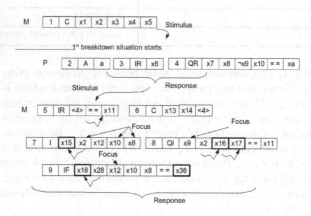

Fig. 3. The conversation in blocks from message 1 till 9

At message 6, C (i.e., Confirm), x13; 'do not know' and x14; '*this*' is where M is confirming to P that he does not know of this problem. At message 7, I (i.e., Inform) x15 x2 x12 x10 x8, M is then informing that now P is shown as 'offline' on M's roster list. x2 is associated to x15 a new primitive to the LHS where the new primitive is another item of the class 'presence'- that is x15 'offline'. x2, x10 and x8 are labeled as 'focus' because both have re-appeared more than once. At message 8, QI (i.e., Query-if) x9 x2 x16 x17 = x11, M queries if P is now online. The focus has changed from x10 'rooster' to a more specific item x9 that is 'online'. The focus of P is associated in parallel associated to a more general object, x16 that is the 'BuddySpace' IM itself. Now the primitives x16 is associated to x17, tool 'BuddySpace' to time 'now'. It shows a kind of symmetrical exchanges in solving the problem; whereby the *presence* (*from online to offline*) has now been *associated* to the *tool in time*. To be more precise, the presence is now being associated to the main 'object', class 'BuddySpace' that is the instant messaging tool to a class 'time', of item 'now'. The alternatives are starting to be narrowed down. At message 9, IF (i.e., Inform-if) x18 x12 x2 x10 x8= = x36, M asks P to inform if M is shown on P's roster as 'green'. The same rule applies where x12 'show-on' has become a focus for M at that moment. M is now associating the primitives x12, x2, x10, x8 to x36; the class 'icon', with item x36 'green'. Now, M is focused on the color of P's icon on the Buddyspace. The tagging is conducted in a backtracking manner. When a primitive is in *focus*, it is an 'object' for the speaker.

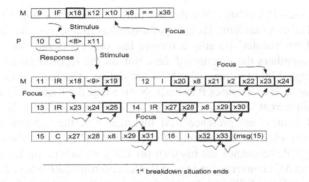

Fig. 4. The conversation blocks from message 11 till 16

Every object part has a subject part where the subject is a referential to the object (refer to Section 2 to again for the notion on object and subject).

Refer to Fig. 4. At message 12, M communicates with I (i.e., Inform), x20, x8, x21, x2, x22, x23, x24. M is referring both to the action and the feature of the BuddySpace. The focus is x23 'icon'. The icon is then the *object*. The feature of the icon is further attributed as having the 'concept' of x24 'eyeball'. Next, at message 13, M communicates with IR (i.e., Inform-ref), x23, x24, x25 that is informing where the icon is. x23 'icon' is associated to x24 *a location*, 'is-at', x25 'top'. At message 14, M communicates with IR (i.e, Inform-ref), x27, x28, x8, x29, x30. M is informing some of icon features. x27 'which', associated to x28 'shown', then to x8 'm', is referencing the information of rooster's function that x29 'user', to x30 'all'. These sequences suggest that M is "actively perceiving" *tied to a focus* while *associating this focus* to what he already knows about the features. The next step is to organize the variables we have identified during the analyses into Fig. 2 model to classify the contexts into punctuations.

Refer to Table 2. We observe the flow of the conversations, for every response of a user (i.e., M or P) we identify the stimulus (e.g., rooster, offline, green). In order to tag whether the user is still speaking about the same subject is to observe the focus

Table 2. Stimulus, focus, context

Message number	Speaker	External Stimulus/Internal Stimulus	'Focus'	Context
2-4	P	m, ¬online, rooster	M	Presence
5-9	M	m, p, offline, green	P, rooster, m, online	Diagnose
11-16	M	Icon, eyeball, users	Icon, m, user, all	Solution
17-19	P	P, icon, grey,	P, icon	Presence
20-21	M	Grey, P, status	Status	Tutorial
22-23	P	status, global	Global	Presence
24-30	M	P, global, states, own-view	Own-view, states	Tutorial

(e.g., user M, user P, eyeball). We discuss only message 2-4 and 5-9. We look at message 2-4. The external stimulus is hypothesized as m and ¬online, and the internal stimulus could be 'rooster' because a rooster has objects (icons, user lists) with its functions. P remembers the function of the color on the Rooster (what it means) and hence has prompted him to query why M is not online. The focus is on M, because it is the *icon color of M* that causes P to react. Notice that the focus is actually inclusion of the external/internal stimulus (following again Fig. 2 model). We classify this punctuation of context as 'presence". At message 5-9, the external stimulus is P, offline and green whereas the internal stimulus is M (M knows about his presence problem through P, he cannot see his own presence as offline on his own Rooster). The focus during M's conversation is user P. His communicative acts during this time were inform, confirm, followed by query if, and then inform-if. These patterns suggest that he is firstly diagnosing to confirm the presence problem. Therefore we classify this punctuation of context as 'diagnose'. On the other hand, notice that P's context remains the same, 'presence'. He is focused on the problem of presence and what it *means by presence* based on the tool functions. We summarize this section. There are two general occurrences taking place. Firstly, M acknowledged that the context of problem is unknown to him and we witness from message 5 till 9, the *interaction is punctuated* in a *certain manner*. M is 'debugging' the context while always focused on the BuddySpace user interface. Next, from message 11 till 16 another sort of punctuation emerged. M is informing an alternative to reach P even if P/M is shown as offline- he is informing P while exploring this alternative.

6 Discussions

In our work, context was used in parallel. Firstly, using a hierarchy of learning and communication tied to situated cognition to model context. Secondly based on this modeling, we analyze conversations in breakdown situations to understand what could possibly construe a 'punctuation of context' from streams of events. There are several generalities that emerged during the observations. The conversation structures are always being *re-sequenced through out* the *time* in making *associations* to *specific items* (e.g., global status, user P, user M, offline, online). These items re-appeared during the breakdown situations while user M is solving the problem. While he is solving the problem, he *relates* the *specific items* to *certain features* of the BuddySpace. It appears to be a complex interchanging idea of *focus*. M is seeking to what he is 'actively perceiving' on the user interface. The way he solve the problems seems to be *tied* to his *current focus* and this influences how he is making *associations* between the *old primitives* to the *new primitives*. Whenever the context is changing at different point of moment, the old items extend to the new items, and it is *contextualized* at the moment. The association of the old to new primitives suggests that M is seeking alternatives *through remembering, forming association* that are then *contextualized arising rather simultaneously*. The changes in sequences are always 'situated'. These observations are suggesting that perhaps the context *context/environment* for the people is *categorical* through *perception* and *conception* [6]. The re-sequencing of the items suggests that the categorization is occurring at *different levels of learning* [4]. That is during the occurrences, there is a complex interplay of *knowing a conception*, and *seeking an alternative to an unknown conception-* making association between the two. It is still unknown to us how the *learning* is *occurring at different levels moment by moment-* e.g., how each item is being re-sequenced as responses. For example, in learning I. Whenever user M sees a 'label' that marks the *context* as 'unknown', has his interaction been punctuated or is it occurring within every step that the conversation is being articulated? We realize that the analyses are very preliminary specifically focused on one person's conversation structures. Nonetheless to understand and relate this act to cognition theories appears to be very complex. The purpose of the work is to build an assistive communication tool for scientific collaboration. In order to know exactly how the assistive system can be designed, we look into conversation structures and using contexts to help identify possible patterns that differentiate breakdown contexts to non-breakdown contexts. An example of what the assistive technology can do is to learn the patterns and to point to where a possible breakdown might occur during collaboration or whenever a breakdown has occurred, to help users 'get out' of breakdown situation. Hence, much of the future work will be devoted to continue modeling the context using the communication model (section 5) and refining it on the remaining corpus as a continuation to the previous [2],[3] and current analyses.

References

1. Binti Abdullah, N.N.: A theoretical framework for the analysis of actual human collaboration on the Web. Phd dissertation (2006), Link: http://honiden-lab.ex.nii.ac.jp/ bintiabd/
2. Binti Abdullah, N.N.: Analysis and Synthesis of Agent Communicative Behaviors. Towards the Learning GRID: advances in Human Learning Services. In: Ritrovato, P., Cerri, S. (eds.) Frontiers in Artificial Intelligence and Applications, vol. 19(9-10), pp. 1015–1041. Taylor and Francis, New York (2005)
3. Binti Abdullah, N.N., Cerri, S.A.: Some preliminary results on the: The induction of communication protocols. In: Cognitive Science 27th Annual Meeting, July 20-23, Stresa, Italy, pp. 268–274 (2005)
4. Bateson, G.: Steps to an ecology of mind. Chandler and Publications Co. (1972)
5. Clancey, W.J.: What we are learning about communication protocols (2001), http://www.spaceref.com/news/viewsr.html?pid=3280
6. Clancey, W.J.: Situated Cognition: On Human Knowledge and Computer Representations. Cambridge University Press, Cambridge (1997)
7. Eisenstadt, M., Komzak, J., Cerri, S.: Enhanced Presence and Messaging for Large-Scale e-Learning. In: the Proceedings of the 3rd International Conference Symposium on the Tele-Education and Life Long Learning (Teleduc'04) (2004)
8. Fipa-Acl.: Foundation for Intelligent Physical Agent. Agent communication Language: Communicative Acts Specification Library (2002)
9. HMP. NASA Haughton-Mars Project.: (2001) Link: http://www.marsonearth.org/about
10. Leont'ev, A.N.: Psychic Reflection, Ch. 2. In: Activity, Consciousness, and Personality. Psychology in the USSR, Problems of Dialectical Materialism. Progress Publishers (1978)
11. Matsumoto, N., Tokosumi, A.: Context Building Through Socially-Supported Belief. In: Dey, A.K., Kokinov, B., Leake, D.B., Turner, R. (eds.) CONTEXT 2005. LNCS (LNAI), vol. 3554, pp. 316–325. Springer, Heidelberg (2005)
12. Plucker, J.: Social Cognitive Theory (1999), Link.: http://www.indiana.edu/~edpsych/p540lectures/sct/index_files/vs_document.htm

Using Context for the Extraction of Relational Views*

Cristiana Bolchini, Elisa Quintarelli, Rosalba Rossato, and Letizia Tanca

Dip. Elettronica e Informatica, Politecnico di Milano
P.zza L. da Vinci, 32 - 20133 Milano, Italy
{bolchini, quintare, rossato, tanca}@elet.polimi.it

Abstract. The paper presents an approach for automatically extracting views from a relational database schema, based on the knowledge of the application domain. In order to achieve such result, the possible contexts emerging from the application domain are identified and, starting from the representation of the characterizing dimensions, a sequence of operations is applied to the schema to derive the portion of interest or, as we say, to *tailor the schema* with respect to each possible context. We introduce the tailoring operators as well as the method to compose partial views to obtain the final ones; a running example is used to lead the reader through the steps of the proposed methodology.

1 Introduction

The notion of "context" has received a lot of attention in the last years, due to the perception that context has often a significant impact on the way humans (or machines) act and on how they interpret things; furthermore, a change in context causes a transformation in the experience that is going to be lived. The word itself, derived from the Latin *con* (with or together) and *texere* (to weave), is descriptive; a context is not just a profile, it is an active process dealing with the way we *weave* our experience *together* to give it meaning. In general, the things we see or do remain unchanged, but the perception is different.

When dealing with the reality of *information management*, context plays a significant role in determining what portion of the entire information is relevant with respect to the ambient conditions. Furthermore, effective data access and management support is indispensable both when considering the huge amount of data usually available, which may confuse the user if not opportunely filtered, and when dealing with devices equipped with reduced resources where only the most valuable data should be kept.

Given this scenario, we propose a context-driven approach to extract data views, based on a) the identification of the context dimensions and their values with respect to the current application scenario, b) the definition of a set of operations to be applied to the entire data set in order to determine the portions of data (partial views) related to the context elements, and c) the combination of such partial views to obtain the data view associated with each possible context.

In this paper we focus the attention on relational databases, and on the extraction of relational views over them; yet, the methodology itself has a broader spectrum. The aim

* This work has been partially funded by projects MIUR-PRIN ESTEEM and MIUR-FIRB ARTDECO.

B. Kokinov et al. (Eds.): CONTEXT 2007, LNAI 4635, pp. 108–121, 2007.
© Springer-Verlag Berlin Heidelberg 2007

is to provide support to the designer of data management applications, be them related to huge (e. g., in data warehousing) or to a very small amount of data (e. g., in portable, lightweight data management systems), in determining and creating the various views to be used in the different contexts, by following a systematic approach. Such a structured methodology also allows to keep the complexity of the operation at an acceptable level and to facilitate maintenance when new context dimensions or values come into play.

These issues of context definition and context-aware view extractions are nowadays particularly investigated, due to the necessity of rationalizing the access to too much information, in articulated application scenarios. A detailed discussion on related work is presented in Section 5.

The rest of this paper is organized as follows. Section 2 illustrates in detail the goal of this approach, highlighting the main contribution of our work and introducing the adopted case study. Section 3 presents the two strategies for view definition, investigating their benefits and limitations, also with respect to the perception the designer has of the application scenario and data. In Section 4 the methodology is applied to the example scenario, walking the reader through the main phases to the result; related work is discussed in Section 5, whereas concluding remarks and considerations on future work are drawn in the last section.

2 Goals and Contributions

Let us consider the relational database of a large real estate agency that conducts negotiations related to flats, shops and houses located in different areas of the city.

The agency database stores data related to customers, estates, owners, and about its own agents. Moreover, when an agent enters into a contract with a customer, the information about the sale (or rent) contract is stored in the database. Our objective is designing a number of views, to be made available to different possible actors of the scenario: supervisors, agents, buyers and sellers. Supervisors are typically managers who are responsible for the agency business at a high level; supervisors are often the first to be in touch with the sellers, who establish the first contact with the top levels of the agency; subsequently, supervisors assign the sale to one or more agents, who will be in charge for it. The agents are also the first contacts for possible buyers of the estates assigned to them. The agency promotes its sales by various means, among which a Web site, which contains information for possible sellers and buyers, whose views are also to be designed over the corporate database.

The first step of the proposed approach consists in specifying the ambient dimensions characterizing the possible contexts in this application scenario, also listing the expected values, according to the methodology presented in [1].

More precisely, our context model, called *Context Dimension Tree*, is an extension of the context model presented in [2], and is used to systematically describe the user needs, and to capture the context the user is acting in. It plays a fundamental role in tailoring the target application data according to the user information needs. Once the possible contexts have been designed, each must be connected with the corresponding view definition. In this way, once the context becomes current, the view is computed

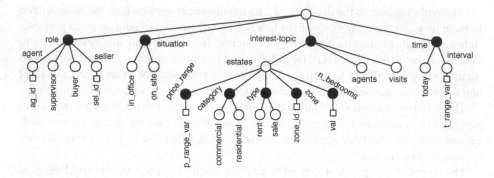

Fig. 1. The Context Dimension Tree

and delivered to the user. The various ways to operate such design-time connection are the subject of this paper.

The tree can be specified in several ways; in particular we propose an ontological representation in the OWL language [3], and an XML representation based on a DTD [4]. In the Context Dimension Tree, the root's children are the *context dimensions* which capture the different characteristics of the users and of the context they are acting in; by specifying a value for each dimension, a point in the multidimensional space representing the possible contexts is identified, a *context element*. A dimension value can be further analyzed with respect to different viewpoints, generating a subtree in its turn. However deep the tree, the complex structure originating from the composition of the Context Dimension Tree elements is called a *context* or *chunk configuration*, and determines a portion of the entire data set, i.e., a *chunk*, specified at design-time, to be selected later, at run-time, when the corresponding context becomes active. Black nodes represent dimensions and sub-dimensions, while white nodes represent the values they can assume, and more precisely, a context element is a concept node (white node), such as the supervisor, or a dimension node with a variable (black node) price_range(p_range_var), elements that determine a point in the space of all possible contexts.

A collection of one or more chunks constitutes the view the system makes available for the user when he or she is in a particular context. Fig. 1 shows the contexts we have elaborated for our real estate agency. The result is quite intuitive, we refer the interested reader to [5] for a more in-depth discussion on the Context Dimension Tree model.

It is worth noting that, in general, the Context Dimension Tree can be designed independently of the data schema. In the present application scenario, the single agency database is composed by the tables reported in Fig. 2.

Let us consider the particular situation of an agent who is currently at the office, and needs to check the sales of residential estates located in a certain area that have been concluded today. Thus, the current context (or chunk configuration) C is composed by the nodes

⟨{agent($ag_id)}, {in_office}, {today}, {residential, sale, zone($zone_id)}⟩

allowing the selection of the information related to the interesting sales.

OWNER(<u>IdOwner</u>, Name, Surname, Type, Address,City, PhoneNumber)
ESTATE(<u>IdEstate</u>, IdOwner, Category, Area, City, Province, RoomsNumber,
        Bedrooms, Garage, SquareMeters, Sheet, CadastralMap)
CUSTOMER(<u>IdCustomer</u>, Name, Surname, Type, Budget, Address, City, PhoneNum)
AGENT(<u>IdA</u>gent, Name, Surname, Office, Address,City,Phone)
AGENDA(<u>IdAgent, Data, Hour</u>, IdEstate, ClientName)
VISIT(<u>IdEstate, IdAgent, IdCustomer, Date</u>, VisitDuration)
SALES(<u>IdEstate, IdAgent, IdCustomer, Date</u>, AgreePrice, Status)
RENT(<u>IdEstate, IdAgent, IdCustomer, Date</u>, RatePrice, Status, Duration)

Fig. 2. The database schema

Such configuration must be associated at design time with the (definition of the) piece of data which must become available when C occurs, and the same must be done for each possible (and reasonable) chunk configuration. Note that the instantiation of the parameter $zone\_id$ is fed to the system at run time (e.g. with the value "Piola"). For this purpose, our context model provides *variables*, graphically represented as small squares attached to concept nodes of the Context Dimension Tree, to be suitably used by the run-time system.

Thus, at design time, once the tree has been defined, the list of its chunk configurations is combinatorially derived. Note that not all possible combinations make sense for a given scenario; the model allows the expression of constraints or preferences on the allowed combinations of the dimension values, thus the meaningless ones are not generated. We do not further elaborate on constraints, which are thoroughly dealt with in [5].

The subsequent work of the designer can take two different directions, one more time-consuming but allowing for a more precise view production, the second one more automatic but more prone to possible errors, thus to be verified a-posteriori.

When the first strategy is adopted, once the chunk configurations are combinatorially derived the designer associates each of them with the corresponding portion of the information domain schema. This can be done by directly writing a query in the language supported by the underlying database, or by selecting these portions by means of a graphical interface which will derive the corresponding view. This process is already supported by a tool we have developed [6]. However, as it can be expected, even after excluding the meaningless configurations, a medium-size Context Dimension Tree originates a huge number of chunk configurations, thus the task of associating relevant chunks to each of them is unpractical.

According to the second strategy, the designer must select the schema portion to be associated with *each context element*, and then the system will combine them within each chunk configuration. The possible combination policies involve the use of different combination operators, such as intersection or union, and the designer should choose different association methods according to the chosen operators.

The next section presents the two proposed strategies, discussing benefits and limitations.

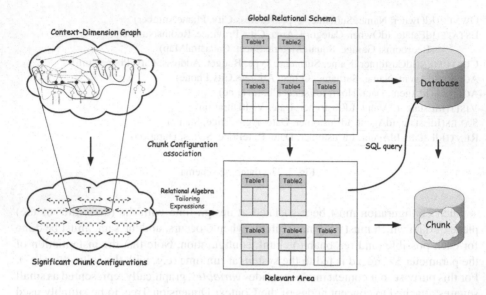

Fig. 3. The Configuration-based mapping strategy

3   Strategies for View Definition

In this section we describe our proposal to define a context-dependent view – expressed as a set of relational algebra expressions – for each chunk configuration. To achieve this goal we have developed two possible strategies: the *configuration-based mapping* and the *value-based mapping*.

Configuration-based mapping

The mapping specifies, for each context (i. e., chunk configuration) C, the set of queries that define the portion of the global database useful for that context. In particular, the designer associates with each chunk configuration the schema chunk (i.e., the view) that s/he deems significant for that specific configuration. Fig. 3 shows the dynamics of the configuration-based mapping strategy.

Example 1. As an example, let us now consider the chunk configuration of the previous section:

$$C = \langle\{\{\texttt{agent(\$ag\_id)}\}, \{\texttt{in\_office}\}, \{\texttt{today}\}, \{\texttt{residential}, \texttt{sale}, \texttt{zone(\$zone\_id)}\}\}\rangle$$

According to the configuration-based mapping, the designer has to select the portion of the global database that is relevant for the current context. In this example, a possible chunk associated with the considered chunk configuration is:

$$\mathcal{R}el(C) = \sigma_{(Category=\text{``Residential''} \land Area=\$zone\_id)}(\text{ESTATE}) \bowtie$$
$$(\sigma_{Date=\$TODAY}(\text{SALE}) \bowtie \text{CUSTOMER}) \qquad \square$$

This strategy has two main disadvantages: (1) the number of chunk configurations for real applications is quite high (e.g., in the present example there are 816 significant contexts), thus, this strategy requires a lot of effort at design time because the designer has

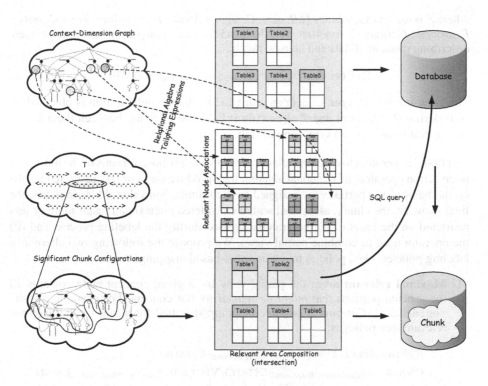

Fig. 4. The Value-based mapping strategy

to manually specify all the views for the chunk configurations resulting from the context model of the target application; (2) if the context model changes, e.g. if a new concept is inserted, a high number of new chunk configurations will have to be generated from its combination with the other concepts, and the designer will have to redefine all the mappings for these.

Value-based mapping

With this strategy, the designer maps each concept node of the tree to a portion (called partial view) of the relational schema. To achieve this goal, he/she labels each node of the Context Dimension Tree with a set of relational algebra expressions that, applied to the global database, allow to define the partial views for the considered node. In the following we refer to this step as *labeling phase*.

After the labeling phase, the view related to each specific chunk configuration is automatically obtained by combining the partial views of its concept nodes. The dynamics of this second strategy is depicted in Fig. 4.

Example 2. For example, the buyer *role* is mapped to a view describing both commercial and residential flats and houses, that is, the ESTATE table deprived of the IdOwner and CadastralMap attributes, which are not interesting for prospective buyers. Formally:

$$\mathcal{R}el(\text{buyer}) = \{\Pi_Z \text{ESTATE}\}$$

where Z is the set of attributes $\{IdEstate, Category, Area, City, Province, RoomsNumber, Bedrooms, Garage, SquareMeters\}$. The residential *category* is a relational view describing residential flats and houses, that is:

$$\mathcal{R}el(\texttt{residential}) = \{\sigma_{Category="Residential"}\text{ESTATE}\}$$

The view for the $\langle\{\texttt{buyer}\}, \_, \_, \{\texttt{residential}\}\rangle$ chunk configuration is obtained by considering $\mathcal{R}el(\texttt{buyer})$ and $\mathcal{R}el(\texttt{residential})$ and applying between them a suitable operator for (partial) view composition. □

As possible operators to combine relational views, we propose variants of the union and intersection operators of relational algebra; they produce more or less restricted results on the basis of the partial view assigned to each dimension value. More in detail, the final view, i.e. the chunk, associated with a considered context can result more or less restricted on the basis of (i) the granularity used during the labeling process and (ii) the operator used to combine partial views. We propose the following two alternative labeling policies – i.e., policies to define value-based mappings.

1. **Maximal relevant area:** the partial view for a given concept node contains all the schema portions that *might be related* to that concept. For example, for the residential *Category* a possible mapping specified by means of the maximal relevant area policy is:

    $\mathcal{R}el(\texttt{residential}) = \{\sigma_{Category="Residential"}\text{ESTATE},$

    OWNER $\ltimes (\sigma_{Category="Residential"}\text{ESTATE}),$ VISIT $\ltimes (\sigma_{Category="Residential"}\text{ESTATE}),$

    SALES $\ltimes (\sigma_{Category="Residential"}\text{ESTATE}),$ RENT $\ltimes (\sigma_{Category="Residential"}\text{ESTATE}),$

    AGENDA $\ltimes (\sigma_{Category="Residential"}\text{ESTATE}) \}$

    According to the spirit of the maximal relevant area policy, in this example the view associated with the residential *Category* contains all the information that is related, in some way, to residential properties; that is, besides the ESTATE table with the specific selection conditions, the view also contains all the further information related to residential flats and houses included in the OWNER, VISIT, SALES, RENT, and AGENDA tables.

2. **Minimal relevant area:** the value-based mapping of a given concept node only specifies the data that *are strictly needed* for that concept.
    For the residential *Category*, the minimal relevant area policy would choose the view: $\mathcal{R}el(\texttt{residential}) = \{\sigma_{Category="Residential"}\text{ESTATE}\}$ which only chooses the tuples of the ESTATE table that refer to residential properties.

It is worth remarking that the hierarchical structure of the Context Dimension Tree has been designed with the idea that lower-level concept nodes correspond, in the data schema, to smaller portions of data, thus the detail level of the data selected while descending the subtree related to each context dimension increases. Thus, it is desirable that the partial view for a node n contain the partial view of each descendant m of n; i.e. $\mathcal{R}el(n) \supseteq \mathcal{R}el(m)$.

According to our experience, we mean the maximal area policy to assign the widest view for each node of the Context Dimension Tree; consequently, for the designer who

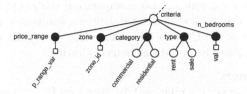

Fig. 5. The portion of the Context Dimension Tree that describes `criteria` information related to estates

applies this policy, it is more natural to perform the labeling phase by navigating the Context Dimension Tree *top-down* (from the root to the leaves). This actually means that the partial view for the root node is the entire database, and, in general, the partial view for any node m is defined by restricting its parent's partial view. Thus, the labeling phase is performed by navigating the Context Dimension Tree top-down and by specifying for each node m a view $(\mathcal{R}el(m))$ over the (previously defined) $(\mathcal{R}el(n))$ of its parent n.

Example 3. Let us now focus our attention on the subpart of the Context Dimension Tree shown in Fig. 5. Consider the maximal area policy; the partial view for the `criteria` *interest-topic* is a view containing all the information related to flats and houses. Formally:

$$\mathcal{R}el(\texttt{criteria}) = \{\text{ESTATE}, \text{OWNER}, \text{VISIT}, \text{SALES}, \text{RENT}, \text{AGENDA}\}$$

The partial view for the `residential` *category* (that is the same one reported for the maximal relevant area policy) is a set of views restricting $\mathcal{R}el(\texttt{criteria})$ only to information about the residential estates:

$$\mathcal{R}el(\texttt{residential}) = \{\sigma_{Category=\text{"Residential"}}\text{ESTATE}, \text{OWNER} \ltimes (\sigma_{Category=\text{"Residential"}}\text{ESTATE})$$

$$\text{VISIT} \ltimes (\sigma_{Category=\text{"Residential"}}\text{ESTATE}), \text{SALES} \ltimes (\sigma_{Category=\text{"Residential"}}\text{ESTATE}),$$

$$\text{RENT} \ltimes (\sigma_{Category=\text{"Residential"}}\text{ESTATE}), \text{AGENDA} \ltimes (\sigma_{Category=\text{"Residential"}}\text{ESTATE})\} \qquad \square$$

By contrast, the minimal area policy should be used when the designer prefers to assign the minimal partial chunk for each node of the Context Dimension Tree; in this case, to be adherent with the spirit of the Context Dimension Tree, it is recommended, when this policy has been chosen by the designer, to perform the labeling phase by navigating the Context Dimension Tree *bottom-up*. This means that the mappings are defined starting from the leaf nodes and the view of a non-leaf node can be obtained by composing the views associated with its children. The composition can be realized by using the union operator and possibly adding additional portions of the global database that the designer considers useful for the more general (non-leaf) concept. For example, when using the minimal policy, $\mathcal{R}el(\texttt{criteria})$ can be obtained by combining $\mathcal{R}el(\texttt{price\_range})$, $\mathcal{R}el(\texttt{zone})$, $\mathcal{R}el(\texttt{category})$, $\mathcal{R}el(\texttt{type})$, and $\mathcal{R}el(\texttt{n\_bedrooms})$.

Since the choice, on the designer's part, of a different labeling policy gives rise to different kinds of mappings, also different operators should be used in the two cases to combine the partial views. These operators can be applied for two purposes: (i) to derive the chunk associated with a chunk configuration, starting from the partial views, and (ii) to define the partial view associated with non-leaf nodes, as discussed for the bottom-up navigation of the Context Dimension Tree during the labeling phase. The operators and their use will be introduced in the following.

Combination Operators

The context-defined views on a relational database may be written by using relational algebra or, equivalently, in SQL, as shown in Section 4. In order to compose different views, and automatically obtain the view for a given context, we need to introduce a suite of new algebraic operators which work on *sets of relations*, which have been formally defined in [7], and whose intuition is provided in the following.

Let $\mathcal{A}$ and $\mathcal{B}$ be two sets of relations, and $S_{\mathcal{A}}$ and $S_{\mathcal{B}}$ the corresponding sets of relational schemata.

Double Union operator: the double union operator $\mathcal{A} \uplus \mathcal{B}$, of $\mathcal{A}$ and $\mathcal{B}$, returns the union of the set of all relations R_i whose schema is in $(S_{\mathcal{A}} - S_{\mathcal{B}}) \cup (S_{\mathcal{B}} - S_{\mathcal{A}})$ and a sort of intersection between R_A and R_B, for each pair of relations $R_A \in \mathcal{A}$ and $R_B \in \mathcal{B}$ having the same schema [1].

Example 4. Assume the labeling of the residential *category* and the buyer *role* reported in the Example 2 (minimal area policy). The view associated with the chunk configuration $\mathsf{C} = \langle \{\mathtt{buyer}\}, \_, \_, \{\mathtt{residential}\} \rangle$ obtained by applying the Double Union operator between $\mathcal{R}el(\mathtt{buyer})$ and $\mathcal{R}el(\mathtt{residential})$ is the following:

$$\mathcal{R}el(\mathsf{C}) = \mathcal{R}el(\mathtt{buyer}) \uplus \mathcal{R}el(\mathtt{residential}) = \sigma_{Category=\text{``Residential''}}(\Pi_Z(\text{ESTATE}))$$

where Z is the set of attributes {*IdEstate, Category, Area, City, Province, RoomsNumber, Bedrooms, Garage, SquareMeters*}.   □

Example 5. Assume the same relevant area for the residential *category*, and for the agent *role* the minimal relevant area containing his/her data and agenda : $\mathcal{R}el(\mathtt{agent}) = \{\sigma_{IdAgent=\$ag\_id}(\text{AGENT}), \sigma_{IdAgent=\$ag\_id}(\text{AGENDA})\}$. The view associated with the chunk configuration $\mathsf{C} = \langle \{\mathtt{agent}(\$\mathtt{ag\_id})\}, \_, \_, \{\mathtt{residential}\} \rangle$ obtained by applying the Double Union operator between $\mathcal{R}el(\mathtt{agent}(\$\mathtt{ag\_id}))$ and $\mathcal{R}el(\mathtt{residential})$ is:

$$\mathcal{R}el(\mathsf{C}) = \mathcal{R}el(\mathtt{agent}(\$\mathtt{ag\_id})) \uplus \mathcal{R}el(\mathtt{residential})$$

$$= \{\sigma_{IdAgent=\$ag\_id}(\text{AGENT}), \sigma_{IdAgent=\$ag\_id}(\text{AGENDA}), \sigma_{Category=\text{``Residential''}}(\text{ESTATE})\} \quad □$$

Double Intersection operator: the double intersection operator $\cap\!\!\!\cap$ applies the intersection operator $\cap$ of relational algebra to the maximal common subschemata of the pairs of relations R_A and R_B, belonging to $\mathcal{A}$ and $\mathcal{B}$, respectively, where either $\mathrm{Sch}(R_A) \subseteq \mathrm{Sch}(R_B)$ or $\mathrm{Sch}(R_B) \subseteq \mathrm{Sch}(R_A)$.

After this first step, the standard union $\cup$ is recursively applied between pairs of the obtained relations having the same schema, since the Double Intersection can generate several relations with the same schema.

---

[1] In this way we preserve selection conditions which have possibly been applied on the same tables in the definition phase of $\mathcal{A}$ and $\mathcal{B}$.

Example 6. Let us now assume that the maximal area policy is applied. The view associated with the agent *role* is

$$\mathcal{R}el(\text{agent}) = \{\sigma_{IdAgent=\$ag\_id}\,\text{AGENT}, \sigma_{IdAgent=\$ag\_id}\,\text{AGENDA},$$
$$\text{VISIT}, \text{SALES}, \text{RENT}, \text{OWNER}, \text{CUSTOMER}, \text{ESTATE}\}$$

while the view related to `residential` *category* is that reported in Example 3.

Consider now the context of agent $\$ag\_id$ specified by the chunk configuration $C = \langle\{\text{agent}(\$ag\_id)\}, \_, \_, \{\text{residential}\}\rangle$. The chunk obtained by applying the Double Intersection operator between $\mathcal{R}el(\text{agent})$ and $\mathcal{R}el(\text{residential})$ is the following:

$$\mathcal{R}el(C) = \mathcal{R}el(\text{agent}(\$ag\_id)) \Cap \mathcal{R}el(\text{residential})$$
$$= \{\sigma_{Category=\text{``Residential''}}\text{ESTATE}, \text{OWNER} \ltimes (\sigma_{Category=\text{``Residential''}}, \text{ESTATE})$$
$$\text{VISIT} \ltimes (\sigma_{Category=\text{``Residential''}}\text{ESTATE}), \text{SALES} \ltimes (\sigma_{Category=\text{``Residential''}}\text{ESTATE})$$
$$\text{RENT} \ltimes (\sigma_{Category=\text{``Residential''}}\text{ESTATE}),$$
$$(\sigma_{IdAgent=\$ag\_id}(\text{AGENDA})) \ltimes (\sigma_{Category=\text{``Residential''}}\text{ESTATE})\} \qquad \square$$

Note that Double Union and Double Intersection are *commutative* and *associative*.

4 View Extraction

To better illustrate our methodology, in this section we propose a real-world case study about the estate agency scenario introduced in Section 2. Suppose that, by applying the value-based mapping strategy, the designer has associated the following partial views by using the *maximal relevant area policy*:

$$\mathcal{R}el(\text{agent}(\$ag\_id)) = \{\sigma_{IdAgent=\$ag\_id}\text{AGENT}, \sigma_{IdAgent=\$ag\_id}\text{AGENDA},$$
$$\text{VISIT}, \text{SALES}, \text{RENT}, \text{OWNER}, \text{CUSTOMER}, \text{ESTATE}\}$$
$$\mathcal{R}el(\text{Residential}) = \{\sigma_{Category=\text{``Residential''}}\text{ESTATE},$$
$$\text{OWNER} \ltimes (\sigma_{Category=\text{``Residential''}}\text{ESTATE})$$
$$\text{VISIT} \ltimes (\sigma_{Category=\text{``Residential''}}\text{ESTATE})$$
$$\text{SALES} \ltimes (\sigma_{Category=\text{``Residential''}}\text{ESTATE})$$
$$\text{RENT} \ltimes (\sigma_{Category=\text{``Residential''}}\text{ESTATE})\}$$
$$\text{AGENDA} \ltimes (\sigma_{Category=\text{``Residential''}}\text{ESTATE})\}$$
$$\mathcal{R}el(\text{sale}) = \{\text{SALES}, \text{OWNER}, \text{CUSTOMER}, \text{AGENT}, \text{VISIT}\}$$
$$\mathcal{R}el(\text{zone}(\$zone\_id)) = \{\sigma_{Area=\$zone\_id}\text{ESTATE}, \text{SALES} \ltimes (\sigma_{Area=\$zone\_id}\text{ESTATE}),$$
$$\text{RENT} \ltimes (\sigma_{Area=\$zone\_id}\text{ESTATE}), \text{OWNER} \ltimes (\sigma_{Area=\$zone\_id}\text{ESTATE})\}$$

Table 1. The partial views associated with the Agent *role* by using the maximal policy

```
{  create view AgentData(IdAgent,Name,Surname,Office,Address,City,Phone)
       as select * from AGENT where IdAgent=$ag_id;
   create view AgentAgenda(IdAgent,Data,Hour,IdEstate,ClientName)
       as select * from AGENDA where IdAgent=$ag_id;
   VISIT; SALES; RENT; OWNER; CUSTOMER; ESTATE     }
```

Table 2. The partial views associated with the Residential *category* by using the maximal policy

```
{  create view ResidEstate(IdEstate,IdOwner,Category,Area,City,Province,
                          RoomsNumber,BedRooms,Garage,SquareMeters,Sheet,CadastralMap)
     as select * from ESTATE where Category='Residential';
   create view ResidOwner(IdOwner,Name,Surname,Type,Address,City,PhoneNumber)
     as select * from OWNER where IdOwner IN
           (select IdOwner from ESTATE where Category='Residential');
   create view ResidVisit(IdEstate,IdAgent,IdCustomer,Date,VisitDuration)
     as select * from VISIT where IdEstate IN
           (select IdEstate from ESTATE where Category='Residential');
   create view ResidSale(IdEstate,IdAgent,IdCustomer,Date,AgreePrice,Status)
     as select * from SALES where IdEstate IN
           (select IdEstate from ESTATE where Category='Residential');
   create view ResidRent(IdEstate,IdAgent,IdCustomer,Date,RatePrice,Status,Duration)
     as select * from RENT where IdEstate IN
           (select IdEstate from ESTATE where Category='Residential');
   create view ResidAgenda(IdAgent,Date,Hour,IdEstate,ClientName)
     as select * from Agenda where IdEstate IN
           (select IdEstate from ESTATE where Category='Residential') }
```

Table 3. The partial views associated with the Sale *type* by using the maximal policy

{OWNER; CUSTOMER; AGENT; SALES; VISIT }

Table 4. The partial views associated with context element Zone, by using the maximal policy

```
{ create view ZonaEstate(IdEstate,IdOwner,Category,Area,City,Province,
                         RoomsNumber,BedRooms,Garage,SquareMeters,Sheet,CadastralMap)
    as select * from ESTATE where Area = $zone_id;
  create view ZonaSale(IdEstate,IdAgent,IdCustomer,Date,AgreePrice,Status)
    as select * from SALES where IdEstate IN
          (select IdEstate from ESTATE where Area=$zone_id);
  create view ZonaRent(IdEstate,IdAgent,IdCustomer,Date,RatePrice,Status,Duration)
    as select * from RENT where IdEstate IN
          (select IdEstate from ESTATE where Area=$zone_id
          );
  create view ZonaOwner(IdOwner,Name,Surname,Type,Address,City,PhoneNumber)
    as select * from OWNER where IdOwner IN
          (select IdOwner  from ESTATE where Area=$zone_id)}
```

Table 5. The views associated with the chunk configuration ⟨{agent($ag_id)},_,_, {residential, sale, zone($zone_id)}⟩ by using the maximal policy

```
{ create view ResidZonaEstate(IdEstate,IdOwner,Category,Area,City,Province,
                           RoomsNumber,BeedRooms,Garage,SquareMeters,Sheet,CadastralMap)
   as select * from ESTATE where Area = $zone_id AND Category='Residential';
  create view ResidZonaSale(IdEstate,IdAgent,IdCustomer,Date,AgreePrice,Status)
   as select * from SALES where IdEstate IN
          (select IdEstate from ESTATE where Area=$zone_id AND Category='Residential');
  create view ResidZonaOwner(IdOwner,Name,Surname,Type,Address,City,PhoneNumber)
   as select * from OWNER where IdOwner IN
          (select IdOwner from Estate where Area=$zone_id AND Category='Residential')}
```

These partial views can be mapped to a set of CREATE VIEW constructs of SQL or database relations, as shown by the code fragments of Tables 1, 2, 3 and 4. The chunk related to the chunk configuration $\langle$agent($\$$ag_id),_,_,{residential, sale, zone($\$$zone_id)}$\rangle$ can be obtained by applying the ⓜ operator to the partial views as follows:

$$\mathcal{R}el(\langle\text{agent}(\$\text{ag\_id}),\_,\_,\{\text{residential, sale, zone}(\$\text{zone\_id})\}\rangle) =$$
$$\mathcal{R}el(\text{agent}(\$\text{ag\_id})) \text{ⓜ} \mathcal{R}el(\text{residential}) \text{ⓜ} \mathcal{R}el(\text{sale}) \text{ⓜ} \mathcal{R}el(\text{zone}(\$\text{zone\_id}))$$

The translation into a set of SQL views is reported in Table 5.

5   Related Work

Several policies and methodologies for view definition have been suggested in the literature during the past years. More precisely, context and its dimensions have been studied in ([8,9,10,11,12,2]) from several points of views and spanning over interdisciplinary research fields ([13]). The early pioneer models and view-design proposals are for relational databases [14], but more recently, the success of XML has motivated the need of models that are independent of the underlying data model. The problem of view definition for XML has been formalized in [15,16], and some other proposals in the XML area are [17,18].

In the Semantic Web Area some view models based on ontologies have been proposed in [19].

The proposals described in [14,15,16,17,18,19] follow the classical notion of view extraction process and need to be extended to consider also user's activity, tasks, and intentions, in fact, the user's context (see [20,11,21,22]).

When focusing on the relational model of data, a few solutions have been presented to introduce the notion of context in the data being modeled, by means of additional attributes explicitly defining the context (e.g., space and time characteristics) the data belongs to ([23,24,25]); in these situations, the final goal is to make data context-aware, thus context and the data schema need be designed at the same time, foreseeing if not all values, all possible context dimensions.

In [23] the Context Relational Model is presented as an extension of the relational one: the notion of context is treated as a fist-class citizen that must be modeled and can be queried; indeed, in the authors' opinion, attribute values may change under different contexts and may not exist in some other contexts. The approach is different from ours, because we study a technique to tailor data, i.e., extract and elaborate relevant portions of relational databases with respect to a notion of context, and do not propose instance changes on the basis of the context dimension values.

In [26] some conceptual operators are formalized for constructing conceptual context dependent views on XML data. In our opinion, the notion of context we use is much more articulated (mutual exclusive and orthogonal dimensions are modeled) and thus, we need to define operators both to extract views, and to combine partial views; the composition step is required to obtain views suitable to represent the relevant portion of data for a notion of context that depends on more than one dimension.

6   Conclusion and Future Work

In this paper we have presented two complementary context-driven strategies for automatic view design over a relational database schema, with the aim of selecting a portion of the entire system with respect to one of the possible contexts for the application scenario. The methodology adopting these two approaches is based on the definition of the Context Dimension Tree, representing the contexts, and on its labeling, in order to build the views. This context-aware view extraction can be adopted in numerous scenarios, from those where small devices are considered, to those where large amount of data need be filtered to offer a more simplified and efficient access and management.

While the configuration-based scenario is already supported (based on ER and XML), we are currently building a first Java prototype environment to demonstrate the flexibility of our methodology dealing with value-based mappings. It is basically formed by two components: the first one is used to configure the labeling policy and the operators to compose partial views; the second is a graphical interface which allows the designer to assign each node its partial view.

References

1. Bolchini, C., Quintarelli, E.: Filtering mobile data by means of context: a methodology. In: Meersman, R., Tari, Z., Herrero, P. (eds.) On the Move to Meaningful Internet Systems 2006: OTM 2006 Workshops. LNCS, vol. 4278, pp. 1986–1995. Springer, Heidelberg (2006)
2. Bolchini, C., Schreiber, F.A., Tanca, L.: A methodology for very small database design. Information Systems 32(1), 61–82 (2007)
3. McGuinness, D.L., van Harmelen, F.: OWL Web Ontology Language Overview, W3C Recommendation (2004)
4. Bolchini, C., Quintarelli, E.: Filtering mobile data by means of context: a methodology. In: Proc. 2nd Int. Workshop on Context Representation and Reasoning, pp. 13–18 (2006)
5. Bolchini, C., Curino, C., Quintarelli, E., Schreiber, F.A., Tanca, L.: Context information for knowledge reshaping. Int. Journal on Web Engineering and Technology (in print 2007)
6. Bolchini, C., Curino, C.A., Orsi, G., Quintarelli, E., Schreiber, F.A., Tanca, L.: CADD: a tool for context modeling and data tailoring. In: Proc. IEEE/ACM Int. Conf. on Mobile Data Management - Demo Session, pp. 221–223. ACM Press, New York (2007)
7. Bolchini, C., Quintarelli, E., Rossato, R.: Relational data tailoring through view composition (submitted for publication)
8. Lenat, D.: Dimensions of context-space. Technical report, Cycorp. (1998)
9. Dey, A.K.: Understanding and using context. Personal Ubiquitous Comput. 5(1), 4–7 (2001)
10. Benerecetti, M., Bouquet, P., Ghidini, C.: On the dimensions of context dependence: Partiality, approximation, and perspective. In: Proc. 3rd Int.l and Interdisciplinary Conf. on Modeling and Using Context, pp. 59–72. Springer, Heidelberg (2001)
11. Ghidini, C., Giunchiglia, F.: Local Models Semantics, or contextual reasoning=locality+compatibility. Artificial Intellicence 127(2), 221–259 (2001)
12. Strang, T., Linnhoff-Popien, C.: A context modeling survey. In: 1st Int. Workshop on Advanced Context Modelling, Reasoning and Management (2004)
13. Feng, L., Apers, P.M.G., Jonker, W.: Towards context-aware data management for ambient intelligence. In: Galindo, F., Takizawa, M., Traunmüller, R. (eds.) DEXA 2004. LNCS, vol. 3180, pp. 422–431. Springer, Heidelberg (2004)
14. Elmasri, R., Navathe, S.: Fundamentals of database systems, 4th edn. Pearson/Addison Wesley (2004)
15. Abiteboul, S.: On views and xml. In: Proc. 18th ACM SIGACT-SIGMOD-SIGART Symp. on Principles of Database Systems, pp. 1–9 (1999)
16. Cluet, S., Veltri, P., Vodislav, D.: Views in a large scale of XML repository. In: Proc. 27th Int. Conf. on Very Large Data Bases, pp. 271–289 (2001)

17. Zhuge, Y., Garcia-Molina, H.: Graph structured views and their incremental maintenance. In: Proc. IEEE 14th Int. Conf. on Data Engineering, pp. 116–125. IEEE Computer Society Press, Los Alamitos (1998)

18. Liefke, H., Davidson, S.B.: View maintenance for hierarchical semistructured data. In: Kambayashi, Y., Mohania, M.K., Tjoa, A.M. (eds.) DaWaK 2000. LNCS, vol. 1874, pp. 114–125. Springer, Heidelberg (2000)

19. Volz, R., Oberle, D., Studer, R., Staab, S.: Views for light-weight web ontologies. In: Proc. ACM Symp. on Applied Computing, pp. 1168–1173. ACM Press, New York (2003)

20. Jiang, L., Topaloglou, T., Borgida, A., Mylopoulos, J.: Incorporating goal analysis in database design: A case study from biological data management. In: Proc. 14th Italian Symp. on Advanced Database Systems, pp. 14–17 (2006)

21. Rajugan, R., Chang, E., Dillon, T.S.: Ontology views: A theoretical perspective. In: Meersman, R., Tari, Z., Herrero, P. (eds.) On the Move to Meaningful Internet Systems 2006: OTM 2006 Workshops. LNCS, vol. 4278, pp. 1814–1824. Springer, Heidelberg (2006)

22. Wouters, C., Rajugan, R., Dillon, T.S., Rahayu, J.W.R.: Ontology extraction using views for semantic web. In: Web Semantics and Ontology, pp. 1–40. Idea Group Pub. (2005)

23. Roussos, Y., Stavrakas, Y., Pavlaki, V.: Towards a context-aware relational model. In: Proc. Context Representation and Reasoning - CRR'05, pp. 7.1–7.12 (2005)

24. Parent, C., Spaccapietra, S., Zimanyi, E.: Conceptual Modeling for Traditional and Spatio-Temporal Applications - The MADS Approach. Springer, Heidelberg (2006)

25. Stuckenschmidt, H.: Toward multi-viewpoint reasoning with owl ontologies. In: Proc. 3rd European Semantic Web Conference, pp. 259–272 (2006)

26. Rajugan, R., Dillon, T.S., Chang, E., Feng, L.: A Layered View Model for XML Repositories and XML Data Warehouses. In: Proc. IEEE 5th Int. Conf. on Computer and Information Technology, pp. 206–215. IEEE Computer Society Press, Los Alamitos (2005)

Context Modeling: Task Model and Practice Model

Patrick Brézillon

LIP6, University Paris 6
104 avenue du Président Kennedy, 75016, Paris, France
`Patrick.Brezillon@lip6.fr`

Abstract. Contextual Graphs are a context-based formalism used in various real-world applications. They allow a uniform representation of elements of reasoning and of contexts for describing different human tasks such as troubleshooting and interpretation. A contextual graph represents a task realization. Its paths represent the different ways of reaching this realization, each way corresponding to a practice developed by an actor realizing the task. In this paper, we revisit the classical distinction between prescribed and effective tasks, procedures versus practices, logic of functioning versus logic of use, etc. in the light of this formalism. We discuss the position of the practice model with respect to the task model using an example involving troubleshooting a problem with a DVD player and another example involving the collaborative construction of an answer, and place this within the context of some other applications developed in the formalism of Contextual Graphs.

Keywords: Contextual graphs, Reasoning, Task, Activity, Procedures and practices.

1 Introduction

Brézillon and Pomerol [4] defined context as " that which constrains something without intervening in it explicitly." We now consider it by extension as the focus of an actor. Several elements justify this definition, the three main elements being that (1) context is relative to the focus, (2) as the focus evolves , its context evolves too, and (3) context is highly domain-dependent. As a consequence, one cannot speak of context in an abstract way.

Next, we can show that the focus at a given stage allows the division of the context into external knowledge and contextual knowledge [1]. The latter constitutes a kind of tank where the contextual elements are to some extent related to the focus in a flat way, whereas the former has nothing to do with the focus. At this conceptual level, the focus acts as a discriminating factor on knowledge in a similar way as for social networks [2]. The focus evolves because a new event occurs (e.g. an unpredicted event) or as a result of a decision made at the previous stage of the focus. The notion of context impacts more on the relationships between knowledge pieces than upon the pieces themselves.

B. Kokinov et al. (Eds.): CONTEXT 2007, LNAI 4635, pp. 122–135, 2007.
© Springer-Verlag Berlin Heidelberg 2007

At present, our research on context is organized along two axes , namely models of reasoning represented in Contextual Graphs, and knowledge instantiation of a part of contextual knowledge, which is structured within a proceduralized context. The formalism of contextual graphs has been used in several real-world applications. We present two applications along the first axis, addressing the question of a troubleshooting problem with a device (a DVD player in this paper) and the collaborative construction of the answer to a question. These applications allow the explicit identification of differences between the behavior prescribed by the procedures (corresponding to the instructions) and the actors' observed behaviors (users faced with a problem with a device). This is completely in line with the prescribed and effective tasks identified by Leplat [7] and procedures versus practices [1], and can be found in a number of applications such as road safety (an aid for self-evaluation of drivers), in medicine (an aid for users to query reformulation in a grid environment) and in software engineering (for the assembly of software pieces).

Along the second axis, we discuss in a companion paper [3] the relationships between contextual knowledge and the proceduralized context in order to implement them in a computer system. To address the current status of the focus, the actor selects a subset of contextual knowledge called proceduralized context. In terms of contextual knowledge, the proceduralized context is an ordered serics of instantiated contextual elements. The two keywords here are instantiation of contextual elements, which is also the link between the two axes , and comparison of the proceduralized context to a buffer between the focus and contextual knowledge.

In real-world applications, context appears as the "missing link" between domain knowledge and the focus. Brézillon and Brézillon [3] present a study on road safety, the representation of a simple crossroads in terms of a situation dressing. Domain knowledge contains elements like roads, lanes, traffic lights, countryside, city, lights, etc. To define a specific intersection, we must contextualize the domain knowledge ("Place" = "City", "Traffic lights" = no, etc.). Thus, the contextual element "Place" is instantiated to "City" and this implies that some other domain elements become irrelevant (e.g. "Field of corn" is no longer an instantiation of "At the corner of the intersection") and others must be instantiated (e.g. "Type of building at the corner"). This kind of dressing of the intersection corresponds to a contextualization of the situation. This contextualization, and thus we go back to the first axis on reasoning, leads to two types of inferencing rules. The first type concerns integrity constraints. For example, "Period of the day" = "Night" implies that the value "Sunny" is not relevant for the contextual element "Weather." The second type is composed of rules about what a driver must do in a given context. For example, "Period of the day" = "Night" implies that the value "Car lights" must be "Switch on." The latter rules constitute a kind of theoretical model of the behavior that drivers must enact in the specific context (i.e. dressing) of the situation, that is for the given situation dressing, the current focus. Thus, a student can have the same question (What do you do at the crossroads?) but will always have to reanalyze the situation in the light of the contexts generated randomly.

This paper presents the results of a study along the first axis, namely the difference between the task model and the practice model, the former being established by the company (those responsible for producing the highway code and laws in the previous example, or the engineers in the example of the DVD player hereafter), and the latter representing users' understanding of the task (from reading the instructions in the example of the DVD player). Note that the practice model in the DVD player application results from the collective work of a group of Masters students. There are clear differences with contextual graphs that can be produced by the students individually, but this is beyond the scope of this paper.

Hereafter, the paper is organized in the following way. The next section recalls the main characteristics of the context-based formalism of Contextual Graphs. After, we discuss the two types of model (i.e. task model and practice model) that are identified in a Contextual-Graph representation. The two following sections illustrate these notions within the application of troubleshooting a problem with a DVD player and of the collaborative construction of the answer to a question. After, we present briefly the type of results that we obtained in other applications.

2 Contextual Graphs

2.1 Context in Decision Making

In a previous piece of work on incident management for subway lines [9, 5], we showed that context-based reasoning has two parts: diagnosis and action. The diagnosis part analyzes the situation at hand and its context in order to extract the essential facts for the actions. The actions are undertaken in a predictable orderto realize the desired task. Sometimes, actions are undertaken even if the situation is not completely analyzed (or even analyzed at all). For example, a driver puts a vehicle into gear before any action or situation analysis. Other actions are carried out before the proceduralization of a part of contextual knowledge. Thus, diagnosis and actions constitute a continuous interlocked process, not two distinct and successive phases in context-based reasoning. Moreover, actions introduce changes in the situation or in knowledge about the situation, and imply a revision of the diagnosis, and thus of the decision making process itself. As a consequence, there is a need for a context-based formalism for a uniform representation of diagnosis and actions.

Contextual graphs propose a representation of this combination of diagnosis and actions. (A contextual graph represents a process of problem solving or at least a step in the process.) Diagnosis is represented by contextual elements. When a contextual node is encountered, an element of the situation is analyzed. The value of the contextual element, its instantiation, is taken into account as long as the situation is under analysis. Afterwards, this instantiation does not matter in the line of reasoning that can be merged again with the other lines of reasoning corresponding to other instantiations of the contextual element. Thus, contextual graphs allow a wide category of diagnosis/action representations for a given problem solving process.

2.2 The Formalism of Contextual Graphs

Contextual graphs are acyclic due to the time-directed representation and guarantee algorithm termination. Each contextual graph (and any sub-graphs in it) has exactly one root and one end node because the decision making process starts in a state of affairs and ends in another state of affairs (not necessarily with a unique solution on all the paths) and the branches express only different contextually-dependent ways to achieve this goal. This gives the general structure of a spindle to contextual graphs. A path represents a practice developed by an actor, and there are as many paths as practices known by the system.

The elements of a contextual graph are: actions, contextual elements, sub-graphs, activities and parallel action groupings [1]. An action is the building block of contextual graphs. A contextual element is a pair of nodes, a contextual node and a recombination node; a contextual node has one input and N outputs (branches) corresponding to the N instantiations of the contextual element. The recombination node is [N, 1] and represents the moment at which the instantiation of the contextual element does not matter anymore. Sub-graphs are themselves contextual graphs. They are mainly used for obtaining different displays of the contextual graph by aggregation and expansion, as in Sowa's conceptual graphs [12]).

An activity is a particular sub-graph that is identified by actors because it appears in the same way in different problem solving processes. An activity is defined in terms of the actor, situation, task and a set of actions. More precisely, an activity is a sequence of actions executed, in a given situation, in order to achieve a particular task that is to be accomplished by a given actor.

A parallel action grouping expresses the fact (and reduces the complexity of the representation) that several sub-graphs must be crossed before continuing, but the order in which sub-graphs are crossed is not important, and they could even be crossed in parallel. The parallel action grouping could be considered as a kind of "complex context."

3 Task Model and Practice Model

3.1 What Is Represented in a Contextual Graph?

Contextual Graphs constitute a context-based formalism for representing reasoning. They have been used in a large spectrum of domains such as medicine, ergonomics, psychology, the army, information retrieval, computer security, road safety, the law.

In the decision making domain, actors identify an activity as a recurring structure in problem solving. This recurring sub-structure is a complex action in the spirit of the notion of a scheme given in cognitive ergonomics [13] where schemes are intended for completing sub-goals. Each scheme organizes an activity around an object and can call on other schemes to complete specific sub-goals. A scheme can be specified by a name, a goal and a contextual graph representing a decision-making process that allows its goal to be achieved in a context-sensitive way. Both contextual graphs and schemes allow the representation of actors' activity and all its variants (procedures and practices), the integration of automatic learning and adaptation in a system, a clear representation of context in actors' reasoning, and the organization of the actors' activity itself.

More generally, enterprises establish procedures based on their experience in order to guide such reasoning. Procedures are collections of secure action sequences developed to address a given focus in any case. These procedures are decontextualized in order to cover a large class of similar focuses (generally differing by their contexts of occurrence), such as the procedure that a driver must follow when arriving at a crossroads, whatever the specificity of the crossroads and the current status of the driver. Such procedures describe the behavior that actors would adopt to address the focus, a kind of theoretical behavior for the actors (i.e. the task model).

Conversely, the practice model corresponds to the effective behaviors displayed by actors facing the focus in a specific context. Differences between the task model and the practice model arise mainly from a difference in the actors' perception due to different backgrounds. For example, everybody uses a refrigerator without difficulty (practice), but few people are aware of the concepts behind the functioning of a refrigerator (i.e. the second principle of Thermodynamics). Thus, if a problem occurs, the system is considered just like a black box, and the refrigerator is immediately brought to the repairer or thrown out and replaced by a new one.

3.2 Describing Task Execution…

The degree of formalization of the task model depends on the nature of the domain. For example, the subway belongs to the domain of Engineering and different ways to buy a ticket in the subway can be modeled exhaustively. Passengers' characteristics (mood, size, etc.) do not matter. Conversely, road safety is a domain where the focus and its context present a large spectrum of possibilities. For example, a crossroads can have the form of X, T, Y or more elaborated topologies, and laws and rules try to capture only the main features of the crossroads, ignoring the number of exceptions and contextual variants (e.g. driving in the fog). Moreover, drivers may develop some practices not anticipated in the Highway Code. Between these two extreme examples, there are applications where the practice model developed by users is based on a logic of use radically (and sometimes deliberately) different from the task model developed by technicians and based on a logic of functioning. This is the case of the DVD player instructions that is presented in the next section.

3.3 …Is not Executing the Task

Generally there are different methods for the task realization. For example, there are several ways of travelling from Paris to attend a conference in Copenhagen. One method consists of going by car with colleagues because it is the cheapest way. Another method is to take the train because you have time and would like to take time to produce a bibiography and/or to stop in Kaiserslautern first to visit a friend. A third method is to take a plane. Thus, there are three methods for the task "Attend the conference in Copenhagen." The task model, which would describe the actions to execute in this task, will retain a relatively high degree of generality (e.g. register, book an hotel, buy your ticket for the journey) and is not concerned with the choice of methods available to realize the task.

The choice of method depends on different contextual elements, and mainly on the values (instantiations) that these contextual elements have when the task must be realized. For example, I will pay for my plane ticket with an order form from my university or my credit card, depending on what I have in my bank account because I know that my university generally reimburses 3-4 months later (i.e. after the conference, not when I will be paying, 3 months before the conference). Generally, this level of detail is too fine for a procedure but could be essential for the actor.

A final difference between the task model and the practice model is when a new situation arises. This supposes the revision of the whole structure within the task model, when in the practice model this necessitates the addition of a few elements such as a new contextual element and a few actions. Thus, the practice model is incrementally enriched, but may move away from the task model.

4 Example: Troubleshooting a Problem with a DVD Player

This section presents the example of troubleshooting a problem with a DVD player, in the way that this troubleshooting would appear in the user manual for a DVD player [10]. There is a one-page aid for troubleshooting in a 40-page manual. We used the French version for this experiment, but we checked the French translation first against the English version.

4.1 Modeling the Task

We first analyzed the troubleshooting page in terms of contextual graphs by associating an alternative with a contextual element. For example, instructions are written such as "If the TV is not switched on, then first switch on the TV". This instruction can be translated directly into a contextual element "TV power" with two possible instantiations, "On" and "Off". The entire contextual graph for the troubleshooting page is presented in a simplified view in Figure 1 and the detailed part of "Video problem" is shown in Figure 2.

This knowledge structure is called the engineering viewpoint in a top-down way because the task model (i.e. how to initially troubleshoot a problem with a DVD player) relies heavily on domain knowledge and its structure in terms of mechanics, power, audio, video, etc. This is a "logic of functioning" that is represented as exclusive alternatives in the contextual graph because each step in the engineer's reasoning is based on a hypothetical-deductive approach. The user model in this troubleshooting presentation impacts on the level of detail to be provided. For a novice with a supposedly very low level of understanding, one sees "If you do not see a red light at the front of your device, then check if the device is connected to the power source," and to an "expert" with specialized knowledge (e.g. "Change AV") without explaining what AV means.

128   P. Brézillon

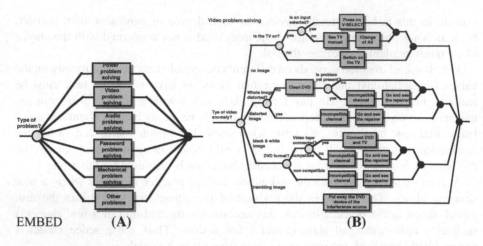

EMBED   (A)   (B)

Fig. 1. Contextual graph for the troubleshooting task for a DVD player (A) and details of the video problem solving process (B)

4.2 Development of a Practice Model

"See a movie on DVD" is a common task for a user. This (normal) task is accomplished regularly by users, and each time with success. Users move from their normal task to the troubleshooting task when a problem occurs at one stage of this routine task. Thus, troubleshooting concerns a given stage of the normal task, knowing that previous stages of the normal task are accomplished correctly.

The instructions for troubleshooting the DVD player were used by a group of seventeen Masters level students (studying context modeling at Paris 6 University). The goal of the experiment was to express in the contextual-graphs formalism their collective understanding of the instructions, not to compare their individual understanding, which was the goal of another experiment, "Buy a ticket for the subway in Paris", presented elsewhere. All the students were aware of how to use a DVD player, although with different perceptions and experience. The result, which is represented in Figure 2, is heavily experience-based. For example, it is natural for them to switch on the TV first before playing a DVD because "I know that the contents of the DVD (i.e. the menu and the movie) are shown on the TV screen." Second I know that the DVD reader is on because the TV and DVD reader are on the same plug. As a result, firstly they contextualize (i.e. use contextual cues) within their environment, and, secondly, they begin a troubleshooting task at the stage of their "See a movie on DVD" task where a discrepancy with what they expect appears. They follow a logic of use, but it is not a bottom-up approach which would contrast with the top-down approach in the task model. For these reasons, the practice model is sequential, and potential problems appear sequentially (mechanical first, etc.) and are ramified when different experiences and/or contexts intervene at each stage.

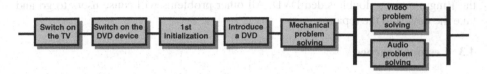

Fig. 2. Contextual graph of the DVD player troubleshooting task realized by users

Figure 2 presents the practice model developed by the students. Whilst the task model has a parallel architecture (see Figure 1A), the practice model has a sequential architecture (see Figure 2). There is also a strong difference at a finer level of description. Users have bought their DVD player, and this operation is not made frequently. Moreover, engineering parameters that are too subtle for the user (e.g. "Is the image completely or only partially distorted?") may lead to the user carrying out the wrong action, which could lead to the destruction of the device. Users then prefer to sum up the technical instructions in one action "Send to the repairer", which, indeed, is also the engineer's conclusion in most cases.

Users know that any action that is not correctly understood or carried out may lead to serious damage to the device, which will then need a more extensive intervention. Thus, users will decide to go and see the repairer. How serious a problem is for the user is a matter of personal interpretation. However, the risk of permanent damage to the device generally stops users from intervening personally, especially if the advice in the manual is written in incomprehensible language. For all these reasons, the solving of the video problem in practice, as represented by the contextual graph in Figure 3, is quite different to the engineer's approach (Figure 1B).

Video diagnosis

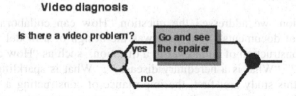

Fig. 3. Detail for the " visual signal? problem" stage of Figure 2 in the practice model for comparison with the same subtask represented in Figure (1B)

Unlike the engineering engineer's? concern, users pay attention to whether the device is under warranty or not, whereas this is not considered in the user manual. Users are also perfectly aware of what to do the first time they install the DVD player. This knowledge relies on their experience and similarity between the new device and devices already installed. A DVD player is like a VCR, it needs a power supply, an image appears on the TV screen, which thus must be switched on and connected to the DVD player, the remote control needs a battery (generally not provided with the device...) and user-device interaction will take place through the TV screen . There is also new information to learn, generally when a stage in the task is new, like the first time the user watches a movie on several DVDs (e.g. The Lord of the Rings) or on a double sided DVD. All other problems will cause users to go and take the device to the repairer.

4.3 Lessons Learned

The paradigm "Divide to conquer" is not applied in the same way in the engineer's logic of functioning and in users' logic of use . In the former, the problem is divided up according to its nature, i.e. domain knowledge (the causes of a mechanical problem are different to the causes of an audio problem). In the latter, the problem is divided chronologically along the normal temporal sequence of actions to be carried out (one first switches on the TV and then the DVD player and implicitly one checks whether there is a power supply problem).

The shared language between engineers and users is very restricted, especially in technical domains. For example, AV1 (audio-video channel 1) and V-SELECT do not belong to the users' language. This is an argument for users to take the DVD player directly to the repairer. Indeed, technical terms are introduced in the rest of the manual and supposed to be shared by the engineer and users, when users read separately (1) the manual for the installation of the device and to learn about its functioning, and (2) the part of the manual concerning troubleshooting on a different day, when it is needed. Moreover, users do not need an extensive knowledge of mechanics, video, etc. to see a movie on a DVD. This is a striking gap between the two viewpoints.

5 Example: Collaborative Answer Construction

5.1 The Experiment

In this application, we addressed the question "How can collaboration improve comprehension of documents?" The goal was the design of a model for the task of collaborative construction of an answer to a question, such as "How does an oyster produce a pearl?" "What is a hereditary disease?", "What is sparkling water?", etc. Two results of this study are: first, the importance of constructing a shared context (expressed as the sub-task of collecting contextual elements) to constructing the answer, and, second, the relative position of cooperation and collaboration to each other. We focus here on the representation of the construction process in a contextual graph, whereas the whole study is presented in [6]. Here, the task model is constructed from practices that are developed and observed by actors.

Eleven groups of two people participated in the experiments, and had sixteen questions to answer. We thus had 176 MP3 files of 90 seconds each to analyze. The two main findings (at least for our purpose here) concern:

- The *Dialog model*, which contains four "building blocks": (a) Repeat or reformulate the question, (b) Find an example, (c) Gather domain knowledge (collection), and (d) Construct the answer either by looking for characteristics or by assembling explanation elements (integration).
- The *constructed-answer model*, which possesses four paths: (a) Neither partner knows the answer, (b) Neither partner knows the whole answer but each has

elements with which to provide an explanation, (c) Co-construction of the answer, (d) One of the partners knows the exact answer and provides it.

Each path in the constructed-answer model represents a practice, such as (like?) a combination of the building blocks identified in the dialog model. Figure 4 represents the contextual graph for the constructed-answer model where all these elements are meet, and Figure 5 gives the detail for the "Activity-1" activity in Figure 4.

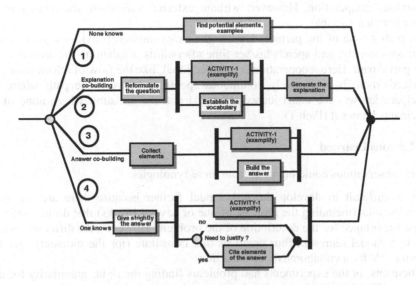

Fig. 4. Contextual Graph of the dialog with four ways to build collaboratively an answer

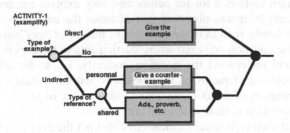

Fig. 5. Details of the "Exemplify" activity in Figure 4

On path 1, neither partner knows the answer. They have no elements of the answer at all. However, they try to utter some rough ideas (for example, a parallel with a known topic or the recall of an advertisement on TV) in order to trigger a constructive reaction from the other.

On path 2, neither partner knows the answer but they think they have elements to generate at least an explanation. Generally, a participant leads the interaction by proposing elements to the other, or asking him/her questions . Explanation generation is a kind of justification or validation to themselves of their general understanding of the question, without trying to construct an answer.

On path 3, both partners have a partial view of the answer, know some of the elements of the answer and assemble them with the elements provided by the other. (In terms of context, this corresponds to the construction of a proceduralized context.) They hold the same position in the construction of the answer, and there is no need for explanations between them or for an external observer. This is a situation of maximal cooperation. However, without external validation, the quality of the answer is rather variable.

On path 4, one of the partners knows the exact answer, provides it immediately and spontaneously, and spends his/her time afterwards explaining the answer to the other participant. Here cooperation is unidirectional, like the flow of information.

Indeed, there is a relatively continuous spectrum between the path where one participant knows the exact answer (Path 4) and the situation where none of the participants knows it (Path 1).

5.2 Lessons Learned

Several observations could be made from these typologies:

• It was difficult to develop the task model further because there are too many combinations (including the absence of one or several blocks) that do not have the same importance for the description of the problem. However, the different paths of the task model represent four practices that constitute (for the moment) four task sub-models for a collaborative construction.

• Participants in the experiments had problems finding the right granularity for their answers. They could also know the answer but not its elements. Thus, a primary difference between the task model and the practice model is that the granularity of the representation matters a lot for actors and may explain variants with the task model. For example, it was observed that at times the answer was given but not using the right words, such as in the example of the use of "gas" instead of "CO_2."

• Repetition of the question occurred when participants in the experiments wished to be sure they had understood the question correctly, i.e. to be able to find some relationships between elements of the questions and contextual elements of their mental representation of the domain. This is also a way of having time to retrieve contextual information in their individual contexts.

• Participants collected contextual elements to construct the answer and determine the granularity for the answer they might construct. Once the level of detail was identified, the selection of pieces of contextual knowledge to use in the proceduralized context was automatic. The level of detail in the answer depended more on what they could assemble than on the level of detail that was indicated implicitly in the question.

6 Other Applications Developed in Contextual Graphs

In the last five years, contextual graphs have been used in several applications.

The first application was for subway monitoring in Paris [5, 9]. The goal was to represent the different ways in which an operator monitored a subway line in an accident situation. The main findings concerned (1) the usual difference between procedure and practice (i.e. prescribed and effective tasks), and (2) the role of activity for describing actor interaction during task realization. In the latter situation, the actors working together have a representation of the task at different representation levels. There is no real task model in this application because procedures are built from experience, as a "compilation" of past successful practices. Indeed, in some sense the task model should be an abstraction of the practice model.

The second application "Buy a Ticket for the subway in Paris" is close to the previous one. We studied more specifically the identification of practices in the practice model from the knowledge that users had of the subway (ranging from an American boy leaving his country and coming to Paris for the first time, to an experienced user living and working in Paris). Here the task model is known in an exhaustive way, and we hoped that the practice model was totally included in the task model. We nevertheless discovered that users organized differently the "building blocks" of the task model and even added new ones (a young American student was looking for a taxi to go to the subway station).

The third application focused on the different ways a user can make use of the contents of a web page [1]. The focus here was on the practice model, not on the task model. The reason was that users' objectives for information retrieval were beyond the simple task model, which could be summed up as (a) click on the link, (b) look for the keywords, and (c) copy the interesting part. Depending on what the user wants to do with the information, the user can copy just the text, a figure, or the entire page if he/she does not currently have the time to read the web page. In a similar way as for the first application, the task model can only be built a posteriori, from the practice model.

The fourth application was developed as part of a national project with seven partners in order to identify how it was possible to improve web sites presenting French scientific and technical culture on museum web sites [14]. In this application, we entered the domain of engineering, as we did for the second application above, a domain where first the task model can be described in a relatively exhaustive way (the goal was to identify all the paths from the home page to the page where the answer to a question was found), and second the practice model can be identified as a sub-model of the task model (other findings from this study will be discussed elsewhere).

Other applications have been carried out (computer security, for the US army, legal, the Revocation of the Edit of Nantes in History), and others are currently under development: road sign interpretation, drivers' behavior modeling, bug management, software design, medical image retrieval on a grid.

7 Conclusion

A contextual graph represents the different methods by which a task can be realized. We have shown that each application leads to special aspects in knowledge representation (the level of detail), man-machine interaction (the need to make different viewpoints compatible), and we have demonstrated the central role played by the human actor, especially when the actor interacts with a system. Other aspects are for future study.

In the application for the subway, a contextual graph represents the different ways in which the person in charge of a subway line solves a problem. The notion of activity has been introduced for representing parts of problem solving (i.e. a sub-graph) appearing recursively in contextual graphs (e.g. "Clear the train of passengers"). Such an activity belongs within the task of the person in charge of the subway line, such as the action to ask the train drive, but this activity is a complex task for the driver (with information on the train, stop at the next station, etc.). Here interaction between two actors is described in a coherent way at different levels of representation. The contextual graph where the activity is replaced by an action represents the task of the person in charge of the line , whereas the same contextual graph with the activity replaced by the corresponding sub-graphs of actions represents the train driver's task.

Shefferd [11] discusses the example of the task "Monitoring a given patient" in medicine that is accomplished by different actors (physicians and nurses) collaboratively, but where each actor is responsible for only a part of the whole task . The tree representation of the Hierarchical Task Analysis can be translated (relatively) easily into a contextual graph. This is another approach to the representation of collaborative work in contextual graphs where the global goal can be divided in distinct subgoals for different actors.

At a political level, the question is "Can we say everything in a practice model when the actors know that the Head of the company does not permit certain actions (e.g. for safety reasons, the subway employee must switch off the power before going onto the tracks. For personal reasons, the employee does not do it to avoid writing an incident report.)

At a strategic level, collaboration can be considered as a minimal expression of cooperation: One leads the interaction and the other only feeds in information (or only agrees), reinforcing the statement of the other. Contextual graphs seem to offer an opportunity for studying and modeling collaboration and cooperation among a group of people. We plan to study the different types of interaction between two groups of actors (more precisely, in the Quidditch game in Harry Potter, in the French team of handball, and interaction between car drivers and pedestrians at a crossroads in a town.)

An explanation is given to: (1) justify a known answer, (2) progress in the co-construction of the answer by sharing elements and their interconnection; (3) when participants are not sure of the granularity required in the answer (e.g. partners speak of 'gas' instead of 'CO2' for sparkling water). The explanation (given instead of an answer) is frequently less precise than an answer (generally at a macro-level), and is often for use between the partners. This gives a new insight into what explanations must be, their role and their direct intervention as part of the task at hand.

This series of lessons learned from the use of contextual graphs as a uniform representation of elements of reasoning and contexts must finally be situated within the second part of our work concerning context as an interface to tailor domain knowledge for a given focus. This second part of the work is presented in a companion paper [3] within the framework of the "situation dressing" of a crossroads. Here the link is that we need to consider contextual elements and their instantiations, and then we have to deal with integrity constraints (at night there is no sun) and with inference rules describing the prescribed behavior of actors in the specific context (provided by instantiations) of the situation. The set of inference rules is certainly related to what we call here the task model.

Acknowledgments. The work presented in this paper is ascribed in the ACC project, which is supported by PREDIT and the French Ministry of Transport , mainly in terms of the funding of a Ph.D.Thesis. We also want to thank the members of the ACC project, especially T. Artières, P.Gallinari and Ch. Tijus. Information on the ACC project can be found at www-poleia.lip6.fr/~jbrezillon. Finally, I would like to thank Jacques Leplat for exciting discussions about his views on prescribed and effective tasks.

References

[1] Brézillon, P.: Task-realization models in Contextual Graphs. In: Dey, A.K., Kokinov, B., Leake, D.B., Turner, R. (eds.) CONTEXT 2005. LNCS (LNAI), vol. 3554, pp. 55–68. Springer, Heidelberg (2005a)

[2] Brézillon, P.: Contextualizations in social networks. In: Schultz, S., Roth-Berghofer, T., Brézillon, P. (eds.) Revue d'Intelligence Artificielle (Special Issue on Applying Context Management) 19(3), 575–594 (2005b)

[3] Brézillon, J., Brézillon, P.: Context modeling: Context as a dressing of a focus. In: Kokinov, B., Richardson, D.C., Roth-Berghofer, T.R., Vieu, L. (eds.) CONTEXT 2007. LNCS (LNAI), vol. 4635, Springer, Heidelberg (2007)

[4] Brézillon, P., Pomerol, J.-Ch.: Contextual knowledge sharing and cooperation in intelligent assistant systems. Le Travail Humain, vol. 62(3), pp. 223–246. PUF, Paris (1999)

[5] Brézillon, P., Cavalcanti, M., Naveiro, R., Pomerol, J.-Ch.: SART: An intelligent assistant for subway control. Pesquisa Operacional. Brazilian Operations Research Society 20(2), 247–268 (2000)

[6] Brézillon, P., Drai-Zerbib, V., Baccino, T., Therouanne, T.: Modeling collaborative construction of an answer by contextual graphs. In: Proceedings of IPMU, Paris, France, (May 11-13, 2006)

[7] Leplat, J.: Regards sur l'activité en situation de travail - Contribution à la psychologie ergonomique. Presses Universitaires de France, Paris (1997)

[8] Leplat, J., Hoc, J.M.: Tâche et activité dans l'analyse psychologique des situations. Cahiers de Psychologie Cognitive 3, 49–63 (1983)

[9] Pomerol, J.-C., Brézillon, P., Pasquier, L.: Operational knowledge representation for practical decision making. Journal of Management Information Systems 18(4), 101–116 (2002)

[10] Scott: Owner's manual. Lecteur plt de DVD/VCD/MP3/CD, Model N° DSX510 (2005)

[11] Shefferd, A.: Hierarchical Task Analysis. Taylor & Francis, London (2001)

[12] Sowa, J.F.: Knowledge Representation: Logical, Philosophical, and Computational Foundations. Brooks Cole Publishing Co., Pacific Grove (2000)

[13] Vergnaud, G.: Concepts et schèmes dans la théorie opératoire de la représentation. Les Représentation, Psychologie Française 30(3), 245–252 (1985)

[14] WebCSTI: Rapport d'avancement des Travaux Lutin (2005), http://www.lutin.utc.fr/pdf/rapport_intermediaire_WebCSTI_Oct_2005.pdf

Context Modeling: Context as a Dressing of a Focus

Juliette Brézillon and Patrick Brézillon

LIP6, University Paris 6, 104 avenue du Président Kennedy, 75016, Paris, France
{Juliette.Brezillon, Patrick.Brezillon}@lip6.fr

Abstract. Contextual Graphs are a context-based formalism used in various real-world applications. They allow a uniform representation of elements of reasoning and of contexts for describing different human tasks such as diagnosis and interpretation. The representation of reasoning by Contextual Graphs supposes an efficient representation of the knowledge associated with a reasoning. Extending the previous view of (1) context relative to a focus, and (2) context as composed of external knowledge and contextual knowledge, in this paper we go a step further by proposing a description of the focus in terms of the instantiation of the contextual elements, which are drawn from domain knowledge. We present the results of this study in a real-world application that we are working on currently, namely the self-evaluation of drivers' behaviors in a situation presented within a large spectrum of contexts.

Keywords: Knowledge representation, Contextual knowledge, Proceduralized context, Road safety, Drivers' behavior modeling, self-training.

1 Introduction

Brézillon and Pomerol [5] defined context as "that which constrains something without intervening in it explicitly." We now consider the "something" by extension as a focus for an actor. Several elements justify this definition, the three main elements being that (1) context is relative to the focus, (2) as the focus evolves, its context evolves too, and (3) context is highly domain-dependent. As a consequence, one cannot speak of context in an abstract way.

Next, we can show that the focus allows the division of context into external knowledge and contextual knowledge [3]. The latter constitutes a kind of tank where the contextual elements are to some extent related to the focus in a flat way, whereas the former has nothing to do with it. At this conceptual level, the focus acts as a discriminating factor on knowledge, like in social networks [4]. The focus evolves because a new event occurs (e.g. an unpredicted event) or as a result of a decision made at the previous stage of the focus. Consequently, the notion of context impacts more on the relationships between knowledge pieces than upon the pieces themselves.

At present, our research on context is organized along two axes, namely reasoning as represented in Contextual Graphs, and knowledge as represented through the instantiation of a part of contextual knowledge. The formalism of contextual graphs

B. Kokinov et al. (Eds.): CONTEXT 2007, LNAI 4635, pp. 136–149, 2007.

has been used in several real-world applications. In this paper, we present an application addressing the question "How can we model context as a dressing of a focus?", which allows the identification of differences between the behavior prescribed by procedures and the effective behaviors of actors. This is completely in line with the prescribed and effective tasks identified by Leplat [13]. We observe this situation in our applications such as road safety (an aid for drivers' self-evaluation), medicine (an aid for users to query reformulation in a grid environment) and software engineering (for form filling and for the assembly of pieces of software).

The second axis tries to go beyond the distinction between external and contextual knowledge. To address the current status of the focus, the actor selects a subset of contextual knowledge that is assembled, organized, and structured within a proceduralized context. In terms of Contextual Graphs, the proceduralized context is an ordered series of instantiated contextual elements. The two keywords here are, first, instantiation, which is also the link between the two axes , and, second, the comparison of the proceduralized context to a buffer between the focus and contextual knowledge.

Applying these observations to real-world applications, context acts like an interface between domain knowledge and the focus. We investigated a problem in road safety, namely the representation of a simple crossroad in terms of a situation dressing. Domain knowledge contains elements like roads, lanes, traffic lights, countryside, city, lights, etc. To define a specific intersection, we must contextualize domain knowledge ("Place" = "City", "Traffic lights" = "No", etc.). Thus, when an element like "Place" is instantiated by "City," some other domain elements become irrelevant (e.g. "Type of field at the corner") and others must be instantiated (e.g. "Type of building at the corner" must be defined by the number of floors, the color, where the door is, etc.). This kind of dressing corresponds to a contextualization of the situation (i.e. the intersection). This contextualization, and thus we go back to the first axis on reasoning, leads to two types of inferencing rules. The first type concerns integrity constraints (e.g. "Period of the day" = "Night" implies that it is not daylight in France). The second type is composed of rules about what one must do in a given context (e.g. "Period of the day" = "Night" implies that "Car lights" must be instantiated to "Switch on"). This constitutes the theoretical behavior that actors must display in the specific context of the situation, that is for the given situation dressing.

In this paper we discuss the relationships between the focus and its context in the framework of our application for road safety. More precisely, we study how contextual elements, relying on domain ontology, could define what is necessary for the focus to be defined.

Hereafter, this paper is organized as follows: in Section 2, we present briefly the ACC project in which this work is ascribed. In section 3, we show that context and situation are two different concepts: the context of a situation appearing like "a set of instantiated contextual elements". In section 4, we explain that viewing context as instantiated contextual elements facilitates the definition of a situation dressing, and in Section 5 we explain the modeling of drivers' behaviors. We conclude by giving some possible extensions for this approach.

2 "Behavior Dressing" and "Situation Dressing"

2.1 GADGET

The GADGET project (this is the acronym for "Guarding Automobile Drivers through Guidance Education and Technology") is a European project on road safety [10]. It proposes a representation of drivers' behaviors at four levels. This project originates in the work of van der Molen and Bötticher [11] who split driving tasks and driving behavior into three hierarchical levels: a Strategic level, a Maneuvering or tactical level, and a Control or operational level. In the GADGET matrix, later also referred to as the GDE matrix [14], a fourth level – the Political level – was added above the other three. Our work assumes that the GADGET methodology must be considered with a contextual dimension too. The GADGET variables, which allow the description of car-driving activity, are contextual elements for drivers' behaviors. This arises from the fact that variables like "Traffic regulation" and "Travel planning" are contextual elements that may constrain the focus (e.g. "Drive slowly because you're not in a hurry"). Our objective is to improve the GADGET representation of drivers' behaviors to produce a coherent and complete picture, thanks to the notion of context. Another assumption is that a decision support system would benefit from a driver's experience when it fails to assimilate the driver's behavior to a known behavior. The system could identify a good or bad behavior for the driver. When it fails and cannot identify a driver's behavior, it enters a learning phase for the unknown behavior and for the acquisition of missing knowledge. Once the driver's behavior is identified, the system evaluates if this behavior leads either to a normal or a critical situation. In the latter situation, the system may propose a change of behavior to the driver by explaining how to move from this potentially dangerous behavior to a safer behavior (and thus go back to a normal situation), and then it is the driver who will learn something.

2.2 "Behavior Dressing"as an Extension of GADGET

The first step of our work was to supplement the variables used in the GADGET methodology. In this section, we introduce the variables that we added. According to our viewpoint, the missing variables were:

- Personal variables relating to the driver, such as his/her gender, age, type of employment, whether or not he/she had passed his/her driving license first time , how long he/she has ha a license, how much he/she drives daily, and if he/she is a professional driver, the type of driving work.
- Motivational variables relating to driving, like whether or not the driver is trying to save gasoline, whether or not the driver always drives as quickly as possible , whether or not the driver always tries to avoid damaging the car , whether he/she drives to relax, and whether the driver likes car races.
- Variables dealing with climatic conditions, such as whether or not the driver likes to drive in the rain , in the fog , or when there is snow or ice.

- Variables describing the driver's physical or emotional state, such as whether or not he/she is tired or stressed , etc.
- Variables describing the driving environment, such as whether or not the driver takes care of children and animals on the road , or if there are animals or children or adults with him/her in the car.
- Variables describing the car, such as its color (insurance companies say that drivers of red cars are aggressive), if the driver takes care of the car, if the driver considers the car as a functional object or a family member, the make of car, the type of vehicle (car, bike, motorbike, bus) and if the car is a company car.

All these variables are not GADGET variables, whereas we think they are important for the description of driving activity. For example, the "gender" variable was not present in descriptions of driving activity; however studies show that women and men do not drive in the same way. All the personal variables that we included are important because they describe the driving experience and the driver's social background, even if they are not directly related to the driving task itself. They were not previously taken into account whereas a person who drives every day for his job, for example, does not drive in the same way as a person who drives only for vacations.

The second step of our work was to model the driver's behavior simultaneously at the four levels of the GADGET methodology. We found in the literature that most of the studies based on the GADGET methodology focused on one level. For example, one study focused on the driver's reaction time at the operational level. Another study focused on the driver's mental representation of the road at the tactical level.

We make the assumption that in order to model the driving task, it is necessary to take into account all four levels of the GADGET matrix. Indeed, in a hierarchical structure, all the upper levels influence the lower levels. For example, if the driver is under time pressure, he/she will not drive as he/she usually does, and maybe he/she will take some risks that he/she wouldn't normally take . If we model this case at the tactical level for example, we just model the fact that the driver is taking serious risks whilst driving, so we will say that he/she is a dangerous driver, and we will not consider that he/she is very stressed.

To take into account all the levels at the same time, we proceed as follows: we consider all the GADGET variables independently of the levels where they are, and regroup them by type of variable. There are two kinds of classification: the variables are repeated (this has a direct influence on the highest level) or the variables describe the same aspect of the driving task.

All the variables are related to some extent to the driver's behavior (the focus), but not all the variables concern a specific driver. Thus, the next step is to see how the contextual elements (i.e. the variables) relating to a specific driver are instantiated, that is what the value of these contextual elements is for that specific driver. The key point here is not that the contextual elements are instantiated but how these instantiations are interrelated. This is what we call the proceduralized context [5].

Thus, this work has two objectives: (1) identification of classes of driver from real data (driving behaviors), and (2) identification of the class corresponding to a given driver.

2.3 "Situation Dressing"

We propose to model driving behavior using a dual approach. First, there is a global approach, which uses the presentation of choices made by other drivers with a similar profile (e.g. choice of method, choice between alternatives) for the same task. This type of modeling considers a driver as a "collective being", that is modeled from a set of users or user categories acting in a similar way [1, 7, 15]. Such a driver model can be described using a network of concepts and relationships between these concepts (e.g. Bayesian nets or hidden Markovian models). Second, a local (or specific) approach considers the driver using the role he/she plays, the behavior he/she displays, the driving task, the situation and the contexts in which these occur. Thus, the driver is represented as:

- A "variable being," because the driver may have different goals and behaviors during the accomplishment of the task ,
- A "unique being," because the driver has specific knowledge, centers of interest, expressed preferences, etc., and
- The being responsible for a driving task that has been contextualized.

The association with a cognitive (local) approach allows the problem to be placed within a larger space, which mainly concerns the representation of the driving situation the driver faces. In other words, we are trying to model driving behaviors from a dual viewpoint: an external view of the driver (from a driver classification, a behavior typology, etc.) and a direct, internal view of the given driver. Our intuition is that qualified driving behavior must rely on the driver's double objective and subjective approaches, using:

- A typology of drivers (Which type of driver am I? Which type of driver should I be?)
- A typology of situations (normal, critical and pre-critical situations)
- A typology of practices (How do I drive? How should I drive?).

Thus, a driver accomplishing a driving task is considered as a triple{driver, situation, practice}. Such a representation is highly contextualized. Nevertheless, our approach relies on some methodologies already proposed in the literature, especially the GADGET methodology, the scenarios proposed in TRAINER and methodology developed for the training of driving instructors [9]. The driver should be able to tackle the following scenarios:

- Identify the type of behavior (and its associated context) the driver is involved in, to evaluate the degree of danger presented by that behavior, and find a way to regain a normal behavior;
- Identify the situation and the driving context, evaluate how critical the situation is, identify pre-critical situations and find the best way to modify his/her behavior in order to regain a normal driving situation .

- Stay vigilant to the behavior of other drivers, detect an abnormal behavior, evaluate a danger for him/her and consequently adapt his/her behavior. (Note that not all drivers perceive a danger identically.)
- The time constant for the driver's response is an essential parameter in our proposal. For example, being vigilant to other drivers' behaviors is a routine task in driving (with a long time constant), whilst adapting his/her behavior to the danger presented by other drivers may have a very short time constant (often less than one second).

A scenario corresponds to the evolution of a situation (and its context) assimilated to a series of situations. A scenario is a path in the situation space with pre-critical situations playing a role similar to a bifurcation point [17]. A pre-critical situation has two potential successors, a normal situation if the driver correctly modifies the driving plan or a critical situation if the driver does not react correctly.

Driving behaviors are represented in the context-based formalism called Contextual graphs that provide a uniform representation of elements of reasoning and of contexts [3]. The principles of contextual-graph building for driving are the following. A contextual graph represents the different behaviors that a driver may present in a given driving situation (a crossroads in the following case study). A path in this graph represents the driver's behavior in that driving situation for a given context (i.e. instantiated elements like "Status" = "In a hurry" and "Weather" = "Rain"). Contextual elements are instantiated because their value is explicitly considered in the decision making process. A driver can exhibit different behaviors for a given scenario, and the same behavior may appear in different scenarios. Thus, drivers' behaviors are represented in a dual space (situation space and a behavior space), and scenarios are the bridge between these two spaces. An intelligent tutoring system using such a database can (1) identify the driver class to which the user belongs, (2) select a situation in which the user has some weaknesses, (3) establish the scenario for which the user may learn how to modify his behavior, (4) follow the driving task realized by the user and anticipate pre-critical situations that may be encountered by the user, and (5) propose ways of correcting the user's behavior.

Domain knowledge, which defines driving situations, is represented by contextual elements. A single context for the situation is an instantiation of a (large) part of these contextual elements. In the next section we discuss the modeling of the situation and of drivers' behaviors for the crossroads case study.

3 Case Study

3.1 Situation Description

Consider the real traffic situation--a simple crossroads—for which we are trying to analyze all the driving situations that could occur. We assume that only two cars arrive at the crossroads. The Highway Code gives the "driver model": " Give right of way to the car coming from your right." Because the system must support a given driver, we choose to select the viewpoint of the driver of the black car (coming from the bottom in Figure 1). We will analyze all possible scenarios, first, according to where the white car is coming from (from the left, the right or in front of the black car), and second, according to the movements of the two cars (turn left, go straight ahead, or turn right) at the crossroads (see Figure 1).

Domain knowledge corresponding to this situation is described by contextual elements that are organized in a hierarchy with instantiations of some of them. A piece of this hierarchy is given as follows:

Physical elements	(e.g. Environment)
Technical elements	(e.g. Type of crossroad structure)
Moment elements	(e.g. Day)
Driving elements	(e.g. Vehicle)
Human elements	(e.g. Physical aspects)

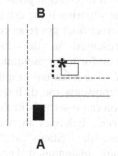

Fig. 1. The chosen driving situation

Such contextual elements allow us to describe the situation at the desired level of detail. According to the hierarchy of domain knowledge, there are various levels of detail in the representation of a situation. For example:

Physical element > Environment > City > Village

The granularity depends on the driver's focus and provides a way to know the driver's level of situation awareness. A driver may not pay attention to the fact that "City" = "Village" and thus may miss some important points he/she needs to take into account in terms of his behavior (e.g. "Reduce speed when driving through a village").

The instantiation of the selected contextual elements (e.g. "Traffic light" = "No") leads us to specify a context for the situation. Changing the instantiation of "Traffic light" = "No" to "Yes" leads us to another context, and the situation, i.e. the crossroads, must be perceived differently by the driver, who must adapt his/her behavior. The instantiation of the contextual elements is a contextualization of the situation. The instantiation set of the contextual elements is called situation dressing.

3.2 Dressing of the Situation

A contextual element has an instance, which can be either a value or another contextual element. This enables us to make explicit the level of detail of the description but supposes a mechanism for acquiring new concepts incrementally because "we don't know what we need before we have to use it" [11]. This leads to a mechanism of incremental acquisition. (We are currently implementing such a piece of software.)

Another consequence is that a contextual element is itself a list of elements, and a recursive one. The situation above is described (very partially) as follows:

> Physical elements
>> Environment =
>>> "Countryside"
>>>> Type of region = "Fields"
>>>> Type of land
>>>> Plant = "None"
>>>> Pasture = "No animal"
>>> "City"
>>> •••

The dressing of a situation represents a context for the "crossroads" situation. Changing one instantiation, e.g. "Field at the right corner of the intersection crossroads" = "Corn field" to the instantiation "Reaped field", leads to another context, and the driver's behavior must be modified (a reaped field lets the user see if the white car coming from the right is approaching the intersection or stopping at the intersection, whereas a corn field means that what is on the right side of the road is not visible .

The situation dressing allows to present the same situation in various contexts (changes of instantiation of any contextual element, or instantiations chosen randomly). Thus, the user must always be careful in analyzing the situation and learn to manage the situation with its context. This is a way of developing situation awareness.

If domain knowledge imposes a structure on contextual elements as discussed above, contextual elements must also obey another organization that depends on the relationships existing between them. We summarize this in Figure 2.

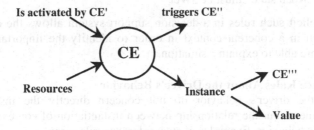

Fig. 2. Relationships between Contextual Elements (CEs)

We already have seen that an instance may be a value or another contextual element (CE). The determination of a value is made from different resources: a sensor (e.g. the temperature), a database (e.g. a user's profile for the user's gender), a computation (e.g. the value of a dollar in euros), or questions to the user (e.g. "Do you like going fast?"). The last point is that the instantiation of a contextual element may lead to another contextual element being triggered or inhibited . For example, choosing "Countryside" implies that "Type of building at the right hand corner" is not relevant, but that it is mandatory to instantiate "Type of field." In the same spirit, the instantiation "Corn" for the contextual element "Type of field" means that (1) corn is tall and hides the view of the white car, (2) visibility is strongly reduced, and (3) the driver must drive carefully. This implies that two types of rules must be considered. In [19], we present a piece of work on the design of a context manager for managing contextual elements.

3.3 Situation Dressing Refinement

3.3.1 Integrity Constraints

Integrity constraints are rules that describe relationships between contextual elements and their instantiation. For example, we can extend the previous example of the "Environment" with rules like:

IF "Item at the right corner" = "Field"
      THEN   Look for "Season"
              IF "Season" = "Summer",
                    THEN look for "Type of field"
                    ELSE "Type of field" = "Reaped"
              IF "Type of field" = "Corn"
                    THEN "Visibility of the road on the right" = " Nil"
                    ELSE "Visibility of the road on the right" = "Good"

(The last line would be refined by taking into account, say, "Weather" (for fog).
Another group of integrity rules concerns the relationships between contextual elements that rely on common sense knowledge. For example:

IF "Moment of the day" = "Night"
      THEN "Weather" cannot be "Sunny"
IF "Weather" = "Rainy"
      THEN "Road state" must be "Wet"

Making explicit such rules in a decision support system allows the consideration of the situation in a coherent context in order to identify the important contextual elements that are able to explain a situation.

3.3.2 Inference Rules About the Driver's Behavior

Rules about the driver's behavior do not concern directly the instantiation of contextual elements but the relationship between instantiation of contextual elements and the driver's behavior. Examples of such inference rules are:

      IF "Road state" = "Wet" or "Weather" = "Fog" or "Visibility" = "Weak"
              THEN "Car speed" = "Reduced" and "Driver status" = "Vigilant"
      IF "Field on the right" = "Reaped"
              THEN "Look to see if a car is coming from the right"
      IF "Sidewalk (Pavement en GB)" = "Small" and "Crowded"
              THEN "Watch to see if a pedestrian in a hurry goes on the pavement into the road"
      IF "Type of day" = "Working day"
              THEN IF "Time" = "Morning" and "Near crossroads" = "School"

THEN "Pay attention to children going to school"
"Anticipate needing to brake quickly"
IF "White car" = " Emergency vehicle"
THEN " Give it right of way"

The model of the theoretical behavior of drivers arriving at a simple intersection in the Highway Code corresponds to the unique rule:

IF "Car on the road to the right" THEN "stop and give it right of way".

This is the rule in the Highway Code that corresponds to the situation only. We have shown here that the contextualization of the situation (it is night, it is raining, etc.) leads to a richer model, not of the drivers but of their behaviors. Context allows consideration of a task within its environment (a contextualized task). Another observation is that if the model of the theoretical behavior is unique for a situation, the model of the "prescribed behavior" of drivers is context-dependent and thus there is a specific model of prescribed behavior for each context. This means that the "distance" between the prescribed task and the actual task can be defined more precisely. With respect to the companion paper [2], we are able to propose a task model (i.e. the prescribed task) that describes a contextualized task. Now we will present the model of drivers' effective behaviors, that provides the second space for describing our problem, alongside the situation space already discussed in this section.

4 Model of Drivers' Behaviors

We represent the evolution of a situation for a given driver as a movement through a series of situations represented in a discrete space of situations. Figure 3 represents five scenarios that can be derived from the first traffic situation given in Figure 1.

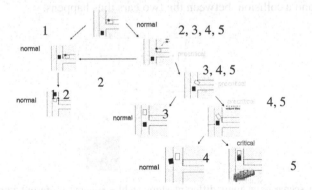

Fig. 3. Graph of all the situations that can be derived from the first one

Scenario 1 corresponds to the normal situation. The black car goes forward and the white car waits until the black car has passed and then turns right after it.

In scenario 2, the white car goes forward a little just to reach the road marking. There are several hypotheses for why the driver of the white car goes forward a little. For example, the driver of the white car might think he/she has time to complete his/her action (turn right before the black car) but abandons the idea rapidly. Another reason could be that the driver wants to look behind the black car to see if any other vehicle is coming. The driver of the black car reduces speed, observes the white car, and, if the white car is no longer moving, decides to maintain his/her driving plan but is careful. Afterwards, the white car turns right, and the second scenario corresponds to the first scenario (see Figure 3).

In scenario 3, the white car goes forwards until the junction markings and the driver decides to act before the black car arrives. Conversely, the driver of the black car had a different interpretation of the situation and anticipated that the other driver would stop at the road marking. However, the driver of the black car is prudent in this situation and is aware of the risk of a critical situation and quickly understands the the driver of the white car's intention when the white car goes forward. Thus, the driver of the black car has time to brake. As we assume that there is no other vehicle in the situation, the driver of the black car can brake easily without posing a risk to the other cars behind him/her. The black car brakes and stops (or at least reduces sufficiently its speed), lets the driver of the white car finish turning, allows some safe distance between the two cars and goes forward, after the white car.

The fourth scenario supposes that, on the one hand, the white car goes forward to pass in front of the black car as in scenario 3, and, on the other hand, the driver of the black car interprets the modified situation differently, thinking that the driver of the white car will wait before moving because he/she does not have right of way. Realizing that the driver of the white car is not behaving as expected, the driver of the black car is surprised and has only a short time to react. The driver of the black car tries to brake, but not quickly enough . To avoid a collision between the two cars, and because there are no other vehicles in the area, the driver of the black decides to overtake the white car and to change lane.

The fifth and last scenario is a variant of the fourth scenario. The driver of the black car tries to brake, but not quickly enough and has no time to change lanes (or can not do it) and a collision between the two cars thus happens.

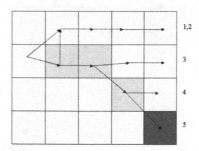

Fig. 4. The five scenarios at their different steps (white squares represent normal situations, pre-critical situations are in grey and the critical situation is in the dark square) in the situation space

Figure 4 gives a representation in the situation space of the different situations and scenarios identified in Figure 3. There is one critical situation and three pre-critical situations (in grey and corresponding to scenarios 2, 3, 4), which leads to five scenarios.

Figure 5 represents drivers'behaviors in the scenarios shown in Figure 4 in the contextual-graphs formalism (The key/caption for Figure 5 is given in Table 1.) Note that the contextual graph contains only the black-car driver's behaviors. The description is more extended (e.g. there are two behaviors that lead to scenario "5") because we have chosen the black-car driver's viewpoint and not the viewpoint of an external observer. This will be the topic of another paper.

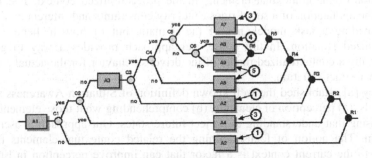

Fig. 5. Contextual graph of the traffic situation (numbers in circles correspond to the five scenarios in Figures 3 and 4). Elements are defined in Table 1.

Table 1. Contextual elements and actions while negotiating the crossroads in Figure 5

Contextual element	
C1	Is the white car stopping?
C2	Is the white car going forward?
C3	Can I let the white car go forward?
C4	Can I overtake the white car on the left?
Action	**Definition**
A1	Maintain the same behavior
A2	Interpret the behavior of the driver of the white car
A3	Note that the driver of the white car is stopping at the road marking
A4	Brake enough to let it go forward
A5	Change lane and overtake
A6	Evaluate the situation
A7	Try to brake strongly

5 Conclusion

This approach is interesting in that a given situation (the crossroads in our study) can be proposed in a large number of contexts. Thus, although the situation is unique, the large spectrum of contexts will force a driver to be attentive all the time and aware of the specificity of the situation each time. We believe that our approach develops a sense of situation awareness within training.

Making context explicit within our application enables user-centered management of domain knowledge. The context is domain knowledge, and the focus guides the distinction between external knowledge and contextual knowledge. The former has nothing to do with the focus (e.g. what is a motorway? in our study), when the former is to some extent related to the focus (e.g. traffic light and lane number). A subset of contextual knowledge is extracted, assembled and constitutes the proceduralized context. This is concretely obtained by combining and inferring relationships between the selected contextual elements. For example, a simple crossroads supposes a special sign before the intersection, but no traffic light. What is important here is that the main distinction between contextual knowledge and the proceduralized context is the instantiation of the contextual elements in the proceduralized context. Instantiation leads to the application of a set of rules (integrity constraints and inference rules), the latter providing a task model, not of the domain, but of how to behave in the contextualized situation. In this sense, our approach provides a way to generate automatically a contextualized model of the driver's behavior for the actual situation, not of the abstract situation.

Endsley [8] established the well-known definition of Situation Awareness with its three levels: (a) perception of elements, (b) comprehending what those elements mean and (c) using that understanding to project future states. Our approach is ascribed in this realm. The notion of focus defining the related contextual elements that are relevant to the current context is a factor that can improve perception in Endsley's first level. Making the distinction between the selected contextual elements and their instantiations explicit may be associated with the second level (i.e. the understanding of the meaning of the elements.) The identification of the rules of "good behavior" (and by contrast of "bad behavior") in the context of the situation allows decision making to be efficient and the third level to be predicted.

This paper gives a new vision of the classical dichotomy "prescribed task versus effective task." We have shown that rules, which are deduced from the instantiation of the contextual elements, lead to a task model that relates to the contextualized situation, not the situation alone. This is important in terms of drivers' behaviors because if the Highway Code addresses the situation (at a simple intersection), the vehicle coming from the right has right of way), the task model that arises from inference rules is able to adapt to the contextualized situation. For example, if the driver coming from your right stops his vehicle and indicates that you can go on, it is not necessary to stop and wait. Thus, the driver will learn a set of operational rules instead of a general rule. In other words, our approach is a means for drivers to develop an efficient model of practice instead of a task model (i.e. a theoretical model). It is more important to learn how to use a rule rather than just to learn the rule.

Acknowledgments. The ACC project is supported by PREDIT GO3 and the French Ministry of Transport (Grants SU-05-276), mainly in terms of the funding of a Ph.D.Thesis. We also want to thank the members of the ACC project, especially T. Artières, P. Gallinari and Ch. Tijus. Information on the ACC project can be found at www-poleia.lip6.fr/~jbrezillon.

References

[1] Blanchard, J., Petitjean, B., Artières, T., Gallinari, P., et al.: Unsystème d'aide à la navigation dans des hypermédias. In: Sloot, P.M.A., Hoekstra, A.G., Priol, T., Reinefeld, A., Bubak, M. (eds.) EGC 2005. LNCS, vol. 3470, Springer, Heidelberg (2005)

[2] Brézillon, P.: Context modeling: Task model and model of practices. In: Kokinov, B., Richardson, D.C., Roth-Berghofer, T.R., Vieu, L. (eds.) CONTEXT 2007. LNCS (LNAI), vol. 4635, Springer, Heidelberg (2007)

[3] Brézillon, P.: Modeling users' practices in contextual graphs. In: David, A. (ed.)Organisation des Connaissances dans les Systèmes d'Informations Orientés Utilisation.Contexte de Veille et d'Intelligence Economique (ISKO-2005). Presse Universitaire deNancy, pp. 77–96 (2005)

[4] Brézillon, P.: Role of context in social networks. In: Proceeding of the 18thInternational FLAIRS Conference, Invited Special Track AI for Social Networks, SocialNetworks in AI, AAAI CD Rom, pp. 20–25 (2005b)

[5] Brézillon, P., Pomerol, J.-Ch.: Contextual knowledge sharing and cooperation inintelligent assistant systems. Le Travail Humain 62(3), 223–246 (1999)

[6] Brézillon, P., Tijus, C.: Increasing The rationality of cognitive tasks withcontextual graphs. In: Proceedings of the 8th European Meeting on Cybernetics and SystemsResearch, Vienna, Austria (April 18-21, 2006)

[7] Brusilovsky, P.: Adaptive hypermedia. In: Kobsa, A. (ed.) User Modeling and User Adapted Interaction,Ten Year Anniversary Issue, vol. 11(1/2), pp. 87–110 (2001)

[8] Endsley, M.R.: Toward a Theory of Situation Awareness in Complex Systems. Human Factors (1995)

[9] Gregersen, N.P., Bartl, G.: Young car drivers: Why are they over represented incar accidents? How can driver training improve their situation. VTI report 409A, Linkoping:Swedish National Road and Transport Institute (2005)

[10] Hatakka, M., Keskinen, E., Gregersen, N.P., Glad, A., Hernetkoski, K.: Fromcontrol of the vehicle to personal self-control; broadening the perspectives to drivereducation. Transportation Research, Part F, pp. 201–215 (2002)

[11] Henninger, S.: The knowledge acquisition trap. In: Proceedings of the IEEE Workshopon Applying Artificial Intelligence to Software Problems: Assessing Promises and Pitfalls(CAIA-92), Monterey, pp. 51–57. IEEE Computer Society Press, Los Alamitos (1992)

[12] Laird, J.E., Newell, A.: Knowledge level learning in SOAR. In: Proceedings of the Sixth National Conference on Artificial Intelligence, pp. 499–504 (1987)

[13] Leplat, J.: Regards sur l'activité en situation de travail -Contribution à la psychologie ergonomique. Presses Universitaires de France, Paris (1997)

[14] Peräaho, M., Keskinen, E., Hatakka, M.: Driver Competence in a HierarchicalPerspective; Implication for Driver Education. University of Turku, Traffic Research, Turku 2003 (2003)

[15] Pohl, W., Nick, A.: Machine Learning and Knowledge Representation in theLabour Approach to User Modeling. In: Proceedings of the 7th International Conference onUser Modeling, Banff, Canada, pp. 197–188 (2000)

[16] Siegrist, S.: Rapport GADGET, Formation et évaluation du conducteur, obtentiondu permis de conduire. In: S. Siegrist (ed.) Vers une gestion théoriquement fondée du risque routier des jeunesconducteurs. Résultats du projet européen GADGET -Groupe de travail N°3, Berne (1999)

[17] Thom, R.: Stabilité structurelle et morphogénèse. Essai d'une théorie générale desmodèles. Inter Editions, Paris (1972)

[18] Van der Molen, H.H., Bötticher, A.M.T.: A hierarchical risk model for trafficparticipants. Ergonomics (1988)

[19] Vieira, V., Tedesco, P., Salgado, A.C., Brézillon, P.: Investigating the specifics of contextual elements management: The CEManTIKA approach. In: Kokinov, B., Richardson, D.C., Roth-Berghofer, T.R., Vieu, L. (eds.) CONTEXT 2007. LNCS (LNAI), vol. 4635, Springer, Heidelberg (2007)

Service-Context Unified Knowledge Representation for Autonomic Adaptation

Marcel Cremene[1] and Michel Riveill[2]

[1] Technical University of Cluj-Napoca,
Cluj-Napoca, Romania
cremene@com.utcluj.ro
[2] University of Nice,
Sophia-Antipolis, France
riveill@unice.fr

Abstract. Autonomic computing is a very ambitious domain dealing with issues such as system self-management, proactive services and adaptation to unpredicted situations. The development of ubiquitous computing have shown also the importance of adapting the services to their *context*. In general, a service cannot adapt autonomously to its context beyond the limits fixed a priori by its developer. In order to overcome this limitation, we propose a dynamically updatable service-context model (knowledge representation) that enables an adaptation platform to diagnose the service adequacy to context and automatically search for solutions in order to correct the inadequacy.

1 Introduction

1.1 Background and Motivation

Autonomic computing [1], [2] is a new and very ambitious direction in software. Its main goal is to enable the computing systems to manage themselves according to 'high-level' objectives expressed by human operators. The most important issues that motivate the interest for autonomic computing are described below.

System complexity management. Due to the telecommunication/hardware advance and spreading in the last years, the services are today ubiquitous. We consider that a computing system includes not only software services but also the context [3]: infrastructure, environment, users. The services, their infrastructure (machines, networks, etc.) and the user needs are in continuous evolution and diversification. This evolution leads also to a high complexity making more difficult for the human operators to manage such systems. As explained in [1], the system maintenance costs are usually very high, some of the problems are caused also by human errors. That is why we need solutions for automatic system management.

Proactive services. Today, we create software services that respect precisely what the developer specified a priori, at the service creation moment. This means that

B. Kokinov et al. (Eds.): CONTEXT 2007, LNAI 4635, pp. 150–163, 2007.
© Springer-Verlag Berlin Heidelberg 2007

a service is somehow limited because it cannot evolve autonomously. In order to pass beyond this limitation, the services must be proactive [4]. By proactive service we understand here a service able to autonomously discover and propose to user new possible features. An example is a service that discovers and uses new components appeared after the service creation or proposes to user new features if the context changes.

Adaptation to unpredicted situations. It is impossible for the developer to completely anticipate the system evolution at the creation moment. User preferences, physical resources, physical and social environment may change dynamically and unpredictably, especially in open environments [5] such as mobile, ubiquitous systems. New context elements relevant for the service may appear a posteriori and they must be somehow used even if the developer has not anticipate them.

1.2 Problem

In our opinion, the main problem comes from the fact that the system does not have an 'understanding' about itself; thus, it is not able to autonomously evolve. The only one that understands how the system works is the developer. That is the reason why the majority of the adaptive platforms existing today require a human operator to specify service and context-specific adaptation rules and strategies. The rules and the strategies are in general not reusable because they are too related to the low level, service-specific and context-specific aspects.

1.3 Objective and Approach

Our objective is to increase the autonomy of the ubiquitous adaptive systems. The developer role must be minimized, the user may guide the adaptation process if necessary but without any knowledge about the low level, service-specific aspects. Our approach is inspired by a combination between the Artificial Intelligence (AI) perspective about the knowledge and the classical closed-loop control [6] from the Control Theory. This combination is depicted in the figure 1. The

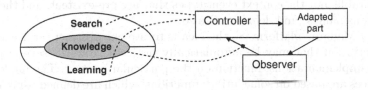

Fig. 1. Artificial Intelligence and Closed-Loop Control

central aspect for the AI domain is the knowledge representation. The solution search is a way to explore the knowledge in order to find solutions and the learning goal is to acquire and adjust the knowledge in order to improve the system. The closed-loop control principle is widely used in automatics and robotics and consider a system as composed by three parts: a) the adapted part (will be the service for us) that is reconfigurable; b) the observer part that collects information about the system state (service and context) and c) the controller part that takes decisions about the needed reconfigurations. The connection between these two domains, as we can see in the figure 1, is that the observer part must extract, generate and update the knowledge, while the controller part is responsible with solution search and learning. The first and most important problem that needs to be solved is to propose a knowledge representation model for the system, composed in our case by the service and its context.

1.4   Paper Outline

This paper is organized as it follows: the next section contains a brief state of the art, section three presents the proposed solution for autonomic adaptation: general architecture, service-context model, service to context adequacy checking, and a solution search example. Section four describes the prototype that we have implemented in order to test our model. The last section presents discussions, conclusions and future work.

2   A Brief Study of Several Existent Adaptive Solutions

In this section, we analyze first some existent context-aware adaptive platforms in order to see if they offer autonomic adaptation. We discuss shortly about the knowledge representation in the AI domain and then we conclude.

Context-aware adaptive platforms. According to [7], in a completely unanticipated system, the answers to questions like *when, where, what* and *how* to reconfigure are known only at runtime. But even the "Chisel" [7] system that claims to be 'completely unanticipated' requires a human operator for modifying the rules/strategies. This fact means that a human operator and not the system, establish when the service is adapted and what the system must do in each situation. Another limitation of this proposal is that only the rules are reconfigurable, not the context event types that are pre-existent, and the strategies/actions names (and definitions) also.

In the "Madam" platform [8], the idea is to use one abstract service architecture description that may be automatically projected towards several possible concrete implementations, function on the particular context. The implementation choices are based on some 'utility functions' which are defined using rules. A similar idea is proposed in [5]. The utility functions are service-specific and they must by specified by the developer and this is a not very simple task. In this case, we have the same situation that is not suitable for autonomic computing: the use of service-specific rules/functions defined by the service developer. Another limitation is that the choice is limited to the pre-existent component implementations and a new, dynamical component insertion in the abstract architecture is not taken into account.

The "Rainbow" architecture [9] propose to separate clearly the adapted system and the adaptation control parts. This fact leads to a more flexible architecture. Still, from the autonomy point of view, the problem comes from the fact that the *adaptation control part* is generally based on rules and strategies that are service-specific, predetermined and developer-made. We have analyzed other several context-aware systems such as: "MobiPADS" [10], "Gaia" [11], "K-component" [12] and we have found the same control principle. Most of existent context-aware systems are not able to discover autonomously new context elements, rules and strategies. The context is not discovered but established by the developer, meaning that a new context cannot be automatically taken into account.

Artificial Intelligence. In order to be able to use existent AI algorithms, we need to find an appropriate knowledge representation for our system. General knowledge representation models are: graphs, rules, procedures, workflows, objects (OOP), symbols and symbol-based logic, weights (neural networks), ontology, semantic graphs, chromozoms (genetic algorithms) and others. The knowledge representation model must be dynamically extensible. The solution search and learning issues depends a lot on the model type. For instance, genetic algorithms have been used for electrical circuit synthesis [13].

Conclusions of study. We were not able to found a general and complete solution for autonomic adaptation. Actual systems have not reached yet the autonomic level [1]. The manner of implementing the adaptation control part in the existent adaptive systems is not suitable for autonomic adaptation because it is based on a pre-known context, rules and strategies. On the other side, the existent general architectures, based on the closed loop and human nervous system (sensors-brain-muscles) seems to be useful. The adaptation techniques allowing dynamic reconfiguration may be also reused because they are not influencing the adaptation autonomy. The key element allowing autonomic adaptation is the control part. The autonomous system must be able to: discover new context elements, diagnose the service to context adequacy and look for solutions. The user may be also included in the control loop for giving some advices or making some choices.

3   Autonomic Adaptation Solution Based on a Service-Context Model

3.1   General Architecture

Figure 2 depicts the proposed general architecture. The adapted system is based on three planes described below. The arrows indicate the informational flow, the black ones concern the observation and the red ones the control.

Context plane. The context plane includes: the hardware infrastructure I, the environment elements E and the users U. This plane does not corespond to a

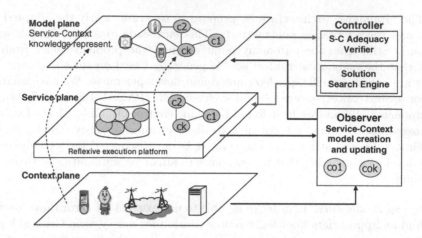

Fig. 2. General architecture for autonomic service adaptation

functional bloc, we use it only for representing the real objects in relation with the service.

Service plane. The service plane contains all the software components. A service is considered as implemented by several interconnected components. Some other components are available in a component repository and may be used in order to adapt the service. We have figured in blue the 'regular' components C1...Ck and in yellow the observer components Co1...Cok. An observer component is a component that enables us to observe (extract information) about the context plane components.

Model plane. The model plane contains the service-context knowledge representation. We are using a graph model because it is similar to the component based model used for the service architecture. The graph is built and updated automatically as the service and context changes. This plane does not corespond to a functional bloc, it just describes the meta-model.

The *adapted part* is the service that is executed on the top of a reflexive platform allowing dynamic reconfiguration. The *Observer* monitors periodically the context and service state and updates dynamically the *service-context model*. The control part uses the service-context model in order to check the service to context adequacy, *S-C Adequacy Verifier* and to look for solutions if necessary, *Solution Search Engine*. The key element of this architecture is the service-context model, which is explained in detail in the next section.

3.2 The Service-Context Model

Software and contextual components. According to the component based approach that we have chosen, a service is described by its component architecture. In order to simplify the model, at the model plan level, we a decompose each complex component (several inputs, several outputs) in several filters, sinks or sources. Another advantage of this approach is the compatibility with the SOA (Service Oriented Architecture) because a service may be seen also as a filter.

The context is represented today using various model types: list of attributes, object oriented models, ontology based models[14], contextual graph[15]. In order to unify the service and context models, we propose to use for service and context the same model type. That means, the context is seen as an architecture composed by *contextual components*: user, terminal, network, environment, etc. Between software components and contextual components two types of interrelations exist: a) *Information exchange*. For instance, the user exchange information with the service through the HMI (Human Machine Interface); and b) *Resources utilization*. For instance, the service uses a certain amount of terminal memory and a certain bit rate of a network.

Profiles. A problem is that actual service and context models do not reveal the service-context interrelations. In order to solve this issue, we introduce the *profile* concept. The profile role is to describe how software and contextual components interact each other. This interactions enable us to check the service-context adequacy. For instance, if a user interacts with a service, it would be normal to use a same language and information type (visual, voice). If a component uses the terminal memory, there must be enough free memory in order to have adequacy.

The profile is a meta-data associated to a component (software or contextual). The profile elements are:

- *Type.* The type may be software or contextual. The software types areregular and observer. The contextual types are: terminal, server machine, network and others. In present we are not using the type but we think it will be useful in association with a future component ontology.
- *Component attributes.* The component attributes are related to the whole component. Examples of such attributes are: memory, CPU, APIs, OS, and they are related usually to the physical and logical resources. Each attribute has a name and a definition domain (values).
- *Flow attributes.* The flow attributes are related to the input and output information flows that enters or goes out through the component ports. These attributes characterize the information content. Examples are: data type, language, compression, delay, bit rate. Each attribute has a name and a definition domain. For each attribute we define a *transfer function* **H**, as for the electrical filters. This function indicates the relation between the output value and the input value for a certain attribute. The **H** function may have parameters that are associated with the component parameters.

The profile enables us to see any component as composed by several superposed filters (sources or sinks, according to "pipe-and-filter" style). From the 'memory' attribute point of view, for instance, the terminal is seen as a memory source and the components are memory sinks. An English to French translation component is a memory sink but also a language filter. If a component affects the information, the component developer must specify this aspect in the component profile, otherwise the adaptation system cannot be aware about the component capabilities.

A scenario. In order to explain easier our model, we use a forum service example built initially for a PDA mobile device and composed by a client (graphical interface) and a server (forum content). The service is implemented using three software components: *TreeViewUI* is a graphical tree viewer that allows the user to see the forum content as a message tree. This component has a HMI and it is installed on the user mobile device. *EditorUI* is a graphical editor allowing the user to compose new messages and send them. This component has also a HMI and it is installed on the user mobile device. *ForumServer* is the forum application server component. This is a business component and it is installed on a server machine. The forum service architecture is depicted in figure 3.

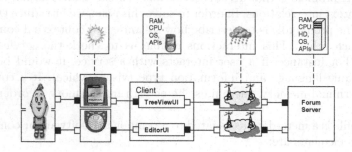

Fig. 3. Service-context unified architecture

Several contextual components are also involved: *User* that interacts with the forum service through its HMI. *Terminal* that includes two components: the display as output device and the keyboard as input device. The terminal devices are interposed between the user and the software components. The terminal screen visibility may be influenced by external factors as the external light for instance. *Network* that connects the terminal with the internet access point and finally with the server machine. Several networks may be concatenated. Uplink and downlink are seen as separated filters. The network bit rate may be influenced by the external conditions like rain. *Server machine* that is a host for the forum server. We may take into account this contextual component for load balancing.

The service-context graph. In order to manipulate the service-context model, we implement it as a graph. The graph depicted in figure 4 corresponds to the architecture depicted in figure 3. For simplifying, in this example we have omitted some relations such as the *Server Forum* resources-oriented relation with the *Server Machine.*

The graph vertices corresponds to software (white) and contextual (gray) components. A node is an object that includes all the profile attributes: component attributes, flow attributes and transfer functions. The graph edges are all

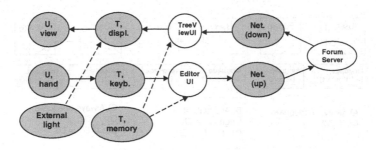

Fig. 4. Service-context graph

oriented and correspond either to information flows (normal arrows) or resource utilization (dotted arrows).

3.3   Service-Context Adequacy

The proposed service-context model is useful only if it allows us to check the service to context adequacy. The first thing is to define what 'adequacy' means using the model terms. In order to do that, we consider two general, service-independent rules. The first concerns the information exchange and the second the resource utilization. These rules and their application are described bellow.

Rule 1: A service S is adequate to its context C if the information exchanged between S and C is compatible

The information flow compatibility is verified separately for each flow attribute (specified in the component profiles). The compatibility validation rule is service-independent: "for each output port interconnected with an input port, the output attribute value must be included in the input interval". For the forum service, if the user (contextual component) produces an information having the 'language' attribute 'FR', but the service input (HMI) requires for the 'language' attribute the value 'EN', we decide that this service is not adequate to its context. This compatibility rule may be applied for any two interconnected components, either software or contextual.

As observation, the semantic information in this case is located in the service and context profiles. This fact helps us to simplify the rules and use generic ones.

Figure 5 describes the service-context adequacy validation for the 'language' attribute.

In case A) the user speaks French so the service requiring English is always inadequate. In the case C) the user speaks English, the service requires English so the service is always adequate. The case B) is the most interesting: the user knows French and English and the service requires English. In this case we need to detect at runtime the user language, impose to the user to use only English or consider the service as inadequate.

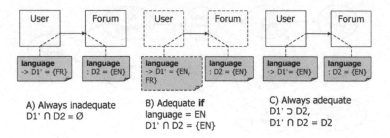

A) Always inadequate
D1' ∩ D2 = ∅

B) Adequate **if**
language = EN
D1' ∩ D2 = {EN}

C) Always adequate
D1' ⊃ D2,
D1' ∩ D2 = D2

Fig. 5. Service-context information exchange based validation

The information flow circulates directly through the interconnections but may suffer modification through the filters. For each attribute, the chain effect is given by the mathematical composition of the transfer functions for each filter in the chain (functions **H** specified in the component profile).

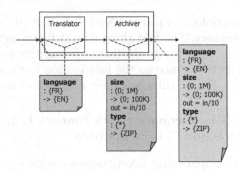

Fig. 6. Information flow composition

Figure 6 depicts the composition operation for two filters: a translator followed by an archiver. If a filter profile does not specify an attribute, we suppose that the filter does not affect that attribute and its output value is equal to its input value. An unspecified function **H** is equivalent to the identity function, this allow us to compose the functions. For instance, the zip archiver does not modify the information language, that means the **H** function for language is the identity function.

As we see in figure 6, the chain flow attributes are given by the reunion of all flow attributes of each filter. If two filters affect a same attribute (fact indicated by their profiles), we use the standard mathematical function composition in order to determine the chain global transfer function. The information composition is analog to signal composition for electrical filters chains.

Observation. In practice we cannot express always easily the filter **H** function (the zip compression factor cannot be known a priori because it is content-dependent). In these cases, the profile will only include the input and output domains for **H**. The output instant value can be also discovered using a probe (observer) component that evaluates the **H** output.

Rule 2: A service is adequate to its context if all the resources required by the service are offered by its context

A service is adequate to its context (physical infrastructure: terminals, machines, networks) if it does not needs more resources than available. The resources nature is generally additive. For instance, if one component takes 100KB memory and another takes 300KB, then the two components will need at least 400KB.

In some cases, the resource utilization does not obey a simple additive relation. For instance, two visual components may be displayed on the same display at the same time or consecutively. The required screen surface is different in the two situations. In order to enable the developer to express different situations, we offer the possibility to use different composition and validation operators, not only the addition and the inferiority. The table from figure 8 depicts several attributes using different composition and validation operators.

3.4   Solution Search and Application

The proposed model allows us to create automatically different service-context configurations and test the service to context adequacy. In order to increase the adaptation speed, the solution search algorithm must use some heuristic. The solution search problem is a complex one and will not be detailed in this paper. We just want to show that our model enables us to do it.

If the inadequacy is caused by a information flow incompatibility, one general solution is to insert an additional filter that is acting like an adapter. A translator is an adapter between two components (software or contextual) "speaking" different languages. The necessary component is searched by its profile: the input/output function of the searched component must solve the inadequacy problem.

The insertion point is searched by verifying the syntactical interface compatibility. As we see in figure 7, the graph model gives us the possibility to follow

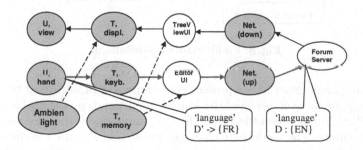

Fig. 7. Solution search for a flow related inadequacy

the information flows. In the forum case, a new language translator filter may be inserted after *EditorUI* output if present on the terminal, or before *ForumServer* input if the translator is a remote web service. The same idea may be used for the service output: a second translation component may be inserted after the *ForumServer* output. As we can see, the model enables us to make distinction between the user ability to write respectively to read (input and output) in English.

In principle, a new filter may be inserted in any point of a filter chain if it's IDL (Interface Definition Language) compatible and if it does not create a new inadequacy because of its profile. An existent filter may be replaced with another one if the same conditions are respected. It remains for future work to find some general and efficient search algorithms that combine several component not only one. A possible solution may come from the AI (Artificial Intelligence) domain, i.e. genetic algorithms which have been used already for electrical circuit synthesis.

3.5   Model Extensibility

The control part, figure 8, uses a common-defined, service-independent table containing the attributes definitions and operators for composition and validation. This table must be created by a human operator and the idea is to have e unique definition for all services. Also, the profile attribute names must be respected by the component developers while describing the profiles. We think that a common attribute ontology is a possible solution.

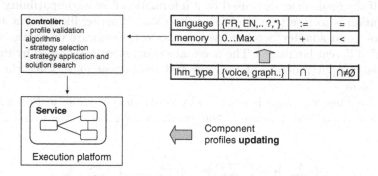

Fig. 8. Profile attributes definitions

Each component must have a profile. The component profiles must be specified by the component developers and the adaptation depends on the profiles content: if an attribute is not present in the profile we cannot check the adequacy for the missing attribute. The model extension requires to add new lines in the attribute table, figure 8 and requires intervention of a human operator. Once added, these definitions may be reused.

For the contextual components, common definitions must be used too. We may have for instance a common ontology defining contextual components, for instance different terminal types with their characteristics.

A drawback of our model is that not only the attribute table must be updated in order to take new attributes into account but also the existing component profiles. The automatical update is still a future work to do.

4 Prototype

The prototype was implemented according to the architecture described in figure 2. The service components are implemented in java, according to CCM (Corba Component Model). We suppose to have all the necessary components. For the translation component, we have used a local proxy for a distant translation web service. Each component has and IDL (Interface Definition Language) description. The service architecture is described using an XML based ADL (Architecture Definition Language). Component profiles are described using a proprietary XML. A deployment engine based on java reflection creates and re-creates the service architecture. Runtime reconfiguration is applied using interaction patterns described using the ISL (Interaction Specification Language) language [16]. The adaptation controller creates the service-context graph (see figure 4) from: ADL, IDLs and component profiles. We use this graph for checking the service to context adequacy and for solution search.

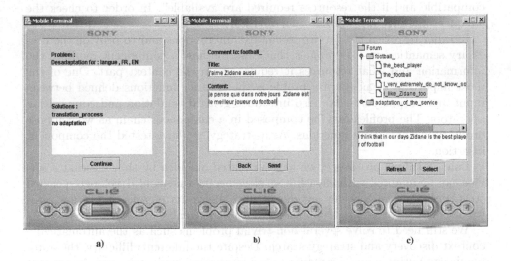

Fig. 9. Forum UI for a PDA device

The figure 9 depicts the forum user interface. The terminal used is a PDA. The user logs in, the platform detects a conflict between the user profile (previously stored) an the service profile because the user language and the service language are different. The platform proposes to user two possibilities: use a translator or leave the service unchanged. Supposing the user chose to use the translator from French to English, his messages are translated. The prototype has two versions: in the first one the user language is supposed to be stored in a database, in the second the language is detected at each message. In the second version the user may write messages in English, French and German and the service is reconfigured for each message, dynamically.

This prototype shows that the forum service may be adapted without using service-specific rules, without indicating the component that must be inserted and without specifying the insertion point (strategy). Instead, the language related inadequacy is discovered by analyzing the service-context model, the required component and the insertion point are searched.

5   Conclusions and Perspectives

In this paper we propose a service-context model allowing autonomic, dynamic adaptation. While most existing adaptation systems use service and context-specific, developer-specified adaptation rules and strategies, in our proposal we replace this by a service-context knowledge representation.

This model represents a knowledge base for the control part that is able to reason about the service to context adequacy and search for adaptation solutions. In our proposal, the rules are high-level defined and service-independent, for instance: "a system is adequate to its context if the information exchanged is compatible and if the resources required are available". In order to check the adequacy we have introduced some operators.

In order to reveal the service to context interactions and to provide the necessary semantics, we use *profiles* that describe how a component modifies the information and what resources it requires from the context part. One of the most important elements of a profile is the transfer functions defined between input and output ports. We also introduce general validation and composition operators. The profiles may be composed in a component chain as we compose ordinary mathematical functions. As a strategy, we have tested the component insertion.

Using a simple prototype, we have validated our idea by showing that a service can be adapted without using service-specific rules and developer-specified strategies, thus we consider our model suitable for autonomic adaptation, even we does not solve all the problems related to this goal.

We still need to solve several non-trivial problems such as the automatically context discovery and strategy search. Despite the inherent difficulty, the autonomic computing domain remains a very interesting field, even more interesting when is combined with the ubiquitous computing. In the future, we intend to focus on the solution search issues: strategy selection, algorithms improvement, AI techniques, feedback based learning, mechanisms allowing us to compare alternative solutions and select the best one.

References

1. Ganek, A.G., Corbi, T.A.: The dawning of the autonomic computing era. IBM Syst. Journal 42(1), 5–18 (2003)
2. Kephart, J.O.: Research challenges of autonomic computing. In: Inverardi, P., Jazayeri, M. (eds.) ICSE 2005. LNCS, vol. 4309, pp. 15–22. Springer, Heidelberg (2006)
3. Dey, A.: Understanding and using context. Personal and Ubiquitous Computing 5(1), 4–7 (2001)
4. Kwon, O., Yoo, K., Suh, E.: ubies: An intelligent expert system for proactive services deploying ubiquitous computing technologies. In: HICSS '05: Proceedings of the Proceedings of the 38th Annual Hawaii International Conference on System Sciences (HICSS'05) - Track 3, Washington, p. 85.2. IEEE Computer Society Press, Los Alamitos (2005)
5. Dubus, J., Merle, P.: Vers l'auto-adaptabilité des architectures logicielles dans les environnements ouverts distribués. In: CAL, pp. 13–29 (2006)
6. Franklin, G., Powell, J.D., Emami-Naeini, A.: Feedback Control of Dynamic Systems. Prentice Hall, New Jersey (2002)
7. J., K.: Completely Unanticipated Dynamic Adaptation of Software. PhD thesis, University of Dublin, Trinity College, Distributed Systems Group (October 2004)
8. Floch, J., Hallsteinsen, S., Stav, E., Eliassen, F., Lund, K., Gjorven, E.: Using architecture models for runtime adaptability. IEEE Software 23(2), 62–70 (2006)
9. Garlan, D., Cheng, S.-W., Huang, A.-C., Schmerl, B., Steenkiste, P.: Rainbow: Architecture-based self-adaptation with reusable infrastructure. Computer 37(10), 46–54 (2004)
10. Chan, A., Chuang, S.-N.: Mobipads: a reflective middleware for context-aware mobile computing. IEEE Transactions on Software Engineering 29(12), 1072–1085 (2003)
11. Roman, M.: An Application Framework for Active Space Applications. PhD thesis, University of Illinois at Urbana-Champaign (2003)
12. Dowling, J., Cahill, V.: The k-component architecture meta-model for self-adaptive software. In: Yonezawa, A., Matsuoka, S. (eds.) Metalevel Architectures and Separation of Crosscutting Concerns. LNCS, vol. 2192, pp. 81–88. Springer, Heidelberg (2001)
13. Lohn, J.D., Colombano, S.P.: A circuit representation technique for automated circuit design. IEEE Transactions on Evolutionary Computation 3(3), 205 (1999)
14. Wang, X.H., Zhang, D.Q., Gu, T., Pung, H.K.: Ontology based context modeling and reasoning using owl. In: PERCOMW '04: Proceedings of the Second IEEE Annual Conference on Pervasive Computing and Communications Workshops, Washington, p. 18. IEEE Computer Society Press, Los Alamitos (2004)
15. Brézillon, P.: Context-based modeling of operators' practices by contextual graphs. In: Bisdorf, R. (ed.) Proceedings of the Human Centered processes, Fond National de la Recherche du Luxembourg, pp. 120–137 (2003)
16. Blay-Fornarino, M., Charfi, A., Emsellem, D., Pinna-Dery, A.-M., Riveill, M.: Software interactions. Journal of Object Technology 3(10), 161–180 (2004)

Goal Reasoning with Context Record Types

Richard Dapoigny and Patrick Barlatier

Université de Savoie, ESIA Laboratoire d'Informatique, Sytèmes, Traitement de
l'Information et de la Connaissance B.P. 806,
F-74016 ANNECY Cedex, France
Phone: +33 450 096529 Fax: +33 450 096559
listic@esia.univ-savoie.fr

Abstract. The concept of goal is central in Artificial Intelligence and its
modelling is a challenging issue. It has been given much attention in areas
such as Requirement Engineering (RE) and Planning and Scheduling,
where its modelling can support formal reasoning through goal types,
goal attributes and relations to other components. However there is a
lack of formalisms able to reason with goal structures in dynamic environments. We claim that a logical framework based on Intuitionistic
Type Theory and more precisely, on Dependent Record Types is able to
address this problem. The formal foundations rely on context modelling
through dependent record types allowing partial knowledge and dynamic
reasoning. For the purpose of goal modelling, we introduce a family of
functions which map Context Record Types to Intentional Record Types
expressing their related actions and goals. A case study in planning illustrates this approach.

1 Introduction

An accumulating body of research suggests that it is profitable to treat human cognition as a system that is primarily concerned with goal management.
More specifically, the symbolic representation of goals, the location of relevant
objects and operations and the construction of plans to achieve them, using objects and operations as components, are part of the process of human cognition.
The implementation of these topics in computing systems has been effective in
Artificial Intelligence (AI) through its sub-disciplines such as Requirement Engineering (RE) or Planning and Scheduling. While the concept of goal is clearly
understood in AI as a final situation to obtain, its representation is subject to
discussion.

Most approaches, in Planning, consider goal representation as a final state or
a set of fluents, which is then decomposed into a sequence of actions to achieve
them. Unfortunately, this goal expression is not general enough to cover all real
life models. Consider for example the scenario in which my objective is to ride a
bike. The final situation is clearly not a state but an atelic situation in which my
location is continuously changing. This argues for the fact that the representation
of goals must include a representation of action (the action which makes this
goal achieved). While many goal classifications have been proposed, there are

B. Kokinov et al. (Eds.): CONTEXT 2007, LNAI 4635, pp. 164–177, 2007.

few approaches focussing on linguistic representation upon which reasoning can take place. However, a structure for goals has been suggested in (24) including a verb and one or more parameters. The existence of a verb in goal structure witnesses the associated process which itself can be expressed as a sequence of actions. Some approaches have given some account of the interrelation between goal engineering and Natural Language Processing (NLP). As underlined in (26), contextual information can be embedded within use case specification as an unambiguous natural language text.

Therefore, the main objective of this paper is to introduce a formal structure for goals with the help of domain ontologies, such as it allows to reason about goal composition in a semantic way. For example, given a global goal sentence and a set of atomic goal expressions, how to derive a sound sequence of primitive goal expressions? For this purpose, we provide a formal semantics for goals in terms of logic and linguistic information that supports rational justifications for planning principles. The definition of goals in terms of Dependent Record Types (DRT[1]) formalizes the intuition that goals are propositions that are preferred to their opposites. More precisely, we are concerned with material processes dealing to a large extent with action verbs. Whereas most approaches in planning focus on a goal expression describing a desired state, a more general perspective (stemming from NLP) would consider an action-based description. As a result, an unifying approach should ground the meaning of goals, that is of verbs, in the structure of the actions they denote together with their effect(s). Section 2 recalls significant goal-oriented approaches in AI. Section 3 draws the basis of a context model based on dependent record types, while section 4 relates these types to an intentional record type made of an action and its related effects including its goal. A case study detailed in section 5 gives an example of their use through a planning algorithm. Finally, section 6 discusses the major benefits of the approach.

2   Goal-Oriented Approaches in AI

The concept of goal which have long been recognized to be an essential component of Artificial Intelligence (AI), appeared also for a wide extent in Requirement Engineering (RE)(18), in planning (14; 27) and more recently, in Semantic Web Service Discovery (9). AI planning systems gain much leverage from means-end reasoning and sub-goal reasoning. The classical formulation of the planning problem requires a description of the agents goal, that is, what behavior is desired. In goal-directed planning, after having adopted goals, the agent searches for ways of achieving them by using goal regression (23). A survey of some alternative approaches to planning in AI showed that the goal-directed planning by itself will not always suffice for finding realistic plans (32). The crude binary distinctions defined by these goals offer no basis for choosing among alternative plans that ensure achievement of goals, and no guidance whatever when no such plans can be found. These insufficiencies pose significant problems for

---

[1] Notice that this abbreviation is distinct from that of NLP.

planning in all realistic situations, where actions have uncertain effects or objectives. Moreover, goals cannot be evaluated directly in terms of their expected values, since goals can be of different scopes, and they can interact with other previously required sub-goals. An important issue in reasoning about plans, processes, and activities holds in the description of the desired goals (or objectives or tasks) as well as which actions (or procedures, or agents) have the capability to achieve them. In planning systems, goals and capabilities are typically described as a predicate with a name and several arguments, and are matched through straightforward variable unification. Some authors in planning (10) have described goals as a flat predicate with a predicate name and several arguments. However, in that case only limited reasoning is done about them. The first step in Semantic Web Service Discovery Services (SWSDS) concentrates on Goal discovery. This activity turns out to find in a repository a predefined goal description corresponding to the user objective since it is assumed that the user is generally unable to formulate a semantically correct goal description. As a result, the first challenge in SWSDS focusses on abstracting goal from user queries. A current solution consists in a mapping from the users' desire to generic goals (16). Goal taxonomies could be used to support more flexible matching approaches exploiting subsumption to relate otherwise disparate descriptions. This is especially important given the recent emphasis on distributed or web-based approaches, where planners, agents, or services need a certain goal accomplished by others, but each of them may have their own way to describe them.

3   Context Modelling

3.1   Intuitionistic Type Theory

While the most significant approaches of context with logic-based models cover a wide spectrum of AI modelling (12; 13; 20; 28; 29), they revealed some difficulty to manage the intensional aspect (some of them present modality as a solution). One important aspect which has been underlined in (12) is the locality principle. This principle stating that different portions of knowledge are defined, is taken as a basis for the context modelling. Then, starting from the observation that physical objects are a central element of process activity and building on recent works (2; 25; 31), we have proposed a context model based on Intuitionistic[2] Type Theory (ITT) for engineering applications. We consider the *context-of* the application, that is, the *context-of* the global goal (since the application is characterized by an objective). The analysis of contextual reasoning requires sound and expressive formalisms. Widely used in NLP (11; 2; 25; 4) and in Programming Languages (3; 5; 22), ITT (19) has been proven to be appropriate to support the linguistic nature of physical situations. The Intuitionistic Type Theory is able to serve as a background for expressing knowledge in AI via Dependent Record Types. In rough words, intuitionism says that only those mathematical concepts that can be demonstrated, or constructed are legitimate.

---

[2] Or Constructive.

ITT exploits both intuitionism and theory of types which provides a rich type system in which any property in predicate logic can be interpreted as a type. It is the basis for important works in logic and AI (theorem provers such as Coq, LEGO, ...), functional languages, logics (linear logic, Martin Löf's Type Theory, ...). One of the major benefits of Type Theory is the proofs-as-programs paradigm[3] which associates a constructive proof with a program realizing the proven formula (15) (see table 1). Another benefit is the computability of any judgement: Intuitionistic Theory of Types is functionally decidable (30). The most fundamental notion of ITT is the typing judgement $a : T$ classifying an object a as being of type T. Examples of typing judgements are:

$x : Animate\_ind$ # x is of type $Animate\_ind$
$s : run(x)$ # $run(x)$ is a type of a proof

Table 1. Proposition as Set

Proposition	Set
$A \wedge B$	$A \times B$, cartesian product
$A \vee B$	$A + B$, disjoint union
$A \rightarrow B$	$A \rightarrow B$, functions from A to B
$(\forall x \in A)B(x)$	$\prod(AB)$, cartesian product of a family $B(x)$ of types indexed on values of type A
$(\exists x \in A)B(x)$	$\sum(AB)$, the disjoint union of a family $B(x)$ of types indexed on values of type A
$\perp$	$\emptyset$

In classical logic, there are only two truth values, by which we mean that every proposition is equal either to *true* or to *false*. In intuitionistic logic, however, this is not the case since we have two possibilities, i.e., *true* and *not yet proven*. As a result, intuitionistic logic is backward compatible with classical logic. The consequences of this choice is that we reject the so-called closed-world assumption and provide some flavor of modality through the second possibility.

3.2 The Context Types

In ITT, a useful innovation is the introduction of dependent types and dependent record types (1; 17). Dependent types are types expressed in terms of data. They are able to express more of what matters about data since they are much more flexible than conventional type systems (i.e., they offer a continuum of precision from the basic assertions up to a complete specification of a problem). As suggested in a previous works (7; 8), the concept of context can be expressed as Dependent Record Types including individuals as well as propositions. Context types (what is possible) are distinguished from context tokens (what is

---

[3] Also known as the Curry-Howard isomorphism.

the realm). They clearly separate the specification of potential contexts through types with their implementation through tokens. A further attraction is that this subdivision also supports ontological engineering for the specification of the applications during the design step. In the framework of physical processes, we introduce the Context Record Type (CRT) expressed by a dependent record type in which the fields detail the physical knowledge (i.e., concepts, their properties and their constraints). Their ability to provide a simple structure that can be reused to specify different kinds of structured semantic objects is a key element of the model.

Definition 1. *A Dependent Record Type is a sequence of fields in which labels l_i correspond to certain types T_i, that is, each successive field can depend on the values of the preceding fields:*

$$C = \begin{bmatrix} l_1 & : T_1 \\ l_2 & : T_2(l_1) \\ \cdots \\ l_n & : T_n(l_1 \ldots l_{n-1}) \end{bmatrix} \tag{1}$$

where the type T_i may depend on the preceding labels $l_1, ..., l_{i-1}$.

A similar definition holds for record tokens where a sequence of values is such that a value v_i can depend on the values of the preceding fields $l_1, ..., l_{i-1}$:

$$c = \begin{bmatrix} l_1 & = v_1 \\ l_2 & = v_2 \\ \cdots \\ l_n & = v_n \end{bmatrix} \tag{2}$$

We can also make use of tabular notation to represent records. The empty sequence $<>$ is a dependent record type and the type T_i is a family of types over the record type $l_1 : T_1, ..., l_{i-1} : T_{i-1}$. Assuming that Γ is a valid context[4], we can express the record type formation rules provided that l is not already declared in R:

$$\frac{}{\Gamma \vdash <> : record - type} \qquad \frac{R : record - type}{\Gamma \vdash R \sqsubseteq <>} \tag{3}$$

$$\frac{\Gamma \vdash R : record - type \quad \Gamma \vdash T : record - type \rightarrow type}{\Gamma \vdash < R, l : T > : record - type} \tag{4}$$

We also assume that the general rules of construction for *Set* and *Prop* types are valid and that primitive syntactic constructions (i.e., equality, functional application and lambda abstraction) hold (for more details see (19)). An important aspect of DRT is that sub-typing is allowed, for example a DRT with additional fields not mentioned in the type is still of that type. CRT can range from the context of a single variable involved in a physical equation to the context of a

---

[4] A valid context in type theory is a sequence $x_1 : T_1, \ldots x_n : T_n$ such that there is a judgment having it as left side of a sequent.

real life situation. Let us consider the initial situation of an air travelling domain in which a traveller (named John) must plan a New-York-Zurich flight.

$$
\underbrace{\begin{bmatrix} x & : Person \\ y & : Ticket \\ p_1 : own(x, y) \\ z & : Flight \\ p_2 : has\_Flight(y, z) \\ t & : DestinationTown \\ p_3 : has\_Destination(z, t) \end{bmatrix}}_{C_1 : Context\ type}
\underbrace{\begin{bmatrix} x & = John \\ y & = t0015JK \\ p_1 = q_1 \\ z & = ZU515 \\ p_2 = q_2 \\ t & = Zurich \\ p_3 = q_3 \end{bmatrix}}_{c_1 : Context\ token}
$$

in which q_1 is a proof of $own(John, t0015JK)$, q_2 is a proof that has_Flight $(John, ZU515)$ and q_3, a proof of $has\_Destination(John, Zurich)$. Since the Curry-Howard isomorphism identifies proofs with programs, it can be used to prove a specification, or in other words, to select which definitions are needed for the specification to work properly. Pre-defined values can be introduced with manifest types (6).

Definition 2. *Given x of type T, $x : T$, a singleton type T_x is such that:*

$$
y : T_x \ \textbf{iff} \ \ y = x \tag{5}
$$

Given a record, a manifest field is a field whose type is a singleton type. We will adopt the notation of (4; 11):

$$
r : \begin{bmatrix} \dots \\ l = x : T \\ \dots \end{bmatrix} \tag{6}
$$

One important aspect of this modelling with CRT is that a context can have any number of fields (there is no upper limit).

3.3 Sub-Typing with Contexts

The extension of a physical context type C to a context type C' corresponds to the process of getting more information. Since in type theory, the analogue of a proposition is the judgement, we can conclude that the judgement in C is lifted to the judgement in C'. The question of sub-typing requires the knowledge of all possible coercions used for a given term and their precise effect, which is untractable in practice. This problem can be avoided by imposing semantic constraints on coercions (1): this is the case in record-based subtyping that we shall adopt here.

Definition 3. *Given two record types C and C', if C' contains at least every label declared in C and if the types of these common labels are in the inclusion relation then C is a subtype of C' which is written:*

$$
C \sqsubseteq C' \tag{7}
$$

Every record token of type C is also a token of type C', since it contains components of appropriate types for all the fields specified in C'. In type theory, the analogue of a proposition is the judgement, and we can conclude that the judgement in C is lifted to the judgement in C'. Type inclusion and corresponding proof rules generalize record type inclusion to dependent record types and propagate it to all the types within the language. For more detail on context sub-typing, see (8). Context by itself doesn't make sense since it must be related to an intentional concept (it is ontologically speaking, a moment universal).

4   Goal Modelling

4.1   Goal Structures

In the following, we assume that capital letters denote types whereas small letters denote tokens. The theory of record types as a part of general type theory allows to define functions and function types providing a version of the typed λ-calculus.

Definition 4. *Given a Context Record Type C, an action can be intuitively described by a family of record types which is a function from records to record types as the λ-abstraction:*

$$\lambda c : C.a : [p_1 :< action\, verb > (\ldots, c.l_i, \ldots) \tag{8}$$

Types are extracted from a local ontology to form the basic DRT of the action concept. Let us consider the air travelling domain described above. A function of the type

$$\lambda c_1 : C_1.a_1 : [p_1 = take\_flight(c_1.x, c_1.z)$$

maps records of the form c_1 into a record of the form:

$$[p_1 = take\_flight(John, ZU515)$$

Ground types generate a simple context in which the respective context types and tokens hold. We assume that each context is related to a single action (the context of the action). We can generalize the previous definition by considering the resulting goal and its related effects in an intentional record. The Intentional Record Type (IRT) can be drawn as a function from a context type to a record type describing both an action, its related intended goal and some propositions resulting from the action on the environment:

$$\lambda c : C.(\begin{bmatrix} a : [p_1 : action\_verb(...) \\ g : [g_1 : ... \\ e : \begin{bmatrix} e_1 : ... \\ e_2 : ... \end{bmatrix} \end{bmatrix}) \tag{9}$$

Notice that while a single action is related to a single context, the IRT may incorporate multiple effects. It can be seen as a link in which an agent observing an action of type $[p_1 : action\_verb(...)$ will predict the existence of a goal of type $[g_1 : ....$ The function in equation 9 is able to express that the intentional record is a consequence of the existence of its context record. In other words, the existence of this context 'causes' the existence of the propositions in the IRT. In summary, if a context is true in a given situation then its related action is executable and the goal is achievable.

Extending the context (e.g., with additional constraints), will lead to a sub-context of an alternate action. Suppose that a context, say c_1 belongs to several context types, e.g., C_1 and C_1' with $C_1 \sqsubseteq C_1'$. We start from the assumption that C_1 and C_1' are respectively mapped to the IRT I_1 and I_1'. Therefore, if we obtain a context c_1, the intuitive decision is to select I_1 rather than I_1' since it contains more specific information (the closest one).

4.2   The Planning Algorithm

The context model can be fruitfully applied to planning problems described by the tuple $P = (S, \Sigma, \mathcal{C}, \mathcal{I}, g)$, where S is the list of initial dynamic constraints (e.g., their values can change during the whole process), Σ stands for the static constraints (at least during the time of the process), $\mathcal{C}$ denotes the set of CRT, $\mathcal{I}$ denotes the set of intentional types, and g the goal to achieve. If $(S, \Sigma, \mathcal{C}, \mathcal{I}, g)$ is a planning problem, then $\Pi(S, \Sigma, \mathcal{C}, \mathcal{I}, g)$ the set of available plans is defined by the following procedure, in which r_i is of type (
$$\begin{bmatrix} a_i : [p_1 : action\_verb(...) \\ g_i : [g_1 : ... \\ e_i : \begin{bmatrix} e_1 : ... \\ e_2 : ... \end{bmatrix} \end{bmatrix}$$
)

(i.e., an intentional type related to the context c_i):

```
function find-plans( S, Σ, C, g)
(let P, p
(for i = 1 to | C |
   (if (consistent Ci < SΣ >)
     ( if (subtype-of g rᵢ.gᵢ)
        (add p rᵢ.aᵢ)
     else
         (for ii = 0 to | C |
            (if ((<> cᵢᵢ cᵢ) and (subtype-of cᵢᵢ ([gᵢ / eᵢ])) and (consistent rᵢᵢ Σ))
               (add p rᵢᵢ.aᵢᵢ))
               ( if (subtype-of g rᵢᵢ.gᵢᵢ))
                  break))))
   (add P p)))
return P)
```

5 Case Study

To illustrate the proposed mechanism, we apply the transportation-planning problem that has been incorporated in the SHOP planner demonstration (21). Briefly, an individual (denoted as "agent") wants to travel from one location to another in a city. Three possible modes of transportation are available: taxi, bus, and foot. Taxi travel involves hailing the taxi, riding to the destination, and paying the driver \$1.50 plus \$1.00 for each mile travelled. Bus travel requires waiting for the right bus, paying the driver (\$1.00), and riding to the destination. Concerning the foot travel, it only involves walking, but the maximum feasible walking distance depends on the weather (it is less or equal to 3 miles in good weather and less or equal to one mile otherwise. Thus, different plans are possible depending on what the layout of the city is, where we start, where we want to go, how much money we have, and what the weather is like.

Domain knowledge is defined through the CRT for each related action and goal. We can express the two primitive goal types corresponding to the two possible context types C_{11} and C_{12} in the first mode of transportation (by foot), with:

$$
\underbrace{\begin{bmatrix}
x & : Location \\
y & : Location \\
z & : Person \\
p_1 & : At(z,x) \\
d_{dest} & : Distance \\
e_1 = good & : Weather \\
dmax = 3 & : Distance \\
p_2 & : d_{dest} <= dmax \\
p_3 & : Has\_dest(z,y)
\end{bmatrix}}_{C_{11}}
\qquad
\underbrace{\begin{bmatrix}
x & : Location \\
y & : Location \\
z & : Person \\
p_1 & : At(z,x) \\
d_{dest} & : Distance \\
e_1 = bad & : Weather \\
dmax = 1 & : Distance \\
p_2 & : d_{dest} <= dmax \\
p_3 & : Has\_dest(z,y)
\end{bmatrix}}_{C_{12}}
$$

$$\lambda c_{11} : C_{11}. \begin{bmatrix} a_{11} : walk(c_{11}.z, c_{11}.y, c_{11}.x) \\ g_{11} : At(c_{11}.z, c_{11}.y) \end{bmatrix}$$

$$\lambda c_{12} : C_{12}. \begin{bmatrix} a_{12} : walk(c_{12}.z, c_{12}.y, c_{12}.x) \\ g_{12} : At(c_{12}.z, c_{12}.y) \end{bmatrix}$$

In a similar way, three primitive goal types are related to the three possible context types C_2, C_3 and C_4 in the second mode of transportation (by bus), with :

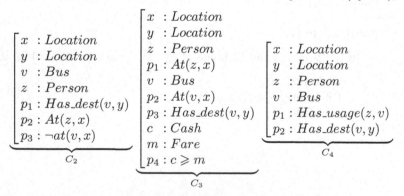

$$
\underbrace{\begin{bmatrix}
x & : Location \\
y & : Location \\
v & : Bus \\
z & : Person \\
p_1 & : Has\_dest(v,y) \\
p_2 & : At(z,x) \\
p_3 & : \neg at(v,x)
\end{bmatrix}}_{C_2}
\quad
\underbrace{\begin{bmatrix}
x & : Location \\
y & : Location \\
z & : Person \\
p_1 & : At(z,x) \\
v & : Bus \\
p_2 & : At(v,x) \\
p_3 & : Has\_dest(v,y) \\
c & : Cash \\
m & : Fare \\
p_4 & : c \geqslant m
\end{bmatrix}}_{C_3}
\quad
\underbrace{\begin{bmatrix}
x & : Location \\
y & : Location \\
z & : Person \\
v & : Bus \\
p_1 & : Has\_usage(z,v) \\
p_2 & : Has\_dest(v,y)
\end{bmatrix}}_{C_4}
$$

$$\lambda c_2 : C_2. \begin{bmatrix} a_2 : wait\_for(c_2.z, c_2.v) \\ g_2 : At(c_2.v, c_2.x) \end{bmatrix}$$

$$\lambda c_3 : C_3. \begin{bmatrix} a_3 : pay\_driver(c_3.z, c_3.m) \\ g_3 : Has\_usage(c_3.z, c_3.v) \end{bmatrix}$$

$$\lambda c_4 : C_4. \begin{bmatrix} a_4 : ride\_bus(c_4.z, c_4.x, c_4.y) \\ g_4 : At(c_4.z, c_4.y) \end{bmatrix}$$

For the third mode of transportation (i.e., taxi), the three primitive goal types are related to the three possible context types C_5, C_6 and C_7 are described by:

$$C_5 = \begin{bmatrix} x & : Location \\ d & : Distance \\ v & : Taxi \\ z & : Person \\ p_1 : At(z, x) \\ p_2 : At\_stand(v, x) \\ c & : Cash \\ m & : Fare \\ p_3 : c \geqslant m + d \end{bmatrix} \quad C_6 = \begin{bmatrix} x & : Location \\ y & : Location \\ z & : Person \\ p_1 : At(z, x) \\ v & : Taxi \\ p_2 : In(z, v) \\ p_3 : Has\_dest(z, y) \end{bmatrix} \quad C_7 = \begin{bmatrix} x & : Location \\ y & : Location \\ d & : Distance \\ z & : Person \\ v & : Taxi \\ p_1 : At(z, y) \\ c & : Cash \\ m & : Fare \\ p_2 : c \geqslant m + d \\ p_3 : At(v, y) \\ p_4 : \neg Paid\_for(z, x, y) \end{bmatrix}$$

$$\lambda c_5 : C_5. \begin{bmatrix} a_5 : hail(c_5.x, c_5.v) \\ g_5 : In(c_5.z, c_5.v) \end{bmatrix}$$

$$\lambda c_6 : C_6. \begin{bmatrix} a_6 : ride\_taxi(c_6.z, c_6.x, c_6.y) \\ g_6 : At(c_6.v, c_6.y) \\ e & : [e_1 : \neg Paid\_for(c_6.z, c_6.x, c_6.y)] \end{bmatrix}$$

$$\lambda c_7 : C_7. \begin{bmatrix} a_7 : pay\_driver(c_7.z, c_7.(m + d)) \\ g_7 : At(c_7.z, c_7.y) \end{bmatrix}$$

The initial situation is described through a list S including dynamic constraints and a list Σ related to static constraints. Note that this separation clearly allows for better performance of the planning algorithm. Due to a lack of space, we only consider 3 problems:

Problem 1. with the global goal "Go to park", the constraints "no cash" and "good weather". The static and dynamic constraints lists are respectively Σ and S_1 such as:

$$\left\{ \begin{array}{ll} x & : Location = downtown \\ e_1 & : Weather = good \\ y_1 & : Location = park \\ y_2 & : Location = uptown \\ y_3 & : Location = suburb \\ dest_1 & : Distance = 2 \\ dest_2 & : Distance = 8 \\ dest_3 & : Distance = 12 \end{array} \right. \left\{ \begin{array}{lll} z & : Person = John \\ v_1 & : Taxi & = Taxi1 \\ v_2 & : Taxi & = Taxi2 \\ b_1 & : Bus & = Bus1 \\ b_2 & : Bus & = Bus2 \\ b_3 & : Bus & = Bus3 \\ m_1 & : fare & = 1 \\ m_2 & : fare & = 1.5 \\ c_1 & : Cash & = 0 \\ c_2 & : Cash & = 12 \\ r_1 & : Prop & = Has\_dest(b_1, \Sigma_1.y_1) \\ r_2 & : Prop & = Has\_dest(b_2, \Sigma_1.y_2) \\ r_3 & : Prop & = Has\_dest(b_3, \Sigma_1.y_3) \\ r_4 & : Prop & = At\_stand(v_1, x) \\ r_5 & : Prop & = At\_stand(v_2, x) \\ r_6 & : Prop & = Has\_priority(v_1) \\ r_7 & : Prop & = \neg At(b_1, x) \\ r_8 & : Prop & = \neg At(b_2, x) \\ r_9 & : Prop & = \neg At(b_3, x) \\ r_{10} & : Prop & = At(z, x) \end{array} \right.$$

The desired goal is expressed through the IRT part: $g : \left[g_G : At(z, y) \right.$ in which z and y_1 have the corresponding values in the constraint list above. Running the algorithm, only c_{11} is true and consistent with $S_1 \Sigma$. Notice that although c_2 is also a potential candidate, c_3 cannot be true since $c_3.p_4$ is not true. Therefore, a single plan $\Pi[1] = \{g_{11}\}$ is available.

Problem 2. The global goal is expressed as "Go to uptown", with "$12 cash" and "good weather". The final destination is $y_2 = uptown$. The dynamic constraints list is the same excepted for the field c with $c = 12$. The first contexts to be true are c_2 and c_5 since they are the only contexts consistent with $< S_2 \Sigma >$. Applying the algorithm, the two possible plans are: $\Pi[1] = \{g2, g3, g4\}$ and $\Pi[2] = \{g5, g6, g7\}$.

Problem 3. The last global goal is "Go to suburb", with "$12 cash" and "good weather". The final destination is now $y_3 = suburb$.

The dynamic constraints list S_3 remains the same as S_2. The first context to be true is c_2 since only $< S_3 \Sigma >$ is consistent with c_2 with the values:

$$c_2 = \left[\begin{array}{l} x = downtown \\ y = suburb \\ v = Bus3 \\ z = John \\ p_1 = Has\_dest(v, y) \\ p_2 = At(z, x) \\ p_3 = \neg At(v, x) \end{array} \right.$$

Finally, the algorithm extracts the single plan, $\Pi[1] = \{g2, g3, g4\}$.

The intuitionistic planner is implemented in LISP. After the plan space is created by the planner, it is possible to rank all the generated plans and the best plan can be automatically chosen according to additional constraint such as minimizing the cost.

6   Conclusion

In this paper, we have exploited the notion of context in type theory to cope with the problems of action-based reasoning and planning. ITT provides a major benefit over the many other AI formalisms used for representing goals, actions and events, including basic first-order formalisms, such as Allen's theory of time, situation or event calculus, ... since it is able to cope with partial knowledge and dynamic knowledge through dependent record types. This approach is suitable to encompass a body of results which have been proposed in action-based reasoning during the last decades such as partial knowledge and the frame problem. The latter doesn't make any sense in ITT with dependent types since records are of a given type, but can have many more fields than this type specifies. The dependent types introduce a simultaneous abstraction property on which context dependence relies. As a result, contexts can be typed and included in the domains of functions as first-class citizens. Moreover, we have shown that such an approach allows to treat intentional propositions like actions and goal in a common type (IRT) expressed as a family of record types. The ability of dependent record types to express any kind of information and to incorporate these representations within a single well-founded theory reveal its powerful aspect. We have given some account of the dynamic capabilities of CRT in the representation of knowledge through their extensions, similar to the lifting operations in (20). In this functional theory, processes are justified by teleological commitments: the theory defines a specific functional role through IRT, for each primitive process that contributes to the task that the theory explains. A first limitation holds in the size of CRT which can affect the complexity of algorithms since contexts are indefinitely extendable. A second limitation comes from the lack of Intelligent User Interface for the system design. For this purpose, further works will include the implementation of a graphical user interface able to serve as a frontal for NLP-based interaction.

Bibliography

[1] Betarte, G.: Type checking dependent (record) types and subtyping. Journal of Functional and Logic Programming 10(2), 137–166 (2000)
[2] Boldini, P.: Formalizing Context in Intuitionistic Type theory. Fundamenta Informaticae 42, 1–23 (2000)
[3] Bove, A., Capretta, V.: Nested General Recursion and Partiality in Type Theory TPHOL R. In: Boulton, R.J., Jackson, P.B. (eds.) TPHOLs 2001. LNCS, vol. 2152, pp. 121–135. Springer, Heidelberg (2001)

[4] Cooper, R.: Records and Record Types in Semantic Theory. Journal of Logic and Computation 15(2), 99–112 (2005)

[5] Coquand, C., Coquand, T.: Structured type theory. In: Workshop on Logical Frameworks and Meta-languages (1999)

[6] Coquand, T., Pollack, R., Takeyama, M.: A Logical Framework with Dependently Typed Records. Fundamenta Informaticae 20, 1–22 (2005)

[7] Dapoigny, R., Barlatier, P.: Dependent Record Types for Dynamic context representation. In: Bramer, M., Coenen, F., Tuson, A. (eds.) Research and Development in Intelligent Systems: Procs. of AI-06, vol. 23, Springer, Heidelberg (2006)

[8] Dapoigny, R., Barlatier, P.: Towards a Context Theory for Context-aware systems. In: Procs. of the 2nd IJCAI Workshop on Artificial Intelligence Techniques for Ambient Intelligence (2007)

[9] Friesen, A., Börger, E.: A High-Level Specification for Semantic Web Service Discovery Services. In: Procs. of the sixth ACM Workshop ICWE'06, pp. 16–23. ACM Press, New York (2006)

[10] Gil, Y.: Description Logics and Planning. AI Magazine 26(2), 73–84 (2005)

[11] Ginzburg, J.: Abstraction and Ontology: Questions as Propositional Abstracts in Type Theory with Records. Journal of Log. Comput. 15(2), 113–130 (2005)

[12] Giunchiglia, F.: Contextual Reasoning. Istituto per la Ricerca Scientifica e Technologica, 9211-9220 (1992)

[13] Ghidini, C., Giunchiglia, F.: Local Models Semantics, or Contextual Reasoning = Locality + Compatibility. Artificial Intelligence 127(2), 221–259 (2001)

[14] Hoffman, G., Breazeal, C.: Collaboration in Human-Robot Teams. In: Procs. of AIAA First Intelligent Systems Technical Conference (2004)

[15] Howard, W.A, Seldin, J.P., Hindley, J.R.: To H.B. Curry: Essays on Combinatory Logic, Lambda Calculus and Formalism. The formulae-as-types notion of construction, pp. 479–490. Academic Press, London (1980)

[16] Keller U., Lara R., Polleres A., Toma I., Kifer M., Fensel D.: WSMO Web Service Discovery DERI International, D5.1 v0.1 (2004)

[17] Kopylov, A.: Dependent Intersection: A New Way of Defining Records in Type Theory. In: Procs. of the 18th Annual IEEE Symposium on Logic in Computer Science, pp. 86–95. IEEE Computer Society Press, Los Alamitos (2003)

[18] Van Lamsweerde, A.: Goal-Oriented Requirements Engineering: A Guided Tour. In: Procs. of the 5th IEEE International Symposium on Requirements Engineering, pp. 249–263. IEEE Computer Society Press, Los Alamitos (2001)

[19] Martin-Lof, P.: Constructive Mathematics and Computer Programming. Methodology and Philosophy of Sciences 6, 153–175 (1982)

[20] McCarthy, J.: Notes on Formalizing Context. In: Procs. of the 13th Int. Joint Conf. on Artificial Intelligence, pp. 555–560 (1993)

[21] Nau, D., Cao, Y., Lotem, A., Munoz-Avila, H.: SHOP: Simple Hierarchical Ordered Planner. In: Procs. of the Sixteenth International Joint Conference on Artificial Intelligence, pp. 968–983 (1999)

[22] Paulson, L.C.: The Foundation of a Generic Theorem Prover. Journal of Automated Reasoning 5, 363–397 (1989)

[23] Pollock, J.: The logical foundations of goal-regression planning in autonomous agents. Artificial Intelligence 106, 267–335 (1998)

[24] Prat, N.: Goal formalisation and classification for requirements engineering. In: Procs. of the Third International Workshop on Requirements Engineering: Foundations of Software Quality, pp. 145–156 (1997)

[25] Ranta, A.: Grammatical Framework: A Type-Theoretical Grammar Formalism. Journal of Functional Programming 14(2), 145–189 (2004)

[26] Rolland, C., Ben Achour, C.: Guiding The Construction Of Textual Use Case Specifications. Data and Knowledge Engineering Journal 25(1-2), 125–160 (1998)

[27] Sirin, E., Parsia, B., Wu, D., Hendler, J., Nau, D.: HTN planning for web service composition using SHOP2. Journal of Web Semantics 1(4), 377–396 (2004)

[28] Thomason, R.H.: Representing and Reasoning with Context. In: Calmet, J., Plaza, J. (eds.) AISC 1998. LNCS (LNAI), vol. 1476, pp. 29–41. Springer, Heidelberg (1998)

[29] Thomason, R.H.: Type theoretic foundations for context, part 1: Contexts as complex typetheoretic objects. In: Bouquet, P., Serafini, L., Brézillon, P., Benercetti, M., Castellani, F. (eds.) CONTEXT 1999. LNCS (LNAI), vol. 1688, pp. 352–374. Springer, Heidelberg (1999)

[30] Valentini, S.: Decidability in Intuitionistic Type Theory is functionally decidable. Mathematical Logic 42, 300–304 (1996)

[31] Villadsen, J.: Multi-dimensional Type Theory: Rules, Categories, and Combinators for Syntax and Semantics. In: Christiansen, H., et al. (eds.) Int. Workshop on Constraint Solving and Language Processing, pp. 160–165 (2004)

[32] Weld, D.: Recent advances in AI planning. AI Magazine 20(2), 93–123 (1999)

Context-Oriented Domain Analysis

Brecht Desmet, Jorge Vallejos, Pascal Costanza,
Wolfgang De Meuter, and Theo D'Hondt

Programming Technology Lab, Vrije Universiteit Brussel,
Pleinlaan 2, B-1050 Brussel, Belgium

Abstract. Context-aware systems are software systems which adapt
their behaviour according to the context of use. The requirements engineering phase is recognized as a primordial step to develop robust
implementations of context-aware systems since it establishes a comprehensive understanding of the problem space. This paper proposes the
Context-Oriented Domain Analysis (CODA) model which is a specialized approach for analyzing, structuring, and formalizing the software
requirements of context-aware systems.

1 Introduction

The Ambient Intelligence vision (IST Advisory Group, 2003) describes scenarios
in which people are pervasively surrounded by interconnected embedded and
mobile devices. As the context of such devices continuously changes over time,
context-aware systems adapt their behaviour accordingly in order to suit the
user's expectations more closely. The robust implementation of context-aware
systems is founded on a comprehensive understanding of the problem domain at
the early stages of software development. Requirements engineering is specifically
concerned with producing specifications for software systems that satisfy the
stakeholders needs and can be implemented, deployed, and maintained.

Traditional methods in requirements engineering, like use cases [1], aim at
capturing functional requirements by looking at the interactions between actors
and systems. Our practical experiments however point out that these methods
do not closely match the niche domain of context-aware systems. This is mainly
caused by the fact that context-aware systems add a new dimension to the actor-
system interaction by incorporating additional information from the (physical
or software) environment: so-called *context information*. We define the latter as
any piece of information which is computationally accessible. [2]

Such a refined parameterization of the actor-system interaction has a strong
impact on the specification of functional requirements. Whereas in monolithic applications, an actor's action typically corresponds to a single behaviour, context-
aware systems have multiple behavioural variations associated to a single action.
The choice of the appropriate variation is determined by the context in which
the system is used.

We claim that as soon as context-aware requirements become the rule rather
than the exception, more adequate modelling techniques are required to capture

B. Kokinov et al. (Eds.): CONTEXT 2007, LNAI 4635, pp. 178–191, 2007.

the contextual influence on software systems. The contribution of this paper consists of a new modelling approach, called Context-Oriented Domain Analysis (CODA), which is a systematic approach for gathering requirements of context-aware systems. CODA is intended to be relatively simple and concise to lower the accessibility barrier for various kinds of stakeholders while being expressive enough to evolve towards the solution space. In contrast to general-purpose methods for requirements analysis, like use cases, goal models [3], or problem frames [4], CODA is solely specialized for context-aware (functional and non-functional) requirements.

This paper is organised as follows. Section 2 presents a context-aware scenario which is used throughout this paper. Next, in Section 3, we explain the CODA approach thoroughly by means of this context-aware scenario. We validate our approach in Section 4 by showing how the various concepts of CODA can be mapped to decision tables. Finally, Section 6 identifies some future work and gives the conclusion.

2   Motivating Example: Context-Aware Cell Phone

We introduce an intelligent cell phone as an illustration of a context-aware system. In the following subsections, we briefly discuss the *requirements* of this context-aware cell phone in an *informal manner*. We take up again these requirements in Section 3 to illustrate our proposed CODA approach.

2.1   Basic Behaviour

We first present the default context-unaware behaviour of the cell phone which we call the *basic behaviour*. This behaviour consists of the following functionalities:

- Incoming communication (R1)
    - play ring sound whenever somebody calls or sends a message (R1.1);
    - provide the means to answer phone calls and read messages (R1.2);
- Outgoing communication (R2)
    - provide means to make phone calls and send messages (R2.1);
    - use default mobile connection for outgoing communication (R2.2);
- Shared by incoming and outgoing communication (R3)
    - maintain a contact list and journal (R3.1).

2.2   Behavioural Variations

We now increase the user experience of this cell phone by making it context-aware. In the following requirements description, we introduce some behaviour which deviates from the basic behaviour, depending on the context in which the cell phone is used. First, we present a group of behavioural variations which affect the *Incoming Communication* (R1).

- If the battery level is low, ignore all phone calls except for contacts classified as VIP (R1.3).
- If the time is between 11pm and 8am, activate the answering machine for incoming phone calls and the auto-reply service for messages. Add voice and text messages to the journal. (R1.4) The outcome of this behaviour is one of the following cases:
  - Everything turned out ok (R1.4.1).
  - A predefined list of callers can circumvent the answering machine by pressing the # button e.g. for emergency reasons (R1.4.2).
  - If the answering machine is unavailable because there is no memory left for voice messages, the cell phone gives an auditive signal (R1.4.3).
- If the user is in a meeting, redirect all calls and messages to the secretary (R1.5).

Next, there is a series of behavioural variations which affect the *Outgoing Communication*:

- The user can switch on a service which counts the amount of outgoing communication. This information is interesting e.g. for estimating costs. The concrete behaviour depends on the type of outgoing communication. (R2.3)
  - In case of phone call, measure the duration of the calls (R2.3.1).
  - In case of messages, count the number of sent data packages (R2.3.2).
- If there is a WiFi connection available, it is tried to make phone calls or send messages via VoIP since this is cheaper for the user (R2.4).
- If there is a GPRS connection available, it is tried to send messages using TCP/IP also since this is cheaper (R2.5).

In general, switches between behaviour are only possible between incoming or outgoing phone calls or messages (R4).

3   Principles of CODA

Context-Oriented Domain Analysis (CODA) is an approach for modelling context-aware software requirements in a structured, well-defined, and unambiguous way. The CODA model enforces software engineers to think of context-aware systems as pieces of basic context-unaware behaviour which can be refined. The driving force of the refinement is the context in which the system is used. We therefore prefer the term *context-dependent adaptation* which is defined as follows: *A unit of behaviour which adapts a subpart of a software system only if an associated context condition is satisfied.* The principle of distinguishing basic behaviour and context-dependent adaptations lays at the heart of our CODA approach.

In this paper, we apply our CODA approach to the requirements description of a context-aware cell phone (cfr. Section 2), yielding the CODA diagram of Figure 1. In the following, we discuss the vocabularium of CODA by means of this concrete example.

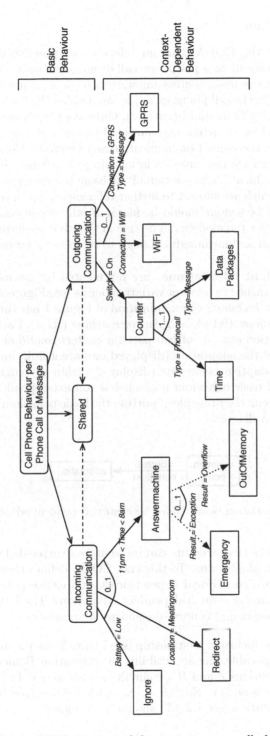

Fig. 1. CODA diagram of the context-aware cell phone

3.1   Vocabularium

The root node of the CODA diagram refers to all possible combinations of context-aware behaviour on a per phone call or message basis. The topmost levels always contain the basic context-unaware behaviour, represented by means of rounded boxes. In the cell phone example, we divided the basic behaviour into three parts: *Incoming Communication* (R1), *Outgoing Communication* (R2), and *Shared* (R3). All these subparts are connected to the root via the "consists of" relationship (—➤). *Incoming Communication* and *Outgoing Communication* are connected to *Shared* via the "uses" relationship (-➤). Since these are the leaf nodes of the hierarchical decomposition of the basic behaviour, we also call them *variation points* which are subject to further refinement. The level of granularity to which the basic behaviour should be hierarchically decomposed is an important design choice for the modeller. The rule of thumb is to decompose until the leaf nodes are small and meaningful enough to serve as variation points.

Context-dependent adaptations. are represented by means of rectangular boxes which are attached to relevant variation points (see Figure 2). For example, the variation point *Incoming Communication* of Figure 1 has three refinements: *Ignore* (R1.3), *Redirect* (R1.5), and *Answermachine* (R1.4). Each such context-dependent adaptation consists of two parts: a *context condition* which specifies the applicability of the adaptation (displayed on parent link) and a *label* which summarizes the adaptive behaviour (displayed within rectangular box). It is not allowed to add basic behaviour nodes below context-dependent adaptations, since this would break the principle of putting the basic behaviour at the topmost levels of the CODA diagram.

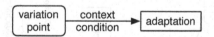

Fig. 2. Variation point refined by context-dependent adaptation

Relationships. The tree structure can be recursively expanded with additional context-dependent adaptations. To this end, CODA defines three kinds of relationships: inclusions, conditional dependencies, and choice points. The former two operate only among context-dependent adapations. The latter can be used among variation points and context-dependent adaptations.

– **Inclusion.** The inclusion relationship (see Figure 3) means that only if adaptation A is applicable, the applicability of adaptation B should be verified. Possibly, adaptations A and B are simultaneously active. For example, if the counter switch is on (i.e. *Switch = On*), either *Time* (see R2.3.1) or *Data Packages* adaptation (see R2.3.2) should be included.

- **Conditional dependency.** The conditional dependency relationship (see Figure 4) has a temporal character: If the return value of adaptation A equals r, then B should be executed subsequently. For example, if the special button # is pressed (i.e. $Result = Exception$) while using the answering machine, callers can circumvent the answering machine (see R1.4.2). Or, if the memory of the answering machine is full (i.e. $Result = Overflow$), some signal starts ringing (R1.4.3).

Fig. 3. Inclusion   **Fig. 4.** Conditional dependency

- **Choice point.** Variation points and context-dependent adaptations can have multiple context-dependent adaptations associated to them. For example, *Incoming Communication* is refined by *Ignore*, *Redirect*, and *Answermachine*. Although the three adaptations can be simultaneously applicable (i.e. $Battery = Low$ while $Location = Meetingroom$ while $11pm < Time < 8am$), the adaptations are semantically conflicting (i.e. one cannot ignore and redirect phone calls simultaneously). Since it is the responsibility of a context-aware system to *choose* a non-conflicting set of adaptations out of a set of available candidates, we use the term *choice point* to mark such places in our CODA diagram. They are graphically denoted with $\wedge$.
  Choice points have a *multiplicity* associated to them. This is a pair consisting of the minimal and maximal number of adaptations to be activated. For example, the variation point *Incoming Communication* has multiplicity "0...1" which means that at most one context-dependent adaptation can be activated, i.e. either *Ignore*, *Redirect*, or *Answermachine*.

3.2   Resolution Strategies

In case of semantic interactions at choice points, a context-aware system should be able to make autonomous decisions based on some user-defined policy. For example, in Figure 1, if $Battery = Low$ and $Location = Meetingroom$, both *Ignore* and *Redirect* adaptations are applicable. However, the multiplicity of the choice point indicates that at most one adaptation can be activated. For these situations, we incorporate the ability to associate *resolution strategies* [5] with choice points. These strategies unambiguously describe which context-dependent adaptations should be activated or deactivated in case of semantic interactions.

   CODA incorporates by default four resolution strategies: priority, frequency, timestamps, and case-by-case which are discussed in the remainder of this section. From our experience, these strategies seem to appear frequently for a wide range of scenarios. However, they are not universal. We therefore allow modellers

to combine or refine existing strategies and define new strategies whenever necessary. Graphically, resolution strategies are represented by means of UML-style
stereotypes [6] which are attached to choice points.

Case-by-case. The most straightforward option is to enumerate all possible
interactions and their resolutions using relationships like exclusion, inclusion,
etc. Case-by-case is considered as the default strategy and does not require the
mentioning of a stereotype. The details of this resolution strategy are discussed
thoroughly in Section 3.3.

Priority. A commonly used strategy is to associate priorities with the alternatives. Priorities are good because they are the easiest way to understand by
most stakeholders. For example, Figure 5 associates a priority with each context-
dependent adaptation. These priorities are graphically represented by means of
circles. If multiple adaptations are applicable, the one with the highest priority
will be elected. Unfortunately, priorities are not an all-round solution because of
limited expressiveness.

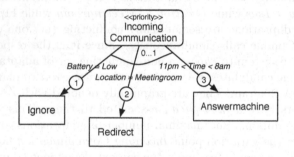

Fig. 5. Priority resolution strategy

Frequency. The frequency strategy is an adaptive method which selects context-
dependent adaptations based on their frequency of use in the past.

Timestamps. One can associate time stamps to context values to keep track
of the order in which the context evolves. A possible timestamp strategy is to
give preference to the most recent context information.

3.3   Vocabularium of Case-by-Case Resolution Strategy

If the user preference does not match an overall resolution strategy (like frequency, priorities, or timestamps), one can use the case-by-case strategy which
is more like a *general-purpose approach.* The idea of this strategy is to add *cross-
reference relationships* among interacting context-dependent adaptations to the
CODA diagram. For example, Figure 6 is an extension of the CODA diagram

of Figure 1 which exhibits an example of the case-by-case resolution strategy. The new relationships are put in bold for clarification. In the remainder of this section, we discuss the semantics of these relationships.

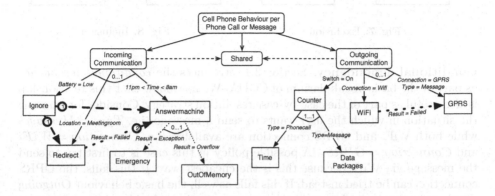

Fig. 6. CODA diagram of context-aware cell phone extended with an example of case-by-case resolution strategy

Independence. All adaptations that do not have a specific relationship specified are defined as being *independent*. This means that they do not semantically interfere with other adaptations. For example, as derived from Figure 6, it is possible that *Switch = On* while *Connection = WiFi*, so both *Counter* and *WiFi* adaptations are active, operating independently.

Exclusion and Inclusion. An adaptation can *exclude* or *include* another one. This is respectively presented in Figure 7 and 8 with a dashed (in case of exclusion) and full (in case of inclusion) arrow between interacting context-dependent adaptations. Their semantics are as follows:

– **Exclusion.** If both adaptations W and Z are applicable, W is activated and Z is deactivated.
– **Inclusion.** If adaptation W is applicable (either because the context condition a is true or because W is included by another adaptation), adaptation Z should also be active at the same time regardless of the thruth value of context condition b. The distinguishing feature between the inclusion defined in Section 3.1 and the inclusion defined here is that the latter operates cross-referencing.

The CODA diagram of Figure 6 contains an illustration of an exclusion: Ignoring a phone call or message excludes both the redirection and answering machine adaptation. This is represented by means of a dashed arrow from *Ignore* to *Redirect* and *Answermachine*.

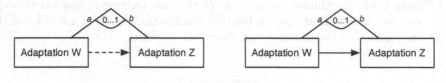

Fig. 7. Exclusion   **Fig. 8.** Inclusion

Conditional dependency. Section 3.1 introduces the *conditional dependency* as part of the basic vocabularium of CODA. We now show that this relationship is also useful as part of the case-by-case resolution strategy. Consider for example the situation in which the user wants to send a message (i.e. $Type = Message$) while both WiFi and GPRS connection are available (i.e. $Connection = WiFi$ and $Connection = GPRS$). A possible policy in this case is to first try to send the message via WiFi because this is the cheapest way. If this fails, the GPRS connection can be tried instead. If this fails as well, the basic behaviour *Outgoing Communication* is used to send the message via the default mobile connection. This user policy is concretized in Figure 6 by means of a cross-referencing dotted arrow from *WiFi* to *GPRS*.

The same policy is applied to the *Redirect* and *Answermachine* adaptations: If the redirection of the phone call fails (e.g. secretary is not available), the caller gets in touch with the answering machine. Priorities are added to the various relationships that are used among the *Ignore*, *Redirect*, and *Answermachine* adaptations to avoid ambiguities. For example, if $Battery = Low$, $Location = Meetingroom$, and $11pm < Time < 8am$ simultaneously, only the exclusions between *Ignore-Redirect* and *Ignore-Answermachine* are applicable.

4   Validation

4.1   Design Rationale

The vocabularium of CODA is intentionally kept concise since we want it to be *accessible for various kinds of stakeholders* including end users, domain experts, application developers, etc. Special attention has been paid to the expressiveness of the CODA model: It tries to be *as human-friendly as possible* by avoiding "enumeration like" descriptions and working with high-level abstractions instead. In this way, CODA offers a high-level view on the runtime contextual variability of a software system without burdening the stakeholders with low-level technical details.

CODA can be used by requirement analysts as an *instrument for communication* with clients to grasp the problem domain. It is furthermore an important *document of reference* for designers and implementors to better understand the technical challenges. Our CODA approach has already proven its usefulness for modelling a wide variety of context-aware scenarios going from intelligent vending machines, domotic systems, and shopping guidance systems to advanced user interfaces.

4.2 Mapping to Decision Tables

Although CODA might seem as being far removed from the solution space, since it has a well-defined syntax and semantics, it can be easily mapped to decision tables [7] which brings it very close to the computational level. For example, Tables 1 and 2 reflect the CODA diagram of Figure 6. Each decision table corresponds to a particular variation point of the CODA diagram. In our particular example, we distinguish *Incoming Communication* and *Outgoing Communication.*

The columns of the decision tables contain an enumeration of all possible context situations (at the top) and the associated actions (at the bottom). The actions represent the adaptations of CODA. Strictly speaking, we should always include an action called "basic behaviour," but we omit this for clarity reasons. Furthermore, Table 2 is incomplete because the case in which *Switch = Off* is not included - also for clarity reasons.

The mapping of CODA to decision tables is a *lossy transformation.* This is because the high-level concepts (e.g. multiplicities, resolution strategies, etc.) of CODA are translated to plain enumerations of yes/no-questions. Although such a mapping is important to evolve towards the solution space, the decision tables themselves are not useful for humans to understand the insights of the problem domain.

In the following, we validate our CODA approach by describing in high-level terms how it can be mapped to decision tables. The transformation algorithm has been implemented in Java using an XML representation of CODA. To this end, we developed an XML Schema Definition which provides *concrete syntax for CODA.* Furthermore, the mapping of CODA to decision tables creates a *formal basis for the semantics of CODA.*

1. Create a decision table per variation point in CODA which is the root of a disjunct subtree.

Table 1. Decision table for incoming communication

Conditions	s_1	s_2	s_3	s_4	s_5	s_6	s_7	s_8	s_9	s_{10}	s_{11}	s_{12}	s_{13}
Battery is low	N	Y	N	N	N	N	Y	Y	N	N	N	N	Y
Location is meetingroom	N	N	Y	N	N	N	Y	N	Y	Y	Y	Y	Y
Time is at night	N	N	N	Y	Y	Y	N	Y	Y	Y	Y	Y	Y
Answermachine returns OK				Y	N	N				Y	N	N	
Answermachine returns Exception				N	Y	N				N	Y	N	
Answermachine returns Overflow				N	N	Y				N	N	Y	
Redirection succeeded (Y) or failed (N)									Y	N	N	N	
Actions													
Ignore		×					×	×					×
Redirect			×						×	×	×	×	
Answermachine				×	×	×				×	×	×	
cond-dep Answermachine → Emergency					×						×		
cond-dep Answermachine → OutOfMemory						×						×	
cond-dep Redirect → Answermachine										×	×	×	

Table 2. Decision table for outgoing communication

Conditions	s_1	s_2	s_3	s_4	s_5	s_6	s_7	s_8	s_9
Switch is on	Y	Y	Y	Y	Y	Y	Y	Y	Y
Connection is WiFi	N	N	Y	Y	N	N	Y	Y	Y
Connection is GPRS	N	N	N	N	Y	Y	Y	Y	Y
Type phone call (Y) or message (N)	Y	N	Y	N	Y	N	Y	N	N
WiFi call/message fails								N	Y
Actions									
Counter	×	×	×	×	×	×	×	×	×
Time	×		×		×		×		
Data Packages		×		×		×		×	×
WiFi			×	×			×	×	×
GPRS							×		×
cond-dep WiFi → GPRS									×

2. Place all context conditions of the CODA diagram in the conditions column of the decision table.
3. Generate all possible yes/no combinations of the context conditions. Redundancy should be avoided.[1]
4. The following rules apply for the generation of actions in the decision table:
   - All context-dependent adaptations which have a *full arrow* as parent link (i.e. either a refinement or inclusion) correspond to a *single action*.
   - Context-dependent adaptations with a *dotted arrow* as parent link (i.e. conditional dependency) are translated to an action called "cond-dep from-adaptation → to-adaptation".
   - It is possible that a context-dependent adaptation has *both a full and dotted arrow* as parent link which implies the definition of two different actions.
5. For each possible context description in column s_i of the decision table, perform the following steps.
   (a) Let n be the variation point of a particular decision table. Furthermore, let solution set $S = \emptyset$.
   (b) At choice point n, determine the set A of applicable (b, p, a) triples based on the context description s_i. The variable b is the root node (i.e. variation point or context-dependent adaptation), p is the parent link type (i.e. full or dotted arrow) and a is the applicable context-dependent adaptation.
   (c) Verify if A fulfills the multiplicity constraint. If not, the resolution strategy associated with choice point n should be applied to A.
   (d) Add set A to the solution set S. Recursively call step (5b) for all $n = a : (b, p, a) \in A$.
   (e) Per (b, p, a) triple of the solution set S, mark the corresponding actions. If $p = dotted$, the appropriate action "cond-dep $b → a$" should be marked.

---

[1] For example, if $\neg(11pm < Time < 8am)$, it is not necessary to include all yes/no combinations of the return values OK, Exception, and Overflow.

5   Related Work

5.1   CODA Versus FODA

The CODA approach is heavily inspired by the already existing Feature-Oriented Domain Analysis used in product-line development. The FODA modelling approach is originally proposed by Kang et al. [8] to model a family of related software products in a very concise manner. Although the CODA diagram looks syntactically very close to FODA, the overall aim of CODA and the semantics of its building blocks differ significantly. Table 3 contains a detailed comparison between CODA and FODA based on the following characteristics:

Goal. What is the intended purpose of the model?
Concept. What does the model describe?
Commonalities and Variabilities. Software variability in general can be characterized by means of common and variable elements. What is the concrete meaning of these elements?
Actor. Who uses the model?
Mode. Is the model a static or dynamic analysis?

Table 3. Comparison of CODA and FODA

Characteristic	FODA	CODA
Full name	feature-oriented domain analysis	context-oriented domain analysis
Goal	product-line development	context-aware systems
Concept	all possible product variations of a family of related products	context-aware behavioural variations within (a subpart of) a single system
Commonalities	behaviour shared by all family members of product	basic context-unaware behaviour which is always applicable, but might be refined
Variabilities	*feature*: any prominent and distinctive aspect or characteristic that is visible to various stakeholders	*context-dependent adaptation*: behaviour refinement of some basic behaviour that is only applicable if a certain context condition is satisfied
Actor	software designer decides on a feature composition	the software system itself makes autonomous decisions about the composition of basic behaviour and context-dependent adaptations based on context conditions, multiplicities and resolution strategies
Mode	*static analysis*: describes static properties of features which enable the generation of all product variations at compile time	*dynamic analysis*: contains context conditions, conditional dependencies and resolution strategies which enable automatic run-time computation of behavioural variations based on context information

5.2 State Charts

Proposals like [9] and [10] already identified the importance of a sound formal basis to develop robust context-aware systems. Central to their approach is the use of state charts (or activity diagrams) to model the application domain. The conceptual difference between CODA and state charts is the way of thinking that is induced. Whereas in CODA one thinks in terms of (hierarchical decomposition of) basic behaviour and refinements of this behaviour at certain variation points, statecharts are about states (e.g. denote a particular way of behaving) and transitions between them.

Strictly speaking, all concepts of CODA can be imitated with state charts simply because state charts are turing complete. However, the concern of CODA is not *what* can be modelled, but *how*. In that regard, we observe that the vocabularium of state charts do not include concepts like multiplicities, resolution strategies at choice points, inclusions, and exclusions. In CODA, these concepts are crucial for establishing a high-level view on the problem space.

6 Conclusion and Future Work

Context-oriented domain analysis is an approach for identifying and modelling *context-aware software requirements*, which is a niche domain within the field of requirements analysis. It enforces modellers to think in terms of *basic context-unaware behaviour* which can be further refined by means of *context-dependent adaptations* at certain *variation points*. A context-dependent adaptation is a unit of behaviour that adapts a subpart of a software system only if a certain context condition is satisfied. By context, we mean every piece of information which is computationally accessible.

This work identifies a number of relationships that may exist among context-dependent adaptations. A context-dependent adaptation can *include* another adaptation which means that the applicability of the second adaptation is verified only if the first one is activated. Next, a context-dependent adaptation can *conditionally depend on* another adaptation. In this case, the applicability of the second adaptation depends on the result of the first adaptation, yielding a sequential execution. We finally introduce the notion of a *choice point* which is a variation point or context-dependent adaptation which has multiple adaptations associated to it. Optionally, one can associate a *resolution strategy* to deal with semantically interacting adaptations.

The CODA approach can be represented in three ways: *Graphically*, where the system's basic behaviour and its context-dependent adaptations are presented in a tree structure; *Textually*, using XML technology to declaratively write down CODA diagrams; and *Structurally*, where the semantics of CODA elements are mapped to decision tables.

The aim of the CODA approach is to have a concise modelling language for context-aware systems which is accessible to various kinds of stakeholders. Since CODA has a well-defined syntax and semantics, it possesses a sound basis for evolving towards the solution space. However, a deeper understanding of the mapping from CODA to the computational level is still under investigation. In this regard, we believe that the mapping of CODA to decision tables is an important step in the right direction.

References

1. Bittner, K.: Use Case Modeling. Addison-Wesley Longman Publishing Co. Inc, Boston, MA, USA (2002)
2. Hirschfeld, R., Costanza, P., Nierstrasz, O.: Context-oriented Programming. Submitted to Journal of Object Technology (2007)
3. Dardenne, A., van Lamsweerde, A., Fickas, S.: Goal-directed requirements acquisition. In: 6IWSSD: Selected Papers of the Sixth International Workshop on Software Specification and Design, pp. 3–50. Elsevier Science Publishers B. V, Amsterdam (1993)
4. Jackson, M.: Problem frames: analyzing and structuring software development problems. Addison-Wesley Longman Publishing Co. Inc. Boston, MA, USA (2001)
5. Steels, L.: Kennissystemen. Addison-Wesley, Reading, MA, USA (1992)
6. Fowler, M.: UML Distilled: A Brief Guide to the Standard Object Modeling Language. Addison-Wesley Longman Publishing Co. Inc. Boston, MA, USA (2003)
7. Feagus, R.M.: Decision tables - an application analyst/programmer's view. Data Processing 12, 85–109 (1967)
8. Kang, K., Cohen, S., Hess, J., Novak, W., Peterson, S.: Feature-Oriented Domain Analysis (FODA) Feasibility Study. Technical Report CMU/SEI-90-TR-21, Software Engineering Institute, Carnegie Mellon University (November 1990)
9. Hinze, A., Malik, P., Malik, R.: Interaction design for a mobile context-aware system using discrete event modelling. In: ACSC '06: Proceedings of the 29th Australasian Computer Science Conference, pp. 257–266, Darlinghurst, Australia, Australia, Australian Computer Society, Inc. (2006)
10. Mahoney, M., Elrad, T.: Distributing statecharts to handle pervasive crosscutting concerns. In: Building Software for Pervasive Computing Workshop at OOPSLA '05, San Diego, CA (October 2005)

A Semantics for Changing Frames of Mind

Karl Devooght[1,2]

[1] France Télécom R&D, 2 avenue Pierre Marzin, 22300 Lannion, France
[2] LLI-IRISA, 49 rue Kerampont, 22300 Lannion, France
karl.devooght@orange-ftgroup.com

Abstract. In intentional systems, dynamic attitudes of an agent are characterized around the notion of action. Possible-world semantics presents an intuitive manner in order to model such attitudes. An action is basically a change from a mental state to another mental state. In this paper, we argue that action that changes not only mental state but also mental context needs a semantics more expressive. In this perspective, we propose a semantics that combines possible-world and a context-oriented semantics, called Local Models Semantics.

1 Introduction

Imagine that Tom is married and has a daughter. Consider also he is a mechanic. One day, he is working in his garage when he is informed that his daughter is sick and that he has to fetch her from school. This causes Tom to stop working and then leaves.

If Tom was an intentional agent, most the existing approaches [1,13,15] would recommend that we define a (logical) model describing Tom's mental state and how his mental state changes over time. Such a model usually based on a semantics inherited from possible-world semantics introduced by Kripke. This semantics provides an intuitive base to give interpretations for different mental attitudes (composing agent's mental states) like informational attitudes (e.g. knowledge, belief), motivational attitudes (e.g. goal, desire), and dynamic attitudes (e.g. feasibility of an action).

Our interest is in this last kind of attitudes. In most cases, dynamic attitudes are focussed on the notion of *action* (or *event*). Action is basically a change from a state to another state. So, characterizing an action in a mental state requires us at least to define its pre-conditions and its effects. The number of effects are often supposed small and limited such that the differences between the two action-related states are considered to be *minimal*. The question now is: is this semantical consideration suitable for actions involving for instance:

– a change of agent roles ?

In our example, Tom being told his daughter is sick is an illustration of an action which involves a change of agent roles. Indeed, before Tom was told, it is intuitively admitted that Tom fills a mechanic role while afterwards he fills a father role. In these cases, there is certainly a change of mental states but mainly

B. Kokinov et al. (Eds.): CONTEXT 2007, LNAI 4635, pp. 192–205, 2007.

a change of mental contexts, which we call *frames of mind*, where minimal change cannot adequately be applied. In this paper, we propose a semantics in which actions can change mental states as well as mental contexts. In this perspective, we combine possible-world semantics and a context-oriented semantics, called local models semantics introduced by Giunchiglia et al. [6].

Concretely, in section 2, we describes possible-world semantics for knowledge and action inspired from Sadek's work[15]. In section 3, we present local models semantics initially devoted to contextual reasoning. We then propose in section 4 a semantics combining both mental states and contexts. Also, we introduce two types of action changing frames of mind that we call contextual decreasing and increasing actions. We show that the sequence of both of them enables us to express, for instance, the change of agent roles. In section 5, we illustrate the proposed semantics on an example. In doing so we consider the variability of agent awareness.

2   Possible-Worlds Semantics

In this section, we briefly review possible-worlds semantics for belief and action. The interested reader is encouraged to consult references such as [2,10,11].

The intuitive idea behind possible-worlds model is that, besides the true state of state of affairs, there are a number of other possible states of affairs, or possible worlds. In order to formalize this idea, we first need a language. We stick to propositional logic here, since most of issues we are interested in dealing with stand at this level. So, besides the standard connectives such as $\land$, $\neg$, and $\lor$ from propositional logic, we also need some way to represent belief. We do this by increasing the language with the *modal* operator B. A formula such as $B\phi$ is read "agent believes ϕ".

Formally, we start with a set Φ of primitive propositions and close off under negation, conjunction and the modal operator B_i. Thus, if ϕ and ψ are formulae in the language, then so are $\neg\phi$, $\phi \land \psi$, and $B\phi$. Connectives such as $\rightarrow$ and $\lor$ are also defined in terms of $\neg$ and $\land$ as usual. Note that we are considering a mono-agent situation here because we are concerned about simplifying notation in this paper, but multi-agent situations can be easily envisaged.

Kripke structures provide an interesting formal tool for giving semantics to this language. A Kripke structure M is a tuple (S, R, π), where S is a set of *states* or *possible worlds*, π is an assignment of truth values to the primitive propositions p for each state $s \in S$ (so that $\pi(s,p) \in \{\text{true}, \text{false}\}$, and R is a set of binary relation on S (see Figure 1). Among these relations, an *epistemic* relation, noted $\mathcal{B}$, is often associated with agent belief. Intuitively, $(s,t) \in \mathcal{B}$, if in state s, agent considers t possible (i.e. if s were the actual state of the world, agent considers state t a possible state of the world).

As well as the possibility of epistemic statements, Kripke structures can be used in order to capture in an intuitive manner dynamic aspects of an agent. For example, this semantics carries over naturally to dynamic logics [7], dialog-oriented logics [14,15] and game logics [12]. Most of these approaches centralize their dynamic representation around the notion of *action*. In Kripke structures, an (atomic) action is basically qualified as a change of state between state before its execution and the state after its execution. So, in order to catch such a characterization of an action, one generally introduces a *feasibility*-operator related to the state-before and a *done*-operator related to the state-after. A feasibility-operator reflects the feasibility of an agent to execute the related action and is a natural way to formulate the pre-conditions of an action. Besides, a done-operator enables to state that an agent has just done an action and to express the effects of this latter.

Formally, we accomplish this by borrowing two operators *feasible* and *done* from Sadek's works [15]. Let us call *Act* a set of actions. If ϕ is a formula and an action $a \in Act$, then so are $Feasible(a,\phi)$ and $Done(a,\phi)$. A formula such as $Feasible(a,\phi)$ is read "an action a is feasible and ϕ is true after its execution", while a formula such as $Done(a,\phi)$ is read "an action a has just been done before ϕ was true". In terms of Kripke semantics, we need to consider an action relation on S for each action a in the scope of the model. We note such a relation $\mathcal{E}_\alpha$ (where a is an action). Intuitively, $((s,t) \in \mathcal{E}_\alpha$, if in state s, agent considers t as an outcome state after performing the action a.

We now define a relation $\models$, where $M,s \models \phi$ is read "ϕ is *true*, or *satisfied*, in state s of structure M":

$$M, s \models true$$
$$M, s \models p, \text{ where p is a primitive proposition iff } \pi(p, s) = \mathbf{true}$$
$$M, s \models \neg\phi \text{ iff } M, s \not\models \phi$$
$$M, s \models \phi \wedge \psi \text{ iff } M, s \models \phi \text{ and } M, s \models \psi$$
$$M, s \models B\phi \text{ iff } M, t \models \phi \text{ for all } t \text{ such that} (s, t) \in \mathcal{B}$$
$$M, s \models Feasible(\alpha, \phi) \text{ iff } M, t \models \phi \text{ such that } (s, t) \in \mathcal{E}_\alpha$$
$$M, s \models Done(\alpha, \phi) \text{ iff } M, t \models \phi \text{ such that } (t, s) \in \mathcal{E}_\alpha$$

The belief clause is designed to capture that the agent believes ϕ if ϕ is true in all possible worlds that the agent thinks possible. Note also that the feasible and done clauses depend on an event-accessibility relation dedicated for a particular action.

We say a formula ϕ is *valid in M* if $M,s \models \phi$ for all states s in M; ϕ is *satisfiable in M* if $M,s \models \phi$ for some state s in M. We say ϕ is *valid* (respectively *satisfiable*) if it is valid in all (respectively some) Kripke structures.

Specifying action requires to point out what its *pre-conditions* and its *effects* are. Action pre-conditions (sometimes called qualifications) regroup the set of necessary and sufficient conditions for performing the action. Formally, we may obtain them by the following formula:

$$\phi \rightarrow Feasible(\alpha)$$

where ϕ refers to the conjunction of all pre-conditions of the action α. Note that Feasible(α) is equivalent to Feasible($\alpha,true$).In a symmetric way, action effects (sometimes called post-conditions) regroup the set of conditions necessarily true just after the action execution. Formally, we may express them by the following formula:

$$Done(\alpha) \rightarrow \phi$$

where ϕ refers to an effect of α. Note that Done(α) is equivalent to Done($\alpha,true$). Specifying all effects of an action runs up against the ramification problem. This problem is related to the resoluteness of the thorough set of action effects. Most of approaches circumvent it by imposing some policy of *minimal change* on states linked to the action. More precisely, minimal change means that the state before and after the action execution differ from a small set of facts (which are in fact the specified effects of the action). As in practice the number of action effects is small and limited (e.g., communicative action), this hypothesis is often relevant.

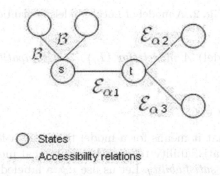

○ States
── Accessibility relations

Fig. 1. A model of Possible-World Semantics

3   Local Models Semantics

In [6], Giunchiglia and Ghidini proposed a semantics, called *Local Models Semantics* motivated as a foundation for a contextual reasoning. The approach is based on two principles: *locality* and *compatibility*. Locality says that reasoning uses only part of what is potentially available. The part being used while reasoning is called *context*. Compatibility conveys that there is *compatibility* among the reasoning performed in different contexts.

Let us describe it formally. Let $\{L_i\}_{i \in I}$ a family of languages (describing what is true in a context) defined over a set of indexes I. Let $\overline{M}_i$ be the class of all the models of L_i. We call $m \in \overline{M}_i$, a local model (of L_i). A *compatibility sequence* **c** (for $\{L_i\}$) is a sequence :

$$\mathbf{c} = \langle \mathbf{c}_0, \mathbf{c}_1, \cdots, \mathbf{c}_i, \cdots \rangle$$

where, for each $i \in I$, $\mathbf{c}_i$ is a subset of $\overline{M}_i$. A *compatibility relation* **C** is a set **C** of compatibility sequences **c**. So, a *model* is a compatibility relation which contains at least a compatibility sequence and does not contain the compatibility sequence of empty sets (see Figure 2). A model $\mathbf{C}$ is a *(weak) chain model* if all the $\mathbf{c}$ in $\mathbf{C}$ are (weak) chains. A compatibility sequence $\mathbf{c}$ is a *(weak)chain* if $|\mathbf{c}_i| = 1$ (≤ 1) for each i in I.

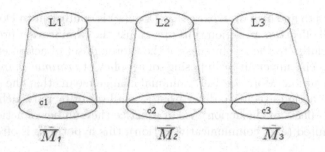

Fig. 2. A model of Local Models Semantics

Definition 1. (Model) *A model (for $\{L_i\}$) is a compatibility relation $\mathbf{C}$ such that:*

1. $\mathbf{C} \neq \emptyset$
2. $\langle \emptyset, \emptyset, \cdots, \emptyset, \cdots \rangle \notin \mathbf{C}$

One can now say what it means for a model to satisfy a formula of a language L_i. Let $\models_{cl}$ be the satisfiability relation between local models and formulas of L_i. We call $\models_{cl}$ *local satisfiability*. Let us use $i{:}\phi$, a labeled L_i-formula, to mean ϕ and that ϕ is a formula of L_i. This notation allows us to keep track of the context we are talking about. Then we have the following *satisfiability* definition:

Definition 2. (Satisfiability) *Let $\mathbf{C} = \{\mathbf{c}\}$ with $\mathbf{c} = \langle \mathbf{c}_0, \mathbf{c}_1, \cdots, \mathbf{c}_i, \cdots \rangle$ be a model and $i{:}\phi$ a formula. $\mathbf{C}$ satisfies $i{:}\phi$, noted $\mathbf{C} \models i{:}\phi$, if for all $\mathbf{c} \in \mathbf{C}$*

$$\mathbf{c}_i \models \phi$$

where $\mathbf{c}_i \models \phi$ if, for all $m \in \mathbf{c}_i$, $m \models_{cl} \phi$

The notion of *validity* is obvious: a formula $i{:}\phi$ is valid, noted $\models i : \phi$, if all models satisfy $i{:}\phi$. What is more interesting is the notion of *logical consequence* (see Definition 3) which allows assumptions and conclusion from distinct languages. Given a set of labelled formula Γ, Γ_j denotes the set of formula $\{\gamma \mid j{:}\gamma \in \Gamma\}$.

Definition 3. (Logical Consequence) *A formula $i{:}\phi$ is a logical consequence of a set of formulae Γ w.r.t. a model $\mathbf{C}$, noted $\Gamma \models_{\mathbf{C}} i{:}\phi$, if every sequence $\mathbf{c} \in \mathbf{C}$ satisfies:*

$$\forall j \in I, j \neq i, \mathbf{c}_i \models \Gamma_j \Longrightarrow$$
$$(\forall m \in \mathbf{c}_i, m \models_{cl} \Gamma_i \Longrightarrow m \models_{cl} \phi)$$

This semantic was proved to be adapted to the formal system allowing multiple contexts (introduced by Giunchiglia [5]), called *Multicontext System (MC System)* where contexts are formalized proof-theoretically.

4 Changing Frames of Mind

Before introducing our approach, let us expose our motivations. In section two, we emphasized the possibility to represent dynamic aspects of agent into a Kripke structure. We do so by means of the notion of action. Recall that an action is basically specified as a change of mental state. Besides, to characterize action by mental notions, pre-conditions and effects can be expressed by using feasible and done operators.

Now, the question we ask ourselves is: can this representation (in possible-world semantics) embody actions involving not only a change of mental state but a change of mental context (or what we call changes a *frame of mind*)?

In order to illustrate such an action and what we mean intuitively by changing the frame of mind, let us reuse the introduction's example. Tom is a mechanic. One day, he is working in this garage (and is actually changing a car wheel) when he is informed that his daughter is sick and that he has to fetch her from school, which causes Tom to stop working and then leaves.

In this example, we identify two of Tom's frames of mind related to two roles he may play. The first frame of mind refers to his role of mechanic and the second one refers to his role as a father who has to take care of his children. Then, two actions take place: changing a car's wheel and passing on the message to Tom. What we want to highlight is that these two actions have different levels of consequences (or effects) on Tom's internal state. On the one hand, changing a car wheel would basically imply that the car wheel is changed. Although this action succeeds in *evolving* Tom's internal state (i.e. moving on from one state to another state), he still finds himself in the same frame of mind as before the execution of the action. That is, he is still filling his role as a mechanic. On the other hand, what being told entails certainly Tom's internal state to be evolved but furthermore to be *restructured*. Indeed, after the execution of this action, Tom does not behave as a mechanician anymore but as a father. Subsequently, one may say that Tom has changed his frame of mind.

Keeping our question in mind and based on this running example, we argue that action representation in possible-world semantics are not suitable for actions changing frames of mind. We see three important reasons in order to justify that. First, recall that actions in possible-world semantics are generally specified under the minimal change principle. Thus, a small and limited number of changes are expected between states before and after action executions. Intuitively, that does not match with actions implying a change of frame of mind since the action effects will include at least all the elements describing the new frame of mind (for instance, all of elements such as knowledge, rules of behavior, etc that Tom's role of father underlies). Second, Kripke structure is grounded on a single language (and then, on an overall related domain). So, in the case we plan to consider several possible agent frames of mind, that means that they have to be defined so that all frames of mind merge into every single world. For instance, if Tom is working in his garage, he is in a mechanic frame of mind. This frame of mind is expressed in Tom's internal state at the same time as a father frame of mind. However, Tom needs to mentally focus himself only on the mechanic frame of mind. We, therefore, need to deal with what Tom is *aware* of. A possible solution is to augment the language by an awareness operator as Fagin and Halpern proposed in [3]. In our example, that would enable to stand that elements specifying the Tom's mechanician frame of mind are aware by him and other ones are not. Nevertheless, we think that there is no obvious reason to keep an explicit track in Tom's reasoning process of what he is *not* aware. Third, possible-world semantics has an implicit representation of context through the change of states. So, there is no easy way to distinguish between the two kinds of actions we mentioned in our example. In fact, since we don't know whether the state before and after action execution belong to the same frame of mind, we cannot assert whether this action has involved a change of frame of mind (e.g., action of telling Tom his daughter is sick).

What we wish to show is that we need a semantics (1) based in some way on possible-world semantics and (2) building on an explicit representation of context since our conviction is that can bring a more expressive semantics (2.1) giving a better interpretation of actions changing frames of mind and (2.2) coping with the three issues.

In section 3, we introduced Local Models Semantics. Such a semantics provides an explicit representation of context (as required in point (2)). So, in the next sections, we aim at providing a semantics combining possible-world semantics (as required in point (1)) and local models semantics which fills the points (2.1) and (2.2).

4.1 Combining Possible-World and Local Models Semantics

The interesting point of local models semantics is the fact there is no constraint on the nature of local models. So, although possible-world and local models semantics are opposed, nothing stops us to combine them by stating local models as Kripke models (as described in section 2). Let us suppose a local models semantics with classes of models $\overline{M}_i$. In this semantics, some $\overline{M}_i$ correspond to *frames of mind*. Recall that the idea behind this is to give a good interpretation of a transition from a frame of mind to another one by means of action. We will do this by using the compatibility relation like an "event-accessibility relation" between frames of mind.

Before that, we ask ourselves on what model types of $\overline{M}_i$ does the compatibility relation have to stay on. In our case, we wish the compatibility to lie on states (or possible worlds) of a Kripke model rather on a Kripke model itself. An obvious reason is that even if we attempt to model actions that change frames of mind, such an action still remains a change of state. So, compatibility has to include this aspect. *Pointed Kripke model* offer a solution in this perspective. A pointed Kripke model is basically a pair (M,s) consisting of a Kripke model M

and a state s of M (on which compatibility can relies on now). Let us suppose that all $\overline{M}_i$ are classes of pointed Kripke models. Note that using pointed Kripke models does not prevent us from using possible-world semantics. Intuitively, a distinction of action types appears now between those (1) qualifying a change of state inside a self frame of mind and those (2) qualifying of state from two different frames of mind.

Furthermore, we borrow a Kokinov's view [8,9](from his dynamic theory of context) applied on frames of mind. We consider a frame of mind as *an implicit intrinsic internal context being considered as the dynamic fuzzy of all memory elements (mental representations or operations) accessible for mental processing at a particular instant of time.* Such a view is consistent with classes of (pointed) Kripke models. Kripke models are internal since they refer to a subject's current mental state within which their behavior is generated, intrinsic since these models based on possible worlds underlies a global cognitive process described as the evolution of the system over time, and finally implicit since they do not have any trace of a representation of some context itself in the language(i.e. to represent the context as an object).

In keeping Kokinov, a frame of mind is *implicitly represented by the distribution of activation over the set of all memory elements. Each pattern of activation represents a specific context.* So, a frame of mind can change (to another frame of mind) according to the activation of these specific contexts. These contexts may regroup elements of *memory* (e.g., beliefs) or elements of *reasoning* (e.g., behavioral rules). In Tom's example, the roles of mechanician and father may be such contexts since they influence Tom's frame of mind at times. Let us called this kind of context mark-context. More precisely, a *mark-context* is a specific and local context (in the Kokinov's sense). We base ourselves on it in order to deduce the changes from one frame of mind to another frame of mind. In other words, the resulting frame of mind is such that the mark-context is activated into it.

The semantic structure we are basing our model is a local models semantics where classes of local models may be formed from one of the two complementary kind of considered context: frame of mind and mark context (see Figure 3). Frame of mind is an implicit, intrinsic and internal context and represents the global cognitive process. This frame of mind may evolve *locally* by means of actions of type (1). It may also take another form by means of actions of type (2) and, in this case, the changes depend on a mark context. Formally, our semantic model is a model in the sense of Giunchiglia et al. [6] where the set of index I is the union of the set of index I_F for frames of mind and the set of index I_M for mark contexts. Let us call these models *frame mind* models (FM-model). So, a FM-model is defined as follows.

Definition 4. (FM-Model) *A FM-model (for the set of modal languages* [1] *$\{L_i\}_{i \in I}$) is a compatibility relation* **C** *such that:*

1. C is a weak chain model

---

[1] Introduced in section 2.

2. $I = I_F \bigcup I_M$

3. $\overline{M}_i$ *are classes of pointed Kripke models*

It is more interesting to characterize actions of type (2) which will require to be constrained and, consequently, clarify the purpose of such models. For the rest of the paper, considered models are FM-models.

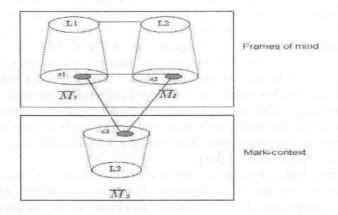

Fig. 3. A model of the considered semantic

4.2   Contextual Increasing and Decreasing Actions

We wish to introduce two types of actions that change frames of mind: contextual *increasing* and *decreasing* actions. Recall that these actions have to express a transition from a state of a frame of mind to a state of another frame of mind and, by consequence, will characterized locally in both states. Recall also that this transition is strongly related to a mark-context. So, a contextual increasing action is an action that have the effect of "activating" the related mark-context. Consequently, it involves a change of frame of mind where the resulting frame of mind includes the elements of the mark-context. On the contrary, a contextual decreasing action deactivates the mark-context and entails a resulting frame of mind excluding the elements of the mark-context.

Formally, let us suppose $(M,s) \in \overline{M}_i$ for a particular $i \in I_F$. We redefine the set of action Act of M as $Act = Act_{local} \cup Act_{contextual}$ where Act_{local} is the set of standard (and local) actions (described in section 2). $Act_{contextual}$ is itself the union of $Act_{c-increasing}$ and $Act_{c-decreasing}$ which are respectively the set of contextual increasing and contextual decreasing actions. Each action from $Act_{contextual}$ has three parameters which point out respectively the frame of mind index of the state before the action execution, the frame of mind index of the state after the action execution and the index of the mark-context. We will note these indexes *from*, *to* and *mark* and suppose that (M,s) contains such sets of indexes.

We now define the feasible and done operators for these actions. If ϕ is a formula and an action $a \in Act_{contextual}$, then so are $Feasible(a(from, to, mark), \phi)$ and $Done(a(from, to, mark), \phi)$. Let us extend the (local) satisfiability relation $\models$ of (M,s) (recall (M,s) is a local model) in the following way:

$M, s \models Feasible(\alpha(from, to, mark), \phi)$ iff

$\forall \mathbf{c} \in \mathbf{C}, \mathbf{c} = \langle \cdots, \mathbf{c}_{from}, \cdots, \mathbf{c}_{to}, \cdots, \mathbf{c}_{mark}, \cdots \rangle$ such that

$\mathbf{c}_{from} = \{(M, s)\}, \mathbf{c}_{to} = \{(M', s')\}$ and $M', s' \models \phi$, and

$\mathbf{c}_{mark} \neq \emptyset$

$M, s \models Done(\alpha(from, to, mark), \phi)$ iff

$\forall \mathbf{c} \in \mathbf{C}, \mathbf{c} = \langle \cdots, \mathbf{c}_{from}, \cdots, \mathbf{c}_{to}, \cdots, \mathbf{c}_{mark}, \cdots \rangle$ such that

$\mathbf{c}_{to} = \{(M, s)\}, \mathbf{c}_{from} = \{(M', s')\}$ and $M', s' \models \phi$, and

$\mathbf{c}_{mark} \neq \emptyset$

The first clause says that an action of $Act_{contextual}$ is feasible (after which ϕ is true) if and only if in all compatibility sequences (included in the compatibility relation $\mathbf{C}$) where the local model (M,s) is represented as a model from which the action α is executed (i.e. related to the index $from$), (1) (M,s) is compatible with (M',s') (which is actually the state after action α execution) and (2) ϕ is true in (M',s'), and (3) there exists a model from the related mark-context compatible with (M,s) and (M',s'). Similar interpretation can be made for the second clause. The difference is that (M,s) is in this case a model represented as a model on which the action is executed (i.e. related to the index to).

Note that the local satisfiability of theses two clauses are pretty unusual. Instead of basing their interpretation upon local elements (e.g., accessibility relations) of the model structure, we do it at a global level with the compatibility relation of this model with other models. The interesting compensation of that is that we give now a clear characterization of action changing frames of mind and thus a clear distinction between actions of Act_{local} and $Act_{contextual}$.

A natural question is how to express pre-conditions and effects for actions of $Act_{c-increasing}$ and $Act_{c-decreasing}$. We argue that pre-conditions and effects may be defined by taking into account (1) local formulae as for local actions and (2) formulae from the related mark-context. For example, in the case of (1), Tom's boss allows him to fetch his daughter may be a local formula as a necessary pre-condition in order to allow Tom to fill his role of father and thus to fetch her. Such a pre-condition depends on the current state of Tom's frame of mind.In the case of (2), having a daughter may be a pre-condition which is better related to the mark-context representing the father role for Tom.

This is on the last kind of formulae that we are interested in in the scope of actions of $Act_{contextual}$. Note that we do not aim to give *the* solution defining pre-conditions and effects of such actions. We propose, at most, *a* solution that highlights the potential expressiveness of this semantics to more easily specify different kinds of pre-conditions and effects from those traditionally proposed (i.e. $\phi \rightarrow Feasible(\alpha)$ and $Done(\alpha) \rightarrow \phi$).

Let us start with actions of $Act_{c-increasing}$. A contextual increasing action is an action executed from a state of a particular frame of mind having the effect of reaching a state of a another frame of mind into which a related mark-context is activated. For example, in our running example, there is such an action activating the father role of Tom.

We propose a *consistency hypothesis* as a necessary pre-condition of feasibility for this kind of action. Intuitively, this hypothesis holds when for any formula ϕ satisfied in the mark-context, either ϕ is not in the language related to the initial frame of mind or $\neg\phi$ is not satisfied in the current state of this frame. Formally, that can be described as following:

Definition 5. (Consistency Hypothesis) *Suppose* $from,to \in I_F$ *and* $mark \in I_M$. *Suppose* $\alpha \in Act_{c-increasing}$. *Suppose* ψ *the conjunction of all* α *local pre-conditions. The consistency hypothesis holds if and only if:*

$$\text{If for any } \phi \text{ such that } \models mark{:}\phi,$$
$$\text{and } \models from{:}\psi \rightarrow Feasible(\alpha(from,to,mark))$$
$$\text{then either } \phi \notin L_{from} \text{ or } \not\models from{:}\neg\phi$$

Concretely, this hypothesis says that filling Tom's father role requires that each element describing this role are either not into the language of the current Tom's frame of mind or consistent with his current mental state.

Now, if we suppose that the consistency hypothesis holds for feasibility, the effects of such an action is to activate the related mark-context in a new frame of mind. We propose an *all-effects hypothesis* as specifying the action effects. This hypothesis holds when for every formula ϕ satisfied in the mark-context, ϕ is an effect of the action into the resulting frame of mind. Formally, that can be described as follows:

Definition 6. (All-effects Hypothesis) *Suppose* $from,to \in I_F$ *and* $mark \in I_M$. *Suppose* $\alpha \in Act_{c-increasing}$. *The all-effects hypothesis holds iff:*

$$\text{If for every } \phi \text{ such that } \models mark{:}\phi,$$
$$\text{then } \models to{:}done(\alpha(from,to,mark)) \rightarrow \phi$$

In other words, this hypothesis says that activating Tom's father role implies integrating every elements describing this role into Tom's (new) current frame of mind.

On the contrary, a contextual decreasing action is an action executed from a state of a particular frame of mind having the effect to reach a state of a another frame of mind into which a related mark-context is inactivated. For example, in our running example, there is such an action deactivating the mechanician role of Tom.

Pre-conditions depending on the related mark-context are not taken into account here. In fact, the goal is to remove elements of the mark-context from the current frame of mind. The problem occurs at the level of the action effects. The question is: what do we have to remove from it? A simple hypothesis, we call

all-effect-back hypothesis is to remove all the formulae ϕ satisfied in the mark-context from the current frame of mind. In other words, all ϕ will not belong to the language of the resulting frame of mind. We know that this hypothesis is quite weak since initial mark-context elements may entail new others elements (by deduction, for example). Nevertheless, this hypothesis is at least the most minimal hypothesis as part of the inactivation of the mark-context. Note also that this hypothesis is applicable if and only if the domains of all mark-contexts are disjoints. Indeed, a formula ϕ satisfied in the current frame of mind may be shared by several mark-contexts. Anyway, we formalize this hypothesis as follows:

Definition 7. (All-effects-back Hypothesis) *Suppose* $from, to \in I_F$ *and* $mark \in I_M$. *Suppose* $\alpha \in Act_{d-increasing}$. *The all-effects hypothesis holds iff:*

> *If for every ϕ such that*
> $\models mark{:}\phi$ *and* $\models to{:}done(\alpha(from, to, mark))$,
> *then* $\phi \notin L_{to}$

Basically, this hypothesis says that inactivating Tom's mechanic role implies to remove every element describing this role from Tom's (new) current frame of mind.

To sum up, we proposed to characterize two kinds of actions changing frames of mind: contextual increasing and decreasing actions. We do this by giving a particular interpretation of the feasibility and done operator for these actions. Such an interpretation is situated at the level of compatibility between frames of mind and mark-contexts. We presented possible hypotheses in order to characterize these actions at this level. In the next section, we show the utility of such a semantics on an example based on agent awareness.

5   Example

Let us suppose Tom visiting museum. Suppose he wanders in order to see paintings and all these paintings call up for Tom one motif: the sea. The key idea is that when Tom sees the sea on a particular painting, that activates a memory space dedicated to this theme.

Let us suppose $\overline{M}_{m-sea}$ representing mark-contexts for the sea memory space. Let us imagine in particular the following formulae satisfied in these models:

$$\models m\text{-sea}{:}B \ sea \wedge B \ sand \rightarrow B \ beach$$

The clause means that believing one sees sea and sand on the painting implies believing one sees a beach.

Now, we may imagine two types of Tom's frame of mind. The first one is when Tom is just wandering without being front of a particular painting. The second one is when Tom is looking at a painting calling up for him the sea theme. Let us represent respectively these frames of mind by $\overline{M}_{f-idle}$ and $\overline{M}_{f-sea}$.

Such considerations allow us to define a model based on our semantics. The different mentioned classes of models are included such that $I_F = \{f\text{-}idle, f\text{-}sea\}$ and $I_M = \{m\text{-}sea\}$. We also guess that consistency, all-effects and all-effects-back hypothesis stand for this model.

In our example, we consider two actions: $e_{i-sea} \in Act_{c-increasing}$ of $\overline{M}_{f-idle}$ and $e_{d-sea} \in \in Act_{c-decreasing}$ of $\overline{M}_{f-sea}$. e_{i-sea} is an action executed from the $f\text{-}idle$ frame of mind which implies the activation of the mark-context related to the sea mark-context. e_{d-sea} is an action executed from the $f - sea$ frame of mark which implies the inactivation of the sea mark-context.

Let suppose that $\models f\text{-}idle$: $Bsea \rightarrow \text{Feasible}(e_{i-sea})$. If $\text{Feasible}(e_{i-sea})$ can be deduced, we have $\models$ f-sea:done(e_{i-sea}). By the all-effects hypothesis, the $f\text{-}sea$ frame of mark satisfied $B\ sea \wedge B\ sand \rightarrow B\ beach$ (i.e. $\models$ done(e_{i-sea}) $\rightarrow (B\ sea \wedge B\ sand \rightarrow B\ beach)$. What that shows is the activation of $m\text{-}sea$ mark-context into the $f\text{-}sea$ frame of mind.

An analog way can be applied for e_{d-sea}. Let suppose that $\models f - sea$: $\neg B\ sea \rightarrow \text{Feasible}(e_{d-sea})$. If $\text{Feasible}(e_{d-sea})$ can be deduced, we have $\models$ f-idle:done(e_{d-sea}). By the all-effects-back hypothesis, $B\ sea \wedge B\ sand \rightarrow B\ beach$ (i.e. $\models$ done$(e_{i-sea}) \rightarrow (B\ sea \wedge B\ sand \rightarrow B\ beach)$ is not into the language of L_{f-idle}. So, this formula is not in the scope of the $f\text{-}idle$ frame of mark. What that shows is the inactivation of $m\text{-}sea$ mark-context into the $f\text{-}idle$ frame of mind.

6   Conclusion

In this paper, we propose a semantics resulting from the combination of possible-world and Local Models semantics. Such a semantics enables us to characterize actions changing frames of mind while traditional characterization of actions can still be considered at a local level. Besides, characterization of actions that (de)active ate a mark-context like roles, memory spaces, etc. They highlights the possibility to express semantically the change of frames of mind.

References

1. Cohen, P.R., Levesque, H.J.: Intention is choice with commitment. Computer Science Dept. University of Toronto, Toronto (1990)
2. Chellas, B.F.: Modal logic. Cambridge University Press, Cambridge (1980)
3. Fagin, R., Halpern, J.Y.: Belief, Awareness, and Limited Reasoning. AI 34, 39–76 (1988)
4. Ghidini, C.: Modelling (un)bounded beliefs. In: Bouquet, P., Serafini, L., Brézillon, P., Benercetti, M., Castellani, F. (eds.) CONTEXT 1999. LNCS (LNAI), vol. 1688, pp. 145–158. Springer, Heidelberg (1999)
5. Giunchiglia, F.: Contextual reasoning. Technical Report 9211–20, Istituto per la Ricerca Scientifica e Technoligica, Trento, Italy (1992)
6. Giunchiglia, F., Ghidini, C.: Local Models semantics, or contextual reasoning = locality + compatibility. In: KR, pp. 282–291 (1998)
7. Harel, D.: Dynamic logic, pp. 497–604. Reidel (1984)

8. Kokinov, B.N.: A dynamic approach to context modeling. In: Proceedings of the IJCAI-95 Workshop on Modeling Context in Knowledge representation and Reasoning. LAFORIA (1995)

9. Kokinov, B.N.: A dynamic theory of implicit context. In: Proceedings of the Second European Conference on Cognitive Science, University of Manchester Press (1997)

10. Kripke, S.: Naming and Necessity. Harvard University Press, Cambridge (1972)

11. Kripke, S.: Semantical considerations on modal logics. Acta philosophica fennica 16, 83–94 (1963)

12. Pauly, M., Parikh, R.: Game Logic - An Overview. Studia Logica 75(2), 165–182 (2003)

13. Rao, A.S., Georgeff, M.P.: BDI agents: From theory to practice. In: proceedings of the First International Conference Multi-Agent Systems, pp. 312–319 (1995)

14. Sadek, M.D.: Attitudes mentales et interaction rationnelle: vers une théorie formelle de la communication, PhD in computer sciences, Université Rennes I (1991)

15. Sadek, M.D.: Communication theory = rationality principles + communicative act models. In: AAAI'94 - Workshop on Planning for InterAgent Communication (1994)

The Influence of Task Contexts on the Decision-Making of Humans and Computers

Ya'akov Gal[1,2], Barbara Grosz[2], Avi Pfeffer[2], Stuart Shieber[2], and Alex Allain[3]

[1] MIT Computer Science and Artificial Intelligence Laboratory, Cambridge MA 02139
[2] Harvard School of Engineering and Applied Sciences, Cambridge MA 02138
[3] Liquid Machines, Inc., Waltham MA 02451

Abstract. Many environments in which people and computer agents interact involve deploying resources to accomplish tasks and satisfy goals. This paper investigates the way that the context in which decisions are made affects the behavior of people and the performance of computer agents that interact with people in such environments. It presents experiments that measured negotiation behavior in two different types of settings. One setting was a task context that made explicit the relationships among goals, (sub)tasks and resources. The other setting was a completely abstract context in which only the payoffs for the decision choices were listed. Results show that people are more helpful, less selfish, and less competitive when making decisions in task contexts than when making them in completely abstract contexts. Further, their overall performance was better in task contexts. A predictive computational model that was trained on data obtained in the task context outperformed a model that was trained under the abstract context. These results indicate that taking context into account is essential for the design of computer agents that will interact well with people.

1 Introduction

Technology has opened up vast opportunities for computer agents to interact with people in such increasingly diverse applications as online auctions, elderly care systems, disaster relief operations, and system administrator groups [1,10]. While these applications differ broadly in size, scope, and complexity, they are similar in that they involve people and computers working together in *task settings*, in which the participants fulfill *goals* by carrying out *tasks* requiring the use of *resources*. Participants may need to cooperate, negotiate, or perform other group actions in order to achieve the goals, requiring their reasoning about the potential and likely behaviors of other participants. For computer agents to interact successfully with people in such mixed human-computer task settings, they need to meet people's expectations of teammates.

For example, in the domain of care of elderly patients, the physical challenges and health problems of this population typically require a team of caretakers—not only doctors and nurses, but also home health aides, housekeepers, family members. Current medical care depends on computer systems for scheduling and tracking prescriptions; computers, of a very small scale, are also key elements of pacemakers and other implantable medical devices. Thus, the agents involved in elder care are both human and computer-based; they come from different organizations and have different roles. As the

B. Kokinov et al. (Eds.): CONTEXT 2007, LNAI 4635, pp. 206–219, 2007.
© Springer-Verlag Berlin Heidelberg 2007

computer agents involved in such care become more sophisticated and more of them become connected to the care of a single individual, the need for abilities to coordinate and work as team members will become important.

In designing computer agents for such settings, it is thus important to understand the decision-making strategies people deploy when they interact with others and to evaluate various computational strategies for interacting with people. Formally modeling the behavior of people, and in particular their decision-making behaviors, raises significant challenges for computer-agent design.

To investigate the influence of task contexts on decision-making, we deployed a conceptually simple but expressive game called Colored Trails (CT) [4]. CT explicitly manifests goals, tasks, and resources in a way that is compelling to people, yet abstracts away from a complicated underlying domain. By embedding decision-making within a task context, CT enables investigators to focus on people's decision-making strategies, rather than specifying and reasoning about individual domain complexities.

CT differs significantly from the highly abstracted settings typically used in behavioral economics, such as decision trees or normal form tables. These forms completely hide the underlying relationship between tasks, goals, and resources and fully specify payoffs for players from potential strategies. We call this abstract representation a *table context*. Game-theoretic tools can be applied in such games to provide an idealized notion of appropriate decision-making behavior. The decisions engendered by CT games can also be described as a table of payoffs, enabling to contrast between task and table contexts use to embed the same decision.

We analyzed people's behavior in terms of various social criteria, for which we give a precise definition in terms of the CT game. We show that people presented with identical decision-making problems in the task context and the table context perform strikingly differently, both qualitatively and quantitatively. When making decisions in the task context, people are more helpful, less competitive and less game-theoretic than when making decisions in the table context. Surprisingly, the results also indicate that the task context improves people's overall performance.

To evaluate the effects of these differences for computer agents that interact with people, we trained predictive models on data obtained in both types of contexts. The models explicitly represented social factors that have been shown to affect people's behavior [3]. Most importantly, the model trained on data obtained in the task context outperformed the model trained on data obtained in the table context. In addition, overall performance was better when the context was task-oriented, rather than payoff-oriented.

For designers of intelligent agents, the important lesson of these experiments is that the design of computer agents that will operate in mixed human-computer settings must consider how the decisions presented to people will be contextualized and reflect the human decision-making process in that context, not merely in a purely idealized (even if theoretically equivalent) manner. As much as we might like it, there is no way for computer agents to escape into pure game theory when participating in mixed systems.

2 Empirical Methodology

This section describes the two types of context, task context and table context, we investigated and the experiments conducted in those settings.

In the *task* context, a 2-player CT game was played on a 4x4 board of colored squares with a set of chips. One square on the board was designated as the goal square. Each player's icon was initially located in a random, non-goal position. To move to an adjacent square a played needed to surrender a chip in the color of that square. Players were issued four colored chips. They had full view of the board and each others' chips, and thus they had complete knowledge of the game situation.

Players were designated one of two roles: *proposer* players could offer some subset of their chips to be exchanged with some subset of the chips of responder players; *responder* players could in turn accept or reject proposers' offers. If no offer was made, or if the offer was declined, then both players were left with their initial allocation of chips. Chip exchanges were enforced by the game controller: after the negotiation ended, both players were automatically moved as close as possible to the goal square.

The scoring function for players depended solely on their own performance: 100 points for reaching the goal; 10 points for each tile left in a player's possession; 15 points deducted for any square in the shortest path between player's final position and the goal-square. These parameters were chosen so that getting to the goal was by far the most important component, but if an player could not get to the goal it was preferable to get as close to the goal as possible. The score that each player received if no offer was made was identical to the score each player received if the offer was rejected by the deliberator. We refer to this score as the *no negotiation alternative* and to the score that each player received if the offer was accepted by the deliberator as the *proposed outcome* score.

Snapshots of the CT GUI of one of the games used in the experiment is shown in Figure 1. The Main Window panel, shown in Figure 1a, includes the board game, the goal square, represented by an icon displaying the letter *G*, and two icons, "me" and "sun", representing the location of the two players on the board at the onset of the game.[1] The bottom part of the Main Window panel, titled "chips", shows the chip distributions for the players. In the game shown here, both players lack sufficient chips to get to the goal square. A proposer uses the Propose Exchange panel, shown in Figure 1b, to make an offer to a responder. The Path Finder panel, shown in Figure 1c, provides decision support tools to be used during the game. It displays a list of path suggestions to the goal, the missing chips required to fulfill each path, and the best position the agent can reach relative to its scoring function. Agents can view this information for the chip set that is currently in their possession, or for any hypothetical chip set for each of the players.

The *table* context consisted of a completely abstract representation of a CT game as a list of potential offers that could be selected by the proposer player. Each offer was represented as a pair of payoffs for the proposer and the responder. Figure 2 shows a snapshot of a game in this representation as seen from the point of view of a proposer player. Each cell in the table represents an offer, and selecting a cell corresponds

---

[1] CT colors have been converted to grey scale in this figure.

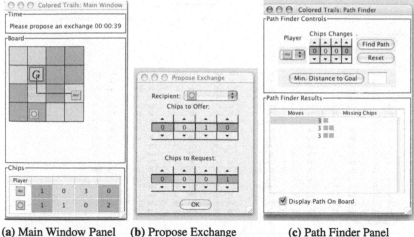

(a) Main Window Panel   (b) Propose Exchange   (c) Path Finder Panel
(onset of game)   Panel

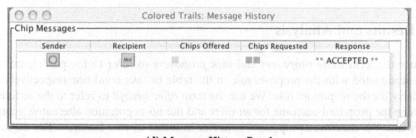

(d) Message History Panel

Fig. 1. Snapshots of Interaction in a Task Context

to choosing the offer associated with its payoffs. One of the cells represents the no-negotiation alternative, which is presented as the default outcome of the interaction.

A total of 32 subjects participated in the experiment, equally divided between the two conditions. They interacted with each other for 96 rounds. Participants in the task condition interacted with each other using the CT environment, whereas those in the table condition interacted with each other using the payoff matrix representation. Participants only interacted with others in their condition group; they were not provided any information about each other. In both conditions, participants were compensated in a manner that depended solely on their individual scores, aggregated over all rounds of interaction.

For each CT round that was played in the task condition, an equivalent round was played in the table condition, in the sense that the payoff pair at the intersection of each row and column represented the score in the CT round for the corresponding offer and response. For example, the payoff matrix shown in Figure 2 is equivalent to the CT game shown in Figure 1.

You are a proposer.

Proposal Phase. Time left: 162

Please choose the default outcome or one of the alternative offers in the table. If you do not choose an offer by the time limit, the result will be the default outcome.

Default outcome:
You Other
○ 180 65

Possible offers:

You	Other		You	Other		You	Other		You	Other		You	Other		You	Other		You	Other		You	Other
180	170		190	55		75	170		55	190		200	40		180	170		75	170		190	55
200	40		190	55		55	190		190	55		65	180		65	180		75	170		45	200
200	45		190	50		65	180		85	160		190	160		180	170		75	170		55	190
210	35		170	180		65	180		190	160		55	190		180	170		55	190		170	75
160	190		190	55		45	200		170	75		85	160		180	170		45	200		190	55
55	190		75	170		200	45		190	55		65	180		200	45		170	180		65	180
55	190		190	160		210	30		180	170		210	30		190	55		200	150		210	35
190	55		190	50		200	150		200	45		160	190		200	45		65	180		210	35
45	200		65	180		95	150		220	20		170	180		190	55		170	75		65	180
65	180		75	170		170	75		85	160		75	170		75	170		190	55		170	180
200	45		150	200		210	30		55	190		85	160		65	180		170	75		160	190
65	180		170	180		170	180		190	160		190	160		190	55		160	190		190	55
200	45		75	170		45	200		170	180		200	45		170	180		35	210			
170	75		180	60		190	55		65	180		170	180		200	40		190	160			
75	170		190	50		160	190		200	40		85	160		200	45		180	170			
180	170		180	170		75	170		200	45		160	85		190	160		180	170			
55	190		190	55		170	180		65	180		55	190		190	160		55	190			

Sorted by
⦿ Original Order
○ Your Benefit Descending
○ Other Benefit Descending

Propose Selected Outcome

Fig. 2. Snapshot of an Interaction in a Table Context

3 Results and Analysis

We use the term *table proposers* and *task proposers* to refer to the participants that were designated with the proposer role in the table or task condition respectively and similarly for the responder role. We use the term *offer benefit* to refer to the difference between the proposed outcome for an offer and the no-negotiation alternative score of the round. We measured proposers' behavior in terms of two features: The degree to which proposers were *selfish* or *helpful* was defined in terms of the average offer benefit they proposed for themselves or for responders, respectively; the degree to which proposers were *competitive* was defined in terms of the difference between the average offer benefit they proposed for themselves and the offer benefit they provided to responders. Although we have given a psychological interpretation to these features, we do not imply that they are independent. For example, proposers can exhibit both a degree of selfishness and a degree of helpfulness based on the average benefit of their offers.

3.1 The Effect of Contexts on Human Behavior

Table 1 presents the average offer benefit to participants in both task and table condition for each role designation. Table proposers offered significantly more benefit to

Table 1. Average Benefit of Offer

	Offer Benefit to		Num.
	Proposer	Responder	acceptances
Task	82.3	**47.6**	62 (77%)
Table	**98**	36	69 (77%)

themselves than did task proposers (t-test $p < 0.05$). Also, table proposers offered significantly less benefit to table responders than task proposers offered to task responders (t-test $p < 0.01$). Thus, the task context had the effect of making proposers more helpful and less selfish when interacting with responders.

The difference between the average offer benefit to proposers and to responders is positive in both conditions (t-test $p < 0.05$). Although in both conditions proposers are competitive, the offer difference was larger in the table condition than in the task condition (t-test $p < 0.05$). Thus, on average table proposers were more competitive than task proposers. We hypothesized that table proposers made competitive offers more often than did task proposers. To test this hypothesis, we performed a within-round comparison of the offer benefit in both conditions. Table 2 presents the number of rounds in which the difference between the proposed benefit for proposers and responders was positive (column "Proposer > Responder") and the number of rounds in which this difference was negative (column "Proposer < Responder"). As shown by the table, table proposers made offers that benefited themselves over responders significantly more often than task proposers (chi-square $p < 0.05$). These results confirm that table proposers are more likely to be competitive than proposers.

Table 2 also shows that 62% of all offers made by table proposers benefited *themselves* more than table responders, while 60% of all offers made by task proposers benefited task *responders* more than themselves (chi-square $p < 0.05$). This striking result indicates that task proposers were helpful more often than they were selfish, whereas table proposers were selfish more often than they were helpful.

Table 2. Frequency of Competitive Offers

	Proposer > Responder	Proposer < Responder
Task	26 (27%)	**51** (60%)
Table	**60** (62%)	24 (28%)

Having established that the context in which decisions are made affected the behavior of proposers, we investigated whether it affected the behavior of responders. It is more difficult to perform within-round comparisons of responder behavior across task and table conditions, because the decision of whether to accept or reject an offer depends on the exchange offered by proposers. For the same round, this exchange may be different for task and table conditions. As shown in Table 1, there was no difference in the ratio of exchanges accepted by responders (77%) between conditions. However, this result does not mean that responders were not affected by context; as also shown in Table 1, they were responding to exchanges that were more helpful to them in the task condition. We expected this pattern to hold for accepted offers as well; thus, we expected that the offers that were *accepted* by responders were more helpful to them in the task condition than in the table condition.

Table 3 shows the exchange benefit to proposers and responders averaged over all accepted proposals, as well as the total accumulated benefit in each condition. The benefit to responders from accepted proposals was significantly higher in the task condition than in the table condition, and conversely for the proposers (t-test $p < 0.05$). These

Table 3. Average Benefit for Accepted Exchanges

	Proposer	Responder	Total
Task	79.5	**56.4**	135.9
Table	**85.6**	40.7	126.3

results indicated that task responders outperformed table responders, whereas table proposers outperformed task proposers. Interestingly, as the rightmost column shows, the total performance (combined proposers and responders scores) was higher in the task condition than in the table condition. The benefit for accepted exchanges is a measurement of performance, because the outcome of each round of interaction was fully determined by the action of the responder (t-test $p < 0.1$). Although this result was not significant at the $p < 0.05$ confidence interval, the trend it indicates suggests that task context has a positive effect on the combined performance of participants.

To compare between the benefits of proposed and accepted exchanges, we plotted the average benefit to proposer and responder from these offers in both conditions, as shown in Figure 3. We define the *discrepancy* between two offers to be the Euclidean distance between the two points representing the benefits of the offers to proposers and responders. As apparent from the figure, the discrepancy between proposed and accepted offers was significantly smaller in the task condition than in the idealized condition (t-test $p < 0.05$). This result suggests that on average, task proposers were more accurate at estimating the offers that were likely to be accepted by responders.

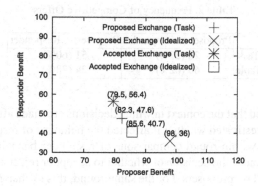

Fig. 3. Benefit for Proposed Exchanges vs. Accepted Exchanges

Also shown in Figure 3 is that in both conditions, accepted offers were more beneficial to responders than proposed offers; also in both conditions, accepted offers were less beneficial to proposers than proposed offers. This result suggests that responders expected proposers to be more helpful and less selfish in both conditions; this aligns with our findings that players were competitive across task and idealized contexts. However, the difference between the benefit to responders from proposed and accepted offers was significantly greater in the task condition than in the idealized condition. Similarly, the difference between the benefit to proposers from proposed and accepted offers was significantly greater in the idealized condition than in the task condition. This implies that in the idealized condition, responders expect proposers to be less selfish, while in the task condition, responders expect proposers to be more helpful. A possible explanation is that the task context induced responders to expect more help from proposers than the idealized context.

3.2 Discussion of Alternative Explanations

To address the question of whether the difference in behavior can be explained by the lack of an explicit representation of payoff in the task condition, we ran an experiment that used the CT game, but allowed subjects to view the payoffs for potential offers for all players. This intermediate representation preserves the task context as well as displaying the payoff function for both players. Results using the same set of games as in the original experiment show that there was no significant difference in the average benefit allocated to proposers and responders in this intermediate representation than in the task condition.

In addition, we ruled out the effect of cognitive demands on subjects by including decision support tools for both modes of decision representation. In the CT game, subjects could use the PathFinder panel, shown in Figure 1c to query the system for suggestions about the best paths to take given any hypothetical chip distribution. When presented with a table of payoffs in the table condition, subjects could sort the table by their own, or the others' benefit. In this way, subjects were allowed to focus on the interaction rather than on the cognitive complexity of the decision-making.

3.3 Comparison with Game Theoretic Strategies

We now turn to a comparison between the offers that were made in each condition and the offers dictated by the exchange corresponding to the Nash equilibrium strategy. We use the term *NE exchange* of a round to refer to the exchange prescribed by the Nash equilibrium strategy profile for the round. This exchange offers the maximum benefit for the proposer, out of the set of all of the exchanges that offer non-negative benefits to the responder. In our scenarios, the NE exchange generally amounted to selfish, unhelpful, competitive offers.

We expected table proposers to be more likely to offer NE exchanges than task proposers. Table 4 shows the number of NE offers made by proposers in both conditions. The proportion of NE offers was significantly higher in the table condition (59%) than in the task condition (15%) (chi-square $t < 0.01$).

To compare the extent to which the exchanges made by proposers in the two type of contexts differed from the NE exchange, we plotted the average benefit offered by NE

Table 4. Frequency of Nash Equilibrium Offers

	Num.. offers
Task	13 (15%)
Table	57 (59%)

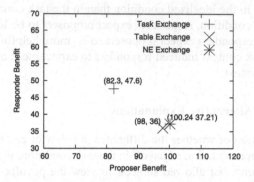

Fig. 4. Benefit from Proposed Exchanges vs. NE Exchanges

exchanges and by proposed exchanges for both task and table conditions, as shown in Figure 4.

The difference between the average benefit to responders from the NE offer and the average proposed exchange was close to zero in the table condition, and large and positive in the task condition (t-test $p < 0.05$). Similarly, the difference between the benefit to proposers from the NE offer and the average proposed exchange was close to zero in the table condition, and large and negative in the task condition (t-test $p < 0.05$). The Euclidean distance between the two points representing the NE benefit to proposers and responders was significantly larger in the task condition than in the table condition. In fact, there was no statistically significant difference between offers in the table condition and NE offers. These results are strikingly significant, showing that participants who make decisions in the table condition are more likely to follow the game-theoretic paradigm.

There is a discrepancy between these findings and those of the behavioral economic studies, which show that people do *not* generally adhere to game theoretic equilibria, and display variance within their play. Several differences between the structure of the negotiation scenario used in our experiments and the games traditionally used in behavioral economics may explain this difference. First, our scenario presented participants with some guaranteed reward (the no-negotiation alternative) if agreement was not reached at the end of the interaction. Traditional behavioral economic games do not provide such reward. (For example, if no agreement is reached in the ultimatum game, both players end up empty handed.) It is possible that in table contexts, proposers saw fit to make selfish exchanges, because they could always fall back on their guaranteed outcome if that offer was rejected.[2] Second, each interaction in our experiment varied which player needed the other to get to the goal. In some rounds, both players were mutually dependent on each other. In traditional behavioral economic experiments, players' dependencies are static. A possible hypothesis, worthy of further investigation, is that table participants were more likely to follow game theoretic equilibria in one type of dependency but not in others.

---

[2] This phenomenon, deemed the "endowment effect", has been documented in the psychology literature [6]).

4 The Effect of Contexts on Learner Agents

This section presents results that indicate the effects of task contexts on the performance of computer systems that learn a model of people's negotiation behavior. Using the data collected from the task and table contexts, we trained a computational model for predicting the actions of human proposers. We adopted the model proposed by Gal and Pfeffer [2] for predicting people's bidding behavior in multi-attribute negotiation. In this model, proposals are generated by converting people's utility functions into a stochastic function that assigns a probability to each potential exchange at each round of interaction.

At each round of interaction k, the inputs to the model were NN_P^k and NN_R^k, the no-negotiation alternative scores for the proposer and responder, and $PO_P^k(x)$ and $PO_R^k(x)$, the proposed outcome scores for the proposer and responder for a potential exchange x. We omit the superscript k when it is clear from context. Using these features, we can define the following social factors for the proposer agent, denoted s_1, s_2, s_3 that match the features we used to analyze human behavior in the Section 3.

- Selfishness measures the extent to which proposers cared about their individual benefit.

$$s_1(x) = PO_P(x) - NN_P$$

- Helpfulness measures the extent to which proposers were interested in the welfare of the group as a whole, as well as their own benefit.

$$s_2(x) = (PO_P(x) + PO_R) - (NN_P + NN_R)$$

- Competitiveness measures the extent to which proposers cared to do better than others. Such participants were willing to sacrifice some of their own benefit in order to increase this difference.

$$s_3(x) = (PO_P(x) - NN_P) - (PO_R(x) - NN_R)$$

For each potential exchange x_j, we defined a "social" utility function $u(x_j)$ for a general proposer player that is a weighted sum of the features defined above:

$$u(x_j) = \sum_{i=1}^{3} w_i \cdot s_i(x_j)$$

where w_i denotes the weight associated with social factor s_i.

This utility function is transformed into a stochastic model that assigns a probability to each possible exchange at each round of interaction. A soft-max function is used to make the likelihood of each exchange proportional to the likelihood of other possible exchanges. This model is well suited for capturing certain aspects of human behavior: The stochasticity of the soft-max function allows for proposers to deviate from choosing the action associated with the highest utility, but in a controlled way. In addition, the likelihood of choosing an exchange that incurs a high social utility will increase if there are few other similar exchanges that incur high utility, and will decrease if there are many other similar exchanges.

The model parameters, represented by the feature weights $w_1, \ldots, w_3$ were trained using supervised learning. The labeled training set consisted of the exchanges made by proposers in the task and table conditions. Each instance consisted of pairs of possible exchanges (x_*, x_j), where x_* was the offer made by the proposer, and x_j is any other possible exchange. To estimate the feature weights of the utility function, we used a gradient-descent technique that learned to predict the probability of a chosen offer x_* given any other offer x_j as follows:

$$P(x_* \text{ chosen} \mid x_* \text{ or } x_j \text{ chosen}, \mathbf{s}_*, \mathbf{s}_j) = \frac{1}{1 + e^{u(x_*) - u(x_l)}}$$

Here, $\mathbf{s}_*$ denotes the social factors associated with the offer that was proposed. This probability represents the likelihood of selecting x_* in the training set, given x_j. The error function to minimize is defined as the extent to which the model is not a perfect predictor of this concept,

$$err_j = 1 - P(x_* \text{ chosen} \mid x_* \text{ or } x_j \text{ chosen } .\mathbf{s}_*, \mathbf{s}_j)$$

Taking the derivative of this function, we obtain the following update rule for the features $\mathbf{w}$, where α is a constant learning rate, and $\mathbf{d} = \mathbf{s}_* - \mathbf{s}_j$.

$$\mathbf{w} = \mathbf{w} + \alpha(err_j)^2 \cdot (1 - err_j) \cdot \mathbf{d}$$

We learned separate models for the task and table contexts. In both cases, we trained and tested the algorithms separately, using ten-fold cross validation. We obtained the following average posterior parameter values for the features selfishness, helpfulness and competitiveness in each condition.

Condition	Learned weights
Task	$(5.20, 3.2, 0.40)$
Table	$(8.20, 1.3, 8)$

As shown in the table, both task proposers and table proposers are selfish, in the sense that they place high weight on their own benefit. However, table proposers assign higher weight to their own benefit than do task proposers, suggesting they are more selfish than task proposers. Task proposers also assign a higher weight to helpfulness and significantly lower weight to competitiveness than table proposers. These values align with the trends reported in the Results and Analysis section.

We evaluated both models on test sets comprised of held out data from both task and table conditions. We report the average negative log likelihood for all models in the following table as computed using ten-fold cross validation. A lower value for this criteria means that the test set was given a higher likelihood by the model.

Training / Testing Condition	Average Log Likelihood
Task / Task	0.144
Table / Task	1.2
Table / Table	0.220
Task / Table	1.2

As shown by the table, the model trained and tested on the task condition was able to fit the data better than the model trained and tested in the table condition, indicating that computer agents participating in mixed human-computer task settings must model human performance in a way that reflects the context under which the decision was made.

In addition, the model trained in the task condition outperformed the model trained in a table context when both models were evaluated in task contexts. (And conversely for the model trained in the table condition.) The extent to which both models underperformed when evaluated in the context they were not trained on was similar for both conditions. These results clearly imply that the context in which decisions are placed affects the performance of computer models that learn to interact with people.

5 Related Work

A series of studies spawned by the seminal work of Tversky and Kahneman [11,7] show that the way decisions, outcomes, and choices are described to people influence their behavior, and these different "framings" fundamentally affect people's perceptions and conceptualizations. For example, people's decision-making is sensitive to the presentation of outcomes as losses or wins and to the presence of alternative choices [12]. In addition, decisions are influenced by the labeling of interactions with terms that carry cultural or social associations [8]. Some of these framing effects (e.g., presence of alternatives) abstract away from domain specifics, while others (e.g., social associations) typically rely on real world or domain knowledge and experience, sometimes quite subtly. Both types of framing effect may be investigated using CT. For example, we have conducted a preliminary study of the effects of social relationships on decision-making in CT [9].

Our work is fundamentally different from work that addresses the effects of graphical versus tabular representations on people's decision-making [13,5]. This work has shown that performance on particular tasks is enhanced when there is a good match between the mode used to represent a task and the cognitive resources required to complete it. It aims to present information in a way that provides good "cognitive fit", a vivid representation that overcomes the constraints of human information processing. In contrast, we examine whether the structural features that are inherent in task contexts, such as the relationship between goals and resources, affect people's decision-making. We do not address the cognitive-load implications of different contexts or with their mode of representation. In fact, we control for the effects of cognitive load in both task and table settings by providing participants with decision-support tools.

Lastly, recent work on modeling the social factors that affect people's decision-making behavior have concentrated on task contexts only [9,3]. This work extends these approaches by comparing models of decision-making in task contexts and table contexts.

6 Conclusion and Future Work

We have shown that when making decisions placed in the context of a task setting, people behave more helpfully, less selfishly, and less competitively than when making decisions in the context of a table of payoffs. Further, people are significantly more likely to behave according to game theoretic equilibria in table contexts, which has a negative effect on their performance, compared to their behavior in task contexts. Moreover, people do not behave differently in task contexts when they are given access to the possible payoffs for themselves and others. We induced predictive models of the decision-making processes, showing that when learning in task contexts, computer players are better at predicting people's behavior than when learning in completely abstract contexts.

The results reported in this study suggest that when building a system for human-computer interaction, placing the decisions in task contexts will improve the performance of both people and computer agents that learn from people. Therefore, designers of systems that involve people and computers interacting together need to decide how to appropriately contextualize the decisions they present to participants.

While our experiments were performed in a relatively simple and flat task context, the fact that differences were found in this context suggest that it is likely there will be even greater ones in more complex settings. Our results provide a guideline for agent designers, specifically that the right context should be used when investigating human decision-making processes. We have presented an infrastructure for conducting such an investigation, and a methodology for how it might be done.

Acknowledgments

Development and dissemination of the Colored Trails formalism is supported in part by the National Science Foundation under Grant No. CNS-0453923 and IIS-0222892.

References

1. Das, R., Hanson, J.E., Kephart, J.O., Tesauro, G.: Agent-human interactions in the continuous double auction. In: Nebel, B. (ed.) Proc. 17th International Joint Conference on Artificial Intelligence (IJCAI'01) (2001)
2. Gal, Y., Pfeffer, A.: Predicting people's bidding behavior in negotiation. In: Stone, P., Weiss, G. (eds.) Proc. 5th International Joint Conference on Multi-agent Systems (AAMAS'06) (2006)
3. Gal, Y., Pfeffer, A., Marzo, F., Grosz, B.: Learning social preferences in games. In: Proc. 19th National Conference on Artificial Intelligence (AAAI'04) (2004)
4. Grosz, B., Kraus, S., Talman, S., Stossel, B.: The influence of social dependencies on decision-making. Initial investigations with a new game. In: Kudenko, D., Kazakov, D., Alonso, E. (eds.) Adaptive Agents and Multi-Agent Systems II. LNCS (LNAI), vol. 3394, Springer, Heidelberg (2005)

5. Jarvenpaa, S.L.: The effect of task demands and graphical format on information processing strategies. Management Science 35(3), 285–303 (1989)
6. Kahneman, D., Knetsch, J.L., Thaler, R.H.: The endowment effect, loss aversion, and status quo bias. Journal of Economic Perspectives 5, 193–206 (1991)
7. Kahneman, D., Tversky, A. (eds.): Choices, Values, and Frames. Cambridge University Press, Cambridge (2000)
8. Liberman, V., Samuels, S., Ross, L.: The name of the game: Predictive power of reputation vs. situational labels in dertermining prisoners' dilemma game moves
9. Marzo, F., Gal, Y., Grosz, B., Pfeffer, A.: Social preferences in relational contexts. In: Fourth Conference in Collective Intentionality (2005)
10. Pollack, M.E.: Intelligent technology for an aging population: The use of AI to assist elders with cognitive impairment. AI Magazine 26(9) (2006)
11. Tversky, A., Kahneman, D.: The framing of decisions and the psychology of choice. Science 211, 452–458 (1981)
12. Tversky, A., Simonson, I.:
13. Vessey, I.: Cognitive fit: A theory-based analysis of the graphs versus tables literature. Decision Sciences 22(2), 219–240 (1991)

Context and Design Agents

John S. Gero[1] and Gregory J. Smith[2]

[1] Krasnow Institute for Advanced Study and Volgenau School of Information
Technology and Engineering, George Mason University, USA
[2] Key Centre of Design Computing and Cognition, University of Sydney, Australia
john@johngero.com,g_smith@arch.usyd.edu.au

Abstract. Informal notions of context often imply much more than that captured in many computational formalisms of it. The view presented in this paper, built on our understanding of designing, is of context being larger than any one agent's representation of it. This paper describes how for an agent's reasoning about context it is the current situation that determines what the agent's interpretations of context are, not the reverse. The paper presents a typical scenario involving collaborating, sketching designers.

1 Introduction

Context is one of those words, like "life" [1], for which there is no universally accepted definition. Akman and Surav [2] on "context":

> "denotation of the word has become murkier as its uses have been extended in many directions and deliver the now widespread opinion that context has become some sort of conceptual garbage can "

Benerecetti et al. [3] on "context":

> "It is sort of commonplace to say that any representation is context dependent. By this, it is generally meant that the content of a representation cannot be established by simply composing the content of its parts"

Fields like AI present context formalisms that tend to mean much less by "context" than less formal, common sense descriptions would indicate. In this paper we present a view that builds on our understanding designers and design agents. Designing is the conscious effort to impose meaningful order [4, quoting Victor Papenek]. Conceptual designing is an early phase of design characterised by abstractness and an incomplete understanding of the problem and/or solution [5]. Designers cope with this by exploring the space of design requirements at the same time as they begin to try and understand the space of conceptual designs. Such designing has been labelled creative when the space of possible designs must be extended before a satisfactory design is found. This is achieved by interacting with the media of the conceptual designs as exemplified by Schön's [6]

B. Kokinov et al. (Eds.): CONTEXT 2007, LNAI 4635, pp. 220–233, 2007.
© Springer-Verlag Berlin Heidelberg 2007

"conversation with the medium". In this paper we start from our understanding of designing, describing a view of context that is bigger than any one agent's representation of it. We also describe how for agents to reason contextually, it is the situation that determines what interpretations of context are and not the reverse. A situation is a rich set of ideas and an interpreted context is the lesser by comparison. We finish by presenting a typical scenario involving collaborating, sketching designers.

2   Outside the Box

The best known AI approach to context would likely be that of McCarthy [7]. This defines a relation $ist(c\, p)$ asserting that a proposition p is true in context c. Context here is an abstract, first-class mathematical entity in the style of a fluent. The "attitude" taken by McCarthy is a "computer science or engineering one":

> "it seems unlikely that this study will result in a unique conclusion about *what context is*" [7, emphasis is McCarthy's].

What *ist* does is introduce some *mathematical* context dependence. We don't find this to be very satisfying, partly because not saying what something is risks formalising the wrong thing and partly because we believe that this approach misses something important. Benerecetti et al. are correct: just saying that a representation is context dependent probably doesn't say much by itself.

The metaphor for context that Benerecetti et al. borrow is a box. Inside a box are expressions and outside of the box are parameters with values. Something inside the box is context-dependent when you need something outside of the box to determine what it means. Good examples are natural language texts using indexicals, like "I saw her yesterday".

The obvious question is why place some expressions outside of the box and some inside? One answer is that techniques like using indexicals have clear benefits not only to language but to an agent's interactions generally (think of deictic references). According to Perry, indexicals are expressions whose designation shifts from context to context. Consider the sentence "now I will tell her". The designation of *now* is [8]:

$$(u \text{ designates } t) \iff \exists x \,(x \text{ is the speaker of } u \,\wedge$$
$$x \text{ directs } u \text{ at } t \text{ during part of } t)$$

So by this metaphor the $(u$ designates $t)$ goes in the box as does, presumably, the rule from the right of the if-and-only-if symbol. What the x, u and t designate go outside of the box. Now meaning is a property of types of expressions rather than of individuals, whereas content is a property of individuals [8]. So the meaning of $(u$ designates $t)$ is understood without having anything outside of the box, but the content of $(u$ designates $t)$ is only understood when x, u and t are known.

Another problem is that what (x is the speaker of u) and (x directs $u \ldots$) mean have their own contextual concerns, as do any objects associated with this meaning. Further, the context at the time of writing or speaking "now I will tell her" will differ from the context at the time of hearing or reading it even if the communicating parties designate x, u and t as the same external entities. Hence the concern of Derrida that "a context is never absolutely determinable, or rather ... its determination is never certain or saturated" [9].

Dewey [10] described context as having a number of aspects that can be collectively called background and selective interest. Ekbia and Maguitman [11] summarise this nicely with the graph reproduced as Figure 1. Background context influences the behaviour of an agent without it being the target of explicit reasoning. A good example, in this case of existential background context, are the un-modelled environmental influences on a sensor. Such background context is anything that influences behaviour that the agent does not explicitly reason on. The context of an agent's experiences is context of the system, and that which an agent reasons as being the context is the interpreted context. There is

$$\text{context} \begin{cases} \text{background} \begin{cases} \text{spatial} \\ \text{temporal} \begin{cases} \text{intellectual} \\ \text{existential} \end{cases} \end{cases} \\ \text{selective interest} \end{cases}$$

Fig. 1. Aspects of context, after [11]

background context but it is partly in the agent and partly not. Selective interest is the attention and subjective biases of an agent:

> "Everything which exists may be supposed to have its own unduplicated manner of acting and reacting, even atoms and electrons, although these individual traits are submerged in statistical statement. But in any event that which I have designated selective interest is a unique manner of entering into interaction with other things" [10].

Much work on context uses natural language as examples. The risk is that such texts come supplied in a symbolic form and consequently "what is context" gets recast as deciding the content and meaning of those symbols.

To see why we consider this to be a problem, consider designing tasks. Figure 2 is an example of a designer thinking with pen and paper [12]. Such drawings may contain visual and non-visual signifiers plus other shapes that are not intended to signify anything. They do not come pre-supplied in symbolic form. These sketching activities are part of dialogue between the designer and the drawing; they are of a dialogue even if nobody else is present as the designer sketches. Drawings like this are often part of a sequence and have contexts that are part of the process of conceptual designing and of communicating. There are sequences of sketching actions within one drawing and there are sequences of past drawings that the designer may or may not refer back to. The following is the architect and engineer Santiago Calatrava describing how he designs:

"To start with you see the thing in your mind and it doesn't exist on paper and then you start making simple sketches and organizing things and then you start doing layer after layer ... it is very much a dialogue" [13].

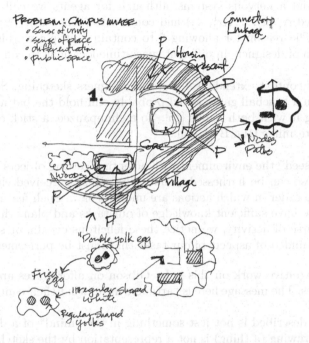

Fig. 2. Designer drawing, taken from [14], of a conceptual design of a proposed site

The drawing of Figure 2 includes text labels that highlight a design metaphor in use (of providing a "sense of unity" to distinct artifacts via a "double yolk egg" metaphor) but this certainly need not be the case. In a collaborative designing session such sketches will constitute a conversation along with the concurrent verbal communication and so the text labels may not be included. Shapes in such sketches need not depict two or three dimensional forms and need not be associated with concepts in the concurrent verbal communication, if there is one.

"In many cases their drawings contributed relatively little to the meaning simultaneously conveyed verbally, and in most cases the drawing made almost no sense at all when viewed out of the context of the conversation" [13].

Neither of these drawings comes supplied as a particular sequence of symbols to be interpreted, and both involve visual signifiers (sketched shapes) and non-visual signifiers (text). Even to a single designer there are many ways to look at these sketches, and research evidence suggests that designers "get inspiration and ideas from their drawings that they did not imagine in advance" [12]. Each designer interprets the context according to the situation as they understand it.

We can step back from designers and drawings by modelling designers as agents interacting with one or more worlds. The environment ξ is taken to be a set of entities aggregated into one or more worlds. Some of these entities are agents (denoted $\mathfrak{a}_1, \mathfrak{a}_2, \ldots$) and some are things (denoted $\gamma_1, \gamma_2, \ldots$). Designers have bodies and a nervous systems, although for agents we call these agent-things (denoted $\alpha_1^1, \alpha_1^2, \ldots, \alpha_2^1, \ldots$) and constructs (denoted $\beta_1^1, \beta_1^2, \ldots, \beta_2^1, \ldots$) respectively. The reason for allowing ξ to contain multiple worlds is to allow the description of designers in different space-time locations to collaborate via a virtual world.

The role of context extends well beyond designers sketching. Someone who had never seen a baseball game would probably still hold the bat at the correct end and swing it with both hands [15]. To a chimpanzee, a stick can be a tool for collecting termites [16]. By Kirsh:

> "Agents "seed" the environment with attention-getting objects or structures. These can be harnessed to not only reduce perceived choice but to bias the order in which actions are undertaken ... Such features work because we have sufficient knowledge of our tasks and plans that when, in the course of activity, we notice these felicitous events, or surprises, we are reminded of aspects of our tasks that must be performed" [17].

The classic cognitive work on this is by Gibson on affordances and the use of contextual cues. The message here is "artifacts mean what their contexts permit" [15].

Context as described is not just something in the "mind" of a designer. The context of a drawing (a thing) is not a representation by the sketching designer (agent); it emerges from interactions between the designers, from what is currently on the drawing, from the sequence of sketch acts until now, and from other recent drawings that led to the currently attended one. It also emerges from that coffee that Mungo did not get this morning, from Boris noticing that the sun shining through that dirty window makes a nice pattern, from ...; that is, from influences of other entities on the agents, whether they are aware of them or not. Viewing context in these terms means viewing it as emerging from the aggregation of interacting entities that is ξ. The context is to do with entities in the environment that influence entities with which the agents interact.

Consider a transducer in a sensor as an example from a different domain. There may be many environmental influences and other effects that may not be in the model of the sensor but which nevertheless are part of the context of sensing the environment. Such effects were highlighted by Beer in his dynamical systems agent model [18]. They include effects of variations in temperature, pressure, viscosity etc.; limits and drifts in zero or sensitivity; invalid assumptions of linearity or similar, noise, interference, hysteresis or aliasing; use beyond designed limits; mechanical wear; and so on. The same idea goes for the CPU and the memory of the agent (temperature limits and nonlinearities, etc.) - all of these are influenced by the environment.

At the location and time at which Figure 2 was drawn there was a context that was of the system of interacting agents (designers) and non-agent things (paper, pens, and so on) that was that world at that time. For that set of designers at that particular time and location there was a context, but each designer had their own view of the situation and so their own interpretation of the context. So we come to a crucial consideration in our view: that there are contexts, there are situations, and there are interpretations of contexts.

The difference between situations and contexts are that a situation is a characteristic of a system of interacting agents and things but it does not exist without there being an agent present to interpret it. If I strike a tuning fork, waves of air pressure result. If I ping a sonar, waves of water pressure result. These are part of the context but neither of these waves are sounds. Sound requires a sensor (an ear or microphone) and perception, and interpreting sequences of sounds as music requires conceptual reasoning. Now agents are embodied in world(s) that they can only experience indirectly via sensors and effectors. That being so, it must be the agent that individuates what is in the environment and situations must be interpretations of an agent. Recognising that there is a situation is like recognising that there is music, and so requires an agent: situations are of the system but exist only within agents.

So there is a context, but as agents individuate what is in the environment, there is for each agent an interpreted context. An interpreted context is those representations whose designations depend on the situation. Notice that we distinguish the interpreted context of an agent from the situation for that agent. An interpreted context is something that the agent is involved in and is something of a passive notion. A situation is something that the agent is involved with and is something of an active notion. But what is this context? We could try to say something like "the context for agent a_i is all of those entities that influence the behaviour of a_i but that it is not necessarily aware of or is not focused on". The problem is that it is an agent that individuates what is in the environment so we prefer to talk of how the agent is coupled to its environment. We want a description of context that suits our constructive, situated notions of agency and that tends to notions of processes rather than to a reductionist enumeration of environmental objects and properties. The basis of our views on agency, memory and context are experiences.

Dewey described the quality of an experience as having two aspects called continuity and interaction:

> "The principle of continuity of experience means that every experience both takes up something from those which have gone before and modifies in some way the quality of those which come after" [19]

> "Experience does not simply go on inside a person. It does go on there ... but this is not the whole of the story. Every genuine experience has an

active side which changes in some degree the objective conditions under which experiences are had" [19]

An experience is only an experience if it is of an embodied agent. It is to do with interaction of the agent with an environment. An experience is also not something static; it is dynamic and is of certain kinds of entities that are coupled to their environment. A coupling between ξ and an agent-thing α_i is an e-experience (an exogenously generated experience) of $\mathfrak{a}_i$. An example is robot navigation experiences involving sonar sensual experiences and motion effectual experiences. Denote an experience of agent $\mathfrak{a}_i$ as e_i^k. An e-experience involves entities perturbing each other, where one of the entities is an α_i and the other is either another agent $\mathfrak{a}_j \neq \mathfrak{a}_i$ or a thing γ_m. A coupling in $\mathfrak{a}_i$ between the agent-thing α_i and agent constructs $\{\beta_i^j\}$ is an a-experience (an autogenously generated experience) of $\mathfrak{a}_i$. An a-experience also involves entities in an agent perturbing each other, where one of the entities is an α_i but where the others are constructs $\{\beta_i^j\}$.

For one experience to perturb another requires two things: that experiences can have parts that are themselves experiences, and that some experiences can be parts of multiple experiences. An experience that is a part of, but not identical to, another experience is a proper part. An experience with no proper parts is atomic. If the experience is temporally atomic but spatially not, we call it an event (Something spatially atomic but temporally not is an entity). Two experiences with one or more common parts are said to overlap. Experiences that perturb each other must overlap. Experiences are disjoint if they never overlap. An experience e^x is emergent[1] from experiences $\{e^y | y \neq x\}$ if:

- e^x is a part of the sum of $\{e^y | y \neq x\}$
- No part of e^x, including itself, is a part of any e^y (for $y \neq x$)

We write $e^x \sqsubseteq e^y$ to mean "experience e^x is a part of experience e^y". We write $e^x \sqsubset e^y$ to mean "experience e^x is a proper part of experience e^y". We write $e^x \bigcirc e^y$ to mean "experience e^x overlaps experience e^y". So

$$e^x \sqsubset e^y \mathrel{\widehat{=}} (e^x \sqsubseteq e^y \wedge e^x \neq e^y)$$
$$e^x \bigcirc e^y \mathrel{\widehat{=}} (\exists e^z \bullet e^z \sqsubseteq e^x \wedge e^z \sqsubseteq e^y)$$
$$perturbs(e^x, e^y) \implies e^x \bigcirc e^y$$

These relations can be generalised to processes in the manner of [20]. Let the type of experiences of $\mathfrak{a}_i$ be E_i such that $e_i^1, e_i^2, \ldots \in \mathsf{E}_i$. Let P be the type of processes of entities or processes emerging from interactions of entities. Given these, we say that a coupling of an e-experience of $\mathfrak{a}_i$ is where some part of an experience of $\mathfrak{a}_i$ overlaps a process not of $\mathfrak{a}_i$. Let $exp(\mathfrak{a}_i) \in \mathbb{P}\mathsf{E}$ find the experiences of agent $\mathfrak{a}_i$, where $\mathbb{P}$ denotes a power set. Let $is\_eexp(\mathfrak{a}_i, e_i)$ be true only if e_i

---

[1] This formulation of process emergence is derived from [20], where it is defined more precisely, as are the part-of and overlap relations.

is an e-experience of agent $\mathfrak{a}_i$, and let $is\_aexp(\mathfrak{a}_i, e_i)$ be true only if e_i is an a-experience of agent $\mathfrak{a}_i$.

$$is\_eexp(\mathfrak{a}_i, e_i) \iff \exists p \in \mathsf{P} \bullet p \notin exp(\mathfrak{a}_i) \wedge p \bigcirc e_i$$
$$is\_aexp(\mathfrak{a}_i, e_i) \iff e_i \in exp(\mathfrak{a}_i) \wedge \neg is\_eexp(\mathfrak{a}_i, e_i)$$

These e-experience overlaps may be of sensors (causally from the environment to the agent) or effectors (causally from the agent to the environment).

The notions of an agent at time t are its experiences restricted to that time. A trajectory is these $n \in \mathsf{N}_i$ changing over time. These notions are what an experience is if we fixate it at a particular time $t \in \tau$. The fixation is a function from E_i onto a subspace that has meaning to the agent. We use the word "notion" to maintain independence from any particular kind of agent representation. Any subset of N is a notion, including $\emptyset$ and N_i itself, as is the intersection of two notions, and a notion may itself contain other notions.

We are now in a position to say what we believe context to be. Let $path(e, p)$ be true only if there is from e to p a sequence of overlapping experiences and processes. Then the context is

$$context = \bigcup_{i \in agents} context(\mathfrak{a}_i)$$
$$context(\mathfrak{a}_i) = \{e : \mathsf{E}_i; p : \mathsf{P} \mid e \in exp(\mathfrak{a}_i) \wedge path(e, p) \bullet p\}$$

Sensing and effecting processes of things and other agents are parts of e-experiences, and interpreting sketch processes (such as of ink on paper) as depicted objects are parts of a-experiences. These processes and experiences are part of the context of the interaction of an agent with its environment.

The situation current at a time is an influence on how the world is viewed and so will direct the attention of the agent to some of the interpretations in the a-experiences of that time. Notice that the situation is not "a view of the world"; it is a process that changes how the world gets viewed. Let a target experience be that experience if the role of the situation is ignored, and call it $e_i^{k\emptyset}$ (the un-situated experience). The experience e_i^k is the target experience after the influence of the situation with respect to one or more other experiences are included. That is, in this document an experience is situated unless it is explicitly denoted otherwise such as in $e_i^{k\emptyset}$. The type of situations is Ψ such that $\psi_i^1, \psi_i^2, \ldots \in \Psi_i$. The type of experiences of $\mathfrak{a}_i$ is E, so situations Ψ_i are functions from notions N_i and experience E_i to a result that is also a E_i.

$$\Psi_i : \mathsf{N}_i \to \mathsf{E}_i \to \mathsf{E}_i$$

The current situation as seen by an experience $e_i^{k\emptyset}$ is one or more functions Ψ that each use another experience to influence this one.

Given these we say that background context is that part of context that is not selective by an agent. Selective context is those situated a-experiences that the agent is attending to. Without going into more detail here we just say that it is some of those a-experiences that depend on the situation for their values. For agent $\mathfrak{a}_i$,

$$selective(\mathfrak{a}_i) \subseteq \{e_1, e_2 : \mathsf{E}_i; n : \mathsf{N}_i$$
$$| \; (\exists \psi \bullet e_1 \in exp(\mathfrak{a}_i) \wedge e_2 = \psi(n, e_1) \wedge is_a exp(\mathfrak{a}_i, e_2))$$
$$\bullet \; e_2\}$$
$$background(\mathfrak{a}_i) = context(\mathfrak{a}_i) - selective(\mathfrak{a}_i)$$
$$interpcontext(\mathfrak{a}_i) =$$
$$\{e : \mathsf{E}_i \; | \; is\_aexp(\mathfrak{a}_i, e) \bullet e\} \cap (selective(\mathfrak{a}_i) \cup background(\mathfrak{a}_i))$$

Akman and Surav [2], quoted earlier, are two of a number of researchers seeking to formalise ideas like context in terms of the "situations" of Situation Theory. That theory has some notions that we find to be appealing, such as that an environment is individuated by an agent into objects on the basis of perceived uniformities. An object is a uniformity across situations, where a uniformity is a locally predictive coherence [21]. However that which situation-theorists call a "situation" we regard as a mathematical entity along the lines of McCarthy's "context". Perhaps it should be given another name along the lines of "fluent". Situation-theorists like Barwise [22] and Devlin [23] tend to be realists: there is a "real world" that agents are situated in, that world is objectively a certain way, and a situation theory expression is a description of how that world actually is.

> "Situations are parts of the world and the information an agent has about a given situation at any moment will be just a part of all the information that is theoretically available ... situations are taken to be real, actual parts of the world, and the basic properties and relations the situation semantics deals with are taken to be real uniformities across situations (and not bits of language, ideas, sets of n-tuples, functions, or some other mathematical abstractions)" [23].

This idea that situations are actual parts of the world is one that we do not accept. To us a situation is something constructed by an agent, and a context is something that emerges from the aggregation of agents and things that is the environment but that which agents have no direct access to. We do not accept a Situation Theory notion of "situation", neither do we accept a Situation Theory notion of "context".

3   Experiences and Interpreted Contexts

For descriptive purposes we build this section around an invented design scenario inspired by our past experiences (such as [24]) with protocol sessions involving real designers and by Figure 2. The reason for inventing a scenario is that the size and complexity of a real scenario would obscure what is important in these descriptions. In this section, descriptions of the scenario are disguised *by this font*.

There are two designers collaborating on a design task. The brief is for the design of buildings and other artifacts on a site at a university campus that is to be publicly accessible. The functions required of these artifacts are disparate but broadly divide in two groups, so the groups should be differentiated some how. An overall sense of unity and place is required despite how disparate the artifacts composing it may seem.

There are two designers, and we model designers as agents, so there are at least two agents that we can denote as $\mathfrak{a}_1$ and $\mathfrak{a}_2$.

One designer is sketching, of which Figure 2 is the most recent drawing. Both designers are communicating verbally. Both designers are communicating non-verbally by looking and at the sketches and gesturing.

Apart from $\mathfrak{a}_1$ and $\mathfrak{a}_2$, ξ contains things. Among these things are the sketches $\{\gamma_s^k\}$ and a pen γ_p. We only need consider one world for this scenario, which we denote ω_o for "the world that contains the office".

$$\{\mathfrak{a}_1, \mathfrak{a}_2, \gamma_p, \gamma_s^1 \ldots \gamma_s^k\} \subseteq \omega_o \subseteq \xi$$

Let γ_s^k be the last of these sketches to have been drawn and let it be as shown as Figure 3.

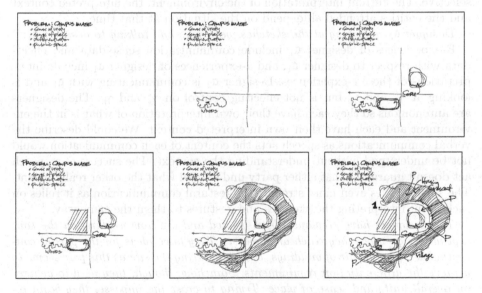

Fig. 3. Thing γ_s^k shown as six frames of the process of sketching that led to Figure 2. The sequence is of time increasing left-to-right starting from the top-left.

Designer $\mathfrak{a}_1$ is sketching on γ_s^k and so controls the depiction of text and non-text signifiers on that drawing.

Providing that $\mathfrak{a}_1$ isn't sketching randomly, $\mathfrak{a}_1$ must be both reasoning and interacting with γ_p and γ_s^k. The agent is experiencing this interaction and reasoning. Designer $\mathfrak{a}_1$ looks at the drawing and at the tip of the pen as they sketch. So there are sensor couplings (process overlaps) from both pen and paper processes to e-experiences, and there are effector couplings from e-experiences to pen-processes. Consider the fourth frame of Figure 3. At that time there are a number of processes that overlap the visual sensor e-experiences of $\mathfrak{a}_1$: processes of the paper, the pen, the existing ink on paper (third frame), the new ink on paper and so on. This includes processes that clearly are attributable to particular things as well as well as emergent processes; the same applies to experiences. The sketched characters "woods" and the corresponding shape that appears at the second frame are example processes or parts of processes of γ_s^k. There are also processes that overlap the effector e-experiences controlling γ_p. Further, other less obvious processes influence the behaviour of the paper, pen and designer, and other even less obvious processes influence these in turn. Sensing and effecting these processes are part of an e-experience, and interpreting them as depicted objects are parts of a-experiences. These processes and experiences are part of the context of this interaction, distinct from the processes of "woods" noted above. The situation current at the time of the fourth frame will direct the attention of the agent at that time to some of the interpretations in the a-experiences of that time. These are the selective interest $selective(\mathfrak{a}_1)$, and the background is those processes and experiences of $context(\mathfrak{a}_1)$ that are not selective. The current interpretation of the environment, the interpreted context and the entities attended all depend on the situation at that time.

Designer $\mathfrak{a}_2$ is looking at the sketches, gesturing and talking to designer $\mathfrak{a}_1$.

E-experiences of designer $\mathfrak{a}_1$ include communication sense-data and effect-data with respect to designer $\mathfrak{a}_1$, and a-experiences of designer $\mathfrak{a}_1$ include interpretations of these e-experiences. Designer $\mathfrak{a}_2$ is communicating with $\mathfrak{a}_1$ and is looking at γ_s^k and γ_p but is not effecting control on γ_s^k and γ_p. The designers are autonomous so they each have their own interpretation of what is in the environment and each have their own interpreted context. We could describe the verbal communications as speech acts the content of each communication would not be understood without understanding the context. The success of a speech act doesn't guarantee that either party understood what the other really meant. The same applies even more strongly for gestural communication as it relies on each agent interpreting the sketches and gestures to them the same way.

The designers have previously been briefed and are now working on the conceptual design when they reach an impasse. They have ideas for the partial conceptual design of a pair of buildings, and structuring the site as this pair seems to achieve the differentiation requirements. Somehow, though, they need to achieve an overall unity and sense of place. Trying to cross the impasse, they begin reframing.

Reframing is one of the techniques used in creative designing when an impasse is reached. One important way of reframing is suggesting and following alternative metaphors for a situation [15]. A-experiences of the designers are constructed "on the fly in a situated way" [24]. Applied to the reframing example, this is

– partly bottom-up as a sketching designer thinking with pen and paper, and
– partly top-down by recognising a change in the current situation by shifting an analogy or metaphor.

This works by suggesting and following up different analogies and alternative metaphors for a situation. The case of Figure 2 is applying a visual metaphor. A metaphor change may be a case trying to re-interpret an entity using different concepts but sketching and perception are situated, interactive processes that these visual metaphors rely on. Visual metaphors are subjective and rely on the interpretation of the viewer in the current situation. They are not objective, observer-independent interpretations [15]. a_2 may suggest the double yolk egg metaphor and a_1 may sketch it but that doesn't guarantee that they understand either the suggestion or the sketch the same way. Further, if the site being designed was built it would be its visitors that judged the meaning of the built artifacts. The visitors may or may not be aware of the metaphor; indeed, the designers may or may not prefer it that way.

> "Designers may well convince themselves that they have "found" a metaphor, but it may well mean nothing to users unless it brings familiarity to the design" [15].

Perhaps a_1 and a_2 want it to look that way, or perhaps the metaphor was just a device to bridge the impasse.

Designer a_1 notices in the sketch (Figure 3 frame 3) a pair of similar cores surrounded by "whitespace", and that triggers a different way of thinking about core/yolk and whitespace/white.

Work by Suwa et al. [24] shows that unexpected visuo-spatial discoveries and cues can trigger different interpretations of the functions supported by a design. Expressing the designer protocols of Suwa in our terms, we could say that there are four kinds of experiences:

1. Physical experiences: e-experiences perturbed by external processes or a-experiences; approximate Suwa's physical actions such as depicting shapes, looking at previous depictions, gestures and movements of the pen.
2. Perceptual experiences: e-experiences perturbed by e-experiences; approximate Suwa's perceptual actions such as attending to spatial relations and comparing depicted elements.
3. Functional experiences: a-experiences; approximate Suwa's functional actions such as exploring design issues between artifacts and considering the psychological reactions of people. They may be perturbed by physical experiences or by perceptual experiences.
4. Conceptual experiences: a-experiences; approximate Suwa's conceptual actions making aesthetic evaluations, setting goals and recalling knowledge.

Knowledge, strategies and goals sometimes trigger design actions, but physical or perceptual actions also trigger design actions.

As designers a_1 and a_2 looking at, gesturing and sketch on γ_s^k they interpret the world w_o of γ_p and γ_s^k whilst concurrently imagining a world w_o' that is yet to exist.

Designing as an activity is more complex than sketching a representation of existing artifacts because the sketching designer must imagine a world that is yet to exist. There is, as described, the world ω_o containing $\mathfrak{a}_1, \mathfrak{a}_2, \gamma_p, \gamma_s^k$ and so on. There is a context with respect to ω_o as well as an interpreted context of each designer. There are also, for each designer, one or more imagined worlds. Further, if the designers are collaborating across space or time in our world there may be an additional virtual world.

What is imagined depends on the situation and each designer interprets γ_s^k as a building site with existing buildings, the woods, the shape of the crescent for the housing, etc. according to their interpretation of the current metaphor and context. Some of this interpretation is of those a-experiences that are what the agent is currently attending to, and so the agent's selective interest depend on the situation and changes over time.

4   Conclusion

The use of context by many that study linguistics and AI is impoverished compared to the notions needed to describe activities like designing. Such formalisms tend to mean much less by "context" than less formal, common sense descriptions would indicate. Some mean much more by context but, in our view, often conflate contexts with situations by describing the benefits of situated action and reasoning but by then labelling this as context. Our view follow from work on understanding designers and design agents. These are interesting not only because of their potential for developing systems and tools for designers but also because designing is notoriously difficult to describe in cognitive or AI terms. Our view is that context is bigger than any one agents representation of it, and that when agents reason contextually it is the situation that determines what interpretations of context are and not the reverse. A situation is a rich set of ideas and an interpreted context is the lesser by comparison.

Acknowledgements

This research is funded by the Australian Research Council, grant number DP0559885. Also thanks to Owen MacIndoe for discussions and feedback.

References

1. Boden, M.A.: The intellectual context of artificial life. In: Boden, M.A. (ed.) The Philosophy of Artificial Life, pp. 1–35. Oxford University Press, Oxford (1996)
2. Akman, V., Surav, M.: The use of situation theory in context modeling. Computational Intelligence 13(3), 427–438 (1997)
3. Benerecetti, M., Bouquet, P., Ghidini, C.: Contextual reasoning distilled. Journal of Experimental and Theoretical Artificial Intelligence 12, 279–305 (2000)
4. Margolin, V.: Design Discourse: History, Theory, Criticism. University of Chicago Press (1986)
5. Gero, J.S.: Towards a model of designing which includes its situatedness. In: Grabowski, H., Rude, S., Grein, G. (eds.) Universal Design Theory, pp. 47–55. Shaker Verlag (1998)

6. Schön, D.A., Wiggins, D.: Kinds of seeing and their functions in designing. Design Studies 13(2), 135–156 (1992)
7. McCarthy, J.: Notes on formalizing contexts. In: Kehler, T., Rosenschein, S. (eds.) Proceedings of the Fifth National Conference on Artificial Intelligence, Los Altos, California, pp. 555–560. Morgan Kaufmann, San Francisco (1986)
8. Perry, J.: Indexicals and demonstratives. In: Hale, R., Wright, C. (eds.) Companion to the Philosophy of Language, Blackwell, Oxford (1997)
9. Derrida, J.: Signature event context. In: Kamuf, P. (ed.) A Derrida Reader, pp. 82–111. Columbia University Press (1991)
10. Dewey, J.: Context and thought. University of California Publications in Philosophy 12(3), (1931) Reprinted in John Dewey: The Later Works, 1929–1953, vol. 6: 1931–1932, Southern Illinois University, pp. 3–21 (1984)
11. Ekbia, H.R., Maguitman, A.G.: Context and relevance: A pragmatic approach. In: Akman, V., Bouquet, P., Thomason, R.H., Young, R.A. (eds.) CONTEXT 2001. LNCS (LNAI), vol. 2116, pp. 156–169. Springer, Heidelberg (2001)
12. Lawson, B.: How Designers Think: The Design Process Demystified, 4th edn. Architectural Press (2006)
13. Lawson, B.: Design in Mind. Butterworth - Heinemann (1994)
14. Laseau, P.: Graphic Thinking for Architects and Designers, 2nd edn. John Wiley and Sons, Chichester (2001)
15. Krippendorff, K.: The Semantic Turn: A New Foundation For Design. Taylor and Francis, Abington (2006)
16. The Science Show: Jane Goodall and chimpanzees. ABC Radio National (January 13, 2007), http://www.abc.net.au/rn/scienceshow/stories/2007/1810596.htm
17. Kirsh, D.: The intelligent use of space. Artificial Intelligence 73, 31–68 (1995)
18. Beer, R.D.: A dynamical systems perspective on agent-environment interaction. Artificial Intelligence 72, 173–215 (1995)
19. Dewey, J.: Experience and Education. Collier (1938) (Reprinted in 1963)
20. Seibt, J.: Free process theory: Towards a typology of occurrings. Axiomathes 14, 23–55 (2004)
21. Seligman, J.: Perspectives in situation theory. In: Cooper, R., (ed.) Situation Theory and Its Applications. Stanford University, pp. 147–191 (1990)
22. Barwise, J.: The Situation in Logic. CSLI (1989)
23. Devlin, K.: Situation theory and situation semantics. In: Gabbay, D.M., Woods, J. (eds.) Handbook of the History of Logic. Logic and the Modalities in the Twentieth Century, vol. 6, pp. 601–664. Elsevier, Amsterdam (2006)
24. Suwa, M., Purcell, T., Gero, J.S.: Macroscopic analysis of design processes based on a scheme for coding designers' cognitive actions. Design Studies 19, 455–483 (1998)

On Relating Heterogeneous Elements from Different Ontologies

Chiara Ghidini[1], Luciano Serafini[1], and Sergio Tessaris[2]

[1] FBK-irst. Via Sommarive 18 Povo, 38050,Trento, Italy
[2] Free University of Bozen - Bolzano. Piazza Domenicani 3. 39100 Bolzano, Italy
ghidini@itc.it, serafini@itc.it, tessaris@inf.unibz.it

Abstract. In the extensive usage of ontologies envisaged by the Semantic Web there is a compelling need for expressing mappings between different elements of heterogeneous ontologies. State of the art languages for ontology mapping enable to express semantic relations between homogeneous components of different ontologies; namely, they allow to map concepts into concepts, individuals into individuals, and properties into properties. In many real world cases this is not enough; for example when relations in an ontology correspond to a class in another ontology (i.e. reification of relations). To support this kind of interoperability we need therefore richer mapping languages, offering constructs for the representation of *heterogeneous mappings*. In this paper, we propose an extension of Distributed Description Logics (DDL) with mappings between concepts and relations. We provide a semantics of the proposed extension and sound and complete characterisation of the effects of these mappings in terms of the new ontological knowledge they entail.

1 Introduction

Most of the formalisms for distributed ontology integration based on the p2p architecture provide a language (hereafter called *mapping language*) able to express semantic relations between concepts belonging to different ontologies. These formalisms can express that a concept C in Ontology 1 is equivalent (less general than, more general than) a concept D in Ontology 2 (see [15] for a survey). Few mapping languages allow also to express semantic relations between properties in different ontologies [9,10,4], and thus state that a relation R in Ontology 1 is equivalent (less general than, more general than) a relation S in Ontology 2. These type of mappings are able to cope a large, but not the totality of the heterogeneity between ontologies.

Assume, for instance, that a knowledge engineer builds an ontology of family unions containing the binary relations `marriedWith` and `partnerOf` between two persons. Suppose also that a second ontology engineer, asked to design a ontology for the same purpose, declares a concept `Marriage`, whose instances are the actual civil or religious marriages and the concept `civilUnion`, whose instances are all the civil unions. We can easily see that while the first ontology prefers to model unions as relations, the second represents them as concepts.

B. Kokinov et al. (Eds.): CONTEXT 2007, LNAI 4635, pp. 234–247, 2007.
© Springer-Verlag Berlin Heidelberg 2007

Despite this difference of style in modelling, the concept `Marriage` and the relation `marriedWith` represent the same (or a very similar) real world aspect, and similarly with `partnerOf` and `civilUnion`. For instance, we can expect that for all married couples in the first ontology, there is a corresponding marriage element in the second ontology, and similarly for the civil unions. To reconcile the semantic difference between the two heterogeneous representations we need a mapping language that allows to map concept of one ontology to relations of another ontology.

Motivated by these observations, Ghidini and Serafini have illustrated in [11] the need of expressive mapping languages that must incorporate not only *homogeneous mappings*, that is mappings between concepts and mappings between relations of different ontologies, but also *heterogeneous mappings*, that is mappings between concepts and relations in the sense illustrated above. They present a preliminary investigation on how to define such expressive mapping language in the framework of Distributed Description Logics (DDL) [14], a refinement of the multi-context logic presented in [8,9] to the DL-based framework for the formal representation of ontology, but they do not go beyond preliminary statements and definitions, especially in the case of heterogeneous mappings. In [10] the authors take a step forward and present a proposal and an algorithm for the representation and reasoning with *homogeneous mappings*. In this paper we continue this stream of work by addressing the more complex task of representing and reasoning with *heterogeneous mappings* (as well as *homogeneous mappings*) which represent a specific relation between heterogeneous ontologies, namely the correspondence between a concept and a relation. Thus the goals of this paper are: (i) to extend the framework of DDL, introducing mechanisms for the representation of *heterogeneous mappings* between different ontologies, (ii) to define a clear semantics for the proposed mapping language, and (iii) to investigate the logical properties of the proposed mapping language.

2   A Rich Language for Mappings

Description Logic (DL) has been advocated as the suitable formal tool to represent and reason about ontologies. Distributed Description Logic (DDL) [14] is a *natural* generalisation of the DL framework designed to formalise multiple ontologies *pairwise* linked by semantic mappings. In DDL, ontologies correspond to description logic theories (T-boxes), while semantic mappings correspond to collections of *bridge rules* ($\mathfrak{B}$).

In the following we recall the basic definitions of DDL as defined in [14,11], and we provide a new semantics for heterogeneous mappings.

2.1   Distributed Description Logics: The Syntax

Given a non empty set I of indexes, used to identify ontologies, let $\{\mathcal{DL}_i\}_{i \in I}$ be a collection of description logics[1]. For each $i \in I$ let us denote a T-box of

---

[1] We assume familiarity with Description Logic and related reasoning systems, described in [1].

$\mathcal{DL}_i$ as $\mathcal{T}_i$. In this paper, we assume that each $\mathcal{DL}_i$ is description logic weaker or at most equivalent to $\mathcal{ALCQI}_b$, which corresponds to $\mathcal{ALCQI}$ with role union, conjunction and difference (see [17]). Because of lack of space, we omit the precise description of $\mathcal{ALCQI}_b$, and we assume that the reader is familiar with DDL as described in [14].

We call $\mathbf{T} = \{\mathcal{T}_i\}_{i \in I}$ a family of T-Boxes indexed by I. Intuitively, $\mathcal{T}_i$ is the description logic formalization of the i-th ontology. To make every description distinct, we will prefix it with the index of ontology it belongs to. For instance, the concept C that occurs in the i-th ontology is denoted as $i : C$. Similarly, $i : C \sqsubseteq D$ denotes the fact that the axiom $C \sqsubseteq D$ is being considered in the i-th ontology.

Semantic mappings between different ontologies are expressed via collections of *bridge rules*. In the following we use A, B, C and D as place-holders for concepts and R, S, P and Q as place-holders for roles. We instead use X and Y to denote both concepts and roles.

Definition 1 (Homogeneous Bridge rules). *An homogeneous bridge rule from i to j is an expression defined as follows:*

$$i : X \xrightarrow{\sqsubseteq} j : Y \qquad \text{(into bridge rule)} \qquad (1)$$

$$i : X \xrightarrow{\sqsupseteq} j : Y \qquad \text{(onto bridge rule)} \qquad (2)$$

where X and Y are either concepts of $\mathcal{DL}_i$ and $\mathcal{DL}_j$ respectively, or roles of $\mathcal{DL}_i$ and $\mathcal{DL}_j$ respectively.

Bridge rules do not represent semantic relations stated from an external *objective* point of view. Indeed, there is no such global view in the web. Instead, bridge rules from i to j express relations between i and j viewed from the *subjective* point of view of the j-th ontology.

Bridge rules (1) and (2) with X and Y instantiated as concepts have been studied in [14]. Hereafter we will call them *concept-into-concept* and *concept-onto-concept* bridge rules. The concept-into-concept bridge rule $i : X \xrightarrow{\sqsubseteq} j : Y$ states that, from the j-th point of view the concept X in i is less general than its local concept Y. Similarly, the concept-onto-concept bridge rule $i : X \xrightarrow{\sqsupseteq} j : Y$ expresses the fact that, according to j, X in i is more general than Y in j. Therefore, bridge rules from i to j provide the possibility of translating into j's ontology (under some approximation) the concepts of a foreign i's ontology. Note, that since bridge rules reflect a subjective point of view, bridge rules from j to i are not necessarily the inverse of the rules from i to j, and in fact bridge rules from i to j do not force the existence of bridge rules in the opposite direction. Thus, the bridge rule

$$i : \mathsf{Article} \xrightarrow{\sqsupseteq} j : \mathsf{ConferencePaper}$$

expresses the fact that, according to ontology j, the concept $\mathsf{Article}$ in ontology i is more general than its local concept $\mathsf{ConferencePapers}$, while

$$i : \mathsf{Article} \xrightarrow{\sqsubseteq} j : \mathsf{Article} \qquad\qquad i : \mathsf{Article} \xrightarrow{\sqsupseteq} j : \mathsf{Article}$$

say that, according to ontology j, the concept Article in ontology j is equivalent to its local concept Article. Bridge rules (1) and (2) instantiated as bridge rules between roles (hereafter *role-into-role* and *role-onto-role* bridge rules) formalize the analogous intuition for roles. For example, the bridge rule:

$$i : \texttt{marriedInChurchWith} \xrightarrow{\ \sqsubseteq\ } j : \texttt{marriedWith}$$

says that according to ontology j, the relation $\texttt{marriedInChurchWith}$ in ontology i is less general than its own relation $\texttt{marriedWith}$.

Definition 2 (Heterogeneous bridge rule). *An heterogeneous bridge rule from i to j is an expression defined as follows:*

$$i : R \xrightarrow{\ \sqsubseteq\ } j : C \qquad \text{(role-into-concept bridge rule)} \qquad (3)$$

$$i : R \xrightarrow{\ \sqsupseteq\ } j : C \qquad \text{(role-onto-concept bridge rule)} \qquad (4)$$

$$i : C \xrightarrow{\ \sqsubseteq\ } j : R \qquad \text{(concept-into-role bridge rule)} \qquad (5)$$

$$i : C \xrightarrow{\ \sqsupseteq\ } j : R \qquad \text{(concept-onto-role bridge rule)} \qquad (6)$$

where R is a role and C is a concept.

Bridge rules (3) and (4) state that, from the j-th point of view the role R in i is less general, resp. more general, than its local concept C. Similarly, bridge rules (5) and (6) state that, from the j-th point of view the concept C in i is less general, resp. more general, than its local role R. Thus, the bridge rule

$$i : \texttt{marriedInChurchWith} \xrightarrow{\ \sqsubseteq\ } j : \texttt{Marriage}$$

expresses the fact that, according to ontology j, the relation $\texttt{marriedInChurchWith}$ in ontology i is less general than its local concept $\texttt{Marriage}$, while

$$i : \texttt{civilUnion} \xrightarrow{\ \sqsubseteq\ } j : \texttt{partnerOf}$$
$$i : \texttt{civilUnion} \xrightarrow{\ \sqsupseteq\ } j : \texttt{partnerOf}$$

say that, according to ontology j, the concept $\texttt{civilUnion}$ in ontology j is equivalent to its local relation $\texttt{partnerOf}$.

Definition 3 (Distributed T-box). *A distributed T-box (DTB) $\mathfrak{T} = \langle \{\mathcal{T}_i\}_{i \in I}, \mathfrak{B} \rangle$ consists of a collection $\{\mathcal{T}_i\}_{i \in I}$ of T-boxes, and a collection $\mathfrak{B} = \{\mathfrak{B}_{ij}\}_{i \neq j \in I}$ of bridge rules between them.*

2.2   Distributed Description Logics: The Semantics

The semantic of DDL, which is a refinement of Local Models Semantics [8,9], assigns to each ontology $\mathcal{T}_i$ a *local interpretation domain*. The first component of an interpretation of a DTB is a family of interpretations $\{\mathcal{I}_i\}_{i \in I}$, one for each T-box $\mathcal{T}_i$. Each $\mathcal{I}_i$ is called a *local interpretation* and consists of a *possibly empty* domain $\Delta^{\mathcal{I}_i}$ and a valuation function $\cdot^{\mathcal{I}_i}$, which maps every concept to a subset of $\Delta^{\mathcal{I}_i}$, and every role to a subset of $\Delta^{\mathcal{I}_i} \times \Delta^{\mathcal{I}_i}$. The interpretation on the empty domain is used to provide a semantics for distributed T-boxes in which some of the local T-boxes are inconsistent. We do not describe this aspect of DDL further. The interested reader can refer to [14].

The second component of the DDL semantics are families of domain relations. Domain relations define how the different T-box interact and are necessary to define the satisfiability of bridge rules.

Definition 4 (Domain relation). *A* domain relation r_{ij} *from i to j is a subset of $\Delta^{\mathcal{I}_i} \times \Delta^{\mathcal{I}_j}$. We use $r_{ij}(d)$ to denote $\{d' \in \Delta^{\mathcal{I}_j} \mid \langle d, d' \rangle \in r_{ij}\}$; for any subset D of $\Delta^{\mathcal{I}_i}$, we use $r_{ij}(D)$ to denote $\bigcup_{d \in D} r_{ij}(d)$; for any $R \subseteq \Delta^{\mathcal{I}_i} \times \Delta^{\mathcal{I}_i}$ we use $r_{ij}(R)$ to denote $\bigcup_{\langle d,d' \rangle \in R} r_{ij}(d) \times r_{ij}(d')$.*

A domain relation r_{ij} represents a possible way of mapping the elements of $\Delta^{\mathcal{I}_i}$ into its domain $\Delta^{\mathcal{I}_j}$, seen from j's perspective. For instance, if $\Delta^{\mathcal{I}_1}$ and $\Delta^{\mathcal{I}_2}$ are the representation of time as Rationals and as Naturals, r_{ij} could be the round off function, or some other approximation relation. This function has to be conservative w.r.t., the order relations defined on Rationals and Naturals. Domain relation is used to interpret homogeneous bridge rules according with the following definition.

Definition 5 (Satisfiability of homogeneous bridge rules). *The domain relation r_{ij} satisfies a homogeneous bridge rule w.r.t., $\mathcal{I}_i$ and $\mathcal{I}_j$, in symbols $\langle \mathcal{I}_i, r_{ij}, \mathcal{I}_j \rangle \models br$, according with the following definition:*

1. $\langle \mathcal{I}_i, r_{ij}, \mathcal{I}_j \rangle \models i : X \xrightarrow{\sqsubseteq} j : Y$, *if* $r_{ij}(X^{\mathcal{I}_i}) \subseteq Y^{\mathcal{I}_j}$
2. $\langle \mathcal{I}_i, r_{ij}, \mathcal{I}_j \rangle \models i : X \xrightarrow{\sqsupseteq} j : Y$, *if* $r_{ij}(X^{\mathcal{I}_i}) \supseteq Y^{\mathcal{I}_j}$

where X and Y are either two concepts or two roles.

Domain relations do not provide sufficient information to evaluate the satisfiability of heterogeneous mappings. Intuitively, an heterogeneous bridge rule between a relation R and a concept C connects a pair of objects related by R with an object which is in C. This suggests that, to evaluate heterogeneous bridge rules from roles in i to concepts in j we need a relation that maps triples of the form $\langle object\_1, relation\_name, object\_2 \rangle$ from ontology i into objects of $\Delta^{\mathcal{I}_j}$. As an example we would like to map a triple $\langle \texttt{John}, \texttt{marriedWith}, \texttt{Mary} \rangle$ of elements from the first ontology into the marriage $\texttt{m123}$ of the second ontology, with the intuitive meaning that $\texttt{m123}$ is the marriage which correspond to the married couple composed of $\texttt{John}$ and $\texttt{Mary}$. We first formally introduce the triples $\langle object\_1, relation\_name, object\_2 \rangle$ for a given ontology i.

Definition 6 (Admissible Triples). *Let $\mathcal{I}_i$ be a local interpretation $\langle \Delta^{\mathcal{I}_i}, \cdot^{\mathcal{I}_i} \rangle$ for $\mathcal{DL}_i$. Let $\mathcal{R}$ be the set of all atomic relations relations of $\mathcal{DL}_i$. We indicate with $\Sigma^{\mathcal{I}_i}$ the set of all triples $\langle x_1, X, x_2 \rangle$ such that $x_1, x_2 \in \Delta^{\mathcal{I}_i}$; $X \in \mathcal{R}$; and $(x_1, x_2) \in X^{\mathcal{I}_i}$.*

Intuitively, $\langle \texttt{John}, \texttt{marriedWith}, \texttt{Mary} \rangle$ is an admissible triple in $\Sigma^{\mathcal{I}_i}$ if $\texttt{John}$ is married with $\texttt{Mary}$, or more formally if the pair $(\texttt{John}, \texttt{Mary})$ belongs to the interpretation of $\texttt{marriedWith}$ in $\mathcal{I}_i$.

Definition 7 (Concept-role and role-concept domain relation). *A concept-role domain relation cr_{ij} from i to j is a subset of $\Delta^{\mathcal{I}_i} \times \Sigma^{\mathcal{I}_j}$. A role-concept domain relation rc_{ij} from i to j is a subset of $\Sigma^{\mathcal{I}_i} \times \Delta^{\mathcal{I}_j}$.*

The domain relation rc_{ij} represents a possible way of mapping pairs of $R^{\mathcal{I}_i}$ into elements of $\Delta^{\mathcal{I}_j}$, seen from j's perspective. For instance,

$$(\langle \texttt{John}, \texttt{marriedWith}, \texttt{Mary} \rangle, \texttt{m123}) \in cr_{ij} \tag{7}$$

represents the fact that $\texttt{m123}$ is an object in ontology j corresponding to the marriage between $\texttt{John}$ and $\texttt{Mary}$ in ontology i, while

$$(\langle \texttt{John}, \texttt{dancePartnerOf}, \texttt{Mary} \rangle, \texttt{couple124}) \in cr_{ij} \tag{8}$$

represents the fact that $\texttt{couple124}$ is an object in ontology j corresponding to the pair of dancers composed of $\texttt{John}$ and $\texttt{Mary}$ (e.g., used to record results for dance competitions). This example emphasises one of the main characteristics of the concept-role and role-concept domain relations, that is the possibility for the same pair of objects in an ontology to correspond to different elements in another ontology because they belong to different relations. As shown in the example above we want to be able to "reify" the fact that $\texttt{John}$ is married with $\texttt{Mary}$ in the element $\texttt{m123}$, and the fact that $\texttt{John}$ dances with $\texttt{Mary}$ in the different object $\texttt{couple124}$.

Definition 8 (Satisfiability of heterogeneous bridge rules). *The role-concept domain relation rc_{ij} satisfies a role-(into/onto)-concept bridge rule w.r.t., $\mathcal{I}_i$ and $\mathcal{I}_j$, in symbols $\langle \mathcal{I}_i, rc_{ij}, \mathcal{I}_j \rangle \models br$, according with the following definition:*

1. $(\mathcal{I}_i, rc_{ij}, \mathcal{I}_j) \models i : R \xrightarrow{\sqsubseteq} j : C$ *if for all $(x_1, x_2) \in R^{\mathcal{I}_i}$ and for all pairs $((x_1, X, x_2), x) \in rc_{ij}$ with $X^{\mathcal{I}_i} \subseteq R^{\mathcal{I}_i}$, we have that $x \in C^{\mathcal{I}_j}$*

2. $(\mathcal{I}_i, rc_{ij}, \mathcal{I}_j) \models i : R \xrightarrow{\sqsupseteq} j : C$ *if for all $x \in C^{\mathcal{I}_j}$ there is a pair $((x_1, X, x_2), x) \in rc_{ij}$, such that $X^{\mathcal{I}_i} \subseteq R^{\mathcal{I}_i}$.*

The concept-role domain relation cr_{ij} satisfies a concept-(into/onto)-role bridge rule w.r.t., $\mathcal{I}_i$ and $\mathcal{I}_j$, in symbols $\langle \mathcal{I}_i, cr_{ij}, \mathcal{I}_j \rangle \models br$, according with the following definition:

3. $(\mathcal{I}_i, cr_{ij}, \mathcal{I}_j) \models i : C \xrightarrow{\sqsubseteq} j : R$ *if for all $x \in C^{\mathcal{I}_i}$, and for all pairs $(x, \langle x_1, X, x_2 \rangle) \in cr_{ij}$, it is true that $X^{\mathcal{I}_j} \subseteq R^{\mathcal{I}_j}$;*

4. $(\mathcal{I}_i, cr_{ij}, \mathcal{I}_j) \models i : C \xrightarrow{\sqsupseteq} j : R$ *if for all $(x_1, x_2) \in R^{\mathcal{I}_j}$ there is a pair $(x, \langle x_1, X, x_2 \rangle) \in cr_{ij}$, such that $X^{\mathcal{I}_j} \subseteq R^{\mathcal{I}_j}$ and $x \in C^{\mathcal{I}_i}$.*

Satisfiability of a role-into-concept bridge rule forces the role-concept domain relation cr_{ij} to map pair of elements (x_1, x_2) which belong to $R^{\mathcal{I}_i}$ into elements

x in $C^{\mathcal{I}_j}$. Note that, from the definition of role-concept domain relation two arbitrary objects y_1 and y_2 could occur in a pair $(\langle y_1, X, y_2 \rangle, y)$ with X different from R itself but such that $X^{\mathcal{I}_i} \subseteq R^{\mathcal{I}_i}$, Thus also this pair (y_1, y_2) belongs to $R^{\mathcal{I}_i}$ and we have to force also y to be in $C^{\mathcal{I}_j}$. In other words, we can say that satisfiability of a role-into-concept bridge rule forces the role-concept domain relation to map pairs of elements (x_1, x_2) which belong to R, or to any of its subroles X, into elements x in $C^{\mathcal{I}_i}$.

Consider the bridge rule

$$i : \mathtt{marriedWith} \xrightarrow{\ \sqsubseteq\ } j : \mathtt{Marriage} \tag{9}$$

Let (John, Mary) and (Philip,Joanna) be two married couples such that $\mathcal{I}_i \models$ marriedWith(John, Mary) and $\mathcal{I}_i \models$ marriedInChurchWith(Philip, Joanna), with $\mathcal{I}_i \models$ marriedInChurchWith $\sqsubseteq$ marriedWith. Let the concept-role domain relation cr_{ji} contain (only) the two pairs

$$(\langle \mathtt{John}, \mathtt{marriedWith}, \mathtt{Mary} \rangle, \mathtt{m123}) \tag{10}$$

$$(\langle \mathtt{Philip}, \mathtt{marriedInChurchWith}, \mathtt{Joanna} \rangle, \mathtt{e345}) \tag{11}$$

Bridge rule (9) is satisfied if both m123 and e345 are instances of Marriage.

Satisfiability of a role-onto-concept bridge rule forces the role-concept domain relation cr_{ij} to identify a corresponding pre-image (x_1, x_2) in $R^{\mathcal{I}_i}$ (or in any of its sub-roles) for all x in $C^{\mathcal{I}_j}$. Thus the bridge rule

$$i : \mathtt{marriedWith} \xrightarrow{\ \sqsupseteq\ } j : \mathtt{Marriage} \tag{12}$$

is satisfied by the pairs (10) and (10) above, under the assumption that m123 and e345 are the only elements in Marriage$^{\mathcal{I}_j}$. The satisfiability of concept-into/onto-roles bridge rules is analogous.

The effects of all the bridge rules introduced in this Section are studied in detail in Section 3. We only want to emphasise here one of the interesting characteristics of the heterogeneous mappings by means of an example. Assume we have an ontology i containing three relations marriedWith, marriedInChurchWith and dancePartnerOf. Assume also that there is an ontology j containing three concepts Marriage, ReligiousMarriage, and DanceCouple, which intuitively describe the same "real word entities" of the three relations of ontology i. Assume we want to capture this correspondence by means of the following heterogeneous bridge rules:

$$i : \mathtt{marriedWith} \xrightarrow{\ \equiv\ } j : \mathtt{Marriage} \tag{13}$$

$$i : \mathtt{marriedInChurchWith} \xrightarrow{\ \equiv\ } j : \mathtt{ReligiousMarriage} \tag{14}$$

$$i : \mathtt{dancePartnerOf} \xrightarrow{\ \equiv\ } j : \mathtt{DanceCouple} \tag{15}$$

Assume also that $\mathcal{I}_i \models$ marriedInChurchWith $\sqsubseteq$ marriedWith. Then we would like to propagate the hierarchical relation of subsumption between these two roles into the analogous hierarchical relation between the corresponding concepts, that is $\mathcal{I}_j \models$ ReligiousMarriage $\sqsubseteq$ Marriage. This fact is guaranteed by applying the rule (19) at page 243. On the contrary, assume that `marriedWith` and `dancePartnerOf` are not related by any subsumption relation (as we do not want to impose that all married couple dance together or that all dancing couples are married to each other) but assume they only have a non-empty intersection. In this case we do not want to propagate this information by inferring that `Marriage` has a non empty intersection with `DanceCouple`, as intuitively an identifier of a `Marriage` is never an identifier of a `DanceCouple`, even if they concern the same pair of persons. The usage of admissible triples in the role-concept domain relation gives us the possibility to obtain this by allowing the same pair of objects in an ontology to correspond to different elements in another ontology because they belong to different roles, as shown in (7) and (8).

Definition 9 (Distributed interpretation). *A distributed interpretation $\mathfrak{J}$ of a DTB $\mathfrak{T}$ consists of the 4-tuple $\mathfrak{J} = \langle \{\mathcal{I}_i\}_{i \in I}, \{r_{ij}\}_{i \neq j \in I}, \{cr_{ij}\}_{i \neq j \in I}, \{rc_{ij}\}_{i \neq j \in I} \rangle$*

Definition 10 (Satisfiability of a Distributed T-box). *A distributed interpretation $\mathfrak{J}$ satisfies the elements of a DTB $\mathfrak{T}$ according to the following clauses: for every $i, j \in I$*

1. $\mathfrak{J} \models i : A \sqsubseteq B$, if $\mathcal{I}_i \models A \sqsubseteq B$
2. $\mathfrak{J} \models \mathcal{T}_i$, if $\mathfrak{J} \models i : A \sqsubseteq B$ for all $A \sqsubseteq B$ in $\mathcal{T}_i$
3. $\mathfrak{J} \models \mathfrak{B}_{ij}$, if
   - *$\langle \mathcal{I}_i, r_{ij}, \mathcal{I}_j \rangle$ satisfies all the homogeneous bridge rules in $\mathfrak{B}_{ij}$,*
   - *$\langle \mathcal{I}_i, cr_{ij}, \mathcal{I}_j \rangle$ satisfies all the concept-to-role bridge rules in $\mathfrak{B}_{ij}$,*
   - *$\langle \mathcal{I}_i, rc_{ij}, \mathcal{I}_j \rangle$ satisfies all the role-to-concept bridge rules in $\mathfrak{B}_{ij}$*
4. $\mathfrak{J} \models \mathfrak{T}$, if for every $i, j \in I$, $\mathfrak{J} \models \mathcal{T}_i$ and $\mathfrak{J} \models \mathfrak{B}_{ij}$

Definition 11 (Distributed Entailment and Satisfiability). *$\mathfrak{T} \models i : A \sqsubseteq B$ (read as "$\mathfrak{T}$ entails $i : A \sqsubseteq B$") if for every $\mathfrak{J}$, $\mathfrak{J} \models \mathfrak{T}$ implies $\mathfrak{J} \models_d i : A \sqsubseteq B$. $\mathfrak{T}$ is satisfiable if there exists a $\mathfrak{J}$ such that $\mathfrak{J} \models \mathfrak{T}$. Concept $i : A$ is satisfiable with respect to $\mathfrak{T}$ if there is a $\mathfrak{J}$ such that $\mathfrak{J} \models \mathfrak{T}$ and $A^{\mathcal{I}_i} \neq \emptyset$.*

3   The Effects of Mappings

An important characteristic of mappings specified by DDL bridge rules is that they are directional, in the sense that they are defined from a source ontology O_s to a target ontology O_t, and they allow to transfer knowledge only from O_s to O_t, without any undesired back-flow effect. In this section we show that the semantic of mappings defined in the previous Section fulfills this requirement. Furthermore we characterize the effects of the bridge rules in terms of the knowledge they allow to propagate from O_s to O_t.

We start by characterizing the effects of mappings of a simple DTB $\langle \mathcal{T}_i, \mathcal{T}_j, \mathfrak{B}_{ij} \rangle$, composed of two T-boxes $\mathcal{T}_i$ and $\mathcal{T}_j$ and a set of bridge rules $\mathfrak{B}_{ij}$ from i to j. The first important property we prove is *directionality*:

Proposition 1. *$\langle \mathcal{T}_i, \mathcal{T}_j, \mathfrak{B}_{ij} \rangle \models i : X \sqsubseteq Y$ if and only if $\mathcal{T}_i \models X \sqsubseteq Y$.*

The proof can be found in [7]. According to Proposition 1, bridge rules from i to j affect only the logical consequences in j, and leave the consequences in i unchanged. In the following we characterise the knowledge propagated from i (the source) to j (the target) using a set of *propagation rules* of the form:

$$\frac{\text{axioms in } i \quad \text{bridge rules from } i \text{ to } j}{\text{axiom in } j}$$

which must be read as: if $\mathcal{T}_i$ entails all the axioms in i, and $\mathfrak{B}_{ij}$ contains the bridge rules from i to j, then $\langle \mathcal{T}_i, \mathcal{T}_j, \mathfrak{B}_{ij} \rangle$ satisfies axioms in j.

3.1 Propagation of the Concept Hierarchy

The propagation of the concept hierarchy forced by mappings between concepts and is widely described in [14]. The simplest version of this effect is described by the following rule:

$$\frac{i : A \sqsubseteq B \qquad i : A \xrightarrow{\sqsupseteq} j : C \qquad i : B \xrightarrow{\sqsubseteq} j : D}{j : C \sqsubseteq D} \tag{16}$$

where A, B, C and D are concepts.

Proposition 2 (Concept into/onto concept). *Rule (16) is sound.*

Proof. Let $y \in C^{\mathcal{I}_j}$. From the satisfiability of $i : A \xrightarrow{\sqsupseteq} j : C$ there is an object $x \in A^{\mathcal{I}_i}$ such that $(x, y) \in r_{ij}$. From the hypothesis we know that $\mathcal{T}_i \models A \sqsubseteq B$, and thus $x \in B^{\mathcal{I}_i}$, and from the satisfiability of $i : B \xrightarrow{\sqsubseteq} j : D$ we have that $y \in D^{\mathcal{I}_j}$. Thus $\mathcal{T}_j \models C \sqsubseteq D$.

3.2 Propagation of the Role Hierarchy

The first effect of mappings between roles concern the propagation of the role hierarchy across ontologies. If $P \sqsubseteq Q$ is a fact of the T-box $\mathcal{T}_i$, then the effect of the bridge rules $i : P \xrightarrow{\sqsupseteq} j : R$ and $i : Q \xrightarrow{\sqsubseteq} j : S$ is that $R \sqsubseteq S$ is a fact in $\mathcal{T}_j$. Formally, we describe this effect by means of the following rule:

$$\frac{i : P \sqsubseteq Q, \qquad i : P \xrightarrow{\sqsupseteq} j : R \qquad i : Q \xrightarrow{\sqsubseteq} j : S}{j : R \sqsubseteq S} \tag{17}$$

where each P, Q, R, and S is either a role or an inverse role. This rule can be obtained from rule (b) in Figure 1 by setting $l = 1, p = 0, m = 0$.

Proposition 3 (Role into/onto role). *Rule (17) is sound.*

Proof. Let $(y_1, y_2) \in R^{\mathcal{I}_j}$. From the satisfiability of $i : P \xrightarrow{\sqsupseteq} j : R$ there is a pair $(x_1, x_2) \in P^{\mathcal{I}_i}$ such that $(x_1, y_1) \in r_{ij}$ and $(x_2, y_2) \in r_{ij}$. From the hypothesis we know that $\mathcal{T}_i \models P \sqsubseteq Q$, and thus $(x_1, x_2) \in Q^{\mathcal{I}_i}$, and from the satisfiability of $i : Q \xrightarrow{\sqsubseteq} j : S$ we have that $(y_1, y_2) \in S^{\mathcal{I}_j}$. Thus $\mathcal{T}_j \models R \sqsubseteq S$.

3.3 Propagation of the Role Domain and of the Range Restriction

The effect of the combination of mappings between roles and mappings between concepts is the propagation of domain and range among relations linked by role-onto-role mappings. The simplest version of this rule is the following:

$$\frac{i : \exists P.\top \sqsubseteq B \qquad i : P \xrightarrow{\ \sqsupseteq\ } j : R \qquad i : B \xrightarrow{\ \sqsubseteq\ } j : D}{j : \exists R.\top \sqsubseteq D} \tag{18}$$

where P, R are roles and B, D are concepts.

The rule above says that if the domain of P is contained in B and the appropriate bridge rules hold, then we can infer that the domain of R is contained in D. A similar rule allows to obtain $j : \exists R^-.\top \sqsubseteq D$ from $i : \exists P^-.\top \sqsubseteq B$ with the same bridge rules, thus expressing the propagation of the range restriction. Rule (18) can be obtained from rule (b) in Figure 1 by setting $l = 0, p = 0, m = 1$. Analogously the rule for range restriction can be obtained by setting $l = 0, p = 1, m = 0$.

Proposition 4 (Role domain and range restriction). *Rule (18) is sound.*

Proof. Let $y_1 \in \exists R.\top^{\mathcal{I}_j}$. Thus there is an object $y_2 \in \Delta^{\mathcal{I}_j}$ such that $(y_1, y_2) \in R^{\mathcal{I}_j}$. From the satisfiability of $i : P \xrightarrow{\ \sqsupseteq\ } j : R$ there is a $(x_1, x_2) \in P^{\mathcal{I}_i}$ such that $(x_1, y_1) \in r_{ij}$ and $(x_2, y_2) \in r_{ij}$. From the hypothesis we know that $\mathcal{T}_i \models \exists P.\top \sqsubseteq B$, and thus $x_1 \in B^{\mathcal{I}_i}$, and from the satisfiability of $i : B \xrightarrow{\ \sqsubseteq\ } j : D$ we have that $y_1 \in D^{\mathcal{I}_j}$. Thus $\mathcal{T}_j \models \exists R.\top \sqsubseteq D$. Similarly for the range restriction. ∎

3.4 Propagation of Role Hierarchy into Concept Hierarchy

The first effect of the heterogeneous bridge rules mapping roles into/onto corresponding concepts is the propagation of the subsumption relations between these role into subsumption relations between the corresponding concepts. The simplest form of this rule is:

$$\frac{i : P \xrightarrow{\ \sqsupseteq\ } j : C \qquad i : Q \xrightarrow{\ \sqsubseteq\ } j : D \qquad i : P \sqsubseteq Q}{j : C \sqsubseteq D} \tag{19}$$

Proposition 5 (Role hierarchy into concept hierarchy). *Rule (19) is sound.*

Proof. Let $x \in C^{\mathcal{I}_j}$. From the satisfiability of $i : P \xrightarrow{\ \sqsupseteq\ } j : C$, there is a triple (x_1, X, x_2) in $\Sigma_{\mathcal{I}_i}$ such that $(x, \langle x_1, X, x_2 \rangle) \in rc_{ij}$ with $X^{\mathcal{I}_i} \sqsubseteq P^{\mathcal{I}_i}$. $(x_1, x_2) \in X^{\mathcal{I}_i}$ from the definition of admissible triple. Since $\mathcal{I}_i \models P \sqsubseteq Q$, we have that $(x_1, x_2) \in Q^{\mathcal{I}_i}$. From the satisfiability of the into-bridge rule $i : Q \xrightarrow{\ \sqsubseteq\ } j : D$, we can conclude that $x \in H^{\mathcal{I}_j}$.

3.5   Propagation of Concept Hierarchy into Role Hierarchy

An effect analogous to the one above is the propagation of the concept hierarchy into the role hierarchy. The simplest form of this rule is:

$$
\frac{i : A \xrightarrow{\; \sqsupseteq \;} j : R \qquad i : B \xrightarrow{\; \sqsubseteq \;} j : S \qquad i : A \sqsubseteq B}{j : R \sqsubseteq S}
\tag{20}
$$

Proposition 6 (Concept hierarchy into role hierarchy). *Rule (20) is sound.*

Proof. Let $(x_1, x_2) \in R^{\mathcal{I}_j}$. From the satisfiability of the onto-bridge rule $i : A \xrightarrow{\sqsupseteq} j : R$ there must be a triple $\langle x_1, X, x_2 \rangle$ of $\Sigma^{\mathcal{I}_j}$ and an $x \in A^{\mathcal{I}_i}$, such that $X^{\mathcal{I}_j} \sqsubseteq R^{\mathcal{I}_j}$, and $(x, \langle x_1, X, x_2 \rangle) \in cr_{ij}$. The fact $\mathcal{I}_i \models A \sqsubseteq B$ implies that $x \in B^{\mathcal{I}_i}$ and, from the satisfiability of the into-bridge rule $i : B \xrightarrow{\sqsubseteq} j : S$, we can conclude that $X^{\mathcal{I}_j} \sqsubseteq S^{\mathcal{I}_j}$, and therefore that $(x_1, x_2) \in S^{\mathcal{I}_j}$.

The general form of rules (16)–(20) is given in Figure 1. The expression $\bigsqcup_{k=1}^{n} S_k$ with $n = 0$ in rule (d) represents the empty role $R_\perp$, which is obtained with the axiom $\top \sqsubseteq \forall R_\perp . \perp$.

Given a set of bridge rules $\mathfrak{B}_{ij}$ from $\mathcal{DL}_i$ to $\mathcal{DL}_j$, we have defined five different rules, shown in Figure 1, which take as input a T-box $\mathcal{T}_i$ in $\mathcal{DL}_i$ and produce a T-box $\mathcal{T}_j$ in $\mathcal{DL}_j$. Starting from these rules we define an operator $\mathfrak{B}_{ij}(\cdot)$, taking as input $\mathcal{T}_i$ and producing a T-box $\mathcal{T}_j$, enriched with the conclusions of rules (a)–(d) in Figure 1.

Theorem 1 (Soundness and Completeness of $\mathfrak{B}_{ij}(\cdot)$). *Let $\mathfrak{T}_{ij} = \langle \mathcal{T}_i, \mathcal{T}_j, \mathfrak{B}_{ij} \rangle$ be a distributed T-box, where $\mathcal{T}_i$ and $\mathcal{T}_j$ are expressed in the $\mathcal{ALCQI}_b$ descriptive language. Then $\mathfrak{T}_{ij} \models j : X \sqsubseteq Y \Longleftrightarrow \mathcal{T}_j \cup \mathfrak{B}_{ij}(\mathcal{T}_i) \models X \sqsubseteq Y$.*

The proof can be found in [7]. The generalisation of the axiomatization for an arbitrary network of ontologies can be obtained following the technique used in [14].

As a final remark we can notice that the combination of homogeneous and heterogeneous bridge rules does not generate any effect in the logic proposed in this paper. This because the domain relation and the concept-role and role-concept domain relations do not affect each other. The investigation of more complex heterogeneous bridge rules, which can lead to this sort of interaction is left for future work. An additional open point concerns the extension of our framework in order to account for transitive roles. It is well known that the unrestricted interaction between number restriction and transitivity is a source of indecidability; moreover, the bridge rules may infer additional subsumption relations among the roles. Therefore, guaranteeing appropriate restrictions to ensure decidability is no longer a matter of analysing the "static" role hierarchy (e.g., a in the case of $\mathcal{SHIQ}$).

$$\frac{i : A \sqsubseteq \bigsqcup_{k=1}^{n} B_k \qquad i : A \xrightarrow{\sqsupseteq} j : C \qquad i : B_k \xrightarrow{\sqsubseteq} j : D_k, \text{ for } 1 \leq k \leq n}{j : C \sqsubseteq \bigsqcup_{k=1}^{n} D_k}$$

(a) Generalisation of rule (16).

$$\frac{i : \exists (P \sqcap \neg(\bigsqcup_{h=0}^{l} Q_h)) . (\neg \bigsqcup_{h=0}^{p} A_h) \sqsubseteq (\bigsqcup_{h=0}^{m} B_h) \qquad i : P \xrightarrow{\sqsupseteq} j : R \qquad i : Q_h \xrightarrow{\sqsubseteq} j : S_h, \text{ for } 1 \leq h \leq l \qquad i : A_h \xrightarrow{\sqsubseteq} j : C_h, \text{ for } 1 \leq h \leq p \qquad i : B_h \xrightarrow{\sqsubseteq} j : D_h, \text{ for } 1 \leq h \leq m}{j : \exists (R \sqcap \neg(\bigsqcup_{h=1}^{l} S_h)) . (\neg \bigsqcup_{h=1}^{p} C_h) \sqsubseteq (\bigsqcup_{k=1}^{m} D_k)}$$

(b) Generalisation of rules (17) and (18).

$$\frac{i : P \sqsubseteq Q \qquad i : P \xrightarrow{\sqsupseteq} j : C \qquad i : Q \xrightarrow{\sqsubseteq} j : D}{j : C \sqsubseteq D} \qquad \frac{i : P \sqsubseteq \bot_R \qquad i : P \xrightarrow{\sqsupseteq} j : C}{j : C \sqsubseteq \bot}$$

(c) Generalisation of rule (19).

$$\frac{i : A \sqsubseteq \bigsqcup_{k=1}^{n} B_k \qquad i : A \xrightarrow{\sqsupseteq} j : R \qquad i : B_k \xrightarrow{\sqsubseteq} j : S_k, \text{ for } 1 \leq k \leq n}{j : R \sqsubseteq \bigsqcup_{k=1}^{n} S_k}$$

(d) Generalisation of rule (20).

Fig. 1. General version of propagation rules

4 Related Work and Concluding Remarks

Recently, several proposals go in the direction of providing semantic mapping among different ontologies (e.g. [16,14,3,9]). However, to the best of our knowledge there is no specific work on heterogeneous mappings as described in this paper. This in spite of the fact that there are several attempts at providing some sort of mappings relating non-homogeneous elements. For example in [4], it is possible to express the mapping

$$\forall x. (\exists y. R(x, y) \rightarrow C(x)) \tag{21}$$

while, in the original version of DDL (see [14]), an analogous mappings can be established by means of the formula

$$1 : \exists R.\top \xrightarrow{\sqsubseteq} 2 : C \tag{22}$$

Note that both cases cannot be considered heterogeneous mappings because they relates the domain of the relation R with the concept C. The limits of these approaches can be highlighted by the following example.

Assume we want to impose that the relation `marriedWith` in ontology i is equivalent to the concept `Marriage` in ontology j, and we only have mappings as in Equation (22). Then, we can only state expressions of the form:

$$i : \exists \mathtt{marriedWith}.\top \xrightarrow{\sqsubseteq} j : \mathtt{Marriage} \qquad i : \exists \mathtt{marriedWith}.\top \xrightarrow{\sqsupseteq} j : \mathtt{Marriage}$$

But these mappings express something rather different from our initial goal as they map single elements of a couple into marriages. Moreover, assume we also have a bridge rule mappings wives in ontology i into women in ontology j as follows:

$$i : \mathsf{Wife} \xrightarrow{\sqsubseteq} j : \mathsf{Woman}$$

together with the axiom Wife $\sqsubseteq$ $\exists$IsMarried.$\top$ in ontology i stating that a wife is a married entity. From all this we can infer in ontology j that a wife is a marriage, i.e., Wife $\sqsubseteq$ Marriage. The problem in this approach lies in the fact that in mapping the two ontologies, we have identified the participants of a relation, (the married person) with the relation itself (the marriage).

In the same spirit of the above cited approaches, but in the area of federated databases, the work described in [2] provides a formalisation of heterogeneous mappings between concepts and relations. In this work the authors define five types of correspondences between concepts and properties, and provide the semantics of these correspondences as follows, where A is a concept and R is a property (i.e. binary relation);

Relation	Semantics
A is equivalent to R	$\forall x.(A(x) \leftrightarrow \exists y.R(y,x))$
A is more general to R	$\forall x.(\exists y.R(y,x) \rightarrow A(x))$
A is less general to R	$\forall x.(A(x) \rightarrow \exists y.R(y,x))$
A and R do overlap	$\exists x.(A(x) \wedge \exists y.R(y,x))$
A and R do not overlap	$\forall x.(A(x) \rightarrow \neg \exists y.R(y,x))$

This semantics is similar to the encoding described in Equation (21). The only difference is that they considers the range of the relation instead of the domain. Therefore, this approach suffers of the same limitations described early on.

The work presented in this paper is clearly connected to the well known modelling process of *reification* (aka *objectification*) adopted in UML or ORM (see [12,13]). As described in [12], this corresponds to think of certain relationship instances as objects. In UML this is supported by means of *association classes*, while in Entity-Relationship diagram this is often mediated by means of *weak entities*. Note that these modelling paradigms do not support rich inter-schema axioms in the spirit of ontology mappings as described in [16].

There are other modelling formalisms which enable the bridging between relations and classes in the context of Description Logics. In particular, the work on $\mathcal{DLR}$ (see [5]), specifically w.r.t. the technique for encoding n-ary relations within a standard Description Logic, and [6]. The advantage of our approach lies in the fact that the local semantics (i.e. the underlying semantics of the single ontology languages) does not need to be modified in order to consider the global semantics of the system. Specifically, there is no need to provide an explicit reification of relations since this is incorporated into the global semantics.

The language and the semantics presented in this paper constitute a genuine contribution in the direction of the integration of heterogeneous ontologies. The language proposed in this paper makes it possible to directly bind a concept with a relation in a different ontology, and vice-versa. At the semantic level we have introduced a domain relation that maps pairs of object appearing in a relation into objects and vice-versa. This also constitute a novelty in the semantics of knowledge integration. Finally we have shown soundness and completeness of the effects of the mappings and we leave the study of decidability and the definition of a reasoning algorithm for future work.

References

1. Baader, F., Calvanese, D., McGuinness, D.L., Nardi, D., Patel-Schneider, P.F.: The Description Logic Handbook: Theory, Implementation, and Applications. Cambridge University Press, Cambridge (2003)
2. Blanco, J.M., Illarramendi, A., Goñi, A.: Building a federated database system: An approach using a knowledge base system. International Journal of Intelligent and Cooperative Information Systems 3(4), 415–455 (1994)
3. Bouquet, P., Giunchiglia, F., van Harmelen, F., Serafini, L., Stuckenschmidt, H.: C-OWL: Contextualizing ontologies. In: Fensel, D., Sycara, K.P., Mylopoulos, J. (eds.) ISWC 2003. LNCS, vol. 2870, pp. 164–179. Springer, Heidelberg (2003)
4. Calvanese, D., De Giacomo, G., Lenzerini, M., Rosati, R.: Logical foundations of peer-to-peer data integration. In: 23rd ACM SIGACT SIGMOD SIGART Sym. on Principles of Database Systems (PODS 2004), pp. 241–251. ACM Press, New York (2004)
5. Calvanese, D., Berardi, D., De Giacomo, G.: Reasoning on uml class diagrams. Artificial Intelligence 1(168), 70–118 (2005)
6. Calvanese, D., De Giacomo, G., Lenzerini, M.: Structured objects: Modeling and reasoning. In: Ling, T.-W., Vieille, L., Mendelzon, A.O. (eds.) Deductive and Object-Oriented Databases. LNCS, vol. 1013, pp. 229–246. Springer, Heidelberg (1995)
7. Ghidini, C., Serafini, L., Tessaris, S.: On relating heterogeneous elements from different ontologies. Technical report, KRDB. Free universiry of Bozen-Bolzano (2007) http://www.inf.unibz.it/krdb/pub/index.php
8. Ghidini, C., Giunchiglia, F.: Local models semantics, or contextual reasoning = locality + compatibility. Artificial Intelligence 127(2), 221–259 (2001)
9. Ghidini, C., Serafini, L.: Distributed First Order Logics. In: Frontiers Of Combining Systems 2, Studies in Logic and Computation, pp. 121–140. Research Studies Press (1998)
10. Ghidini, C., Serafini, L.: Mapping properties of heterogeneous ontologies. In: Proceedings of the 1st International Workshop on Modular Ontologies (WoMo-06), vol. 232 of CEUR Workshop Proceedings (2006), http://ceur-ws.org/Vol-232
11. Ghidini, C., Serafini, L.: Reconciling concepts and relations in heterogeneous ontologies. In: Sure, Y., Domingue, J. (eds.) ESWC 2006. LNCS, vol. 4011, pp. 11–14. Springer, Heidelberg (2006)
12. Halpin, T.: Objectification of relationships. In: Proceedings of the 10th International IfIP WG8.1 Workshop on Exploring Modeling Methods in Systems Analysis and Design (EMMSAD'05) (2005)
13. Rumbaugh, J., Jacobson, I., Booch, G. (eds.): The Unified Language Reference Manual. Addison-Wesley, Reading (1999)
14. Serafini, L., Borgida, A., Tamilin, A.: Aspects of distributed and modular ontology reasoning. In: Proceedings of the Nineteenth International Joint Conference on Artificial Intelligence (IJCAI-05), pp. 570–575 (2005)
15. Serafini, L., Stuckenschmidt, H., Wache, H.: A formal investigation of mapping language for terminological knowledge. In: 19th Joint Conference on Artificial Intelligence (IJCAI-05), pp. 576–581 (2005)
16. Stuckenschmidt, H., Uschold, M.: Representation of semantic mappings. In: Semantic Interoperability and Integration, number 04391 in Dagstuhl Seminar Proceedings. Internationales Begegnungs- und Forschungszentrum (IBFI), Schloss Dagstuhl, Germany (2005)
17. Tobies, S.: Complexity Results and Practical Algorithms for Logics in Knowledge Representation. PhD thesis, RWTH Aachen, Germany (2001)

ReCQ: Real-World Context-Aware Querying

Shun Hattori, Taro Tezuka, Hiroaki Ohshima, Satoshi Oyama,
Junpei Kawamoto, Keishi Tajima, and Katsumi Tanaka

Department of Social Informatics, Graduate School of Informatics, Kyoto University
Yoshida-Honmachi, Sakyo, Kyoto 606-8501, Japan
{hattori,tezuka,ohshima,oyama}@dl.kuis.kyoto-u.ac.jp,
{kawamoto,tajima,tanaka}@dl.kuis.kyoto-u.ac.jp

Abstract. This paper proposes a method of context-aware querying in
mobile/ubiquitous Web searches, which provides mobile users with four
capabilities: (1) context-aware keyphrase inference to help them input
a keyphrase as a part of their keyword-based query, (2) context-aware
subtopic tree generation to help them specify their information demand
on one subtopic, (3) discovery of comparable keyphrases to their original
query to help them make better decisions, and (4) meta vertical search
focused on one subtopic to make the retrieval results more precise.

1 Introduction

We have been able to access information anywhere and at any time in our daily
lives as well as at home or while working at the office, with the exponential
growth of information available on the Web and advances in mobile/ubiquitous
computing environments. It is especially crucial to obtain better retrieval results
in mobile computing environments, because mobile devices often have inferior
I/O user interfaces and there is little time to leisurely browse for information
while moving or undertaking various activities in the real world. However, the
original queries by mobile users tend to be so short and ambiguous that existing
mobile Web search engines cannot accurately deduce their information demands,
and this thus presents too many irrelevant retrieval results.

A number of different approaches have already been proposed for closing the
gap between user queries and demands in the field of IR (Information Retrieval):
query modifications such as query expansion [1], query relaxation [2] or query
substitutions [3], automatic classification and visualization of the retrieval results
by clustering [4], and written or spoken natural language querying [5].

We propose a **ReCQ** system for mobile/ubiquitous Web searches in this paper, which allows mobile users to seek out more precise information by using
Real-world Context-aware Queries based on their original query and real-world
contexts such as current geographic location through the following four functions:

(1) context-aware keyphrase inference,
(2) subtopic tree generation and context-aware re-formation,
(3) discovery of comparable keyphrases from the Web, and
(4) meta vertical search focused on one subtopic.

B. Kokinov et al. (Eds.): CONTEXT 2007, LNAI 4635, pp. 248–262, 2007.

2   Overview of ReCQ System

We give an overview of our proposed context-aware system for mobile/ubiquitous Web searches in this section, called ReCQ (Real-world Context-aware Querying), which mainly consists of the four following functional capabilities.

Function 1. Context-aware Keyphrase Inference
infers what keyphrase mobile users will try to input as a part of their keyword-based query from its initial substring (e.g., "d" or "da") which they have already input and their current place name (e.g., "bookstore") as a real-world context, and offers its several candidate keyphrases (as shown in Fig. 1(a)). Mobile users can effectively input their query by selecting one from these. We will describe this in more detail in Section 3.

Function 2. Context-aware Subtopic Tree Generation
generates a tree structure of subtopics (e.g., "book" and "movie") for a keyphrase (e.g., "da vinci code") which mobile users have input by clustering non-personal query logs, and re-forms it adapted to their current place name (as shown in Fig. 1(b)). Mobile users can disambiguate their query by selecting one subtopic. We will describe this in more detail in Section 4.

Function 3. Discovery of Comparable Keyphrases
discovers comparable keyphrases to an original one (e.g., "da vinci code") on a selected subtopic (e.g., "book") by mining the Web (as shown in Fig. 1(c)). Mobile users can search with alternative queries as well as the original query and make better decisions. We will describe this in more detail in Section 5.

Function 4. Meta Vertical Search focused on Subtopic
finds a Web site to retrieve information on a specific topic and only searches only the site for a user query, by submitting [intitle:q AND site:url] to Google's Web search engine [6] where their query, q, and one of its subtopics, s, are given and url is one of the higher-ranked URLs googled by [s AND "search"]. Mobile users can obtain more acute results.

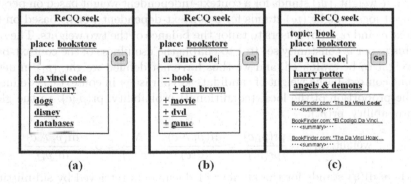

(a)   (b)   (c)

Fig. 1. Overview of our Real-world Context-aware Querying (ReCQ) system

3   Context-Aware Keyphrase Inference

Mobile users have a lot of trouble in inputting a keyphrase as a part of their keyword-based query in mobile/ubiquitous computing environments because of their inferior input interfaces available to them. Therefore, keyphrase inference is a very important capability for these people. Conventional methods often rank candidate keyphrases which match a substring input at the beginning by users based on their personal input logs. However, their input log of a keyphrase does not often contain contextual information about the situation in which they input the keyphrase, except for time. Consequently, even if they want to finally input a different keyphrase and have already input the same substring in different situations, they would be offered quite the same ordered candidate keyphrases independent of each situation. We propose a method of keyphrase inference based on real-world contexts such as the name of the place mobile users are currently located at, in order to infer what keyphrase they try to input more adequately dependent on their situation.

3.1   Method and Configuration

Our method of inferring what keyphrase mobile users try to input as a part of their query from its initial substring which they have already input as well as the name of their current GPS-based location, consists of the following steps:

Step 1. Listing of Candidates for Inferred Keyphrases
When an input substring, s, and a selected context expression, c, are given, all the whole keyphrases that match substring s at the beginning are placed on the candidate list from dictionaries of keyphrases.

Step 2. Weighting of Candidates for Inferred Keyphrases
The synthetic weight of each candidate keyphrase, p_i, for a substring, s, that a mobile user, u, has input in a context, c, is essentially calculated as:

$$\text{weight}_{u,c}(p_i) := (1 - \alpha_u) \cdot \text{weight}_u(p_i) + \alpha_u \cdot \text{weight}_c(p_i),$$

where $\text{weight}_u(p_i)$ stands for a context-independent weight based on personal input logs, $\text{weight}_c(p_i)$ stands for a context-dependent weight based on context c, and α_u allows users to tailor the balance of the two weights. The α_u in this paper is constantly set to 1 to enable the usefulness of the context-based weight to be evaluated, and we thus have not defined $\text{weight}_u(p_i)$ in detail. The context-based weight of candidate keyphrase p_i in context c is defined as the proportion of the local (conditional) probability, $\text{pr}(p_i|c)$, to the global probability, $\text{pr}(p_i)$:

$$\text{weight}_c(p_i) := \frac{\text{pr}(p_i|c)}{\text{pr}(p_i)} = \frac{\text{df}(p_i \wedge c)}{\text{df}(c)} \cdot \frac{N}{\text{df}(p_i)} = \beta_c \cdot \frac{\text{df}(p_i \wedge c)}{\text{df}(p_i)},$$

where $\text{df}(q)$ stands for the number of documents retrieved by submitting a query, q, to a search engine, N stands for the entire number of documents in the corpus of the search engine, and $\beta_c = N/\text{df}(c)$ stands for a certain constant value when context c is given.

3.2   Experimental Results

We demonstrate from several experimental results that context-aware keyphrase inferences are more suitable than context-independent keyphrase inferences for mobile Web searches and that our proposed method can infer differently ordered keyphrases dependent on all contexts within which mobile users are situated.

We collected about 260 candidate keyphrases in Step 1 for each alphabetic letter by submitting just it and 26 strings of any letter following it (e.g., "d" and from "da" to "dz") to Google Suggest [7], which offers at most 10 queries inferred from a users' given substring independent of their contexts such as current location. In Step 2, we calculated our context-based weight, $weight_c(p_i)$, for each pair of candidate keyphrases, p_i, and context expressions, c, by using Google Web Search [6] as a corpus of documents. We used five context expressions such as "at * bookstore", "at * cd store", "in * school", "in * theater" and "at * zoo", where * stands for the wild card operator supported by Google.

Table 1 compares our proposed context-aware keyphrase inference to Google Suggest as a context-independent keyphrase inference, for an initial "d" to mobile users within all each context. The top 10 candidate keyphrases ranked with our method differ depending on the contexts unlike Google Suggest, and it is obviously better than Google Suggest except for the context "at * zoo".

Table 1. Comparison of our context-aware keyphrase inference to Google Suggest in context-independent keyphrase inference for "d" initially given in five contexts

	Google Suggest		Context: "at*bookstore"		Context: "at*cd store"
1	dictionary	1	**da vinci code**	1	**dj shadow**
2	dell	2	**drudge report**	2	**dvd**
3	dictionary.com	3	**dc comics**	3	**disney channel**
4	debenhams	4	**desperate housewives**	4	**da vinci code**
5	disney	5	**drudge**	5	driving directions
6	disney channel	6	**dwell**	6	**download**
7	deal or no deal	7	**dnc**	7	**dungeons and dragons**
8	dillards	8	**dreamweaver**	8	dc metro
9	dixons	9	dg time	9	dunkin donuts
10	dhl	10	**dts**	10	**dj tiesto**

	Context: "in*school"		Context: "in*theater"		Context: "at*zoo"
1	da vinci code	1	dish network	1	ds games
2	dallas cowboys	2	dfw airport	2	da vinci code
3	dyspraxia	3	direct tv	3	dunkin donuts
4	drudge report	4	**da vinci code**	4	dallas cowboys
5	**dunkin donuts**	5	dyson vacuum	5	desperate housewives
6	**dating sites**	6	disney channel	6	dc metro
7	**disney channel**	7	drudge report	7	drudge report
8	**dictionary.com**	8	**daniel craig**	8	**dog breeds**
9	dish network	9	**desperate housewives**	9	dating sites
10	desperate housewives	10	dc metro	10	disney channel

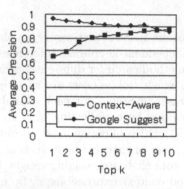

Fig. 2. For "at * bookstore"

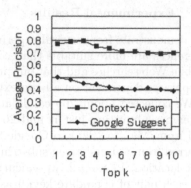

Fig. 3. For "at * cd store"

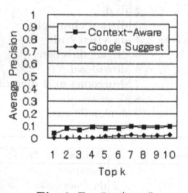

Fig. 4. For "in * school"

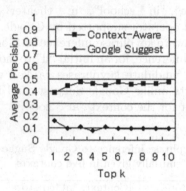

Fig. 5. For "in * theater"

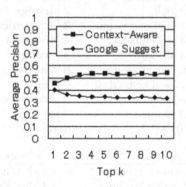

Fig. 6. For "at * zoo"

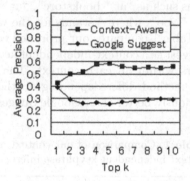

Fig. 7. For five contexts

Fig. 2 to 6 compares our context-aware keyphrase inference and Google Suggest as a context-independent keyphrase inference on the top k average precision for each context, and Fig. 7 compares them on the top k average precision in total. Our method is only inferior for "at * bookstore". The results for "at * zoo" are very poor, but one reason for this is that about 260 candidate keyphrases for each alphabetic letter rarely include names of animals. For example, if the candidate keyphrases for the initially given "d" include "dog", "dinosaur", and "dolphin", they are respectively ranked as the 1st, 7th, and 10th. Therefore, our method only has to exhaustively accumulate candidate keyphrases for each initially given string, and offers more precise results for most contexts.

4 Context-Aware Subtopic Tree Generation

The original queries by mobile users tend to be more ambiguous than their actual information demands. Therefore, one important capability is to close the gap by refining their queries. Semantically related terms to the user query are offered by most conventional methods for query expansion, based on relevance between terms in a target corpus, but do not always include the subtopic terms that users demand to refine their original query. We propose a method of generating subtopics in a tree structure by using non-personal query logs and of re-forming the tree based on users' real-world contexts such as the name of the place where they currently are, in order to offer exhaustive and categorized subtopics for their original queries. This is similar to the approach taken by Kawamoto *et al.*, although their method has aimed at supporting collaborative searches [8].

4.1 Method and Configuration

Our method of generating a tree structure of subtopics on a query (or a keyphrase possibly) given by mobile users based on non-personal query logs and of re-forming these based on their current place name, consists of the following steps:

Step 1. Listing of Subtopics
    When a keyword-based query, q, and a context expression, c, are given, keyword-based expressions which co-occur with the query in non-personal query logs and also the root query itself are placed on the subtopic list, S.
Step 2. Categorization of Subtopics in Tree
    A keyword-based expression, s_i ($\in S$), on the subtopic list is a child of the other expression, s_p ($\in S - s_i$), on the subtopic list, if and only if the dependence of the expression s_i on its parental expression s_p ranks the highest of the other expressions on the subtopic list:

$$s_i \in S(s_p) \texttt{ iff } \text{depend}(s_i; s_p) = \max \; \{\text{depend}(s_i; s_j)|s_j \in S - s_i\},$$

$$\text{depend}(s_i; s_j) := \begin{cases} \dfrac{\text{df}_{(s_i \wedge q)}}{\text{df}_{(q)}} - \dfrac{\text{df}_{(s_i)}}{N}, & \texttt{if } s_j - q, \\ \dfrac{\text{df}_{(s_i \wedge s_j \wedge q)}}{\text{df}_{(s_i \wedge q)}} - \dfrac{\text{df}_{(s_i \wedge s_j \wedge q)}}{\text{df}_{(s_j \wedge q)}}, & \texttt{otherwise.} \end{cases}$$

The children, $S(q)$, of root q are definitely determined to be the direct children, $S^*(q)$, of the root query, while the children, $S(s_i)$, of an expression s_i except for the root do not always be the direct children of the expression. Next, each new subtopic list, $S' := S(s_j^*)$, of a direct child, s_j^* ($\in S^*(q)$), of the current root and new root $q' := [q$ AND $s_j^*]$ are processed as above.

Step 3. Context-aware Re-formation of Subtopic Tree

For each set of direct children, $S^*(s_i)$, of an expression, s_i ($\in S$), on the subtopic list, our context-based weight of a child, s_j ($\in S^*(s_i)$), in context c is calculated like as in Step 2 in Section 3.1:

$$\text{weight}_{q,c}(s_j) := \text{weight}_c(s_j \wedge q) \simeq \frac{\text{df}(s_j \wedge q \wedge c)}{\text{df}(s_j \wedge q)}.$$

4.2 Experimental Results

We demonstrate that our method could offer the exhaustive and categorized subtopics for mobile-user queries. Fig. 8 compares our proposed subtopic tree with Vivisimo [9] for a user query "da vinci code" and a context "bookstore", which is a commercial Web clustering system to place search results into folders that represent a subtopic. All the main subtopic-phrases of "da vinci code" such as "book", "movie", "dvd" and "game" appear in our proposed subtopic tree.

Subtopic Tree Using Query Logs:

⊙ ···"book" (0.01603)
   ⊕ ···"author" (0.01714)
   ⊕ ···"book"&"review" (0.01609)
   ⊕ ···"audio book" (0.01371)
   ⊕ ···"book"&"summary" (0.010)
   ⊕ ···"dan brown" (0.00844)
   ⋮
⊕ ···"game" (0.01073)
⊕ ···"movie" (0.00977)
⊕ ···"dvd" (0.00975)

Vivisimo's Clustering:

⊕ ···**Dan Brown**
⊕ ···**Reviews**
⊕ ···**Opus**
⊕ ···**Image**
⊕ ···**Answers**
⊕ ···**Da Vinci Code Movie**
⊕ ···**Cast, Film**
⊕ ···**Breaking The Da Vinci Code**
⊕ ···**Conspiracy**
⊕ ···**Apple, Louvre Museum**

Fig. 8. Comparison of our subtopic tree and Vivisimo's clusters (Query q = "da vinci code" and Context c = "bookstore")

Subtopic Tree Using Query Logs:

⊙ ···"play station" (0.00972)
   ⊕ ···"play station 3" (0.00833)
   ⊕ ···"ps3" (0.00176)
   ⋮
⊕ ···"psp" (0.00226)
⊕ ···"digital camera" (0.00217)
⊕ ···"vaio" (0.00211)
⊕ ···"tv" (0.001811)
⊕ ···"ericsson" (0.00118)
⊕ ···"pictures" (0.00056)

Vivisimo's Clustering:

⊕ ···**Sony BMG**
⊕ ···**Rootkit**
⊕ ···**Sony Pictures**
⊕ ···**Screenshots, Game**
⊕ ···**Sony Music**
⊕ ···**Global**
⊕ ···**Electronics**
⊕ ···**Downloads**
⊕ ···**PSP**
⊕ ···**Mobile, Sony Ericsson**

Fig. 9. Comparison of our subtopic tree and Vivisimo's clusters (Query q = "sony" and Context c = "game store")

The directory for "book" is opened, because the context-based weight of "book" within the context "bookstore" ranks the highest of those in the direct children of the user query. Our method offers more exhaustive subtopics in this case.

Fig. 9 compares them for a user query "sony" and a context "game store". The directories for "play station" and "psp" had better enter in the directory for "game", but it was not in the top 100 query expressions that co-occurred with "sony" by Overture's Keyword Selector Tool [10] in September 2006.

5   Discovering Comparable Keyphrases from the Web

Mobile users occasionally search the Web for information on making decisions on whether or not to do a certain activity (e.g., buy this book), but they are usually not aware of the alternatives to their original activity, if any. Therefore, one important capability is to remind mobile users about alternative activities. We propose a method of discovering context-aware comparable keyphrases from the Web in order to offer the alternatives to mobile-user queries.

5.1   Method and Configuration

When a mandatory single keyphrase as a target object of discovery and an optional keyword-based expression (possibly a single word) as its context are given, our method discovers comparable keyphrases to the object keyphrase within the certain context from the Web.

Although Google Sets [11] is a web-based tool for discovering comparable phrases for an object, we cannot currently condition the object by using one of its various aspects. However, the method proposed by Ohshima *et al.* [12] allows us to do so. Their approach is based on the following two assumptions:

(1)   the conjunction "or" connects two comparable keyphrases,
(2)   if two keyphrases p_1 and p_2 are comparable, there are both "p_1 or p_2" and "p_2 or p_1" patterns in a target corpus of documents such as the Web.

Our method adapts these assumptions and consists of the following steps:

Step 1. Extraction of Candidates for Comparable Keyphrases
   When object keyphrase p and context expression c are given, the top k sets are retrieved by the queries, ["p or" AND c] and ["or p" AND c], in a conventional Web search engine such as Google [6]. The k in the experiments described below is set to 100. Each retrieval set of a Web page consists of its title, snippet (brief summary), and URL. The results retrieved by Google Blog Search [13] sorted by date of upload are also taken into account so that fresher comparable keyphrases are not missed. The text between "p or" and its immediate following separator such as ".", ",", "?", ")" and "or" in the top k sets of the title and snippet, that consists of fewer words than a certain threshold value, is regarded as the candidate for comparable keyphrases to the object keyphrase, p, within the context, c.

Step 2. Weighting of Candidates for Comparable Keyphrases

The weight of each p_i candidate for comparable keyphrases to the object keyphrase, p, within the context, c, is calculated in [12] as:

$$\text{weight}_{p,c}(p_i) := \sqrt{\text{df}^A_{p,c}(p_i) \cdot \text{df}^B_{p,c}(p_i)},$$

$$\text{df}^A_{p,c}(p_i) := \text{df}(\,[\text{``}p \ or \ p_i\text{''AND } c]\,),$$

$$\text{df}^B_{p,c}(p_i) := \text{df}(\,[\text{``}p_i \ or \ p\text{''AND } c]\,),$$

where $\text{df}(q)$ stands for the number of documents retrieved by submitting a keyword-based query, q, to a search engine. However, the above function has some problems. Even when either $\text{df}^A_{p,c}(p_i)$ or $\text{df}^B_{p,c}(p_i)$ is much smaller, if it is not zero and its another is sufficiently great, the $\text{weight}_{p,c}(p_i)$ also becomes greater. For example, $\sqrt{10 \cdot 10} < \sqrt{1 \cdot 1000}$. Therefore, we adopted the following function for weighting each candidate to solve this problem:

$$\text{weight}'_{p,c}(p_i) := \min_{p,c}(p_i) + \left(1 - \frac{\min_{p,c}(p_i)}{\max_{p,c}(p_i)} \right),$$

$$\min_{p,c}(p_i) := \min \ \{\text{df}^A_{p,c}(p_i), \text{df}^B_{p,c}(p_i)\},$$

$$\max_{p,c}(p_i) := \max \ \{\text{df}^A_{p,c}(p_i), \text{df}^B_{p,c}(p_i)\}.$$

5.2   Interface from the Previous Module of ReCQ

The input from the previous step of our ReCQ system includes a query, q, which consists of ordered keyphrases p_i typed into the search box and subtopic words selected from the subtopic tree of the original query by the search user:

$$q = [\ p_1 \ \text{AND} \ p_2 \ \text{AND} \ \cdots \ \text{AND} \ p_n \ ].$$

The object for discovering comparable keyphrases must be represented by a single keyphrase in order to adopt our method in the previous subsection. Therefore, if a query input into the search box consists of multiple keyphrases (i.e, $n \geq 2$), our ReCQ system must select a single query keyphrase from these as the object of discovery and regard both the other query keyphrases and the subtopic words as its subtopic expression.

The appropriateness of a keyphrase, p_i, in a query, q, for the object of discovering comparable keyphrases is calculated based on the following heuristics:

More proper keyphrase p_i with greater $\text{length}(p_i)$ and smaller $\text{ord}_q(p_i)$ in query expression q is more appropriate for the object of discovery.

where

- $\text{prop}(p_i) \in \{0,1\}$: whether or not the keyphrase p_i is a proper noun,
- $\text{length}(p_i) \in \mathcal{N}^+$: the number of words that comprise the keyphrase p_i,

– $\mathrm{ord}_q(p_i) \in \mathcal{N}^+$: the ordinal number i of the keyphrase p_i in the query q.

Let us assume that a mobile user has input ["book" AND "da vinci code"] as a query in the search box of our ReCQ system and has selected none from its subtopics in a tree structure. Because "da vinci code" is greater on the order but more proper and greater on the length than "book", our ReCQ system regards "da vinci code" as more appropriate for the target keyphrase of discovery and then tries to discover the comparable keyphrases for "da vinci code" within the context that is represented by the remaining keyphrase, "book". Examples discovered in this case include "harry potter" and "angels and demons".

5.3   Experimental Results

We demonstrate that our method can discover the comparable keyphrases to mobile-user queries within contexts by conducting several experiments.

Table 2 shows the experimental results for the target object "da vinci code" and three typical subtopics for it such as "book", "movie", and "game". The candidate keyphrases acceptable for each context are listed in boldface. Although "da vinci" and "dan brown" are not acceptable as comparable keyphrases to "da

Table 2. Comparable keyphrases to object ($p =$"da vinci code")

Context $c = \phi$				Context $c = $ "book"			
Candidate p_i	$\mathrm{df}^A_{p,c}$	$\mathrm{df}^B_{p,c}$	$w'_{p,c}$	Candidate p_i	$\mathrm{df}^A_{p,c}$	$\mathrm{df}^B_{p,c}$	$w'_{p,c}$
harry potter	303	97	97.68	**harry potter**	262	72	72.73
angels and demons	489	43	43.91	**angels and demons**	148	33	33.87
dan brown	19	13	13.32	dan brown	13	10	10.23
fanaa	7	23	7.70	da vinci	12	7	7.42
bible	7	23	7.70	**the bible**	35	4	4.89
da vinci	18	7	7.61	bible	4	13	4.69
the bible	39	4	4.90	**national treasure**	8	4	4.50
talladega nights	4	16	4.75	**map of bones**	3	17	3.82
map of bones	3	20	3.85	**the kite runner**	3	1	1.66
the passion of christ	5	1	1.80	**kite runner**	2	1	1.50
Context $c = $ "movie"				Context $c = $ "game"			
Candidate p_i	$\mathrm{df}^A_{p,c}$	$\mathrm{df}^B_{p,c}$	$w'_{p,c}$	Candidate p_i	$\mathrm{df}^A_{p,c}$	$\mathrm{df}^B_{p,c}$	$w'_{p,c}$
harry potter	43	51	43.16	**harry potter**	38	49	38.22
dan brown	13	8	8.38	angels and demons	57	30	30.47
da vinci	10	6	6.40	**national treasure**	0	7	7.22
the bible	28	4	4.86	dan brown	10	5	5.5
over the hedge	8	4	4.50	bible	3	6	3.50
fanaa	3	19	3.84	da vinci	6	3	3.50
map of bones	3	9	3.66	**mi3**	2	5	2.60
Mission Impossible 3	4	3	3.25	**jfk assassination**	1	4	1.75
bible	2	21	2.90	Men	3	1	1.67
king kong	2	1	1.50	**king kong**	1	1	1.00

Table 3. Comparable keyphrases to object ($p =$ "sony")

Context $c = \phi$				Context $c =$ "tv"			
Candidate p_i	$df_{p,c}^A$	$df_{p,c}^B$	$w'_{p,c}$	Candidate p_i	$df_{p,c}^A$	$df_{p,c}^B$	$w'_{p,c}$
microsoft	50700	27800	27800.45	microsoft	29900	18300	18300.39
nintendo	31500	16800	16800.47	**panasonic**	14500	11200	11200.23
panasonic	22700	15400	15400.32	nintendo	20400	9590	9590.53
canon	11400	10600	10600.07	**sharp**	1010	866	866.14
ms	10200	9580	9580.06	**toshiba**	16600	762	762.95
dell	21600	982	982.95	**samsung**	840	659	659.22
samsung	9860	955	955.90	**dell**	887	506	506.43
toshiba	26200	912	912.97	**philips**	9340	384	384.96
sandisk	1100	725	725.34	**hp**	351	11700	351.97
apple	679	970	679.30	warner	18100	111	111.99
Context $c =$ "music"				Context $c =$ "game"			
Candidate p_i	$df_{p,c}^A$	$df_{p,c}^B$	$w'_{p,c}$	Candidate p_i	$df_{p,c}^A$	$df_{p,c}^B$	$w'_{p,c}$
microsoft	26900	14600	14600.46	**microsoft**	46000	24400	24400.47
canon	86500	1690	1690.98	**nintendo**	28900	16500	16500.43
panasonic	11700	996	996.91	**ms**	9690	9470	9470.02
nintendo	16700	895	895.95	panasonic	10500	9080	9080.14
toshiba	573	585	573.02	**sega**	2940	23100	2940.87
xbox	531	4410	531.88	**xbox**	681	1160	681.41
samsung	542	522	522.04	samsung	716	634	634.11
philips	992	381	381.62	hp	523	7830	523.93
apple	376	609	376.38	dell	18300	502	502.97
pioneer	1340	268	268.80	**ea**	827	358	358.57

vinci code", they are fatally included in any top 10 lists. However, almost all the other keyphrases discovered for the contexts are expected to be acceptable.

Table 3 shows the experimental results for the target object "sony" and three typical subtopics for it such as "tv", "music", and "game". Although there are

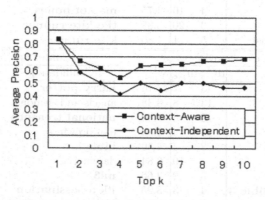

Fig. 10. Comparison of context-aware and context-independent comparable keyphrase discoveries on top k average precision

fewer acceptable keyphrases for the context "game", they have already been discovered exhaustively. We inferred that such results for each context are adversely affected by co-occurrence in other contexts from "microsoft", "nintendo" and "samsung" being included in any top 10 lists.

Fig. 10 compares context-dependent and context-independent comparable keyphrase discoveries on top k average precision. This demonstrates that the effectiveness of reflecting the contexts of a target object on discovering its comparable keyphrases from the Web.

6 Related Work

6.1 Mobile and Context-Aware Information Retrieval

This work is very much related to the research fields of Mobile Information Retrieval [14,15] and Context-Aware Retrieval [16,17] of information for mobile and ubiquitous/pervasive computing environments. Consequently, we introduce some of related works in these fields in this section.

SAP-IR [18] is an efficient IR technique that combines situation-based adaptation and profile-based personalization, and which consists of three components: context-action data collection, user-profile generation, and SAP-IR request generation. SAP-IR applies data mining techniques to generating user profiles which reflect their behaviors, interests, and intentions in all situations, based on their usage history, which is a set of usage-history tuples of context data, action data, and action-related data. When an initial IR request is issued by a mobile user, it is intercepted and modified to generate a SAP-IR request based on user profiles and the current context. Our work is similar to SAP-IR in terms of applying the real-world contexts of mobile users to refining their queries. However, we propose a generalized query refinement by mining the Web, while SAP-IR proposed a personalized query refinement by analyzing user profiles.

Jimminy [19] is a wearable personal note-taking and note-archiving system, which automatically presents the archived notes to the wearers based on their current location and people in the nearby area surrounding him/her as real-world contexts, and the subject-line and content of any current note being written such as information-world contexts. Our work is similar to Jimminy in terms of leveraging the current geographic location as a real-world context. However, we utilize the real-world contexts of mobile users to refine the original query that they submitted to mobile Web search engines, while Jimminy utilizes these to present information related (annotated directly) to them.

6.2 Vertical Search

General-purpose search engines such as Google [6] cannot always satisfy the demands of mobile users searching the Web for specific information on a given subtopic. Many domain-specific search engines, also known as Vertical Search engines, have been built to facilitate more efficient searches in particular domains. They usually provide more precise results and more customizable functions.

Focused Crawler [20] locates Web pages relevant to a pre-defined set of topics based on example pages provided by the user, and also analyzes the link structures among the collected pages. NanoSearch or NanoSpider [21] is a server-side or client-side vertical Web search engine for the nanotechnology domain. The vertical spider for NanoSearch collects pages by following links on each page it has collected, using a simple breadth-first search algorithm. The spider stops after a specified number of pages have been collected. Our work is similar to these in terms of vertical searches. However, when a user query and a subtopic are given, our proposed meta vertical search first finds vertical search engines that focus on the subtopic and then submits the user query to them.

7 Conclusion and Future Work

We proposed our **ReCQ** system for mobile/ubiquitous Web searches in this paper, which allows mobile users to seek out more precise information anywhere at any time by refining Real-world Context-aware Queries based on both their original query and real-world contexts such as their current geographic location through the following four functional capabilities:

(1) Context-aware Keyphrase Inference
    for helping mobile users to input a keyphrase as a part of their keyword-based query more efficiently compared to context-independent keyphrase inference,
(2) Subtopic Tree Generation and Context-aware Re-formation
    for helping mobile users to specify their information demands on one subtopic more efficiently compared to offering terms related to their query,
(3) Discovering Comparable Keyphrases from the Web
    for helping mobile users to know about the alternatives and make better decisions compared to searching the Web for only their original query, and
(4) Meta Vertical Search Focused on One Subtopic by User Query
    for making the retrieval results more precise compared to meta general-purpose searches by using both a user query and one subtopic for it.

We plan to develop a prototype system for mobile/ubiquitous Web searches in the near future based on our proposed methods, and evaluate it in more detail. We would also like to challenge to utilize not only current but also past continuous and/or prospective real-world contexts, and to personalize context-based weightings based on user profiles and/or personal query logs.

Acknowledgments. This work was supported in part by a MEXT the 21st Century Center of Excellence (COE) Program on the "Informatics Research Center for Development of Knowledge Society Infrastructure" (Leader: Katsumi Tanaka, 2002–2006), a MEXT Grant for "Software Technologies for Search and Integration across Heterogeneous-Media Archives" for the "Development of Fundamental Software Technologies for Digital Archives" (Project Leader: Katsumi Tanaka), and a MEXT Grant-in-Aid for Scientific Research on Priority Areas: "Cyber Infrastructure for the Information-explosion Era" and Planning Research on "Contents Fusion and Seamless Search for Information Explosion" (Project Leader: Katsumi Tanaka, A01-00-02, Grant#: 18049041).

References

1. Xu, J., Croft, W.B.: Query Expansion Using Local and Global Document Analysis. In: Proc. of the 19th Annual International ACM SIGIR Conference on Research and Development in Information Retrieval, pp. 4–11. ACM Press, New York (1996)
2. Mirzadeh, N., Ricci, F., Bansal, M.: Supporting User Query Relaxation in a Recommender System. In: Bauknecht, K., Bichler, M., Pröll, B. (eds.) EC-Web 2004. LNCS, vol. 3182, pp. 31–40. Springer, Heidelberg (2004)
3. Jones, R., Rey, B., Madani, O., Greiner, W.: Generating Query Substitutions. In: Proc. of the 15th International Conference on WWW, pp. 387–396 (2006)
4. Cutting, D.R., Karger, D.R., Pedersen, J.O., Tukey, J.W.: Scatter/Gather: A Cluster-based Approach to Browsing Large Document Collections. In: Proceedings of the 15th ACM International Conference on Research and Development in Information Retrieval (SIGIR'92), pp. 318–329. ACM Press, New York (1992)
5. Chang, E., Seide, F., Meng, H.M., Chen, Z., Shi, Y., Li, Y.C.: A System for Spoken Query Information Retrieval on Mobile Devices. IEEE Transactions on Speech and Audio Processing 10, 531–541 (2002)
6. Google Web Search (2007), http://www.google.com/
7. Google Suggest (2007), http://labs.google.com/suggest/
8. Kawamoto, J., Tanaka, K., Tajima, K.: Supporting of Group Search by Extracting Search Intention from the Query Log and the Navigation History. In: Proceedings of the IEICE 18th Data Engineering WorkShop (DEWS'07) (2007)
9. Vivisimo (2006), http://vivisimo.com/
10. Overture's Keyword Selector Tool (2007), http://inventory.overture.com/d/searchinventory/suggestion/
11. Google Sets (2007), http://labs.google.com/sets/
12. Ohshima, H., Oyama, S., Tanaka, K.: Searching Coordinate Terms with Their Context from the Web. In: Aberer, K., Peng, Z., Rundensteiner, E.A., Zhang, Y., Li, X. (eds.) WISE 2006. LNCS, vol. 4255, pp. 40–47. Springer, Heidelberg (2006)
13. Google Blog Search (2007), http://blogsearch.google.com/
14. Kawai, H., Akamine, S., Kida, K., Matsuda, K., Fukushima, T.: Development and Evaluation of the WithAir Mobile Search Engine. In: Proc. of the 11th International Conference on World Wide Web (WWW'02), Poster-ID:102 (2002)
15. Jose, J.M., Downes, S.: Evaluation of Mobile Information Retrieval Strategies. In: Proc. of the 5th ACM/IEEE-CS Joint Conference on Digital Libraries, p. 411 (2005)
16. Brown, P.J., Jones, G.J.F.: Context-Aware Retrieval: Exploring a New Environment for Information Retrieval and Information Filtering. Personal and Ubiquitous Computing 5, 253–263 (2001)
17. Jones, G.J.F., Brown, P.J.: Context Aware Retrieval for Ubiquitous Computing Environments. In: Crestani, F., Dunlop, M.D., Mizzaro, S. (eds.) Mobile and Ubiquitous Information Access. LNCS, vol. 2954, pp. 227–243. Springer, Heidelberg (2004)
18. Yau, S.S., Liu, H., Huang, D., Yao, Y.: Situation-Aware Personalized Information Retrieval for Mobile Internet. In: Proc. of the 27th Annual International Computer Software and Applications Conference (COMPSAC'03), pp. 638–645 (2003)

19. Rhodes, B.: Using Physical Context for Just-in-Time Information Retrieval. IEEE Transactions on Computers 52, 1011–1014 (2003)
20. Chakrabarti, S., van den Berg, M., Dom, B.: Focused Crawling: A New Approach to Topic-Specific Web Resource Discovery. Computer Networks 31, 1623–1640 (1999)
21. Chau, M., Chen, H., Qin, J., Zhou, Y., Qin, Y., Sung, W.K., McDonald, D.: Comparison of Two Approaches to Building a Vertical Search Tool: A Case Study in the Nanotechnology Domain. In: Proceedings of the 2nd ACM/IEEE-CS Joint Conference on Digital Libraries (JCDL'02), pp. 135–144. ACM Press, New York (2002)

Objective vs. Subjective Scales: The Challenge That the Scale Type Poses to the JUDGEMAP Model of Context Sensitive Judgment

Penka Hristova, Georgi Petkov, and Boicho Kokinov

Central and East European Center for Cognitive Science, Department of Cognitive Science and Psychology, New Bulgarian University, 21 Montevideo Street, Sofia 1618, Bulgaria

Abstract. The paper presents a computational model of context sensitive judgment, called JUDGEMAP, which has been developed for modeling *judgment on a subjective scale*. This paper presents an attempt to apply the same model to the case of *judgment on an objective scale*. This is a big challenge since the behavioral data are showing the opposite type of effects. Thus we have repeatedly obtained *contrast effects of irrelevant information*, when judging on a subjective scale. In the experiment described here we obtained an *assimilation effect* in exactly the same conditions except that the scale was objective. Without any changes of the model we run the corresponding simulations and there are a good and bad news. The bad news is that we did not obtain the assimilation effect, but the good news is that the contrast effect disappeared. The paper discusses possible reasons for these results and possible ways to improve the model.

Keywords: judgment, context effects, assimilation, contrast, analogy-making, cognitive modeling, psychological experimentation, cognitive architectures.

1 Introduction

The present research focuses on the mechanisms behind contextually sensitive judgment. Many experimental results in the field of judgment demonstrate a particular shift in ratings depending on the context. The two main contextual effects usually found in such studies are called contrast (a shift in judgment away from the context) and assimilation (a shift in judgment toward the context).

Unfortunately, the existing empirical studies could not unambiguously determine the conditions under which contrast and assimilation appear. This uncertainty calls into question the contextual nature of judgment in general, that is, whether the two contextual effects are systematic or can be considered as a noise.

Definitely, there is no consensus among the researchers in the field about the causes of contextual effects in judgment. Is there one particular factor that produces contrast and assimilation under specific circumstances or, probably, there are several different factors that contribute to the contextual effects? Finally, it is also possible that these factors compete with each other and the outcome becomes not easily predictable.

B. Kokinov et al. (Eds.): CONTEXT 2007, LNAI 4635, pp. 263–276, 2007.

A profitable step to overcome the current state of affairs may be an explanation of contextual influences in terms of the cognitive mechanisms that cause them. This was exactly the view-point taken by the JUDGEMAP project. Its aim was to suggest several mechanisms that may account for contextual effects in judgment on a subjective scale.

2 JUDGEMAP Model

Instead of modeling explicitly all effects in a judgment task, the JUDGEMAP project starts from a different perspective. We defined several principles that we assume to be central for the cognitive system, and then the attempt was to model the specific task for judgment on the basis of these principles.

We assume: First, that human memory is associative; second, that context is not just a source of noise, but is necessary for a flexible and at the same time effective reasoning; and third, that the ability for mapping (in particular, analogy-making) is not just a specific human capability, but is essential for cognition.

All these principles are integrated and implemented in the cognitive architecture DUAL [11, 12]. It is a multi-agent system that combines connectionist and symbolic mechanisms. The memory is represented with a localist semantic network. Each DUAL-agent 'stands for' something, but even very small pieces of knowledge are represented with a huge number of interconnected DUAL-agents. The sources of activation are two special nodes, called INPUT and GOAL, which represent respectively the environment and the goals of the system. The activation level of the agents, however, does not represent in any way the meaning of the agents, but their relevance to the current context. Thus, the context is defined as the overall pattern of activation that dynamically and continuously changes in response to the environment.

Each DUAL-agent can perform restricted number of symbolic operations. In particular, it can exchange messages with its neighbors; can modify its links; and can create new DUAL-agents. All symbolic operations, however, have a 'price' that should be paid by activation. Thus, the higher the relevance of a certain agent is, the faster it works [11, 12].

The AMBR model [9, 10, 13] is a DUAL-based model for analogy-making. After attachment of the description of the target situation on the GOAL node, the activation spreads from the particular instances to the corresponding concepts and close associations, and then back to some past instances, stored in memory. All relevant instances send markers, which spread upwards in the class hierarchy. If two markers cross somewhere, a hypothesis for correspondence between their origins emerges, i.e. the respective marker-origins are assumed to be analogous, because they have common super-class. The speed of marker spreading reflects the relevance of the respective agents and thus only small number of relevant hypotheses is created. There are other mechanisms for structural correspondence that ensure the systematicity of the mapping. On one hand, there are mechanisms for creation of other hypotheses. For example, if two relations are analogous, than their respective arguments should also be analogous; if two instances are analogous, then their respective concepts should be analogous, etc. On the other hand, inhibitory links between the competing hypotheses emerge. If one and the same element has two or more hypotheses, these hypotheses are assumed to be inconsistent with each other because of the constraint for one-to-one mapping.

Thus, locally and asynchronously many interconnected hypotheses emerge. The result of the relaxation of the network of hypotheses is considered as a final analogy.

JUDGEMAP model [14, 23, 24] is a DUAL-based model of judgment on a scale, highly integrated with AMBR. It is designed under the assumption that the process of judgment on a scale is a process of mapping between a set of stimuli and the set of the available ratings. During this mapping the main constraint is that stimulus with higher magnitude should receive higher rating.

The representation of the stimulus that should be judged is attached to the GOAL node. The scale is represented with a chain of interconnected agents standing for the respective ratings and is attached to the INPUT node. The task of judgment is represented with several already created correspondences, attached to the GOAL node: 1) On one hand, the concept of the stimuli should correspond to the concept of the ratings; 2) On the other hand, the relation for higher magnitude should correspond to the relation for higher rating. Moreover, in order to ensure that the scale will have interval (not only range) properties, higher order relations that compare differences between magnitudes and differences between ratings are also built.

JUDGEMAP models judgment using some mechanisms inherited from the AMBR model and a few new ones. The model treats the judgment process as a result of a structural mapping between two sets. One of the sets is called comparison set. It consists of the target stimulus together with some similar memorized stimuli and the recently judged ones. The main mechanism for construction of the comparison set is the spreading activation mechanism. The second set consists of the available ratings. Note, however, that one and the same stimulus could be judged within different comparison sets, depending on the context, and thus it can receive different rating. Moreover, the context influences the set of the rating too. All ratings have their activation level that changes dynamically during the process of judgment. For example, the ratings of the recently judged stimulus would be more active than the rest. Because of the chain-like organization of the scale, this higher activation would spread to the neighbors of the recently used rating. In general, one of the important characteristics of the JUDGMAP model is its context sensitivity.

Thus, when the target stimulus is presented to the model to be judged, it serves as a source of activation that spreads through the conceptual system and extracts similar exemplars from memory, together with their ratings. The relevant to the task magnitude of the target stimulus is compared to the magnitudes of the elements from the comparison set and thus new agents, who represent the differences between stimuli, emerge. Due to the mechanisms for structural correspondences, the comparisons between the target stimulus and the memorized ones serve as justifications for creation of hypotheses for correspondence between the target stimulus and various ratings. The justifications for a certain hypothesis support it, whereas the inconsistent hypotheses inhibit each other. As a result of the relaxation of this constraint-satisfaction network, one of the hypotheses wins against its competitors and the respective rating is interpreted as the response of the model.

The JUDGEMAP model successfully simulated many of the phenomena in human judgment, found in psychological experiments. In particular, it captures the range and the frequency effects, i.e., the tendency to use all available ratings and to use them approximately equal times [24]. The model also simulates the sequential assimilation effect, and replicates these results with two-dimensional stimuli [24]. In addition, JUDGEMAP was also used for modeling choice between alternatives and successfully replicates some psychologically validated phenomena [23].

3   JUDGEMAP's Prediction and Its Testing

When people judge skewed set of stimuli, they tend to shift their ratings in the direction, opposite to the skew. This is the well-known frequency effect [21, 22]. With other words, suppose that people should judge the lengths of lines, but the short lines dominate. In this case people would overestimate all lengths, thus tending to use all ratings almost equal times.

JUDGEMAP successfully simulated this result because of the pressure for one-to-one mapping (Fig.1). If there are numerous short lines, it is more probably the short lines to dominate in the comparison set. Thus, the small ratings would be more frequently used. Now, suppose that there are competing hypotheses for judging a certain target stimulus with the ratings 3 and 4. Keeping everything else equal, suppose that there are more lines in the comparison set that were already judged with 3 than with 4. Then the target stimulus would be judged with 4, because of the inhibitory links between hypotheses that connect one and the same rating with different stimuli. Note, however, that this mechanism is inherited from the AMBR model for analogy-making and is not specifically designed for simulating the frequency effect. As a result, the JUDGEMAP model was able to replicate the frequency effect, when the judged stimulus set is a skewed one.

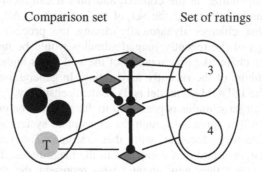

Comparison set   Set of ratings

Fig. 1. The mechanism for one-to-one mapping, inherited from the AMBR model causes the hypotheses for the more often used ratings to receive more inhibition and hence, if a positively skewed set is presented, it is a tendency the stimuli to be overestimated

Suppose, however, that the whole set of stimuli is uniformly distributed, but it can be separated into two skewed sets according to a dimension that is irrelevant to the task. For example, let people should judge the lengths of uniformly distributed lines, but let the lines differ in their color. Half of the lines are positively skewed and are green, whereas the other half are negatively skewed and are red (Fig. 2).

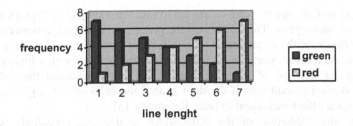

Fig. 2. An example of uniformly distributed set of lines, where each line length is presented for judgment equal number of times. The frequency of the line presentation, however, depends on the line's color. Short lines were presented more often in green, depicted with black lines on the figure, while long lines – more often in red, depicted with the gray textured bars on the figure.

According to the JUDGEMAP model when a green line is to be judged, the activation would spread to the concept 'green' and then back to some of the green instances. Thus, there would be more green lines in the comparison set. However, because the subset of the green lines is positively skewed, it is more probable the short lines to dominate in the comparison set. Thus, because of the frequency principle, the target line would be overestimated. On the contrary, if a red line should be judged, it is more probably the long red lines to dominate the comparison set, and hence, the target red line would be underestimated.

Thus, the JUDGEMAP's prediction is that the green lines would be judged with higher ratings that the red ones with exactly the same length. This particular prediction of the model was successfully simulated and replicated with a psychological experiment [14]. Participants and the JUDGEMAP rated the length of lines on a 7-point scale. The shorter lines were presented more often in green color, while the longer lines were presented more often in red color, thus forming respectively, positively and negatively skewed distributions of lines.

Surprisingly enough we obtained a similar in size difference in judgments of the target green and red lines from people (0.046) and from the model's simulation (0.053). Although this difference was small in size it was significant for both the simulation and the psychological experiment. Thus, the prediction of the JUDGEMAP model was considered to be experimentally confirmed.

The same effect of the irrelevant color on judgment of line length was robustly replicated in several subsequent experiments. We found the same small though significant effect of color on judgment of line length, when the lines were presented at random positions on the screen [6] and also for a very short time [7]. Moreover, in all subsequent experiments the color was counterbalanced across the groups in order to be sure that the effect of irrelevant line color is not due to a specific perceptual length illusion of the green and red colors used in all of our experiments. We didn't found any evidence for such perceptual distortions in our experiments.

In addition, the same effect of irrelevant-to-the-task dimension was found in judgment of abstract stimuli [7, 8]. We used the same design but changed the stimuli from simple green and red lines to much more abstract green and red digits, standing for a particular target characteristic. For example, in one of the experiments participants were asked to judge the age of a hypothetical man on the bases of a number from 10 to 75 that appeared on the screen [7]. Each number represented the age of a person. Participants were instructed to rate, on a subjective 7-point scale, how old a man of such age is. The numbers were green or red and were skewed in such a way that digits with a particular color formed positive or negative stimulus distribution. As a result, participants judged the same number with a higher rank (i.e. as standing for the age of an older man) if the number shared the color of the positively skewed stimuli than if the digit shared the color of the negatively skewed ones. The same effect was found in price judgments [8].

In sum, the prediction of the JUDGMAP model was repeatedly tested and confirmed within a series of experiments. In all of them we obtain the same effect of irrelevant dimension in judgment on a subjective scale, i.e. stimuli ratings were pushed away from the context of irrelevant-to-the-task information.

4   The Importance of the Type of Scale

This result was quite successful in a way, since the same contrast effect of the context of irrelevant information was repeatedly demonstrated within a series of experiment with the same design. Unfortunately, Goldstone [5] reported an effect in opposite direction (assimilation) of an irrelevant stimulus dimension on judgment of object's color in an experiment with comparable design. Participants in Goldstone's experiment were asked to reproduce the color of the object on the screen and were influenced by the irrelevant-to-the-task shape of the objects. Basically, their color judgments were assimilated toward the prototype of the category to which the objects belong, depending on their shape. For example, if the object's shape belongs to the category of more reddish objects, the reproduced color was more reddish than the reproduced color of an identically colored object that belongs to a different shape, and hence, color category. Goldstone [4, 5] assumes that irrelevant information influences the judgment process relatively early in information processing and discuses the possibility for this effect to be a form of perceptual learning phenomena. Goldstone [4] argues that contextual manipulation of the irrelevant stimulus dimension may cause on-line detectors build up, responsible for the effect interest.

There are, however, several crucial differences in the experimental designs used by Goldstone [5] and in our case [7, 8, 14]. First, Goldstone manipulated only the range of the stimulus distribution, while we usually manipulate the frequency of the stimulus distribution with respect to irrelevant-to-the-task stimulus dimension. This difference, however, could not reverse the contextual effect of interest, since both stimulus range and stimulus frequency result in contrast from the context of stimulus set [21, 22]. Such contrast from the range and/or the frequency of the stimulus set was reported many times in experiments, manipulating the range and/or the frequency of the relevant stimulus dimension [21, 22]. Moreover, there is enough empirical evidence, showing that manipulation of the range of the stimulus set with respect to irrelevant stimulus dimension also results in contrast effect [1, 17, 18, 19, 20, 26]. Hence, manipulation of the range rather than the frequency of the stimuli do not seem to be able to reverse the effect of irrelevant stimulus dimension. The second crucial distinction in the experimental designs consists in the type of scale (objective vs. subjective scale), used by Goldstone [5] and in our case [7, 8, 14] This second difference between the designs should be considered much more carefully, since there are researchers, arguing that subjective and objective scales may cause opposite contextual effects. Objective scales are considered to be more likely to produce assimilation effects than subjective scales [3, 5, 15, 16, 27, 28]. Although this claim is based on experiments that manipulate the context of the stimulus set with respect to a stimulus relevant (i.e., judged) dimension and there is no theoretical explicit explanation of the way the scale may influence judgment in such a crucial manner, it seems important to test the possible influence of the scale on the direction of contextual shift.

4.1 Psychological Experiment Judgment on an Objective Scale

We decided to test how the scale influences the effect of irrelevant-to-the-task dimension on judgment of line length. In this manner we hope to be able to isolate only the effect of the objective scale judgment, since we have enough data on judgment of line length on a 7-point scale. That is why, in this experiment we asked participants to judge line length in millimeters.

Method
Design. The within subject independent variable were color (varying at 2 levels). The group counterbalanced the experimental design so that the positively and the negatively skewed stimuli to be presented were either in green or in red. The dependent variable was the mean rating of line lengths in millimeters.

Stimuli. 14 color lines that vary from 180 pixels to 505 pixels with an increment of 25 pixels were presented 8 times each forming a basic set of 112 trials. Each line was presented either in red or in green. The frequency distribution of green lines in the first experimental group was positively skewed, while of the red lines – negatively skewed. In the second experimental group the presentation of lines was just on the opposite, i.e., red lines formed a positively skewed distribution and green lines formed a negatively skewed one. The frequency of the positively and negatively skewed lines is presented in Table 1.

Procedure. Each line was presented horizontally on a gray background in a random position on the screen. The procedure for randomization of the position of each line on an iMac screen was programmed in PsyScope [2]. The participants were instructed to rate each line in millimeters. The experimenter writes down participant's answer and changes the slight manually. The experiment was conducted in sound-proved booths and lasted around 15 minutes for each participant.

Participants. 39 students (24 female and 15 male) from New Bulgarian University participated in the experiment. Participants' age varied between 19 and 36 years. All participants were paid 0.5 euro for taking part in the experiment. There were 19 students in group 1 and 20 students in group 2.

Results and Discussion. The data was averaged by item (14 lengths). Each participant had 28 mean judgments (14 lines*2 colors). The color was analyzed as a within-subject factor, while the group was a between-subject factor. As in all of ours previous experiments, the Repeated Measurement Analyses showed a non-significant main effect of the group: $F(1, 37) = 1.166$, $p=0.287$ which means that it does not matter whether the red or the green color is positively skewed. Thus, the results from the two

Table 1. Frequency and color of the lines for a block of 112 trials, where lines with *color P* were positively skewed and lines with *color N* were negatively skewed

Lines	*Length in pixels*	Number of the lines with *color P* (Positively skewed distribution)	Number of the lines with *color N* (Negatively skewed distribution)
1;2	180;205	7	1
3;4	230;255	6	2
5;6	280;305	5	3
7;8	330;355	4	4
9;10	380;405	3	5
11;12	430;455	2	6
13;14	480;505	1	7

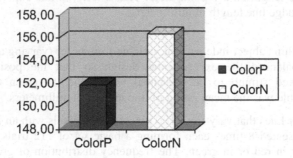

Fig. 3. Mean ratings of the *lines* for each color in millimeters. The black bar stands for ratings of the positively skewed lines, while gray-textured bar – for negatively skewed lines.

groups were accumulated and we use *color P* to indicate a positively skewed distribution and *color N* to indicate a negatively skewed distribution in all further analyses.

The main effect of the irrelevant dimension (color *P* vs. color *N*) on rating of the 14 lines was significant, as estimated with the Repeated Measurement Analysis: F (1, 37) =7.569, p=0.009, the effect size (ES) = 0.170. The difference between the mean judgment of positively skewed lines (151.906) and the mean judgment of negatively skewed lines (156.396) was 4.490 mm. Negatively skewed lines were rated higher than positively skewed lines despite the fact that they were equal in length (Fig. 3).

In conclusion, obviously, the scale reverses the effect of irrelevant dimension. The context of irrelevant-to-the-task dimension assimilated the estimated line lengths in millimeters in contrast to the effect of the irrelevant dimension in judgment of line length on a 7-point scale. This result could hardly be described by the JUDGEMAP model, since the model presupposes that judgment is a process of mapping and hence, assumes that the scale is predefined.

If we assume, however, that there is a qualitative difference between the objective and subjective scales, some empirical results cannot be explained. In particular, Wedell, Parducci & Geiselman [29] found that when people judge on a 100-point but subjective scale, the contrastive frequency effect disappeared.

Thus, an alternative possibility is to think about the objective scales as subjective ones, but having much more ratings. Moreover, in the case of length judgments of lines shown on a computer screen, we have an implicit predefined limit of the possible lengths in millimeters, since the screen has a constant width. Thus, a speculative prediction of the JUDGEMAP model is that if the scale consists of too many ratings, because of the limitations of spreading activation, only small part of the scale would be active in any particular moment. Hence, if a certain stimulus should be judged, and if the stimuli with high magnitudes dominate in the comparison set, then only the high ratings of the scale would be active. As a result, the well-simulated contrast effect would appear, but only relative to the active part of the scale. Considered with respect to the whole scale, however, the effect can be exactly the opposite one, namely assimilation.

4.2 Simulation with JUDGEMAP Judgment on a Hundred-Point Scale

This simulation tested the specific prediction of the JUDGEMAP model that the irrelevant dimension will influence the judgment on a hundred point scale. A set of 112 lines was designed. Each line was represented with a coalition of three DUAL-agents – one for the line itself, one for its length, and one for its color. The whole set consists of seven groups of lines. There were eight lines with an equal length in each group. Thus, in the first group there were eight lines with a length 100; in the second one – eight lines with a length 200, etc. In the last group there were eight lines with a length 1400. According to the line's color, however, the distribution was more complex. In the first 2 groups there were seven green and one red line in each group; in the second 2 groups – six red and two green lines in each group; etc. In the last two groups there were one green and seven red lines in each group (see Table 1).

Thus, the overall set was uniformly distributed, but it consists of two skewed subsets according to the line's color, which is completely irrelevant to the task property. In summary we used the same set as in the subjective scale simulations.

The scale was represented with a set of hundred ratings, interconnected each one with its neighbors. There were also associative links between the neighbor ratings that can be divided to 10, i.e., between 10th and 20th, between 20th and 30th, etc. All 100 ratings were instances of one concept of scale itself. There were, however, only few opposite links from the concept to the ratings of 10, 50, and 90, thus simulating several 'favorite' numbers. The same method for activating the scale was used in all JUDGEMAP simulations, since without the opposite links from the scale concept to some specific scale values no ratings could be activated at all.

The task was represented with a correspondence between the concepts of longer line and of higher rating. The whole set of 112 lines was judged 30 times, each time all of the lines were judged sequentially in a random order.

Results and Discussion. The data was analyzed in the same way as in the psychological experiment. The difference between the mean judgment of positively skewed lines (48.907) and the mean judgment of negatively skewed lines (50.359) was 1.452 on 100-hundred scale, but the main effect of the color on rating of the 14 lines was non-significant, as estimated with the Repeated Measurement Analysis: $F (1, 29) =1.686, p=0.204$.

The significant assimilative effect to the direction of the skew, received in the psychological experiment, was not replicated. The contrast effect, however, simulated with a seven-point scale, also disappeared. This result is in line with the experiment of Wedell Parducci & Geiselman [29], which demonstrates that, the role of the stimulus skew (i.e., the pressure of frequency principle) decreases when the number of the available rating increases.

Obviously, however, there was an extremely high bias of the opposite links from the scale concept to the ratings 10, 50, and 90. It can be noticed in Figure 4 that JUDGEMAP prefers these ratings and their neighbors much more often than the other ratings. In other words, the main problem of the simulation was that JUDGEMAP could not successfully support the appropriate parts of the scale active enough. The main difference between the results of the simulations with 7-point and 100-point scales was that in the first case all ratings were active enough, whereas in the second case they are not. When judging on a 7-point scale most of the ratings participate in the competition and the small difference in their activation level causes small effects like the sequential assimilation. When judging on a 100-point scale, however, the activation was not enough to support all ratings (and should not be!). The main source of activation in this case was the opposite links, thus extremely increasing the bias that they press.

Thus, one possibility for JUDGEMAP to simulate assimilative effect when judging on an objective scale, using the same mechanisms as when judging on a subjective one, is to find another representation of the scale. For example, we may assign randomly the opposite connections from the scale concept to the scale ratings, avoiding in such a way the observed high bias in the 100-point scale simulation. In this manner we may overcome the JUDGEMAP's preference to use mainly the rating around the scale values (i.e., rating 10, 50 and 100 in the reported simulation) that receive activation from the 100-scale concept. However, even random, the opposite links would press too high bias.

Another possibility for JUDGEMAP model to simulate the observed assimilation in judgment on objective scale is to think that when people judge on an objective scale, they do not use any predefined "chain"[1] of possible answers, but rather generate the ratings. Thus, if each time JUDGEMAP generates a new rating, there would not be a need for inhibitory links between hypotheses that connect one and the same rating with different stimuli. Thus, the pressure for one-to-one mapping, which is the main source of the contrast effects in judgment on a seven-point scale, would be eliminated. How exactly to generate these new ratings, however, is still an open question for us. Although the idea that people use different strategies when judging on a subjective or on an objective scale seems reasonable the main idea of the JUDGEMAP model is to demonstrate how different cognitive phenomena can be explained as an emergent result of a limited number of basic mechanisms (more precisely, the mechanisms for analogical mapping).

---

[1] In all JUDGEMAP simulations the scale was represented as a "chain" of interconnected nodes, where each node, standing for a particular scale value is connected with associative links to its neighbors. For example, rating "3" is connected with associative links to rating "2" and respectively, to rating "4", rating "4" is connected to rating "3" and rating "5" etc.

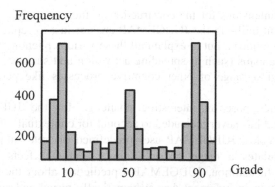

Fig. 4. The frequency distribution of the ratings, given by JUDGMAP

They are, however, other alternative possibilities. One of them is to think about additional mappings between the target stimulus and the elements of the comparison set. During such type of mappings, the ratings of the memorized stimuli would be transferred with appropriate modifications. Suppose that the target stimulus that a person has to judge reminds him/her of another stimulus that he/she has already judged or just remembers its absolute value. Then, a person may just transfer the rating of the known stimulus to the similar new one. Let's think for a while about our green positively skewed and red negatively skewed lines, although the possibility that a particular line may remind you about another one does not sound quite realistic. Suppose, however, that you judge the length in millimeters of a green target line. The target line may remind you about another green line of approximately the same length that you have already estimated as being 200 millimeters. Then you may just transfer the rating of the previously judged "similar" line to the new one, probably with slight modifications depending on the degree of similarity between the length of the old and the new line. Moreover, since the green lines were positively skewed, there is higher probability that the target green line may remind you about a short green line. Thus, the ratings of the green lines would be biased toward the lower part of the scale, while the rating of the red lines – toward the upper scale values. In this manner, we may increase the probability for assimilation toward the context of irrelevant dimension, but only for judgment on a scale that has more values than the system may simultaneously keep in the WM. Judgment on a 7-point scale would not be substantially affected by this transfer mechanism, since the pressure for one-to-one mapping would be still strong enough to overcome the possible assimilation introduced by this transfer mechanism. An attempt to implement transfer mechanisms in the AMBR model was already made [25], and these mechanisms can be used in the judgment task, namely to explain why the scale was able to reverse the effect of context in the psychological experiments.

4 Conclusions

The idea that people perform judgments relative to a set of comparable elements is not new or surprising. According to the JUDGEMAP model, however, people use even irrelevant dimensions for the construction of the comparison set. Furthermore, our main efforts in building the JUDGEMAP are not just to replicate some specific psychological phenomena, but to explain all these various phenomena in terms of the same basic mechanisms (such as spreading activation and structure mapping), which are also basic for a range of other cognitive processes like perception, analogy, memory.

Objective scales pose an interesting challenge for the JUDGEMAP model, although the model has never pretended to account for contextual effects in judgments on this kind of scales. JUDGEMAP uses predefined discrete subjective scales and successfully simulates a range of well-known context effects on judgment on subjective scale. In addition, JUDGEMAP's prediction about the role of irrelevant stimulus information in judgment was systematically tested and confirmed within a series of psychological experiments.

The idea, however, that the type of scale reverses the context effect because of different underlying mechanisms [5, 15, 16, 27, 28] challenges in an important way some basic assumptions of JUDGEMAP. The model assumes and successfully demonstrates that one and the same basic mechanisms may be used for judgment, analogy-making, choice-making [23] and even partially for perception [25]. Thus, it seems reasonable to suggest that the same mechanisms may also account for judgment on objective scale.

Our first attempt to model assimilation toward the context of irrelevant dimension, without any changes in the model, failed. In the previous section, we outlined several possible opportunities to extend the JUDGEMAP model in order it to be also able to explain judgment on objective scale without any essential changes in the model's mechanisms and assumptions. In summary the main idea would be to add a mechanism for rating transfer (based on direct comparison – analogical mapping between an already evaluated stimulus and the target one) and to solve the problem of realistic representation of large scales. The analogy transfer will be a new mechanism for hypothesis building in both the subjective and objective scales. It can potentially contribute to assimilation effects in both cases. The difference would be in the role of inhibitory links in both cases. In the case of subjective scales there is a pressure to use the whole scale and thus the role of competition between the hypotheses should be higher (and leads to contrast), while in the case of objective scales no such competition is required. The good news from the current simulation is that with large scales the contrast effect disappears. Thus if the two mechanisms (competition between hypotheses leading to contrast and hypothesis formation based on the ratings of similar stimuli leading to assimilation) are co-existing in both subjective and objective scales and working against each other, in large objective scales only the assimilation effect will persist and this would explain the overall assimilation effect. This has yet to be tested with a further development of the JUDGEMAP model.

Acknowledgments. This work is supported by the Project ANALOGY: Humans – the Analogy-Making Species, financed by the FP6 NEST Programme of the European Commission.(Contr. No 029088).

References

1. Arieh, Marks, L.: Context effects in visual length perception. Role of ocular, retinal, and spatial location. Perception & Psychophysics 64(3), 478–492 (2002)
2. Cohen, MacWhinney, Flatt, Provost: PsyScope: An Interactive Graphic System for designing and controlling experiments in Psychology Laboratory Using Macintosh Computers. Behavior Research, Methods, Instruments and Computers 25, 257–271 (1993)
3. Foti, Hauenstein: Processing Demands and the Effects of Prior Impression on Subsequent Judgments: Clarifying the Assimilation/Contrast Debate. Organizational Behavior and Human Decision Processes 56, 167–189 (1993)
4. Goldstone, R.: Perceptual Learning. Annual Review of Psychology 49, 585–612 (1998)
5. Goldstone, R.: Effects of Categorization on Color Perception. Psychological Science 6(5), 298–304 (1995)
6. Hristova, P., Kokinov, B.: Perceptual Learning vs. Context-Sensitive Retrieval: Why do people judge green lines to be shorter/longer than red lines of the same length? Do they perceive them differently or do they retrieve a biased set of alternatives in their comparison set? In: Proceedings of the Second European Cognitive Science Conference (in press)
7. Hristova, P., Kokinov, B.: A Common Mechanism Is Possibly Underlying the Shift in Perceptual and Conceptual Judgment Produced by Irrelevant Information. In: Proceedings of the 28th Annual Conference of the Cognitive Science Society, Erlbaum, Hillsdale, NJ (2006)
8. Hristova, P., Petkov, G., Kokinov, B.: Influence of Irrelevant Information on Price Judgment. In: Proceedings of the International Conference on Cognitive Economics, NBU Press (2005)
9. Kokinov, B.: Associative Memory-Based Reasoning: How to Represent and Retrieve Cases. In: O'Shea, T., Sgurev, V. (eds.) Artificial Intelligence III: Methodology, Systems, Applications, Elsevier, Amsterdam (1988)
10. Kokinov, B.: A Hybrid Model of Reasoning by Analogy. In: Holyoak, K., Barnden, J. (eds.) Advances in Connectionist and Mental Computation Theory. Analogical Connections, Ablex, Norwood (1994a)
11. Kokinov, B.: The DUAL Cognitive Architecture. A Hybrid Multi-Agent Approach. In: Cohn, A. (ed.) Proceedings of the Eleventh European Conference of Artificial Intelligence, John Wiley & Sons, Ltd. London (1994b)
12. Kokinov, B.: The Context-Sensitive Architecture DUAL. In: Proceedings of the Sixteenth Annual Conference of the Cognitive Science Society. LEA, Hillsdale (1994c)
13. Kokinov, B., Petrov, A.: Integration of Memory and Reasoning in Analogy-Making: The AMBR Model. In: Gentner, D., Holyoak, K., Kokinov, B. (eds.) The Analogical Mind: Perspectives from Cognitive Science, MIT Press, Cambridge, MA (2001)
14. Kokinov, B., Hristova, P., Petkov, G.: Does Irrelevant Information Play a Role in Judgment? In: Proceedings of the 26th Annual Conference of the Cognitive Science Society, pp. 720–725. Erlbaum, Hillsdale, Mahwah (2004)
15. Lockhead, King: A Memory Model of Sequential Effects in Scaling Tasks. Journal of Experimental Psychology: Human Perception and Performance 3, 461–473 (1983)
16. Manis, Nelson, Shedler: Stereotypes and Social Judgment: Extremity, Assimilation and Contrast. Journal of Personality and Social Psychology 55, 28–36 (1988)
17. Marks, L.: The slippery context effect in psychophysics: Intensive, extensive, and qualitative continua. Perception and Psychophysics 51, 187–198 (1992)
18. Marks, L.: Recalibrating the auditory system: The perception of loudness. Journal of Experimental Psychology: Human Perception and Performance 20, 382–396 (1994)

19. Marks, L., Armstrong: Visual and haptic representations of space. In: Inui, McClelland (eds.) Attention and Performance XVI: Information Integration in perception and communication, MIT Press, Cambridge (1996)
20. Marks, L., Warner: Slippery context effect and critical bands. Journal of Experimental Psychology: Human Perception and Performance 17, 986–996 (1991)
21. Parducci, A.: Category Judgment: A Range-Frequency model. Psychological Review 72(6), 407–418 (1965)
22. Parducci, A.: Contextual Effects: A Range-Frequency Analysis, Handbook of Perception, vol. 2. Academic Press, NY (1974)
23. Petkov, G.: Modeling Analogy-Making, Judgment, and Choice with Same Basic Mechanisms. In: Fum, D., Missier, F., Stocco, A., Goliardiche, E. (eds.) Proceedings of the Seventh International Conference on Cognitive Modeling, pp. 220–225 (2006)
24. Petkov, G.: Judgment as Mapping (JUDGEMAP2). In: Proceedings of the Doctoral Consortium at the Fifth International and Interdisciplinary Conference on Modeling and Using Context. Technical Report LIP 2005/007 of the Laboratoire d'Informatique de Paris 6, pp. 95–104 (2005), URL http://www.lip6.fr
25. Petkov, G., Kiryazov, K., Grinberg, M., Kokinov, B.: Modeling Top-Down Perception and Analogical Transfer with Single Anticipatory Mechanism. In: Proceedings of the Second European Cognitive Science Conference (in press)
26. Rankin, Marks, L.: Differential context effects in chemosensation: Role of perceptual similarity and neural communality. Chemical Senses 25, 747–759 (2000)
27. Ward: Critical Bands and Mixed-Frequency Scaling: Sequential Dependencies, Equal Loudness Contours, and Power Function Exponents. Perception and Psychophysics 47, 551–562 (1990)
28. Weddel: Methods for Determining the Locus of Context Effects in Judgment. In: Caverni, Fabre, Gonzales (eds.) Cognitive Biases, New York, Elsevier Science Publishers, Amsterdam (1990)
29. Wedell, Parducci, Geiselman: A Formal Analysis of Ratings of Physical Attractiveness: Successive Contrast and Simultaneous Assimilation. Journal of Experimental Social Psychology 23, 230–249 (1987)

Similarity Measurement in Context

Carsten Keßler

Institute for Geoinformatics, University of Münster, Germany
carsten.kessler@uni-muenster.de

Abstract. Context plays a crucial role when measuring the similarity of two concepts. Nonetheless, the modelling of context has been mostly neglected in existing similarity measurement theories. In this paper, we explore the influence of context in existing similarity measurement approaches for the geospatial domain, focussing on whether and how these approaches account for it. Based on these observations, the processing of context during similarity measurement is analysed, and general implementation issues, especially ease of integration into existing reasoning systems and computability, are discussed. The results of the different analyses are then combined into a generic set of characteristics of context for similarity measurement, with regard to the geospatial domain.

Keywords: Similarity measurement, context, geospatial concepts.

1 Introduction and Motivation

The importance of context for similarity measurement has long been observed and is beyond dispute. In fact, context is required for similarity measures to make sense in the first place. As Murphy and Medin put it, "the relative weighting of a feature [...] varies with the stimulus context and task, so that there is no unique answer to the question of how similar one object is to another" [18], p.292. As an example, imagine being asked to compare two buildings in New York City: the Chrysler Building and the Radio City Music Hall. The answer depends on whether you are currently talking about functional aspects, which makes both very dissimilar – or whether you are talking about architectural styles, which results in a high similarity of the two Art Deco buildings. To that effect, measuring similarity without taking context into consideration is in most cases useless [10].

Even so, the actual modeling and incorporation of context into similarity measurement has mostly been neglected or appears as future work in the literature. Existing similarity theories [9] produce satisfying results in psychological experiments. However, it must be noted that these experiments are carefully designed such that the subject's similarity ratings are not biased due to environmental – i.e. contextual – influences [23]. Such an isolated perspective on similarity has two drawbacks: on the one hand, it is based on unrealistic preconditions, as people's similarity ratings in everyday situations are always influenced by their current context; on the other hand, such theories are missing the chance to utilize contextual information to make similarity measurements more accurate and tailored to the situation of an individual.

B. Kokinov et al. (Eds.): CONTEXT 2007, LNAI 4635, pp. 277–290, 2007.
© Springer-Verlag Berlin Heidelberg 2007

The motivation of this paper is to improve similarity measurements by explicitly integrating context. Such an integrated model would allow for more precise queries, not only retrieving the *generic* similarity of two concepts or individuals, but directly referring to the respects which need to be taken into consideration. Concerning applications using similarity measurement, contextual information can be useful to clarify ambiguous situations, e.g. when searching knowledge bases by query concepts. In such search scenarios, the knowledge base typically contains a lot of information that is insignificant for a comparison. The context can specify what information needs to be considered, and what is out of scope for the current task.

To develop a useful context model, "we must attain a better understanding of what context is" [4], p.2. We are thus interested in a definition of context that is application-driven, i.e. that allows us to figure out what context parameters are important for a particular comparison task. The specific aim of this paper is hence a notion that helps putting context for similarity measurement into computational practice. The long-term objective is the development of a tool which supports developers in assessing the influence of the available context parameters on the overall similarity measurement.

This paper focuses on the geospatial domain because there is a big interest in context for similarity measurement within this research area. On the one hand, similarity measurement has been an important field of research within the community during the last years, e.g. to enhance retrieval of geographic information, or to integrate heterogeneous spatial data sources [12, 20]. On the other hand, location is an important aspect of context and plays a crucial role in different applications such as location based services (LBS) or mobile decision support systems [22, 25]. An improved understanding of context for similarity measurement in the geospatial domain can thus contribute to further developments in various branches of this research field. Nonetheless, the anticipated results are expected to be largely transferable to other application areas for similarity measurement.

The remaining part of the paper is organized as follows: We first present relevant related work from the fields of similarity measurement and context. Three applications of similarity measurement from the geospatial domain are then analyzed regarding their incorporation of context. Finally, a definition of context for similarity measurement, and formal characteristics of context are presented, followed by conclusions and open research questions.

2   Related Work

This section presents relevant related work from the fields of similarity measurement and from other research areas with an interest in contextual information. A generic definition of context is presented as a starting point for a notion of context for similarity measurement.

2.1   Similarity Measurement

Similarity measurement theories stem from research on the human ability to intuitively determine how similar two objects are, and to put those similarity ratings in relation (e.g. "computer science is more similar to mathematics than geography"). There are two main interests within this research area: on the one hand, psychologists aim at understanding and modeling how humans rate similarity; on the other hand, the artificial intelligence (AI) community is interested in designing formal – and thus computable – methods for ambiguous reasoning tasks; however, integrated approaches that take both perspectives into account are rare. Although the basic idea of similarity measurements is to reflect human ratings, the design of cognitively adequate algorithms that reproduce the human similarity rating process is difficult in practice. This is not only because of a lack of understanding concerning the underlying cognitive processes, but also because existing knowledge representations such as ontologies focus on formalizing knowledge, rather than matching the mental concept representations of human agents. Hence, the focus of this paper is on the AI perspective of similarity measurement, striving for cognitively plausible results which match human similarity ratings; the discussion whether the applied methods that lead to those results correspond to human cognitive processes is thus secondary.

From the psychological perspective, there are different approaches to similarity measurement, relying on different ways of representing concepts. Similarity in feature-based approaches can be computed in such representations following different strategies, for example counting (and possibly weighting) common features, and integrating structural similarity [27]. Geometry-based approaches, in contrast, assign dimensions with a geometric or topologic structure to the concepts which represent their properties [8]. All concepts are thus placed in an n-dimensional space, which allows for similarity measurement based on the semantic distance between two concepts. Network models put the stress on the edges in the network, and are mostly used to reproduce similarity ratings from human subject tests. Independent of the approach chosen for concept representation, similarity values are usually normalized to values between 0 (completely dissimilar) and 1 (identical). Although this list is not complete[1], it is sufficient to show what different preconditions a generic notion of context must be able to adapt to.

2.2 Defining Context

Any definition of context is heavily dependent on the field of application, as shown by the analysis of 150 different definitions by Bazire and Brézillon [2]. Looking at definitions within the field of computer science, the literature mostly falls back on enumerations of examples. In other cases, the definitions are too specific to be transferable to similarity measurement [19]. A generic definition of context for ubiquitous computing is presented in [4], pp.3-4:

"Context is any information that can be used to characterise the situation of an entity. An entity is a person, place, or object that is considered relevant to the interaction between a user and an application, including the user and applications themselves."

The central aspects in this definition are *identity* (user), *activity* (interaction with an application), *location* and *time* (as the temporal constraints of a certain situation) [4]. This list does not claim completeness, nor do all of the aspects always play a role, as

---

[1] For a comprehensive list of similarity theories, see [9].

will be shown. The definition will serve as a starting point for this paper, since it is from a related field of research, yet still generic enough to be transferred to similarity measurement for the geospatial domain. We will develop a more specific definition for similarity measurement throughout this paper.

3 Similarity and Context in the Geospatial Domain

In this section, we analyze three different approaches for similarity measurement in the geospatial domain. The chosen scenarios stem from research publications and represent a broad range of applications for similarity measurement in this scientific field, both in terms of concept representation method and kind of application. The objective of this review is to show which aspects of context play a role in the presented use cases, and to point out which of them have been considered in the corresponding approaches. For this purpose, the categories identity, activity, location and time from the definition in section 2.2 are used for reference. Moreover, this review demonstrates the need for context in similarity measurement, as none of the presented tasks can be completed satisfyingly without taking context into consideration.

3.1 Comparing Geospatial Features

Rodríguez and Egenhofer (2004) introduce the Matching-Distance Similarity Measure (MDSM) [24], an approach for the comparison of geospatial features in ontologies. MDSM is a weighted sum of the similarities of two concepts' parts, functions and attributes, extending Tversky's ratio model [27]. It allows for asymmetric similarity measurement, as the perceived similarity of a to b is not always the same as the similarity of b to a. This fact is either based on the varying prominence of the instances at hand (e.g. the Kaufmann Concert Hall is more similar to the Radio City Music Hall than vice versa) [13, 27], or on the comparison of sub- and super-concepts (e.g. Concert Halls are more similar to Buildings than vice versa) [5].

MDSM explicitly includes context, modeling it as a set of tuples consisting of operations and their arguments. This information is processed in two manners: First, the domain of application is determined by selecting all features that are ontologically related to the operations' arguments. Second, weights for mereological, functional and attributional similarity are derived from the context. These weights can be calculated based on variability (focusing on a feature's informativeness) or on commonality (focusing on how characteristic a feature is for the application domain).

The notion of context included in MDSM is based on the assumption that all relevant contextual information is immanent in the task the user wants to perform – the activity, using the terminology of our current context definition. However, referring to the other aspects of the definition, spatial and temporal constraints are not supported by this context view. This limitation is based on the structure of the underlying ontology, which lacks spatial and temporal information. The user preferences are represented through the operations selected for the context. Looking at the examples given in the paper, such as "the user's intention is to play a sport", location and time provide important contextual information: a system that considers a more detailed form of context could reduce the domain of application to locations in the user's vicinity, and opening times could be considered. A user model would even allow for a weighting by the user's preferences, e.g. higher weighting of swimming pools than soccer fields. It must, however, be noted that the ontology used in the paper does not contain individuals; consequently, instance-specific information (location, opening times) cannot be considered in the measurements. Although the notion of context in MDSM could be refined by further information, it introduced the first inclusion of context for similarity measurement in the geospatial domain.

3.2 Geographic Information Retrieval

Janowicz (2006) introduces Sim-DL, a similarity theory for concepts specified in the $\mathcal{ALCNR}$ description logic (DL) [11]. The development of Sim-DL aims at closing the gap between similarity theories from psychological research and formal knowledge representations used in the AI community. Similarity in Sim-DL is asymmetric and calculated as the normalized weighted sum of the similarities of all descriptions of two concepts. The similarity of the single parts is the overlap of their concept descriptions in normal form. Comparable to the approach presented in the previous section, contextual information is used in Sim-DL to specify the domain of application. Moreover, weights are used to express the impact of a part on the overall similarity. The method for determining weights is not specified within Sim-DL.

Context is explicitly stated together with the search concept when starting a similarity query. The author uses the example of "botels" in Amsterdam to illustrate the SIM-DL approach. When measuring whether botels are conceptually closer to hotels or to boat houses, the user explicitly states that the context for this comparison should be, for example, housing. Accordingly, all concepts within the knowledge base related to housing are used for the similarity measurement. Concepts which are related to the query concept, but not related to housing (such as tub or water taxi), are not taken into consideration. Regarding our current definition of context, the main question is how to model identity, location and time, which cannot be represented in $\mathcal{ALCNR}$ (activity is represented through the choice of the domain of application). As the author points out, $\mathcal{ALCNR}$ is not expressive enough, e.g. to explicitly state geographic locations (which requires concrete domains), but only topological relationships. Likewise, temporal relations can be expressed, but no specific points in time. This lack of expressiveness limits what can be said about instances. Moreover, reasoning in description logics is expensive concerning computation time, even on simple knowledge bases with only a few concepts. To improve this, more efficient reasoning algorithms for DL are required. Consequently, Sim-DL is an approach to similarity measurement with a limited notion of context which is compatible with AI knowledge representations, but which still has limitations in practice.

3.3 Landmark Selection for Pedestrian Navigation

Raubal (2004) [21] presents a formalization of Gärdenfors' conceptual spaces [8], a theory from cognitive semantics accounting for the fact that different people may have different understandings of the same expressions. Conceptual spaces are sets of quality dimensions with a geometric or topologic structure. Concepts are represented as regions in such a space (instances as points, respectively), allowing for similarity measurements based on semantic distance. Raubal formalizes Gärdenfors' model as conceptual vector spaces, employing z-transformations to standardize the values for dimensions of the space. As opposed to the approaches presented above, similarity is calculated at the instance level in this case.

The approach is demonstrated by using a pedestrian navigation scenario, where user and system[2] have different conceptualizations of landmarks. For example, the system's conceptualization may include information about buildings' historical importance, which is irrelevant to most users. Such semantic gaps are closed via transformations and projections between the corresponding vector space representations.

The conceptual spaces approach includes various aspects of context. Conceptual spaces are centered on the user, so that there is a detailed user model at hand, i.e. the user's conceptual space. Moreover, the paper introduces methods to match this user profile with external conceptualizations, which can be utilized to extend existing systems with user profiles, and to match between different systems. The choice of a landmark at every decision point during the navigation task is context-dependent: Among the landmarks available at a decision point, the most distinct one is chosen, i.e. the landmark with the largest semantic distance to the landmark prototype. The prototype is an imaginary landmark instance, calculated as the combination of the mean values for each dimension. Beyond user and location, the author discusses temporal aspects of context. For the scenario, the time of day is crucial. If a landmark sticks out because of its color, it is salient during daytime, but not at night [28]. The different contexts are represented by weightings on the dimensions of the conceptual space, for example the color is assigned a high weight for the daytime context, and a low one for the nighttime context.

Comparing the presented approach to our current definition of context, only activity is not explicitly modeled, whereas user, location and time are already included. However, this is mostly due to the use case chosen, which includes a fixed activity (pedestrian navigation). Contextual aspects depending on the task could easily be included by adapting the weights. The limitations of this approach are based on the requirement for every quality to be at least ordered in some way; data on the nominal scale cannot be represented properly[3] [14]. Moreover, conceptual spaces have only been used for small numbers of dimensions so far, and the scenarios were mostly of limited complexity. Further research is required to demonstrate how this approach can be applied in more complex situations.

3.4 Summary

The three approaches presented in this section embark on different strategies for concept representation and similarity measurement, and also for the inclusion of context. Nonetheless, they share the idea of assigning weights to the single factors that go into a similarity measurement to reflect a specific context. Accordingly, these

---

[2] More precisely, the system reflects the system designer's conceptualization.

[3] It is possible to integrate nominal values by creating a Boolean dimension for every one, but this easily leads to a large number of dimensions, rendering the whole approach impracticable.

weights have a big impact on the overall result of the measurement. Rodríguez & Egenhofer have analyzed two different strategies – commonality and variability – for the different scenarios in their paper. Although the change of strategy did not alter the overall ranking drastically, the commonality approach (which puts the stress on common features) produces more variation in the results. From a cognitive perspective, this approach seems to be the more plausible one compared to the variability strategy, since psychological research has found that people appear to focus on commonalties, also referred to as the *max effect* [17].

Context is also used to determine the domain of application. This is either done by automatic extraction of concepts from the user's query [24], or by explicit statement of context concepts [11]. In both cases, these concepts are used to select all related concepts from the knowledge base as the domain of application. It is remarkable that none of the presented approaches allow for the inclusion of additional contextual information that is not already present in the knowledge base, because the essential idea of context in other fields of research is mostly to add supplementary information to what is already known. In some cases, context is even regarded as completely external to the knowledge base [6].

Concerning the similarity measurement itself, all approaches assume the existence of a common understanding of the basic terms of the knowledge base, usually defined in a shared vocabulary such as a top level ontology. As the presented strategies only select context from within the knowledge base, this applies also to the context. In conclusion, it must be pointed out that all of the presented approaches were focusing on the similarity theory itself, and that context was only a part of the theory. The notions of context engaged within the theories are thus not complete, but show how context can generally be integrated in the similarity measurement process.

4 Context for Similarity Measurement Applications

In this section, we present the requirements and constraints for context in similarity measurement applications. Following from those theoretical and practical prerequisites, a definition of context for similarity measurement is given, and a set of generic properties for this notion of context is formalized.

4.1 General Requirements

The observations from section 3 have shown that it is not possible to come up with a fixed context model for similarity measurement in the geospatial domain. The context parameters that play a role depend to a great extent on the application. Although the categories identity, activity, location and time have been used for the analysis, these categories are not of great help. On the one hand, they are too generic, since *every* contextual parameter can be squeezed into one of those categories. On the other hand, they do not say anything about the relevance of these categories for a comparison task.

Apart from the relevance of concepts, the question of how to obtain data for those parameters plays a big role in practice. Aspects of context that are not available in the knowledge base must either be captured automatically, or, if this is not possible, explicitly provided by the user. Collection of context information by user input is a usability issue and must be balanced in every case. The formalization of the knowledge base is also important for the context model [2]. As we have seen in section 3, the context must in any case be in the same form of representation as the knowledge base; otherwise, it is not possible to integrate both. For example, providing additional contextual information, formalized in the Web Ontology Language (OWL) [16], for an application built on conceptual spaces would be hard to utilize, since both are based on very different kinds of concept representation. Moreover, the context must refer to the same shared vocabulary as the knowledge base to enable integration, where the knowledge base can also serve as the shared vocabulary. Such integration also allows for comparison of different contexts. Intuitively, a similarity measurement should produce similar results under similar contexts. This behavior could also be observed in MSDM: changes in the strategy for selection of weights, resulting in slight changes to the context, caused only small changes in the outcome of the similarity measurement.

Research on similarity measurement has lead to the development of models that produce reliable results. Accordingly, context should be established as an add-on to existing similarity theories – instead of inventing yet another similarity theory. Specific context models are heavily depending on different aspects of the application, even within the specific field of similarity measurement; nonetheless, it is still possible to make generic statements about context for similarity measurement. The next sections will give an overview of the typical environment for contextual information, and then define context for similarity measurement on a generic level, which provides the basic conditions for specific context models built for applications.

4.2 The Context Processing Chain

Applications that make use of contextual information generally follow a certain process chain when completing a task for the user. For a context-aware similarity application, this chain starts when the user defines the kind of problem he wants to solve. These problems are composed of comparisons of concept pairs at the lowest level. Such a query may be augmented with an explicit context statement, but parts of the context can also be automatically extracted[4] and then interactively refined by the user. Time and location, for example, are contextual aspects which can easily be captured automatically.

After this first initialization step, the user query and the context information have to be aligned with the knowledge base, i.e. it must be checked whether the knowledge base already contains all context information provided with the query. If this is not the case, the additional information must be "injected" to the knowledge base, relying on a shared vocabulary for alignment. The domain of application is then a subset of this extended knowledge base, consisting of those parts of the knowledge base that are conceptually related to the context. Within the domain of application, weights are assigned to the concept in the next step. The steps completed so far can be regarded as

---

[4] Techniques for automatic context extraction are beyond the scope of this paper. First solutions, which can partly be transferred to similarity measurement applications, can be found in [15] for context-aware web search engines, and in [3] for ubiquitous computing.

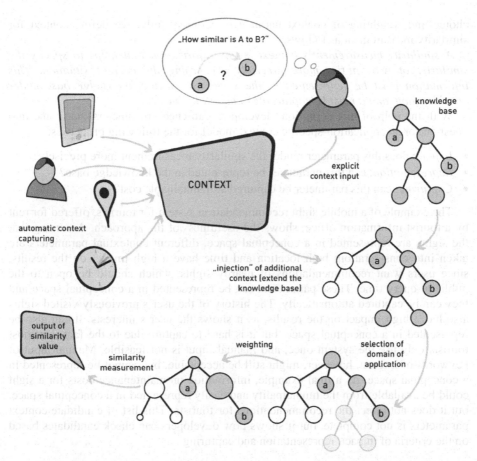

Fig. 1. The overview of the context processing chain uses a tree-structured knowledge base for reasons of simplicity. The general sequence of the process remains the same for other kinds of knowledge base representation.

a preparation for the actual similarity measurement, which is then carried out on the weighted domain of application. The method applied for similarity measurement again depends on the kind of knowledge representation. For complex queries, several iterations of this process may be required, until the results are finally presented to the user. Such results may, for example, consist of a ranked list of the most similar concepts compared to the query concept. Figure 1 shows on overview of the context processing

4.3 Definition of Context for Similarity Measurement

A generic definition of context was given in section 2.2, focusing on the four elements identity, activity, location and time. As explained in the previous section, this definition is not useful for similarity measurement, as it does not support the choice and weighting of context parameters. Consequently, we define context for similarity measurement as follows:

A similarity measurement's context is any information that helps to specify the similarity of two entities more precisely concerning the current situation. This information must be represented in the same way as the knowledge base under consideration, and it must be capturable at maintainable cost.

With the help of this definition, developers can check parameters that come into question for an application-specific context model for the following properties:

- *Impact*: does this parameter render the similarity measurement more precisely?
- *Representation*: can this parameter be represented in the knowledge base?
- *Capturing*: can this parameter be captured at maintainable cost?

The example of a mobile sight recommendation system for tourists, offered for rent by a tourist information office, shows the usefulness of the approach. Assuming that the sights are represented in a conceptual space, different contextual parameters are taken into consideration: both location and time have a high impact on the results, since users want recommendations of nearby sights, which should be open to the public at query time. These parameters can be represented in a conceptual space and they can be captured automatically. The history of the user's previously visited sights also has a high impact on the results, as it shows the user's interests. It can also be represented in a conceptual space, but it is hard to capture due to the fact that most tourists only use the system once, and manual input is not feasible. Manual input of keywords of interest, however, might still be acceptable, but cannot be represented in a conceptual space. As a final example, information on maintenance costs for a sight could be available from the municipality and easily represented in a conceptual space, but it does not affect the recommendations for tourists. This list of candidate context parameters is not complete, but it shows how developers can check candidates based on the criteria of impact, representation and capturing.

4.4 Generic Characteristics of Context for Similarity Measurement

Although we do not propose a specific formalized context model here, as this would have to be tailored both to the application and to the model of concept representation used in the knowledge base, it is still possible to formalize a set of generic characteristics of context. This affects especially the relationships between context, knowledge base and domain of application. Those characteristics will be shown in the following, referring to a similarity task with query concept a and target concept b, as this is the underlying operation for all complex similarity measurement tasks.

The following statements assume the existence of a similarity theory based on a language L with symbols and grammar, which allows for the construction of complex concepts and relationships among instances. Both the knowledge base K and the context C are expressed in L, and are assumed to be consistent in the following. As illustrated in section 4.2, it cannot always be assumed that all contextual information is already present in the knowledge base. Accordingly, we define an extended knowledge base K_E as the union of K with context C (note that K_E may be equal to K, if the context is already completely covered by the knowledge base):

$$K_E = C \bigcup K \tag{1}$$

K_E is also assumed to be consistent. As mentioned in section 4.1, a shared vocabulary is required to make sure that a connection between context and knowledge base can be established. Accordingly, the existence of at least one concept which is part of both the knowledge base and the context is required:

$$C \bigcap K \neq \varnothing \tag{2}$$

Going back to the definition of context for similarity measurement given in section 4.3, the impact of a potential context parameter (i.e. a concept c) for the overall similarity is crucial for the decision whether to include it in a context model for a specific application. The minimum impact is represented by an application-dependent constant δ, so that all potential context parameters can be checked against this threshold value. The final context then includes all parameters with an impact greater than δ, where the impact is defined as the mean difference between a similarity measurement in a context *with* the parameter compared to one *without* the parameter:

$$C = \{c \mid imp(c) > \delta\} \tag{3}$$

$$imp(c_n) = \frac{\sum \mid sim_{(c_n \in c)}(a,b) - sim_{(c_n \in c)}(a,b) \mid}{\mid C \mid} \tag{4}$$

Following the process illustrated in section 4.2, the extended knowledge base K_E is then used to determine the domain of application D from the extended knowledge base. The domain of application then consists of all concepts c from K_E that are used to define either a or b. To enable this step, the language L must support subsumption:

$$D = \{c \in K_E \mid c \sqsupseteq a \sqcup c \sqsupseteq b\} \tag{5}$$

Besides the sets of concepts introduced so far, there exists a function w which assigns weights to the concepts c in the domain of application, reflecting the importance of every concept in a given context. The sum of all weights is 1:

$$w : D \times D \to [0,1], \sum w = 1 \tag{6}$$

Similarity is then a function that computes a similarity value between 0 and 1 for a pair of query and target concepts from the weighted domain of application D_W:

$$sim(q,t) : D_w \times D_w \to [0,1] \tag{7}$$

As the context is itself represented in the same form as the knowledge base, different contexts can be compared using a context-free comparison, where the domain of application comprises the whole context (without any reduction or addition), and the weights are all equal. This can be used to formalize the statement from section 4.1: the more similar two contexts are, the less a similarity measurement should change under those two contexts. In other words, the difference between the results of a similarity measurement in two different contexts converges to 0 with a growing similarity of the two contexts:

$$\lim_{sim(C_1,C_2)\to1} sim_{C_1}(a,b) - sim_{C_2}(a,b) = 0 \tag{8}$$

The characteristics presented above are independent of the actual knowledge representation; however, subsumption has been taken for granted here, which cannot be assumed in general, but is supported by common languages for knowledge representation such as OWL. Together with the definition of context presented in section 4.3, they provide a generic foundation for the design of application-specific context models for similarity measurement.

5 Conclusions and Future Work

A proper incorporation of context into similarity measurement has mostly been neglected so far, missing the chance to disambiguate similarity measurements and to tailor them to specific situations. In this paper, we have analyzed three approaches to similarity measurement in the geospatial domain and discussed the influence of context on the corresponding use cases. Accordingly, the context models included in the similarity theories at hand were analyzed.

Based on the broad range of models for concept representation and corresponding methods for similarity measurement, a definition of context for similarity measurement was presented. The definition provides application developers with a notion of context that supports the selection of context parameters for similarity measurement applications, based on impact of the parameters, compatibility with the knowledge base (representation), and practicability (capturing). This is in line with the analysis of general requirements for a context model (consistency and compatibility with knowledge base) and the way context is processed when a similarity measurement is completed. The definition of context was finally complemented with a set of formal characteristics of context on an abstract level.

Future research should focus on context model implementations which put the generic findings of this paper into practice, to enable research on specific problems at the application level. Specifically, robust methods for the assignment of weights to the parts of the domain of application must be developed, depending on the current context. Newly developed methods must then be verified in human subject tests to evaluate whether the results correspond to user ratings. Sensitivity analyses are required to show which context parameters have the biggest influence to the overall similarity. Options for combination with other strategies for context parameter selection, for example based on granularity [26] or on cognitive processes [7], need to be investigated. More research is also required concerning the integration with existing knowledge base and reasoning systems. This is especially crucial as it is unlikely that existing knowledge bases will be converted to new formats required for similarity measurement, causing additional work for developers. Instead, such new functionality must be compatible with widely used representation languages such as OWL. Concerning the research on context for similarity measurement in general, the differences between similarity among instances, concepts and whole knowledge bases requires further research, as context comes in different flavors depending on what is compared [1].

The next steps within this research will be the development of a context-enabled similarity server as part of the SimCat project (http://sim-dl.sourceforge.net). The server will then be used for different use cases for context and similarity measurement. The first scenario planned for implementation is a portal for cyclists, allowing for context-dependent comparison of bike routes.

Acknowledgements

This research is funded by the German Research Foundation (DFG) under the project "Semantic Similarity Measurement for Role-Governed Geospatial Categories". Special thanks go to Martin Raubal and Krzysztof Janowicz for helpful comments.

References

1. Albertoni, R., De Martino, M.: Semantic Similarity of Ontology Instances Tailored on the Application Context. In: Meersman, R., Tari, Z. (eds.) On the Move to Meaningful Internet Systems 2006: CoopIS, DOA, GADA, and ODBASE. LNCS, vol. 4275, Springer, Heidelberg (2006)
2. Bazire, M., Brézillon, P.: Understanding Context Before Using It. In: Dey, A.K., Kokinov, B., Leake, D.B., Turner, R. (eds.) CONTEXT 2005. LNCS (LNAI), vol. 3554, Springer, Heidelberg (2005)
3. Chen, G., Kotz, D.: Context Aggregation and Dissemination in Ubiquitous Computing Systems. In: Proceedings of the Fourth IEEE Workshop on Mobile Computing Systems and Applications, IEEE Computer Society Press, Los Alamitos (2002)
4. Dey, A.K.,, Abowd, G.D.: Towards a Better Understanding of Context and Context-Awareness. In: CHI 2000 Workshop on the What, Who, Where, When, Why and How of Context-Awareness. The Hague, The Netherlands (2000)
5. Egenhofer, M.J., Mark, D.M.: Naive Geography. In: Kuhn, W., Frank, A.U. (eds.) COSIT 1995. LNCS, vol. 988, Springer, Heidelberg (1995)
6. Ehrig, M., et al.: Similarity for Ontologies - A Comprehensive Framework. In: ECIS, Regensburg, Germany (2005)
7. Freksa, C., Klippel, A., Winter, S.: Invisible Geography-A Cognitive Perspective on Spatial Context. In: Spatial Cognition: Specialization and Integration 2007, Schloss Dagstuhl, Germany (2007)
8. Gärdenfors, P.: Conceptual Spaces - The Geometry of Thought. MIT Press, Cambridge (2000)
9. Goldstone, R.L., Son, J.: Similarity. In: Holyoak, K., Morrison, R. (eds.) Cambridge Handbook of Thinking and Reasoning, pp. 13–36. Cambridge University Press, Cambridge (2005)
10. Goodman, N.: Seven strictures on similarity In: Goodman, N. (ed.) Problems and projects, pp. 437–447 Bobbs-Merrill, New York (1972)
11. Janowicz, K.: Sim-DL: Towards a Semantic Similarity Measurement Theory for the Description Logic ALCNR in Geographic Information Retrieval. In: Meersman, R., Tari, Z., Herrero, P. (eds.) On the Move to Meaningful Internet Systems 2006: OTM 2006 Workshops. LNCS, vol. 4277, Springer, Heidelberg (2006)

12. Janowicz, K.: Similarity-Based Retrieval for Geospatial Semantic Web Services Specified using the Web Service Modeling Language (WSML-Core). In: The Geospatial Web - How Geo-Browsers, Social Software and the Web 2.0 are Shaping the Network Society, Springer, Heidelberg (2007) (forthcoming)
13. Johannesson, M.: Modelling Asymmetric Similarity with Prominence. British Journal of Mathematical and Statistical Psychology 53, 121–139 (2000)
14. Keßler, C.: Conceptual Spaces for Data Descriptions. In: The Cognitive Approach to Modeling Environments (CAME), Workshop at GIScience 2006, Münster, Germany: SFB/TR 8 Report No. 009-08/2006 (2006)
15. Kraft, R., Maghoul, F., Chang, Y.Q.C.C.: Contextual Search at the Point of Inspiration. In: Proceedings of the 14th Conference on Information and Knowledge Management (CIKM), Bremen, Germany, ACM Press, New York (2005)
16. McGuinness, D.L., van Harmelen, F.: OWL Web Ontology Language Overview. In: W3C Recommendation, pp. 2003–2004 (2004)
17. Medin, D., Goldstone, R., Gentner, D.: Respects for similarity. Psychological Review 100(2), 254–278 (1993)
18. Murphy, G.L., Medin, D.L.: The role of theories in conceptual coherence. Psychological Review 92(3), 289–316 (1985)
19. Pascoe, J.: Adding generic contextual capabilities to wearable computers. In: Second International Symposium on Wearable Computers (ISWC'98) (1998)
20. Quix, C., et al.: Matching schemas for geographical information systems using semantic information. In: Meersman, R., Tari, Z., Herrero, P. (eds.) On the Move to Meaningful Internet Systems 2006: OTM 2006 Workshops. LNCS, vol. 4277/4278, Springer, Heidelberg (2006)
21. Raubal, M.: Formalizing Conceptual Spaces. In: Formal Ontology in Information Systems, Proceedings of the Third International Conference (FOIS 2004), IOS Press, Amsterdam (2004)
22. Rinner, C., Raubal, M.: Personalized Multi-Criteria Decision Strategies in Location-Based Decision Support. Journal of Geographic Information Sciences 10(2), 149–156 (2004)
23. Rissland, E.L.: AI and Similarity. IEEE Intelligent Systems 21(3), 39–49 (2006)
24. Rodríguez, A., Egenhofer, M.: Comparing Geospatial Entity Classes: An Asymmetric and Context-Dependent Similarity Measure. International Journal of Geographical Information Science 18(3), 229–256 (2004)
25. Schiller, J., Voisard, A.: Location Based Services. Morgan Kaufmann Publishers Inc., San Francisco (2004)
26. Schmidtke, H.R.: Granularity as a Parameter of Context. In: Dey, A.K., Kokinov, B., Leake, D.B., Turner, R. (eds.) CONTEXT 2005. LNCS (LNAI), vol. 3554, Springer, Heidelberg (2005)
27. Tversky, A.: Features of Similarity. Psychological Review 84(4), 327–352 (1977)
28. Winter, S., Raubal, M., Nothegger, C.: Focalizing Measures of Salience for Wayfinding, in Map-based Mobile Services - Theories. In: Meng, L., Zipf, A., Reichenbacher, T. (eds.) Methods and Implementations, pp. 127–142. Springer, Heidelberg (2005)

Delimited Continuations in Operating Systems

Oleg Kiselyov[1] and Chung-chieh Shan[2]

[1] FNMOC
oleg@pobox.com
[2] Rutgers University
ccshan@rutgers.edu

Abstract. *Delimited continuations* are the meanings of delimited evaluation contexts in programming languages. We show they offer a uniform view of many scenarios that arise in systems programming, such as a request for a system service, an event handler for input/output, a snapshot of a process, a file system being read and updated, and a Web page. Explicitly recognizing these uses of delimited continuations helps us design a system of concurrent, isolated transactions where desirable features such as snapshots, undo, copy-on-write, reconciliation, and interposition fall out by default. It also lets us take advantage of efficient implementation techniques from programming-language research. The Zipper File System prototypes these ideas.

1 Introduction

One notion of context that pervades programming-language research is that of *evaluation contexts*. If one part of a program is currently running (that is, being evaluated), then the rest of the program is expecting the result from that part, typically waiting for it. This rest of the program is the evaluation context of the running part. For example, in the program "$1 + 2 \times 3$", the evaluation context of the multiplication "2×3" is the rest of the program "$1 + $".

The meaning of an evaluation context is a function that maps a result value to an answer. For example, the meaning of the evaluation context "$1 + $" is the increment function, so it maps the result value 6 to the answer 7. Similarly, in a program that opens a file and summarizes its contents, the meaning of the evaluation context of the opening of the file is a function that maps a handle for a file to a summary of its contents. This function is called a *continuation*.

A continuation is *delimited* when it produces an intermediate answer rather than the final outcome of the entire computation. For example, the increment function is a delimited continuation when taken as the meaning of "$1 + $" in the program "print($1 + 2 \times 3$)". Similarly, we treat a function from file handles to content summaries as a delimited continuation when we view the summarization program as part of an operating system that reaches its final outcome only when the computer shuts down months later. The *delimiter* (or *prompt*) is the boundary between the producer of the intermediate answer (such as the summarization program) and the rest of the system.

B. Kokinov et al. (Eds.): CONTEXT 2007, LNAI 4635, pp. 291–302, 2007.

Many uses have been discovered for the concept of continuations [1]: in the semantic theory of programming languages [2,3], as a practical strategy for their design and implementation [4,5], and in natural-language semantics [6,7]. In operating-system research, continuations are poorly known and seldom used explicitly. In this paper, we cross the boundary between operating systems and programming languages to argue by examples that continuations, especially delimited ones, pervade operating systems—if only implicitly. We contend that systems programmers should recognize the applications of delimited continuations, so as to design systems with sensible defaults and implement them using efficient techniques from the literature.

One example of delimited continuations appears in the interaction between an operating system and a user program running under its management. From time to time, the user program may request a service from the kernel of the operating system, for example to read a file. When the kernel receives a request for a system service, it first saves the state, or *execution context*, of the user process. After processing the request, the kernel resumes the process, passing it the reply. If the request takes some time to process, such as when data must be fetched from a hard drive, the operating system may let some other user process run in the meantime and only resume the original user process when the hard drive is done. We can think of the execution context as a function that maps the kernel's reply to the outcome of the user process. This function is a delimited continuation; the delimiter in this case is the boundary between the user process and the rest of the system.

Saving the execution context for a process to be resumed later is called *capturing* the continuation of the process [8]. Usually a captured continuation is invoked exactly once, but sometimes it is invoked multiple times. For example, a typical operating system offers services for a process to duplicate ("fork") itself into two parallel processes or to save a snapshot of itself to be restored in the future. Other times the captured continuation is never invoked, such as when a process invokes the "exit" service to destruct itself. Two or more continuations that invoke each other once each are called *coroutines*. For example, in the PDP-7 Unix operating system, the shell and other user processes transfer control to each other as coroutines (using the "exec" system service [9]).

The concept of an operating-system kernel has found its way into the programming-language literature, for instance to describe in a modular and rigorous way what *side effects* such as state, exceptions, input/output, and backtracking mean [10,11,12]. A recurring idea in that work is that of a *central authority* [13], mediating interactions between a program, which performs computations, and the external world, which provides resources such as files. A computation yields either a value or a side effect. A side effect is a request to the central authority to perform an action (such as reading a file), paired with a continuation function that accepts the result of the action and resumes the computation.

In practical systems programming, continuations are best known for writing concurrent programs [8,14,15,16,17,18,19,20], distributed programs [21,22,23], and Web programs [24,25,26,27,28,29]. In these and many other applications, the programmer codes the handling of events [30] in *continuation-passing style*, whether or not the programmer is aware of the fact. With awareness, continuations have guided the design of a network protocol that does not require the server to track the state of each connection, and is thus more scalable, easier to migrate, and more resistant to denial-of-service attacks [31].

This paper focuses on a less-known use of continuations: file systems. We stress *transactional* file systems, which treat each operation such as changing, deleting, or renaming a file as a *transaction*, and where a transaction can be undone (that is, rolled back). Our Zipper File System manages each connection between it and its users as a delimited continuation, so it is natural and easy to implement *copy on write*: each user appears to have exclusive use of a separate file system, but the parts that are identical across users are actually stored only once and shared until one user changes its "copy" to be different.

Section 2 gives two examples of delimited continuations in systems programming in more detail. Section 3 describes our Zipper File System. Section 4 reviews the benefits we reap of recognizing continuations explicitly.

2   Instances of Continuations

We give two examples of delimited continuations: a user process requesting a system service, and traversing a data structure. The examples seem unrelated, yet use the same programming-language facility (notated CC below), thus simplifying their implementation. We have built the Zipper File System as a working prototype of both examples. Our prototype and illustrative code below are written in Haskell, a high-level general-purpose programming language, because it is suitable for operating systems [32] and its notation is concise and close to mathematical specification.

2.1   System Calls

The first example is a user process that invokes a system service. As sketched above, the process captures its current continuation and sends it to the kernel along with the requested action. The code below defines a data structure `Req r` that combines the continuation and the action.

```
data Req r = Exit
           | Read (Char -> CC r (Req r))
           | Write Char (() -> CC r (Req r))
```

The possible actions defined are `Exit`, `Read`, and `Write`. An `Exit` request means to destruct the process: it contains no continuation because the process is done. A `Read` request means to read a character: it contains a continuation that accepts the `Character` read, yields as the answer another request (usually `Exit`), and may issue more requests during the computation. The type of this continuation, `Char -> CC r (Req r)`, reflects the fact that the continuation may issue more requests: `CC r` marks the type of a computation that may incur side effects, so the type CC r (Req r) means a computation that yields Req r after possibly incurring side effects. (The parameter r is a *region label* [33,34] and does not concern us here.) A Write request means to write a character: it contains the Character to write, along with a continuation that accepts nothing; hence the type () -> CC r (Req r).

Using these services, we can program a simple user process cat to copy the input to the output.

```
service p req = shiftP p (\k -> return (req k))

cat p = do input <- service p Read
           service p (Write input)
           cat p
```

The function service initiates a *system call*: cat invokes service to request reading and writing services from the kernel.

The variable p above is a control delimiter: it represents the boundary between the user process and the kernel, delimiting the continuation in a request from the user process to the kernel. In the definition of service above, the expression shiftP p (\k -> ...) means for the user process to capture the delimited continuation up to the delimiter p and call it k. Because p delimits the user process from the kernel, the delimited continuation k is precisely the execution context of the user process. The subexpression return (req k) means for the user process to exit to the kernel with a new request data structure containing the captured delimited continuation k.

We now turn from how a user process initiates a request to how the operating-system kernel handles the request. The kernel handles system calls in a function called interpret, which takes three arguments.

1. The record world represents the state of the whole operating system. It includes, among other fields, the *job queue*, a collection of processes waiting to run.
2. The *process control block* pcb describes various resources allocated to the current process, such as network connections called *sockets*. Sockets constitute the input and output channels of the process.
3. The request from the process, of type Req r, specifies how the process exited along with whether and how it should be resumed.

The function interpret is invoked by the *scheduler*, another component of the operating system. The scheduler passes an old world to interpret and receives in return an updated world, then chooses the next process to run from those in the updated job queue.

Let us examine how interpret implements Exit and Read actions. An Exit request is handled by disposing of the process' resources, such as by closing its socket. The process itself never resumes, and the memory it uses can be reclaimed right away, because no continuation in the system refers to the process anymore. The process control block can be reclaimed as well.

```
interpret world pcb Exit = do liftIO (sClose (psocket pcb))
                            return world
```

Reading a character may take a long time, and other user processes should be allowed to run in the meantime. Thus the kernel does not respond to a Read request immediately. Rather, the interpret function creates a record of the pending read on the socket and appends the record to the job queue. It then returns the world with the updated job queue to the scheduler.

```
interpret world pcb (Read k) = return world
  {jobQueue = jobQueue world ++ [JQBlockedOnRead pcb k]}
```

The kernel keeps track of the process waiting for a character only by storing the process' continuation in the record of pending read. When the kernel receives data from a socket, it locates any associated read-pending request in the job queue and resumes the blocked process by invoking the function resume below.

```
resume world (JQBlockedOnRead pcb k) received_character =
  do req <- k received_character
     interpret world pcb req
```

The function extracts the continuation k of the suspended process and passes it the received_character, thus resuming the process. The process eventually returns another request req, which is interpreted as above.

This example shows how a process that just yielded control (to the kernel) is a continuation [14]. We have in fact implemented delimited continuations in the Perl 5 programming language by representing them as server processes that yield control until they receive a client connection. Although the mathematical meaning of a delimited continuation is a function that maps request values from a client to response answers from the server, the function is represented by data structures [35] and so can be saved into a file or sent to remote hosts. To save a captured continuation to be reused later is to take a snapshot of a process, or to *checkpoint* it.

The control delimiter p in the code above delimits the kernel from a user process. The same kind of delimiters can be used by a user process such as a debugger to run a subcomputation in a sandbox and intercept requests from the sandbox before forwarding them to the kernel. This *interposition* facility falls out from our view of requests as containing delimited continuations.

2.2 Data Traversal

The second, seemingly unrelated example of delimited continuations is the traversal and update of a complex data structure. For simplicity, instead of a directory tree, we consider here a binary tree in which each node either contains two branches or is a leaf node labeled by an integer.

```
data Tree = Leaf Int | Node Tree Tree
```

We define an operation to traverse the leaves of the tree, perhaps returning a new, updated version for some of them.

```
traverse :: Monad m => (Int -> m (Maybe Int)) -> Tree -> m Tree
traverse visit l@(Leaf n) = do result <- visit n
                               return (maybe l Leaf result)
traverse visit (Node l r) = do l <- traverse visit l
                               r <- traverse visit r
                               return (Node l r)
```

The first argument to the `traverse` function, `visit`, is itself a function, of type `Int -> m (Maybe Int)`. It takes the integer label of the current leaf node and returns either `Nothing` or a new label with which to update the node. For example, the following code makes a tree like `tree1` except all leaf labels less than 2 are replaced with 5.

```
traverse (\n -> return (if n < 2 then Just 5 else Nothing)) tree1
```

The update is *nondestructive*: the old `tree1` is intact and may be regarded as a snapshot of the data before the update. If `tree1` is not used further in the computation, the system will reclaim the storage space it occupies. To use `tree1` further, on the other hand, is to "undo" the update. The nondestructive update takes little more memory than a destructive update would, because the new tree *shares* any unmodified data with the old tree. That is, `traverse` performs copy-on-write. (The code above actually only shares unmodified *leaves* among traversals. A slight modification of the code, implemented in the Zipper File System, lets us share unmodified *branches* as well.)

Another benefit of the nondestructive update performed by `traverse` is *isolation*: any other computation using `tree1` at the same time will be unaffected by our update and may proceed concurrently. Two concurrent traversals that wish to know of each other's updates must exchange them, possibly through a common arbiter—the operating-system kernel—using the same system-call interface based on delimited continuations discussed in Section 2.1. The arbiter may reconcile or reject the updates and report the result to the concurrent traversals. The outcome does not depend on the order in which the updates are performed— that is, we avoid *race conditions*—because nondestructive updates do not modify the same original version of the data that they share. Nondestructive updates of the same sort are used in distributed revision control and in robust distributed telecom software [36].

For reading and updating a file, file system, process tree, or database, an interface like `traverse` is a more appropriate access primitive than the *cursor*-based (or *handle*-based) interface more prevalent today, in that the traversal interface eliminates the risk of forgetting to dispose of a cursor or trying to use a cursor already disposed of [37]. The traversal interface is no less expressive: when the cursor-based access is truly required, it can be automatically obtained from the traversal interface using delimited continuations, as we now explain.

The *zipper* [38] data-type `Z r` is what is commonly called a database cursor or file handle.

```
data Z r = Done Tree | Yet Int (Maybe Int -> CC r (Z r))
```

A zipper's state is either **Done** or **Yet**. A **Done** zipper has finished traversing the old tree and holds a new tree. A **Yet** zipper represents an unfinished traversal and holds the current leaf label (**Int**) and a continuation to advance the traversal (**Maybe Int -> CC r (Z r)**).

The zipper provides the following interface. The **open** function begins a traversal on an initial tree. The **curr** function reads the current leaf label. The **next** function advances the traversal, whereas **write** updates the current leaf label then advances the traversal. The **close** function finishes the traversal and returns the new tree.

```
open :: Tree -> CC r (Z r)
open tree = promptP (\p -> let visit n = shiftP p (return . Yet n)
                           in liftM Done (traverse visit tree))

curr :: Z r -> Int
curr (Yet n _) = n

next :: Z r -> CC r (Z r)
next (Yet _ k) = k Nothing

write :: Int -> Z r -> CC r (Z r)
write n (Yet _ k) = k (Just n)

close :: Z r -> CC r Tree
close (Done tree) = return tree
close z = next z >>= close
```

The sample program below uses these functions to add the first leaf label to the second leaf label.

```
test2 = runCC (do z1 <- open tree1
                  let s1 = curr z1
                  z2 <- next z1
                  let s2 = curr z2
                  z3 <- write (s1+s2) z2
                  close z3)
```

This programming style is like using a database cursor or file handle, except the functions **next** and **write** are nondestructive and return new zippers (z2 and z3 above) to reflect the new state of the tree. Using the old zippers (z1 and z2), we can recall any past state of the traversal, undoing the updates after that point. If we do not use the old zippers, the system will reclaim the storage space they occupy. As before, different zippers from the same traversal share data by copy-on-write. To save a captured continuation to be reused later is to take a *snapshot* of the data.

3   The Zipper File System

The Zipper File System is a prototype file server and operating system. It consists of only about 1000 lines of Haskell code, about half of which implements delimited continuations and zippers. It provides multitasking, exception handling, and transactional storage all using delimited continuations. More information, including complete source code, is available online at http://okmij.org/ftp/Computation/Continuations.html#zipper-fs

Storage in the Zipper File System is a data structure much like the `Tree` above, except leaves contain file data and tree nodes have an arbitrary number of branches, identified by string names that serve the same role as directory and file names in a conventional file system. The system exports the traversal and zipper operations described above as an interface for client access. A simple kernel manages *shell* processes, each of which lets a user access this interface over a network connection. Multiple users may connect at the same time and use commands such as `ls` (list directory contents), `cat` (display directory contents), `cd` (work in another directory), `touch` (create a file), `mkdir` (create a directory), `rm` (delete), `mv` (move), `cp` (copy), and `echo` (write a literal string to a file). Thanks to the copy-on-write semantics that arises naturally from the use of delimited continuations, the `cp` (copy) command need only establish sharing between two locations in the file system, not copy any actual file data. Unlike in the Unix operating system, one can traverse sequentially to the *next* node from any node.

The kernel uses delimited continuations to provide system calls and schedule which user process to run next. The *type system* isolates the processes from each other and prevents them from performing input/output or changing global state except by issuing a request to the kernel. Thus any processor can potentially be scheduled to run any process without worrying about the undesirable interactions that often result when two processes access the same memory at the same time. This protection is similar to that among Unix processes, except we enforce it by programming-language types in software rather than a memory-management unit in hardware.

For a user of the Zipper File System, what most sets it apart is the transactional semantics of its storage. The user can undo mistakes such as deleting a directory or truncating a file. Moreover, multiple users are completely isolated from each other: each network connection appears to expose exclusive use of a separate file system, as if every operation always occurs before or after every other operation, never concurrently. Data unmodified by two clients are shared across them. These features all come for free with the zipper.

As with database transactions, a client may announce its update by "committing" it. The commit request is handled by a central authority, which examines the update and accepts or rejects it, with no risk of race conditions. Any transaction system needs a conflict resolution mechanism such as versioning, patching, or manual intervention. Our system resolves conflicts in the central authority that maintains the global state, rather than in user processes, which cannot

change the global state directly. The conflict-resolution policies are thus easier
to implement.

4   Conclusion

We have described how the Zipper File System explicitly uses delimited continuations for multitasking and storage. For storage, delimited continuations make
it natural and easy to provide a transactional semantics, complete isolation, and
sequential traversal. For multitasking, delimited continuations make it natural
and easy to schedule processes for execution, respond to input and output events,
and handle exceptions. In both applications, delimited continuations avail us of
the state of the art in implementation techniques, such as copy-on-write and
stack segmentation [39,40,41].

The recent surge of operating systems and file systems implemented in high-
level programming languages [32,42,43] find their roots in earlier systems such
as Multics, Inferno, and SPIN. Our work shows how delimited continuations
are particularly helpful, especially in conjunction with types that describe the
shape of data and effect of code in detail. We use such types to sandbox processes,
isolate transactions, prevent race conditions, improve scalability to multiple processors, and obviate the user-kernel boundary in hardware.

We treat the file system, which is usually thought of as a persistent data
structure, as an ongoing traversal process that communicates with the outside
world as a coroutine. More generally, data as small as a single integer variable can
be profitably treated as a process with which to exchange messages [44,45]. These
alternating viewpoints between process and data prompt us to ask: could the
vision of persistent virtual memory pioneered by Multics be relevant in today's
world of ubiquitous memory management units?

Any software component can interact with the rest of the world using delimited continuations. When the continuations are isolated by restrictions on side
effects, the interaction naturally and easily supports snapshots, undo, and reconciliation. Thus to use an operating system can and should be to navigate a virtual
file system containing the history and transcript of all potential interactions.

References

1. Reynolds, J.C.: The discoveries of continuations. Lisp and Symbolic Computation 6, 233–247 (1993)
2. Strachey, C., Wadsworth, C.P.: Continuations: A mathematical semantics for handling full jumps. Higher-Order and Symbolic Computation 13, 135–152 (2000)
3. Fischer, M.J.: Lambda-calculus schemata. Lisp and Symbolic Computation 6, 259–
   288 (1993)
4 Kelsey, R., Clinger, W.D., Rees, J., Abelson, H., Dybvig, R.K., Haynes, C.T.,
   Rozas, G.J., Adams IV, N.I., Friedman, D.P., Kohlbecker, E., Steele, G.L., Bart-
   ley, D.H., Halstead, R., Oxley, D., Sussman, G.J., Brooks, G., Hanson, C., Pitman,
   K.M., Wand, M.: Revised⁵ report on the algorithmic language Scheme. Higher-
   Order and Symbolic Computation 11, 7–105 (1998) Also as ACM SIGPLAN Notices 33(9), 26–76

5. Steele, Jr., G.L.: RABBIT: A compiler for SCHEME. Master's thesis, Department of Electrical Engineering and Computer Science, Massachusetts Institute of Technology, Also as Memo 474, Artificial Intelligence Laboratory, Massachusetts Institute of Technology (1978)
6. Shan, C.c., Barker, C.: Explaining crossover and superiority as left-to-right evaluation. Linguistics and Philosophy 29, 91–134 (2006)
7. Barker, C., Shan, C.c.: Types as graphs: Continuations in type logical grammar. Journal of Logic, Language and Information 15, 331–370 (2006)
8. Wand, M.: Continuation-based multiprocessing revisited. Higher-Order and Symbolic Computation, 283 (1999)
9. Ritchie, D.M.: The Evolution of the Unix Time-sharing System. AT&T Bell Laboratories Technical Journal 63, 1577–1593 (1984)
10. Sitaram, D., Felleisen, M.: Control delimiters and their hierarchies. Lisp and Symbolic Computation 3, 67–99 (1990)
11. Kiselyov, O.: How to remove a dynamic prompt: Static and dynamic delimited continuation operators are equally expressible. Technical Report 611, Computer Science Department, Indiana University (2005)
12. Kiselyov, O., Shan, C.c., Friedman, D.P., Sabry, A.: Backtracking, interleaving, and terminating monad transformers (functional pearl). In: ICFP '05: Proceedings of the ACM International Conference on Functional Programming, pp. 192–203. ACM Press, New York (2005)
13. Cartwright, R., Felleisen, M.: Extensible denotational language specifications. In: Hagiya, M., Mitchell, J.C. (eds.) TACS 1994. LNCS, vol. 789, pp. 244–272. Springer, Heidelberg (1994)
14. Kumar, S., Bruggeman, C., Dybvig, R.K.: Threads yield continuations. Lisp and Symbolic Computation 10(2), 223–236 (1998)
15. Dybvig, R.K., Hieb, R.: Continuations and concurrency. In: Proceedings of the Second ACM SIGPLAN Symposium on Principles and Practice of Parallel Programming, pp. 128–136. ACM Press, New York (1990)
16. Dybvig, R.K., Hieb, R.: Engines from continuations. Journal of Computer Languages 14(2), 109–123 (1989)
17. Shivers, O.: Continuations and threads: Expressing machine concurrency directly in advanced languages. In: Proceedings of the Second ACM SIGPLAN Workshop on Continuations, ACM Press, New York (1997)
18. Haynes, C.T., Friedman, D.P., Wand, M.: Obtaining coroutines with continuations. Journal of Computer Languages 11, 143–153 (1986)
19. Li, P., Zdancewic, S.: A language-based approach to unifying events and threads (2006), http://www.cis.upenn.edu/~stevez/papers/LZ06b.pdf
20. Adya, A., Howell, J., Theimer, M., Bolosky, W.J., Douceur, J.R.: Cooperative task management without manual stack management, or, event-driven programming is not the opposite of threaded programming. In: Proceedings of the 2002 USENIX Annual Technical Conference, USENIX, pp. 289–302 (2002)
21. Sumii, E.: An implementation of transparent migration on standard Scheme. In: Felleisen, M. (ed.) Proceedings of the Workshop on Scheme and Functional Programming. Number 00-368 in Tech. Rep. Department of Computer Science, Rice University, pp. 61–63 (2000)
22. Sewell, P., Leifer, J.J., Wansbrough, K., Zappa Nardelli, F., Allen-Williams, M., Habouzit, P., Vafeiadis, V.: Acute: High-level programming language design for distributed computation. In: ICFP '05: Proceedings of the ACM International Conference on Functional Programming, pp. 15–26. ACM Press, New York (2005)

23. Murphy VII, T., Crary, K., Harper, R.: Distributed control flow with classical modal logic. In: Ong, C.H.L. (ed.) CSL 2005. LNCS, vol. 3634, pp. 51–69. Springer, Heidelberg (2005)
24. Queinnec, C.: Continuations and web servers. Higher-Order and Symbolic Computation 17, 277–295 (2004)
25. Graunke, P.T.: Web Interactions. PhD thesis, College of Computer Science, Northeastern University (2003)
26. Colomba, A.: SISCweb: A framework to facilitate writing stateful Scheme web applications in a J2EE environment (2007), http://siscweb.sf.net/
27. Balat, V., et al.: Ocsigen: A Web server and a programming framework providing a new way to create dynamic Web sites (2007), http://www.ocsigen.org
28. Belapurkar, A.: Use continuations to develop complex Web applications. IBM developerWorks (2004)
29. Krishnamurthi, S., Hopkins, P.W., McCarthy, J., Graunke, P.T., Pettyjohn, G., Felleisen, M.: Implementation and use of the PLT Scheme Web server. Higher-Order and Symbolic Computation (2007)
30. Williams, N.J.: An implementation of scheduler activations on the NetBSD operating system. In: Proceedings of the FREENIX Track: USENIX Annual Technical Conference, Berkeley, CA, USENIX (2002) pp. 99–108 (2002)
31. Shieh, A., Myers, A., Sirer, E.G.: Trickles: A stateless transport protocol. Summaries of OSDI'04. USENIX;login (2004) 6th Symposium on Operating Systems Design and Implementation, OSDI'04. vol. 30(2) p. 66, Work-in-Progress Reports (2005)
32. Hallgren, T., Jones, M.P., Leslie, R., Tolmach, A.P.: A principled approach to operating system construction in Haskell. In: Danvy, O., Pierce, B.C. (eds.) Proceedings of the 10th ACM SIGPLAN International Conference on Functional Programming, ICFP 2005, Tallinn, Estonia, September 26-28, 2005, pp. 116–128. ACM Press, New York (2005)
33. Launchbury, J., Peyton Jones, S.L.: State in Haskell. Lisp and Symbolic Computation 8, 293–341 (1995)
34. Moggi, E., Sabry, A.: Monadic encapsulation of effects: A revised approach (extended version). Journal of Functional Programming 11, 591–627 (2001)
35. Danvy, O., Nielsen, L.R.: Defunctionalization at work. In: Proceedings of the 3rd International Conference on Principles and Practice of Declarative Programming, pp. 162–174. ACM Press, New York (2001)
36. Nyström, J.H., Trinder, P.W., King, D.J.: Are high-level languages suitable for robust telecoms software? In: Winther, R., Gran, B.A., Dahll, G. (eds.) SAFECOMP 2005. LNCS, vol. 3688, pp. 275–288. Springer, Heidelberg (2005)
37. Kiselyov, O.: General ways to traverse collections (2004),
    http://okmij.org/ftp/Scheme/enumerators-callcc.html
    http://okmij.org/ftp/Computation/Continuations.html
38. Huet, G.: The zipper. Journal of Functional Programming 7, 549–554 (1997)
39. Clinger, W.D., Hartheimer, A., Ost, E,M : Implementation strategies for continuations. Higher-Order and Symbolic Computation 12, 7–45 (1999)
40. Bruggeman, C., Waddell, O., Dybvig, R.K.: Representing control in the presence of one-shot continuations. In: ACM SIGPLAN 1996 Conference on Programming Language Design and Implementation, ACM Press, New York (1996)
41. Gasbichler, M., Sperber, M.: Final shift for call/cc: Direct implementation of shift and reset. In: ICFP '02: Proceedings of the ACM International Conference on Functional Programming, pp. 271–282. ACM Press, New York (2002)

42. Derrin, P., Elphinstone, K., Klein, G., Cock, D., Chakravarty, M.M.T.: Running the manual: an approach to high-assurance microkernel development. In: Haskell '06: Proceedings of the 2006 ACM SIGPLAN workshop on Haskell, pp. 60–71. ACM Press, New York (2006)
43. Jones, I., et al.: Halfs, a Haskell filesystem (2006), http://www.haskell.org/halfs/
44. Ernst, E.: Method mixins. Report PB-557, Department of Computer Science, University of Aarhus, Denmark (2002)
45. Van Roy, P.: Convergence in language design: A case of lightning striking four times in the same place. In: Hagiya, M., Wadler, P. (eds.) FLOPS 2006. LNCS, vol. 3945, pp. 2–12. Springer, Heidelberg (2006)

Explanations and Context
in Ambient Intelligent Systems

Anders Kofod-Petersen and Jörg Cassens

Department of Computer and Information Science (IDI),
Norwegian University of Science and Technology (NTNU),
7491 Trondheim, Norway
{anderpe,cassens}@idi.ntnu.no
http://www.idi.ntnu.no/

Abstract. Ambient intelligent systems are context aware by perceiving and reasoning about their environment, they perceive the needs of their users and proactively respond to these needs by being context sensitive. Users do not interact with these systems by traditional means only, but also through behavioural interfaces. This combination of mixed initiative systems and unconventional interfaces puts strong requirements on the explanatory capabilities of any system. The work presented here focuses on explaining the behaviour of an ambient intelligent systems to its users. It demonstrates how explanations can be combined with context to deal with the different types of explanations that are required for a meaningful interaction of a system and its users.

1 Introduction

Recent insights into both ubiquitous and pervasive computing have lead to the realisation that to achieve the scenarios and visions proposed, systems must be viewed as more complex than initially argued by Weiser [1]. This has lead to the developments jointly labelled as *ambient intelligence* [2]. The explicit focus on intelligence stands in stark contrast to the original argument by Weiser, where: "no revolution in artificial intelligence is needed – just the proper embedding of computers into the everyday world" [1, p. 3].

The core of an ambient intelligent systems is the ability to appreciate the system's environment, be aware of persons in this environment, and respond intelligently to their needs. To realise the abilities of an ambient intelligent system, three main areas of responsibility can be identified [3]: first, the initial responsibility of *perceiving* the world that the system inhabits; second, the responsibility of being aware of the environment and reason about ongoing situations, which traditionally has been labelled as *context awareness*; and third, exhibit appropriate behaviour in ongoing situations by being *context sensitive* [3,4].

Arguably one of the most important aspects of an ongoing situation is the activity that is occurring. For an ambient intelligent system to function it must be able to reason about its own, as well as other ongoing activities. Systems that aim at exhibiting the properties connected with ambient intelligence must

B. Kokinov et al. (Eds.): CONTEXT 2007, LNAI 4635, pp. 303–316, 2007.

be more than mere reactive systems, where deliberation and reasoning plays an important part.

Marx [5] demonstrates this difference by arguing that even though a spider conducts operations that resemble those of a weaver, and a bee humbles many an architect, there is a significant difference between them. Even the worst architects raise the structures in their imagination before they are erected in reality. At the end of each labour-process, we get a result that already existed in the imagination of the labourer. The labourer not only affects the materials used, but also realises a purpose that gives the law to his modus operandi, and to which the labourer's will must be subordinated. Besides the exertion of the bodily organs, the process demands that, during the whole operation, the workman will be steadily in consonance with his purpose. This means close attention. The less he is attracted by the nature of the work, and the mode in which it is carried on, and the less, therefore, he enjoys it as something which gives play to his bodily and mental powers, the more close his attention is forced to be.

The elementary factors of the labour-process are: i) the personal activity of the labourer, ii) the subject of the work, and iii) its instruments.

This is also the starting point for activity theory. To capture the activity related aspects of any situation, activity theory [6,7] can be used to acquire and model the relevant knowledge. Briefly, activity theory considers activities as a set of actions and operations on an object. These actions and operations are conducted by a labourer, or subject, to achieve an already imagined outcome. The subject's actions and operations are mediated by the use of certain instruments, or artefacts. We will elaborate on this later.

According to Turing [8], one indication that a system *is* intelligent is its ability to *appear* intelligent; i.e. by passing the Turing test. Therefore, we need to understand what makes humans appear intelligent.

Following Kant, human understanding has as a necessary constituent the ability to conceptualise perceived phenomena (structured through 'categories of understanding') through an active, discursive process of making sense of the intuitive perception [9, p. 58].

In later works, Kant gives us a more detailed description of his understanding of human reason. He makes clear that the human ability of reasoning has perceptivity (attentio), abstraction (abstractio), and reflection (reflexio) as its necessary preconditions [10, p. 138].

Further on, it is important to note that the ability of human beings to act freely, the ability to initiate a causal chain from freedom, is coupled with his ability to act morally (Kant describes freedom as the ratio essendi of the moral law, while the moral law is the ratio cognoscendi of freedom [11, p. 4]). Kant couples the ability to act morally (and thus freely) with the ability to give a rational explanation of the behaviour in his categorical imperative – "Act so that the maxim of thy will can always at the same time hold good as a principle of universal legislation" [11, p. 30]. Therefore, we can ascribe the ability of explaining ones behaviour and motives to every rational being, that means to every intelligent entity. We therefore count explanatory capabilities, in particular the ability to explain ones own understanding of the world and ones own behaviour, as a necessary precondition for appearing intelligent.

2 Background

One approach to realising intelligent behaviour is by employing *case-based reasoning* [12]. This method springs from understanding reasoning as an explanation process [13]. Our understanding of common occurrences assists us in comprehending stories, in such a way that details omitted or assumed implicitly do not make a story incomprehensible for us. Our general knowledge about situations, the expectations, and the behaviour which should be exhibited are stored in what has been referred to in psychology as *scripts* [14], which are closely related to the concept of *schema* [15,16].

Sørmo et al. [17] present a framework for explanations in intelligent systems with a special focus on case-based reasoning. Specifically, they identify five goals that explanations can satisfy. The goal of *transparency* is concerned with the system's ability to explain how an answer was reached. *Justification* deals with the ability to explain why the answer is good. When dealing with the importance of a question asked, *relevance* is the goal that must be satisfied. *Conceptualization* is the goal that handles the meaning of concepts. Finally, *learning* is in itself a goal, as it teaches us about the domain in question. These goals are defined from the perspective of a human user. His expectation on what constitutes a good explanation is situation dependend and has a historic dimension (compare e.g. Leake [18]).

Roth-Berghofer has explored some fundamental issues with different useful kinds of explanations and their connection to the different knowledge containers of a case-based reasoning system [19]. Based on earlier findings from natural language explanations in expert systems, five different kinds of explanation are identified: *conceptual explanations*, which map unknown new concepts to known ones, *why-explanations* describing causes or justifications, *how-explanations* depicting causal chains for an event, *purpose-explanations* describing the purpose or use of something, and *cognitive explanations* predicting the behaviour of intelligent systems. Roth-Berghofer, further on, ties these different kinds of explanation to the different knowledge containers of case-based reasoning systems [20], namely case base, similarity measure, adaptation knowledge, and vocabulary.

Building on these two works, we have earlier started to investigate a combined framework of user goals and explanation kinds [21]. The goal of this work was to outline a design methodology that starts from an analysis of usage scenarios in order to be able to identify possible expectations a user might have towards the explanatory capabilities of an intelligent system. The requirements recognised can further on be used to identify which kind of knowledge has to be represented in the system, and which knowledge containers are best suited for this task. In this work, we have identified the need for a socio-psychological analysis of workplaces in order to be able to design systems that can meaningful engage in socio-technical interactions.

In order to further explore the assumed advantages of designing systems from a socio-technical perspective, we have later on investigated the use of theories from industrial and organisational psychology in designing a case-based reasoning system geared towards ambient intelligence. The work presented here shows how the user-centric explanation goals can be satisfied by relating kinds of explanations in context awareness and context sensitivity with a socio-technical approach to modelling context.

3   Use of Activity Theory as a Means to Model Context

We have published some work on using activity theory to model context awareness [22,23]. Although we have discussed the use of this theoretical framework to help understand when to deliver an explanation [24], we have not previously explored how to make use of the same theoretical framework for designing explanatory capabilities for context aware systems. We will now outline how these deficiencies can be overcome.

First in this section, we will give a short summary of aspects of activity theory that are important for this work. See [25] for a short introduction to activity theory and [26,27] for deeper coverage. The theoretical foundations of activity theory in general can be found in the works of Vygotsky and Leont'ev [6,7,28].

Activity theory is a descriptive tool to help understand the unity of consciousness and activity. Its focus lies on individual and collective work practice. Some of its basic properties are:

- **Hierarchical structure of activity:** Activities (the topmost category) are composed of goal-directed actions. These actions are performed consciously. Actions, in turn, consist of non-conscious operations.
  If an action fails, the operations comprising the action can get conceptualised and might become conscious actions in the next attempt to reach the overall goal. This is referred to as a *breakdown situation*.
- **Object-orientedness:** Objective and socially or culturally defined properties. Our way of doing work is grounded in a praxis which is shared by our co-workers and determined by tradition. The way an artefact is used and the division of labour influences the design. Hence, artefacts pass on the specific praxis they are designed for.
- **Mediation:** Human activity is mediated by tools, language, etc. The artefacts as such are not the object of our activities, but appear already as socio-cultural entities.
- **Continuous Development:** Both the tools used and the activity itself are constantly reshaped. Tools reflects accumulated social knowledge, hence they transport social history back into the activity and to the user.
- **Distinction between internal and external activities:** Traditional cognitive psychology focuses on what is denoted internal activities in activity theory, but it is emphasised that these mental processes cannot be properly

understood when separated from external activities, that is the interaction with the outside world.

We have used an expanded model of activity theory, the Cultural Historical Activity Theory (CHAT, compare e.g. [29,30]), in order to analyse the use of technical artefacts as instruments for achieving a predefined goal in the work process as well as the role of social components, like the division of labour and community rules.

We have linked these different aspects of an activity to related categories of context in order to build a psychologically plausible context model. At the same time, we have used the model to guide our analysis of the work processes to be modeled into the system. However, we have not exploited all of the above mentioned aspects of activity theory in order to gain insight into the expectations and needs of the prospective users with regard to explanations.

4   Explanations and Context

The term explanation can have different foci. Either as goals that explanations can satisfy or as kinds of explanations that can be given. In addition, Leake identifies three different facets of explanations within the context of case-based reasoning [31]:

- Using explanations to support the case-based reasoning process
- Generating explanations by case-based reasoning
- Using cases for explaining system results to an external user

With our notion of user goals, we can subsume the last two facets as both being targeted towards the user of the system. In our understanding, showing the case to the user is a special case of 'generating explanations by case-based reasoning', making use of the case-based reasoning assumption that similar problems have similar solutions. Provided that the user has some knowledge about the similarity function and that the case structure is understandable by the user, the displayed case acts as an explanation to the user (see e.g. [17,32]). We are left with two functions of an explanation, as described in [33]: first, enhancing and promoting the reasoning process. Second, delivering some knowledge about the reasoning process, its results, or implication to the user. We call the first aspect the *system centric view* on explanation and the second one the *user centric view* on explanation:[1]

- Explanation as **part of the reasoning process** itself.
  Example: a knowledge intensive case-based reasoning system can use its domain knowledge to explain the absence/variation of feature values.
- Giving explanations of the found solution, its application, or the reasoning process **to the user**.
  Example: in an engine failure diagnosis system, the user gets an explanation on why a particular case was matched.

---

[1] This distinction is valid not only for case-based reasoning systems.

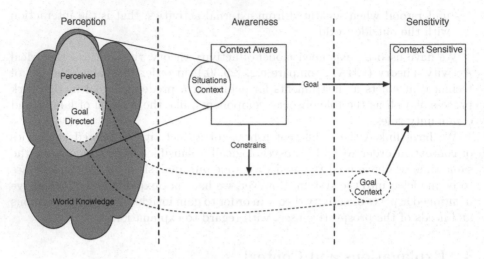

Fig. 1. Dual use of Context

We have earlier argued that an ambient intelligent system consists of three layers, each with its own responsibility [3]. The top layer is responsible for *perceiving* the world and order the perceived data into a coherent context structure on which reasoning is possible. The awareness layer is responsible for assessing the context and classify an ongoing situation. This layer demonstrates the ability of *context awareness*. Finally, the third layer is responsible for selecting and executing suitable behaviour based on the classification done in the awareness layer. This ability is referred to as *context sensitivity*.

In this architecture, context serves two purposes. Initially it is used as a focussing lens on the part of the world that can be perceived. Here the context limits the parts of the knowledge that the system uses to classify the situation. The second use of context is in the context sensitivity layer, where context is viewed as a lens that focuses the part of the system's knowledge that is to be used to satisfy the goal of the situation.

Figure 1 depicts the dual use of context. Initially the Situation Context is what the context aware part uses to execute the case-based reasoning process that classifies the situation. Once the situation has been classified a suitable goal for this situation is found. This goal further limits the part of the context that is necessary for the context sensitivity part to exhibit appropriate behaviour. The goal as well as the context are made available to the context sensitivity part, as is indicated by the Goal arrow and the Goal Context in the figure.

For the purpose of this paper we will disregard the perception layer of the architecture as the perception layer demonstrates no reasoning capabilities, and only structures perceived data syntactically. Following our earlier arguments introduced in [3], we identify these two aspects as two distinct steps in the reasoning process:

Table 1. Context and Explanations

	Context Awareness	Context Sensitivity
System Centric	Generate an explanation to recognise the situation	Identify the behaviour the system should expose
User Centric	Elucidate why the system identifies a particular situation	Explicate why a certain behaviour was chosen

- **Context Awareness:** Trying to detect which situation the system is in. *Example:* An ambient intelligent system for supporting health personnel figures out that the user is on a ward-round because of the time of the day, the location, and the other persons present.
- **Context Sensitivity:** Acting according to the situation the system thinks it is in. *Example:* the same system fetches the newest versions of electronic patient records of all patients in the room from the hospital systems. When the user stands close to the bed of a patient, the system automatically displays them.

Combining these views on explanation and on context, we end up with two dimensions of inquiry as depicted in Table 1. This table shows the four different areas where explanations can be required, divided into a system centric and user centric view.

In the system centric view where explanations are a part of the reasoning process it is possible to initially generate an explanation used to *recognise* the situation. In this step we are using explanations to find out what situation we are in, by explaining similarities between a new situation and previously experienced situations. Following the recognition of a situation we can now use explanations to identify appropriate behaviour.

When dealing with the user centric view we can initially use explanations to elucidate why the system assumes that we are in a certain situation. The system can use all available sources of knowledge in order to gain the user's confidence in its capabilities. In the situation where the the system is required to explicate the behaviour that it exhibits, the explanation is used to explain why it takes a specific action.

As described above, activity theory has been used to recognise contextual facets of a work situation. By integrating the knowledge necessary for supporting the different explanatory goals of the user with this contextual information, the explanatory capabilities of the system are coupled with the different contexts. Hence, the hypothesis is that this explanatory knowledge will indeed primarily be used in the appropriate context.

We will now explore the relations between the basic properties of activity theory and explanation goals.

Hierarchical structure of activity: The fact that activities are hierarchically structured, and that changes in these structures occur, facilitates certain explanation goals. Actions that are performed often will be transformed into operations. Vice versa, if an anticipated outcome of an operation does not occur, non-conscious operation will become conscious actions. This is called a breakdown situation. The explanatory capabilities of a system should support this. In fact two goals are relevant in these situations:

- **Transparency:** If parts of the non-conscious operations are carried out by artefacts, the system might need sufficient knowledge to explain the artefacts inner working in case of a breakdown.
- **Relevance:** If an artefact involved in an action can behave differently than expected, it should be made clear why the unexpected behaviour occurred.

Object-orientedness: In the activity theoretical sense of the term object-oriented, the meaning of this term is twofold. On one hand, it highlights that all human activities have an objective, a goal, and therefore points towards the mental part of an activity. On the other hand, it refers to the fact that this mental objectives are directed towards the physical world. This holds for automated processes insofar as the automation already assumes a goal, and is supposed to support this goal:

- **Transparency:** It should be possible for a system to explain its relation to the physical processes.
- **Justification:** An intelligent system should be able to explain its goals to the user.

Mediation: Every activity will incorporate some tools, be it physical (like machinery) or psychological artefacts (like language). If parts of the activity are carried out by an intelligent artefact, this artefact both acts as a mediator in the physical world and as a mediator of the psychological processes of the user:

- **Justification:** The system should be able to explain the connection between its actions and the reasoning process.

Continuous development: The aspect of continuous development deals with the continuous change in the way we interact with the world. Both the user's activities and the artefacts used are changing. It should be noted that this includes the necessity for an intelligent system to adopt to changes over time:

- **Learning:** The system should be able to support the user's learning processes. If the system is extended, or new capabilities are included, the system should be able to act as teacher. It should therefore incorporate knowledge about how the new component facilitates the problem solving process.

Distinction between internal and external activities: Activity theory tries to overcome the dichotomy of mental processes and the outside world by focussing on the relation between internal and external activities. It is therefore crucial that the system supports the user in building an understanding of the artefacts used.

- **Conceptualisation:** The system should support the user's understanding of it by providing means of explaining its own world model to him.

Not all explanation goals can be satisfied by an activity theoretical perspective alone. Some goals can only be satisfied by inspecting other parts of the knowledge model, either in all cases or for certain situations. As an example, when recognising a situation the transparency goal can be satisfied by supplying a trace of the reasoning process used for classification. The different sources of knowledge required to satisfy the different goals will be further discussed in the following section.

5   Identifying Explanations Kinds from Goals

With the combination of explanations and context described above it is now possible to identify different kinds of explanations by identifying the explanation goals of the user. The four different areas where explanations can be required are shown in Table 1. For the purpose of this paper we will focus on the user centric perspective where explanations are used to elucidate why the system identifies a particular situation and to explicate why a certain behaviour was chosen.

As we have stated before, users do not interact with an ambient intelligent system by traditional means only but also through behavioural interfaces. This means also that if the system gets everything right, it should be unobtrusive and supportive. The main situations where explanations are necessary are when something goes wrong, i.e. the system does not recognise the correct context or follows a path of actions which the user perceives as wrong, unusual, or unexpected. So while we do not dismiss the option that a user wants some explanation from the system even if it does what the user expects, we do not focus on this aspect in this paper. But it has to be kept in mind that the system's explanatory capabilities should also cover its ability to explain itself when nothing goes wrong. This is of special importance during the beginning of the use of the system in order to gain the user's trust into the system.

We would also like to point out that we have chosen not to consider the learning goal in this paper. The learning goal is specifically targeted towards educational systems. The goal of such a system is typically not only to find a good solution to a problem, but to explain the solution process to the user in a way that will increase his understanding of the domain. We do not consider this type of systems at the time being.

5.1   Context Awareness

In case of the context aware user centric perspective the system might *misclassify* a situation. In this case the system must satisfy the goals of *transparency*, *justification* and *conceptualisation*. In case of *transparency* and *justification* they explain the process through which the classification was reached. The choice between a *transparency* or *justification* goal is governed by the user's proficiency level. Where an expert user will require *transparency*, a novice user requires *justification*[2]. These two goals map to the 'how' and 'why' explanation kinds, where 'how' explains the causal chain of events leading to the classification, and 'why' justifies why the system thinks that the answer is good. The knowledge required to supply these kinds of explanations is found within the reasoning method, e.g. similarity measures in case-based reasoning.

5.2   Context Sensitivity

When dealing with the context sensitive user centric perspective, the system has two main situations in which explicating is required (not counting the situation where the system exhibits flawless behaviour). These two main situations are when the system exhibits *wrong behaviour* for the situation, and when it exhibits *unexpected behaviour*. Both of these situations can result in a breakdown situation as defined by activity theory. In case of a *wrong behaviour* the system's goal is not in line with the user's goal, any operations performed by the user will fail and become actions, thus a breakdown situation is occurring. In this case, the system displaying wrong behaviour must satisfy the same goals as when misclassifying the situation. This means that the *transparency/justification* goals must be satisfied. As with the case of misclassification, these goals map to the 'why' and 'how' kinds, which require knowledge about the reasoning process employed. In addition, the hierarchical structure principle in activity theory can guide the process through which these goals are satisfied.

From a user perspective, the system can *behave unexpectedly* in several different manners: it can request an *unexpected action* from the users, non-user actions can be performed by a *new or alternative person* or by a *new or unexpected artefact*.

When the system requests a *new action* from the user, a breakdown situation occurs, and the user must respond consciously. Again, the goals of *transparency/justification* must be satisfied. In addition, the system must satisfy the *relevance* goal by explaining the relevance of the requested action, and in case of previously unperformed actions *conceptualization* is required. The hierarchical structure principle in activity theory can guide the process through which the *transparency/justification* and *relevance* goals are satisfied, whereas the *conceptualization* goal can be satisfied by inspecting the specific domain model. The *relevance* goal maps to the 'purpose' kind where an explanation of the purpose of the requested action gives the relevance. Finally the *conceptualization* goal maps to the 'conceptualization' kind, mapping unknown concepts to known ones.

If a non-user action is performed by a *new or alternative artefact*, three goals must be satisfied: *transparency/justification, relevance* and *conceptualization*. The mediation principle in activity theory can guide the process where the *transparency/justification* goal is satisfied, whereas the *relevance* and *conceptualization* goals are satisfied by inspecting the specific domain model. As aforementioned the *transparency/justification* goals map to the 'why' and 'how' kinds and the *conceptualization* goal maps to the 'conceptualization' kind. In the case

---

[2] This separation will be used consistently throughout the rest of the paper.

of the *relevance* goal, this maps to the 'purpose' kind when dealing with alternative artefacts by describing the purpose of this artefact. When dealing with a new artefact, the *relevance* goal also maps to the 'conceptualization' kind.

For non-user actions performed by a *new or alternative person*, the description is similar to the one for artefacts. However, one important distinction exists. In the activity theoretical part of the knowledge model persons are part of the community that cooperates with the user through a division of labour. However, our current modelling of persons and roles does not distinguish between the two. Thus, even though an action is performed by a new or alternative person, the fact that the role is unchanged means that the activity as viewed from the system is unchanged. This is contrary to the way artefacts are perceived, where using a new or alternative artefact to perform an action will result in a change in the activity. This means that no activity theoretical principle can guide the satisfaction of the goals, thus other parts of the knowledge model must be inspected.

6 Example

We will briefly investigate the relations between context and explanation by the means of an example. Let us consider the following scenario: We have a case-based diagnostic system for aircraft failures. An engineer is equipped with an intelligent mobile assistant and one of his tasks is to diagnose the probable causes of engine problems. Let us assume that the engineer is working both at his home base and at line stations where faults have occurred.

Scenario 1 – Misclassified Context: Let us assume that our engineer is going to work with the head of engineering on a new schedule for sending engineers to line stations. He is doing administrative work and not working on technical problems. The time of this meeting, however, is at a time where there is usually a briefing with all engineers, and the system also recognises that some of the other people usually participating at this meeting are present. However, instead of being in a meeting room, we are at the office of the head of the engineering group, a fact which contradicts the assumption of being in the briefing. The system might now explain away this unusual facet by generalising that both the meeting room and the office are rooms and that an office to a certain degree serves the same purpose as a meeting room. Therefore, the system assumes that we are in a briefing and delivers fault information about the airplanes which are scheduled to be worked on.

When this error becomes obvious to the engineer, he might want to check why the system displayed this kind of information. So we are in the *explicate* phase of Table 1. If he is an expert user of the system, he might have an interest what lead to the problem, so his goal is *transparency*. The kind of explanation helpful is a 'why' explanation, in particular one where the system displays the best matched cases and that it has classified the office as a general kind of room.

Scenario 2 – New Artefact Used: Let us now assume that the engineer is working on a diagnostic task and, in the course of this task, needs access to some performance data. This is recognised by the system. The knowledge source usually used for this kind of data is temporarily not available, so the system queries a different system which was added recently. This comes as a suprise to the engineer who was not aware of neither the unavailability of the first system nor the existence of the second.

The engineer now wants to know why the data from the new system is helpfull, he has a *relevance* goal. This can be supported by a 'purpose' kind of explanation, and by inspecting its own domain knowledge, the system can describe the purpose of the new data source, for example by explaining that the new data source is a backup system for performance data.

7 Summary and Future Work

This paper builds on a view of ambient intelligence encompassing first an understanding of the situation (context awareness) and then decisions on behaviour (context sensitivity). It has been argued that in both phases, explanations can be viewed from a system centric as well as a user centric perspective. It has further been described how explanations play a key role in ambient intelligent systems as a necessary prerequisite for a system being perceived as intelligent by human users.

The conceptual framework presented here describes how explanations can be used in the different parts of an ambient intelligent system. Further on, it describes how knowledge about requirements for explanations which can fulfil different user goals can be gained. We have introduced a means of taking user goals into account which is both psychologically plausible and in line with the tradition in context aware computing.

We have further on outlined how an understanding for user goals can be obtained both from an activity theoretic analysis of the activity environment and from the general and domain specific knowledge encompassed in the system at hand.

We have described how different user goals for explanations are related to different kinds of explanation and by this have outlined what knowledge a system has to contain in order to fulfil the user's goals. However, we have not yet tied this into a detailed methodology for intelligent systems design.

The three layered conceptual architecture (perception – awareness – sensitivity) combined with our conceptual model of explanations in ambient intelligence gives a foundation for the development of explanation aware applications. The different goals a user might have towards explanations together with their mapping to kinds and the inclusion of socio-technical analytic methods help us integrating the explanatory capabilities of the application at an early stage of the design process.

Our current implementation of an ambient intelligent case-based reasoning system can cater to the system centric perspective of explanations to some degree, but this has to be developed further. Regarding the user centric perspective, the current application does support the transparency, conceptualization and justification goals, where the latter is only supported partially due to the underlying issues with plausible inheritance in the current Java implementation. For the other goals, further implementation work is necessary.

Another aspect that deserves further attention is our model of the division of labour. In order to reconcile our view on artifacts and humans, we have to find ways to integrate the modelling of different persons as subjects into our generic context model.

Additionally, we want to augment existing design guidelines with methods for the analysis of social aspects which can lead to a better understanding of the environment in which the ambient intelligent system has to function than ad-hoc methods can give. It is also important to note that we have not yet fully utilised some aspects of our theoretical foundations in organisational psychology, like the notions of breakdown situations or functional organs in activity theory, or the use of semiotics for the organisation of the user interface itself.

References

1. Weiser, M.: The computer for the 21st century. Scientific American, 94–104 (1991)
2. Ducatel, K., Bogdanowicz, M., Scapolo, F., Leijten, J., Burgelman, J.C.: ISTAG scenarios for ambient intelligence in 2010. Technical report, IST Advisory Group (2001)
3. Kofod-Petersen, A., Aamodt, A.: Contextualised ambient intelligence through case-based reasoning. In: Roth-Berghofer, T.R., Göker, M.H., Güvenir, H.A. (eds.) EC-CBR 2006. LNCS (LNAI), vol. 4106, pp. 211–225. Springer, Heidelberg (2006)
4. Yau, S.S., Wang, Y., Karim, F.: Development of situation-aware application software for ubiquitous computing environments. In: 29th Annual International Computer Software and Applications Conference (COMPSAC'02), Edinburgh, Scotland, vol. 1, pp. 107–112. IEEE Computer Society, Los Alamitos (2002)
5. Marx, K.: Das Kapital, Band 1: Der Produktionsprozeß des Kapitals. In: Marx Engels Werke (MEW), vol. 23, Dietz-Verlag, Berlin (1867)
6. Vygotski, L.S.: Mind in Society. Harvard University Press, Cambridge (1978)
7. Leont'ev, A.N.: Activity, Consciousness, and Personality. Prentice-Hall, Englewood Cliffs (1978)
8. Turing, A.: Computing machinery and intelligence. Mind LIX, 433–460 (1950)
9. Kant, I.: Kritik der reinen Vernunft (2. Auflage). Akademie (1787)
10. Kant, I.: Anthropologie in pragmatischer Hinsicht. Akademie (1798)
11. Kant, I.: Kritik der praktischen Vernunft. Akademie (1788)
12. Aamodt, A., Plaza, E.: Case-based reasoning: Foundational issues, methodological variations, and system approaches. AI Communications 7, 39–59 (1994)
13. Schank, R.C.: Explanation Patterens – Understanding Mechanically and Creatively. Lawrence Erlbaum, New York (1086)
14. Schank, R,, Abolson, R.: Scripts, Plans, Goals and Understanding. Lawrence Erlbaum, Mahwah (1977)
15. Bartlett, F.C.: Remembering: A study in Experimental and Social Psychology. Cambridge University Press, Cambridge (1932)
16. Rumelhart, D.E.: Schemata: The building blocks of cognition. In: Spiro, R.J., Bruve, B., Brewer, W.F. (eds.) Theoretical Issues in Reading and Comprehension, Lawrence Erlbaum Assoc. Inc., Mahwah (1980)

17. Sørmo, F., Cassens, J., Aamodt, A.: Explanation in case-based reasoning – perspectives and goals. Artificial Intelligence Review 24, 109–143 (2005)
18. Leake, D.B.: Goal-based explanation evaluation. In: Goal-Driven Learning, pp. 251–285. MIT Press, Cambridge (1995)
19. Roth-Berghofer, T.R.: Explanations and case-based reasoning: Foundational issues. In: Funk, P., González Calero, P.A. (eds.) ECCBR 2004. LNCS (LNAI), vol. 3155, pp. 389–403. Springer, Heidelberg (2004)
20. Richter, M.M.: The knowledge contained in similarity measures. In: Aamodt, A., Veloso, M.M. (eds.) Case-Based Reasoning Research and Development. LNCS(LNAI), vol. 1010, Springer, Heidelberg (1995)
21. Roth-Berghofer, T.R., Cassens, J.: Mapping goals and kinds of explanations to the knowledge containers of case-based reasoning systems. In: Muñoz-Ávila, H., Ricci, F. (eds.) ICCBR 2005. LNCS (LNAI), vol. 3620, pp. 451–464. Springer, Heidelberg (2005)
22. Kofod-Petersen, A., Cassens, J.: Using activity theory to model context awareness. In: Roth-Berghofer, T.R., Schulz, S., Leake, D.B. (eds.) MRC 2005. LNCS (LNAI), vol. 3946, pp. 1–17. Springer, Heidelberg (2006)
23. Cassens, J., Kofod-Petersen, A.: Using activity theory to model context awareness: a qualitative case study. In: Sutcliffe, G.C.J., Goebel, R.G. (eds.) Proceedings of the Nineteenth International Florida Artificial Intelligence Research Society Conference, Melbourne Beach, pp. 619–624. AAAI Press, Stanford (2006)
24. Cassens, J.: Knowing what to explain and when. In: Gervás, P., Gupta, K.M. (eds.) Proceedings of the ECCBR 2004 Workshops. Number 142-04 in Technical Report of the Departamento de Sistemas Informáticos y Programación, Universidad Complutense de Madrid, Madrid, pp. 97–104 (2004)
25. Nardi, B.A.: A brief introduction to activity theory. KI – Künstliche Intelligenz, 35–36 (2003)
26. Bødker, S.: Activity theory as a challenge to systems design. In: Nissen, H.E., Klein, H., Hirschheim, R. (eds.) Information Systems Research: Contemporary Approaches and Emergent Traditions. North Holland, pp. 551–564 (1991)
27. Nardi, B.A. (ed.): Context and Consciousness. MIT Press, Cambridge (1996)
28. Vygotski, L.S.: Ausgewählte Schriften Bd. 1: Arbeiten zu theoretischen und methodologischen Problemen der Psychologie. Pahl-Rugenstein, Köln (1985)
29. Kutti, K.: Activity theory as a potential framework for human-computer interaction research [27] 17–44
30. Mwanza, D.: Mind the gap: Activity theory and design. Technical Report KMI-TR-95, Knowledge Media Institute, The Open University, Milton Keynes (2000)
31. Leake, D.B.: Workshop introduction: ECCBR-04 workshop on explanation in CBR. Slides last access 22.02.2007 (2004), https://www.cs.tcd.ie/research_groups/mlg/ecbrws2004/
32. Cunningham, P., Doyle, D., Loughrey, J.: An evaluation of the usefulness of case-based reasoning explanation. In: Ashley, K.D., Bridge, D.G. (eds.) ICCBR 2003. LNCS(LNAI), vol. 2689, pp. 122–130. Springer, Heidelberg (2003)
33. Aamodt, A.: A Knowledge-intensive, Integrated Approach to Problem Solving and Sustained Learning. PhD thesis, University of Trondheim, Norwegian Institute of Technology, Department of Computer Science, University Microfilms PUB 92-08460 (1991)

Context-Sensitivity of Human Memory: Episode Connectivity and Its Influence on Memory Reconstruction

Boicho Kokinov, Georgi Petkov, and Nadezhda Petrova

Central and East European Center for Cognitive Science,
Department of Cognitive Science and Psychology,
New Bulgarian University, 21 Montevideo Street, Sofia 1618, Bulgaria

Abstract. This paper is testing a DUAL-based model of memory. The model assumes decentralized representation of episodes as a coalition of agents and analogical transfer processes as the basis for memory reconstruction of our past. It is a model of active reconstruction thereby allowing memory insertions and blending of episodes. The experiment explores the role of the degree of internal connectivity of the coalition representing the episode on the outcome of the reconstruction process. It demonstrates that the more the links between the elements of the episode are, the higher the number of details we recall, and the lesser the intruded elements and the context influence.

Keywords: Cognitive Science, Psychology, Cognitive Modeling, Episodic Memory, Context effects.

1 Introduction

Even though human memory has been studied for more than 100 years now, we still do not have a clear understanding of how it works. There are two main metaphors for human memory used over this century (and the millenniums before that): the *storehouse* metaphor and the *paleontologist* metaphor. According to the first metaphor human memory is a "storage" where "memory traces" are "collected" and later on "retrieved". According to the second metaphor human memory is an active process of "constructing the past" (Neisser, 1967) – that is why this approach is also called "constructivist approach" (Bartlett, 1932, Schacter, 1995, 1999, Kokinov, Hirst, 2003). These two metaphors are still being in use and are still the basis of the main accounts of human memory.

In this paper we will discuss the possible mechanisms underlying episodic memory, i.e. memory for events, instances, and experiences. There are a number of models of episodic memory that can be classified according to two factors: whether they are more or less abstract (mathematical models, computational symbolic models, or biologically-oriented connectionist models) and whether they follow the storehouse or the paleontologist metaphor. There is a correlation between these two dimensions and as a rule the mathematical and symbolic models of memory are predominantly based on the storehouse metaphor, while the connectionist models tend to be more of a constructivist type, but this is not necessarily the case.

B. Kokinov et al. (Eds.): CONTEXT 2007, LNAI 4635, pp. 317–329, 2007.

In the short review that follows two important characteristics will be taken into account: the capabilities of the models to *explain false, illusory memories* (Deese, 1959, Loftus 1977, 1979, 2003, Roediger & McDermott, 1995, Schacter, 1995, 1999, Kokinov & Hirst, 2003), i.e. to explain not only the successfully recalled events, and the failure to recall some details, but also the cases of inserting elements in the recalled events that have never happened, as well as blending of two or more different episodes; and the capabilities of the models to *explain context-sensitivity of human memory* (Davies & Thomson, 1988, Smith, 1988), i.e. the tendency to recall an event easier when in the same environment or in the same internal state than in a changed environment or state; to recognize a face easier when the person is in the same setting, dressed the same way, doing the same activities, etc.; to recall different aspects of an event depending on the specific context of recall.

There are many models of episodic memory. These include the SAM model (Raaijmakers & Shiffrin, 1981), the REM model (Shiffrin, & Steyvers, 1997), the MINERVA2 model (Hintzman, 1984, 1986, 1988), the CHARM model (Metcalfe, 1982, 1985, 1990), the TODAM2 model (Murdock, 1982, 1983, 1993, 1995), the Complementary Learning Systems (CLS) model (McClelland, McNaughton, & O'Reilly, 1995, Norman, & O'Reilly, 2003), the ACT-R model (Anderson, 1993, Anderson & Lebiere, 1998). These models have been successfully used to account for various aspects of memory for list of words both in recognition and recall tasks. We are, however, interested in explaining the recall of complex episodes.

Except for the ACT-R model, all other models share a basic assumption which is that "memory traces" are represented by feature vectors. This is fine when lists of words has to be remembered, however, it becomes problematic when memorizing real-world episodes which include not only items and features, but also relations between the objects and participants. The relational information becomes even more important when analogy-making is involved (Gentner, 1983) and episodes are often used for transferring knowledge from old to new situations. ACT-R uses structured representations (chunks) and thus allows for representing this relational information. One may argue that the associative information in the "memory images" of SAM is relational in nature, and this is certainly true, but it is a very specific case and cannot be used for representing complex relational knowledge about the episodes.

Most of these models would account for the known context effects. Incorporating environmental information in the feature vector (or the chunk) and trying to find the best match to the retrieval cue (which may involve environmental features as well) results in a context-sensitive recall and/or recognition. In this way they account for the fact that people recall some words from the lists in one context, but not in others. Most of them, however, will not be able to account for context sensitive event recall, i.e. for the fact that different aspects of the episode might be reported on different occasions. This is because retrieval of an episode is all-or-non phenomenon according to these models – either the models finds the corresponding vector or not. Some models fix this problem by postulating a stochastic process by which some of the features in the feature vector might be unsuccessfully recovered or randomly changed during the recall and thus reproduced wrongly. Basically these models tend to ignore this issue since they were designed for explaining memory for word rather than for complex episodes.

It would be even more difficult for most models to explain false, illusory memory since most of them are based on the storehouse paradigm. Still some of these models explicitly attack this issue. Thus, for example, the CHARM model has been used to simulate some of Loftus' (Loftus 1977, 1979, 2003, Loftus et al, 1995) experimental results showing that human memory blends two similar events. TODAM2 should also be able to simulate these results since it is very similar in nature – both models assume that all memory traces are transformed (e.g. by convolution) and added to a single LTM vector. In this way the interference between two similar vectors results in blending between them. The CLS model (McClelland, 1995) has also been able to simulate blending of simple sentences which is even more interesting since the blending is produced at retrieval, i.e. it is constructed.

The next section describes a model of human episodic memory that was designed in order to face all these challenges: to be able to represent complex relational structure, to explain the constructive nature of human memory, and to account for its context sensitivity.

2 DUAL-Based Model of Episodic Memory

DUAL is a general cognitive architecture (Kokinov, 1994b, 1994c) developed in order to provide an integrated platform for building models of various cognitive processes that will interact with each other. Several models have been built so far on its bases: the AMBR model of analogy-making and memory (Kokinov, 1988, 1994a, Kokinov & Petrov, 2001, Grinberg & Kokinov, 2003), the JUDGEMAP model of judgment (Kokinov, Hristova, Petkov, 2004, Petkov, 2006), the PEAN model of perception (Nestor, Kokinov, 2004) and the newest integrated model of analogy and perception (Petkov, et al., 2007).

DUAL is a multi-agent system that combines the connectionist and symbolic approaches at the micro level. Each DUAL-based system consists of a big number of simple micro-agents each of which is hybrid. The symbolic part of the micro-agent represents a small piece of knowledge – a separate aspect of a proposition, of an episode or a concept, and its connectionist part represents the level of relevance of that piece of knowledge to the current context. In this way knowledge is represented by symbol structures in a decentralized fashion – knowledge is distributed over coalitions of agents. On the other hand, context and relevance are represented by the pattern of activation over the entire set of micro-agents.

Long term memory (LTM) corresponds to the whole set of micro-agents, while working memory (WM) corresponds to the set of micro-agent that are activated above a certain threshold at a given moment of time. Only the agents which are in WM are performing symbolic operations. Moreover, the speed of their symbolic processing depends on their activation level, thus the more active the agents are the faster they process the information and therefore have greater influence on the computational process. Cognitive processes are emerging in DUAL as a result of the local interactions among the micro-agents. There is no central control on the processes. Everything emerges from the message exchanges between simple micro-agents.

Episodes are represented by coalitions of agents, i.e. agents that are linked together and exchange activation supporting each other. Each agent in the coalition represents either an aspect of the episode (an object, a person, a feature) or a relations between aspects of the episode (relation between two persons or objects, an action performed by someone, etc.). The agent representing an object can be linked to the agent representing its feature and vice versa, the agent representing a relation is linked to the agents representing its arguments, etc. In this way the coalition is a kind of subnetwork of the network of the knowledge represented in LTM. Some coalitions are loosely connected since there are not many links between the agents (either there are few relations among the objects in the scene, or they were not encoded). These coalitions are quite vulnerable, i.e. it could easily happen that only few elements of the coalition are activated (and the activation cannot spread to the rest of the coalition because of the few links within it) and thus the cognitive model will spontaneously recall only a few aspects of the episode. On the other hand, some coalitions consist of strongly interconnected agents and these coalitions will be quite robust – as soon as some agents are activated all other members of the coalition become active as well because of the numerous excitatory links (Figure 1).

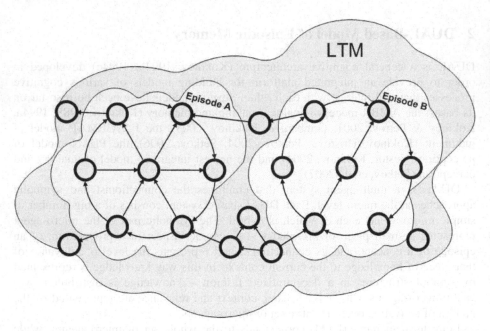

Fig. 1. Episodes are represented as coalitions of interconnected agents in LTM. Some episodes are robust (e.g. Episode A in this picture) – they consist of highly interconnected agents, while others are vulnerable (e.g. Episode B in this picture) – they consist of loosely connected agents.

The events and situations are represented in a hierarchical order. Thus, suppose for example, that several sets of pictures are presented at the computer screen during a psychological experiment. The participation in the experiment will be represented as an episode and each set of pictures will be represented as a sub-episode. In turn, each concrete picture is a sub-episode of the sub-episode, etc.

Recall is modeled in two ways in DUAL. Spontaneous free recall is a result of simple spreading activation. Activation starts from agents representing the immediately perceived aspects of the environment (connected to the INPUT node) and the goals of the system (connected to the GOAL node). The result of the spreading activation entirely depends on the initial activation (residual from some priming task and perceptual) and the pattern of connectivity. Cued recall is modeled as a kind of superficial analogy being sought. The probe is considered as a target and the AMBR analogy-making mechanisms are responsible for finding the closest base, and for the mapping and transfer processes. The model simulated blending of dissimilar episodes (Grinberg & Kokinov, 2003) which was a very surprising result. No other model or theory has ever claimed that dissimilar episodes can be blended. Taken as a strong prediction of the model, it has been experimentally tested and confirmed (Kokinov & Zareva, 2001, Zareva & Kokinov, 2003).

A number of other predictions fall out of the model. Consider the two coalitions presented in Figure 2. They represent the same objects participating in the two episodes. In the first case there are a number of relations between the objects thus connecting them into a strong and robust coalition, while in the second case there are no relations between the objects and they are bound together into a coalition only by the fact that all of them were present at the same place – in the lab. This second coalition will be weaker and more vulnerable. What are the consequences of this difference?

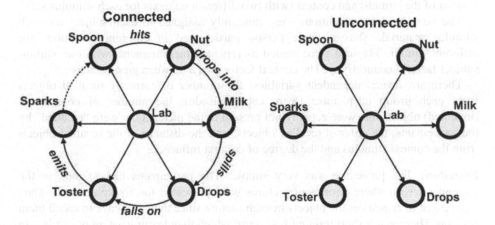

Fig. 2. An example of strongly connected and weakly connected coalition. In the strongly connected version there are relations between each two objects in the scene, while in the weakly connected version there are no relations among the objects (except for the spatial relations which are not depicted).

Predictions

Firstly, the first episode should be expected to be easier for recall: when activating some of the elements of the coalition the activation will spread easily to the rest and most of them will be activated as well. Therefore we should expect more elements of the episode to be reported.

Secondly, it would be easier for intruders from other episodes to be integrated into the weak coalition than into the robust one, since in the robust coalition all elements will be highly active because of the strong links among them and they will easily win the competition with the potential intruders, while in a weak coalition the intruders may easily become more active and win over its own members. Therefore less constructed illusory elements should be expected in the case of strong coalition than in the case of a weak one.

Finally, context effects should be stronger in the second case, since the coalition is unstable and even a single unrelated cue can change the activation levels and thus produce a bias towards the recall of associatively related elements of the episode.

4   Psychological Experiment: Testing the Model's Prediction

The experiment described in this section tests the predictions of the DUAL-based model of episodic memory by designing strongly connected and weakly connected episodes and testing the effect of the connectedness on various variables.

4.1   Method

Design. The experiment has a 2x2 mixed design. The independent variables are connectedness (with two levels – strongly connected version and weakly connected version of the stimuli) and context (with two different contexts for each stimulus set).

The connectedness conditions were randomly assigned to each subject for each stimulus material. Thus a single person participated in different conditions for different stimuli. The data were treated as repeated measurements with one within-subject factor – connectivity. The context factor was a between groups factor.

There are several dependent variables: the number of correctly recalled objects from each group of pictures (from each episode); the number of constructed (invented) objects that were actually not present in the pictures but were "recalled" by the participants; the order of recalled objects; and the distance of the recalled objects from the context stimulus and the degree of context influence.

Procedure. The procedure was very simple. The participants had to look at the computer screen where a series of pictures were presented for 3 seconds each. They were asked to remember the objects in each picture since they will have to recall them later on. There was a short training session in which they learnt what an object is – in order to eliminate parts of objects and their properties and relations from the list of to be remembered and recalled things. We asked them to focus on the objects only.

Then they participated in another experiment for 15 minutes in which they had to evaluate the length of line segments on a 7 point scale. This is a distracter task, which aims to shift their attention to a different field in order to be sure that they cannot hold the pictures or objects in their WM. So, if after that they would be able to recall some objects they should come from LTM.

The third session was a cued recall test. On a sheet of paper the participants had to write the list of objects they remember from the corresponding group. The first element of the group was present on the answer sheet and served as a cue for the rest of the group.

Fig. 3. Examples of the stimulus material: (left column) the strongly connected version, and (right column) the weakly connected version

Stimuli. Three sets of pictures have been used each of them consisting of 12 pictures. On each picture there are three objects, and each object is repeated on three pictures. Thus in each set of 12 pictures which is considered as an episode in our case, there are 12 different objects altogether. Each such set of 12 objects is presented in either a strongly connected version, or in a weakly connected one.

In the weakly connected version (see the right column in Figure 3) simply the three objects were not related in any meaningful way on the screen. In the strongly connected version (see the left column in Figure 3) the three objects interact in a meaningful way. The scenes were designed not to evoke schematic knowledge (prototypical events) thus the relations were quite strange and could not be used to predict what will happen next. The purpose of these relations was to make the representation of the episode a closed connected chain of objects and in this way to become a strong coalition.

The context stimuli were designed to be associatively linked to one of the objects in the corresponding set of pictures (Figure 4). Thus for example the "gift" is associatively linked to the "bottle of champagne", while the "bread" is associatively linked to "toaster". The idea is that presenting the context element "gift" the participants will be more likely to recall those elements that are associatively linked to it, and its neighbors, than when presented with "bread". This manipulation was designed to study the fine context effects on the content of the recalled episodes.

spoon, ...

spoon, ...

Fig. 4. Examples of the answer forms containing pictures of the context stimuli: gift and bread, together with the cue

Participants. 48 students from the New Bulgarian University participated in the experiment. Each of them participated in both the strongly connected and weakly connected condition, but each of them participated in only one context condition for each picture set.

4.2 Results

The data were aggregated for each participant and each condition (averaged over the items, i.e. over groups of objects to be remembered) and thus we obtained two measurements for each of them: for strongly connected and weakly connected episodes.

Thus repeated measurements ANOVA revealed a significant main effect of connectedness on the number of correctly recalled objects (F(1, 47) = 36.483, p<0.001) – Figure 5.

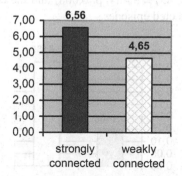

Fig. 5. Mean number of correctly recalled elements of the episode depending on the connectedness of the episode (out of 12 objects)

The main effect of connectedness on the number of falsely constructed elements of the episode (illusory memory) was also significant (F(1, 47) = 5.905, p=0.019) – see Figure 6.

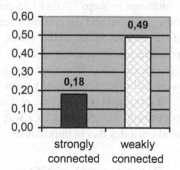

Fig. 6. Mean number of constructed (inserted illusory) elements of the episode depending on the connectedness of the episode

The next step was to analyze the main effect of connectedness on context influence. Context influence was measured in the following way: for each recalled element and for each of the two contexts 10 independent judges rated on a 7 point scale how closely associated the listed element and the context element are. In this way we obtained an average associative distance between each generated word and the context element. Then we calculated the difference between the two distances and called it context influence. The bigger this difference is the higher the context influence is, i.e. in the two different contexts subjects generated very different elements – one close to context 1 and the other to context 2. If the difference would be zero, then subjects would have generated the very same list of elements, or elements that are equally close to both contexts. It turned out that the main effect of connectedness on context influence is marginally significant (F(1, 45) = 3.484, p=0.068) and the context influence is higher in the case of weakly connected episodes.

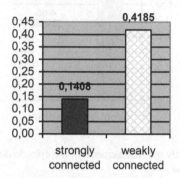

Fig. 7. How connectedness moderates context influence? Average context influence in the case of strongly connected episodes and weakly connected episodes

Finally, the order of recall of the episode elements was analyzed. A new variable was introduced which is called "distance in steps" – this is a measure of how many steps there are between the previously recalled and the currently recalled element if we follow the order of presentation of the objects in the initial slides. If the participants exactly follow the order of initial presentation the average distance in steps for their recall list will be 1. Of course, this is not the case. However, the participants in the strongly connected episodes group were following significantly more closely the initial order of presentation (F(1, 43) = 10.431, p=0.002). This is because they can use the represented causal relations between the elements as a way of traversing the episode, while in the weakly connected episodes this is impossible.

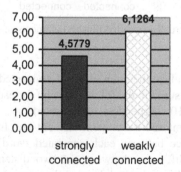

Fig. 8. Strongly connected episodes tend to be recalled to a greater degree in the same order as presented than the weakly connected episodes

4 Conclusions

All of the predictions of the DUAL-based model of memory were confirmed (in one case only marginally). Strongly connected episodes make the recall easier – participants recall a bigger number of correct objects, a smaller number of incorrect (inserted) objects and they tend to recall them more closely following the order of presentation of the objects. At the same time strongly connected episodes are less influenced by context, while weakly connected episodes tend to be recalled in a context-dependent manner (the content of the episode is changing with context).

This is only a first step in a long journey. A number of additional questions arise out of this experiment. Although we tried to push away the schematic knowledge from this experiment by designing strange, unconventional situations, we can still not be sure that schematic knowledge has not been involved to certain degree. One way to explore this further would be to explicitly manipulate the degree of conventionality of the relations between the objects. Highly conventional relations are expected to chunk the whole episode into a single whole and thus make it much easier to remember, they should contribute to higher number of correct recalls, but also a higher number of false (illusory) recalls if a prototypical object is missing from the presented situation. And also context effects should be smaller or even nonexistent with prototypical situations.

The DUAL-based model of episodic memory presented here allows for a much more detailed analysis of the content of the episode representation, especially of the internal structure of the episode. Most models of memory ignore this structure, but as we see from the experimental data, the structure plays an important role for successful recall, for the specific content we recall, and is characteristic for the degree of constructivist illusions and context influence imposed on recall.

Acknowledgments. This work is supported by the Project ANALOGY: Humans – the Analogy-Making Species, financed by the FP6 NEST Programme of the European Commission.(Contr. No 029088).

References

1. Anderson, J.R., Lebiere, C.: The Atomic Components of Thought. Erlbaum, Mahwah (1998)
2. Anderson, J.R.: Rules of the Mind. Erlbaum, Hillsdale (1993)
3. Bartlett, F.C.: Remembering: A Study in Experimental and Social Psychology. Cambridge University Press, Cambridge (1932)
4. Davies, G., Thomson, D.: Memory in context: Context in memory. John Wiley & Sons, Chichester (1988)
5. Deese, J.: On the prediction of occurrence of particular verbal intrusions in immediate recall. Journal of Experimental Psychology 58, 17–22 (1959)
6. Dodson, C.S., Koutstaal, W., Schacter, D.L.: Escape from illusion: Reducing false memories. Trends in Cognitive Science 4, 391–397 (2000)
7. Gentner, D.: Structure-mapping: A theoretical framework for analogy. Cognitive Science 7, 155–170 (1983)
8. Grinberg, M., Kokinov, B.: Simulation of Episode Blending in the AMBR Model. In: Proceedings of the 4th European Cognitive Science Conference, Lawrence Erlbaum, Hillsdale (2003)

9. Gillund, G., Shiffrin, R.M.: A retrieval model for both recognition and recall. Psychological Review 91, 1–65 (1984)
10. Grinberg, M., Kokinov, B.: Analogy-Based Episode Blending in AMBR. In: Kokinov, B., Hirst, W. (eds.) Constructive Memory, NBU Press, Sofia (2003)
11. Hintzman, D.L.: MINERVA 2: A simulation model of human memory. Behavior Research Methods, Instruments, & Computers 16, 96–101 (1984)
12. Hintzman, D.L.: Schema abstraction in a multiple-trace memory model. Psychological Review 93, 411–428 (1986)
13. Hintzman, D.L.: Judgments of frequency and recognition memory in a multiple-trace memory model. Psychological Review 95, 528–551 (1988)
14. Kokinov, B.: Associative Memory-Based Reasoning: How to Represent and Retrieve Cases. In: O'Shea, T., Sgurev, V. (eds.) Artificial Intelligence III: Methodology, Systems, Applications, Elsevier, Amsterdam (1988)
15. Kokinov, B.: A Hybrid Model of Reasoning by Analogy. In: Holyoak, K., Barnden, J. (eds.) Advances in Connectionist and Mental Computation Theory, Analogical Connections, vol. 2, Ablex, Norwood (1994a)
16. Kokinov, B.: The DUAL Cognitive Architecture. A Hybrid Multi-Agent Approach. In: Cohn, A. (ed.) Proceedings of the Eleventh European Conference of Artificial Intelligence, John Wiley & Sons, London (1994b)
17. Kokinov, B.: The Context-Sensitive Architecture DUAL. In: Proceedings of the Sixteenth Annual Conference of the Cognitive Science Society. LEA , Hillsdale (1994c)
18. Kokinov, B.: The Mechanisms of Episode Construction and Blending in DUAL and AMBR: Interaction Between Memory and Analogy. In: Kokinov, B., Hirst, W. (eds.) Constructive Memory, NBU Press, Sofia (2003)
19. Kokinov, B., Grinberg, M.: Simulating Context Effects in Problem Solving with AMBR. In: Akman, V., Bouquet, P., Thomason, R.H., Young, R.A. (eds.) CONTEXT 2001. LNCS (LNAI), vol. 2116, pp. 221–234. Springer, Heidelberg (2001)
20. Kokinov, B., Hirst, W. (eds.): Constructive Memory. NBU Press, Sofia (2003)
21. Kokinov, B., Hristova, P., Petkov, G.: Does Irrelevant Information Play a Role in Judgment? In: Proceedings of the 26th Annual Conference of the Cognitive Science Society, Lawrence Erlbaum, Hillsdale (2004)
22. Kokinov, B., Petrov, A.: Integration of Memory and Reasoning in Analogy-Making: The AMBR Model. In: Gentner, D., Holyoak, K., Kokinov, B. (eds.) The Analogical Mind: Perspectives from Cognitive Science, MIT Press, Cambridge (2001)
23. Kokinov, B., Zareva-Toncheva, N.: Episode Blending as Result of Analogical Problem Solving. In: Proceedings of the 23rd Annual Conference of the Cognitive Science Society, Lawrence Erlbaum, Hillsdale (2001)
24. Loftus, E.: Shifting human color memory. Memory and Cognition 5, 696–699 (1977)
25. Loftus, E.: Eyewitness testimony. Harvard University Press, Cambridge (1979)
26. Loftus, E., Feldman, J., Dashiell, R.: The reality of illusory memories. In: Schacter, D. (ed.) Memory distortions: How minds, brains, and societies reconstruct the past, Harvard University Press, Cambridge (1995)
27. Loftus, E.: Our changeable memories: Legal and practical implications. Nature Review Neuroscience 4(3), 231–234 (2003)
28. Loftus, E., Pickrell, J.: The formation of false memories. Psychiatric Annals 25, 720–725 (1995)
29. McClelland, J.L., McNaughton, B.L., O'Reilly, R.C.: Why there are complementary learning systems in the hyppocampus and neocortex: Insights from the successes and failures of connectionists models of learning and memory. Psychological Review 102, 419–457 (1995)

30. McClelland, J.L.: Constructive memory and memory distortions: a parallel distributed processing approach. In: Schacter, D. (ed.) Memory Distortion, pp. 69–90. Harvard University Press, Cambridge (1995)
31. Norman, K.A., O'Reilly, R.C.: Modeling hippocampal and neocortical contributions to recognition memory. A complementary-learning-systems approach. Psychological Review 104, 611–646 (2003)
32. Murdock Jr., B.B.: A theory for the storage and retrieval of item and associative information. Psychological Review 89, 609–626 (1982)
33. Murdock Jr., B.B.: A distributed memory model for serial-order information. Psychological Review 90, 316–338 (1983)
34. Murdock Jr., B.B.: TODAM2: a model for the storage and retrieval of item, associative, and serial-order information. Psychological Review 100, 183–203 (1993)
35. Murdock Jr., B.B.: Developing TODAM: three models for serial-order information. Memory & Cognition 23, 631–645 (1995)
36. Neisser, U.: Cognitive psychology. Appleton Century Crofts, New York (1967)
37. Nestor, A., Kokinov, B.: Towards Active Vision in the DUAL Cognitive Architecture. International Journal on Information Theories & Applications 11(1), 9–15 (2004)
38. Petkov, G.: Modeling Analogy-Making, Judgment, and Choice with Same Basic Mechanisms. In: Fum, D., Missier, F., Stocco, A., Goliardiche, E. (eds.) Proceedings of the Seventh International Conference on Cognitive Modeling. pp. 220–225 (2006)
39. Petkov, G., Kiryazov, K., Grinberg, M., Kokinov, B.: Modeling Top-Down Perception and Analogical Transfer with Single Anticipatory Mechanism. In: Proceedings of the Second European Cognitive Science Conference (2007)
40. Raaijmakers, J.G.W., Shiffrin, R.M.: SAM: A theory of probabilistic search of associative memory. In: Bower, G.H. (ed.) The psychology of learning and motivation, vol. 14, pp. 207–262. Academic Press, New York (1980)
41. Raaijmakers, J.G.W., Shiffrin, R.M.: Search of associative memory. Psychological Review 88, 93–134 (1981)
42. Ryan, L., Nadel, L., Keil, K., Putnam, K., Schnyer, D., Trouard, T., Moscovitch, M.: The hippocampal complex and retrieval of recent and very remote autobiographical memories: Evidence from functional magnetic resonance imaging in neurologically intact people. Hippocampus 11, 707–714 (2001)
43. Roediger, McDermott.: Creating false memories: Remembering words not presented in lists. Journal of Experimental Psychology: Learning, Memory, & Cognition 21(4), 803–814 (1995)
44. Schacter, D.L. (ed.): Memory distortion: how minds, brains, and societies reconstruct the past. Harvard University Press, Cambridge (1995)
45. Schacter, D.L.: The seven sins of memory: insights from psychology and cognitive neuroscience. American Psychologist 54, 182–203 (1999)
46. Shiffrin, R.M., Steyvers, M.: A model for recognition memory: REM – retrieving effectively from memory. Psychonomic Bulletin and Review 4, 145–166 (1997)
47. Smith, S.: Environmental context-dependent memory. In: Davies, G., Thomson, D. (eds.) Memory in context: Context in memory, John Wiley & Sons, Chichester (1988)
48. Zareva, N., Kokinov, B.: Blending of Non-Similar Episodes as a Result of Analogical Mapping with a Third One. In: Proceedings of the 25th Annual Conference of the Cognitive Science Society, Lawrence Erlbaum, Hillsdale (2003)

Enhancing Just-in-Time E-Learning Through Machine Learning on Desktop Context Sensors

Robert Lokaiczyk, Andreas Faatz, Arne Beckhaus, and Manuel Goertz

SAP Research CEC Darmstadt
Bleichstr. 8
64283 Darmstadt, Germany
{robert.lokaiczyk, andreas.faatz, arne.beckhaus, manuel.goertz}@sap.com

Abstract. The objective of novel e-learning strategies is to educate the learner during his actual work process. We focus on this new approach of in-place and in-time e-learning, which offers learning resources right in time the user is in need for it. A crucial factor for those modern task-oriented e-learning software is the user's context. To deliver learning resources to the user, which are both suitable and helpful with regards to the user's current work situation and his competencies, the application always has to consider the learner's actual work task, his environment, and history. In this paper, we present an architecture for the work task prediction, evaluate different machine learning algorithms in depth by their accuracy for that purpose and discuss the integration in our e-learning environment. This validates the possible usage in real-world business scenarios.

1 Introduction

The goal of our research project APOSDLE[1] (see [10]) is to enhance the productivity of knowledge workers by integrating learning, teaching, and working. It is believed that the traditional 'learn first, apply later'-approach is not suitable to today's dynamic knowledge economy. It should be substituted by an interweaved learning paradigm and an understanding of life-long learning. APOSDLE is one means of supporting this shift in learning paradigms and can help to increase knowledge workers' productivity at the electronic workplace.

APOSDLE is not only a concept but a software system as well. Currently, there are often different systems for communication, knowledge management, and other business tasks. APOSDLE intends to unify these workspaces in one software system [11]. That way, users can act as informal teachers while

---

[1] APOSDLE (**A**dvanced **P**rocess-**O**riented **S**elf-**D**irected **L**earning **E**nvironment) is partially funded under the 6th framework programme (FP6) for R&D of the European Commission within the Information Society Technologies (IST) work program 2004 under contract no. IST-027023.

B. Kokinov et al. (Eds.): CONTEXT 2007, LNAI 4635, pp. 330–341, 2007.

communicating. For example, the content shared during collaboration is enriched with meta information and stored as so-called knowledge artefacts. Thus, learning material need not be explicitly created in a time-consuming and costly manner. Learners can rather rely on up-to-date and informal knowledge suited to work processes they want to master next.

In order to support this and many other aspects of the integration of learning, teaching, and working, APOSDLE needs to be aware of a user's current working task. This meta-information is to be retrieved automatically and unobtrusively using low-level context information as indicators. The applicability of traditional machine learning algorithms to this problem is the subject of this paper.

The paper is structured as follows: First, we give an introduction to novel e-learning concepts and propose some innovations to overcome the limits of existing approaches. This is necessary to comprehend the background and objectives of our e-learning environment. The main section 3 shows a formalization of context for desktop environments and derives features (Section 3.1) out of desktop context, which can be used as input for machine learning (ML) algorithms. We define preprocessing steps for those features in section 3.2 and use them in a variety of ML algorithms to predict the actual user's work task (Section 3.3). The evaluation according to accuracy is located in section 4 right before the related work section. The conclusions in section 6 summarize the findings of this paper and give an extensive outlook on potential improvements and extensions.

2   Goal and Requirements

The goal of the APOSDLE task predictor is to know the active task of the user at any point in time. Whereby task is a defined unit of work consisting of activities to reach a certain goal. The problem of task determination is perceived as a machine learning task. When first using APOSDLE, the system is untrained and the user needs to specify the task he works on from a predefined list of business tasks (manual selection). During this work process the APOSDLE context monitor logs any desktop events reflecting the user's actions. These include keyboard presses, application launches, document full texts, etc. That way, tagged training material of user's work streams with the task name as class label are collected and as soon as enough material is gathered APOSDLE trains a ML model of the user's work task in this business process. The optimal result is achieved when the user continues to work and s/he does not need to manually notify the system of task switches anymore. The APOSLDE task predictor automatically classifies the active tasks using continously recorded event streams (automated selection). Whenever classification detects a change in tasks, the APOSDLE e-learning environment displays a list of associated learning resources which provide the user with context-aware learning material suitable for his current work task. The whole scenario is depicted in Figure 1.

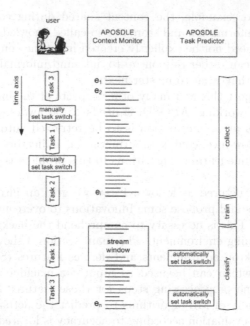

Fig. 1. Application Scenario

Some of the most important requirements for the APOSDLE e-learning environment, which were elicited by application users, are:

- overall unobtrusiveness to the user
- real-time recommendation of suitable learning material
- process orientation of work
- low memory and CPU usage
- support for Windows desktop environment

These requirements and soft goals lead to modifications in a traditional e-learning architecture. Thereout results the need for a holistic context model with extensive context sensors and high training speed and prediction accurracy of the ML algorithms. The necessary modifications to fulfill those requirements are discussed in section 3, since they are primary success factors for the usage in real-world e-learning scenarios in a business setting.

3   Approach

3.1   Features

To our understanding, context is the environmental setting of the user's current work situation. We define context indicators technically as low-level user and system events that are collected from the user's computer desktop and serve as

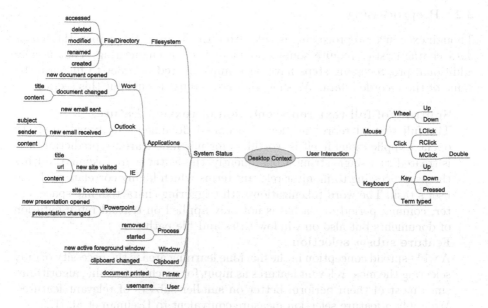

Fig. 2. Overview: Desktop Context Sensors

input for the APOSDLE task predictor. Our set of context sensors is summarized in Figure 2.

The context information is gathered by software hooks which operate on a operating system level. Figure 3 illustrates this process. The Windows operating system translates many system events to messages. For example, an application is notified of a mouse click by receiving a *WM_LBUTTONDOWN* message. These messages can be intercepted by the APOSDLE context monitor by setting a hook in the message queue of the system via a Windows kernel function. That way, it forwards all messages to the target application after unobtrusively logging the user's work. Unobtrusively means hereby, that the user is not bothered during his work since in contrary to other approaches no explicit input or selection of context data is necessary.

Our overall hypothesis is, that those sensors provide good indicators for a certain work situation (work task). This will be evaluated in Section 4.

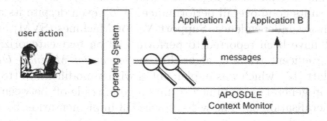

Fig. 3. Event Stream Generation

3.2 Preprocessing

Though excessive preprocessing is not within the focus of this paper, the sensor data characteristics require some amount of feature engineering. That is why additional preprocessing steps have been implemented in order to increase the value of the recorded data. We show the basic steps throughout this section.

- **Splitting of full text representation of textual features**
  The full textual representation of accessed documents or typed input to opened applications itself is worthless for machine learning prediction if it is treated as a single string. Consequently, the features are tokenized during the preprocessing to monitor relevant terms which highly correlate with the user's task. The word tokenization with triggering characters like space, enter, comma, period or slashes is not only applied on textual representation of documents but also on window titles and file paths.
- **Feature subset selection**
  A wide-spread conception in the machine learning area is the necessity of only selecting the most relevant features as input for machine learning algorithms, since most of them perform better on smaller subsets of relevant features. We apply a feature selection measure equivalent to Breiman et al. [1].
- **Filtering frequent and noisy events**
  Some system events appear very frequently and can be seen as noise in the event stream, since they do not correlate to the user's work task. Those events include for example file access to operating system libaries and swap files or filesystem events not initiated by the user, e.g. caused by anti virus software etc. Those noisy events are simply filtered out from the event stream and should therefore lesser influence the task prediction [12].

3.3 Prediction

The input data's event stream character poses a challenge to the application of traditional machine learning algorithms. The challenge in machine learning to both generalize well and not overfit constitutes the need for performance measures like accuracy and coverage. Moreover, it is also crucial to perform classification and training in reasonable time amounts due to scenario constraints. The machine learning algorithms we implemented and tested are of the types decision tree learning, rule learning, Naïve Bayes, and Support Vector Machines. In addition, one stream-based algorithm was evaluated. Naïve Bayes (NB) was choosen due to its good overall performance [7] [5], even despite its assumption of class condition independence. Support Vector Machines (SVM) are machine learners that have been reported to perform well on text categorization problems [9]. One efficent training algorithm is *Sequential Minimal Optimization* (SMO) by Platt [13], which was implemented with a modification [18] in APOS-DLE. SVMs in general are assumed to find a good trade-off between overfitting und over-generalisation [2]. The well-known ID3 implementation by Ross Quinlan [17] [15] was choosen as concrete instance of decision tree learners, since it avoids overfitting by a pruning strategy [16]. One of the first successful learning techniques was rule learning [3]. Since it also generates human-readable classification rules and the efficiency and competitiveness was proven by its authors, the incremental reduced error pruning [6] (IREP) algorithm was also choosen for implementation. The fifth and last classifier evaluated is—in contrast to the first four ones—a truly stream-based one. We implemented an Euclidian Distance Classificator (abbreviation: Euclid). Any unseen stream window is classified with the class label (task name) whose average feature vector lies closest to the feature vector of the new sample in terms of the Euclidean distance measure $D(\mathbf{x}, \mathbf{x}') = \sqrt{\sum_{i=1}^{n}(\mathbf{x}_i - \mathbf{x}_i')^2}$. This classifier perfectly suits the APOSDLE requirements of low memory usage and high classification performance. Most APOSDLE implementations of machine learning algorithms have been validated against those of the open source project named Weka [8] in order to validate their correctness.

4 Evaluation

In order to evaluate the APOSDLE task prediction in general and the five learning algorithms in particular, a scenario was created that resembles the real use cases well. As evaluation scenario for task prediction we used a modeled business process of a sample application domain. We decided to model business tasks like *market analysis, product design and specification, find and contact suppliers, contract placement* and *triggering production* in a sequential process model formulated in the project's process description language YAWL.[2] Synthetic training data generation is not applicable to this problem since the specific streaming data with an inherent task model are difficult to mimic. Therefore, the evaluation solely occurred on multiple hours of real data recorded by a student in an evaluation scenario of varying repetitions of the defined tasks. Since the requirements of the APOSDLE project presume small amounts of training data in the real application scenario, the effort of recording real data for evaluation can be judged as reasonable. The next subsections present the findings of the resulting sequence of experiments.

4.1 Accuracy Values

An important requirement of the APOSDLE task prediction is its suitability to situations where labeled training material is sparse. Therefore, the dependence of the implemented algorithms on data availability has been evaluated. Figure 4 shows that all algorithms perform worse when provided with less training material.

The highest gain can be observed for Naïve Bayes. Euclid and IREP are influenced to the smallest degree by the training material availability. Starting at 200 samples, the relations between all algorithms are rather stable. SMO performs best in all scenarios. For the analyzed domain, the trade-off between classification accuracy and cost of collecting labeled data can be maximized with

---

[2] Yet Another Workflow Language. See *http://yawlfoundation.org*.

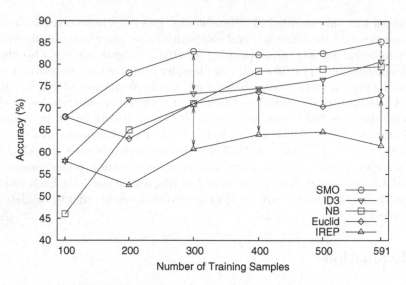

Fig. 4. Effect of Training Material Size on Accuracy

SMO and 300 training samples. This amount is as low as 20 minutes of recording per task (i.e. target label) and yields classification accuracies of 83%.

4.2 Effect of Window Size

The choice of the window size (Figure 1) which serves as input to the ML algorithm influences the learning task to a high degree. Since this component aggregates events to stream windows, it determines the number of samples that are made available to the learner. Short slices lead to large amounts of samples but small window sizes and vice versa.

Additionally, there are application case restrictions to stream window determination. A minimum of 5 seconds and a maximum of 30 seconds shall not be exceeded in order to prevent too frequent or too infrequent task switches. Our implementation is capable of meeting these requirements and has been evaluated for optimal parameters in terms of stream window determination.

Figure 5 reveals that all classifiers perform better when provided with long stream windows. SMO profits most, whereas IREP is rather indifferent. While the two min/max time intervall combinations of 20/30 and 5/30 are nearly the same, it can be concluded that making use of the highest flexibility between 5 and 30 seconds performs best. With this setting, our stream window determination algorithm chooses where to slice inbetween these wide bounds and cuts the window after meaningful events (e.g. application starts, changes in word application content). This suits the application scenario perfectly since it allows both fast detection of task switches and stability of forecast. In a real world application, it might be advisable to adjust these limits to the user's computer experience. For novices with unpracticed, slow PC usage, the limits might need to be increased.

Despite the rather high accuracy values in Figure 5, this performance measure is not ideally suited to the APOSDLE task prediction. It only reflects the performance of classical machine learning algorithms. However, when using the APOSDLE system, the user is not interested in the percentage of correctly classified stream windows but in the fraction of time with a correctly selected task. Even when providing 100% accurately classified stream windows, the automatic task detection always lags behind by the length of a stream window. This bias becomes relevant in scenarios with frequent task switches since the APOSDLE system shows the old task until the first stream window is fully recorded and processed. This effect justifies an upper bound on the stream window's length. Nevertheless, the accuracy measure is suitable to this evaluation as long as it is kept in mind that users might experience a lower performance.

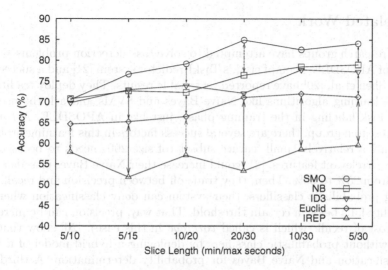

Fig. 5. Effect of Stream Window on Accuracy

4.3   Effect of Preprocessing

Figure 6 plots the difference in accuracies of the full configuration compared to a configuration where the tested preprocessor has been left out. The ends of the vertical lines represent maximum and minimum on the 10 cross-validation runs. The top and bottom of the bars represent the 3rd and 1st quantil and the line inbetween is the average of all 10 runs.

It can be observed that filtering system file events has little influence on the overall accuracy. Only decision tree and rule learners seem to make use of this information. Splitting of user file events into file name parts and subdirectories has a positive effect though still not being statistically significant. Figure 6 also reveals that splitting of window titles does not have an effect on accuracy. We assume that this is due to the fact that terms in window titles are often also terms in the application content itself and therefore not influence the prediction.

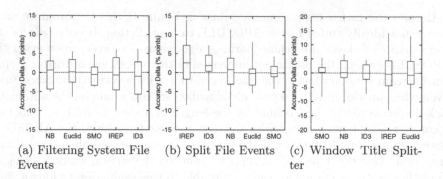

(a) Filtering System File Events   (b) Split File Events   (c) Window Title Splitter

Fig. 6. Effect of Preprocessing on Accuracy

5   Related Work

Several research groups have attempted to solve task detection problems similar to that of APOSDLE. Stumpf et al.'s TaskPredictor system [21] and a succeeding work of Shen et al. [20] have reported reasonable results. They deploy traditional machine learning algorithms like Naïve Bayes and SVMs and ask the user for explicit task labeling in the training phase, just like in APOSDLE. According to this research group, there are several success factors in this learning problem. First, only a relatively small feature subset (of size 200) needs to be used. By removing irrelevant features, [21] could increase their Naïve Bayes classifier's accuracy from 25% to 60%. Then, they trade off between precision and recall. Due to using probabilistic classifiers, their system can deny classification when the probability falls below a certain threshold. That way, precision can be increased at the cost of recall (which is called *coverage* in this case). [20] show that one can do without probabilistic classifiers by deploying a hybrid model of a SVM for classification and Naïve Bayes for probability determination. A third and last success factor of these two works is the stream window determination. A cut is performed only if the active application or the document therein changes (including site changes in internet browsers). [21] and [20] report that noise is a problem inherent in this learning scenario. Not only do several tasks access the same resources (windows, files, etc.) but there are also many different ways to fulfill a task. Additionally, task switches are fuzzy in the learning phase since the user might not know when exactly to indicate the task change (e.g. before an old application is closed, after a new application is launched, or inbetween).

Other researchers have accessed the problem from a different perspective. Schwarz and Roth-Berghofer [19] used a case-based-reasoning approach but do not provide an evaluation. Oliver et al. [12] do without any manual training by the user but utilize unsupervised clustering of tasks instead.

While the approaches of [21] and [20] give promising results for the objective of this paper, [19] and [12] can be seen to be out of its scope since they do not access the problem from a classical machine learning classification perspective.

6 Summary and Outlook

This paper proved the applicability of classical machine learning algorithms for user task prediction with low-level operating system events as indicators for a certain work task. Unlike other works (see Section 5), we have achieved accuracy values of over 85% with nearly full coverage[3]. In addition we fulfill the real-world requirements defined in section 3. Consequently, we distinct significantly from related work by:

- exploiting a more holistic context model using additional, previously neglected context sensors
- evaluating a broader spectrum of ML-algorithms with regard to their suitability
- integrating the task prediction in a real-world e-learning application
- suiting multiple real-world requirements for productive usage
- having reached a high prediction accurracy on our testing dataset despite the need to give a prediction of the user's task at any point in time

The evaluation of the machine learning algorithms revealed that the support vector machine implementation SMO performs best in terms of accuracy. Its high computational requirement in the training phase can be satisfied in the APOSDLE scenario by learning over night. Further recommendations regarding a priority list of algorithms and the minimal training requirements are illustrated in Figure 4. However, these results are limited to a special application domain and are inparticulary dependant on our recorded training dataset. Therefore they must not be generalized before being confirmed in larger field tests.

Despite these positive results, there is still room for improvement of the APOSDLE context-aware e-learning architecture. Most importantly, scientific advances on stream based machine learning schemes have not been analyzed in this paper. These algorithms might perform better than the traditional algorithms implemented here. The results of a basic stream algorithm, Euclidean Distance Classification, were not competitive, but still proved that even simple stream based algorithms can achieve reasonable accuracies. Another potential improvement could be achieved by exploiting stream characteristics by means of feature engineering. That way, traditional machine learning algorithms could make use of additional information inherent in the data sequence.

Further improvement of the low-level operating system sensors that provide the input to the machine learning task might be another source of advance. The more information they contain the better results can be expected from machine learning. Most importantly, the mouse hook should make available any mouse click and move events together with control names and types, text under the mouse cursor, and an indicator of mouse usage. Mouse usage can be helpful to identify graphics tasks like digital image manipulation or creation of presentations. Analogously, a frequency indicator for keyboard usage could help to

---

[3] The APOSDLE task predictor has a classification result at any point of time—except immediately after its launch when the first stream window is still recorded.

identify tasks that involve a lot of typing, like word processing. New types of desirable sensors are support for full text access with more application-specific sensors (like Microsoft Excel, Adobe Reader, and Firefox) and possibly other more generic, application-independent content and interaction sensors.

The classification algorithms could be enhanced by using ensemble techniques. A first implementation of an ensemble classifier makes use of the flexible packaging capabilities of our system architecture. However, it did not yet yield a performance gain in a first test configuration. Further experiments should therefore test whether assignment of different weights to events is useful in other setups. Other ensemble techniques that combine different classifiers should also be considered. Dietterich gives a good overview of these techniques in [4].

In spite of the positive preliminary evaluation conducted in this paper, the APOSDLE task prediction still has to prove its performance in a larger field study. Several application domains with users of different computer experience and varying numbers of work process tasks need to be considered. Since these data are not yet available from ongoing user studies, the evaluation in this paper was limited to one scenario. Consequently, one of the next tasks is evaluating whether varying application domains with their text domains yield performance differences in context-dependant task prediction.

References

[1] Brunk, C.A., Pazzani, M.J.: An Investigation of Noise-Tolerant Relational Concept Learning Algorithms. In: Proceedings of the 8th International Workshop on Machine Learning, vol. 961, pp. 389–393 (1991)

[2] Burges, C.J.C.: A Tutorial on Support Vector Machines for Pattern Recognition. Data Mining and Knowledge Discovery 2(2), 121–167 (1998)

[3] Clark, P., Boswell, R.: Rule Induction with CN2: Some Recent Improvements. In: Proceedings of the Fifth European Working Session on Learning, vol. 482, pp. 151–163 (1991)

[4] Dietterich, T.G.: Ensemble Methods in Machine Learning. In: Kittler, J., Roli, F. (eds.) MCS 2000. LNCS, vol. 1857, pp. 1–15. Springer, Heidelberg (2000)

[5] Domingos, P., Pazzani, M.J.: Beyond Independence: Conditions for the Optimality of the Simple Bayesian Classifier. In: International Conference on Machine Learning, pp. 105–112 (1996)

[6] Fürnkranz, J., Widmer, G.: Incremental Reduced Error Pruning. In: Proceedings the Eleventh International Conference on Machine Learning, New Brunswick, pp. 70–77 (1994)

[7] Han, J., Kamber, M.: Data Mining. Concepts and Techniques. Morgan Kaufmann Publishers, San Francisco (2001)

[8] Ian, E.F., Witten, H.: Data Mining. Hanser Verlag (2001)

[9] Joachims, T.: Text Categorization with Support Vector Machines: Learning with Many Relevant Features. In: Proceedings of the 10th European Conference on Machine Learning, pp. 137–142 (1998)

[10] Lindstaedt, S.N., Ley, T., Mayer, H.: Integrating Working and Learning with APOSDLE. In: Proceedings of the 11th Business Meeting of Forum Neue Medien, November 10-11, 2005, Verlag Forum Neue Medien, Vienna (2005)

[11] Mayer, H., Haas, W., Thallinger, G., Lindstaedt, S., Tochtermann, K.: APOSDLE - Advanced Process-oriented Self-directed Learning Environment. In: Poster Presented on the 2nd European Workshop on the Integration of Knowledge, Semamtic and Digital Media Technologies, 30 November - 01 December (2005)

[12] Oliver, N., Smith, G., Thakkar, C., Surendran, A.C.: Swish: semantic analysis of window titles and switching history. pp. 194–201 (2006)

[13] Platt, J.: Fast Training of Support Vector Machines using Sequential Minimal Optimization. MIT Press, Cambridge (1998)

[14] Platt, J.: Probabilistic Outputs for Support Vector Machines and Comparison to Regularized Likelihood Methods. In: Smola, A.J., Bartlett, P., Schoelkopf, B., Schuurmans, D. (eds.) Advances in Large Margin Classifiers, pp. 61–74. MIT Press, Cambridge (2000)

[15] Quinlan, J.R.: Induction of Decision Trees. Machine Learning 1(1), 81–106 (1986)

[16] Quinlan, J.R.: Simplifying Decision Trees. International Journal of Man-Machine Studies 27(3), 221–234 (1987)

[17] Quinlan, J.R.: Learning decision tree classifiers. ACM Computing Surveys (CSUR) 28(1), 71–72 (1996)

[18] Schölkopf, B., Smola, A.J.: Learning with Kernels. MIT Press, Cambridge (2002)

[19] Schwarz, S., Roth-Berghofer, T.: Towards Goal Elicitation by User Observation. In: Workshop Knowledge and Experience Management anlässlich des GI Fachgruppentreffens Wissensmanagment (FGWM 03) (2003)

[20] Shen, J., Li, L., Dietterich, T.G., Herlocker, J.L.: A hybrid learning system for recognizing user tasks from desktop activities and email messages. In: IUI '06: Proceedings of the 11th international conference on Intelligent user interfaces, pp. 86–92. ACM Press, New York (2006)

[21] Stumpf, S., Bao, X., Dragunov, A., Dietterich, T.G., Herlocker, J., Johnsrude, K., Li, L., Shen, J.: Predicting User Tasks: I Know What You're Doing. In: 20th National Conference on Artificial Intelligence (AAAI-05), Workshop on Human Comprehensible Machine Learning (2005)

Coping with Unconsidered Context of Formalized Knowledge

Stefan Mandl and Bernd Ludwig

Lehrstuhl für Künstliche Intelligenz
Friedrich-Alexander-Universität Erlangen-Nürnberg
{Stefan.Mandl, Bernd.Ludwig}@informatik.uni-erlangen.de

Abstract. The paper focuses on a difficult problem when formalizing knowledge: What about the possible concepts that didn't make it into the formalization? We call such concepts the *unconsidered context* of the formalized knowledge and argue that erroneous and inadequate behavior of systems based on formalized knowledge can be attributed to different states of the unconsidered context; either while formalizing or during application of the formalization. We then propose an automatic strategy to identify different states of unconsidered context inside a given formalization and to classify which parts of the formalization to use in a given application situation. The goal of this work is to uncover unconsidered context by observing sucess and failure of a given system in use. The paper closes with the evaluation of the proposed procedures in an error diagnosis scenario featuring a plan based user interface.

1 Concerning the Unconsidered When Formalizing Knowledge

When formalizing informal knowledge about a problem domain, certain activities have to be performed. On the *Knowledge Management* (KM) side, the yet informal knowledge which is relevant for the problem at hand has to be identified and made accessible. *Knowledge Engineering* (KE) activities prepare the informal knowledge in such a way that it allows for a formal representation. The following activities are listed in [14]:

1. Learn the terminology of the problem domain
2. Cut down on the coverage of the knowledge to be formalized
3. Select representation formalism
4. Create conceptualization
5. Write down the contents using the terminology

Finally the knowledge has to be encoded as a formal system which is expressed in a *Knowledge Representation* (KR) language. In this paper, we restrict our discussions to formalized knowledge which is represented in a logical language – for the experiments, we use Answer-Set-Programming (ASP). As implementation of ASP, we use the Smodels System (see [13] and [18]).

At each level of activities – the KM-, KE-, and KR-levels – things are left behind:

B. Kokinov et al. (Eds.): CONTEXT 2007, LNAI 4635, pp. 342–355, 2007.

- On the KM-Level, knowledge that is not considered important is unconsidered. Furthermore, if the relevant knowledge either cannot be found or is not accessible, it has to be left behind. One typical reason for knowledge not being accessible is the fact that it is often people (experts) who carry the knowledge and hence, when there are other urgent tasks, there is no time to acquire the knowledge from the expert.
- On the KE-Level, the use of a strict terminology and conceptualization allows to focus on the seemingly important concepts to be formalized, but in turn leaving everything behind that is not put into the terminology or modeled in the conceptualization.
- On the KR-Level, statements that cannot be expressed in a certain Knowledge-Representation language have to be approximated with other statements – leaving behind the original statement with the original meaning.

Thus, there is no doubt that no formalization is complete in the sense that everything that could have been said about the problem domain is being considered and included in the formalization. As Genesereth & Nilsson [3] put it:

> Language (probably any language) cannot capture all that we want to say about the world.

Every formlization takes place in a certain context, those parts of the context that are not put into the formalization make up the *unconsidered context* of the formalization.

Unconsidered context has the following properties:

- *Informal* – as the unconsidered parts are not covered by the conceptualization, there is no way to associate formal sentences with them; they have to remain informal.
- *Infinite* – every entity involved in the formalization introduced new backgrounds and perspectives. Even a single individual can easily come up with different opinions about the same subject.
- *Dynamic* – Being unconsidered does not mean that these things do not change; the real world is changing beyond the formalization.

Obviously the dynamics of the unconsidered context are a major problem. If the unconsidered context did not change, there would be little harm. But when it changes, it can influence the correctness of the considered parts of the formalization.

This circumstance has been recognized in the field of Planning. In [11], Mc-Carthy explains the so called *qualification problem* as follows:

> It seemed that in order to fully represent the conditions for the successful performance of an action, an impractical and implausible number of qualifications would have to be included in the sentences expressing them. For example, the successful use of a boat to cross a river requires, if the boat is a rowboat, that the oars and rowlocks be present and unbroken, and that they fit each other. Many other qualifications can be

added, making the rules for using a rowboat almost impossible to apply, and yet anyone will still be able to think of additional requirements not yet stated.

All the qualifications that could have been added are unconsidered context. When the unconsidered context is changing, it can affect both, creating and using the formalized knowledge.

At *system creation time*, different setups of unconsidered context can lead to an inconsistent theory. Such a situation can easily occur when different people with different backgrounds and presuppositions work together on a project. They may agree on the surface-level but when it comes to writing down the knowledge, differences begin to show.

At *runtime*, changing unconsidered context has the potential to cause the formalized knowledge to be plainly wrong!

2   Previous Work

There is surprisingly little prior work on unconsidered context but as the problem is omnipresent when building intelligent systems, there is a lot of work motivated by problems that – we think – could be interpreted as problems actually caused by unconsidered context.

In Machine Learning, there is the problem of 'concept drift in online concept learning' (see for examples [7], or [19]), where, the concept to be learned appears to be changing over the course of time. Such behavior can actually be understood as *hidden context changes* (see [6] or [20]). Hidden context and unconsidered context are similar concepts. While *hidden context* is invisible from the formalization's point of view, *unconsidered context* was not put into the formalization beforehand – we use the term *unconsidered* in order to emphasize the responsibility of the knowledge engineer. Thus, some of the techniques developed for handling concept drift can be adapted to handle unconsidered context; in our work, we try to deal with a more general setting: 1) the proposed techniques are not restricted to online learning and 2) we try to formalize the previously unconsidered and therefore make it possible to reason about unconsidered contexts.

In the mid-1980s Rodney Brooks proposed to build *intelligent systems that contain no representation at all* ([1]) – this is maybe the most forceful reaction to the problems of formalizing knowledge. We do not know if unconsidered context was known to Brooks and explicitly influenced his ideas, but we do know that it causes a lot of problems when building knowledge based systems and henceforth assume that it influenced Brooks at least to some degree.

The field of *context aware computing* (see [17]) is born out of the idea that one has to add more and more sensors in order to improve system performance. Thus, advocates of context aware computing try to reduce the unconsidered context of systems. The major problem with this approach is: there is no real end to it. On the other hand, if failure is not critical and the system approaches close to 100% performance, just making some spurious mistakes in some obscur situations, much is being gained.

In order to increase modularity when building large knowledge bases (like the one described in [8]), *formal context logic* was created. Interestingly, no definition of 'context' is provided:

> *"Contexts are abstract objects. We don't offer a definition, but we will offer some examples."* [12]

Thus, in formal context logic, context is represented *inside* the system as a formal structure while the unconsidered context is located *outside* the system. As (see the next section) our intent is indeed to find a way to make the unconsidered context accessible inside the system (with hindsight, when the system is actually used), formal context logic may serve as a way to represent unconsidered context, but as the context structures used in our system are quite simplistic, formal context logic would have been overkill; we use a much more hands-on approach, at least for the time being.

If something is not unconsidered but seems to be unimportant, it would be nice if we wouldn't have to be concerned with it. There are some subfield that deal with default assumptions, namely Frames and Non-monotonic Reasoning (see [16]). Defaults are related to normality which in turn is related to context.

Belief-Change/Revision (see [2]) and Knowledge Base Refinement (see [4]) deal with different ways of modifying a given theory or knowledge base. The following chapter reveals our plans to follow their footsteps.

3   Coping with Unconsidered Context

3.1   Three Basic Strategies

As mentioned at the end of section 1, the concept of unconsidered context allows for a common understanding of different types of errors, thus techniques for dealing with unconsidered context provide the potential to improve a given erroneous theory. We have found three basic strategies in order to deal with theories that are influenced by the effects of unconsidered context:

1. The most obvious strategy simply is to *formalize again*. Insights that have been gained in the first iteration now help to avoid unfortunate constructions. Typically, in hindsight it is much easier to determine what should have been put into the formalization such that the required tasks can be accomplished.
2. In order to avoid the efforts of a re-formalization (both monetary and time), it is possible to *document the assumptions* the system makes with respect to the unconsidered context. Now the user has to decide whether she should trust answers given by the system.
3. The most ambitious alternative is the *automatic correction* of the given system. As shown in figure 1, from a given set of axioms a set of subsets is created, yielding a set of new systems. In the last step, a classifier function is created which selects the appropriate sub-system for a given query.

Besides the usefulness in itself, automatic correction is also interesting because the two other approaches – re-formalization and documentation – obviously also benefit from an auto-correcting system:

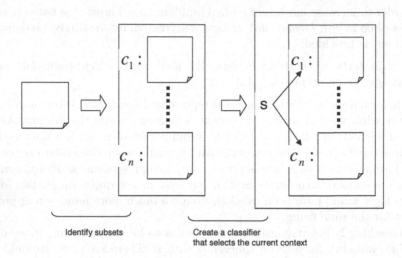

Identify subsets   Create a classifier
                          that selects the current context

Fig. 1. Automatic correction overview

- Auto-correction – by delivering reasonable subsets – provides (indirect) hints on which parameters may be worth to consider for a re-formalization.
- By comparing the identified subsets, it should be possible to determine which queries are safe in the sense that every context answers them in the same way. Then one could provide documentation about the queries that are safe to ask.

Hence, automatic correction is a goal worthy to achieve, whether or not actually delivered systems are to be supplied with an auto-correcting component.

3.2   Identification and Classification

Identification and *classification* of unconsidered context are the two main activities that allow automatic correction. An identification function is mapping from a formalization W to a subset of the set of all subsets $2^{2^{W}}$ of W. Thus, having n Axioms in a declarative theory, there are $2^{2^{n}}$ possible selections, for a set of $n = 6$ elements, there are $18,446,744,073,709,551,616$ subsets of the set of all subsets. Hence, there is no simple generate-and-test approach for identification functions. Therefore, we rely heavily on heuristics and external assumptions about the structure and behavior of the unconsidered context.

In [10] we analyze an online context learning problem. The assumptions are that 1) the sequence of examples adheres to observations made in reality, thus the unconsidered context can only change in ways that are possible in reality. 2) We assumed that every significant different state of the unconsidered context reveals itself by causing different probabilities that certain features show up in observations. In the present paper, we deal with the case when the formalization is given as a set of axioms for a logical theory. Hence, there is no set or sequence of examples. In fact, we actually do require a sequence of test examples – queries with correct answers – for our identification procedure, but not for the given theory where the unconsidered contexts are to be identified.

3.3   An Evolutionary Approach to Identification and Classification

As picture 1 shows, finding the subsets and creating the classifier are conceptually distinct phases. Identification is actually an optimization problem.

When given an objective function the measures the quality of a set of subsets of the consituents of a formalization, we could use a standard genetic algorithm (see [5]) to find close to optimal solutions. The crucial part is the objective function. It could feature various heuristics like:

– The subsets should be distinct.
– The subsets should give different answers on as many queries as possible.
– The subsets should be correct on a given test sequence as long as possible before making an error.

All those heuristics are afflicted by the problem that they are ad-hoc; one does not know when to use them or not. A better founded heuristic function is presented in the next subsection.

3.4   Combining Identification and Classification

The general idea can be captured with the slogan: *There is no reason to identify contexts that cannot be classified later.* We have to understand that identification is one component of a larger system, no matter how good the results of the identification are with respect to some objective function, if the rest of the system cannot facilitate the results of identification, the system still performs weakly.

Hence we propose to take into account the performance of *the complete system*, comprising identification and classification as an objective function for identification. In other words: those identifications are set to have high (in our GA, higher means fitter) fitness, which perform well in conjunction with a given prediction function on a test set.

3.5   Do We Really Identify Unconsidered Context?

Even if the system performance increases, why should we belief that we found different states of unconsidered context? The answer is quite straightforward: If we have a set of subsystems and a way to select subsystems for queries such that the performance increases, then we have adapted the system to things that change outside the system, hence unconsidered context. We are not able to identify *specific* setups of the unconsidered context; we hope to be able to identify *equivalent* setups, the (informal) equivalence relation reads: 'makes the same subset of the given set of axioms a good description of the state of affairs.'

3.6   A Classification Function Based on Actions

If the domain has the concept of *actions* then – because actions actively change the world – it is an obvious choice to base the fitness function on sequences of actions. Given a sequence of $n+1$ actions $a^0, \ldots, a^n$, the *current context* c_i^n is to be determined. This is a task suitable for the well-known Hidden-Markov-Models (HMMs; see [15]).

In order to use a HMM to determine the current context given a sequence of actions, we need to define what kind of *observations* are presented to the HMM. HMMs only deal with observations not actions. In order to overcome this limitation, from the set of all possible actions $\mathcal{A}$ and all possible contexts $\mathcal{C}$, we create the set of observations

$$\mathcal{O} = \mathcal{A} \times \mathcal{C}$$

In the implementation, we use integers to represent members of $\mathcal{O}$ which in turn represent combinations of actions and identified context; hence, we assume that the sets of actions and actions are finite.

The currently active context given an action and a sequence of previous observations is then chosen by comparing the likelyhood – as computed with the HMM – of all possible extensions of the given sequence with observations that contain the given action and choosing the most likely extension, thus obtaining the context.

4   The Coffee-Shop-Logistics (CSL) Diagnosis Domain

In order to evaluate the proposed techniques, we are in an uncomfortable position. On the one hand, we like to evaluate how our techniques perform when unconsidered, invisible parameters are changing; on the other hand, we like to perform a controlled experiment – we want to be sure that improvements do not happen by chance and changes in unconsidered context actually do happen during the evaluation. Therefore we decided to proceed as follows: 1) Create a formal domain (full), 2) decide which concepts should be unconsidered (small). 3) Create examples in the full domain and 4) map them to the small one by eliminating all unconsidered concepts.

The evaluation task is to do *error diagnosis*.

The domain used here is similar to the one described in [9] . There is a coffee-dispenser, a Lego™-Robot and a model train.

A typical history of events is the robot putting a cup under the spout of the coffee-dispenser, the coffee-dispenser filling the cup, the robot putting the cup on the wagon of the train, and the train delivering the cup to some user (see figure 2). The actual actions performed in the domain are not encoded as fixed procedures; instead, there is a model describing the state of the domain. When the user utters a goal like

"A small cup of coffee please"

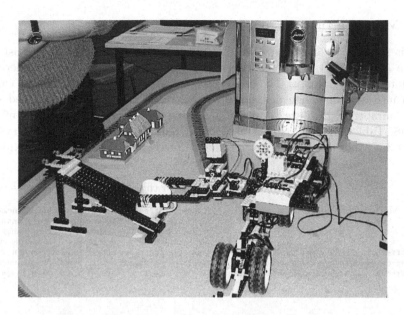

Fig. 2. The real domain which influenced the creation of the diagnosis domain. The robot (center) takes a cup from the ramp, then it will bring it to the coffee dispenser, when the cup is filled, the robot is to put the cup on the train.

the speech signal is (hopefully) and transformed into a formal goal description like:

```
(:goal (and (delivered cup)
            (mode-osc jura)))
```

which is a goal-state description in the planning language PDDL. Then, a planning system creates a plan – a sequence of actions – that when successfully executed will achieve the goal state. The involved speech recognition, natural language understanding and dialog managing technologies are not described in this paper; we assume that somehow a formal PDDL goal description is available. After each plan stepp, the world state is transformed into a list of logical facts. Diagnosis is performed by concatenating this list with another list of axioms suitable for diagnosis and using a model checker to find possible diagnosis. Thus, the system's performance can be evaluated by presenting situations and comparing the system's diagnoses with the true diagnoses. These are obtained from a correct diagnosis theory that operates on the 'full' domain (see page 348).

In order to introduce unconsidered context, we mark some concepts as invisible. Those are still used when planning and creating the diagnosis system to be optimized and when creating the evaluation examples, but they are removed before evaluating the identification and classifications procedure ('small'; see page 348). In order to evaluate the proposed the runtime data is created by a simulator which generates random goals, executes plans, performs diagnosis and records the results in example sequences.

4.1   Modeling the Domain

In this section, we show how the CSL domain was modeled. Table 1 lists the visible (considered) concepts. Please note that actions are also considered as concepts in the domain. Those are used because the *previous* action can be taken into account when defining diagnosis rules. Furthermore, we need some small numbers which we represent by using the symbolic constants n0, n1, ..., n8. Table 2 lists all the visible (considered) predicates used in the system. Table 3 shows the invisible (unconsidered) predicates. Even when we explicitly

Table 1. Considered concepts in the CSL domain

cup	a cup	produce-coffee	action (with obvious meaning)
jura	the coffee dispenser	draw-off-osc	action: produce one small cup
robo	the robot	draw-off-tsc	action: produce two small cups
train	the train	draw-off-obc	action: produce one big cup
draw-off-tbc	action: produce two big cups	take-cup-off-spout	action: (with obvious meaning)
put-cup-on-spout	action: (with obvious meaning)	load-cup-on-waggon	action: (with obvious meaning)
deliver-cup	action: (with obvious meaning)	go-in-place	action: train moves to special location

Table 2. Visible predicates in the CSL domain

under-spout ?c	true when a cup ?c is under the spout
ready ?x	true when coffee dispenser ?x is ready to produce coffee
service-request ?j	true when the self diagnosis of coffee dispenser ?j found an error
empty ?c	is cup ?c empty?
mode-osc ?j	is coffee dispenser ?j in mode 'one small cup'?
mode-tsc ?j	is coffee dispenser ?j in mode 'two small cups'?
mode-obc ?j	is coffee dispenser ?j in mode 'one big cup'?
mode-tbc ?j	is coffee dispenser ?j in mode 'two big cups'?
robo-loaded ?r	true when robot ?r is carrying cup ?c
train-loaded ?t	true when cup ?c is loaded on train ?t
parked ?c	true when cup ?c is in parking position
delivered ?c	true when cup ?c has been delivered
in-place ?t	true when train ?t stands ready
action ?a	true if ?a is the name of the last action performed (see table 1)

provide the diagnosis rules that contain unconsidered concepts, we hesitate from providing a set of diagnosis rules containing only visible concepts. Instead, we use a simulator to create examples that only contain visible concepts. We then use those examples as diagnosis rules. As a matter of fact, such rules are very bad, no generalization is applied. Still, as the number of concepts and predicates in the CLS-domain is very small, we hope to cover enough cases to get reasonable results. The next subsection provides more details on how the visible diagnosis rules are created via the simulator.

Table 3. Unconsidered predicates in the CSL-domain

water-left ?n   ?n is a measure for the amount of water left
coffee-left ?n   ?n is a measure for the amount of beans coffee beans left
cups-left ?n   ?n is the number of cups left

4.2   Using a Simulator to Generate 'Visible' Diagnosis Rules and Evaluation Examples

In order to create diagnosis rules and evaluation examples, we need a corpus of examples. We produce one by following the procedure outline below. As we want to generate data without user interaction, we have to provide additional healing actions that can be taken if a diagnosis indicates a problem. Thus, we are assuming that every diagnosed error can be corrected. The procedure to generate examples contains the following steps:

- randomly select one of a list of possible goals,
- given the current state of the system, create a plan that will achieve the goal,
- execute the plan (action by action),
- after each action, apply the full set of diagnosis rules ,
- record the pair

$$\langle\langle\alpha_1, \ldots, \alpha_n, \text{not } \alpha_{n+1}, \ldots, \text{not } \alpha_{n+m}\rangle, \langle diagnosis_1(X_1), \ldots, diagnosis_k(X_k)\rangle\rangle$$

  but remove any literal that should be unconsidered!
- apply every possible healing actions (we assume that healing actions do not conflict!),
- continue until goal state is reached.

The procedure outlined above is iterated several times in order to create a large body of tuples. Those tuples are used as diagnosis rules and for evaluation. Figure 3 shows the diagnosis rules and therapy rules containing unconsidered parameters. A small fraction of the diagnosis rules obtained in this way (only those concerned with the diagnosis `no_more_coffee`) is shown in figure 4 (note that the diagnosis rules created in this way are not unique which also can be seen in the figure). The unconsidered parameters are used only inside the planning system, the plan executor and the diagnoser – all outputs are deprived of the unconsidered concepts. Thus, we achieve the desired effect: something relevant changes beyond the (small) representation.

To perform the diagnosis, in addition to literals describing the current state and the diagnosis rules, we provide some background knowledge about the domain that restricts the created models to the actually possible cases. We have background knowledge for concepts that cannot be in a model at the same time and rules that forbid models with no diagnoses at all.

Figure 5 illustrates how visible diagnosis rules and evaluation examples are generated.

```
action(deliver_cup) :- diagnosis(no_cup_available).
water_left(n0) :- diagnosis(no_more_water).
coffee_left(n0) :- diagnosis(no_more_coffee).
cups_left(n0) :- diagnosis(no_more_cups_left).

healing(refill_water) :- diagnosis(no_more_water).
healing(refill_coffee) :- diagnosis(no_more_coffee).
healing(bring_new_cup) :- diagnosis(no_cup_available).
healing(provide_new_cups) :- diagnosis(no_more_cups_left).
```

Fig. 3. Diagnosis rules with unconsidered concepts and selection of the appropriate healing actions for a given diagnosis

```
diagnosis(no_more_coffee) :- mode_tsc(jura), in_place(train),
                             mode_osc(jura), under_spout(cup),
                             action(produce_coffee), ready(jura).
no_diagnosis(no_more_coffee) :- mode_tsc(jura), in_place(train),
                                mode_osc(jura), ready(jura),
                                action(load_cup_on_waggon),
                                train_loaded(train, cup).
diagnosis(no_more_coffee) :- mode_tsc(jura), in_place(train),
                             mode_osc(jura), under_spout(cup),
                             action(produce_coffee), ready(jura).
```

Fig. 4. Some of the simulator created diagnosis rules, reduced to visible concepts

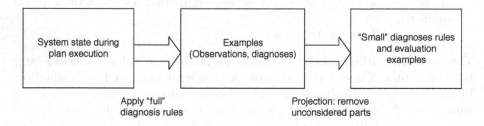

Fig. 5. High level view of visible rule and example generation

In order to evaluate the system, we create a sequence of evaluation examples in the same way as for the diagnosis rules; the major difference is that we keep the examples in sequence and do not remove double entries. Correctness per test t_i is defined to be the fraction of missing and wrong diagnoses, hence given system answers D_{t_i} diagnoses B_{t_i} which are known to be correct, the correctness is

$$\text{Corr}(D_{t_i}|B_{t_i}) = \frac{|B_{t_i} \cap D_{t_i}|}{|B_{t_i} \cup D_{t_i}|}$$

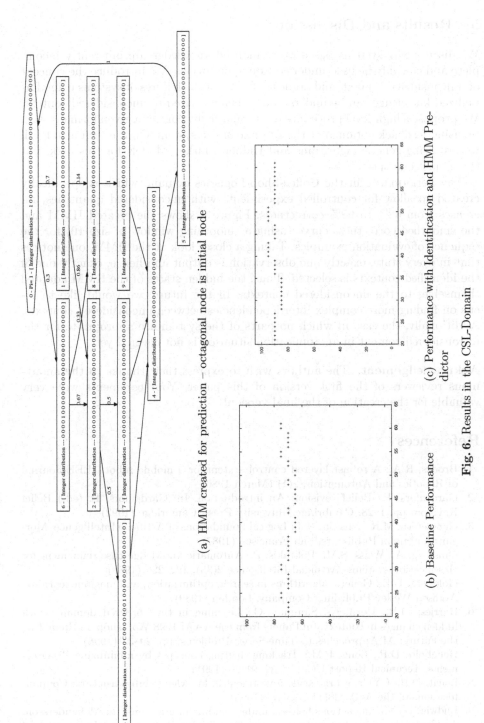

(a) HMM created for prediction – octagonal node is initial node

(b) Baseline Performance

(c) Performance with Identification and HMM Predictor

Fig. 6. Results in the CSL-Domain

5   Results and Discussion

We discuss why systems based on formalized knowledge are inherently incomplete and can only be used under certain assumptions. We introduce the concept of 'unconsidered context' and argue that most of the failures of systems using formalized knowledge can be understood as being related to unconsidered context. We propose a high-level procedure to automatically correct a given formalization by using feedback obtained at the runtime of the system. On the technical level, we are using genetic algorithms and Hidden Markov Models for this task, but this is just one option!

The performance in the Coffee-Shop-Logistics domain, which is specifically created to allow for controlled experiments with unconsidered quantities, increases from 68% to 92% correctness. Figure 6 shows the created HMM and the smoothed correctness curve (using a smoothing window of size 10) for the sequence of evaluation examples. Taking a closer look at the HMM, one notices that in every state, exactly one observation is output and hence, exactly one of the identified contexts is selected. Thus, the hidden states of the HMM adapted themselves to the unconsidered contexts. In the future, we would like to focus on finding more complex interdependencies between unconsidered contexts. Additionally, the case in which no parts of the system are appropriate for the unconsidered context in an application situation is not covered yet.

Acknowledgement. The authors wish to express their thanks to the anonymous reviewers of the first version of this paper. Your comments were very valuable for the creation of the final version!

References

1. Brooks, R.A.: A robust layered control system for a mobile robot. IEEE Journal of Robotics and Automation, 2(1) (March 1986)
2. Gärdenfors, P.: Belief revision: An introduction. In: Gärdenfors, P. (ed.) Belief Revision, pp. 1–28. Cambridge University Press, Cambridge (1992)
3. Genesereth, M.R., Nilsson, N.J.: Logical Foundations of Artificial Intelligence. Morgan Kaufmann Publishers, San Francisco (1987)
4. Ginsberg, A., Weiss, S.M., Politakis, P.: Automatic knowledge base refinement for classification systems. Artificial Intelligence 2(35), 192–226 (1988)
5. Goldberg, D.E.: Genetic algorithms in search, optimization, and machine learning. Addison-Wesley Publishing Company, London (1989)
6. Harries, M.B., Horn, K., Sammut, C.: Learning in time ordered domains with hidden changes in context. In: Papers from the AAAI 1998 Workshop on Predicting the Future: AI Approaches to Time-Series Problems, pp. 29–33 (1998)
7. Helmbold, D.P., Long, P.M.: Tracking drifting concepts by minimizing disagreements. Technical Report UCSC-CRL-91-26 (1991)
8. Lenat, D.B.: CYC: A large-scale investment in knowledge infrastructure. Communications of the ACM 38(11), 33–38 (1995)
9. Ludwig, B.: Tracing actions helps in understanding interactions. In: Alexandersson, J., Knott, A. (eds.) Proceedings of the 7th SIGdial Workshop on Discourse and Dialogue (2006)

10. Mandl, S., Ludwig, B., Schmidt, S., Stoyan, H.: Recurring hidden contexts in online concept learning. In: Workshop on Planning, Learning and Monitoring with Uncertainty in Dynamic Worlds, pp. 25–29 (2006)
11. McCarthy, J.: Circumscription—a form of non-monotonic reasoning. Artificial Intelligence 13, 27–39 (1980)
12. McCarthy, J.: Notes on formalizing context. In: Proceedings of the Thirteenth International Joint Conference on Artificial Intelligence, vol. 1, pp. 555–560 (1993)
13. Niemelä, I., Simons, P., Syrjänen, T.: Smodels: a system for answer set programming. In: Proceedings of the 8th International Workshop on Non-Monotonic Reasoning (April 2000)
14. Puppe, F., Stoyan, H., Studer, R.: Knowledge engineering. In: Görz, G., Rollinger, C.-R., Schneeberger, J. (eds.) Handbuch der Künstlichen Intelligenz, ch. 15, pp. 599–641. Oldenbourg Verlag, München (2003)
15. Rabiner, L.R.: A tutorial on hidden markov models and selected applications in speech recognition. In: Proceedings of the IEEE, vol. 77 (1989)
16. Reiter, R.: Nonmonotonic reasoning. Annual Review of Computer Science 2, 147–186 (1987)
17. Schmidt, A.: Ubiquitous Computing — Computing in Context. PhD thesis, Lancaster University (2002)
18. Simons, P.: Extending and implementing the stable model semantics, Research Report 58, Helsinki University of Technology, Helsinki, Finland (2000)
19. Widmer, G., Kubat, M.: Learning flexible concepts from streams of examples: FLORA 2. In: European Conference on Artificial Intelligence, pp. 463–467 (1992)
20. Widmer, G., Kubat, M.: Learning in the presence of concept drift and hidden contexts. Machine Learning 23(1), 69–101 (1996)

OCCAM: Ontology-Based Computational Contextual Analysis and Modeling

Srini Narayanan[*], Katie Sievers[**], and Steve Maiorano[**]

International Computer Science Institute (ICSI) and University of California, Berkeley
1947 Center Street, Berkeley, California 94704
snarayan@icsi.berkeley.edu

Abstract. The ability to model cognitive agents depends crucially on being able to encode and infer with contextual information at many levels (such as situational, psychological, social, organizational, political levels). We present initial results from a novel computational framework, Coordinated Probabilistic Relational Models (CPRM), that can potentially model the combined impact of multiple contextual information sources for analysis and prediction.

Keywords: Bayesian modeling, cognitive models, agent models, computational sociology.

1 Introduction

The ability to capture contextual influences formally (where context includes social structures, practices, and norms) is of great importance in today's globalized and multi-cultural environment, not only to foster intercultural understanding but also to provide a collaborative and computationally tractable way to predict potential conflicts and crises. Current modeling tools are primarily based on mining patterns from data and ignore important social, psychological, and cultural dimensions that often determine cause, motivation, and intent. Knowledge pertaining to cultural factors is informally (if at all) applied based on an individual's instinct and is neither indicative of corporate experience nor shared. There is thus a pressing need to enhance the current analysis and policy-making framework with tools that operationalize the acquisition and use of the best cultural and social scientific data and make available this knowledge to a collaborative process.

This paper reports on initial steps and preliminary results addressing this state of affairs. Specifically we address the following issues.

- How do we systematize the encoding and application of psychological, social/cultural factors, norms, and practices to analysis and prediction?
- Can we formally model the impact of context for analysis? Our focus is on formal operational models that support analysis, explanation, and prediction.

---

[*] Srini Narayanan is the contact author.
[**] Katie Sievers and Steve Maiorano are affiliated with the Advanced Behavioral Sciences Group (ABSG) of the United States Government.

B. Kokinov et al. (Eds.): CONTEXT 2007, LNAI 4635, pp. 356–368, 2007.

- Can we apply our methodology to support cross-cultural comparisons? We are exploring formal techniques that can shed light on highly sensitive factors, and important cultural similarities and differences that condition possible outcomes and responses of different groups in specific situations.
- Of central concern in today's world is the rapid operationalization of knowledge so we can bring it to bear on cross-cultural analysis. Here we are exploring ontology-based tools for knowledge entry as well as use advanced semantic extraction technology to mine relevant social and cultural information from different media sources including open media.

The rest of the paper is organized as follows. First, we state the background assumptions, findings, and research that guide our model building and analysis efforts. This is followed by a description of the computational modeling and simulation framework. We report on preliminary results from the application of the computational tools to two case studies involving motivational and cultural context for analysis and prediction. The first of the two models is based on an extensive threat assessment framework developed at the Monterey Institute for International Studies (MIIS). The goal of this model is to automate via a computer simulation a factor analysis protocol where the outcome variable is the likelihood of specific groups attacking critical infrastructure targets. A second model predicts the impact of specific international policies on coca-eradication efforts in the context of two similar countries, Bolivia and Peru. Of specific interest here was to identify similarities and differences in predicted response between the two countries and compare the model predictions to actual responses of the two countries.

2 Background

The early view of sociologists that cultural context was a "seamless web" [3], unitary and internally coherent across groups and situations has given way to the realization that depicts culture as fragmented across groups and inconsistent across its manifestations. The current view of culture is as complex structures that constitute resources that can be put to strategic use. Once we acknowledge that culture is inconsistent, it becomes crucial to identify units of cultural analysis and to focus attention upon the relations among them. Similarly, once we acknowledge that people behave as if they use culture strategically, it follows that the cultures into which people are socialized leave much opportunity for choice and variation. Thus our attention turns to ways in which differing cultural frames or understandings may be contextually cued.

Research from a variety of disciplines [2, 3, 7, 8, 9, 10, 11, 14, 15, 16] has focused on study and formalization of psychological and cultural framings and their situational evocation[1]. A great deal of convergent results from Cognitive Science, Sociology, Anthropology, and Neuroscience indicates that complex concepts are not categorical (cannot be defined by necessary and sufficient conditions).[2] Instead

---

[1] For more information on linguistic and cultural frames see http://framenet.icsi.berkeley.edu. For neural underpinnings and computational models see http://www.icsi.berkeley.edu/NTL.

[2] An illustrative example is the concept *mother* with possible members including birth mother, biological mother, genetic mother, nurturant mother, surrogate mother, stepmother, etc.

complex concepts exhibit a radial structure often with a prototypical member and a number of mappings and extensions [14, 15, 16]. Prototypes of categories could arise from various considerations including a) being a central category (others relate to it; amble and swagger relate to the prototype walk), b) being an essential feature that meets a folk theory (birds have feathers, lay eggs), c) being a typical case (sparrow is a typical bird), d) being an ideal positive social standard ("parent) or an anti-ideal negative social standard ("terrorist"), e) a stereotype (set of assumed attributes as in dumb blonde) or f) a salient exemplar (second world war as a just war).

Abstract concepts (such as democracy, freedom, love, mathematical concepts) are often metaphorically mapped from more experiential domains such as *force, spatial motion, and social cognition*. There is a lot of cross-cultural metaphoric knowledge that relies on distinctions in the experiential socio-cultural groundings of abstract and contested concepts [9, 10].

Over the last decade, we have been building models of conceptual acquisition and use which exploit these findings [4, 11, 12] on the structure of complex conceptual categories. Such models have been formalized and used to encode complex metaphors, frames and grammatical constructions [7, 8, 9]. We now describe the use of these models to provide a realistic framework for encoding complex motivational, and socio-cultural knowledge for use in analysis and prediction.

From the computational modeling perspective, we situate our efforts in the much larger matrix of tools and techniques that have or potentially can be applied to modeling context in all its forms. Table 1 shows the various modeling frameworks and their capability to capture contextual background (including social and cultural) knowledge. Previous attempts to incorporate social and cultural knowledge include ad-hoc approaches including individual intuition, dynamic system theory, cellular automata or artificial evolution techniques, rational actor theories, game theoretic techniques, Bayesian analysis, and logical techniques. Each of these approaches addresses some aspects concerning the modeling and use of socio-cultural knowledge. For instance, game theoretic agents are able to model fairly complex social agents capable of sequential and iterative decision making in the presence of other social actors in an uncertain environment. However, the rational actor model which provides the theoretical underpinnings, has questionable ability in terms of modeling actual human motivation and intent which has led to a variety of divergences between theoretical predictions and actual data. Cellular automata and evolutionary techniques (including artificial life) capture the essential property of *emergence* in complex systems, where collaborative and competitive behavior between multiple agents (usually multiple generations of agents) leads to hierarchies, coalitions, segregations and other complex arrangements manifest in human groups. However, these approaches are notoriously hard to analyze and have yet to take into account the structural complexity of cognitive agents.

Hence there is a need to unify these approaches and synthesize a new technique that is able to account for and utilize the observations that a) social knowledge is not categorical and requires the use of prototypes and radial categories, b) human perception, motivation, and social practices are fundamental, not epiphenomenal, and c) events and actors change, evolve, and adapt dynamically.

Table 1. Shown above are the various approaches used to model complex scenarios that include emergent behavior, dynamic situations with imprecise and incomplete information, where multiple social actors engage in decision making and coalition formation in the pursuit of shared interests and goal. Graphical models here include Bayes Nets, DBN based models as well as undirected models including Markov Random Fields (MRF) and Conditional Random Field Models (CRF). They also include standard neural networks trained using back-propagation techniques (Multi-layer Perceptrons) and recursive networks (SRN). Cellular Automata models include swarm intelligence models as well as spatial density function models. Hybrid CPRM are extended CPRM which incorpate both discrete and continuous state.

Technique	Basic Technology	Complexity of Social Actors	Learning Adaptation	Continuous State	Dealing with incomplete information
Non-Linear Dynamic Systems	Differential Equations	low	low	yes	no
Stochastic Processes	Markov/Queuing models	Low/ Medium	Low-high	partial	Medium
Graphical Models	Bayesian Networks, MRF, CRF	medium	high	partial	medium
Cellular Automata	Evolution rules for agents	low	high	no	low
Social Networks	Graph analysis (small world)	medium	med	no	medium
Game Theory	Rational actor model	high	low	no	medium
Multi-Agent systems	Distributed AI/swarms/ Artificial life	high	low	no	medium
Qualitative Techniques	Naïve Physics	medium	low	partial	high
Hybrid Automata	Hybrid-system theory	medium	low	yes	high
ICSI Hybrid CPRM	**Bayesian Hybrid-system theory**	**high**	**med**	**yes**	**high**

For several years we been developing a novel computational framework called Coordinated Probabilistic Relational Models (CPRM). The CPRM modeling framework is unique in being explicitly designed to model complex psychological, social, and cognitive context and the software program implementing the framework is capable of constructing a faithful, robust, flexible, interactive, and graphical computer simulation of the entire decision process. The framework is faithful in that it accurately models the process threads, event models and decision processes in the analysis protocols; robust in the sense of doing so over a wide range of parameter settings; flexible in being able to generate the best hypothesis consistent with partial, incomplete, and mutable data; interactive in that the system operation and parameter settings can be interactively changed while the software program is executing, and hypothetical ``what-if'' simulations performed; and graphical in that the model is a formal graphical structure that supports visualization of the decision process as well as exact quantitative analysis.

3 Modeling Approach

Modern inference systems deal with the ambiguity and uncertainty inherent in any large, real-word domain using probabilistic reasoning. Such models have many advantages, including the ability to deal with missing and uncertain data. Bayesian

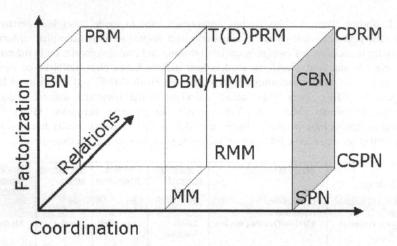

Fig. 1. Probabilistic Inference: The space of models. The origin corresponds to pure statistical models that are based on attribute value vectors (such as vector space models). The x-axis represents increasing sophistication is handling dynamics (from sequences to fully branching dynamics). The y-axis represents graph properties of the model and the use of independencies to make inference tractable (as in graphical models). The z-axis (into the plane) represents modelling expressiveness moving from propositional to fully relational representations.

networks have worked extremely well in moderate sized cases, but do not scale to situations of the size and complexity needed here to model analyze and infer aspects of complex systems. In general, reasoning about complex event structure, ambiguity, and dynamics requires modeling coordinated temporal processes and complex, structured states. A significant amount of work has gone into different aspects of overall problem.

Figure 1 maps out the space of relevant probabilistic modeling and inference techniques along three basic dimensions (extended from the description in (Anderson *et al.* 2002) [1]). The dimension along the x-axis (left-right) depicts the increasing dynamic component. In Figure 1, the x-axis corresponds to the complexity of the dynamics modeled, the y-axis (vertical going up) to the complexity of the state representation and the z-axis (into the plane) the richness of the relations. The origin of the space is an unstructured probabilistic state vector representation with no explicit temporal or relational information. Moving to the right along the x-axis, we get to linear temporal models of sequences. Markov Models (MM) are the most widely used technique to model such simple sequential processes. However, Markov models are fairly inflexible and representationally inadequate as models of actions. Moving further right, we arrive at a set of well developed graphical modeling approaches (such as Stochastic Petri Nets (SPN)) designed to model distributed dynamic systems with complex coordination, concurrency and resource constraints.

Moving from the origin up along the y-axis, we have Factor Models, Markov Random Fields (MRF) (the undirected version) and Bayes Nets (BN) (the directed version). Temporally extended Bayes Nets (TBNs, also called DBNs) model each time step in a sequence as a BN and links between state variables at different time steps capture the temporal dependencies between variables. Moving rightward,

Coordinated Bayes Nets (CBNs) [12] combine the expressive action modeling framework provided by the SPN or CSPN (SPN with objects) based representation with the ability to model complex states provided by the BN framework. This model of action and its use in reasoning about actions was illustrated in [11, 12]. PRMs [16] extend the Bayes Net formalism to allow specification of a probability distribution over a set of relational interpretations.

We have been developing a novel computational framework called Coordinated Probabilistic Relational Models (CPRM) which result from a complete integration of PRM and our extended Hybrid Petri nets (HySPN), and are suitable for building and learning formal models of complex systems. The CPRM modeling framework comes out of a larger project at Berkeley that has been building neurally plausible computational models of cognitive and social phenomena (such language, motivation, intent) for over two decades (http://www.icsi.berkeley.edu/NTL). As far as we know, CPRM models are unique in their ability to model, learn and reason evidentially about dynamically evolving events in complex, uncertain environments.

Currently, an initial implementation of the framework (described in [11] and henceforth referred to as the ICSI simulator) has demonstrated the capability to go beyond finding generic and often trivial patterns in data to discerning correlations and activity that reflects purpose and intention. The simulator is the reasoning component of a question-answering system, AQUINAS (Answering Questions Using INference And Semantics) [13], designed to provide answers to complex questions requiring justification, causal inference, and hypothetical reasoning. An essential requirement for systems that attempt complex causal inference about purpose and intent is the ability to model context specific information in an uncertain, partially observable environment.

This paper reports on our first attempts to use the ICSI simulator to formally model the various process threads and the contextual influence of multiple uncertain systemic, social, organizational, and psychological factors. Analysts can interactively manipulate and conduct "what-if" simulations to assess the sensitivity of individual factors or combinations of factors on the likelihood of specific threat hypotheses and attacks.

4 Initial Results

We report on two case studies relating to the use of the model. The first represents work performed in conjunction with the Monterey Institute for International Studies (MIIS) and is based on making operational in a computer model an elaborate threat assessment framework developed at MIIS. The goal here was to replicate in a computer model the decision making process that individual analysts engaged in to evaluate the threat potential of specific cases involving specific groups. The second model was an attempt to capture complex social and cultural factors, combine their contextual influence with other physical, systemic, and motivational information sources supporting different hypotheses in a probabilistic framework. The goal here was to be able to explore the explanatory power of these different information sources in predicting similarities and differences in the response of different nation-states (in this case Bolivia and Peru) to specific international policy objectives (in this case coca-eradication).

4.1 An Operational Model of Motivation and Intent for Threat Assessment

One application resulted in the first operational model of the Determinants Effecting Critical Infrastructure Decisions (DECIDe) threat assesment framework developed by Gary Ackerman and his group (then at the Monterey Institute for International Studies (MIIS)). The DECIDe Framework is based on a "contributing factors approach" that: 1) lays out the key elements (factors) that shape a terrorist group's targeting decision(s); 2) indicates the major relationships and interplay between these factors; and 3) makes clear their direct influences on target selection. The factors and sub-factors used in the framework, as well as the relationships between them, are based upon the conclusions and hypotheses drawn from the literature assessment, case studies of past attacks on critical infrastructure and analysis of data contained in the database of attacks on critical infrastructure. As a first test of our approach, we successfully constructed prototype models of the various MIIS analyses processes and were able to capture the richness of the inter-factor relationships encoded in the DECIDe framework in a computational model that could be used for prediction as well as for training and dissemination.

At the highest level of analysis (see Figure 2), the model consists of a set of classes that model the various factor clusters (such as ideology and psychological factors, group dynamics, past activity, organizational structure and life cycle status, and technical expertise). The clusters are related to each other which are correlations between the different classes. For instance, knowing the ideology of a group can provide some information about the type of target the group is likely to select. Direct correlations are represented as conditional probability distributions which quantify the distribution over values of a child class given an assignment of values to the parent class. The algorithms for inference go backward and forward on the network updating the values of query variables (a subset of the network) given evidence on any another subset of variables.

CPRM models are able to reason at multiple levels of evidence and model specificity including detailed process and agent interactions (see Figure 3). The lower level analysis process models the detailed decomposition of individual factors and their inter-relationships. For instance the ideology of a group is composed by their ethnic and political makeup, their attitude towards killing combatants, themselves, or innocent people, etc. The PRM framework allows us to represent and infer with probabilistic relations at multiple levels of granularity. This, we believe, is an essential requirement for dealing with contextual information in any domain. Being able to make use of partially specified or incomplete information requires aggregation of information.

Figure 4 shows the finest level of encoding of the specific events pertaining to an attack taken from the MIIS Critic database. The model is built automatically from the database and provides the analyst a detailed simulation of the events leading to and constituting the attack, and the consequences of the attack. The analyst can query the model in various ways including interactively changing some or all of the events, participants, actions, times, synchronization points, etc and running the modified simulation to make predictions.

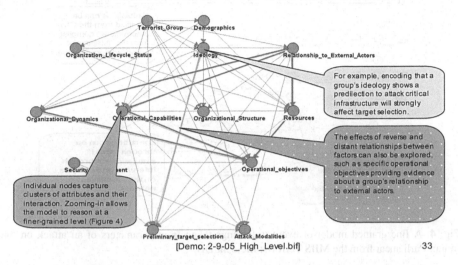

Fig. 2. A formal graphical model of the MIIS threat assessment process. Shown is the highest level of the DECIDe framework with the various factors and the outcome variable (Preliminary_target_selection). Each of these factors represents an aggregation of information from more fine grained analysis (see Figure 3 and Figure 4).

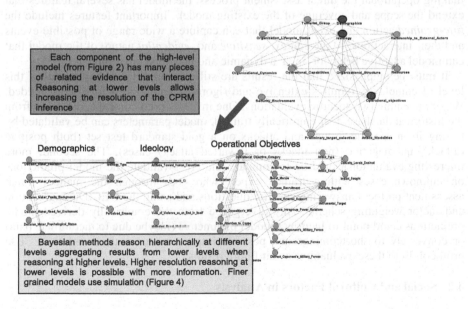

Fig. 3. A lower level probabilistic network for increased resolution of reasoning

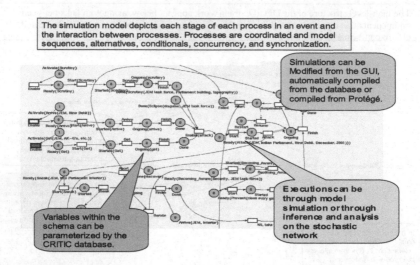

Fig. 4. A fine grained model of event unfoldings taken from parameters of an attack on the Indian Parliament from the MIIS Terrorist Incident DB

We were able to successfully build the model of threat assessment that faithfully modeled all the factors and their inter-relationships as encoded in the DECIDe protocol developed by MIIS. Besides the obvious advantage of systematizing and making operational the threat assessment process, the model has several features that extend the scope and coverage of the existing model. Important features include the *fine-grained* action and event model that can capture a wide range of possible events and their interactions; b) the *context-sensitive* and *evidential* nature of the model that can model adaptive behavior in a a dynamic and uncertain environment.

It must be emphasized that the results are still preliminary and any model of this level of complexity requires extensive and rigorous evaluation before being fielded. We are planning two specific evaluations. One involves predicting specific cases from the historical database. Our empirically trained, model parameters can be validated by testing it on specific groups and attacks on a gold standard test set (both positive (attack) and negative (non-attacks or thwarted attack) cases). The second, more interesting evaluation would be to compare and cross-validate the model predictions on unknown cases with a trained expert who goes through the manual threat assessment protocol answering specific questions and using the DECIDe aggregation and factor weighting scheme. Any divergence from the empirically derived model predictions could point to incorrect model parameters (maybe due to incomplete data) or conversely to shortcomings and possible improvements in the current DECIDe protocol. Both these evaluations await future results.

4.2 Social and Cultural Factors in Analysis

Social and cultural context is one of the fundamental determinants of human behavior. In general, model building and automated analysis incorporating social and cultural context is at its infancy, partly because systematic delineation and treatment of socio-cultural factors and practices has proven extremely hard. Does the CPRM framework facilitate in any way the encoding and use of social and cultural factors in analysis and prediction?

We took the first tests on testing the utility of our approach by applying the modeling framework to predict the role of cultural and social factors regarding the production and use of coca in Bolivia (especially after election of Bolivian President Evo Morales in December 2005). Specifically, we asked the question of our model "How do cultural, social, and political factors impact coca eradication efforts?"

	Bolivia	Peru
Education	Adult literacy rate- 87% Primary school attendance- 77.5% Secondary school attendance- 56.5% Source: UNICEF	Adult literacy rate- 88% Primary school attendance- 95.5 % Secondary school attendance- 48% Source: UNICEF
Religion (Catholic, Protestant)	90% Catholic 10% Protestant Source: CIA World Factbook, http://www.providence.edu/las/ Statistics.htm	85% Catholic 10% Protestant other/none- 5% Source: CIA World Factbook,
Ethnicity (Indigenous, mestizo, white)	Quechua- 30% Mestizo-30 % Aymara-25% White- 15% Source: CIA World Factbook	Amerindian Population45% Mestizo- 37% White- 15% Black, Japanese, Chinese & other- 3% Source: CIA World Factbook
Residence (urban/rural)	Urban- 64% Rural- 36% Source: Bolivia National Institute of Statistics (INE)	Urban- 74% Rural- 26% Source: UNICEF
Economic status	Population below $1 per day- 14% Gross National Income per capita- $960	Population below $1 per day- 18% Gross National Income per capita- $2,360 (Note: GNI per capita for the US is $41,400)
Nutrition	Children under 5 suffering from underweight-8%. Children under 5 suffering from stunted growth (due to poor nutrition)- 27%	underweight- 7% stunted growth (malnutrition)- 25%
Government position re: coca eradication	Current government is strongly against coca eradication. Morales operates on a policy of "Coca yes, Cocaine no"	Garcia government aims to continue coca eradication. Past conflicts between coca growers and the government Coca growers marching on the capital
Political strength of coca growers (cocaleros)	Well organized, fairly strong political constituency.	Well organized, it is unclear how much political clout this group has
Cocalero perception of government attitudes re: coca	Government is working for the cocaleros. Morales a cocalero himself, so having his role in office immediately allows cocaleros to see themselves as part of the govt. However he will have to make good on his promises to reduce eradication in order to keep their support.	Garcia's policy is to continue coca eradications although it is unclear at this point what sort of relationship he will try to create with the coca growers.

Fig. 5. Shown above are some of the relevant factors and activities bearing on Bolivian and Peruvian reponses to a coca eradication policy. Analysts generate a table of this form which is translated into an ontology (using Protege (http://protege.stanford.edu)) which is then automatically compiled into a graphical model for testing, validation, predictions and inference. Notice that some factors have quantitative values while others have qualitative descriptions.

To answer the question, analyst and anthropologist Katie Sievers came up with a set of relevant *Social/Cultural Factors, Economic Factors, and Political Factors*. We used the framework to model the various factors and to compute the joint impact of the different kinds of factors on coca eradication efforts? We also used the model to predictions differences in responses to coca-eradication efforts between Bolivia and Peru.

Figure 5 shows a fragment of the information used (culled from literature and on-line sources by anthropologist Katie Sievers) to construct a model for the scenario of interest. We modeled the different parameters (social, economic, political) by culling evidence from a variety of sources. We instantiated the model, encoded it using the ICSI simulator, and computed the effect of the parameters on the outcome variable (response to a coca eradication policy). Analysts can directly interact with the model GUI and study the effect of perturbations or study the sensitivity of different parameters on the strength of different hypotheses. The modeling framework combines the information and generates the best hypothesis (MAP estimate) for the outcome variables (in this case the support for positive or negative attitudes toward coca eradication programs). Once in the modeling framework, various formal techniques (such as KL divergence, mutual information, sensitivity analysis) can be performed to detect similarities and differences between different social groups/actors/cultures.

Our approach enables us to design and apply formal algorithms for sensitivity and perturbation analysis, divergence in highly sensitive variables including computing *mutual information and KL-divergence* between the two structured networks that capture the multiple factors concerning Bolivia and Peru.

Our results predict greater acceptance of coca eradication efforts in Peru compared to Bolivia. While social factors are similar the political factors dominate. Such factors included the different values for the variables {*Leader background, position, attitude*}. An important result of the analysis was the prediction that *ethnic distribution* of voters was extremely important as a differentiator. This is initially counter-intuitive since the ethnic distribution of the two countries is fairly similar. However, on closer examination the prediction was made due to the combination of two factors:

1) The *indigenous groups* have a small majority in Bolivia (55%) while they are a large minority (45%) in Peru.
2) *Indigenous groups* are much more likely (odds ratio 4: 1) to vote for coca production than the *mestizo* and *white* groups.

Of course, this is only interesting if we knew the actual voting patterns and percentages in the two country elections. We did not have the information at modeling time and assumed that everyone voted. Whatever the ground truth is in terms of voting percentages, the model prediction is informative since it suggests a potentially important information gathering need. Clearly, if future investigation reveals comparable high voting patterns in the two countries, various ongoing interventions (for example religious and missionary activities or targeted educational policies) could be revaluated and their potential impact on public opinion seen in a new light. One central lesson from this modeling exercise was that it was the combination of factors that is predictive. No single factor is sufficiently predictive.

Our initial results suggest that the technology and graphical modeling approach can encode and evaluate the impact of other socio-cultural factors such as education, religion, ethnicity, nutrition, and economic status. We must emphasize that these results are still preliminary and the problem of systematically comparing the impact of social and cultural context on differential policy responses is a complex and important topic which is still at its infancy. What we found iteresting is that our modeling results are able to indicate that despite the degree of similarity of the above-mentioned factors in Bolivia and Peru, the attitudes toward coca are different. Our results are able to suggest reasons at a deep level for this seeming anomaly. There is ongoing work based on collaborations that is extending these preliminary results to investigate issues of scalability and coverage of the basic approach.

5 Conclusion

Dealing with context is a fundamental requirement in modeling cognitive agents. We are interested in using the modeling framework and simulator to encode a variety of scenarios that incorporate social, economic, and cultural factors, activities, and practice and evaluate the impact of this information on the analytic decision process. In selecting scenarios, identifying relevant socio-cultural processes, and in evaluating the model, we plan to continue our close cooperation with anthropologists and sociologists. Model building, evaluation, and training/dissemination are inherently iterative processes. The CPRM framework enables the analyst to interact with the model in various ways including dynamically (asynchronously at run time) changing some or all of the factors, events, participants, actions, times, synchronization points, etc and running the modified simulation to make predictions. Our ultimate goal is to produce a robust software package and methodology that can enhance the current toolkits available to the modeler (Table 1).

One important effect of having a graphical model is the ability to use parameter estimation techniques to directly estimate the quantitative influence and interdependencies between factors and ultimately the contribution of various factors to the outcome variable (threat potential). This allows a data driven approach to computing factor influence which could be compared to the specific conditional independence assumptions and manually generated weighting schemes in the original model (when there is data).

Evaluation of models continues to be a vexing issue. An obvious measure is the ability of the framework to encode a wide variety of rich scenarios which incorporate systemic, social and motivational context. Other measures include a) incremental knowledge and data reuse in terms of the additional effort required to model and analyze new cases, and b) the case with which contextual knowledge can be entered, analyzed, and modified using both the ICSI simulator GUI and the OWL-based ontology editors (such as Protégé (using OWL-S)) that directly compile to CPRM models.

Acknowledgments. Thanks to John DeNero for building the first models of the MIIS threat assessment scenarios and protocols. We acknowledge the support of NSF, DARPA under the DAML program, and DTO under the AQUAINT program.

References

1. Anderson, C.R., Domingos, P., Weld, D.S.: Relational Markov Models and their Application to Adaptive Web Navigation. In: Proceedings of the Eighth ACM SIGKDD International Conference on Knowledge Discovery and Data Mining (KDD-2002) (2002)
2. Aziz-Zadeh, Fiebach, L.C., Narayanan, S., Feldman, J., Dodge, E., Ivry, R.B.: Modulation of the FFA and PPA by language related to faces and places. Social Neuroscience (2006) (to appear)
3. DiMaggio, Paul: Culture and cognition. Annual Review of Sociology 23, 263–288 (1997)
4. Gedigian, M., Bryant, J., Narayanan, S., Ciric, B.: Catching Metaphors. In: Scalable Natural Language Understanding Conference, Boston (May 2006)
5. Feldman, J., Narayanan, S.: Embodied Meaning in a Neural Theory of Language. Brain and Language 89, 385–392 (2004), http://www.icsi.berkeley.edu/%7Esnarayan/B+L.pdf
6. Fillmore, C.J.: The case for case. In: Bach, Harms (eds.) Universals in Linguistic Theory, New York, Holt, Rinehart, Winston, pp. 1–88 (1968)
7. Fillmore, C.J.: Frame semantics and the nature of language. In: Annals of the New York Academy of Sciences: Conference on the Origin and Development of Language and Sp 2003 (1980) with Johnson, M. Metaphors We Live By. University of Chicago Press. 2003 edition contains an 'Afterword' (1976)
8. Lakoff, G.: Women, Fire, and Dangerous Things: What Categories Reveal About the Mind. University of Chicago Press, Chicago (1987)
9. Lakoff, G.: Moral Politics. University of Chicago Press, Chicago (1989)
10. Lakoff, G., Johnson, M.: Philosophy In The Flesh: the Embodied Mind and its Challenge to Western Thought. Basic Book (1999)
11. Narayanan, S.: Reasoning About Actions in Narrative Undertanding. In: Proceedings of the International Joint Conference on Artificial Intelligence (IJCAI '99), Stockholm, August 1-6, pp. 350–358. Morgan Kaufmann, San Francisco (1999)
12. Narayanan, S.: Moving Right Along: A Computational Model of Metaphoric Reasoning about Events. In: Proceedings of the National Conference on Artificial Intelligence (AAAI '99), Orlando, Florida, July 18-22, pp. 121–128. AAAI Press, California (1999)
13. Narayanan, S., Harabagiu, S.: Question Answering based on Semantic Structures. In: International Conference on Computational Linguistics (COLING 2004), Geneva, Switzerland (August 22-29, 2004)
14. Eleanor, R.: Prototype classification and logical classification: The two systems. In: Scholnick, E. New Trends in Cognitive Representation: Challenges to Piaget's Theory, pp. 73–86. Lawrence Erlbaum Associates, Hillsdale (1983)
15. Eleanor, R., Mervis, C.: Categorization of Natural Objects. Annual Review of Psychology 32, 89–113 (1981)
16. Eleanor, R., Lloyd, B. (eds.): Cognition and Categorization. Lawrence Erlbaum Associates, Hillsdale (1978)
17. Pfeffer, A.: Probabilistic Reasoning for Complex Systems, A.J. Pfeffer. PhD Thesis, Stanford University (January 2000)
18. Scheffczyk, J., Baker, C.F., Narayanan, S.: Ontology-based Reasoning about Lexical Resources, Ontology and Lexical Resources. In: Natural Language Processing, Cambridge University Press, Cambridge (2006) (earlier version presented at OntoLex 2006, Genoa, Italy, May 2006) (to appear)

User Profiling with Hierarchical Context: An e-Retailer Case Study

Cosimo Palmisano[1], Alexander Tuzhilin[2], and Michele Gorgoglione[1]

[1] Politecnico di Bari, Management Dept.,
c.palmisano@poliba.it m.gorgoglione@poliba.it
[2] New York University, Stern Business School, IOMS Dept.,
atuzhili@stern.nyu.edu

Abstract. In e-commerce applications, no systematic research has been provided to evaluate if the use of a detailed and rich contextual representation improves the user modeling predictive performances. An underestimated issue is also evaluating if context could be inferred by existing customer data off-line, in spite of getting the customer involved on-line in the gathering process. In this paper, we address those problems, defining context as "the intent of" a customer purchase. To this aim, we collected data containing rich contextual information, hierarchically structured, by developing a special-purpose browser. The experimental results show that the finer the granularity of contextual information the better is the modeling of customers' behavior. Representing the context in a hierarchical structure is a necessary condition, for inferring the context off-line, but it's not a sufficient one.

Keywords: E-commerce, context hierarchy, context inference.

1 Introduction

In his interview at AMA (American Management Association) P.K. Prahalad [25] stated that "the ability to reach out and touch customers anywhere at anytime means that companies must deliver not just competitive products but also unique, real-time customer experiences shaped by *customer context*" and that this would be the next main issue for the CRM practitioners. There exists substantial anecdotal evidence in the press and the popular literature that supports Prahalad's observation, including scientific literature in the field of customer profiling and recommendation systems. For example, the director of personalization at one of the major on-line retailing companies once received a nasty email from the CEO telling him that he should either fix his personalization system or lose his job. The CEO's email was prompted by a customer's complaint that the company's personalization system was making offensive assumptions about the lifestyle of this customer and was recommending inappropriate products to that person. Upon a closer examination, it was discovered that the customer once bought an item as a gift for his friend, and the personalization system started recommending related products to that customer making implicit assumptions about his lifestyles, which infuriated that customer. This true story is

B. Kokinov et al. (Eds.): CONTEXT 2007, LNAI 4635, pp. 369–383, 2007.

very symptomatic of problems pertaining to many personalization systems that often predict customer behavior from the registration and the purchasing information of online customers without studying the contexts in which these purchases are made. In the previous example, if the system knew that the purchase was made in the context of a gift, this transaction should have been discarded from inferring that customer's behavior, and the whole problem would have been avoided. Getting such contextual data characterizing the circumstances in which purchasing or other on line transactions took place, such as the "intent of" a purchase, special payment conditions, economic climate and the customer's geographic location, is not easy in many e-commerce applications. For instance, it may not be practical to ask the customer about the purpose of his/her purchase because of privacy and some technological constraints. Therefore, before acquiring such contextual information, it is necessary to provide hard scientific evidence that this contextual information indeed makes a significant difference in building better customer models. In our prior work [12], we addressed this problem and demonstrated that (a) contextual information matters in the sense that it facilitates building better personalized predictive models of customer behavior, and (b) granularity of contextual information also matters, i.e., the more granular and the more specific the contextual information is, the better we can predict customers' behavior. However, the contextual information usually does not come as a set of various alternatives, such as buying a product for yourself or as a gift. Usually, it is organized in the form of a context hierarchy, where coarser types of context are partitioned into progressively finer levels of contextual information.

In this paper, we study the questions of whether (a) it is feasible to infer these whole hierarchies of context from the data and, (b) whether the inferred hierarchical models outperform individual-level models of contextual knowledge. We show that the more we know about the context of a transaction, the better we can predict the customer's behavior. We also show in our experiments that it is possible to infer the contextual information of a transaction with a reasonable degree of accuracy.

Answering these questions has relevant managerial implications. In fact, acquiring contextual knowledge is costly in terms of privacy and technological issues and this cost is even higher if this knowledge is represented by complex structures. Providing a systematic analysis about this research issue is important to evaluate what is the better approach to make this knowledge useful and the gathering process of rich contextual knowledge as worth as possible.

2 Literature Review

In our previous work on context [12] we addressed the problem of investigating if contextual information indeed makes a significant difference in building better customer models in e-commerce applications. To this aim we collected experimental purchasing data of customers and the "intent of purchase" was gathered as contextual information. The overall contextual purchasing option was defined by a tree-shaped hierarchical structure where the root was the coarser representation of the contextual information and the leaves the finer knowledge representation. After collecting all the purchasing data, we built predictive models of purchasing behavior for the contextual and un-contextual cases under different experimental settings. The more relevant settings for our research purposes were: the degree of contextual information and the granularity of customer segments. In the first case the aim was to evaluate how the prediction performances change at different levels of contextual knowledge. In the second one the aim was to evaluate at which unit of analysis we get better predictive performances. In this prior work has been demonstrated that (a) contextual information matters in the sense that it facilitates building better personalized predictive models of customer behavior, and (b) granularity of contextual information also matters, i.e., the more granular and more specific the contextual information is, the better we can predict customers' behavior.

The basic hypothesis of the previous work was that contextual information is available and ready to be used to label each transaction; but it's not always the case. In many situations context could not be easily available and its gathering can be too expensive because of privacy concerns and various other considerations. In those cases, one possibility would be to infer the context from existing data off-line, thus reducing the costs of collecting it on-line, and avoiding user intervention in data collection. This issue was not investigated in our previous work and will be investigated in this paper. In particular the differences in performance between inferring a single level of context and inferring the whole hierarchy of contextual knowledge will be systematically evaluated.

Scholars in marketing have maintained that the purchasing process is contingent upon the context in which the transaction takes place. The same customer can adopt different decision strategies and prefer different products or brands depending on the context [6], [17], [22]. According to [20], "consumers vary in their decision-making rules because of the usage situation, the use of the good or service (for family, for gift, for self) and purchase situation (catalog sale, in-store shelf selection, and sales person aided purchase)." Therefore accurate prediction of consumers' preference undoubtedly depends upon the degree to which we have incorporated the relevant contextual information. Those statements have been also supported by the results of our previous work. The importance of including contextual information in recommender systems has also been demonstrated in [2], where a multidimensional approach to recommender systems is presented. In general, it is possible to assert that the ability of exploiting the knowledge of context is expected to increase the potential of many applications aimed at delivering services to users [1]. Other contributions to the context paradigm have been provided in information retrieval [7] [19], web browsing personalization systems [13], [31], Web services [23]. Most of this work has also tried to determine how to improve the use of context by applying different representations of contextual knowledge using taxonomies, hierarchical structures model or semantic web appliances. In [7] Bothorel and Chavalier propose the click stream data as an identification criterion and create a rich context for providing clues to recommend relevant web pages links to an unknown user. In [13] the use of Semantic Web is suggested for facilitating the capture of knowledge regarding users' context, and supporting the performance of web searching tasks. In [31] Zhu et al. introduced the notion of structured contexts and show its effectiveness using a lightweight ontology to provide a structure for representing contexts in an online price comparison example.

In e-commerce, the concept of a context is associated with Contextual marketing which is the strategy of providing personalized information (advertisements, banners, offers) to customers at the point of need in real time, [16], [21].

If the concept of customer and that of transaction are broadened to embrace any user interacting with a company or an application to get a service, then the importance of knowing the context is recognized in other fields and applications. For instance, context-aware systems are designed to exploit the contextual information available to better serve the user [9], and to adapt to changes in the context. In [24] is introduced the concept of primitive context as the basic context abstraction for formalising and reasoning about context in a consistent and conceptually simple way.

All the web and context-aware examples cited have the common characteristics of reasoning about situations in which contextual knowledge exists, is reliable and has been represented in different structures. But the reliability of contextual data in certain industrial situations is very expensive in terms of technological investments and privacy concerns. E-commerce is a typical example of a sector where privacy concerns and technological constraints are really high. Therefore, it is important to determine how strategic it is to acquire the contextual information, when modeling the behavior of a customer [8], [9]. So far scholars, belonging to different fields, have addressed the problem of inferring the contextual data off line, in spite of getting the user involved in the gathering process. One approach to context recognition and inference is based on supervised learning which requires the intervention of an expert, or the user, at some point of the process to label contexts or define the user needs in a given context. A second compelling opportunity is setting up an unsupervised learning stage to learn associations between contexts and user needs without explicit user intervention. An example of contextual knowledge inference has been studied in [28] by the concept of "granularity". They demonstrate increasing the level of granularity of spatial and temporal context data tends to provide good inferential properties in their natural language processing application. Another example of contexts inference is applied in text documents [11], where the aim of the work is to infer context taxonomy for locating the right documents by using contextual indexing or contextual reasoning. Other researchers have applied a comparative approach in order to experimentally evaluate if the inference problem is feasible in an un-supervised way or not. In [10] an unsupervised learning approach to context recognition has been compared to supervised models. Another example of comparison between contextual inference using supervised and unsupervised technique is provided in [26]. This paper describes how probabilistic graphical models learned with different Acyclic Directed Graphs could exploit context represented as statistical dependences. In [26] a supervised approach developed by the expert is useful to elaborate the more efficient Bayesian Network for improving predictive performances. The main statement is that even if many unsupervised algorithms for drawing more efficient probabilistic graphical models are available, they still require an assistance of the expert. We will take the main idea provided in [26] in the OCR field of application in order to be expanded and enhanced for the e-commerce domain where all those research aspects, related to context have been underestimated.

3 Problem Formulation

In the literature, context has had several alternative definitions in different fields and applications. The Webster's dictionary [29] defines context as "conditions or circumstances which affect some thing." In the data mining community, context is defined as those events which characterize the life of a customer and can determine a change in his/her preferences, status (e.g., prospect to actual), and affect the customer's value for a company [5]. In the context-aware systems literature, context was initially defined as the location of the user, the identity of people near the user, the objects around, and the changes in these elements [27]. In [4] a corpus of 150 definitions referring to different domains of cognitive sciences and related disciplines has been analyzed. In the field of e-commerce, the context has been defined as "the intent of" a purchase made by a customer, as supported by the anecdotal evidence provided at the beginning of this work. The same customer may buy from the same on line account different products for different reasons: a book for improving his/her personal work skills, a book as a gift for a partner, or an electronic device for his/her personal hobby. When the intent of the purchase varies, the user behavior is also supposed to change. As in the example, this kind of contextual information may be useful for building better user profiles and providing more accurate on-line recommendations. Given our definition of context, the problem can be formulated as follows.

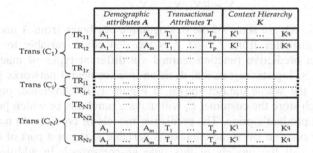

Fig. 1. User model-data structure

Let C be the customer base represented by N customers. Each customer C_i is defined by the set of m demographic attributes $A = \{A_1, A_2,..., A_m\}$, and a set of r transactions $Trans(C_i) = \{TR_{i1}, TR_{i2}, ...,TR_{ir}\}$, where each transaction TR_{ij} performed by customer C_i is defined by a set of transactional attributes $T = \{T_1, T_2, ...,T_p\}$. In addition, we also have a set of contextual attributes K associated with each transaction TR_{ir}. The table specifying all this demographic, transactional and contextual information about customers is presented in Figure 1. In general the set of contextual attributes K can have a complex structure reflecting the complex nature of this information. However, in this paper, we assume that domain K is defined by a set of q attributes $K^1,..., K^q$ having a hierarchical tree-shaped structure associated with it. In the tree structure the root represents the coarsest contextual knowledge while the leaves are the finest representation of the context, as in Figure 2. The values taken by attribute K^q define the finest (more granular) degree of contextual knowledge while K^l the coarsest. For example, a customer C_i can be defined by the demographic attributes $A=\{IDuser,\ Name,\ Age,\ Income\}$, by the set of five transactions made by C_i, $Trans(C_i)=\{TR_1,\ TR_2,\ TR_3,\ TR_4,\ TR_5\}$, each transaction defined by the transactional attributes $T=\{ProductID,\ StoreID,\ Price,\ TransactionTime\}$ and finally by a set of contextual attributes K describing the context ("the intent of") of each purchase.

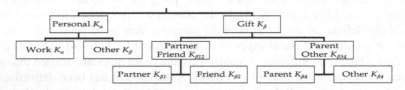

Fig. 2. Contextual hierarchy information for a purchasing transaction

Finally, the customer base C can be partitioned into several segments [15], [18] by computing h summary statistics $S_i=\{S_{i1},\ S_{i2},\ ...,S_{ih}\}$ for customer C_i over the transactions made by that customer, each S_{ij} being defined as a statistics on some of the attribute in T across the transactions $Trans(C_i)$. Then customers can be clustered into segments in the space defined by these statistics. A model of customer behavior can be built in the following general form:

$$Y = f(X_1, X_2,..., X_p) . \tag{1}$$

where $X_1, X_2,..., X_p$ are some of the demographic attributes from A and some of the transactional attributes from T, and Y is the dependent variable to be predicted. Function f is a predictive function learned via different types of machine learning methods, such as logistic regression, decision trees or neural networks [30], that will be learned on the whole dataset shown in Figure 1. For instance, one may try to predict in which store the customer C_i will make a purchase, or which product will be bought, or the product's price. The predictive models of type (1) do not assume any contextual information since the contextual variable K is not a part of these models. Therefore, we call the models of this type *un-contextual*. In addition, we define *contextual* counterparts of predictive models (1), the model taking the following form:

$$Y = f_{K^q=\alpha}(X_1, X_2,..., X_p) . \tag{2}$$

In model (2) only the transactions associated with the context $K^q=a$ are used for building the model. For example, if the model is built for the computer science faculty from University X, where $K^l="gift"$, this means that only the *gift-related* transactions made by the CS faculty are used for building the model. Then the meaning of the expression "*context matters*" is that the contextual predictive models of type (2) *significantly* outperform in terms of predictive accuracy the un-contextual models of type (1) across different degrees of contextual knowledge [12]. The following two models are the formalization of the inferring process:

$$K^q = f(X_1, X_2,..., X_p) . \tag{3a}$$

$$K^{Hier} = f(X_1, X_2,..., X_p) . \tag{3b}$$

In model (3a) and (3b) the dependent variable, i.e. the variable to be predicted, is the contextual information. In Figure 3(a) and 3(b) the structures of the networks are presented for exploiting context represented as statistical dependencies; in each graph the structure is fixed and we only estimate its parameters. The use of graphical models for presenting contextual knowledge has been studied in [14], [26]. In model (3a) one contextual attribute per time is inferred. For instance, in the coarsest context degree each transaction is labeled with K^I, in the finest degree of contextual knowledge with K^3. In model (3b) the aim is to evaluate how the model can infer K^q using *the whole hierarchy* of context, rather than a single level of contextual knowledge (each transaction will be labeled with q contextual attributes K^I, K^2,..., K^q). For models (3a) and (3b) the predictive function f is defined as a Naïve Bayes (NB) network (Figure 3(a)) and a Bayesian Network (BN) in figure 3(b), respectively. In model (3b) hierarchy K^{Hier} consists of q variables (K^I,..., K^q) organized as shown in Figure 3(b), and where the last variable is K^q which is the same dependent variable as in the NB model (3a). Both BN and NB predict the same contextual variable K^q. We expect that by dropping the independence hypothesis of the NB model we should get better inference results for the model defined by (3b) in Figure 3(b). Another expectation is that the output of both models will be strictly influenced by the trade-offs between modeling error due to overly strict independence assumptions and estimation error of models that are too elaborate for the size of the available training set. Those expectations will be considered when the results of the comparison between the predictive performance of models (3a) and (3b) are analyzed.

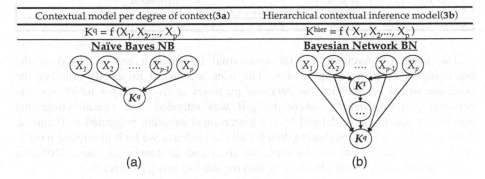

Contextual model per degree of context(**3a**)	Hierarchical contextual inference model(**3b**)
$K^q = f(X_1, X_2,..., X_p)$	$K^{hier} = f(X_1, X_2,..., X_p)$
Naïve Bayes NB	**Bayesian Network BN**
(a)	(b)

Fig. 3. Contextual Inference models

4   Experimental Setup

Since contextually rich datasets suitable for building personalized customer models are not readily available, as was explained in Section 1, we had to collect such data by ourselves in order to conduct our study. To this aim we developed a special-purpose browser to help users navigate a well-known e-commerce retail portal and purchase products on its site. This browser was made available to a group of student. Once a product was selected by a student in order to be purchased, the browser recorded the selected item, the purchasing price and other useful characteristics of the transaction.

In addition, the student had to specify the *context* ("intent of") in which the purchase was made. The data was pre-processed by excluding the students who made less than 40 transactions. The resulting number of students having at least 40 transactions was 556, and the total number of purchasing transactions for these students was 31,925. For each customer (student) we collected the following *demographic* data: age, previous studies, marital status, and composition of the family, place of living, hobbies and whether the student owned a car. The car ownership was used as a proxy for the income. The *transactional* data included item purchased, price, day, time, session duration, number of clicks per connection, and the time elapsed for each web page. The data set structure is described in Table 1.

Table 1. Data set structure

Demographic data A_i	Type	Values/range
1. Gender	Boolean	Male/Female
2. Age	Numerical	18-31
3. High School descr.	Nominal	Grammar, Professional, Private
4. Student description	Nominal	Outside, Traveling, Resident
5. Personal Car	Boolean	Yes/No
6. Hobby	Nominal	Reading, Dancing, Music, Electronics, Sports, Movies, Traveling, Informatics, Cooking, Cars, Arts, Photography, Collections, Fashion
Transactional data T_i	Type	Values/range
1. Visit Duration	Numerical	0-919 sec.
2. Price	Numerical	1-2000 $
3. N. of clicks	Numerical	1-35
4. Weekday	Boolean	Weekday/weekend
5. Store	Nominal	Electronics, home/garden, featured, Kid/baby, book/music, new
6.Purchase description	Boolean	Yes/No

The intent of purchase, i.e. the contextual information was collected at the beginning of each browsing session. The user was asked to specify whether the purchase would be intended for *personal* purposes or as a *gift, for which* specific personal purpose, and *for whom* the gift was intended. The overall contextual purchasing options were defined by the hierarchical structure presented in Figure 2. After collecting all the purchasing data for all the students, we built predictive models of their purchasing behavior for the contextual and un-contextual cases. Different experimental settings were obtained by varying the following parameters:

1. *Degree of contextual information.* The contextual models can be built by considering few values of K (rough knowledge of context) or as many as available (finer knowledge.)
2. *Granularity of customer segments.* A total of 4 unit of analysis have been used ranging from a single segment containing aggregated customer base to the 1-to-1 case when all the segments contain transactions of each single customer. Two intermediate levels included 100 segments and 10 segments. A predictive model is built for a cluster of customers.
3. *Types of predictive models.* We considered four different types of data mining classifiers modeling the function f, including decision trees and decision rules (JRip, J48, PART, NBTree) [30]. Those classifiers are trained and validated on the whole dataset.

4. *Dependent variables*. 3 transactional variables have been used for predicting customers' behavior (the positive or negative ending of each transaction, the day of the transaction, the store where the customer will purchase).

5. *Performance measures*. For providing statistical measurement of how well the classification functions correctly identifies or excludes a condition we used the predictive accuracy and the area under the ROC curve [30] as performance measures of predictive models.

For the contextual inference process we built predictive models of type (3a) and (3b) under different experimental settings. In the last case (hierarchical contextual model) the number of parameters is reduced: it has been used only one predictive function (BN and NB) in spite of four and the dependent variable is the context itself and not a transactional attribute. All the other settings are the same (degree of context, granularity of market, performance measures). The degree of contextual information is defined as follows.

The contextual information K is structured in a three-level hierarchy $(q=3)$, as shown in Figure 2, from a rough to a finer degree of knowledge. The contextual structures are deployed as follows. In the first level, the contextual variable K^1 takes two different values: K_α="*personal*" and K_β="*gift*". In the third and finer level K^3, the "*personal*" context is split in $K_{\alpha 1}$="*personal for work*" and $K_{\alpha 2}$="*personal for other purposes*", the "gift" context is split in $K_{\beta 1}$="*gift for partner*", $K_{\beta 2}$="*gift for friends*", $K_{\beta 3}$="*gift for parents*" and $K_{\beta 4}$="*gift for others*". In the second level, four values are aggregated in two resulting in $K_{\beta 12}$="*gift for partner and friends*" and $K_{\beta 34}$="*gift for parent and other*", respectively.

5 Results

Given the number of experimental settings, resulting in a high number of contextual versus un-contextual comparisons, the more concise way to compare contextual model to the un-contextual one is computing the relative difference between the performance values as:

$$(\text{Performance}_{con} - \text{Performance}_{unc}) / \text{Performance}_{unc} . \tag{4}$$

where *con* refers to the contextual models and *unc* to the un-contextual model. A positive value means that the contextual model outperforms the un-contextual and viceversa. In both plots in Figure 4 are represented different degrees of contextual knowledge (from coarsest to finer) on the horizontal axis and on the vertical axis is measured the relative difference in performance averaged across all the experimental settings. In Figure 4(a) each of the four lines is plotted calculating performance formulation (4) where each line represents one level of customer segments. Figure 4(a) shows that the contextual models outperform the un-contextual for each type of customer segmentation. It also shows that in almost all cases of customer granularity, the curves representing the value of (4) are monotone, i.e. the finer the context degree the higher the value of (4). The graph also demonstrates that in most cases finer segmentation of the customer base leads to higher performance improvement when a contextual model is used instead of un-contextual. In fact, with the individual models of customers ("Single" in Fig. 4(a)) significantly outperform all other cases achieving

11% performance improvement for the finest granularity of contextual information ("Degree 3" in Fig. 4(a)).

Figure 4(b) presents the comparison between contextual and un-contextual models with respect to the degrees of contextual information but this time we have relaxed the market granularity assumption. In order to have a clearer representation, the positive values of (4) are computed separately from the negative values, and the absolute values are plotted in the graphs. The solid line plots the positive values of (4) per degree of context, while the dashed line plots the negative values of (4) in absolute terms. For the positive occurrence of (4) in Figure 4(b), the plot shows that the performance measure grows from the coarsest to the finest degree of contextual knowledge. In the negative occurrences of (4), there are stable and low performances.

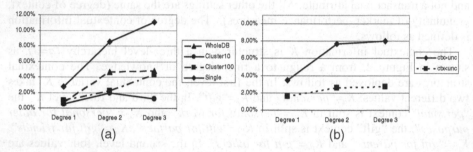

(a)   (b)

Fig. 4. Relative difference of performance per degree of context

Reporting the statistical significance of each comparison would have been impossible because of the large number of them (1152 in total). Figure 5 presents a summary of the statistical significance tests by reporting the percentage of comparisons with a statistical significance higher than 95%. A Wilcoxon test [3] was used for testing the null hypothesis (no difference between the two averages). In the graph the percentage of statistically significant comparisons are plotted against the degree of contextual information (on the x-axis) and for each customer granularity level (specified by different curves), for the cases in which the contextual models dominate the un-contextual.

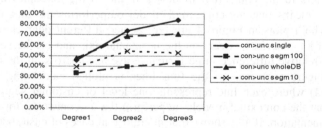

Fig. 5. Percentage of statistical significant comparisons

The values in Figure 5 are computed as follows: for each degree of context, the number of significant comparisons is divided by the overall number of comparisons and each line represents a different degree of customer granularity. For example, point 72% for Degree 2 for the "con>un-con single" line means that, fixing the experimental condition for the degree of context at second level and for customer granularity at single customer unit of analysis, the 72% of the possible comparisons where contextual outperform un-contextual are statistically significant. The number of statistically significant experiments where the contextual models outperform the uncontextual increases with the degree of knowledge of context and this is true per each customer granularity level (all curves are monotone). In particular, the best results are obtained when the single customer is the unit of analysis ("con>unc single" line in figure 5). The number of statistically significant experiments rises from 48% at the coarsest degree of contextual knowledge to 82% for the finest degree.

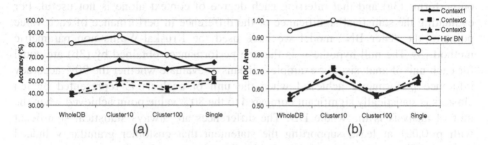

Fig. 6. Inference model performances per customer granularity

Figure 6 shows the results for the contextual inference problem. Both figures have been drawn applying the models (3a) and (3b). In Figure 6(a) performances is measured by the accuracy and in Figure 6(b) by the ROC area. The lines labeled as "context1", "context2" and "context3" are the plots of the inference performances achieved applying the model (3a) per each degree of context (K^1, K^2, K^3). The solid line with empty circles (specified by "Hier BN") represents the plot of the performance for model (3b) learned by the BN in Figure 3(b). Each line is plotted per degree of customer granularity (x-axis). In both figures the hierarchical model (3b) clearly outperforms each one of the models (3a), achieving high performance results, in particular the accuracy reaches the maximum value of 90% and the ROC area reaches the level of 100%. In both cases the maximum performance value was achieved when the unit of analysis is ten clusters of customers. Those results demonstrate that inferring the whole hierarchy of contextual knowledge in our experiment outperforms the approach in which each level per time is inferred. Moreover, trying to infer one level per time does not provide any improvement when the degree of contextual knowledge increases; for instance in the accuracy plot the inference of the coarsest degree of context it's higher than finer levels ("context1" outperforms "context2" and "context3"). Another interesting result is that the peak of performance achieved by the "Hier BN" at cluster 10 unit of analysis. This result shows that better inference performances can be achieved for a particular unit of analysis.

In terms of statistical significance we have evaluated two different aspects: the difference in performance between each of the four lines of the graph, and the difference in performance of each results of the "Hier BN" line. With the Friedman test (Non Parametric Repeated Measure Anova) [3] we have tested the null hypothesis that the performances of each of the four lines of the graphs are equal. For example, it means to evaluate how statistically significant is the difference in performance between the "context1" line and the "context2" and all possible combinations between all the shapes. The results are always statistically significant for the accuracy with $p<0,001$ at least. For the ROC area, the difference between the "Hier BN" and each of the single context lines is statistical significant ($p<0,0001$), while the difference in performance between each of the lines built with model (3a) are not. The results statistically support the statement that the hierarchical inference model (3b) outperforms (3a) and that inferring each degree of context alone is not useful. For evaluating the statistical significance of the difference in performance of each value point of the "Hier BN" model we have used the Kruskal-Wallis non parametric method [3]. The null hypothesis is that the performances obtained by (3b) are equal for each unit of analysis. For example it means to evaluate whether the 90% accuracy inference performance achieved when the unit of analysis is represented by ten clusters is statistically significant compared to the 80% value point achieved when the unit of analysis is the whole DB. The differences are always statistical significant with $p<0,001$ at least, supporting the statement that customer granularity indeed makes a difference in performing hierarchical inference models.

6 Discussions of Results

The results described in Section 5 present empirical evidence that the models built by taking into account rich contextual information usually provide better predictive performance in e-commerce applications. More specifically, the main conclusions of our study can be summarized as follows:

1. The degree of contextual information matters. The more we know about the context of a transaction, the better we can predict the customer's behavior.
2. Inferring the context is feasible. The predictive accuracy by which context is inferred may reach the value of 90%, and inferring the whole context hierarchy structure is better than inferring one hierarchical level per time.

Each point is discussed in detail below.

1. The degree of contextual information matters: the finer the knowledge about the context of a transaction, the better the predictive performance of a customer's behavior. As we move to finer degrees of contextual information, we observe higher values of performance gain. On average, as shown in Figure 4, knowing the finest degree of context leads to the highest gains in performance, growing from 3.5% (when K takes two values) to 8% (when K takes six values), in the cases in which the contextual models dominate the un-contextual. On the other hand, gathering finer degrees of contextual information can lead to a decrease in performance in those settings in which the un-contextual model dominates the contextual. However, the loss is moderate (1.63% to 2.75%). The same evidence is provided by studying the statistical significance of the experimental results, as shown in Figure 5. Whatever the unit of analysis the number of statistically significant events grows when the degree of the contextual information grows and the contextual models dominate the un-contextual. The highest variations occur when the unit of analysis is the single customer. In fact, in this setting there is no case in which the un-contextual model outperforms the contextual models and the difference is statistically significant.

2. *The inferring process is feasible.* The results depicted in Figure 6 show that the inference of context from existing data is possible and inferring the whole context hierarchy structure is better than inferring one hierarchical level per time. In fact, predicting just the coarsest degree of context is on average 15% more accurate than the other two degrees. Inferring the whole hierarchy structure provides outstanding results, compared to the model (3a) but also in absolute terms. A 90% value of predictive accuracy and a value of 1 for the ROC area are definitely good enough for considering the opportunity of inferring the context off-line instead of getting the user involved in the process of gathering contextual information.

Another interesting result is related to the market granularity. The highest values of performances in inferring the context hierarchy is reached when the unit of analysis is a relatively low number of large customers segments (ten clusters). On the other hand, the highest value of accuracy in predicting customers' behavior (2) is reached when the unit of analysis is the single customer. This means that the hierarchical context inference model (3b) needs a large amount of data for inferring the context and this large amount of information can be provided in less granular market segments, while in model (2) the contextual effects get stronger when we build progressively smaller segments of customers, because providing contextual information, customer transactions pertaining to a particular context are reduced, making fewer data points to fit the model, while homogeneity of these transactions increases, making it easier to predict more accurately customer behavior in similar contexts.

Interpreting the inference results in the light of the literature on Bayesian probabilistic models leads to the following conclusions:

- The model (3b), relaxing the independence condition of NB models, remarkably well captures the inner dependencies between the attributes and the context without errors, as shown in Figure 6(a and b). In our case, the "expert supervision" in building the BN of model (3b) provides so efficient results that one should reject the opportunity of getting the customer involved in the process of gathering contextual information.
- Given the complexity of the network in (3b), the requested size of data for leveraging the trade off between the complexity of the network and the size of the sample needed for inferring the context is reached at some intermediate clustering level ("Cluster10" in Figure 6(a and b)).

Finally we can generalize that the inferring process is reliable only if the data analyst can properly select a good model, such as hierarchical BN and identifies proper segmentation level to make the best inference about the context.

References

1. Aaltonen, A., Huuskonen, P., Lehikoinen, J.: Context Awareness Perspectives for Mobile Personal Media. In: Aaltonen, Lehikoinen: Personal and Ubiquitous Computing (2005)
2. Adomavicius, G., Tuzhilin, A., Sankaranarayanan, R., Sen, S.: Incorporating Contextual Information in Recommender Systems Using a Multidimensional Approach. ACM Transactions on Information Systems 23(1), 103–145 (2005)
3. Barnes, J.W.: Statistical Analysis for Engineers and Scientists. McGraw-Hill, New York (1994)
4. Bazire, M., Brézillon, P.: Understanding Context Before Using It. In: Dey, A.K., Kokinov, B., Leake, D.B., Turner, R. (eds.) CONTEXT 2005. LNCS (LNAI), vol. 3554, Springer, Heidelberg (2005)
5. Berry, A., Linoff, G.: Data Mining Techniques: For Marketing, Sales, and Customer Support. Wiley Computer Publishing, New York (1997)
6. Bettman, J.R., Luce, M.F., Payne, J.W.: Consumer Decision Making: A Constructive Perspective. In: Tedeschi, M. (ed.) Consumer Behavior and Decision Making, pp. 1–42 (1991)
7. Bothorel, C., Chevalier, K.: How to Use Enriched Browsing Context to Personalize Web Site Access. In: Blackburn, P., Ghidini, C., Turner, R.M., Giunchiglia, F. (eds.) CONTEXT 2003. LNCS, vol. 2680, pp. 23–25. Springer, Heidelberg (2003)
8. Chen, G., Kotz, D.: A Survey of Context-Aware Mobile Computing Research. Department of Computer Science, Dartmouth College, Technical report (2000)
9. Dey, A.K., Abowd, G.D., Salber, D.: A Conceptual Framework and a Toolkit for Supporting the Rapid Prototyping of Context-Aware Applications. HCI 16(2), 97–166 (2001)
10. Flanagan, J.A.: Unsupervised clustering of context data and learning user requirements for a mobile device. In: Dey, A.K., Kokinov, B., Leake, D.B., Turner, R. (eds.) CONTEXT 2005. LNCS (LNAI), vol. 3554, Springer, Heidelberg (2005)
11. Fortu, O., Moldovan, D.: Identification of Textual Contexts. In: Dey, A.K., Kokinov, B., Leake, D.B., Turner, R. (eds.) CONTEXT 2005. LNCS (LNAI), vol. 3554, Springer, Heidelberg (2005)
12. Gorgoglione, M., Palmisano, C., Tuzhilin, A.: Personalization in Context: Does Context Matter When Building Personalized Customer Models? In: Perner, P. (ed.) ICDM 2006. LNCS (LNAI), vol. 4065, Springer, Heidelberg (2006)
13. Heath, T., Motta, E., Dzbor, M.: Uses of Contextual Information to Support Online Tasks. In: 1st AKT Doctoral Symposium, Milton Keynes, UK
14. Heckerman, D.: A tutorial on learning with Bayesian networks. Technical report, Microsoft Research, Redmond, Washington (1995)
15. Jiang, T., Tuzhilin, A.: Segmenting Customers from Population to Individuals: Does 1-to-1 Keep Your Customers Forever? IEEE TKDE 18(10), 1297–1311 (2006)
16. Kenny, D., Marshall, J.F.: Contextual marketing: the real business of the Internet, Harvard Business Review, 119–125 (2000)
17. Klein, N.M., Yadav, M.S.: Context Effects on Effort and Accuracy in Choice: an Enquiry into Adaptive Decision Making. Journal of Consumer Research 15(4) (1989)
18. Kotler, P.: Marketing Management. Prentice Hall, London (2003)
19. Leake David, B., Maguitman, A.G., Reichherzer, T.: Exploiting Rich Context: An Incremental Approach to Context-Based Web Search. In: Dey, A.K., Kokinov, B., Leake, D.B., Turner, R. (eds.) CONTEXT 2005. LNCS (LNAI), vol. 3554, pp. 254–267. Springer, Heidelberg (2005)

20. Lilien, G.L., Kotler, P., Moorthy, S.K.: Marketing Models. Prentice Hall, Englewood Cliffs (1992)
21. Luo, X.: The Performance Implications of Contextual Marketing for Business-to-Consumer Electronic Commerce: An Empirical Investigation. J. of Database Marketing 10(3) (2003)
22. Lussier, J.G., Olshavsky, R.W.: Task Complexity and Contingent Processing in Brand Choice. Journal of Consumer Research, 154–165 (1979)
23. Maamar, Z., Benslimane, D., Narendra, N.C.: What can context do for web services? Communications of the ACM 49(12), 98–103 (2006)
24. Pappas, A., Hailes, S., Giaffreda, R.: A design model for context-aware services based on primitive contexts. In: First International Workshop on Advanced Context Modelling, Reasoning And Management UbiComp (2004)
25. Prahalad, C.K.: Beyond CRM: C.K. Prahalad Predicts Customer Context is the next Big Thing. American Management Association MwWorld (2004)
26. Sarkar, P., Nagy, G., Veeramachaneni, S.: Modeling context as statistical dependence. In: Fifth International and Interdisciplinary Conference on Modeling and Using Context (2005)
27. Schilit, B., Theimer, M.: Disseminating active map information to mobile Hosts. IEEE Network 8(5), 22–32 (1994)
28. Schmidtke, H.R.: Granularity as a parameter of context. In: Dey, A.K., Kokinov, B., Leake, D.B., Turner, R. (eds.) CONTEXT 2005. LNCS (LNAI), vol. 3554, Springer, Heidelberg (2005)
29. Webster's new twentieth century dictionary of the English language (1980)
30. Witten, H., Frank, E.: Data Mining: Practical machine learning tools and techniques, 2nd edn. Morgan Kaufmann, San Francisco (2005)
31. Zhu, H., Madnick, S.E.: Structured Contexts with Lightweight Ontology. MIT Sloan Research Paper No. 4620-06 (2006)

Context-Aware Security Management System
for Pervasive Computing Environment*

Seon-Ho Park, Young-Ju Han, and Tai-Myoung Chung

Internet Management Technology Laboratory,
School of Information and Communication Engineering,
Sungkyunkwan University,
300 Cheoncheon-dong, Jangan-gu,
Suwon-si, Gyeonggi-do 440-746, Republic of Korea
{shpark,yjhan}@imtl.skku.ac.kr, tmchung@ece.skku.ac.kr

Abstract. This paper presents the context based authentication and
authorization management system for security management in the pervasive computing environment. we explored security considerations of
the pervasive computing environment. The proposed system adopts the
context-role based access control model as access control model for enforcement of access control service based on various context information. We also studied the methodology to apply partial credential to
user authentication. We introduce the authentication confidence index
for applying the partial credential to authentication mechanisms. The
authentication confidence index is also used for user-role activation in
the access control service. This paper shows comparison between our
system and related works, such as Cerberus and CASA.

Keywords: pervasive computing, context aware, authentication, context
role based access control, partial credential.

1 Introduction

The rapid growth of computing devices and networking technologies has enabled
to transplant computing devices and networking infrastructure to human life
space. In addition, mobile hand-held devices, such as PDAs and mobile phones,
and context sensing devices, such as various sensors and camera, are enabling
the construction of pervasive computing environments in which devices, software agents, and services are all expected to seamlessly integrate and cooperate in support of human objectives-anticipating needs, negotiating for service,
acting on our behalf, and delivering services in an anywhere, anytime fashion.
Traditional computing devices and applications are independent each other and

* This research was supported by the MIC(Ministry of Information and Communication), Korea, under the ITRC(Information Technology Research Center) support
program supervised by the IITA(Institute of Information Technology Advancement)
(IITA-2006-C1090-0603-0028).

B. Kokinov et al. (Eds.): CONTEXT 2007, LNAI 4635, pp. 384–396, 2007.

are separated from human activities and environmental states. In the pervasive computing environment, however, computing devices and applications can easily inter-operate each other and interact with human activities by context-awareness[1,2,3].

From a security perspective, the pervasive computing environment has new security challenges, because it has several features which are different from traditional computing environment, such as context awareness and pervasively deployment of various computing devices [1,4,5]. For the solution to the new security challenges of the pervasive computing environment, we propose the COBAR system that enables a management and an enforcement of context-based security policies. This system provices partial credential based user authentication and context-based access control. Security services of COBAR system is based on CRBAC (Context-Role Based Access Control) model, ACI (Authentication Confidence Index) and location-aware authentication for supporting context-aware security management.

The remainder of this paper is composed as follows. Section 2 explores security challenges of pervasive computing environment. In section 3, we discuss an overview of the COBAR system. Section 4 illustrates security models and services that the COBAR system provides. Section 5 illustrates an architecture and functions of core components of the COBAR system. In section 6, we discuss an implementation of the COBAR system and show the process of the security service of the COBAR system. In section 7 we explore related works and compare the COBAR system with them. Section 8 concludes the paper.

2   Security Challenges of Pervasive Computing Environment

The most important core technique of the pervasive computing environment is the context-awareness. The context-awareness enables the system to provide dynamically automatic intelligent services to the users. In such a computing environment, the context information as well as users and system entities must be considered as an important factor of the security policy. And, the relationship between the context information and users or/and system entities is also considered as an important requirement for the security policy management. Traditional security policies and mechanisms have a subject-centric feature. Therefore traditional security policies and mechanisms are inadequate for pervasive computing environment. This section illustrates several security considerations for the security management of the pervasive computing environment[1,4,5].

The user authentication of the pervasive computing environment has two problems which are the usability problem and the management problem of various authentication mechanisms that have different credential degree. In pervasive computing environment, computers are available in huge numbers, embedded in every day artifacts, like phones, furniture, cars, and buildings. Hence, each user can use many personal computing devices, and at the same time, the same publicly available device can be used by many users. The many-to-many relationship between users and computers causes some usability challenges for user authentication. Common user authentication schemes involve user to directly request for the identification verification of users. However, in the pervasive computing environment that has many pervasive computing devices, users would need to directly request the conduct of authentication to all pervasively available computers before (s)he could start using them. The solution to this problem is very important to efficiently achieve "ubiquitous" non-intrusive and transparent user authentication in the pervasive computing environment.

The second problem is about management of various many authentication mechanisms that have different confidence level. In the pervasive computing environment, many authentication devices such as PDA, smart badge and fingerprint scanner, and authentication protocols such as Challenge-Response, user name-password, Digital signatures and Kerberos is used to authenticate users and system entities. These various authentication methods have different confidence level. Unlike traditional computing system using simply one authentication mechanism, the pervasive computing system can use multi-authentication for secure and active service. Therefore, the mechanism to manage the different credential degree of various authentication mechanisms is required in the pervasive computing environment.

Another security challenge is about the access control policy. Traditional access control policies and mechanisms are based on only the subject(users, processors) information. For example, in the Access Control List(ACL) which is a very commonly used as an access control mechanism, a permission to access resources or services is controlled by checking for the membership in the access control list associated with each object. This method is, however, inadequate for context-aware applications of pervasive computing environment, because it cannot consider the context information. Granting the access to the user without taking the user's current context into consideration can compromise the security as the user's access privileges not only depend on the identifier of the user, but also on the user location and the user's internal and environmental states. Thus, in the pervasive computing environment, to support a secure context-aware service and a security policy based on varied context information, we must take a context based access control policy into consideration. In addition, the tool which can manage the complex security policy rule sets which contain various and large context information must be implemented [1].

3   COBAR System Overview

The COBAR system aims to provide the partial credential based authentication and the context-aware access control service and manage well-structured security policies to efficiently reflect organization structure. The COBAR system must catch every communications and operations of all entities in the pervasive computing environment so as to control all security services, therefore the COBAR must be deployed as AAA server, by adding accounting management to

COBAR, or embedded in home gateway(home server), for example, in the home network system.

The security service of COBAR includes a user authentication and an access control. The access control of the COBAR is based on the Context-Role Based Access Control model. The model has all advantages of RBAC and also enables the management of the context-based access control policy. The user authentication of the COBAR manages user authentication information using the ACI value. The ACI value is used to manage differentiated confidence level of various authentication mechanisms. The ACI value can also be used for the user-role activation in the access control part. The detailed explanation about security models of COBAR is talked in the following section 4.

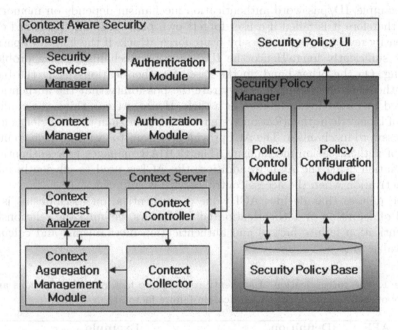

Fig. 1. The COBAR system overview

Figure 1 shows the high-level overview of the COBAR system. The Context Aware Security Manager(CASM) provides security services including a user authentication and an access control and manages security sessions in the pervasive system. Providing security services and managing security sessions are controlled by context Information and the CASM must apply context information dynamically changed to security sessions. If the change of context information is not dynamically applied to security sessions, the compromise of security can be occurred. The Context Server(CS) collects and manages context information to provide it to the CASM. The gathered context is aggregated and managed based on the context management policy, and the policy is defined in the Security Policy Manager. The Security Policy Manager(SPM) manages security policies, and provides policies to the CASM and the CS. The Security Policy UI provides web-based interface to configure and manage the security policies to security manager. The detailed explanation about components of the COBAR architecture is discussed in section 5.

4   Security Models of COBAR System

4.1   Authentication Confidence Index

The COBAR system applies different confidence level to each user authentication mechanism using the Authentication Confidence Index(ACI). Every authentication mechanism has the different confidence level based on its features. For example, ID/password authentication mechanism depends on memory of a user, therefore it is failed if a user forgets own password. The password can be also easily revealed to attackers by brute-force attack, if the length of password is not sufficiently long. Hence the ID/password mechanism has a problem of copying. On the other hand, in the case of authentications using the biometric authentication system, it is very rare the possibility that the authentication is failed by forgetting, a forgery, or a theft. Hence, we can think the confidence level of biometric authentication system to be higher than the confidence level of ID/password mechanism. The ACI provides a means to evaluate each confidence level of authentication mechanisms. The COBAR manages user authentication information using the ACI. In addition, the ACI is used to efficiently manage role activation when the access control service is enforced.

The process that decides ACI value of authentication mechanisms is composed of definition of authentication failure factors, defining the relationship of authentication failure factors and authentication mechanisms, and calculating ACI values.

Table 1. The categorization of authentication failure factors and definitions and examples of each factor (AFF: authentication failure factors)

AFF	Definition	Example
Loss (or forgetting)	The possibility of danger that the authentication material is lost or user forgets it.	When a user lost his smart or forgot his password
Duplication	The possibility of danger that an attacker duplicates user's authentication material.	Copying a password or a grid card
Theft	The possibility of danger that the authentication material is stolen or guessed	When the smart card was stolen or the password was guessed by the attacker.
Transformation (or Modification)	The possibility of danger that the authentication material is modified by attacker or transformation by itself.	A transformation of biometric information or modifying a password that transmitted over the network.

Table 1 shows authentication failure factors that we defined. The failure of a user authentication is occurred by the user's abnormal behaviors or by an attacker's malicious behaviors. The former is occurred by the user's forgetting, loss, or transformation of authentication materials and the latter is occurred by a duplication, a theft, a modification of authentication materials by the attacker. These authentication failure factors affect the result of the user authentication. Hence we decide ACI values of authentication mechanisms by defining relationships between the authentication failure factors and authentication mechanisms.

The next step of defining the authentication failure factors is to calculate the ACI value using them. The ACI calculation method can be also various. For example, the fuzzy logic or the probabilistic approach can be used for the ACI calculation. We have used the probabilistic approach. The following formula is our algorithm of the probabilistic approach for the ACI calculation.

$$P_{aci} = 1 - \frac{1}{m} \sum_{i=1}^{m} P(e_i), (m = |E|, e_i \in E)$$

E is the set of authentication failure factors and $P(e)$ is the probability value of a certain failure factor. P_{aci} is the ACI value of the authentication mechanism and $|E|$ is the number of elements of E. The algorithm means that the average of probability values of failure factors is the failure rate of certain authentication mechanism and so subtracting it from 1 which is the highest ACI value is the ACI value of certain authentication mechanism.

We calculated ACI values of several popular authentication mechanisms using the above definition of the authentication failure factors and the ACI calculation formula.

In the case of the ID/Password, it has four failure factors, "loss", "duplication", "theft", "transformation". Suppose that the loss rate is 0.9, the duplication rate is 0.6, the theft rate is 0.6, and the transformation rate is 0.5. The ACI is 0.35.

In the case of the Smart Card, it has strong possibilities of "loss", "theft", and "modification". Suppose that the loss rate is 0.7, the duplication rate is 0.0, the theft rate is 0.7, and modification rate is 0.5. The ACI is about 0.58.

In the case of the Fingerprint authentication, there is not much possibility of "loss" and "theft" occurring, but it can be affected by "duplication" and "transformation". Suppose that the loss rate is 0.0, the duplication rate is 0.2, the theft rate is 0.0, and the transformation rate is 0.2. The ACI is 0.9.

The ACI calculation depends on features and contexts of the system, therefore the system administrator must define authentication failure factors and calculation algorithm for applying the ACI to the system when the COBAR system is deployed.

4.2 Context-Role Based Access Control

We use the CRBAC [1] model to define, manage, and enforce an access control policy based on context relating to an access control service. The CRBAC has features of traditional RBAC [7,8] since it is extended model of RBAC. Therefore, it enables security manager to define and manage the well-structured security policies that efficiently reflect organization's structure using features of RBAC such as the role-hierarchy and the constraint for the separation of duty(SoD). The CRBAC model adds a notion of context-role to a traditional role based access control in order to apply security-sensitive context information to a security policy and an access control decision. The context-role represents environmental state of the system by a mapping of the context-roles and the context information.

The role activation is very important and has to be carefully executed, since the principal of the SoD may be violated because of many-to-many relationship of users and roles. We solve this problem by means of relationship between the strength of permission that a role has and an ACI level of authenticated user. Allowing a user that possesses higher ACI to have stronger permission is very natural behavior, because the ACI means a confidence level of authenticated user. The COBAR provides function to assign appropriate activation level to every user roles and only users which have higher ACI value than activation level of certain role are able to activate the role.

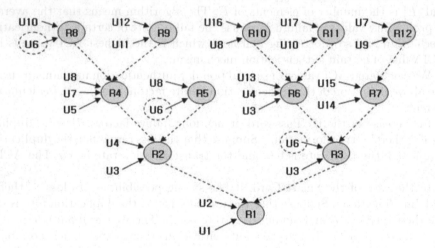

Fig. 2. An example of a user role hierarchy tree and assignment relationships of users and roles

Example 1. Figure 2 is an example of a user role hierarchy tree and relationship of assignment of users and user roles. A user U6 is assigned to role R3, R5, and R8. These roles have a different set of permissions and sensitive levels of each set of per-missions are different respectively. We assume that U6 can be authenticated by means of an ID/password, a smart card, and a fingerprint. ACI values of these authentication mechanisms are calculated in section 4.1. We can assign appropriate ACI level to each role to configure a condition for role activation. Let us assign respectively 0.3, 0.5, and 0.8 to R3, R5, and R8. To active these roles, users are authenticated with ACI value that is higher than activation level of respective roles. If a user U6 is authenticated by means of ID/password, only R3 is activated and R5 and R8 are not activated for U6. Similarly, if U6 is authenticated using the smart card, R3 and R5 are activated but R8 is not activated for U6.

COBAR provides APIs that define the relationship between entities of the system and components of CRBAC. For example, relationships of user and user-role, context and context-role, and object/operation and permission must be defined before defining access control policy.

5 Architecture of COBAR System

This section describes detailed architecture and functions of core components of COBAR system. The CASM is core component of COBAR system. The CASM provides context aware security services which are the user authentication and the access control, the security service session management, and the management of authentication devices and protocols. Because context aware security services require context information, the CASM also provides the management

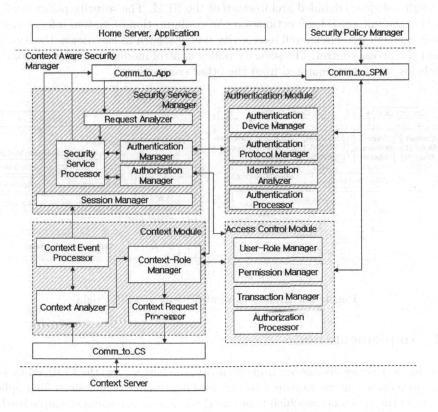

Fig. 3. The Architecture of CASM

function of context information and the monitoring function of the context change. Figure 3 shows a detailed design of CASM.

The security service manager (SSM) manages security services. The SSM analyzes the request of security services, manages the authentication module and the access control module, and conducts the security session management after enforcement of access control. The authentication module (AM) enforces a user authentication and manages authentication mechanisms. The access control module (ACM) enforces the access control of authenticated users based on the CRBAC mechanism. The context module (CM) manages the context role activation and provides activated context roles to the ACM.

The CS provides functions for collection and management of context and management of wireless sensor network. Figure 4 shows detailed architecture of the CS(left) and the SPM(right). The context request analyzer analyzes the request which is sent from the CASM. The context collector provides functions about collecting context and management of sensor network. The context controller controls policies about a context management and a context reasoning. The context reasoning module enforces a context reasoning based on policies about the context management.

The SPM manages all security policies for the COBAR system. The right part of figure 4 shows detailed architecture of the SPM. The security policy configuration module provides functions for the configuration of system information of management domain as well as security policies, such as the user authentication and the access control. The security policy control module provides appropriate policies which are requested from the other components.

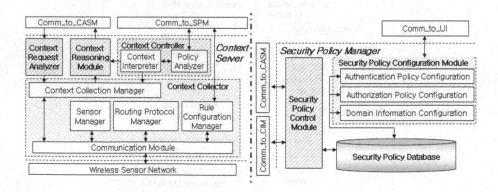

Fig. 4. The Architectures of CS(left) and SPM(right)

6   Implementation

In this section we discuss our implementation, where we use the COBAR system to authenticate users, capture context, and control access decisions for applications of the smart home which is our testbed. The smart home is simple testbed

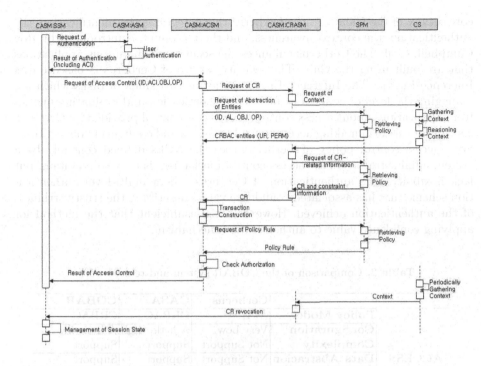

Fig. 5. The process of security service that the COBAR system provides

that is composed several authentication devices, sensor devices that are connected through the wireless network, and a program which simulates the home network system based on a context-awareness. Our authentication devices include smart card, ID/password, and fingerprint scanners. Simulation program includes various appliances such as TV, audio, lamp, humidifier, and so on. We decide to use simulation program to test operations of COBAR system, because it is difficult to implement a real environment for testing of our system and the focus of our work is only security management system. Sensor devices can capture a temperature, humidity, an illumination, and a gas leakage. We also use the temporal information and spatial information as well as context information that are captured sensor devices. The policy of COBAR is configured through the web-based graphical user interface, therefore the policy manager can easily access and manage the security policy.

Figure 5 illustrates the process of the security service that the COBAR system provides.

7   Related Works and Comparison

There are currently two representative researches for security framework of the pervasive computing. One is the Cerberus [9] developed by the University of Illinois. And the other is the CASA [10] developed by the Georgia Tech. As a core service of the Gaia [11], the Cerberus that integrates the identification, the authentication, the context awareness, and the reasoning, is introduced by Roy Campbell, et al. The Cerberus enhances the security of ubiquitous applications that are built using the Gaia. The security service of Cerberus is based on its Inference Engine. The Inference Engine performs two kinds of tasks which are managing the level of confidence for user authentication and evaluating queries from applications about access control. The access control provided by Cerberus considers context in making access control decisions and configuring policy. However, access control policy of Cerberus uses the ACLs defined centrally by a system administrator. These access control mechanism is easy to maintain, but lack flexibility. The authentication of Cerberus uses a multi-level authentication scheme that has associated confidence values describing the trustworthiness of the authentication achieved. However, it is insufficient that the method for applying confidence value to authentication mechanism.

Table 2. Comparison of the COBAR system and related works

		Cerberus	CASA	COBAR
	Policy Model	ACL	GRBAC	CRBAC
ACCESS CONTROL	Configuration Complexity	Very Low Not Support	A little High Support	A little low Support
	Data Abstracion	Not Support	Support	Support
	Reflection of Organization Structure	Difficult	Very easy	Very easy
	Overhead for Policy Storage	Low	Very High	Middle
AUTHENT-ICATION	Partial Credential	Support	Support	Support
	Formulation of Authentication Confidence	Lack	Lack	Support
	Authentication Confidence for Multiple Authentication	Support using simple formulation	There is no formulation	Support using simple formulation

The CASA provides a context-based access control using the GRBAC [12] model for a security of the Aware Home. The GRBAC is an extension of traditional Role-Based Access Control. It enhances traditional RBAC by incorporating the notion of object roles and the notion of environment roles, with the traditional notion of subject roles. An environment role can be based on any system state that the system can accurately collect. Object roles allow us to capture various commonalities among the objects in a system, and use these commonalities to classify the objects into roles. However the GRBAC has some problems. First, the GRBAC is not suitable for large and complex organizations, because of defining too many roles in the system. Second, the RBAC loses its advantage of data abstractions by an object role. The RBAC abstracts the user-level information from the system-level information by the notion of permission which is relationship between objects and operations, because the object role violates, however, the relationship, the data abstraction could not be achieved. In addition, this problem violates user/role and role/permission associations. Finally, the GRBAC has an unnecessary overlapping between environment roles and object roles, because certain physical environmental things can be also objects.

Table 2 shows the summary of the result that we compare the COBAR system with the Cerberus and the CASA.

8   Conclusion

The context-awareness feature of the pervasive computing environment requires new security challenges. A paradigm shift in policy models is needed to move focus from the subject-centricity to the context. We introduce context-based security management system using new security models, such as the context-role based access control model and partial credential based authentication model. We focused implementation of the context-role based access control mechanism which is our previous work. We also proposed formalized algorithm for calculation of ACI value of authentication mechanism. Our system uses this ACI value to improve the role activation process in an access control process.

References

1. Park, S.-H., Han, Y.-J.: Context-Role Based Access Control for Context-Aware Application. In: Gerndt, M., Kranzlmüller, D. (eds.) HPCC 2006. LNCS, vol. 4208, pp. 572–580. Springer, Heidelberg (2006)
2. Korkea-aho, M.: Context-Aware Application Survey, Internetworking Seminar (Tik-110.551), Helsinki University of Technology (April 2000)
3. Schilit, B., Adams, N., et al.: Context-aware computing applications. In: WM-CSA 1994, Santa Cruz, California, pp. 85–90. IEEE Computer Society Press, Los Alamitos (1994)
4. Zhang, G., Parashar, M.: Context-aware Dynamic Access Control for Pervasive Applications. In: 2004 Communication Networks and Distributed Systems Modeling and Simulation Conference (CNDS'04), San Diego, California (January 2004)
5. Convington, M.J., Long, W., et al.: Securing Context-Aware Applications Using Environment Roles. In: SACMAT'01, Chantilly, Virginia (May 3-4, 2001)
6. Moran, T.P., Dourish, P.: Introduction to This Special Issue on Context-Aware Computing. Hunam Computer Interaction 16 (2001)
7. Sandhu, R.S., Coyne, E.J., et al.: Role-Based Access Control Models. IEEE Computer 29(2), 38–47 (1996)
8. Ferraiolo, D.F., Sandhu, R., et al.: Proposed NIST Standard for Role-Based Access Control. ACM Transactions on Information and System Security 4(3) (August 2001)

9. Al-Muhtadi, J., Ranganathan, A., et al.: Cerberus: A Context-Aware SEcurity Scheme for Smart Spaces. In: IEEE International Conference on Pervasive Computing and Communications (PerCom 2003), Dallas-Fort Worth, Texas (March 23-26, 2003)
10. Convington, M.J., Fogla, P., et al.: A Context-Aware Security Architecture for Emerging Applications. In: Proceedings of the 18th Annual Computer Security Applications Conference, p. 249 (2002)
11. Cerqueira, R., Hess, C.K., et al.: Gaia: A Development Infrastructure for Active Spaces. In: Workshop on Application Models and Programming Tools for Ubiquitous Computing (held in conjunction with the UBICOMP (2001)
12. Moyer, M.J., Ahamad, M.: Generalized role based access control. In: Proceedings of the 2001 International Conference on Distributed Computing Systems (ICDCS), Mesa (April 2001)

VIVACE Context Based Search Platform

Romaric Redon[1], Andreas Larsson[2], Richard Leblond[1], and Barthelemy Longueville[1]

[1] EADS France, Innovation works, TCC5 simulation, IT & systems engineering, Marius Terce.
18,31300 Toulouse, France
{romaric.redon, richard.leblond,barthelemy.longueville}@eads.net
[2] Faste Laboratory, Luleå University of Technology, 971 87 Luleå, Sweden
andreas.c.larsson@ltu.se

Abstract. One of the key challenges of knowledge management is to provide the right knowledge to the right person at the right time. To face this challenge, a context based search platform was developed in the frame of the European Integrated Project VIVACE. This platform is based on the identification of a user context and the subsequent pushing of applicable knowledge to that particular user. We introduce a context model to represent the user's context. This context model is used to describe the context of an engineer working in a specific company. Further, we developed means to index available knowledge based on company engineering context and means to search for knowledge applicable to the user's context. Since it is not always possible to describe in which context the knowledge assets should be applied, we added learning capabilities which enable the system to learn the applicability of specific knowledge to a user's context based on user feedback.

Keywords: Knowledge management, context aware systems and applications, context modelling, analogy and case based reasoning.

1 Introduction

This article deals with a presentation of the context based search platform developed in the frame of VIVACE – an Integrated Project within the European Commission's Sixth Framework Programme (FP6). After this introduction Part II provides an outline of the VIVACE project and describes the overall objectives of the Knowledge Enabled Engineering (KEE) Work Package. Part III focuses on KEE modelling activities: knowledge modelling and context modelling. Part IV deals with a detailed description of the concept of context based search and a presentation of the platform capabilities. In Part V the main features of the prototype developed in 2006 are presented as well as early experimentation results. Foreseen short term and longer term perspectives are discussed in part VI. Finally, part VII provides some conclusions.

2 VIVACE Knowledge Enabled Engineering

VIVACE [1] is a €70M Integrated Project in the EC Sixth Framework Programme (FP6). The acronym stands for 'Value Improvement through a Virtual Aeronautical

B. Kokinov et al. (Eds.): CONTEXT 2007, LNAI 4635, pp. 397–410, 2007.

Collaborative Enterprise', with the main project goal to support the design of a complete aircraft, including engines, by providing increased simulation capabilities throughout the product-engineering life cycle. Briefly stated, the goal is to create a 'virtual product' in a 'virtual enterprise' – thereby aiming to achieve a 5% cost reduction in aircraft development and a 5% reduction of the development phase of a new aircraft design combined with a contribution to a 30% reduction in the lead time and 50% reduction in development costs respectively for a new or derivative gas turbine engine.

The Knowledge Enabled Engineering (KEE) Work Package is one of six integrated technical packages that collectively form the Advanced Capabilities subproject (SP3) of VIVACE. Starting from the well-known knowledge management phases (storage, retrieval, reuse, sharing etc.), the main goal is to define and exploit advanced methods that could help companies capture how knowledge is used, and allow them to radically improve their engineering process by leveraging past design experience. The Work Package focuses on providing methods, tools, solutions and training activities that create conditions for the successful integration of knowledge enabling solutions both on the business side and on the technical side of the project's existing application environment of aeronautics. Beyond the consortium, the work promotes and facilitates the consolidation of the vision of a consistent way of building a real 'knowledge-driven' virtual enterprise, starting from the assumption that the developed core system will be applicable independent of the individual company type of business.

KEE can be considered as the exploitation of Knowledge Management within an engineering context, which fundamentally means leveraging knowledge sources in order to enable engineers to complete their work quickly and correctly. Thus, KEE is about providing the right information to the engineer, at the right time, in the right format, in a collaborative environment that promotes learning within the organization, across the supply chain and across the Extended Enterprise. Therefore, the KEE Work Package proposed to design a context based search platform that would enable users to search for knowledge which is applicable to their contexts. This article will focus on the description of the platform even though KEE also produce results in other area such as facilitating knowledge sharing, managing lessons learned, assessing team relationships and assessing maturity in a gated decision process.

3   KEE Modelling Activities

In order to proceed towards the development of a platform that provide applicable engineering knowledge depending on the user's context, a first required step was to specify what we mean by engineering knowledge and user context. The following paragraphs describe the models we introduced in KEE to represent engineering knowledge and user context.

3.1   Engineering Knowledge Modelling

Engineering knowledge deals with knowledge about products, processes and organisations. A key issue is that engineering knowledge is often stored in people's head or diluted with other possibly irrelevant, information in technical documents.

In order to support proper capture of engineering knowledge, methodologies such as CommonKADS[2] and MOKA[3] were proposed. These methodologies enable the building of knowledge models composed of interlinked *Knowledge Elements* (K-El). K-El are pieces of knowledge focusing on specific topics. MOKA introduces different forms to support the capturing and structuring of knowledge about both product and process. Entity and Constraints forms enable the collection of knowledge about product breakdown and product limitations. Activity and rules forms enable the collection of knowledge about process breakdown and flow control. At last Illustration forms could be linked to any of the other forms so as to record any corresponding past experience.

These forms are an example of how to organize structured K-El. Other examples of K-El found in industrial companies may include documents about lessons learnt, best practices, expert manuals or also expert contact information etc.

The smaller the K-El, the more the process of delivery-in-context makes sense. The objective is then to select the right K-El which do apply to the user context. If all K-El are merged in a single big document, and without any possibility to discriminate them, the in-context delivery process will make no sense or will be time consuming. This single big document will be applicable in almost all user contexts, and the individual user will not know (or with delay) which knowledge in the document does really apply to his/her context.

KEE introduces also the concept of *Knowledge Source* (K-Source). A K-Source is a K-El container. Examples of a K-Source could be a simple file repository for managing K-El which are stand alone documents, a web application for managing K-El which are interlinked web pages, or a complex content management system for managing structured interlinked K-El. A K-source usually provides standard capabilities such as index extraction and search capabilities. For a windows file repository, for example these capabilities are provided through Microsoft index server.

3.2 Context Modelling

The objective of this chapter is to describe the work performed in order to represent user context in engineering. The aim was to propose a relevant context model that could easily be understood by engineers and that we can use to quickly develop a platform in order to gain the end-user buy-in.

First of all, it is worth noting that context is still an ill-defined concept such as discussed in [4]. In order to define the context model to use within VIVACE, we investigated two approaches. First a top-down approach which studies existing context models already proposed in the literature and tries to adjust them to fit our needs. Second a bottom-up approach which starts from the study of existing K-El and aims at describing their context of use.

Top-Down Approach. According to Dey et al [5] context is any information that can be used to characterise the situation of an entity. Based on this definition we can propose that engineering context is any information that can be used to characterise the situation of an engineer.

In the literature different context models were proposed, some of them, developed for context representation of mobile users focus more on describing the user's physical context [6] (i.e. his/her current location, device, available resources, etc.), whereas some others include the description of the user's organizational context (role, group membership, tasks, etc.). In this last category, context description model proposed by Kirsch et al. [7] retain our attention. It is based on five viewpoints: space, tool, time, community and process. Several context representation classes are used to describe each viewpoint as shown in the following UML diagram.

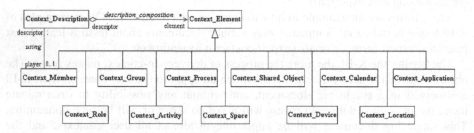

Fig. 1. Kirsch et al. [7] context description model

For KEE use cases, the influence of the user's physical context is not that important: we mainly target engineers working in design offices. Somehow, these engineers always have access to the same resources through the same type of device (i.e. their computer on the network). It means that at a first glance the Context_Space Context_Location, Context_Device representation classes maybe less relevant than the other one for our problem situation.

Bottom-Up Approach. Edmonds [8] says that context is the abstraction of those elements of circumstances in which a model is learnt [...], that allows recognition of new circumstances where the model can be usefully applied. In order to achieve our objective of in-context K-El delivery, we focused on representation of an engineering context, which is the abstraction of those elements of circumstances in which a K-El is learnt [...], that allows recognition of new circumstances where the K-El could be usefully applied. Therefore, we followed recommendations from Longueville et al. [9] to formalize what they call the explicit context. We studied real examples of K-El coming from VIVACE use cases and we identified how to describe their domain of applicability. The result from this bottom-up approach was the identification of relevant context dimensions. Context dimensions are properties or attributes that describe the context. Six context dimensions arose from the analysis: *product*, *activity*, *project*, *gate*, *role* and *discipline*. The domain of applicability for a K-El is described by specifying associated context dimension values. For example, a specific K-El may be applicable for the balancing process (activity) of the blade (product), within the scope of X34 (project) during preliminary design (gate) for a simulation engineer (role) in dynamic analysis (discipline).

We synthesized results coming from both approaches to propose the following UML engineering domain model. Our engineer is identified as a member of an organization; she/he has a role and skills in disciplines and takes part into projects (Community viewpoint). The organization provides her/him with applications running on various devices (Tool viewpoint). she/he performs activities that support product design (Process viewpoint) at a given gate (Time viewpoint) of the project.

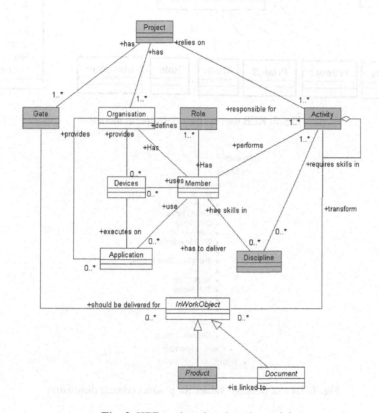

Fig. 2. KEE engineering domain model

According to the results of the bottom-up approach, classes in white were qualified, at a first glance, as less relevant than the other ones for our objective of in-context knowledge delivery. We finally proposed to rely only on six context dimensions to describe the context of our engineer. We introduced context dimension classes to potentially handle complex information associated to each context dimension (e.g. several attributes may be used to describe the product). A simplified context description model with context dimension modelled as attributes was also proposed.

In order to describe a company specific context description model we relied on the simplified context description model and managed the list of possible values for each context dimension in form of a tree. For example, the following tree organizes the list of possible values for the product context dimension for the AVIO company context description model.

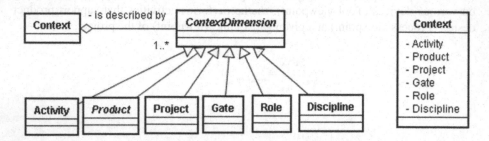

Fig. 3. KEE user context description models

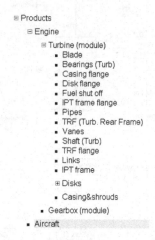

Fig. 4. Tree of possible values for product context dimension

Based on this KEE user context description model, and company context dimensions values, the context of user Daniele working in the AVIO company may be described as follows.

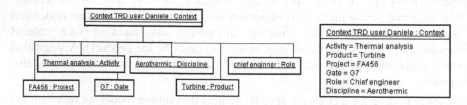

Fig. 5. Description of context of user Daniele working in the AVIO company

4   VIVACE Context Based Search Platform Capabilities

4.1   Overview of VIVACE Context Based Search Platform Capabilities

For the end user, the expected capability of the VIVACE context based search platform is to provide K-El applicable to the user's context described by the following context dimensions: product, activity, project, gate, role and discipline. Therefore, several sub capabilities were developed:

Index K-El on Context. This capability enables the management of the association between a K-El and the different descriptions of contexts in which it was or should be applied.

Context Similarity and K-El Applicability Computation. This capability enables the identification of contexts similar to the user's context, to retrieve K-El which were used in those similar contexts and to compute individual K-El applicability.

At a first glance, these two capabilities may be considered as sufficient for enabling context based search, but since knowledge is not usually indexed on context, the system should include capabilities to learn which knowledge is applicable to which context. Therefore, two new capabilities were developed:

Meta Search in K-Sources. This capability enables searching for K-El in all K-sources through ad-hoc techniques, such as full-text search.

K-EL Applicability Learning and Validation. This capability enables the system to learn that a K-El is applicable to a specific context.

These four capabilities enable a learning process which is shown in the following figure:

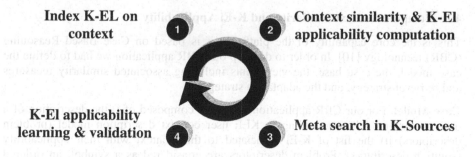

Fig. 6. VIVACE context based search capabilities

The following paragraphs give more detail for each capability

4.2   Index K-El on Context

Indexing K-El on context means to say that a specific K-El is applicable to a specific context with a specific level of applicability. The level of applicability could be an input from the expert or more likely a value computed by the platform itself. In order to index knowledge on context, we specified a *K-El reference and context database* which enables the management of links between contexts and K-El references. A K-El reference is a pointer to a K-El, it contains the K-El identifier and other information such as a title, a description, a type etc.

The platform includes means to specify and deploy K-Source specific extraction and transformation rules that could be launched on a periodic basis. These rules enable interpretation of K-El content in order to generate K-El references and possibly to retrieve context information so as to generate the proper links in the *K-El reference and context database*.

The conceptual data model of the *K-El reference and context database* is shown in the following figure. This model enables i)to manage many to many relationships with associated applicability between K-El references and contexts, ii)to make the distinction between applicability given by an expert and applicability computed/learnt by the system.

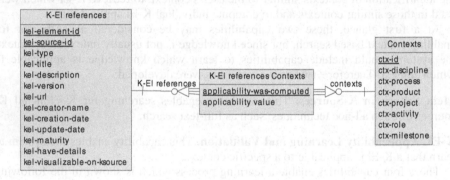

Fig. 7. *K-El reference and context database* conceptual data model

4.3 Compute Context Similarity and K-El Applicability

This is the core capability of the platform; it is based on Case Based Reasoning (CBR) technology [10]. In order to develop our CBR application we had to define the case model, the case base, the viewpoints including associated similarity measures and retrieval strategy, and the adaptation strategy.

Case Model. For our CBR application, a case is composed of i) the description of a user context modelled according to KEE user context description model (problem descriptors) ii) the list of K-El associated to this context with their applicability (solution descriptors). Problem descriptors are considered as a symbol, an ordered symbol or a taxonomy, as described in the following figure:

Case
Activity : Taxonomy
Product : Taxonomy
Project : Taxonomy
Gate : Ordered Symbol
Role : Symbol
Discipline : Symbol
Applicable K-Elements

Fig. 8. Case model

Case Base. The case base is obtained from the *K-El reference and context database* and it contains the description of all the contexts with associated K-EL.

Viewpoints. Viewpoints contain information about weights and similarity measures to use for each descriptor as well as for selection of the retrieval strategy. For our application, default weights were proposed, similarity measures such as taxonomy and similarity matrices were used and nearest neighbour retrieval method was selected.

Adaptation. The result of the nearest neighbour retrieval is a list of similar contexts with associated K-El and their applicability. Depending on i) the frequency of occurrences of a specific K-El in this list of similar contexts, and ii) the K-El applicability for each similar context; the platform computes individual K-El applicability to user's context.

4.4 Meta Search in K-Sources

This capability propagates a full text search request to all K-sources connected to the platform. Then, each K-source relies on its own search capabilities to perform the search (for example Documentum™ based K-sources which will use Documentum™ search capabilities and for WWW K-source search will be performed by ad-hoc web search engine such as Google™. The Results of each K-source search process are then sent back to the platform which aggregates results and possibly adds new K-El reference to the K-El reference and context database.

4.5 Knowledge Applicability Learning and Validation

Users can assess K-El applicability to his/her context. For K-El that result from full-text search, applicability is unknown and the user could decide to quantify applicability to his/her context by valuing a percentage from 0% (not applicable) to 100% (fully applicable). For K-El that result from contextual search, the user could decide to increase or decrease the applicability value which was computed by the system.

The platform should include a validation process to control the user's feedback process. This validation process may be implemented differently from company to company. For example, some companies may wait for 5 users to give feedback in the same direction to automatically validate, whereas others may ask an administrator to validate manually on a periodic basis.

After validation, the *K-El reference and context database* is updated according to users' feedback thus enriching potential results of any later context based search.

5 VIVACE Context Based Search Platform Prototype

5.1 Overview of Platform Architecture and Implementation

A first prototype of the platform was developed in 2006 based on a three-layered architecture:

Portal Layer for enabling a user's context identification and contextual and full text searches. The portal implementation is based on portlet technologies, thus it could be easily integrated into other web applications, such as existing company intranets.

Kernel Layer for enabling context similarity and K-El applicability computation as well as managing the *K-El reference and context database*. The kernel implementation is based on EADS Innovation Works CBR engine.

Knowledge Source Interface (KSI) Layer for enabling extraction and alignment of K-El metadata and multi-source search capabilities. The KSI implementation is based on Documentum ECIS services.

The three different layers were based on open source components (APACHE components and MySQL) and they communicate through web services as shown in the following figure.

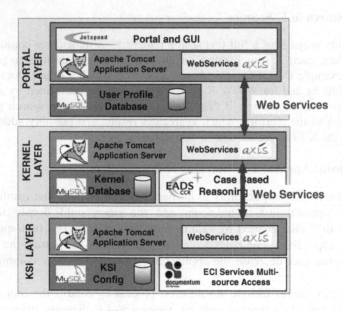

Fig. 9. Platform architecture

5.2 Platform Prototype User Interface

The platform prototype user interface is composed of five main panels:

Context Identification Panel. This panel enables the identification of the user's context through setting appropriate context dimensions values.

Search Panel. This panel enables the launch of the contextual search, which may be combined with complex filter-based K-El metadata and full text search in K-sources.

K-El Browser. This panel enables the browsing of search results

Fig. 10. Search and K-El browser panel

K-El reference and Context Viewer. This panel enables the visualisation of K-El reference and the context in which the K-El are applicable.

K-El Applicability Feedback Form. This panel, which is activated each time the user opens a K-El, enables the user to assess the applicability of the K-El with regard to his/her context.

5.3 Platform Prototype Scenario of Use

This generic scenario provides a walk through of how we envisage the platform being used.

1. User A is working in context Cx
2. Platform provides applicable K-El to user A through context based search.
3. User A accesses K-El reference and he/she could decide to open the K-El. For each opened K-El, the platform requests his/her feedback on K-El applicability.
4. User A is not fully satisfied by K-El obtained in step2, he/she searches for other K-El through a full text search in all K-sources.
5. User A find interesting K-El and he/she records applicability of this K-El to his/her context.
6. User B is working in a context Cy similar to Cx
7. Platform provides applicable K-El to user B. New K-El which were found in step 4 and said to be applicable by user A in step 5 are automatically provided to user B.

5.4 Platform Prototype Experimentation

Based on the VIVACE Turbine Rotor Design (TRD) use case, successful experimentations were conducted by KEE partners to validate the prototype. AVIO experts were involved in the project, they participated in the specification of the TRD context description model and they provided knowledge about similarities between context dimensions values. AVIO internal K-sources and external K-sources, such as the World Wide Web, were connected to the platform.

Results of these first experimentations validate that the platform can help provide the user with applicable knowledge depending on his/her context. Furthermore, promising results were obtained for the indexing of web pages based on context. The platform promotes collective learning about which information available on the web is applicable to which context. Thus, the platform offers promising capabilities to solve the information overload issue that users encounter in engineering activities.

6 Perspectives

6.1 Future Work

Piloting Activities. A piloting phase is scheduled in early 2007 in order to validate the platform in a real industrial environment and to measure associated benefits. The platform will be used by an operational team working on Turbine Rotor Design at AVIO.

SWOT analysis. SWOT analysis aims at evaluating the Strengths, Weaknesses, Opportunities and Threats involved in our proposal. This analysis will rely on consolidated results obtained from the piloting activities and analysis of other proposals for enabling context based search such as for example, those proposed by Kirsh-Pinheiro et al.[11] and David Leake et al.[12].

Context Modelling Enhancement. As described in part III, we based our work on a simplified context description model. The objective is to enhance this context description model in order to take into account i) richer information about existing context dimension (eg context dimension classes rather than attributes, for example, the discipline context dimension class may be described by several attributes such as the name of discipline, the level of expertise, etc.) ii)new context dimension, for example to better describe user profile and tool used iii)latest research results on context modelling.

Context Similarity Computation. The objective is to refine the context similarity computation algorithm to cope with the enhanced context description model and to better exploit existing links between context dimensions in the engineering domain model.

Guidelines Elaboration. As software platform or tool alone will never be an answer to a knowledge management issue, appropriate guidelines focusing on organizational, methodological and behavioural aspects should be elaborated. These guidelines will be used together with the platform to address the challenge of in-context knowledge delivery.

Integration Activities. The platform will be integrated with other advanced capabilities developed in the VIVACE project, such as Engineering Data management [13] (EDM) and Design To Decision Objectives (DTDO). The objective is to provide in-context delivery capabilities for knowledge as well as for product and simulation data. All results should be integrated in the VIVACE toolbox which will be a collaborative engineering environment that will notably raise the level of support for efficient decision making in engineering.

6.2 Research Perspectives

Advanced Context Identification. The objective is to enable automatic or assisted identification of user context. A user's context may be identified through monitoring and analysis of user behaviours, application and data used etc. However, it may not be possible to identify all context dimensions automatically, so the user may still have to set some context dimension values and validate the identified ones.

Knowledge Pushing. The objective is to combine advanced context identification capabilities and context based search capabilities to automatically push applicable knowledge to the user depending on his/her context. In other words, the aim is to develop a pro-active search system that does not necessarily require the user to take the search initiative.

Learning Enterprise. The objectives are twofold: at the software level to enhance and develop users' feedback mechanisms in our platform; at the organizational level to promote a learning culture in which users are eager to provide their feedback for the benefit of others. Nowadays, with participative tools associated to the Web2.0 framework, an efficient learning organization emerges on the web. Enabling this transformation in industry is still a challenge.

7 Conclusion

In order to face the new competitive situation in industrial companies, the design cycle must be shortened and engineers are asked to design right first time. On the one hand, shortening the design cycle leaves less time for the engineer to search for knowledge, on the other hand, the requirement to design right first time increases the need for knowledge search and reuse. The key issue is then to provide the right knowledge to the right user at the right time in the design process.

In order to face this issue we proposed a context based search platform that enables in-context delivery of knowledge. First results of platform experimentation are very promising. The platform enables collective learning of which knowledge is applicable to which context and efficient searching for knowledge applicable to the user context.

We believe that this context based search platform is a first step toward the development of pro-active search systems. Therefore further research work is required in order to develop automatic context identification capabilities and to use them together with context based search capabilities. Nowadays, engineers are often not even aware that there may be some knowledge available to help them, so they do not take the search initiative. For this reason, pro-active search systems that may push applicable knowledge without requiring user initiative are seen as the ultimate answer for supporting engineering activities.

Acknowledgements. The VIVACE integrated project is partly sponsored by the Sixth Framework Programme of the European Community (2002-2006) under priority 4 "Aeronautics and Space" as integrated project AIP3 CT-2003-502917. VIVACE context based search platform was developed by AVIO, EADS IW and Xerox.

References

1. Value Improvement through a Virtual Aeronautical Collaborative Entreprise.: www.vivaceproject.com
2. Schreiber, G., Akkermans, H., Anjewierden, A., de Hoog, R., Shadbolt, N., Van de Velde, W., Wielinga, B.: Knowledge Engineering and Management: the CommonKADS Methodology. MIT Press, Cambridge (2000)
3. Callot, M., Oldham, K., Stokes, M., Godwin, N., Brimble, R., Klein, R., Sellini, F., Merceron, F., Danino, D.: MOKA - Methodology and Tools Oriented to Knowledge based Engineering. Project EP25418 Public report N° 2 (1999)
4. Bazire, M., Brézillon, P.: Understanding Context Before Using It. In: Dey, A.K., Kokinov, B., Leake, D.B., Turner, R. (eds.) CONTEXT 2005. LNCS (LNAI), vol. 3554, Springer, Heidelberg (2005)
5. Dey, A.K, Abowd, G.D.: Toward a Better Understanding of Context and Context Awareness (1999)
6. Lelouma, T., Iayaïda N.: Context Aware Adaptation for Mobile Devices (2004)
7. Kirsch-Pinheiro, M., Villanova-Olivier, M., Gensel, J., Martin, H.: Representing Context for an Adaptive Awareness Mechanism. In: de Vreede, G.-J., Guerrero, L.A., Marín Raventós, G. (eds.) CRIWG 2004. LNCS, vol. 3198, Springer, Heidelberg (2004)
8. Edmonds, B.: The Pragmatic Roots of Context (1999)
9. Longueville, B., Gardoni, M.: A Survey of Context Modeling: Approaches, Theories and Use for Engineering Design Researches. In: Blackburn, P., Ghidini, C., Turner, R.M., Giunchiglia, F. (eds.) CONTEXT 2003. LNCS, vol. 2680, Springer, Heidelberg (2003)
10. Watson, I., Marir, F.: Case based Reasoning: a review. The knowledge Engineering review (1994)
11. Kirsch-Pinheiro, M., Villanova-Olivier, M., Gensel, J., Martin, H.: Context-aware Filtering for Collaborative Web Systems: Adapting the Awareness Information to the User's Context. In: Preneel, B., Tavares, S. (eds.) SAC 2005. LNCS, vol. 3897, Springer, Heidelberg (2006)
12. Leake, D., Maguitman, A., Reichherzer, T.: Exploiting Rich Context: An incremental Approach to Context-Based Web Search. In: Blackburn, P., Ghidini, C., Turner, R.M., Giunchiglia, F. (eds.) CONTEXT 2003. LNCS, vol. 2680, Springer, Heidelberg (2003)
13. Nguyen, V.T., Feru, F., Guellec, P., Yannou, B.: Engineering Data Management for extended enterprise - Context of the European VIVACE Project. In: PLM06 International Conference (2006)

AcroDef: A Quality Measure for Discriminating Expansions of Ambiguous Acronyms

Mathieu Roche and Violaine Prince

LIRMM - UMR 5506, CNRS, Univ. Montpellier 2,
34392 Montpellier Cedex 5 - France

Abstract. This paper presents a set of quality measures to determine the choice of the best expansion for an acronym not defined in the Web page. The method uses statistics computed on Web pages to determine the appropriate expansion. Measures are context-based and rely on the assumption that the most frequent words in the page are related semantically or lexically to the acronym expansion.

1 Introduction

Named Entities Recognition (NER) has become one of the major issues in Information Retrieval (IR), knowledge extraction from texts, classification, question answering (QA), and machine aided translation (MT). The state-of-the art literature in NER mostly focuses on proper names, temporal information, specific expressions in some technical or scientific fields for domain ontologies building, and so forth. A lot of work has been done on the subject, among which on acronyms, seen as particular named entities. Acronyms are very widely used in every type of text, and therefore have to be considered as a research issue as linguistic objects and as named entities.

An **acronym** is composed from the first letters of a set of words, written in uppercase style. This set of words is generally frequently addressed, which explains the need for a shortcut. It is also a specific multiword expression, such as "named entities recognition", abbreviated into NER, sometimes completely domain dependent (as NER or NLP are) and sometimes becoming a commonly used item (such as SARS, AIDS, USA, etc.). In some cases, acronyms become proper names referring to countries or companies (like USA or IBM). However, most of the time, acronyms are domain or period dependent. They are contracted forms of multiword expressions where words might belong to the common language. As contracted forms, they might be highly ambiguous since they are created out of words first letters. For instance NER, the acronym we use for Named Entities Recognition might also represent Nippon Electrical Resources or Natural Environment Restoration. Those are two other possible expansions for the acronym NER. An **expansion** is the set of words that defines the acronym. The word **definition** will also be used as a synonym for expansion in this context.

In all cases, an acronym behaves like a named entity. However, the intrinsic ambiguity in most acronyms enhances the difficulty of finding which exact entity

B. Kokinov et al. (Eds.): CONTEXT 2007, LNAI 4635, pp. 411–424, 2007.

is referred by this artificial name. Literature has been addressing acronym building and expansion (see section "state-of-the art") when the acronym definition is given in the text. However, choosing the right expansion for a given acronym in a given document, if no previous definition has been provided in the text, is an issue definitely belonging to NER, and not yet exhaustively tackled. The difficulty in acronym disambiguation is to automatically choose, as an expansion, the most appropriate set of words. This article tries to deal with this issue by offering a **quality measure** for each candidate expansion. In this context, let us name a a given acronym. For every a which expansion is lacking in a document d, we consider a list of n possible expansions for a: $a^1...a^n$. For instance, if IR is the acronym at stake, we could have $IR^1=$ Information Retrieval, and $IR^2 =$Investor Relations (in finance and communication), and $IR^3 =$Infra Red (in optics and medicine). In a multilingual context, things could become worse, $IR^4 =$ Impôt sur le Revenu (the French expression for income tax). Some web resources exist for providing acronym definitions (as an example, we use the site http://www.sigles.net/, which browses more than $17,000$ sites in 212 countries).

The aim of our approach is to determine k ($k \in [1, n]$) such that a^k is the relevant expansion of a in the document d. To make such a choice, we provide a quality measure, called $AcroDef$, which relies on Web resources. The figure 1 summarizes the applied global process. The presentation is structured as following: section 2 discusses the output of the related literature, section 3 focuses on the quality measure $AcroDef$, where context and web resources are essential characteristics to be taken into account. Section 4 describes some experiments and discusses their results and finally conclusion and perspectives are suggested in 5.

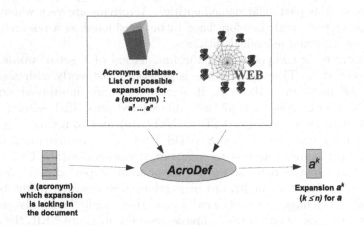

Fig. 1. Global process

2   Acronym Expansion Relevant Literature

Among the several existing methods for acronyms detection and expansion in literature, we present here some significant works. First, acronyms detection within texts is an issue by itself. It involves recognizing a character chain as an acronym and not as an unknown or misspelled word. Most acronyms detecting methods rely on using specific linguistic markers.

Yates' method [19] involves the following steps. First, the sentences are separated by segments using specific markers (brackets, points) as frontiers. The second step compares each word of each segment with the preceding and following segments. Then the couples acronyms/expansions are tested. The candidates acronym/definitions are accepted if the acronym characters correspond to the first letters of the potential definitions words. For example, the pair "IR/Information Retrieval" is a good acronym/expansion candidate. The last step uses specific heuristics to select the relevant candidates. For example, these heuristics rely on the fact that: (1) acronyms length is smaller than their expansion length, (2) they appear in upper case, (3) long expansions of acronyms tend to use "tool-words" such as determiners, prepositions, and so forth.

Other works [4,11] use similar methods, based on the presence of markers associated to specific and linguistically oriented heuristics. Larkey *et al.*'s method [11] uses a search engine to enhance an initial corpus of Web pages useful for acronym detection. To do so, starting from a list of given acronyms, queries are built and submitted to the AltaVista search engine[1]. Queries results are Web pages which URLs are explored, and eventually added to the corpus.

Our method shares with [11] the usage of the Web. However, we do not look for existing expansions in text since we try to determine possible expansion that would be lacking in the text where the acronym is detected. From that point of view, we are closer to works like Turney's [17], which are not specifically about acronyms but which use the Web to define a ranking function. The algorithm PMI-IR (Pointwise Mutual Information and Information Retrieval) described in [17] queries the Web via the AltaVista search engine to determine appropriate synonyms to a given query. For a given word, noted *word*, PMI-IR chooses a synonym among a given list. These selected terms, noted $choice_i$, $i \in [1, n]$, correspond to the TOEFL questions. The aim is to compute the $choice_i$ synonym that gives the better score. To obtain scores, PMI-IR uses several measures based on the proportion of documents where both terms are present. Turney's formula is given below (1): it is one of the basic measures used in [17]. It is inspired from Mutual Information described in section 3.1.

$$score(\ choice_i\ ) = \frac{nb(\ word\ NEAR\ choice_i\ )}{nb(\ choice_i\ )} \tag{1}$$

- $nb(x)$ computes the number of documents containing the word x,
- $NEAR$ (used in the "advanced research" field of AltaVista) is an operator that precises if two words are present in a 10 words wide window.

With this formula (1), the proportion of documents containing both *word* and $choice_i$ (within a 10 words window) is calculated, and compared with the number of documents containing the word $choice_i$. The higher this proportion is,

---

[1] http://www.altavista.com/

the more *word* and *choice$_i$* are seen as synonyms. More sophisticated formulas have also been applied: they take into account the existence of negation in the 10 words windows. For instance, the words "big" and "small" are not synonyms if, in a given window, a negation associated to one of these two words has been detected.

To enhance relevance to the document, our approach tries to take into account the dependencies between the words composing the possible expansions in order to rank them. In that sense, we are close to Daille's approach [7,8]. Also, as defended in next section, we use other quality measures and attempt to relate as much as possible to the context, in order to significatively enhance basic measures.

3 Defining the *AcroDef* Measure

To determine the expansion of an acronym starting from a list of co-occurrences of set of words, our aim is to provide a relevance ranking of this set using statistical measures. The most appropriate definition has to be placed at the top of the list. Therefore an overview of some existing measures is necessary to understand our choice.

3.1 Statistical Measures

Several quality measures in the literature are based on ranking function. They are brought out of various fields: Association rules detection [1,10], terminology extraction [8,13], and so forth. The following are the most widely used.

Mutual Information. One of the most commonly used measures to compute a sort of relationship between the words composing what is called a **co-occurrence** is Church's Mutual Information (MI). The formula is the following [6]:

$$I(x,y) = \log_2 \frac{P(x,y)}{P(x)P(y)} \tag{2}$$

Such a measure tends to extract rare and specific co-occurrences according to [8,13,16]. Let us notice that in this formula (2), the use of the log_2 function is not mandatory, since the latter is strictly growing. Thus, the order of the co-occurrences provided by the measure is not impacted by the application of function log_2. In the case of acronyms expansion, $P(x,y)$ measures the probability of finding couples of words (x,y) where x and y are neighbors, and in this order. For instance, with the acronym IR, x might represent the word "Information" and y the word "Retrieval". It might also be a pair such as "Investor" and "Relations". When simplified, the formula (2) could be written as follows, where nb designates the number of occurrences of words and couples of words:

$$IM(x,y) = \log_2 \frac{nb(x,y)}{nb(x)nb(y)} \tag{3}$$

This measure might be adapted to ternary co-occurrence in the way described by Jacquemin [9]. So, a natural extension of this measure would be applied to acronyms expansions that are composed of n words (formula (4)).

$$IM(x_1, ..., x_n) = \log_2 \frac{nb(x_1, ..., x_n)}{nb(x_1) \times ... \times nb(x_n)} \qquad (4)$$

Cubic Mutual Information. The Cubic Mutual Information is an empirical measure based on MI, that enhances the impact of frequent co-occurrences, something which is absent in the original MI [7]. Such as measure is defined by the following formula (5). Vivaldi *et al.* have estimated that the Cubic MI was the best behaving measure [18].

$$IM3(x, y) = \log_2 \frac{nb(x, y)^3}{nb(x)nb(y)} \qquad (5)$$

This measure is used in several works related to noun or verb terms extraction in texts. As for MI, the measure could be extended as follows:

$$IM3(x_1, ..., x_n) = \log_2 \frac{nb(x_1, ..., x_n)^3}{nb(x_1) \times ... \times nb(x_n)} \qquad (6)$$

Dice's Coefficient. An interesting quality measure is Dice's coefficient [15]. It is defined by the following formula (7).

$$D(x, y) = \frac{2 \times P(x, y)}{P(x) + P(y)} \qquad (7)$$

Similarly to the Cubic MI, Dice's coefficient weakens the impact of rare and often irrelevant co-occurrences [14]. Formula (7) leads directly to formula (8).[2]

$$Dice(x, y) = \frac{2 \times nb(x, y)}{nb(x) + nb(y)} \qquad (8)$$

In Petrovic *et al.*'s article [12], the authors present an extension of the original Dice formula to three elements:

$$Dice(x, y, z) = \frac{3 \times nb(x, y, z)}{nb(x) + nb(y) + nb(z)} \qquad (9)$$

In a natural way, we could extend the preceding formula to n elements as follows:

$$Dice(x_1, ..., x_n) = \frac{n \times nb(x_1, ..., x_n)}{nb(x_1) + ... + nb(x_n)} \qquad (10)$$

We call it **the n extended Dice's formula**. The three measures presented before, MI, Cubic MI and Dice's Coefficient, are important for our measure *AcroDef* characterization. The two following subsections (3.2 and 3.3) describe *AcroDef* in its both variants: The basic measure and the contextual one. *AcroDef* uses Dice's coefficient. Subsection 3.4 shows another variant of *AcroDef* that involves the two other measures MI and Cubic MI.

---

[2] By writing $P(x) = \frac{nb(x)}{nb\_total}$, $P(y) = \frac{nb(y)}{nb\_total}$, $P(x, y) = \frac{nb(x,y)}{nb\_total}$.

3.2 Basic *AcroDef* Measure

Since our work, like many others, relies on Web resources, the nb function used in the preceding measures represents the number of pages provided by the search engine Exalead (http://www.exalead.fr/). The choice of Exalead has been determined by the fact that our test corpus, as explained in section 4 is built out of the Google search engine resulting pages (http://www.google.com/). It was important not to introduce a bias due to a particular engine.

Starting from the n extended Dice's formula (10), and using statistics provided by search engines we propose the basic *AcroDef* measure (formula (11)).

$$BasicAcroDef_{Dice}(a^j) = \frac{\left|\{a_i^j|a_i^j \notin M_{tools}\}_{i\in[1,n]}\right| \times nb(\bigcap_{i=1}^n a_i^j)}{\sum_{i=1}^n nb(a_i^j|a_i^j \notin M_{tools})} \text{ where } n \geq 2 \quad (11)$$

- $\bigcap_{i=1}^n a_i^j$ represents the set of words a_i^j ($i \in [1,n]$) seen as a string (using *brackets* with Exalead and illustrated as follows: $"a_1^j...a_n^j"$).
- M_{tools} is a set of tool-words (prepositions, determiners, etc.). The idea is to detect the pages containing these words as such, since they are not semantically discriminant.
- $|.|$ represents the number of words of the set.

Since we ran most of our experiments in French, we used the acronym "JO" as a basic example. With $a =$ JO, two definitions are available on http://www.sigles.net/:

a^1: **Jeux Olympiques** (Olympic Games) and a^2: **Journal Officiel** (Official Journal)

Let us precise that the resulting pages numbers with both definitions are:

- $a_1^1 \cap a_2^1 =$ **Jeux** $\cap$ **Olympiques**: $366,508$ resulting pages
- $a_1^2 \cap a_2^2 =$ **Journal** $\cap$ **Officiel**: $603,036$ resulting pages

As a matter of fact, the IR acronym has given the following results on the same site:

1. IR^1: **Initiative Républicaine** (Republican Initiative). Domains: *Politics, society*. Language: French.
2. IR^2: **Impôt sur le Revenu** (Income Tax). Domains: *Finance, tax*. Language: French.
3. IR^3: **Infrarouge** (Infrared). Domains: *Research, sciences*. Language: French.
4. IR^4: **Insuffisance Rénale** (Renal Insufficiency). Domains: *Health, sciences*. Language: French.
5. IR^5: **Investor Relations**. Domains: *Communication, finance*. Language: English.
6. all other listed elements contain IR as a subchain either in the acronym or in its expansion.

Let us note that **Information Retrieval** does not appear on this Acronym Dictionary Portal as a well known expansion for IR. This means that domain dependent acronyms really need to be associated to an ontological choice, something that is discussed in the perspectives section of this paper.

Back to our example with "JO", the obtained values with the *BasicAcroDef* formula (11) are very close.[3]

- $BasicAcroDef_{Dice}(\text{JO}^1) = \frac{2 \times nb(\textbf{Jeux} \cap \textbf{Olympiques})}{nb(\textbf{Jeux}) + nb(\textbf{Olympiques})} = \frac{2 \times 366508}{116929964 + 1207545} = 0.0062$

- $BasicAcroDef_{Dice}(\text{JO}^2) = \frac{2 \times nb(\textbf{Journal} \cap \textbf{Officiel})}{nb(\textbf{Journal}) + nb(\textbf{Officiel})} = \frac{2 \times 603036}{178302348 + 28140994} = 0.0058$

Practically this comes back to submitting the three following queries to Exalead: `"Jeux Olympiques"` (Jeux $\cap$ Olympiques), `Jeux` and `Olympiques`. Let us note that more pages result from the query `"Journal Officiel"`, whereas the highest score is obtained with the expansion `"Jeux Olympiques"`.

In languages like French, many noun phrases contain tool words such as determiners or prepositions, and thus, several acronym expansions will be composed of such elements. So, when the definition of an acronym contains a tool word, it is neglected in the formula denominator.

This basic formula does not take the context into account. This is a severe limitation. Therefore, next subsection details a measure that relies on context to define a more relevant expansion choice for a given acronym.

3.3   Contextual *AcroDef* Based on Dice's Coefficient

In this paper, we define the **context** as a set of significant words present in the page where the acronym to expand is found. Of course, other definitions of the context notions have to be considered as extensions to this preliminary approach. However, even in this restricted point of view, several operational expressions of the context could be used:

- the n most frequent words (excepting tool words);
- the n most frequent proper name;
- the n most rare words;
- grammatical (part-of-speech tag) [3] or terminological information [2,8,13] present in the surroundings of the considered item.

A combination of these expressions could also be envisaged. The experiments presented in this article (section 4) use a context represented by the most frequent words, and give satisfying results. Other experiments using several contexts will be proposed in a future work.

Adding contextual information to *BasicAcroDef* (formula (11)) leads to formula (12). The principle underlying this formula is to apply statistical measures on a set of words of a given domain. So, the goal is not to count the dependency between the words of an acronym definition and those of the context, but to restrict the searching space. This restriction is a requirement for the word dependency computation (and not otherwise). The formula is written as follows:

$$AcroDef_{Dice}(a^j) = \frac{\left| \{ a_i^j + C | a_i^j \notin M_{tools} \}_{i \in [1,n]} \right| \times nb(\bigcap_{i=1}^{n} a_i^j + C)}{\sum_{i=1}^{n} nb(a_i^j + C | a_i^j \notin M_{tools})} \tag{12}$$

$$\text{where } n \geq 2$$

---

[3] Queries submitted in December 2006.

In this formula, $a_i^j + C$ represents the pages containing the word a_i^j with all the words of the context C. For this we use the Exalead AND operator. If we take our example $a =$ JO with its two possible expansions (Jeux Olympiques and Journal Officiel), the favored definition with $BasicAcroDef$ is still Jeux Olympiques since it scores 0.0062 against the 0.0058 value for Journal Officiel. If we take as a first context the following $C = \{$loi$\}$ (meaning *law*) then in this case we have:

- $AcroDef_{Dice}(\text{JO}^1) = \frac{2 \times nb((\text{Jeux} \cap \text{Olympiques}) + \text{loi})}{nb(\text{Jeux} + \text{loi}) + nb(\text{Olympiques} + \text{loi})} = 0.018$

- $AcroDef_{Dice}(\text{JO}^2) = \frac{2 \times nb((\text{Journal} \cap \text{Officiel}) + \text{loi})}{nb(\text{Journal} + \text{loi}) + nb(\text{Officiel} + \text{loi})} = 0.159$

Now, the choice of Dice's coefficient for $AcroDef$ either basic or contextual could be questioned as such. Dice's coefficient is known to favor frequent associations, but so does the Cubic MI. And what about MI in the case of acronym expansions? What are its advantages or liabilities? These questions have lead us to attempt a comparison between fundamental measures as variables in the $AcroDef$ quality metrics and is the subject of the following subsection.

3.4   An MI and Cubic MI Based $AcroDef$

In order to provide comparisons between basic measures, the formulas (13) and (14) define the $AcroDef$ measures, respectively based on MI and Cubic MI.

$$AcroDef_{IM}(a^j) = \frac{nb(\bigcap_{i=1}^n a_i^j + C)}{\prod_{i=1}^n nb(a_i^j + C | a_i^j \notin M_{tools})} \text{ where } n \geq 2 \tag{13}$$

$$AcroDef_{IM3}(a^j) = \frac{nb(\bigcap_{i=1}^n a_i^j + C)^3}{\prod_{i=1}^n nb(a_i^j + C | a_i^j \notin M_{tools})} \text{ where } n \geq 2 \tag{14}$$

These different measures that are language independent are tested in the following section dedicated to the experimentation of $AcroDef$ on real data.

4   Experiments

The application, programmed in Perl, contains different parameters, that are: The number of words in the context C, the tool words list, the different quality measures. The following subsections describe the experimental protocol implemented for the system evaluation, with a corpus of a sensible length (see section 4.1) manually built, and a large corpus (see section 4.2). The first is a pre-evaluation corpus, evaluating the feasibility of the method and the measures soundness, and the second is a real "live" corpus, which results correspond to what is expectable from our system.

4.1   Experimenting on a Manually Built Corpus for a Pre-evaluation

To test both feasibility and soundness, we have focused on the study of the "JO" French-based acronym explained before. We have browsed a set of a 100

Web pages containing this acronym, split into 50 pages with "JO" abbreviating `Journal Officiel`, and the 50 remaining for `Jeux Olympiques`. These pages have been obtained as a result of several manual queries with Google's search engine. They contain no expansion of the "JO" acronym, as required for our working hypothesis.[4]

The first task was to clean the corpus by removing the HTML tags and the tool words, deleting punctuation marks and various special characters. Then, to evaluate the various measures defined before, we built the *contingency evaluation matrix* provided in table 1.

Table 1. Contingency evaluation matrix

		Real	
		Journal Officiel	Jeux Olympiques
Prediction	Journal Officiel	a	c
	Jeux Olympiques	b	d

where

- a is the number of pages correctly predicted with the expansion `Journal Officiel`,
- b is the number of pages predicted with the expansion `Jeux Olympiques` but which real expansion is `Journal Officiel`,
- c is the number of pages predicted with the expansion `Journal Officiel` but which real expansion is `Jeux Olympiques`,
- d is the number of pages correctly predicted with the expansion `Jeux Olympiques`.

The system quality is measured by estimating the **error ratio** (ER) corresponding to the number of ill-classified pages divided by the total number of predictions, $ER = \frac{b+c}{a+b+c+d}$. For instance, when using only the *BasicAcroDef* formula (based on Dice's coefficient, and without context) (formula (11)), the best score is always obtained with the `Jeux Olympiques` expansion (see section 3.2). This implies that all pages are classified into the category "Olympic Games", and thus leads to an error ratio of 50% (with $b = d = 50$ and $a = c = 0$). This is why we suggest to use a context composed of one to three words (the most frequent words, different from tool words, in every page). Restricting the evaluation to a maximum of three words context is motivated by the fact that with four words, many queries get no pages as a result.

The results of this preliminary experiments are detailed in table 2. This test set has required 1800 queries to the Exalead search engine[5] with 6 queries per page and 3 test sets of 100 pages each. The workload for building such a test set is heavy and explains why, as a first exploratory task, we restricted our preliminary evaluation to one acronym.

---

[4] We have used for this the subfield "pages containing none of the following words" of the "advanced research" Google functionality.

[5] Experiment lead in December 2006.

Table 2. Error ratio on a pre-evaluation test corpus of 100 Web pages (acronym "JO")

	1 word Context	2 words Context	3 words Context
$AcroDef_{IM}$	47%	45%	42%
$AcroDef_{IM3}$	26%	14%	8%
$AcroDef_{Dice}$	29%	16%	9%

Table 2 shows that measure with a low error ratio are Cubic MI and Dice's Coefficient (as expected). However, the use of both measures is here context-dependent, and the larger the context is, the better the measure behaves. A three words context has a low error ratio with Cubic MI and Dice's measure (respectively 8% and 9%). Most classification errors are caused by the most frequent words that are not related to the domain (words like "tomorrow", "july", "France", etc.). Further, cleaning the HTML pages might be difficult in some cases and might also provoke errors in the expansion prediction.

However, this first evaluation is interesting because it highlights two phenomena:

- It definitely dismisses a simple MI measure, regardless of any context: The error ratio with such a measure is 3 to 5 times the error ratios of its fellow measures.
- The context width has a significant impact on results and the best measures (Cubic MI and Dice) are more sensitive to it than MI.

Since an error ratio of 8% corresponds to a success ratio of 92% then it seems that *a Cubic MI with a three words context might be the best quality measure for an acronym expansion candidate*, when this expansion is absent from the considered document.

This "conclusion" seen as working hypothesis needs to be reinforced. So we tested the three measures on a much larger scale to see whether it still holds. Next section presents an experiment on 1303 texts.

4.2   Experimenting on a Larger Corpus

For this experiment we have used a corpus provided by the Evaluation Conference DEFT'06 (*DÉfi Fouille de Textes*, meaning *Text Mining Challenge*), which is a francophone equivalent of the TREC Conferences. This second edition of the Text Mining Challenge consisted in providing a thematic text segmentation for French written corpora belonging to various domains (politics, law, science). We particularly focused on the law corpus, composed of law articles of the European Union.[6] The 1303 articles (11 Mb) containing the JO acronym are selected. This acronym is generally used in this corpus to refer to precise articles of the Official Journal (for example, references "JO 308 du 18.12.1967" or "JO no L 249 du

---

[6] Corpus available at the following address:
http://www.lri.fr/ia/fdt/DEFT06/corpus/donnees.html

8.9.1988" where JO acronym is not defined). For every law article, we measure if the JO acronym has to be associated with the **Journal Officiel** expansion by using the *AcroDef* measures. Table 3 details the error ratios obtained with this corpus, with a context width varying from one to three words. In this experiment we had to submit 23,454 queries computed as such: 1303 articles, 6 queries per article and 3 test sets for the three context width values (one to three words).

Table 3. Error ratios of the three *AcroDef* measures and the three context widths, using DEFT06 law corpus

	Number of correctly associated acronyms	*ER*
1 word Context		
DefAcro$_{IM}$	190	85.4%
DefAcro$_{IM3}$	1040	20.2%
DefAcro$_{Dice}$	842	35.4%
2 words Context		
DefAcro$_{IM}$	434	66.7%
DefAcro$_{IM3}$	1234	5.3%
DefAcro$_{Dice}$	1200	7.9%
3 words Context		
DefAcro$_{IM}$	650	50.1%
DefAcro$_{IM3}$	1281	1.7%
DefAcro$_{Dice}$	1274	2.2%

Table 3 shows that our method improves its results on a large corpus: With the DEFT06 corpus, the obtained results are very satisfying with our best error ratios around 2%. The context width impact is confirmed: Errors are significantly reduced with a 2 or 3 words context. Moreover, the capabilties of Cubic MI and Dice's coefficient are also confirmed over simple MI: With a 3 words context, their error ratios are respectively 1.7% and 2.2%. These two measures favor frequent co-occurrences. In our case, the number of Web pages sharing an expansion associated to a relevant context is important. As a consequence, a high score is given to measures that return a high number of pages.

One of the possible explanations for such good results on this corpus could be related to the specificity of the DEFT06 corpus: It belongs to a given domain, and the most frequent words constituting contexts are representative of the domain of law. Whereas the pre-evaluation corpus pages, derived from the Web directly through queries, could show up some ambiguities (for instance, texts dealing with the economical consequences of Olympic Games). However, experiments tend to show that, whatever the nature of the corpus is, the *AcroDef* measures with Cubic MI and Dice's coefficient are rather efficient and meaningful.

4.3 Extending Experimentation to Different Couples of Acronyms/Definitions

Ambiguous acronyms are naturally very frequent, and this first study with the French ambiguous "JO" acronym has lead us to attempt a further investigation about the acronyms of the principal French political parties (as one knows, they are rather numerous). The goal of it was to examine the various quality measures with a variable number of suggested definitions. Moreover, the acronyms could be built out of several words (and not only two as in our first set of experiments).

To start the process, we have imported different definitions for the acronyms LCR, PCF, PS, UDF, UMP, FN on the site http://www.sigles.net/ to build an "acronym thesaurus." Without any specific context, these acronyms are naturally recognized by people as political parties names. These definitions are detailed in table 4.[7] The political parties names are in bold.

Table 4. French Political Parties Acronyms Expansions. The parties full names are in bold.

Political acronyms	Expansions	
LCR	**Ligue Communiste Révolutionnaire**	Lettre de Change Relevé
PCF	**Parti Communiste Français**	Paysage Cinématographique Français
	Paysage Culturel Français	Press Club de France
PS	**Parti Socialiste**	Post Scriptum
	Police Secours	Poste de Secours
	Prise de Sang	Premier Secours
	Préfecture de la Sarthe	Préfecture de la Savoie
	Préfecture de la Somme	Passage Supérieur
UDF	**Union pour la Démocratie Française**	Union des Dentistes Français
UMP	**Union pour un Mouvement Populaire**	Urgences Médicales de Paris
FN	**Front National**	Fabrique Nationale
	Fondation Napoléon	

Then we have sent queries to the Google search engine with each of the acronyms and select pages that do not contain their expansions. Then, for each acronym, we have manually extracted the first sites belonging to political parties (about ten per acronym). We have then computed the error rate of this test corpus in order to estimate the number of pages not associated to the definition in the political domain. The obtained results validate these low error rates obtained in the precedent experiments, even with a reduced number of context words. As an example, with a one word context only, the error ratio is less than 4% with the Cubic MI *AcroDef* measure.

5   Conclusion and Perspectives

Acronyms are widely used words that act as proper names for organizations or associations, or as shortcuts in denominating very frequent concepts or notions.

---

[7] The acronyms UDF and UMP having only one expansion on this site, we have explored the Web to find other sites with other definitions.

As such, they are representative of the named entities issue under study in the text mining scientific community. Acronyms recognition is one part of the issue, but ambiguous acronyms expansion, especially when the acronym definition is not present in the considered document, is another. This article offers a set of quality measures to determine the choice of the best expansion for an acronym not defined in the Web page that uses it, the *AcroDef* measure. The method uses statistics computed on Web pages to determine the appropriate definition. Measures are deeply **context-based** and rely on the assumption that the most frequent words in the page are related semantically or lexically to the acronym expansion. The first results are very satisfactory since the relevant acronym expansion is found in 92 to 98% of the time, with a context of three words.

Even few, the errors are explained by the fact that they originate from too general words within contexts. If the most frequent words in the page are highly polysemous, too widely used, or vague, this has an impact on the best expansion choice, since the semantic constraint is looser. If the corpus in which acronyms have to be expansed belongs to a given domain, an interesting perspective would be to use as heuristics domain-based descriptors (proper names, terms), or even better, a domain ontology. As an example, the very specific proper name "Beijing", if added to the measure context, could be very relevant to find pages on Olympic Games (to characterize the Olympic Games in China in 2008). The proper name "China" would be also appropriate but "Beijing" strikes better.

Every method has its limitations and needs to be enhanced. This approach has difficulties in building a context for *AcroDef* when the Web page in which the acronym has been found only contains a short text (a few lines for instance). Context extraction relies on words frequency as a cornerstone for thematic detection, and if words are not numerous, frequency becomes meaningless. An interesting perspective would be to represent documents as semantic vectors defined in [5] to get a thematic information on the text. These vectors project the document on a Roget-based ontology and thus do not need quantities of words to sketch a thematic environment for the acronym. That complementary information, associated with *AcroDef*, would help predicting acronym definitions in the case of short texts.

References

1. Azé, J., Kodratoff, Y.: A study of the effect of noisy data in rule extraction systems. In: Proceedings of EMCSR'02, vol. 2, pp. 781–786 (2002)
2. Bourigault, D., Jacquemin, C.: Term extraction + term clustering: An integrated platform for computer-aided terminology. In: Proceedings of the European Chapter of the Association for Computational Linguistics, pp. 15–22 (1999)
3. Drill, E.: Some advances in transformation-based part of speech tagging. In: AAAI, vol. 1, pp. 722–727 (1994)
4. Chang, J., Schtze, H., Altman, R.: Creating an online dictionary of abbreviations from medline. Journal of the American Medical Informatics Association 9, 612–620 (2002)
5. Chauché, J.: Détermination sémantique en analyse structurelle: une expérience basée sur une définition de distance. In: TA Information, pp. 17–24 (1990)

6. Church, K.W., Hanks, P.: Word association norms, mutual information, and lexicography. Computational Linguistics 16, 22–29 (1990)
7. Daille, B.: Approche mixte pour l'extraction automatique de terminologie: statistiques lexicales et filtres linguistiques. PhD thesis, Université Paris 7 (1994)
8. Daille, B.: Study and Implementation of Combined Techniques for Automatic Extraction of Terminology. In: The Balancing Act: Combining Symbolic and Statistical Approaches to Language, pp. 49–66. MIT Press, Cambridge (1996)
9. Jacquemin, C.: Variation terminologique: Reconnaissance et acquisition automatiques de termes et de leurs variantes en corpus. In: Mémoire d'Habilitation à Diriger des Recherches en informatique fondamentale, Université de Nantes (1997)
10. Lallich, S., Teytaud, O.: Evaluation et validation des règles d'association. Numéro spécial Mesures de qualité pour la fouille des données, Revue des Nouvelles Technologies de l'Information (RNTI), RNTI-E-1 pp. 193–218 (2004)
11. Larkey, L.S., Ogilvie, P., Price, M.A., Tamilio, B.: Acrophile: An automated acronym extractor and server. In: Proceedings of the Fifth ACM International Conference on Digital Libraries, pp. 205–214. ACM Press, New York (2000)
12. Petrovic, S., Snajder, J., Dalbelo-Basic, B., Kolar, M.: Comparison of collocation extraction measures for document indexing. In: Proc of Information Technology Interfaces (ITI), pp. 451–456 (2006)
13. Roche, M., Azé, J., Kodratoff, Y., Sebag, M.: Learning interestingness measures in terminology extraction. a roc-based approach. In: Proceedings of ROC Analysis in AI Workshop (ECAI 2004), pp. 81–88 (2004)
14. Roche, M., Kodratoff, Y.: Pruning Terminology Extracted from a Specialized Corpus for CV Ontology Acquisition. In: Meersman, R., Tari, Z. (eds.) On the Move to Meaningful Internet Systems 2006: CoopIS, DOA, GADA, and ODBASE. LNCS, vol. 4276, pp. 1107–1116. Springer, Heidelberg (2006)
15. Smadja, F., McKeown, K.R., Hatzivassiloglou, V.: Translating collocations for bilingual lexicons: A statistical approach. Computational Linguistics 22(1), 1–38 (1996)
16. Thanopoulos, A., Fakotakis, N., Kokkianakis, G.: Comparative Evaluation of Collocation Extraction Metrics. In: Proceedings of LREC'02, pp. 620–625 (2002)
17. Turney, P.D.: Mining the Web for synonyms: PMI–IR versus LSA on TOEFL. In: Flach, P.A., De Raedt, L. (eds.) ECML 2001. LNCS (LNAI), vol. 2167, pp. 491–502. Springer, Heidelberg (2001)
18. Vivaldi, J., Màrquez, L., Rodríguez, H.: Improving term extraction by system combination using boosting. In: Proceedings of the 12th European Conference on Machine Learning (ECML), pp. 515–526 (2001)
19. Yeates, S.: Automatic extraction of acronyms from text. In: New Zealand Computer Science Research Students' Conference, pp. 117–124 (1999)

Risk Context Effects in Inductive Reasoning: An Experimental and Computational Modeling Study

Kayo Sakamoto and Masanori Nakagawa

Tokyo Institute of Technology, 2-21-1 O-okayama, Meguro-ku, Tokyo, 152-8552, Japan
{sakamoto.k.ad, nakagawa.m.ad}@m.titech.ac.jp

Abstract. Mechanisms that underlie the inductive reasoning process in risk contexts are investigated. Experimental results indicate that people rate the same inductive reasoning argument differently according to the direction of risk aversion. In seeking to provide the most valid explanation of this, two kinds of models based on a Support Vector Machine (SVM) that process different knowledge spaces are proposed and compared. These knowledge spaces—a feature-based space and a category-based space—are both constructed from the soft clustering of the same corpus data. The simulation for the category-based model resulted in a slightly more successful replication of experimental findings for two kinds of risk conditions using two different estimated model parameters than the other simulation. Finally, the cognitive explanation by the category-based model based on a SVM for contextual inductive reasoning is discussed.

Keywords: inductive reasoning, categorization, risk, natural language processing, corpus-based conceptual clustering, Support Vector Machines.

1 Introduction

This study deals with one kind of inductive reasoning argument (e.g., Rips, 1975; Osherson, Smith, Wilkie, Lopez, and Shafir, 1990), such as:

> The person likes wine.
> The person doesn't like beer.
> The person likes champagne.

In this type of argument, its strength (the likelihood of the conclusion below the line given the premises above the line) depends mainly on the entities in each sentence (e.g., "wine", "beer", "champagne") since these sentences share the same basic predicate (e.g., "The person likes ~." and "The person doesn't like ~.").

However in real-world situations, even reasoning-based behavior that involves such a simple argument evaluation can entail some element of risk context. For example, the relatively straightforward situation of giving somebody a present involves some risk. Even if you knew that the person in question likes wine but not beer, could you reasonably infer their reactions toward receiving a bottle of champagne from you? If the person were a close friend, they would be unlikely to

B. Kokinov et al. (Eds.): CONTEXT 2007, LNAI 4635, pp. 425–438, 2007.

take offense if they do not like champagne. Therefore, in this situation, you would be fairly safe in inferring that the person "probably" likes champagnes. On the other hand, when faced with the risk of upsetting your boss, which could have more serious consequences, you might make a different inference, telling yourself how "unlikely" it is that the boss likes champagne. In these different risk contexts, the argument strength should be evaluated differently, which means that human ratings of the argument strength are by nature context-dependent. This study examines the impact of risk contexts on inductive reasoning. While several studies have naturally discussed the context-dependency of inductive reasoning argument (e.g., [3]), they have only addressed the issue with identical entity sets and by changing the predicate. Accordingly, they claim that the information required for similarity computation differs for different predicates, that is, different semantic contexts. The present study, however, reports that identical arguments (consisting of the same premise and conclusion propositions) are rated differently in different situational contexts. Thus, the findings from this study indicate that people modify the same similarity information necessary to rate argument strengths according to the given situational context, which results in different ratings. Especially, the situational contexts treated in the present study entail 'concocted' social evaluations in which argument ratings are scored, and each score is set up to imply the argument rater's social ability. In such a situational context, people tend to avoid the risk of low evaluation about his/her 'concocted' social ability. The present study clarifies the effect of such risk contexts on inductive reasoning argument ratings.

The outline of this study is as follows: First, an experiment is described which indicates that people rate the same inductive reasoning arguments differently according to the direction of risk aversion. Then, two kinds of models based on Support Vector Machine (SVM) which differ in how they explain the mechanisms underlying people's performance in the experiment are proposed and simulation results are compared in terms their fit to the data. Finally, we argue that inductive reasoning in risk contexts is best explained by a category-based model based on SVM which adjusts the similarities for positive premise entities, negative premise entities, and conclusion entities.

2   Experiment

An experiment was conducted to examine whether people's ratings for inductive reasoning arguments are influenced by risk aversion strategies concerning social evaluations. Specifically, we compare participant's ratings under two distinct risk conditions: in the over-estimation risk condition, over-estimated ratings of the argument's likelihood entail a score-decreasing risk, while in the under-estimation risk condition under-estimated ratings entail a score- decreasing risk.

2.1   Method

2.1.1   Participants
77 Japanese undergraduate students, of which 34 were assigned to the over-estimation risk condition, with the remaining 43 being assigned to the under-estimation risk condition.

2.1.2 Task and Condition

The experimental task was rating the likelihood of inductive reasoning arguments on a 7-point scale (e. g., [13], [11]). Unlike the usual inductive reasoning task, each rating was scored according to the variation from a 'concocted' right answer. If a rating corresponded to this right answer, it would score perfectly. In the over-estimation risk condition, as the likelihood rating increased relative to the right answer, the reduction to the score also increased. Conversely, in the under-estimation risk condition, as the likelihood rating decreased relative to the right answer, the more the reduction to the score increased. Score allocations for each condition are shown in Table 1. Participants were told a cover story that their scores imply the person's social ability. In the end of the experiment, the participant's total score rank in the all participants.

Table 1. Allocation of scores in each risk condition

	over 3 points over-estimating	2 points over-estimating	1 point over-estimating	corresponds to the right answer
UNDER	add 0	add 35	add 65	add 100
OVER	minus 100	minus 65	minus 35	add 100

	1 point under-estimating	2 points under-estimating	over 3 points under-estimating
UNDER	minus 35	minus 65	minus 100
OVER	add 65	add 35	add 0

2.1.3 Materials

In the experiment, 4 sets of inductive reasoning arguments were used. Each set contains 8 arguments, and each argument consists of 2 positive premises, one negative premise, and a conclusion. In the 8 arguments of one set, all premises were fixed and combined with each of the 8 conclusions. The premise and conclusion statements all consisted of a combination of a predicate (*Mr. A likes '~'*) and an entity (e. g., *steak*), such as *"Mr. A likes steak."* In the case of negative premises, the predicate involved a negative verbal form, such as *"Mr. A doesn't like Japanese noodles."* The positive and negative premise entities and the conclusion entities in each argument set were selected from those in [15] and [16]. The first of these earlier studies verified that participants can discriminate corpus-derived latent categories in their rating of inductive reasoning arguments, while the second examined whether participants can distinguish between entities of the same latent category based on similarities with positive premise entities or negative premise entities. Those previous studies, however, did not consider the contextual conditions. Accordingly, the concocted right answer for each argument was assigned by referring to stable rating data from the previous studies.

2.1.4 Procedure

All the experimental procedure was controlled in a web application executed in Internet Explorer 6.0 (see Figure 1). Participants joined in the experiment as an exercise in a web application class. The procedure of the web application included an instruction section, 4 argument rating sections, and a final ranking announcement. In the instruction section, participants are given an overview of the experiment: a cover story concerning its purpose (to measure social abilities to guess the preferences of another person), the flow of experiment, and the scoring/ranking system according to each risk condition. During the first argument rating section, unlike the later sections, rating feedback was given. This included the right answer, the participant's rating, the difference between the rating and the right answer, the participant's current score, and the current maximum score. At the end of the first rating section, the participant's were told their interim score and a false ranking (this was the same for all participants). During the subsequent rating sections no rating feedback was provided apart from the interim score which was presented at the end of each section. After all the rating sections were completed, the experiment ended when the participants had been given their final scores and actually computed rankings, followed by debriefing concerning the experiment.

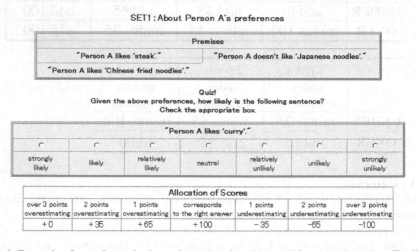

Fig. 1. Example of experiment in the under-estimation risk condition (translated into English)

2.2 Results

Only the data from the three subsequent rating sections (without feedback) were analyzed in terms of differences between the two conditions. Ratings on the 7-point scale were translated into numerical scales (-3 ~ 3). The average ratings over the 3 sets of arguments (24 arguments) were 0.014 (under-estimation risk condition) and -0.138 (over-estimation risk condition) respectively, differing significantly between the two conditions ($p<0.01$). In general, the same tendency was observed for each argument set. These results suggest that participants' ratings are affected by the risk situation: in the over-estimation risk condition, ratings tended to be lower because of the strategy to avoid making over-estimations that might incur a score decrease, while the participant ratings in the under-estimation risk condition tended to be higher due to the strategy to avoid under-estimations that might incur score decrease.

3 Model

3.1 Model's Assumption

The processes of inductive reasoning addressed in this study are assumed to involve a kind of similarity-based temporal categorization that utilizes stable semantic knowledge. For example, the temporal category that "*Mr. A likes*" can be formed from positive and negative premise entities (e. g., "*Mr. A likes steak*", "*Mr. A doesn't like Japanese noodle*" → "*steak*" and "*Japanese noodle*") and applied in making estimations about the likelihood of the conclusions (e. g., "*Mr. A likes pork*" → highly likely) based on the similarity of "*pork*" with "*steak*" and the dissimilarity with "*Japanese noodle*". As Ashby and Maddox [1] propose, the assumptions for a categorization model may consist of three components: internal representation assumptions, retrieval assumptions, and response selection assumptions. The model in this present study also makes three assumptions.

3.1.1 The Internal Representation Assumption
This assumption explains the way in which the stimuli and the contrasting categories (in this study, corresponding to negative premise entities) are represented. In the present model, the entities of premises and conclusions are assumed to be prototypes in a knowledge space ([2]). Previous modeling studies for inductive reasoning have proposed two kinds of knowledge representation in broad terms. One is based on *features* (e.g., [19]), the other is based on *existing categories* ([11], [18]). It is important to compare simulation outcomes concerning these two hypotheses about knowledge representation in terms of their relative data fit. However, feature-based prototype spaces and category-based spaces tend to be difficult to construct for practical simulations: they require a prohibitively large set of feature rating data (number of entities × number of features) for feature-based spaces, and huge numbers of similarity rating data (number of entity combinations) for category-based spaces constructed from category memberships. Accordingly, these previous inductive reasoning models have only been investigated for restricted domains (e.g., animal domain). In contrast to many other inductive reasoning models, the feature space and the category-based space for the present model are therefore constructed from corpus-analysis results that provide feature information and category membership information for an enormous quantity of words.

3.1.2 The Retrieval Assumption
This assumption provides a description of the information that must be collected before a response can be made. For example, the similarity computation between the premise and conclusion entities should be described in terms of this kind of assumption. In the present model, the similarities between the premise and conclusion entities are described by a nonlinear function of simple Euclidean

distances. Previous prototype models have been criticized for their inabilities to resolve the XOR category structure (e.g., [9]]). However, several works have recently shown that nonlinear functions for psychological distances can be a solution to the complex category structures in the prototype model (e.g., [16], [8]). The proposed models in this study have Support Vector Machine (SVM) structures that utilize a kernel method ([21]). Specifically, the kernel functions are assumed to be the nonlinear similarity functions between premise and conclusion entities. Thus, these proposed models show that people can temporally discriminate natural language concepts within a complex semantic structure according to various combinations of positive and negative premise entities (see also [16]).

3.1.3 The Response Selection Assumption

This provides a description about how people select a response after all the relevant information has been collected. In the present model, participants' responses (argument ratings) are assumed to be influenced by the desire to optimize response utility, that is, to choose a response that might not lead to score decreases. Since score decreases might cause the low evaluation of the participant's ability, he/she tries to avoid such a score decreasing risk by adjusting the relevant information collected for the task response. The present model represents such a contextual adjustment by the parameters that denote the balance between the similarities with positive premises and the similarities with negative premises. Specifically, the similarity between positive premise entities and the conclusion and the similarity between negative premise entities and the conclusion are adjusted by these parameters to yield an "optimal" response for the given risk context. The notion of adjusted similarity is frequently seen in earlier categorization models. However, most of those models can be interpreted as the results of selective attention to "context-appropriate" dimensions or features in order to make similarity estimations (e. g., [6], [10], [8], cf. an empirical study, [3]). Thus, the contexts treated in these previous studies are only "semantic" ones. Rather, in the present model, the response decision is assumed to be based on similarity estimations which are themselves biased by "situational" contexts that leads to the participant's risk aversion strategies.

3.2 Model Construction

3.2.1 A Corpus Analysis for Feature-Based and Category-Based Space Construction

Based on the above-mentioned internal representation assumptions, the results of [16]'s soft-clustering analysis of a Japanese corpus were utilized in the construction of a feature-based space to represent premise and conclusion entities, by computing the conditional probabilities of feature words given nouns as the strengths of the relationships between those nouns (entities) and those features. Their method of soft-clustering was similar in structure to popular methods of natural language processing, such as Pereira's method and PLSI ([4], [5], [12]). This method assumes that the co-occurrence probability of a term "N_i" and a term "A_j", $P(N_i, A_j)$, can be represented as equation (1):

$$P(N_i, A_j) = \sum_k P(N_i \mid C_k) P(A_j \mid C_k) P(C_k) \tag{1}$$

where $P(N_i|C_k)$ is the conditional probability of term N_i, given the latent semantic class C_k. Each of the probabilistic parameters in the model, $P(C_k)$, $P(N_i|C_k)$, and $P(A_j|C_k)$ are estimated as values that maximize the likelihood of co-occurrence data measured from a corpus using the EM algorithm ([5]). In this study, the term "N_i" represents a noun, and the term "A_j" represents a feature word, such as a predicate. The number of latent classes was fixed at 200.

For the actual estimations, the word co-occurrence frequencies used were extracted from Japanese newspaper articles, covering a ten-year span (1993-2002) of the Mainichi Shimbun. This co-occurrence frequency data consists of combinations of 21,205 nouns and 83,176 predicates in modification relations. CaboCha ([7]), a Japanese analysis tool for modification relations, was used for extraction.

From the estimated parameters $P(C_k)$, $P(N_i|C_k)$, and $P(A_j|C_k)$, it is possible to compute the conditional probabilities of feature words given particular nouns as follows:

$$P(A_j \mid N_i) = \frac{\sum_k P(A_j \mid C_k) P(N_i \mid C_k) P(C_k)}{\sum_k P(N_i \mid C_k) P(C_k)}, \tag{2}$$

In this study, this conditional probability $P(A_j \mid N_i)$ is assumed as the strengths of the relationships between features and entities. When a certain feature word has a high conditional probability given a particular noun, it is natural that the entity denoted by the noun has the feature indicated by the feature word. Thus, by considering each A as a feature dimension, entities can be represented in the feature-based space constructed from the corpus-analysis results.

From the estimated parameters $P(C_k)$, $P(N_i|C_k)$, it is also possible to compute the membership distribution $P(C_k| N_i)$ as follows:

$$P(C_k \mid N_i) = \frac{P(N_i \mid C_k) P(C_k)}{P(N_i)} = \frac{P(N_i \mid C_k) P(C_k)}{\sum_k P(N_i \mid C_k) P(C_k)}, \tag{3}$$

In this study, the latent class C_k is assumed to be a category that can be described in terms of a typicality gradient ([14]). In fact, most of the estimated latent classes were identified as meaningful categories, as shown in Table 2.

3.2.2 Inductive Reasoning Models Based on Support Vector Machine
Based on the above-mentioned internal representation assumption, retrieval assumption and the response selection assumption, two kinds of models based on Support Vector Machine (SVM: [21]) are proposed. One processes the feature-based representations, while the other processes the category-based representations. Each model has an almost identical structure to that in [16]. The likelihood of a conclusion including entity N_i^c, denoted as $v(N_i^c)$, is represented by the following discrimination function constructed from an SVM based on Gaussian kernel functions:

$$v(N_i^c) = a \, \text{SIM}_+(N_i^c) + b \, \text{SIM}_-(N_i^c) \tag{4}$$

Table 2. Examples of estimated classes and their representative members

Category of Foods (c1)		Category of Valuable assets (c2)		
	P(c1|ni)			P(c2|ni)
1 steak	0.876	1	stock	0.929
2 set meal	0.867	2	government bonds	0.862
3 grain foods	0.811	3	estate	0.791
4 vegetable soup	0.817	4	building estate	0.780
5 meat	0.739	5	real estate	0.757
6 curry	0.734	6	cruiser	0.662
7 Chinese noodle	0.720	7	farmland	0.657
8 pizza	0.716	8	foreign bond	0.628
9 barleycorn	0.594	9	house	0.594
10 rice cake	0.555	10	currency	0.555

where

$$\mathrm{SIM}_+\left(N_i^c\right) = \sum_j^{n^+} e^{-\beta d_{ij}^+}, \tag{5}$$

$$\mathrm{SIM}_-\left(N_i^c\right) = \sum_j^{n^-} e^{-\beta d_{ij}^-}, \tag{6}$$

for the feature-based version,

$$d_{ij}^+ = \sum_k^m \left(P\left(A_k \mid N_i^c\right) - P\left(A_k \mid N_j^+\right)\right)^2, \tag{7}$$

$$d_{ij}^- = \sum_k^m \left(P\left(A_k \mid N_i^c\right) - P\left(A_k \mid N_j^-\right)\right)^2. \tag{8}$$

for the category-based version,

$$d_{ij}^+ = \sum_k^m \left(P\left(C_k \mid N_i^c\right) - P\left(C_k \mid N_j^+\right)\right)^2, \tag{9}$$

$$d_{ij}^- = \sum_k^m \left(P\left(C_k \mid N_i^c\right) - P\left(C_k \mid N_j^-\right)\right)^2. \tag{10}$$

d_{ij}^+ and d_{ij}^- for the feature-based version are functions for word distance based on the feature words (denoted as A_k), while for the category-based version these are word-distance functions based on the latent classes (denoted as C_k). d_{ij}^+ represents the distance between the conclusion entity N_i^c and the positive premise entity N_j^+, while d_{ij}^- represents the distance between the conclusion entity N_i^c and the negative premise entity N_j^-. Here, the number of feature words m is fixed to 20 (out of 83,176), with the assumption that only characteristic feature dimensions for the concerned entities should be utilized. As for the number of categories, the number of categories m is fixed to 20 (out of 200). Each word distance function constructs Gaussian kernel functions, such as $SIM_+(N_i^c)$ and $SIM_-(N_i^c)$, when combined with nonlinear exponential functions and parameter β. For the feature-based version, 10^5 is applied to β, while 10^2 is applied for the category-based version. In this study, these Gaussian kernel functions are regarded as nonlinear similarity functions that reflect the retrieval assumption. $SIM_+(N_i^c)$ represents the similarities between the conclusion entity N_i^c and the positive premise entities, while $SIM_-(N_i^c)$ denotes the similarities between N_i^c and the negative premise entities. Furthermore, a and b are parameters that are estimated from the likelihood of each conclusion (ratings obtained from the experiment). In the present study, these parameters mirror the response selection assumption, and are assumed to play a role as similarity adjusters in making the "optimal" response to a given risk situation.

3.3 Simulations

3.3.1 Simulation Procedure
Simulations were conducted in order to examine the following validities:

I.   The validity of the internal representation assumption.
II.   The validity of the retrieval assumption.
III.   The validity of the response selection assumption.

In the case of (I), the validity of the knowledge space constructed from the corpus-analysis data has already been verified in [17], [15], and [16]. However, the relative validities of the feature-based space and the category-based space have not been sufficiently examined; to remedy that deficient, comparisons are made for how the models fit to the empirical data. In the case of (II), the validity of the nonlinear similarity function is examined. As in the case of (I), the fit between a model and the empirical data can be taken as an index of this validity. In the case of (III), the adjuster parameters for similarities are estimated for each risk condition. The estimated values of the adjuster parameters should be consistent with peoples' risk aversion strategies for each context.

3.3.2 Simulation Results
Table 3 shows the estimated adjuster parameters, a and b, the correlation coefficients between the experimental data and model output values, and the F ratios that

Table 3. Simulation results (**: $p<0.01$)

	Representations			
	Feature-based		**Category-based**	
	Risk conditions			
	UNDER	OVER	UNDER	OVER
parameter a	1.76	1.62	3.77	3.57
parameter b	-1.39	-1.66	-2.98	-3.40
$|b/a|$	0.79	1.02	0.79	0.95
correlation coefficient	**0.59	**0.61	**0.69	**0.71
F **ratio**	**7.26	**8.00	**12.18	**13.09

represent fitness indices for the two versions of the models for each risk condition. As the correlation coefficients and F ratios in this table show, the model estimations for both experimental conditions are significant, and are, therefore, consistent with the internal representation assumption and the retrieval assumption of the models. Specifically, the correlation coefficients of the category-based version are significantly higher than those of the feature-based version for both experimental conditions ($p>0.05$). Therefore, the category-based version shows a better level of fit than the feature-based version, indicating that the category-based representation hypothesis has a relatively higher level of validity. Moreover, the estimated values for parameter a are positive ($a > 0$) while the estimated values for parameter b are negative ($b < 0$) in both conditions for both versions. This is consistent with the model's assumption that the argument ratings are based on the similarities of conclusion entities with positive premise entities and the dissimilarities with negative premise entities. The absolute ratio of the estimated parameters ($|b/a|$) in the over-estimation risk condition is higher than in the under-estimation risk condition. This indicates that, in the proposed model, those parameters fulfill an adjustment role that can account for shifts in argument ratings under different risk conditions. Thus, the estimation results support the validity of the model's response selection assumption—that response decisions based on similarity estimations are biased by risk aversion strategies towards social evaluation contexts in which the participant's social ability is evaluated. In other words, participants in the over-estimation risk condition placed greater emphasis on the conclusion entities' dissimilarities with the negative premise than participants in the under-estimation risk condition. In the over-estimate risk condition, the "optimal" response is one that does not overly stress the conclusion entity's similarity with positive premises. On the other hand, under the under-estimation risk condition, the "optimal" response is the opposite of that in the other condition: namely, one that does not overly stress the conclusion entity's dissimilarity with negative premises.

4 Discussion

The present study adopts two approaches to examining inductive reasoning in risk contexts—an experimental study and the proposal and simulation of computational models. The results of the experiment suggest that peoples' ratings of an argument vary according to the risk context. Thus, when making an over-estimation would incur a risk of the score being reduced, people tend to rate arguments as being less "likely", while the same argument tend to be rated as being more "likely" when there is a risk of an under-estimation incurring the score decreasing. On the other hand, the results from simulations of the proposed models indicate that the model based on SVM that processes corpus-oriented categorical knowledge was more successful in replicating the empirical data than the model which processes corpus-oriented feature knowledge. The replication of empirical data for two kinds of risk conditions was achieved using two different estimated model parameters. Thus, the mechanisms that underlie inductive reasoning would seem to be based on category-based prototypical representations of conceptual knowledge, complex computations of similarity. Especially, the mechanism underlying the risk context effects in inductive reasoning is explained by similarity adjustment based on risk aversion strategies toward social evaluation contexts.

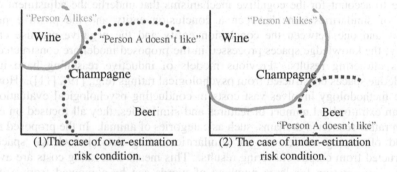

Fig. 2. Similarity adjustment for each risk condition

Figure 2 is a graphic representation of the similarity adjustment mechanism for both risk conditions based on ratings for the following argument:

> Person A likes wines.
> Person A doesn't like beers.
> Person A likes champagnes.

Note that the similarities between entities (distances in the graphic representation) do not change, but rather the response boundaries (the orange and green dashed lines) do change. These changes can be attributed to the difference in the absolute ratio for the estimated parameters $|b/a|$. The relative adjustment sizes (boundary sizes) for the temporal category of "Person A likes" and for the temporal contrast category of "Person A doesn't like" reflect the sizes of the ratio $|b/a|$. Since $|b/a|$ for the over-estimation risk condition is higher than that in the under-estimation risk condition, the relative adjustment size for the temporal category "Person A likes" in the over-estimation risk condition is smaller than that in the under-estimation risk condition. With such a mechanism, the conclusion "Person A likes champagnes" will be less "likely" in the over-estimation risk condition while being more "likely" in the under-estimation risk condition. This effect of different ratios $|b/a|$ is brought by people's risk aversion strategies toward social contexts in which his/her response based on inductive reasoning is evaluated.

This study addressing Rips's [13] types of inductive reasoning (called category-based induction or property induction) in risk contexts is particularly noteworthy in drawing together three particularly interesting interdisciplinary perspectives. First, the present study shows that an identical argument strength in inductive reasoning depends on the risk context that is incorporated as part of the experimental design. Previous studies regarding contextual inductive reasoning have only dealt with arguments that have identical entity sets by changing the predicates (e.g., [3], [20]). Second, the cognitive mechanisms that underlie our empirical findings can be clearly explained by a model based on SVM utilizing a kernel method that was originally inspired by mathematics (e.g., [21]). While it might also be possible to develop a multilayer neural network in order to adequately model inductive reasoning in risk contexts, if evaluated only in terms of data fitting, such a model would, however, be unable to account for the cognitive mechanisms that underlie the adjustment of two kinds of similarities—one between a conclusion entity and the positive premise entities and one between the conclusion entity and the negative premise entities. Finally, the knowledge spaces processed in the proposed model are constructed from corpus clustering results. Previous models of inductive reasoning have utilized knowledge spaces constructed from psychological ratings (e.g., [19], [11]). However, as the methodology involves vast costs in conducting psychological evaluations for such an extra-ordinal number of features and similarities, they all focused on entities within rather restricted domains, such as categories of animal. In the proposed model, instead of relying on features or similarities rating data, knowledge spaces are constructed from corpus-clustering results. This means that rating costs are avoided, because information for large numbers of words can be computed from a corpus. This makes it possible to conduct predictive simulations for many more conclusion entities than those used in the experiment in this paper. Moreover, these predictive simulations can be applied to constructing an induction-based search engine that searches concepts similar to positive examples and dissimilar from negative examples (cf., [15]). Furthermore, since the corpus-based methodology and the computational model treating contextual effects are combined, the present study can be applied to the 'contextual' induction-based search engine that provides appropriate search results to a given search context. For example, considering the previously mentioned situation when you knew that a person likes wine but not beer, and the risk of unsuitable search results is high (e.g., when you are thinking about a present for upsetting boss) this kind of search engine will provide a result eliminating champagne. On the other hand, for another searching situation when you are thinking about a present for your close friend, the search engine will provide a result including champagne. Therefore, the present study that draws together three interdisciplinary perspectives opens up an exiting application possibility.

Acknowledgments. This study was supported by the Tokyo Institute of Technology 21COE Program, "Framework for Systematization and Application of Large-scale Knowledge Resources". Furthermore, the authors would like to thank Dr. T. Joyce, a postdoctoral researcher with the 21COE-LKR, for his critical reading of our manuscripts and valuable comments on an earlier draft.

References

1. Ashby, F.G., Maddox, W.T.: Relations between prototype, examplar, and decision bound models of categorization. Journal of Mathematical Psychology 37, 372–400 (1993)
2. Hampton, J.A.: Polymorphous concepts in semantic memory. Journal of Verbal Learning and Verbal Behavior 18, 441–461 (1979)
3. Heit, E., Rubinstein, J.: Similarity and property effects in inductive reasoning. Journal of Experimental Psychology: Learning, Memory, and Cognition 20, 411–422 (1994)
4. Hofmann, T.: Probabilistic latent semantic indexing. In: Proceedings of the 22nd International Conference on Research and Development in Information Retrieval:SIGIR '99. pp. 50–57 (1999)
5. Kameya, Y., Sato, T.: Computation of probabilistic relationship between concepts and their attributes using a statistical analysis of Japanese corpora. In: Proceedings of Symposium on Large-scale Knowledge Resources: LKR2005 (2005)
6. Kruschke, J.K.: ALCOVE: An exemplar-based connectionist model of category learning. Psychological Review 99, 22–44 (1992)
7. Kudoh, T., Matsumoto, Y.: Japanese Dependency Analysis using Cascaded Chunking. In: Proceedings of the 6th Conference on Natural Language Learning: CoNLL 2002, pp. 63–39 (2002)
8. Matsuka, T., Nickerson, J.V., Jian, J.: A prototype model that learns and generalize Medin, Alton, Edelson, & Frecko (1982) XOR category structure as humans do. In: Proceedings of the Twenty-Eighth Annual Conference of the Cognitive Science Society (2006)
9. Medin, D.L., AltonM., W., Edelson, S.M., Freko, D.: Correlated symptoms and simulated medical classification. Journal of Experimental Psychology: Learning, Memory, and Cognition 8, 37–50 (1982)
10. Nosofsky, R.M.: Attention, similarity, and the identification categorization relationship. Journal of Experimental Psychology: General 115, 39–57 (1986)
11. Osherson, D.N., Smith, E.E., Wilkie, O., Lopez, A., Shafir, E.: Category-Based Induction. Psychological Review 97(2), 185–200 (1990)
12. Pereira, F., Tishby, N., Lee, L.: Distributional clustering of English words. In: Proceedings of the 31st Meeting of the Association for Computational Linguistics, pp. 183–190 (1993)
13. Rips, L.J.: Inductive judgment about netural categories. Journal of Verbal Learning and Verbal Behavior 14, 665–681 (1975)
14. Rosch, E.: On the internal structure of perceptual and semantic categories. In: Moore, T.E. (ed.) Cognitive Development and the Acquisition of Language, pp. 111–144. Academic Press, New York (1973)
15. Sakamoto, K., Terai, A., Nakagawa, M.: Computational Models of Inductive Reasoning and Their Psychological Examination: Towards an Induction-Based Search-Engine. In: Proceedings of the Twenty-Seventh Annual Conference of the Cognitive Science Society, pp. 1907–1912 (2005)

16. Sakamoto, K., Nakagawa, M.: The Effects of negative premise on Inductive reasoning: A psychological experiment and computational modeling study. In: Proceedings of the Twenty-Eighth Annual Conference of the Cognitive Science Society, pp. 2081–2086 (2006)
17. Sakamoto, K., Terai, A., Nakagawa, M.: Computational Models of Inductive Reasoning Using the Statistical Analysis of a Japanese Corpus. The Journal of Cognitive Systems Research (in press) (2007)
18. Sanjana, N.E., Tenenbaum, J.B.: Bayesian models of inductive generalization. In: Becker, S., Thrun, S., Obermayer, K. (eds.) Advances in Neural Processing Systems 15, MIT press, Cambridge, MA (2003)
19. Sloman, A.T.: Feature-Based Induction. Cognitive Psychology 25, 231–280 (1993)
20. Smith, E.E., Shafir, E., Osherson, D.: Similarity, plausibility, and judgment of probability. Cognition 49, 67–96 (1993)
21. Vapnik, V.: The Nature of Statistical Learning Theory. Springer, Heidelberg (1995)

Representing Context in Web Search with Ontological User Profiles

Ahu Sieg, Bamshad Mobasher, and Robin Burke

School of Computer Science, Telecommunication and Information Systems
DePaul University, Chicago, Illinois, USA
{asieg,mobasher,rburke}@cti.depaul.edu

Abstract. One of the key factors for effective personalization of information access is the user context. We propose a framework which integrates several critical elements that make up the user context, namely, the user's short-term behavior, semantic knowledge from ontologies that provide explicit representations of the domain of interest, and long-term user profiles revealing interests and trends. Our proposed approach involves implicitly building ontological user profiles by assigning interest scores to existing concepts in a domain ontology. These profiles are, therefore, maintained and updated as annotated instances of a reference domain ontology. We propose a spreading activation algorithm for maintaining the interest scores in the user profile based on the user's ongoing behavior. Our experimental results show that the user context can be effectively utilized for Web search personalization. Specifically, re-ranking the search results based on interest scores derived from the semantic evidence in an ontological user profile provides better search results by proficiently bringing results closer to the top when they are most relevant to the user.

1 Introduction

Web personalization alleviates the burden of information overload by tailoring the information presented based on an individual user's needs. One of the key factors for accurate personalized information access is user context. A system that does not know who is asking for information and for what purpose will never be able to provide more than very general answers.

Despite their popularity, users' interactions with Web search engines can be characterized as one size fits all [1]. The representation of user preferences, search context, or the task context is generally non-existent in most search engines. Indeed, contextual retrieval has been identified as a long-term challenge in information retrieval. Allan et al. [1] define the problem of *contextual retrieval* as follows: "Combine search technologies and knowledge about query and user context into a single framework in order to provide the most appropriate answer for a user's information needs."

Researchers have long been interested in the many roles of context in a variety of fields including artificial intelligence, context-aware applications, and

B. Kokinov et al. (Eds.): CONTEXT 2007, LNAI 4635, pp. 439–452, 2007.

information retrieval. The notion of *context* may refer to a diverse range of ideas depending on the nature of the work being performed. For example, context-aware mobile search is a search paradigm in which applications can discover and take advantage of contextual information such as user location, time of day, nearby people and devices, and user activity. In PC troubleshooting, context contains low-level state information of computers [2]. In text retrieval, context can be defined as a body of words surrounding a user-selected phrase [3].

While there are many factors that may contribute to the delineation of the user context, here we consider three essential elements that collectively play a critical role in personalized Web information access. These three independent but related elements are the user's short-term information need, such as a query or localized context of current activity, semantic knowledge about the domain being investigated, and the user's profile that captures long-term interests. Each of these elements are considered to be critical sources of contextual evidence, a piece of knowledge that supports the disambiguation of the user's context for information access.

In recent years, personalized search has attracted interest in the research community as a means to decrease search ambiguity and return results that are more likely to be interesting to a particular user and thus providing more effective and efficient information access [4,5,6,7]. In this paper, we present a novel approach for building ontological user profiles by assigning interest scores to existing concepts in a domain ontology. These profiles are maintained and updated as annotated specializations of a pre-existing reference domain ontology. We propose a spreading activation algorithm for maintaining the interest scores in the user profile based on the user's ongoing behavior.

Since the users' interests change over time, we focus on implicit methods for incrementally creating an ontological representation of user profiles. Utilizing annotations, such as an *interest score*, has proven to be successful for the evolution of personal ontologies [8]. Interest scores assigned to topics have also been utilized for taxonomy-driven profile generation in the context of e-commerce recommender systems [9]. Trajkova and Gauch [10] calculate the similarity between the Web pages visited by a user and the concepts in a domain ontology. After annotating each concept with a weight based on an accumulated similarity score, a user profile is created consisting of all concepts with non-zero weights. In our approach, the hierarchical relationship among the concepts is also taken into consideration for building the ontological user profile as we update the annotations for existing concepts using spreading activation.

An ontology is an explicit specification of concepts and relationships that can exist between them [11]. One increasingly popular method to mediate information access is through the use of ontologies [12,13]. Researchers have attempted to utilize ontologies for improving navigation effectiveness as well as personalized Web search and browsing, specifically when combined with the notion of automatically generating semantically enriched ontology-based user profiles [14,13].

Since semantic knowledge is an essential part of the user context, we use a domain ontology as the fundamental source of semantic knowledge in our framework. An ontological approach to user profiling has proven to be successful in addressing the *cold-start problem* in recommender systems where no initial information is available early on upon which to base recommendations [15]. When initially learning user interests, systems perform poorly until enough information has been collected for user profiling. Using ontologies as the basis of the profile allows the initial user behavior to be matched with existing concepts in the domain ontology and relationships between these concepts.

Our experimental results show that the user context can be effectively utilized for Web search personalization. Specifically, re-ranking the search results based on interest scores derived from the semantic evidence in an ontological user profile successfully provides the user with a personalized view of the search results by bringing results closer to the top when they are most relevant to the user.

2   Ontological User Profile as the Context Model

Our context model for a user is represented as an instance of a reference domain ontology in which concepts are annotated by *interest scores* derived and updated implicitly based on the user's information access behavior. We call this representation an *ontological user profile*. Figure 1 depicts a high-level picture of our proposed context model based on an *ontological user profile*.

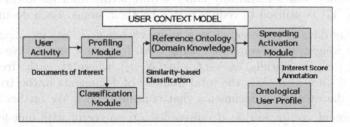

Fig. 1. Ontological User Profile as the Context Model

When disambiguating the context, the domain knowledge inherent in an existing reference ontology is called upon as a source of key domain concepts. The ontological user profile is initially an instance of the reference ontology. Each concept in the user profile is annotated with an *interest score* which has an initial value of one. As the user interacts with the system by selecting or viewing new documents, the ontological user profile is updated and the annotations for existing concepts are modified by spreading activation. Thus, the *user context* is maintained and updated incrementally based on user's ongoing behavior.

Accurate information about the user's interests must be collected and represented with minimal user intervention. This can be done by passively observing the user's browsing behavior over time and collecting Web pages in which the user has shown interest. Several factors, including the frequency of visits to a page, the amount of time spent on the page, and other user actions such as bookmarking a page can be used to automatically collect these documents [16].

Based on the user's behavior over many interactions, the *interest score* can be incremented or decremented based on contextual evidence. Once an *ontological user profile* is constructed, the underlying user context can then be utilized for a variety of information access activities such as searching, browsing, and filtering.

2.1   Representation of Reference Ontology

Our current implementation uses the *Open Directory Project*[1], which is organized into a hierarchy of topics and Web pages that belong to these topics. We utilize the Web pages as training data for the representation of the concepts in the reference ontology. The textual information that can get extracted from Web pages explain the semantics of the concepts and is learned as we build a term vector representation for the concepts.

We create an aggregate representation of the reference ontology by computing a term vector $\vec{n}$ for each concept n in the concept hierarchy. Each concept vector represents, in aggregate form, all individual training documents indexed under that concept, as well as all of its subconcepts.

We begin by constructing a global dictionary of terms extracted from the training documents indexed under each concept. A stop list is used to remove high frequency, but semantically non-relevant terms from the content. Porter stemming [17] is utilized to reduce words to their stems. Each document d in the training data is represented as a term vector $\vec{d} = \langle w_1, w_2, ..., w_k \rangle$, where each term weight, w_i, is computed using term frequency and inverse document frequency [18]. Specifically, $w_i = tf_i * \log(N/n_i)$, where tf_i is the frequency of term i in document d, N is the total number of documents in the training set, and n_i is the number of documents that contain term i. We further normalize each document vector, so that $\vec{d}$ represents a term vector with unit length.

The aggregate representation of the concept hierarchy can be described more formally as follows. Let $S(n)$ be the set of subconcepts under concept n as non-leaf nodes. Also, let $\{d_1^n, d_2^n, ..., d_{k_n}^n\}$ be the individual documents indexed under concept n as leaf nodes. $Docs(n)$, which includes of all of the documents indexed under concept n along with all of the documents indexed under all of the subconcepts of n is defined as:

$$Docs(n) = [\bigcup_{n' \in S(n)} Docs(n')] \cup \{d_1^n, d_2^n, ..., d_{k_n}^n\}$$

The concept term vector $\vec{n}$ is then computed as:

$$\vec{n} = \left[\sum_{d \in Docs(n)} \vec{d} \right] / |Docs(n)|$$

---

[1] http://www.dmoz.org

Thus, $\vec{n}$ represents the centroid of the documents indexed under concept n along with the subconcepts of n. The resulting term vector is normalized into a unit term vector.

2.2 Context Model

The initial user profile is essentially an annotated instance of the reference ontology. Each concept in the user profile is annotated with an *interest score*, which has an initial value of one. Figure 2 depicts a portion an ontological user profile corresponding to the node *Music*. The interest scores for the concepts are updated with spreading activation using an input term vector.

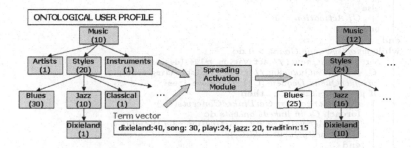

Fig. 2. Portion of an Ontological User Profile where Interest Scores are updated based on Spreading Activation

Each node in the ontological user profile is a pair, $\langle C_j, IS(C_j) \rangle$, where C_j is a concept in the reference ontology and $IS(C_j)$ is the interest score annotation for that concept. The input term vector represents the active interaction of the user, such as a query or localized context of current activity.

Based on the user's information access behavior, let's assume the user has shown interest in *Dixieland Jazz*. Since the input term vector contains terms that appear in the term vector for the *Dixieland* concept, as a result of spreading activation, the interest scores for the *Dixieland, Jazz, Styles*, and *Music* concepts get incremented whereas the interest score for *Blues* gets decreased. The *Spreading Activation* algorithm and the process of updating the interest scores are discussed in detail in the next section.

2.3 Updating User Context by Spreading Activation

We use *Spreading Activation* to incrementally update the *interest score* of the concepts in the user profiles. Therefore, the ontological user profile is treated as the semantic network and the interest scores are updated based on activation values.

Traditionally, the spreading activation methods used in information retrieval are based on the existence of maps specifying the existence of particular relations

Input: Ontological user profile with interest scores and a set of documents
Output: Ontological user profile concepts with updated activation values

$CON = \{C_1, ..., C_n\}$, concepts with interest scores
$IS(C_j)$, interest score
$IS(C_j) = 1$, no interest information available
$I = \{d_1, ..., d_n\}$, user is interested in these documents

foreach $d_i \in I$ do
    Initialize *priorityQueue*;
    foreach $C_j \in CON$ do
        $C_j.Activation = 0$; // Reset activation value

    end
    foreach $C_j \in CON$ do
        Calculate $sim(d_i, C_j)$;
        if $sim(d_i, C_j) > 0$ then
            $C_j.Activation = IS(C_j) * sim(d_i, C_j)$;
            $priorityQueue.Add(C_j)$;
        else
            $C_j.Activation = 0$;
        end
    end
    while $priorityQueue.Count > 0$ do
        Sort *priorityQueue*; // activation values(descending)
        $C_s = priorityQueue[0]$; // first item(spreading concept)
        $priorityQueue.Dequeue(C_s)$; // remove item
        if $passRestrictions(C_s)$ then
            $linkedConcepts = GetLinkedConcepts(C_s)$;
            foreach C_l in *linkedConcepts* do
                $C_l.Activation+ = C_s.Activation * C_l.Weight$;
                $priorityQueue.Add(C_l)$;
            end
        end
    end
end

Algorithm 1. Spreading Activation Algorithm

between terms or concepts [19]. Alani et al. [20] use spreading activation to search ontologies in Ontocopi, which attempts to identify communities of practice in a particular domain. Spreading activation has also been utilized to find related concepts in an ontology given an initial set of concepts and corresponding initial activation values [21].

In our approach, we use a very specific configuration of spreading activation, depicted in Algorithm 1, for the sole purpose of maintaining *interest scores* within a user profile. We assume a model of user behavior can be learned through the passive observation of user's information access activity and Web pages in which the user has shown interest in can automatically be collected for user profiling.

For each iteration, the algorithm has an initial set of concepts from the ontological user profile. These concepts are assigned an initial activation value. The main idea is to activate other concepts following a set of weighted relations during propagation and at the end obtain a set of concepts and their respective activations.

As any given concept propagates its activation to its neighbors, the weight of the relation between the origin concept and the destination concept plays an important role in the amount of activation that is passed through the network. Thus, a one-time computation of the weights for the relations in the network is

Input: Ontological user profile concepts with updated activation values
Output: Ontological user profile concepts with updated interest scores
$CON = \{C_1, ..., C_n\}$, *concepts with interest scores*
$IS(C_j)$, *interest score*
C_j.*Activation, activation value resulting from Spreading Activation*
k, constant

$n = 0$;
foreach $C_j \in CON$ **do**
   | $IS(C_j) = IS(C_j) + C_j$.*Activation*;
   | $n = n + (IS(C_j))^2$; // sum of squared interest scores
   | $n = \sqrt{n}$; // square root of sum of squared interest scores
end
foreach $C_j \in CON$ **do**
   | $IS(C_j) = (IS(C_j) * k)/n$; // normalize to constant length
end

Algorithm 2. Algorithm for the Normalization and Updating of Interest Scores in the Ontological User Profile

needed. Since the nodes are organized into a concept hierarchy derived from the domain ontology, we compute the weights for the relations between each concept and all of its subconcepts using a measure of containment. The containment weight produces a range of values between zero and one such that a value of zero indicates no overlap between the two nodes whereas a value of one indicates complete overlap.

The weight of the relation w_{is} for concept i and one of its subconcepts s is computed as $w_{is} = \frac{\vec{n}_i \cdot \vec{n}_s}{\vec{n}_i \cdot \vec{n}_i}$, where $\vec{n}_i$ is the term vector for concept i and $\vec{n}_s$ is the term vector for subconcept s. Once the weights are computed, we process the weights again to ensure the total sum of the weights of the relations between a concept and all of its subconcepts equals to 1.

The algorithm considers in turn each of the documents assumed to represent the current context. For each iteration of the algorithm, the initial activation value for each concept in the user profile is reset to zero. We compute a term vector for each document d_i and compare the term vector for d_i with the term vectors for each concept C_j in the user profile using a cosine similarity measure. Those concepts with a similarity score, $sim(d_i, C_j)$, greater than zero are added in a priority queue, which is in a non-increasing order with respect to the concepts' activation values. The activation value for concept C_j is assigned to $IS(C_j) * sim(d_i, C_j)$, where $IS(C_j)$ is the existing interest score for the specific concept. The concept with the highest activation value is then removed from the queue and processed. If the current concept passes through restrictions, it propagates its activation to its neighbors. The amount of activation that is propagated to each neighbor is proportional to the weight of the relation. The neighboring concepts which are activated and are not currently in the priority queue are added to queue, which is then reordered. The process repeats itself until there are no further concepts to be processed in the priority queue. The algorithm processes each edge only once. The interest score for each concept in the ontological user profile is then updated using Algorithm 2. First the resulting activation value is added to the existing interest score. The interest scores for all concepts are then treated as a vector, which is normalized to a unit length using a pre-defined constant, k, as the length of the vector. Rather than gradually increasing the interest scores, we utilize normalization so that the interest scores can get decremented as well as getting incremented. The concepts in the ontological user profile are updated with the normalized interest scores.

3   The Contextual Approach for Search Personalization

The Web search personalization aspect of our research is built on the previous work in ARCH [22]. In ARCH, the initial query is modified based on the user's interaction with a concept hierarchy which captures the domain knowledge. This domain knowledge is utilized to disambiguate the user context.

In the present framework, the *user context* is represented using an *ontological user profile*. The characterization of the user's information need and context is an important step towards the goal of information access, but it is only the first step. The accurate representation of the user's context must be turned into actions that assist the user in finding information. Our goal is to utilize the user context to personalize search results by re-ranking the results returned from a search engine for a given query. Figure 3 displays our approach for search personalization based on ontological user profiles.

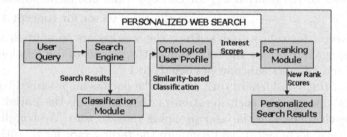

Fig. 3. Personalized Web Search based on Ontological User Profiles

Assuming an ontological user profile with interest scores exists and we have a set of search results, Algorithm 3 is utilized to re-rank the search results based on the interest scores and the semantic evidence in the user profile.

A term vector $\vec{r}$ is computed for each document $r \in R$, where R is the set of search results for a given query. The term weights are obtained using the *tf.idf* formula depicted in Section 2.1. In order to calculate the rank score for each document, first the similarity of the document and the query is computed using a cosine similarity measure. Then, we compute the similarity of the document with each concept in the user profile to identify the best matching concept. Once the best matching concept is identified, a rank score is assigned to the document by multiplying the interest score for the concept, the similarity of the document

Input: Ontological user profile with interest scores and a set of search results
Output: Re-ranked search results

$CON = \{C_1, ..., C_n\}$, *concepts with interest scores*
$IS(C_j)$, *interest score*
$R = \{d_1, ..., d_n\}$, *search results from query q*

foreach $d_i \in R$ **do**
    Calculate $sim(d_i, q)$;
    maxSim = 0;
    foreach $C_j \in CON$ **do**
        Calculate $sim(d_i, C_j)$;
        if $sim(d_i, C_j) \geq maxSim$ **then**
            (Concept)c = C_j;
            maxSim = $sim(d_i, C_j)$;
        end
    end
    Calculate $sim(q, c)$;
    if $IS(c) > 1$ **then**
        rankScore(d_i) = $IS(c) * \alpha * sim(d_i, q) * sim(q, c)$;
    else
        rankScore(d_i) = $IS(c) * sim(d_i, q) * sim(q, c)$;
    end
end
Sort R based on rankScore;

Algorithm 3. Re-ranking Algorithm

to the query, and the similarity of the specific concept to the query. If the interest score for the best matching concept is greater than one, it is further boosted by a tuning parameter α. Once all documents have been processed, the search results are sorted in descending order with respect to this new rank score.

4   Experimental Evaluation

Since the queries of average Web users tend to be short and ambiguous, our goal is to demonstrate that re-ranking based on ontological user profiles can help in disambiguating the user's intent particularly when such queries are used. We measure the effectiveness of re-ranking in terms of *Top-n Recall* and *Top-n Precision*.

4.1   Evaluation Methodology and Experimental Data Sets

As of December 2006, the *Open Directory* contained more than 590,000 concepts. For experimental purposes, we decided to use a branching factor of three with a depth of ten levels in the hierarchy. Our experimental data set contained 506 concepts in the hierarchy and a total of 8857 documents that were indexed under various concepts.

We processed the indexed documents into three separate sets including a *training set*, a *test set*, and a *profile set*. For each concept, we used 60 percent of the associated documents for the training set, 20 percent for the test set, and the remaining 20 percent for the profile set. For all of the data sets, we kept track of which concepts these documents were originally indexed under in the hierarchy. The *training set* was utilized for the representation of the reference ontology, the *profile set* was used for spreading activation, and the *test set* was utilized as the document collection for searching.

The *training set* consisted of 5157 documents which were used for the one-time learning of the reference ontology. The concept terms and corresponding term weights were computed using the formula described in Section 2.1.

Table 1. Sets of Keyword Queries Used in Experiments

Query	# of Terms	Criteria
Set 1	1	highest weighing term in concept term vector
Set 2	2	two highest weighing terms in concept term vector
Set 3	3	three highest weighing terms in concept term vector
Set 4	2 or more	overlapping terms within highest weighing 10 terms

A total of 1675 documents were included in the *test set*, which were used as the document collection for performing our search experiments. Depending on the search query, each document in our collection can be treated as a signal or a noise document. The signal documents are those documents relevant to a particular concept that should be ranked high in the search results for queries related to that concept. The noise documents are those documents that should be ranked low or excluded from the search results.

The *test set* documents that were originally indexed under a specific concept and all of its subconcepts were treated as signal documents for that concept whereas all other test set documents were treated as noise. In order to create an index for the signal and noise documents, a *tf.idf* weight was computed for each term in the document collection using the global dictionary of the reference ontology.

The *profile set* consisted of 2000 documents, which were treated as a representation of specific user interest for a given concept to simulate ontological user profiles. As we performed the automated experiments for each concept/query, only the profile documents that were originally indexed under that specific concept were utilized to build an ontological user profile by updating the interest scores with the spreading activation algorithm.

We constructed keyword queries to be able to run our automated experiments. We decided to extract the query terms from the concept term vectors in the ontology. Each concept term vector was sorted in descending order with respect to term weights. Table 1 depicts the four query sets that were automatically generated for evaluation purposes. Our keyword queries were used to run a number of automated search scenarios for each concept in our reference ontology. The first set of keyword queries contained only one term and included the highest weighing term for each concept. In order to evaluate the search results when a single keyword was typed by the user as the search query, the assumption was that the user was interested in the given concept.

The second set of queries contained two terms including the two highest weighing terms for each concept. The third set of queries were generated using the three highest weighing terms for each concept. As the number of keywords in a query increase, the search query becomes less ambiguous.

Even though one to two keyword queries tend to be vague, we intentionally came up with a fourth query set to focus specifically on ambiguous queries. We generated this query set by computing the overlapping terms using the highest weighing ten terms in each concept term vector. Only the overlapping concepts were included in the experimental set with each query consisting of two or more overlapping terms within these concepts.

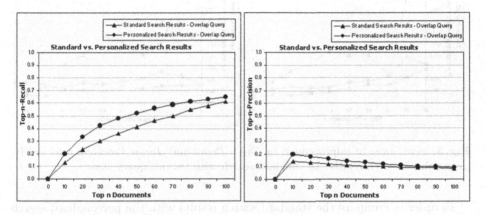

Fig. 4. Average *Top-n Recall* and *Top-n Precision* comparisons between the personalized search and standard search using "overlap queries"

Our evaluation methodology was as follows. We used the system to perform a standard search for each query. As mentioned above, each query was designed for running our experiments for a specific concept. In the case of standard search, a term vector was built using the original keyword(s) in the query text. Removal of stop words and stemming was utilized. Each term in the original query was assigned a weight of 1.0. The search results were retrieved from the test set, the signal and noise document collection, by using a cosine similarity measure for matching. Using an interval of ten, we calculated the *Top-n Recall* and *Top-n Precision* starting with the top one hundred results and going down to top ten search results. The *Top-n Recall* was computed by dividing the number of signal documents that appeared within the top n search results at each interval with the total number of signal documents for the given concept. We also computed the *Top-n Precision* at each interval by dividing the number of signal documents that appeared within the top n results with n.

Next, documents from the profile set were utilized to simulate user interest for the specific concept. For each query, we started with a new instance of the ontological user profile with all interest scores initialized to one. Such a user profile represents a situation where no initial user interest information is available.

We performed our spreading activation algorithm to update interest scores in the ontological user profile.

After building the ontological user profile, we sorted the original search results based on our re-ranking algorithm and computed the *Top-n Recall* and *Top-n Precision* with the personalized results.

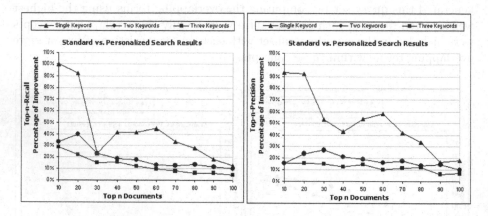

Fig. 5. Percentage of improvement in *Top-n Recall* and *Top-n Precision* achieved by personalized search relative to standard search with various query sizes

In order to compare the standard search results with the personalized search results, we computed the average *Top-n Recall* and *Top-n Precision*, depicted in Figure 4. Our evaluation results verify that using the ontological user profiles for personalizing search results is an effective approach. Especially with the overlap queries, our evaluation results confirm that the ambiguous query terms are disambiguated by the semantic evidence in the ontological user profiles.

We have also computed the percentage of improvement between standard and personalized search for *Top-n Recall* and *Top-n Precision*, depicted in Figure 5. The evaluation results show significant improvement in recall and precision for single keyword queries as well as gradual enhancement for two-term and three-term queries.

As a preliminary evaluation of stability for the user profiles, we used a single profile document for each concept and utilized that document as the input for the spreading activation algorithm for 15 rounds. We utilized the documents in the *profile set* for this experiment. For each concept, we used a profile document that was originally indexed under that specific concept, which we refer to as the signal concept. Our goal was to measure the change in interest scores. Every time a profile document is processed, the interest scores for the concepts in the ontological user profile are updated. Our expectation was that eventually the interest scores for the signal concept should become relatively stable. Figure 6 displays the percentage increase in average interest scores and demonstrates that user profiles potentially become stable.

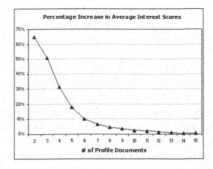

Fig. 6. The average rate of increase in *Interest Scores* as a result of incremental updates

5   Conclusions and Outlook

We have presented a framework for contextual information access using ontologies and demonstrated that the semantic knowledge embedded in an ontology combined with long-term user profiles can be used to effectively tailor search results based on users' interests and preferences. In our future work we plan to evaluate the stability and convergence properties of the ontological profiles as interest scores are updated over consecutive interactions with the system.

References

1. Allan, J., et al.: Challenges in information retrieval and language modeling. ACM SIGIR Forum 37(1), 31–47 (2003)
2. Wen, J., Lao, N., Ma, W.: Probabilistic model for contextual retrieval. In: Proceedings of the 27th Annual International ACM SIGIR Conference on Research and Development in Information Retrieval, SIGIR 2004, Sheffield, UK, pp. 57–63. ACM Press, New York (2004)
3. Finkelstein, L., Gabrilovich, E., Matias, Y., Rivlin, E., Solan, Z., Wolfman, G., Ruppin, E.: Placing search in context: The concept revisited. ACM Transactions on Information Systems 20(1), 116–131 (2002)
4. Singh, A., Nakata, K.: Hierarchical classification of web search results using personalized ontologies. In: Proceedings of the 3rd International Conference on Universal Access in Human-Computer Interaction, HCI International 2005, Las Vegas, NV (July 2005)
5. Shen, X., Tan, B., Zhai, C.: Ucair: Capturing and exploiting context for personalized search. In: Proceedings of the Information Retrieval In Context Workshop, SIGIR IRiX 2005, Salvador, Brazil (August 2005)
6. Aktas, M., Nacar, M., Menczer, F.: Using hyperlink features to personalize web search. In: Advances in Web Mining and Web Usage Analysis, Proceedings of the 6th International Workshop on Knowledge Discovery from the Web, WebKDD 2004, Seattle, WA (August 2004)
7. Liu, F., Yu, C., Meng, W.: Personalized web search for improving retrieval effectiveness. IEEE Transactions on Knowledge and Data Engineering 16(1), 28–40 (2004)

8. Haase, P., Sure, Y., Hotho, A., Schmidt-Thieme, L.: Usage-driven evolution of personalized ontologies. In: Proceedings of the 3rd International Conference on Universal Access in Human-Computer Interaction, HCI International 2005, Las Vegas, NV (July 2005)
9. Ziegler, C., Lausen, G., Schmidt-Thieme, L.: Taxonomy-driven computation of product recommendations. In: ACM International Conference on Information and Knowledge Management, CIKM 2004, Washington, DC (November 2004)
10. Trajkova, J., Gauch, S.: Improving ontology-based user profiles. In: Proceedings of the Recherche d'Information Assistée par Ordinateur, RIAO 2004, University of Avignon (Vaucluse), France pp. 380–389 (April 2004)
11. Gruber, T.R.: Towards principles for the design of ontologies used for knowledge sharing. In: Formal Ontology in Conceptual Analysis and Knowledge Representation, Deventer, The Netherlands (1993)
12. Haav, H., Lubi, T.: A survey of concept-based information retrieval tools on the web. In: 5th East-European Conference, ADBIS 2001, Vilnius, Lithuania, pp. 29–41 (2001)
13. Ravindran, D., Gauch, S.: Exploting hierarchical relationships in conceptual search. In: Proceedings of the 13th International Conference on Information and Knowledge Management, ACM CIKM 2004, Washington DC, ACM Press, New York (2004)
14. Gauch, S., Chaffee, J., Pretschner, A.: Ontology-based personalized search and browsing. Web Intelligence and Agent Systems 1(3-4) (2003)
15. Middleton, S., Shadbolt, N., Roure, D.D.: Capturing interest through inference and visualization: Ontological user profiling in recommender systems. In: Proceedings of the International Conference on Knowledge Capture, K-CAP 2003, Sanibel Island, Florida, pp. 62–69 (2003)
16. Dumais, S., Joachims, T., Bharat, K., Weigend, A.: Implicit measures of user interests and preferences. ACM SIGIR Forum 37(2) (2003)
17. Porter, M.: An algorithm for suffix stripping. Program 14(3), 130–137 (1980)
18. Salton, G., McGill, M.: Introduction to Modern Information Retrieval. McGraw-Hill, New York (1983)
19. Salton, G., Buckley, C.: On the use of spreading activation methods in automatic information. In: Proceedings of the 11th annual international ACM SIGIR conference on Research and Development in Information Retrieval, SIGIR 1988, Grenoble, France, pp. 147–160. ACM Press, New York (1988)
20. Alani, H., O'Hara, K., Shadbolt, N.: Ontocopi: Methods and tools for identifying communities of practice. In: Proceedings of the IFIP 17th World Computer Congress - TC12 Stream on Intelligent Information Processing, Deventer, The Netherlands, The Netherlands, pp. 225–236 (2002)
21. Rocha, C., Schwabe, D., de Aragao, M.P.: A hybrid approach for searching in the semantic web. In: Proceedings of the 13th international conference on World Wide Web, WWW 2004, New York, USA, pp. 374–383 (2004)
22. Sieg, A., Mobasher, B., Lytinen, S., Burke, R.: Using concept hierarchies to enhance user queries in web-based information retrieval. In: Proceedings of the International Conference on Artificial Intelligence and Applications, IASTED 2004, Innsbruck, Austria (February 2004)

Thai Text Coherence Structuring with Coordinating and Subordinating Relations for Text Summarization

Thana Sukvaree[1], Asanee Kawtrakul[1], and Jean Caelen[2]

[1] Department of Computer Engineering, Kasetsart University, Bangkok, Thailand
thanas_spu@hotmail.com, asanee.kawtrakul@nectec.or.th
[2] Laboratory CLIPS, University of Joseph Fourier, Grenoble Cedex 9, France
jean.caelen@imag.fr

Abstract. Text summarization with the consideration of coherence can be achieved by using discourse processing with the Rhetorical Structure Theory (RST). Additional problems on relational ambiguity may arise, especially in Thai. For example, the use of cue words, i.e. "tae/แต่" (meaning "but"), can be identified as a contrast relation or an elaboration relation. Therefore, we propose the reduction of the ambiguity level by reducing the relation types to two, namely Coordinating and Subordinating relation. Our framework is to concentrate on coherence structuring which requires the following 3 steps: (1) identify an attachment point for an incoming discourse unit by using our Adaptive Right-frontier algorithm; (2) extract Coordinating and Subordinating relations through the identification of linguistic coherence features in the lexical and phrasal level, using Bayesian techniques; (3) construct coherence tree structures, The accuracy is 70.45% for the first step, 77.47% and 79.89% for COR and SUBR extraction respectively in the second step and 64.94% in constructing coherent tree of the third.

1 Introduction

Nowadays, there is a high need for automatic text summarization, which is recognized as one of the solutions to tackle the problem of overwhelming amounts of available information. Research in automatic text summarization still requires further developments. Recent research works on the matter focused on the identification of more relevant information from the text to project in the summary. There are two main approaches in achieving this problem: statistical-based approach and knowledge-based one. The statistical-based approach[1,2] often gives incoherent results, which causes further misunderstandings by humans. By contrast, the knowledge-based approach takes this problem into consideration and uses methods of salience extraction from the structure of text representation which is expressed in the form of discourse relation, but requires strong knowledge in creating the text structure[3,4] with the assumption of the result from the salience extraction remaining the same from the source text.

B. Kokinov et al. (Eds.): CONTEXT 2007, LNAI 4635, pp. 453–466, 2007.

In various research papers in summarization, the Rhetorical Structure Theory (RST)[5], is often used to extract salience through the application of knowledge-based approach at discourse level[3,4]. This theory includes explanations on the occurrence of discourse relations and text generation by using tree structures. However, if the RST is used, problems of relation ambiguity would have to be accounted for[6,7]. One cause of ambiguity is that there are too many rhetorical relations to be classified accurately because the definitions are rather vague and do not provide concrete linguistic criteria to look out for in text. Therefore, in our research, we reduce the number of discourse relations to only two Coordinating relation and Subordinating relation according to the Segmented Discourse Representation Theory (SDRT)[8] . Furthermore, we propose a method for constructing a simplified discourse structure by using the right frontier constraint of Polanyi[9] together with the discourse dependency function called "adaptive right frontier". This should produce a discourse structure sufficient to increase the quality of text summarization.

In Section 2 we give a brief overview of the theoretical concepts which bear on our topic. In section 3, we argue the crucial problems in the construction of the discourse trees. Section 4 presents our solution and we describe experiments and results in Section 5. In section 6, we show that the outcome of this research has positive effects on text summarization. Our conclusions are summarized in Section 7.

2   Preliminary

Mann and Thompson[5] have introduced the RST by classifying rhetorical relations (RR) into two categories, namely a paratactic (multi-nucleus) relation and a hypotactic (mono-nucleus) relation[3]. A paratactic relation is defined to be a relationship that exists between two discourse units (du) which have the same value of interest. A hypotactic relation can be defined as a relationship that exists between discourse units where the value of interest is inequivalent. These two types of relation play a role as nuclearity functions for salience extraction in text summarization. By a Nucleus (N), we mean a discourse unit which is more important or has more value of interest. A Satellite (S) is a discourse unit that contains less value of interest. See example in Text-1 and Fig. 1.

Example-1 [Text-1]

S1: The Brown hopper likes to live in the bottom area of the rice plant
S2: and infest the sap in that area
S3: rice plant shows symptoms of dried leaf as if it has been boiled or burnt
S4: which is called "symptom of inconsistent burning".

Because RST proposes too many possible relation such as Elaboration, Explanation, Cause-result, Conditional, Contrast, Sequence, Consequence, Joint, List, Background etc., it is difficult to specify the relations to generate a rhetorical structure. The root of this problem stems from the vagueness of the definition

Table 1. Rhetorical relations classified as paratactic relations and hypotactic relations

Types	Rhetorical Relations
Paratactic (COR)	List, Joint, Cause-Result, Problem-Solution, Topic-Shift, Contrast, ...
Hypotactic (SUBR)	Elaboration, Background, Justify, Evidence, Condition, Explanation, Consequence, Question-Answer, ...

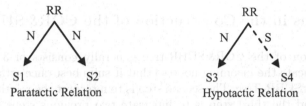

Fig. 1. Paratactic and hypotactic relations in RST

of RST relations. Thus, in this research, we propose to reduce the number of relations to only two, namely subordinating and coordinating relations. These two relations have been well studied in [9,8], A relation $R(\alpha, \beta)$ between α and β is called subordinating if β adds something to what is said in α so that the information expressed by β is in a sense more granular than the information expressed by α. If $R(\alpha, \beta)$ is not subordinating relation then it is the coordinating relation. In addition to these two relations, we would also take nuclearity into account.

If RR is the main set for this discourse rhetorical relation and if we work in accordance with the RST theory, then we would have the following set:

RR = {Elaboration, Cause-Result, Condition, List, Joint, Contrast, Explanation, Evidence, ...}

When considering the way in which we decide over the subsets of RR to be either the Coordinating relation (COR) or Subordinating relation (SUBR), we can make the following subsets (see Table 1).

We obtain two relations: coordination and subordination (Fig. 2.), including all the rhetorical relations in the RST[?]. Thus this concept transforms a space of intentional relations (RST) to the space of coherence relations in the SDRT.

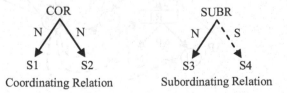

Fig. 2. Coordinating and Subordinating relations with nuclearity

It has the advantage to reduce the complexity of the RR interpretation, e.g. transforming Fig. 1 into Fig. 2. We will elaborate this concept later.

In general, when we take the discourse unit in the tree structure with two discourse relations, following the RST theory, we call this COR&SUBR-tree. The leaves of the tree (the tree end-nodes) comprise of grammatical structures that are elementary discourse units[3] and the internal parts of the tree structure contain relations that exist between the small discourse unit and the complex discourse segment.

3   Problems in the Construction of the COR&SUBR-Tree

The construction of the COR&SUBR-tree generally consists of 3 steps. The first one is to locate the incoming node so that it suits best once attached to the previous COR&SUBR-Tree. The second step is to interpret the relations existing in the text. And the third step is to integrate two previous steps to build up coherent tree. Problems occurring in each step are discussed in the next section.

3.1   Identifying the Connection Between an Incoming Node and the Previous Discourse Tree

This problem is from the point of view of matching, a problem of incoming node (INC) considered to be a part of previous discourse tree (PDT) as in Fig. 3. A possible Attachment Point (AP) that connects the incoming node (INC) with PDT tree consists of AP1, AP2, AP3, AP4 and AP5. Different attachment points will result in different discourse tree structures. This will affect the extract of discourse tree which will cause incorrect text summary.

When considering time complexity of all possible positions, we see that it is in $O(n^2)$. However, this problem can be solved by using Right Frontier algorithm[9] together with linguistic information which decreases time complexity into linear order that we will discuss later.

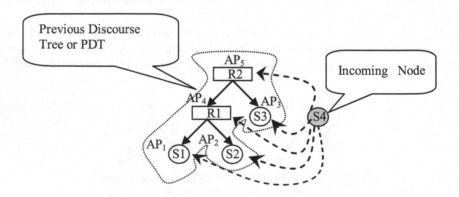

Fig. 3. The possibly APs for S4 attach to PDT

3.2 Problem of Ambiguity in Interpretation of the Discourse Relation

Interpretation of the discourse relation can be in various forms[3,5,6,7]. For example, there are two ways to interpret the discourse in text-1: [S1, S2] is the cause of [S3, S4] which denoted by CR[JT[S1, S], EB[S3, S4]] or the other way is [S3, S4] is a consequence of [S1, S2] which denoted by CSQ[JT[S1,S2], EB[S3,S4]].

Although, T1 and T2 are the same structure but the top label relations of each tree are different in nuclearity, CR (Cause-Result) is multi-nucleus, CSQ (Consequence) is mono-nucleus. If we extract salience from these then will be produced summary in different set.

Our work proposes a solution to those problems by the reduction of relations using a transformation from an n-dimensional space of traditional rhetorical relations into a 2-dimensional space of COR and SUBR. We classify any paratactic relations in RST to coordinating relation in SDRT and classify the hypotactic relations in RST to subordinating relation in SDRT.

The problems of attachment point and ambiguity of discourse relation will affect the extract of salience of text summary from Fig. 3. and Fig. 4. instead of RST tree. The former problem will create different tree structures. The latter will affect nuclearity of RST tree specification which is essential for selecting salience from RST tree. In order to generate the coherent tree, we propose solution to the above problems in the next section.

4 Solution

We describe our solution to discourse tree generation in 2 parts.

4.1 Identifying the Attachment Point of an Appropriate Incoming Node to PDT

This problem is an attachment point problem. The traditional Right Frontier Constraint: RFC[9] only concerns with the anaphoric pronoun. Consequently, RFC cannot solve some of our problems. For example, an incoming EDU (elementary discourse unit[3]) becomes a new topic of content or the segment, and the attachment point does not locate in the right frontier area in PDT[10] Also

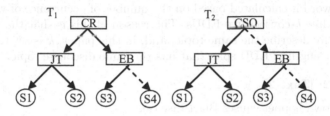

Fig. 4. The problems of multiple interpretations between textual [S1, S2] and [S3, S4]

it could happen that the incoming discourse unit does not have any anaphoric pronoun. Therefore, we propose the algorithm of using Adaptive Right Frontier (ARF) which combines the discourse dependency function (DDF) with the RFC in order to cover these three phenomena.

The DDF is considered having 3 linguistic parameters: Content Relevant (CV), Discourse Marker (DM) and Anaphoric Expression (AE). We use a linear combination model to formulate this function. Let x be a node in PDT, and y be the incoming discourse unit. We define:

$$DDF(x, y) = \alpha CV(x, y) + \beta DM(x, y) + \gamma AE(x, y) \qquad (1)$$

where α, β and γ are weighting constants. To determine whether the incoming discourse unit is a new segment or not, the node in PDT that has maximum value is tested against a predefined threshold, δ. Specifically, if $max_{x \in PDT} DDF(x, y) \geq \delta$, the incoming node will be a node in PDT; otherwise, it will becomes a new segment.

How to compute the parameter of the coherence dependency function: CV, DM and AE

CV (Content Relevance)

Content Relevance is a measurement of the relationship between discourse unit pair whose value is computed form discourse context. Conceptually, we want the high value of CV to mean that discourse unit pair describes the same topic and, vice versa, the low value of CV to mean that they describe different topics. Thus, the value of CV is one component to decide whether the new coming discourse unit should create a new segment or not. To compute this, we define

$$CV(x, y) = sim(f_x, f_y)$$

where f_x and f_y are the foci of the discourse unit x in PDT and the incoming discourse unit discourse unit y respectively. According to B.J. Grosz[11], we use the NP (noun phrase) that precedes the main verb or the agent which has the highest potential of the discourse entities as a focus of the discourse unit. The similarity between the foci f_x and f_y is then computed by using the cosine of the angle between the word vectors in the vector space model[12]. For a fixed collection of corpus, a m-dimensional vector is generated for each word, where m is the number of unique noun word in the corpus. The weight associated with each noun word is calculated based on the number of occurrence of word w_i and w_j in the same k-consecutive EDUs. The reason of this is that the consecutive EDUs usually describe the same topic, and, in this paper, k is set to 3 which is the average length of EDU span that has the same discourse topic.

Example-2: [Text-2]

S1: The Brown hopper causes Blast disease,
S2: especially, this disease always occurs in summer.

S3: spay the insecticide only in the morning,
S4: don't spray the insecticide in the evening.

To compute the word similarity in example 2, we firstly create a set of important words of the corpus which are "Brown hopper", "Blast disease", "summer", "Insecticide", "morning", and "evening". Then, the 6-dimentional vector is generated for each word w_i. The value of j-th dimension is generated by counting the number of time w_i appear together with w_j in the same k-consecutive EDUs; for example, the number of time the word 'summer' appears in the same 3-consecutive EDUs with the word 'morning' is 2 (S1:S2:S3 and S2:S3:S4) and the number of time the word 'Brown hopper' appears in the same 3-consecutive EDUs with the word 'evening' is 0. After obtaining the word vector for all words, we can calculate the similarity between word w_i and w_j by using the inner product of the word vector w_i and w_j, which can be computed from the equation:

$$ sim(w_i, w_j) = \frac{\sum_{k=1}^{m} w_i[k] \dot{w}_j[k]}{\sqrt{\sum_{k=1}^{m} w_i^2[k]} \sqrt{\sum_{k=1}^{m} w_j^2[k]}} $$

DM (Discourse Marker)

DM is the connective device for discourses which plays two roles: the cohesive device and the inference of semantic relation. In this section, we use DM in the first role as the traffic policeman to point out the attachment point of INC. If DM has the signal for the left hand side attach to PDT, such as "(The Brown hopper likes to live in the bottom area of the rice plant)$_{EDU1}$ (and infest the sap in that area)$_{EDU2}$", then its value is +1. On the other hand, if the DM has the signal to create a new segment such as "(In conclusion, agriculture commodity and food standards prepared by ACFS can be applied by all stockholders)$_{EDU1}$ (which can benefit all parties concerned in the industry and the economy as a whole)$_{EDU2}$", then its value is -1. When the DM can not be used to guide the direction of the attachment point, the value will be set to zero. To formulate this, we analysis the corpus and create a set of discourse marker that can be used to guide the attachment point direction namely DM_{left} and DM_{right}. The function used to determine the value of the output is defined as in Equation 2.

$$ DM(x, y) = \begin{cases} +1 & \text{if discourse unit } y \text{ contain a discourse marker in } DM_{left}; \\ -1 & \text{if discourse unit } y \text{ contain a discourse marker in } DM_{right}; \\ 0 & \text{otherwise.} \end{cases} $$

$$ (2) $$

where $DM_{left} - \{$ซึ่ง:which, โดย:by means of, และ:and, หรือ:or, ...$\}$

$DM_{right} = \{$ในที่สุด:finally, สรุปได้ว่า:conclusion, โดยปกติ:normally, ...$\}$

AE (Anaphoric Expression)

AE value describes the strength of the relation between discourse units using anaphoric expression. The intuition of this is that the unit should be related if they describe the same thing. Specifically, the unit that contains the antecedent of the anaphor of the incoming unit should be more related with the incoming unit than the unit that does not contain any antecedent. To compute this, we use anaphora resolution described in [13] to identify antecedent of y. and the value of AE is compute from the number of antecedent of anaphor in y that exists in x.

$$AE(x, y) = \text{the number of antecedent of anaphor in } y \text{ that exists in } x \quad (3)$$

Identifying the attachment point of an incoming discourse unit

Finally, we propose the Adaptive RFC for computing the coherence value to decide the attachment point of the incoming discourse unit in (4)

$$AdaptiveRFC(x, y) = RFC(x, y) + DDF(x, y) \quad (4)$$

where the RFC is the ranking value of the rightmost node of PDT. The RFC value decreases when it is as long as the distance from the bottom of the rightmost of the PDT. The attachment point of an incoming discourse unit is the unit that has maximum adaptive RFC value.

We tested 200 document files about plant diseases in agricultural domain which has 126 discourse markers (COR/SUBR). We used the threshold ? at 0.057 and the coefficient value of (2) with (0.88, 0.47, and 0.55). Maximum Likelihood Estimation (MLE) was used to compute the coefficient numbers of DDF and we adjust a suitable threshold with trial and error method. The accuracy of result in this section can be seen in the experiment and result section. Then, we follow this algorithm in Fig. 5.

```
Build_Up_Tree(text_seg){
  inc_edu = Get_EDU(text_seg)
  while ( inc_edu <> null) {
   If ( tree == null) then   tree <- inc_edu; exit();
   else
     inc_edu = current;
     RFC_nodes = RFC( PDT );
     RFC_node.area = top;
     while  RFC_node.area > bottom
   /* ranking the accessible value to the right frontier node */
       RFC_node.accesible++ ;
     if max(ARFC(RFC_nodes,inc_edu)) > threadhold
       Attach(RFC_nodes,inc_edu)
               /* add  INC to the new node of PDT */
     else { /* introduce the new segment */
       Tree_Space = current ; /*save the old tree */
       inc_node = current; /*set as the new tree */
     } /*  if-max */
  } /* while-inc_edu */
} /* Build_Up_Tree */
```

Fig. 5. Local Tree construction

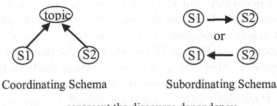

Coordinating Schema   Subordinating Schema

$\longrightarrow$ represent the discourse dependency

Fig. 6. COR/SUBR relationship model

4.2 Discourse Relations Disambiguation by Reducing Transformations Approach

This approach is to use coordinating relation and subordinating relation which have common nuclearity as a connected relation to generate discourse tree. This gives a transformation from a problem in an n-dimensional space of relations in RST to the 2-dimensional space of Coordinating and Subordinating relations which have common nuclearity.

Let RR^n be the set of rhetorical relations having n relations r_k , $k = 1,2, ,n$, where r_k is in R. That is

$$PR^n = \{r_k \in R, k = 1, 2, ..., n\}. \text{ Let } RR^2 = \{r_c = COR, r_s = SUBR\}$$

RR^2 is set of 2 dimension space of 2 semantic relations; COR/SUBR relation. Therefore, they are in accordance with Satisfaction-Precedence/Dominant relation[?] and Coordinating relation/Subordinating relation[9,?] and we denote it with COR and SUBR. To simplify the resolution of the ambiguity problem in n-dimension, we consider just 2 dimensions of COR and SUBR.

We define COR/SUBR properties with nuclearity function of RST.

Definition: Coordinating relation means the relation between discourse topics having the same important interrelated events or objects.

Definition: Subordinating relation means the relation between entity and interrelated proceeding in the form that one proceeding event or object depends on the other. This definition can be explained as shown in Fig. 6.

COR & SUBR recognition

We use Naive Bayes classifier to classify the COR/SUBR relations and Thai discourse cues defined in [14] Semantic noun phrase discourse entities will be used as the features in this learning process. For the discourse cues, considered as the discourse marker in [3], are separated into two groups corresponding with RST's nuclearity as DMCOR , DMSUBR . For example,

$$DM_{COR} = \{\text{"และ:and"} , \text{"หรือ:or"}, \text{"แต่:but"}, \text{"ถ้า-แล้ว:if-then"}, ...\},$$
$$DM_{SUBR} = \{\text{"ซึ่ง:which"} , \text{"โดย:by"}, \text{"ดังนั้น:therefore"}, ...\}$$

However, it is not necessary that there be a discourse marker within a discourse unit. Therefore, we apply DM and the semantic noun phrase discourse entities for COR/SUBR relation recognition. If the discourse entity of the discourse unit pair has hyponym relation in WordNet, then the discourse unit pair has a subordinating relation; otherwise, it is a coordinating relation. For the example, [S1: Blast disease can commonly spread to every parts of Thailand] [S2: It caused by fungus called Pyricularia], the following example, the noun phrase discourse entities are Blast disease, part of Thailand in S1 and fungus in S2. We found that the similarity value of Blast disease - fungus is greater than the other pair. These features computed by supervised learning technique whose annotated data are separated into two sets of COR and SUBR. Each set has 1000 EDU pairs in agricultural domain, and the testing data of each set are 300 EDU pairs. Naive Bayes is applied to calculate the weight of each individual feature. The results of precision and recall are evaluated by an expert. The precision of this experiment is 79/77% for COR/SUB and 76/83% for recall.

4.3   Coherent Tree Construction

As mentioned about local tree construction in section 4.1 and 4.2, we span coherent tree as shown in Fig. 5. We use the bottom-up algorithm to merging local PDT_i where $i = 1$ to n. The local PDT was generated and store into Tree Space in Fig. 5. Then, the discourse relations {COR, SUBR} are identified between local PDT_i and local PDT_j by repeating step 4.2, where the input can be multiple EDU which was selected by nucleus, from leaf to root node of local PDT, to represent the local PDT. For example,

Example-3: [Text-3]

S1: Blast disease can commonly spread to every parts of Thailand
S2: this disease caused by fungus called Pyricularia
S3: which the conidia of this fungus can be blown by the wind
S4: therefore blast disease distribute its through the wind
S5: when the conidia of the fungus settle on various parts, rice that are highly moist
S6: it will sprout in a fiber form, destroying the plant

Fig. 7, illustrates how the representative of local PDT can be derived. The local PDT is the output of algorithm in Fig. 5. From section 2, the nuclearity property has two statuses {N: nucleus denote with line arrow and S: satellite denote with dash line arrow}. We can use nucleus property of discourse relation to decide the representative of individual discourse unit pair. The PDT_j, the discourse unit pair [S2, S3] has relationship with subordinating relation; S2 has a nucleus status and S3 has a satellite status, thus we select S2 as the repres=entative of [S2, S3], denoted with {S2} as parent of [S2, S3]. In the same method, we consider discourse unit pair [S2,S3] and [S4] as subordinating relation, also the {S2} was selected to represent the discourse unit pair [S2, S3] and [S4]. Next, [S1] and [S2, S4] is consecutive discourse unit pair which are

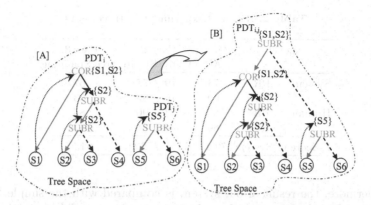

Fig. 7. [A] Representative of local PDT, selected by nucleus property of discourse relations and [B] local PDT Merging

coordinating relation; [S1] and [S2,S4] has a nuclearity property as a nucleus. Therefore, the representative of [S1] and [S2,S4] is {S1,S2}. In the same way, PDT_j , {S5} will be the representative of discourse unit pair [S5,S6]. Finally, we compute the discourse relationship between PDT_i and PDT_j with the method in section 4.2 and the $PDT_{i,j}$ will be generated as a result of this step.

The experiment was maintained under the condition that the input document has one topic which is a plain text. Therefore, this experiment does not cover the case of a long text. And its result will be reported in the next section.

5   Experiment and Result

The experiments were done by testing 200 document files of plant's disease symptoms in agricultural domain. The average edu length is 17.34 words with the total number of 3320 EDUs. The measurement consists three parts. In part-1, we consider the accuracy of the position of an attachment point of incoming EDU. In part-2, we measure the average of accuracy of relation classification between COR and SUBR relations. Finally, we measure accuracy of full coherent tree spanning. In each part, we align the result generated by the system with the result produced by 3 persons, two of which are linguist and another is not. The result is shown in table 2, where PR represents the precision measurement and RC represents the recall measurement. As the F-score of the system in part-1 has an average accuracy of 70.45%, we verify that the causes of almost all errors in this part have been caused by a nonadjacent incoming EDU that crosses over on the left hand side more than 2 distance units. In part-2, there are two numeric results. We interpret this as a result of inadequate features used in the experiment. There are not enough features to distinguish some cases such as cue's ambiguity. Finally, in part-3, we expect that its error results from the propagation error in the previous step. However, the result of the coherent tree spanning is nearly 65% of F-score.

Table 2. Result of experiment in three parts

Level		Part-1: AP	Part-2: COR/SUBR	Part-3: Tree Spanning
System	PR	73	79 / 77	67
	RC	69	76 / 83	63
Human	PR	87	93 / 90	84
	RC	86	90 / 88	82
F-Score of System		70.45	77.47/79.89	64.94

Furthermore, the result of our system is compared with the simple baseline system, based on the answer set from the human judgments. There are three measurements; first is the accuracy of the attachment point, evaluated by counting the newly posited INC at the rightmost branch of the PDT, is 66%, which is below F-Score of the system by 6.74%. Second is the measurement of discourse relations identification (the coordinating relation and the subordinating relation), where any internal nodes are subordinating relation, since this relation mostly occurs more than 79% in corpus. Therefore, only the PR and the RC from subordinating relations are determined as 63% for the PR and 57% for the RC, which is below F-Score of the system by 22.97% and 40.16%, respectively. Third is the determination of the accuracy of the discourse tree spanning process which the baseline system has 49% accuracy, which is below F-Score of the system by 32.53%. In other word, our system have significant outperforms the baseline system in all parts.

6   Application of Coordinating and Subordinating Relations in Text Summarization

After we have generated a coordinating and subordinating structure containing the nuclearity within each a relationship, it is easy to extract the salience unit by using the beam search algorithm based on the nucleus-satellite property and breadth first search policy. For the example, from the nuclearity function we can determine the location of salience in Text-4 as shown in the corresponding leaf nodes of Fig. 8. Then we apply the beam search to extract the salience nodes, as in S1, S6, S7, from the Coherent Tree, T4 (stands for Text-4). By the result of this beam search, the short summary text {S1, S6, and S7} is generated in the first step. The second step: {S2, S3} are added into the previous summary text, following by {S4, S5} and so on, depending on the user desire of the length of summary. However, the coherent characteristic is still in the summary produced.

Example-4 [Text-4]

S1: Soft Rot disease found in almost every growth step,
S2: especially, once lettuces start to bulb.

S3: Initially, softening and water-soaking spots or scales are found.
S4: Afterward, a wound progress widespread
S5: and they cause slimy softening rot with bad smell.
S6: When the disease becomes severe, lettuces are whole-bulb rotten
S7: and their necks become soft when pressed.

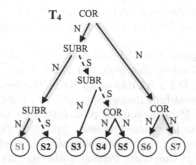

Fig. 8. Salience nodes in the first step of salience extraction on Coherent Tree

7   Conclusion

Our algorithm for the text summarization problem gives a construction of the coherent tree with two COR/SUBR relations. We concentrated in finding a simple method to compute a coherent structure. Consequently, we reduced the n-dimensional space of RST to the 2-dimensional space of COR and SUBR. In this way, we found that evident of features can be increasing more than the individual relation in RST. However, we show how to modify the ARF with forward-backward constrain, which mentions about the closing off status of the previous EDU and a new topic signal of the incoming EDU. These are two important steps before generating the coherent tree. Bayesian techniques are used as tools for recognizing the relations. The results of experiment seems satisfied with our corpus.

The main problem of constructing the coherent tree with COR/SUBR relations in this experiment may result from propagation error in the preceding step. So, we will tune them by adding a temporal feature that relates to positive error significantly.

Acknowledgements

The work described in this paper has been supported by the grant of Franco-Thai project and partially supported by a grant from NECTEC No. NT-B-22-14-12-46-06. The authors would like to present deeply thanks to Jean Caelen to review this work.

References

1. Edmundson, H.P.: New Method in Automatic Extracting. ACM 16(2), 264–285 (1969)
2. Hovy, E., Lin, C.: Automated text summarization in summarist. In: Proceedings of the Workshop on Intelligent Scalable Text Summarization, pp. 18–24 (1977)
3. Marcu, D.: The rhetorical parsing of natural language texts. In: Meeting of the Association for Computational Linguistics, pp. 96–103 (1997)
4. Cristea, D., Postolache, O., Pistol, I.: Summarisation through discourse structure [15], pp. 632–644
5. Mann, W.C., Thompson, S.A.: Rhetorical structure theory: Toward a functional theory of text organization. Text 8(3), 243–281 (1998)
6. Moore, J.D., Pollack, M.E.: A problem for RST: The need for multi-level discourse analysis. Computational Linguistics 18(4), 537–544 (1992)
7. Hovy, E., Maier, E.: Parsimonious or profligate: How many and which discourse structure relations. In: Discourse Processes, pp. 18–24 (1977)
8. Asher, N., Lascarides, A.: Logics of Conversation. Studies in Natural Language Processing. Cambridge University Press, Cambridge (2005)
9. Polanyi, L.: A formal model of the structure of discourse. Journal of Pragmatics 12, 601–638 (1988)
10. Sassen, C., Kühnlein, P.: The right frontier constraint as conditional [15], pp. 222–225
11. Grosz, B.J., Joshi, A.K., Weinstein, S.: Centering: A framework for modeling the local coherence of discourse. Computational Linguistics 21(2), 203–225 (1995)
12. Salton, G., Wong, A., Yang, C.S.: A vector space model for automatic indexing. Commun. ACM 18(11), 613–620 (1975)
13. Kongwa, A., Kawtrakul, A.: Know-what: A development of object-property extraction from thai texts and query system. In: Proceeding of the Sixth Symposium on Natural Language Processing (2005)
14. Wattanamethanont, M., T.S., Kawtrakul, A.: Thai discourse relations recognition by using naive bayes classifier. In: The Proceedings of the Sixth Symposium on Natural Language Processing (2005)
15. Gelbukh, A. (ed.): Computational Linguistics and Intelligent Text Processing. In: Gelbukh, A. (ed.) CICLing 2005. LNCS, vol. 3406, Springer, Heidelberg (2005)

Three Interactions Between Context and Epistemic Locutions

Richmond H. Thomason

Philosophy Department
University of Michigan
Ann Arbor, MI 48109-2110, USA

Abstract. I motivate and formalize three interactions between context and epistemic modalities, discussing (1) the effects of temporal perspective on knowledge of the future, (2) the effects of perceived risk on belief, and (3) the effects of presupposed background information on epistemic 'might'.

1 Introduction

From the start, philosophy has been full of arguments that start off plausibly enough, but that lead, through a series of apparently sound steps, to implausible or even totally unacceptable conclusions. These arguments strike many people—philosophers and nonphilosophers—as puzzles. If the conclusion is unacceptable, there must be a mistake somewhere in the argument. The puzzle will be resolved when the mistake has been identified and explained.

Two sorts of resolution methods stand out as particularly useful in this enterprise: appeals to ambiguity and to context dependence. It is easy to see why a syntactically correct argument—say, an application of *modus ponens*—can be mistaken if an expression is used with one sense in the premises and with quite another sense in the conclusion, or if expressions are used in one context in the premises and another context in the conclusion.[1] And both explanations have been exploited in philosophy.

Of course, the ambiguities and contextual dependencies that are important for philosophy have to be subtle. If they were obvious, there would be no puzzle in the first place; the arguments would obviously be wrong and the solutions would be ready to hand. But although the skeptical arguments of Sextus Empiricus, for example, have conclusions that are obviously wrong, it is very difficult to identify the mistake, and to give a satisfactory explanation of the flaw in the reasoning.

Cartesian demons and evil neurological experimenters are typical protagonists in the philosophy classrooms where problems of this kind are introduced to students. We can imagine experiments where disembodied brains are provided

---

[1] The variable-fixing expression 'let x be' provides a simple and unproblematic example of a contextual fallacy. *Premises:* 'Let x be 2. Then x is even. Let x be 3. Then x is odd.' *Conclusion:* 'x is even and odd.'

B. Kokinov et al. (Eds.): CONTEXT 2007, LNAI 4635, pp. 467–481, 2007.

with experiences just like those of normal people. Since we can't exclude these possibilities, we ourselves might be just such a brain. So, after all, we don't know that we have hands.

Philosophers' unfortunate fondness for ridiculously far-fetched examples of this kind can create a misleading impression that knowledge is problematic only in introductory philosophy classrooms. But the problem is much more general than this. Let's consider some more realistic examples.

Take, for instance, the following two quotations from the Brown Corpus (my underlining added).[2]

(1.1) As for food, Mrs. Henry Louchheim, chairman of this phase, is a globetrotter who knows good food. "New Orleans"? she says, "Of course I've had the best. It is just bad luck that we are having the party in a month with no 'R's, so no oysters. But we have lots of other New Orleans specialties. I know they will be good. We've tried them out on the club chef—or say, he has tried them out on us and we have selected the best".

(1.2) Just a month after the Korean War broke out, the 7th Cavalry was moving into the lines, ready for combat. From then on the Fighting Seventh was in the thick of the bitterest fight in Korea. One night on the Naktong River, Mel Chandler called on that fabled *esprit de corps*. The regiment was dug in on the east side of the river and the North Koreans were steadily building up a concentration of crack troops on the other side. The troopers knew an attack was coming, but they didn't know when, and they felt lonely and depressed.

You can quibble with these claims to knowledge. You could point out that food can spoil unexpectedly—for instance if the refrigeration fails. You could say that the attack would not have happened if the North Korean government suddenly told their troops to stay in place, perhaps because they had arbitrarily and unexpectedly decided to negotiate for peace. Imagine an articulate and persuasive critic pointing out possibilities to Mrs. L in which the food will not be good, citing instance after instance where expert caterers had ordered good food from reliable chefs, but where, through some misfortune, bad food had been served. Under determined criticism of this sort, Mrs. L may well have to withdraw her knowledge claim, even though she may feel that she has been tricked or manipulated into doing so.

Examples of this kind show convincingly that the extreme and far-fetched skeptical examples of which philosophers are so fond are limiting cases of natural cases where perfectly ordinary knowledge claims can be undermined. Why is knowledge useful, if it is so fragile? A diagnosis of the flaw in a troublesome argument is more than a logical exercise; in order to resolve the difficulty, it needs to clarify the nature of knowledge and the role of knowledge claims in communication and reasoning.

---

[2] The Brown Corpus was collected in 1961. It contains over a million words of representative English prose from various genres. I have provided long quotations because the point I want to make, I believe, is better supported by naturally occurring examples that also supply background detail about the reasoning on which the knowledge is based.

In [Lewis, 1979], David Lewis proposed the idea of a "conversational score," and described ways in which conversational acts depend on the score, and can influence it. Two of these dependencies (the possibilities over which a modal auxiliary like 'can' are taken to range, and the standards of accuracy appropriate for an adjective like 'smooth') suggest ways of trying to disarm some well-known philosophical puzzles. These ideas have led to a great deal of activity in the intersection of epistemology and philosophy of language; see [Preyer and Peter, 2005a] for a collection of papers on this topic, and references to others.

As you would expect, the linguistic evidence sheds some additional light, but at the same time adds another layer of complexity to the already complex issues. So the extent to which the philosophical problems are resolved or even illuminated is controversial. Genuine philosophical problems are recalcitrant, even to multi-disciplinary solutions.

Nevertheless, I believe that our best hope for making progress on these problems lies in a multi-disciplinary approach that brings to bear all the areas of Cognitive Science. What I miss in the recent philosophical work on context and epistemology is sufficient attention to reasoning, and to the role of epistemic locutions in realistic examples where the epistemic notions are actually engaged. In fact, many examples in the current literature go beyond typical philosophical examples in their complexity.[3] They involve some minimal stage setting, more than one sentence, and judgments about whether the sentences are appropriate or true. But few of these examples actually show the characters actually engaged in reasoning, and many of them are not entirely realistic.

I also suspect that we might gain more in the long run by relaxing our concentration on large-scale philosophical topics, like the refutation of skepticism. The linguistic work on context and epistemology has revealed unexpected features of locutions like 'know' and 'might', but the most interesting things we have learned seem to be at best distantly related to the original problem. I believe that we can improve our theories by combining models of compositional semantics and domain reasoning with a systematic study of the work done by epistemic concepts in realistic, moderately complex examples of reasoning. These things are well worth doing, even if we remain unable to settle the larger question of philosophical skepticism.

In this paper I will try to illustrate this methodology by considering three cases: knowledge of the future, the effects of risk on belief, and epistemic 'might'.

2   Uncertain Knowledge of the Future

Indeterminist tense logics seek to provide a semantics for tense operators in models that allow multiple future outcomes, giving equal weight to each alternative. Supervaluations, a technique proposed in [van Fraassen, 1969], can be used for this purpose; the idea was first proposed in [Thomason, 1970] and has been taken up and developed by later authors. (See [Belnap, Jr. *et al.*, 2001] and the references therein.) The idea is to first define truth relative to an arbitrarily

---

[3] I am thinking of examples like: "I direct my eyes at a ripe tomato. I see red."

selected future history; a sentence is then said to be true *simpliciter* if it is true relative to all future histories.

To formalize this, we will work with a propositional modal language $\mathcal{L}_1$ that has past and future modalities [P] and [F][4] and a historical necessity operator [H]. Frames and models for this language are defined as follows.

Definition 1. Frames, histories, valuations, models, evaluation points.

A *frame* for indeterministic logic is a pair $\mathcal{F} = \langle M, \preceq \rangle$, where M is a nonempty set (of moments) and $\prec$ is a transitive, antireflexive relation over M such that if $m_1, m_2 \prec m$, then $m_1 \prec m_2$ or $m_2 \prec m_1$ or $m_1 = m_2$.

A *history* h on a frame $\mathcal{F} = \langle M, \preceq \rangle$ is a maximal $\prec$ chain on $\mathcal{F}$. $\mathcal{H}_m$ is the set of histories h of $\mathcal{F}$ such that $m \in h$.

A *valuation* on a frame $\mathcal{F} = \langle M, \preceq \rangle$ is a function V that inputs an atomic formula p and outputs a subset $V(p)$ of M.

A *model* on a set $\mathcal{P}$ of propositional atoms is a pair $\langle \mathcal{F}, V \rangle$, where $\mathcal{F}$ is a frame and V is a valuation of $\mathcal{P}$ on $\mathcal{F}$.

An *evaluation point* (or *e-point*) in a model $\mathcal{M} = \langle M, \preceq \rangle$ is a pair $\langle m, h \rangle$, where h is a history over $\langle M, \preceq \rangle$ and $m \in h$.

The satisfaction relation $\mathcal{M}, m, h \models \phi$ between a model $\mathcal{M} = \langle M, \preceq \rangle$, an e-point in $\mathcal{M}$, and a formula ϕ of $\mathcal{L}_1$ is defined recursively as follows.

Definition 2. $\mathcal{M}, m, h \models \phi$.

1. **Basis:** $\mathcal{M}, m, h \models p$ iff $m \in V(p)$.
2. **Booleans:** Boolean conditions are routine.
3. **Past:** $\mathcal{M}, m, h \models \langle P \rangle \phi$ iff for some $m' \prec m$, $\mathcal{M}, m', h \models \phi$.
   $\mathcal{M}, m, h \models [P]\phi$ iff for all $m' \prec m$, $\mathcal{M}, m', h \models \phi$.
4. **Future:** $\mathcal{M}, m, h \models \langle F \rangle \phi$ iff for some m', $m \prec m'$ and $m' \in h$, $\mathcal{M}, m', h \models \phi$.
   $\mathcal{M}, m, h \models [F]\phi$ iff for all m', $m \prec m'$ and $m' \in h$, $\mathcal{M}, m', h \models \phi$.
5. **Historical Necessity:** $\mathcal{M}, m, h \models [H]\phi$ iff for all h' such that $m \in h'$, $\mathcal{M}, m, h' \models \phi$.

Applying van Fraassen's supervaluation idea to this notion of satisfaction relative to a history provides the following definition of satisfaction *simpliciter*.

Definition 3. $\mathcal{M}, m \models \phi$.

$\mathcal{M}, m \models \phi$ iff for all $h \in \mathcal{H}_m$, $\mathcal{M}, m, h \models \phi$.

In Model $\mathcal{M}_1$, for instance, neither $\langle F \rangle p$ nor $\neg\langle F \rangle p$ is true at m_0 (neither $\mathcal{M}_1, m_0 \models \langle F \rangle p$ nor $\mathcal{M}_1, m_0 \models \neg\langle F \rangle p$) because $\mathcal{M}_1, m_0, h_1 \models \langle F \rangle p$, while $\mathcal{M}_1, m_0, h_1 \models \neg\langle F \rangle p$. But, for the same reason, $[H]\langle F \rangle p$ and $[H]\neg\langle F \rangle p$ are both false at m_0. Related to this is the fact that a formula like $\langle F \rangle p$ is *future-dependent*—its truth at a

---

[4] [F] is "always in the future", [P] is "always in the past." The duals are $\langle F \rangle$, "sometimes in the future," and $\langle P \rangle$, "sometimes in the past."

moment has to be evaluated with respect to a postulated future—whereas $[\textsc{h}]\langle\textsc{f}\rangle p$ is future *in*dependent.

So far, I have simply restated ideas that go back to [Thomason, 1970] and which I hope the reader will be willing to assume as background. Now, however, I want to add a knowledge operator $[\textsc{k}]$ to this temporal language, and to ask whether $[\textsc{k}]\langle\textsc{f}\rangle p$ is future dependent. In effect, we are asking whether, in an indeterministic setting, someone's claim to know something may turn out to have been true in one subsequent scenario, and to have been false in another.

Model $\mathcal{M}_1$:

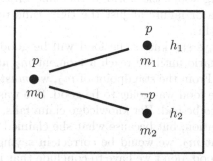

Before we can set out the satisfaction conditions for knowledge, we will need some motivation and philosophical background.

If we are interested in ordinary, human knowledge of the future (rather than the "certain knowledge" that some theologians talk about), it certainly seems as if knowledge can be future-dependent in this way, and hence can be fallible.

Returning to Examples (1.1) and (1.2), cited in Section 1, in which Mrs. Louchheim knows the food will be good and the 7th Cavalry knows the enemy will attack, let's suppose that in both cases things turned out just as expected. Mrs. L found the food to be very good, and the North Koreans attacked the next day across the Naktong. We are told that Mrs. L knew her food, and had sampled the specialties to be served at the party; we can assume that the 7th Cavalry were observing the enemy and the observations were supplemented with other information and evaluated by military intelligence experts.

Consider again the objections that a food-ordering skeptic or a military intelligence skeptic might raise to Mrs. L or the 7th Cavalry. The food skeptic, says, for instance, that New Orleans is hot and the refrigeration can always fail. Depending on details that I haven't supplied, in some cases the objections may be useful; but in many cases we would say they are *beside the point*. I would like to claim that, in calling them beside the point, we are classifying them as inappropriate, rather than (say) as simply mistaken, untrue, or without force, and that the sort of mistake we have in mind here is related to context. I'm sympathetic to those who want to say that attributions of knowledge are relative to standards of justification. Raising an objection to a knowledge claim that only has force if these standards are inappropriately strict is one way of being beside the point.

But others have discussed this matter at some length.[5] I want to investigate a different and, I think, unnoticed additional way in which knowledge has to depend on context. At least, this sort of context dependence is needed if we, and Mrs. L, and the 7th Cavalry, are ever to be in a position to have knowledge about genuine future contingencies.

The problem is this. In each case, the attack on the knowledge claim involves a scenario that apparently is possible, even if far-fetched. In an indeterminist setting, it is plausible to suppose that these are historically possible scenarios. For instance, nothing about the world at the time Mrs. L made her prediction ruled out a refrigerator failure at just the right time to ruin the food for her party. Let us grant this.

At m_0, Mrs. L says she knows the food will be good. But now, let's follow the improbable scenario until we reach a moment m_2 at which spoiled food is served at the party. From the standpoint of m_2, we *must* say that Mrs. L didn't know at m_0 that the food was going to be good. She was wrong because at m_0, the food was going to be bad. Her knowledge claim fails, not because she lacked an adequate justification, but because what she claimed to know was false.

But if later on, at m_2, we would be correct in saying she didn't know that the food would be good, don't we have to conclude that in fact, she didn't know it when she made her claim? At m_2 we can say with certainty that she didn't know at m_0 that the food would be good. But this means that at m_0 her claim to know it would be good was false. So, it seems that at m_0 she can't have known, after all, that the food would be good, even if (luckily) it does turn out to be good.

Note that this attack on the possibility of knowledge has nothing to do with standards of justification—it uses only temporal reasoning, and a semantic characteristic of knowledge—that you can't know things that are false.

This sort of argument against the possibility of uncertain knowledge of the future can be disarmed, but doing so requires developing a rather complex and delicate account of the semantics of future-dependent claims. I do not think that this account could have been worked out without the clarity that comes with formalization and the use of model-theoretic techniques.

First, notice that an argument similar to the one we used to attack knowledge at m_0 can be deployed in terms of truth rather than knowledge. We refer again to Model $\mathcal{M}_1$, and simply consider $\langle F \rangle p$ at m_0. Notice that from the standpoint of m_2, $\neg \langle P \rangle \langle F \rangle p$ is true. But if $\neg \langle P \rangle \langle F \rangle p$ is true at m_2, then (looking back from m_2), $\langle F \rangle p$ should be *false* at m_0, whereas the supervaluational theory we endorsed makes it neither true nor false.

In [MacFarlane, 2002], John MacFarlane addresses the problem of after-the-fact truth by making satisfaction relative to not one, but two moments: a "context of evaluation" and a "context of assessment." The satisfaction scheme then becomes $\mathcal{M}, m, m', h \models \phi$, where m is the moment of evaluation and m' the moment of assessment. And ϕ is true *simpliciter* in $\mathcal{M}$ at $\langle m, m' \rangle$ if $\mathcal{M}, m, m', h \models \phi$

---

[5] See the discussion of this issue in the papers collected in [Preyer and Peter, 2005b], and in the works cited in that volume.

for all $h \in \mathcal{H}_{m'}$—supervaluational truth is reckoned using the histories through the moment of assessment rather than the larger set of histories through the (possibly earlier) moment of evaluation.

In Model $\mathcal{M}_1$, for instance, $\langle F \rangle p$ will be true *simpliciter* at $\langle m_0, m_1 \rangle$ and false *simpliciter* at $\langle m_0, m_2 \rangle$. It will be neither true nor false, however, at $\langle m_0, m_0 \rangle$.

In recent unpublished work [Thomason, 2007], I have proposed a slightly different approach, which uses double-indexing techniques of the sort that go back to [Kaplan, 1978]. According to this theory, the recursive definition of satisfaction is modified as follows, to incorporate MacFarlane's two temporal indices.

Definition 4. $\mathcal{M}, m, m', h \models_1 \phi$.

1. **Basis:** If $\phi \in \mathcal{P}$ then $\mathcal{M}, m, m', h \models_1 \phi$ iff $m \in V(\phi)$.
2. **Booleans:** Boolean conditions are routine.
3. **Past:** $\mathcal{M}, m, m', h \models_1 \langle P \rangle \phi$ iff for some $m_1 \prec m$,
   $\mathcal{M}, m_1, m', h \models_1 \phi$.
   $\mathcal{M}, m, m', h \models_1 [P] \phi$ iff for all $m_1 \prec m$, $\mathcal{M}, m_1, m', h \models_1 \phi$.
4. **Future:** $\mathcal{M}, m, m', h \models_1 \langle F \rangle \phi$ iff for some m_1, $m \prec m_1$ and
   $m_1 \in h$, $\mathcal{M}, m_1, m_2, h \models_1 \phi$, where
   $m_2 = \max(m_1, m')$.
   $\mathcal{M}, m, m', h \models_1 [F] \phi$ iff for all m_1, $m \prec m_1$ and $m_1 \in h$,
   $\mathcal{M}, m_1, m_2, h \models_1 \phi$, where $m_2 = \max(m_1, m')$.
5. **Historical Necessity:** $\mathcal{M}, m, m', h \models_1 [F] \phi$ iff for all h' passing
   through m, $\mathcal{M}, m, m', h' \models_1 \phi$.

We now define truth *simpliciter* by first insisting, as Kaplan does, that evaluation must start at a *normal index*, where the moment of evaluation is the same as the moment of assessment. This gives us a notion of truth relative to a single e-point. We then use supervaluations, considering a formula to be simply true at m when it is true relative to all histories passing through m.

Definition 5. $\mathcal{M}, m, h \models_1 \phi$ and $\mathcal{M}, m \models_1 \phi$.
   $\mathcal{M}, m, h \models_1 \phi$ iff $\mathcal{M}, m, m, h \models_1 \phi$.
   $\mathcal{M}, m \models_1 \phi$ iff $\mathcal{M}, m, h \models_1 \phi$ for all $h \in \mathcal{H}_m$.

For a language with only future and past tenses and historical necessity, this account of truth at a moment does not differ from MacFarlane's. But if truth is added to the language, there are substantive differences from the sort of semantics that MacFarlane recommends. This two-stage approach to satisfaction also helps when a knowledge operator [K] is added.

The standard semantic treatment of knowledge in temporal settings is presented in [Fagin et al., 1995]. This theory uses possible-worlds semantics rather than branching time. A possible world in the Fagin-Halpern-Moses models is analogous to an e-point or moment-history pair in our models. Therefore, in a branching setting, we need to treat an epistemic possibility as an e-point.

In the simplest case (and we do not want to make things more complicated than they need to be), we interpret knowledge at world w using a set K_w of worlds containing w; this interpretation yields the modal logic **S5**. This leads to an altered definition of a frame and to a satisfaction clause for knowledge along the following lines.

Definition 6. Epistemic frames, evaluation pairs, models.

An (epistemic) *frame* for indeterministic logic is a triple $\mathcal{F} = \langle M, \preceq, K \rangle$, where M is a nonempty set (of moments), $\prec$ is a transitive, antireflexive relation over M such that if $m_1, m_1 \prec m$, then $m_1 \prec m_2$ or $m_2 \prec m_1$ or $m_1 = m_2$, and K is a function from e-points in $\mathcal{F}$ to sets of e-points in $\mathcal{F}$, such that $\langle m, h \rangle \in K_{\langle m, h \rangle}$.

Definition 7. $\mathcal{M}, m, m', h \models_1 \phi$, $\mathcal{M}, m, h \models_1 \phi$, and $\mathcal{M}, m \models_1 \phi$.

Clauses 1–5 as in Definition 4.
6. **Knowledge:** $\mathcal{M}, m, m', h \models_1 [\text{K}] \phi$ iff for all $\langle m_1, h' \rangle \in K_{\langle m, h \rangle}$, where h' passes through m', $\mathcal{M}, m_1, m', h' \models_1 \phi$.

$\mathcal{M}, m, h \models_1 \phi$ and $\mathcal{M}, m \models_1 \phi$ are defined as in Definition 5.

The following example will help to clarify how this semantics works in simple cases. We confine histories to only two points of time; the earlier point at which Mrs. L claims to know that the food at the party will be good, and the time at which the food is served. We will use p to mean 'The food at the party is served, and it is good' and q to mean 'The chef is married'. Mrs. L has no idea at any time whether the chef is married. In the actual initial moment, the chef is married and the party has not yet taken place. In all histories, the chef's marital status remains unchanged. Whether or not the chef is married, there is an outcome in which the food is good, and a (far-fetched) outcome in which it is not good. This model actually is a forest consisting of two unconnected trees, but it is easiest to diagram the knowledge relations by unfolding the four histories, as in Model $\mathcal{M}_2$, below.

The diagram shows only knowledge relations at the earlier time. Dashed arrows relate $\langle m_0, h_1 \rangle$ and $\langle m_0, h2 \rangle$ to the e-points that represent e-points compatible with what Mrs. L knows. (To avoid clutter, I have only shown the accessibility relations that indicate what Mrs. L knows at m_0.) In $\langle m_0, h_1 \rangle$, where the food will be good and the chef is married, the only e-points compatible with what she knows are ones in which the food turns out to be good. In the anomalous pair $\langle m_0, h_2 \rangle$ where the food will not be good and the chef is married, all e-points are compatible with her knowledge. The e-points where the food turns out to be good, of course are the ones she expects. The e-point where the food is not good and the chef is married has to be added because of reflexivity. But if this e-point is added, reasonable closure principles involving the independence of the chef's marital state from whether the food will be good compel us to include the e-point where the food is not good and the chef is not married.

In this model, we have $\mathcal{M}_2, m_0, h_1 \models_1 [\text{K}] \langle \text{F} \rangle p$ but $\mathcal{M}_2, m_0, h_2 \models_1 \neg [\text{K}] \langle \text{F} \rangle p$. Therefore, $[\text{K}] \langle \text{F} \rangle p$ is neither true nor false at m_0. On the other hand, we have $\mathcal{M}_2, m_1, h_1 \models_1 \langle \text{P} \rangle [\text{K}] \langle \text{F} \rangle p$. In other words, according to this theory, when Mrs. L said she knew the food would be good what she said was neither true nor false. But after the fact, when things have turned out as she expected, she *knew* it would be good.

Model $\mathcal{M}_2$:

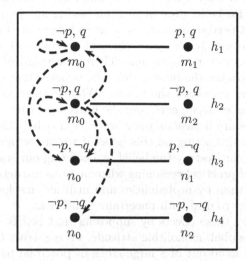

I have only experimented with this theory for a short while, so at this point I put it forward as a tentative suggestion. But I do think that something like this account can be maintained, and that it shows how to develop and defend a view of how knowledge of the future can be uncertain.

Note that it is an essential part of this theory that the semantics of an agent's knowledge is not merely a matter of the agent's psychological state. Mrs. L's psychological state at the e-point where the food will be bad is indistingishable from her state at the e-point where it will be good.

3 Belief, Risk, and Impatience

Belief is (apparently) less dependent on context than knowledge. I might be able to convince Mrs. L that she didn't know the food would be good by elaborating scenarios where it turns out to be bad; but I certainly can't convince her by such arguments that she didn't believe it would be good.

Nevertheless, I think that belief depends on context in other ways, and that sometimes we are able to manipulate these dependencies in order to create or destroy beliefs. I discussed these matters in [Thomason, 1987], so I will be fairly brief here.

Consider a nervous driver at a stop sign at a busy intersection on a dark night. He needs to drive across the intersection. He looks left. A car zooms by from that direction. He looks right. It's clear. He looks left, it's clear. But wait—he can't see what's going on to the right, and doesn't believe it's clear anymore. So he looks right. He repeats the process until he realizes that he'll never get across this way. Time is pressing. But he can't move unless the road is clear. So he lowers his standards, saying to himself "If it was clear to the right a second ago it's clear now." And he hits the gas, hopefully without getting into an accident.

Moral: There are occasions when we can't act without a belief, and in which high standards for belief prevent us from having an appropriate belief. In these cases, an urgent need to act can cause us to lower our standards.

Consider a normal driver approaching an intersection on a dark night. Traffic on the crossroad is very infrequent. There is no sign of a car coming, and as the driver approaches the intersection, she believes there is no car on the other road. But as she get closer she thinks "What if there were—we would crash!" Instantly, her belief disappears, and she brakes her car.

Moral: There are occasions when we have a belief that is well justified, but the consequences of acting on this belief if we are wrong are very harmful. In these cases, we can destroy the belief by changing our standards.

In a theory of practical reasoning where actions are determined by beliefs and desires (rather than by probabilities and utilities) mechanisms of this sort are essential in order to deal with uncertainty and risk.

We can model these effects by supposing that beliefs are local. Rather than appealing to a global, monolithic attitude, we construct belief-like attitudes for the occasion at hand out of a large stock of potential beliefs that can be combined much as we might select and combine propositional axioms for some *ad hoc* purpose. Potential beliefs come with features indicating their provenance and, for instance, the circumstances under which we learned them, and they are sorted according to their entrenchment or plausibility. When we combine potential beliefs into a modality that will guide our actions in a given situation, we can manipulate the beliefs by filtering out less plausible proto-beliefs in the presence of risk, or allowing them in when it is urgent to have a belief of some sort.

The context-dependence that I have indicated in this section is different from the context-dependence I discussed in Section 2. It belongs to a theory of philosophical psychology, or to an agent architecture, rather than to semantics; for semantic purposes, we might well want to relativize the truth of BELIEVE(a, p) to a world w, without distinguishing the features of w that bear on whether BELIEVE(a, p) is true.

However, in understanding how belief can play an effective and flexible role in practical reasoning, it may be important that an agent's belief that p may depend on more than the agent's dispassionate assessment of whether or not p is true. It depends on other psychological factors, and these factors can to some extent be manipulated.

4   Epistemic 'Might'

So-called epistemic modals, and especially the epistemic employment of the modal auxiliary 'might', have attracted attention in the literature on context and epistemology, and the recent literature has disclosed some hitherto unnoticed and interesting features. Here, I want to discuss the apparent dependence of locutions involving 'might' on the speaker's epistemic state. This case was raised as an aside in [Hawthorne, 2004], and has been discussed in [DeRose, 1991], [Egan et al., 2005], [MacFarlane, 2006], and elsewhere. Here I will mainly refer to the account in [Egan et al., 2005].

The examples that are usually mobilized to illustrate the speaker-dependence of 'might' involve overhearers. In the example that [Egan et al., 2005] develop, for instance, Myles (a reporter being interviewed on the radio), asked where Professor Granger is, says "We don't know—she might be in Prague." Professor G, listening to the broadcast while on a beach somewhere in the South Pacific, denies that she might be in Prague. You can elaborate this: if Prof. G calls the station and tells Myles where she is, he will have to admit that he was wrong when he said she might be in Prague.

Various theories have been advanced to account for this. Egan, Hawthorne and Weatherson favor a theory proposed earlier by DeRose (but without some of De Rose's added qualifications, so that the relationship between the speaker and the relevant group is somewhat loose):

> S's assertion of 'it is possible that P' is true if and only if (1) no member of the relevant community knows that P is false and (2) there is no relevant way by which members of the relevant community can come to know that P is false. [DeRose, 1991][pp. 593–594]

I find this account, with its multiple 'relevant's, too vague. As we will see, there are cases when, for practical purposes, there is no way the individual members of the community can come to know P, but, in the appropriate sense, the group knows P. We will need to see how these cases interact with epistemic 'might'.

I will suppose along with many other authors, but without arguing for it, that 'might' is connected as in DeRose's analysis with some sort of group knowledge. The problem, given a group G and knowledge operators [K,a] for each agent $a \in G$, to define the relevant group epistemic operator [K,G].

DeRose's formulation is close to what is usually called *distributed knowledge*; see [Fagin et al., 1995][p. 24]. The definition is this. (I assume a possible worlds semantics that interprets the individual modalities [K,a] by means of a relation R_a over worlds.)

Definition 8. $\mathcal{M}, w \models$ [K,G]ϕ.

$\mathcal{M}, w \models$ [K,G]ϕ iff for all w' such that $\langle w, w' \rangle \in \bigcap_{a \in G} R_a$, $\mathcal{M}, w' \models \phi$.

This amounts to saying that the group d-knows p if p follows from pooled or combined knowledge of the members of G. In fact, a corollary of Definition 8 is that [K,G]ϕ is true in a model if and only if there are formulas $\psi_1, \ldots, \psi_n$ and group members $a_1, \ldots, a_n$ such that [K, a_i]ψ_i is true for each i, $1 \leq i \leq n$, and ϕ is a logical consequence of $\psi_1 \wedge \ldots \wedge \psi_n$. It does *not* assume, however, that the members of G can pool their knowledge freely; there may be constraints on their ability to communicate.

This definition eliminates an element of indeterminacy in DeRose's account. Also, I think, it is more faithful to the facts.

In the rather brief space available, I want to indicate how various hypotheses about 'might' could be explored by developing examples in which the reasoning activities of the participants are brought into the picture. The purpose is to make a plausible case for the fruitful use of such examples.

First, let's return to the Brown Corpus. Epistemic 'might' occurs rather frequently in this corpus (well over 100 instances). The following three examples are representative.

(2.1) Benington recalled that he once told Hartweger that he doubted Gordon would ever play much for him because he seemed to be lacking in all of the accepted basketball skills. After the coach listed all the boy's faults, Hartweger said, "Coach before I leave here, you'll get to like me". Mrs. Benington admired Gordon's spirit and did what she could to persuade her husband that the boy might help the team.

(2.2) The weather bureau has estimated that radioactive fallout from the test might arrive here next week.

(2.3) The heightened tension, in fact, had been a major factor in the President's change of view about the urgency of a meeting with the Soviet leader. He was not going to Vienna to negotiate—the simultaneous announcements in Washington and Moscow last week stressed that no formal negotiations were planned. But Mr. Kennedy had become convinced that a personal confrontation with Mr. Khrushchev might be the only way to prevent catastrophe.

In each of these examples, there is reasoning in the background, either by an individual or a group.

Mrs. B and Mr. B, as a group, were debating the worthiness of various candidates for the basketball team. At the beginning of the debate, we can assume, Mr. B claimed to know the boy would not help the team. In persuading him he was wrong (which in fact, the passage goes on to say, she does), she got him to admit that the boy might help the team. At the beginning of the debate, Mr. B denied MIGHT(p). At the end, he accepted MIGHT(p).

The weather bureau constitutes a deliberating group in Example (2.2). At the outset, there may have been many possibilities: perhaps the fallout will arrive this week, or any of the three subsequent weeks. They gather data and make projections. Week 1 and week 4 are ruled out, and (let us suppose) week 2 gets a less than 40% chance, while week 3 is deemed more likely. The newspaper reports the result of the deliberations using the earlier date, to simplify and perhaps to provide a more impressive warning.

President Kennedy and his advisors deliberated, with the heavy responsibility of avoiding a nuclear war without making the United States seem willing to be influenced by threats. They considered many options. One by one, they discovered powerful arguments against all but one of them. At that point, it seemed to them that there might be only one alternative.

These simple examples make it clear that the status of 'might' can be influenced in the course of a group deliberation. If 'might' is a group epistemic modality, it is one that changes and that sometimes—as in the case of Example (2.1)—can be explicitly negotiated in the course of a dialogue. I conclude that, in presenting examples as data for theories of 'might', we must be very careful to provide enough detail so that we know with exactly which point in the reasoning the 'might' is to be associated.

In Example (2.1), Mr. and Mrs. B begin their negotiation by disagreeing about whether Hartweger might help the team. At the end, Mr. B (let us say) is convinced he was wrong; he sincerely says "I was mistaken; actually, that boy might help the team." At an intermediate point, before he was persuaded but after he began to feel the force of Mrs. B's argument, he may have been genuinely uncertain about whether Hartweger might help the team. This example shows, then, that the members of G may disagree about $[\mathrm{K},\mathrm{G}]p$, and that they can be uncertain about whether $[\mathrm{K},\mathrm{G}]p$. Such facts, of course constrain theories of the meaning of epistemic 'might'.

As a tool in exploring the contours of 'might', I suggest the use of dialogues involving the group solution of constraint satisfaction problems and, in particular, of word puzzles.

Imagine, for instance, a father who has already solved a crossword puzzle and who is helping his young daughter to a solution. The word at $\langle 1, \mathrm{Down}\rangle$ has the clue "a large feline, found in Central America." There are six letters for this word. The girl says "It might be 'jaguar'." The father says "Yes, it might. But look at $\langle 1, \mathrm{Across}\rangle$." The clue is "A small house, often used as a summer home." "Oops," says the girl. "That's 'cottage'—I know that. Are there cougars in Central America?" "Yes," says the father. "I had to check that." "Then the word can't be 'jaguar'," the girl says. "It must be 'cougar'."

Here, less cooperatively, the father could have said "No it couldn't be 'jaguar'. Did you look at $\langle 1, \mathrm{Across}\rangle$?" In the former case, I would say that the relevant operator isn't always knowledge; the father is suspending his knowledge to participate as a partner in the daughter's problem-solving. Egan, Hawthorne and Weatherson consider a similar, but less elaborated example and conclude that the speaker may not always be a member of the group.

The systematic use of information-seeking conversations in relatively structured domains can yield useful evidence. Consider, for instance, the following dialogue.

> Round 1. M to A: "The mystery word is a noun."
> Round 1. M to B: "It has 3 letters."
> Round 1. A to all: "It might be 'mother'."
> Round 1. B to all: "It can't be 'mother' but it might be 'the'."
> Round 1. A to all: "OK, it might be 'car'."
> Round 1. B to all: "Yes, It might be 'car'."
> Round 2. M to A: "It begins with 't'."
> Round 2. M to B: "It ends with 'p'."
> Round 2. A to all: "It might be 'time'."
> Round 2. B to all: "No, but it might be 'cap'."
> Round 2. A to all: "No, it can't be 'cap'. But it might be 'tap'."
> Round 2. B to all: "Yes, it might be."
> Round 3. M to all: "That's right, game's over."

Here, three agents—two guessers A and B, and a moderator M whose job is to reveal constraints—are playing a guessing game. The rules of the game prevent A and B from directly communicating constraints known to them. A can't overhear M's communications to B and B can't overhear M's communications to A. Dialogues of this sort can be used to address issues such as whether a distributed knowledge analysis is more faithful to the facts than DeRose's. But they can be a fruitful and relatively precise instrument, I think, for exploring many other issues having to do with epistemic modals.

5 Conclusion

Although I have been rather brief, I hope that I have managed to make a convincing case for my main points: (1) modeling methods from logic can be helpful in exploring issues in the philosophy and semantics of context and epistemic locutions, and (2) in combination with examples designed to bring the reasoning that 'might' is tracking into prominence, these methods may be able to lead us to improved theories of this interesting and important cluster of phenomena.

References

Belnap Jr. N.D., Perloff, M., Xu, M.: Facing the Future: Agents and Choices in Our Indeterminist World, Oxford University Press, Oxford (2001)

DeRose, K.: Epistemic possibilities. The Philosophical Review 107(2), 581–605 (1991)

Egan, A., Hawthorne, J., Weatherson, B.: Epistemic modals in context. In: Preyer, G., Peter, G. (eds.) Contextualism in Philosophy: Knowledge, Meaning, and Truth, pp. 131–168. Oxford University Press, Oxford (2005)

Fagin, R., Halpern, J.Y., Moses, Y., Vardi, M.Y.: Reasoning about Knowledge. The MIT Press, Cambridge, Massachusetts (1995)

Hawthorne, J.: Knowledge and Lotteries. Oxford University Press, Oxford (2004)

Kaplan, D.: On the logic of demonstratives. Journal of Philosophical Logic 8, 81–98 (1978)

Lewis, D.K.: Scorekeeping in a language game. Journal of Philosophical Logic 8(3), 339–359 (1979)

MacFarlane, J.: Future contingents and relative truth. The Philosophical Quarterly 53(212), 321–336 (2002)

MacFarlane, J.: Epistemic modals are assessment-sensitive. Unpublished manuscript, University of California at Berkeley (2006)

Preyer, G., Peter, G. (eds.): Ontextualism in Philosophy: Knowledge, Meaning, and Truth. Oxford University Press, Oxford (2005)

Preyer, G., Peter, G. (eds.): Contextualism in Philosophy: Knowledge, Meaning, and Truth. Oxford University Press, Oxford (2005)

Thomason, R.H.: Indeterminist time and truth-value gaps. Theoria 36, 246–281 (1970)

Thomason, R.H.: The multiplicity of belief and desire. In: Georgeff, M.P., Lansky, A. (eds.) Reasoning about Actions and Plans, pp. 341–360. Morgan Kaufmann, Los Altos, California (1987)

Thomason, R.H.: Truth after the fact in indeterminist tense logic. Unpublished manuscript, Philosophy Department, University of Michigan. Available from the author (2007)

van Fraassen, B.C.: Presuppositions, supervaluations, and free logic. In: Lambert, K. (ed.) The Logical Way of Doing Things, pp. 67–91. Yale University Press, New Haven, Connecticut (1969)

Do You Believe What Eye Believe?

John M. Tomlinson Jr. and Daniel C. Richardson

University of California at Santa Cruz, Psychology Dept.,
1156 High St. Santa Cruz, CA 95062 USA
otomlins@ucsc.edu, dcr@ucsc.edu

Abstract. Speaker belief is an essential component how interlocutors interact, according to information structure and other theories of conversational interaction. We tested this assumption by investigating unscripted spontaneous speech patterns in an experimental paradigm that manipulated speakers belief states about shared visual information. We found that interlocutors were more likely to use references based on content (rather than appearance) in mismatched belief conditions. Also, final rising pitch contours (*confirmation contours*) seemed to be used more when interlocutors share the same visual common ground. These contours seem to elicit more back-channels than final falling pitch contours. Our results provide evidence that situational variables such as visual common ground strongly effect how speakers create their utterances.

Keywords: prosody; eye tracking; visual common ground; intonation; joint attention.

1 Introduction

Speakers have a large repertoire of devices that aid understanding and orchestrate conversation [1][6][7][8]. These devices can best be thought of as *collateral signals* because of their role in coordinating attention and gauging speakers' intentions in spontaneous conversation ([7][8] refer to these as *primary signals* or *collateral signals* depending on the function whereas [19] refers to these as *natural signals* or *natural signs* depending on their ability to recognize speaker intent; when their functions merge, they are referred to *linguistic signals*). We choose to refer to these devices simply as *collateral signals* because despite whether they are intentional or not, we hypothesize their primary role is the coordination of attention amongst interlocutors.

Collateral signaling helps interlocutors establish common ground, which is mediated by *mutual belief* [7][8]. For example, while writing this paragraph, I believe that you can read, understand English, have some familiarity with specialist psychological terms, and so on. If this were a dialogue, you would give me feedback to the contrary if any of these assumptions were incorrect. This feedback could be explicit, by either a propositional statement or some type of *collateral signal*. Or they could be more implicit signals, using actions such as gesturing and pointing [2][9]. Our study intends to shed light on these linguistic actions that help coordinate joint

B. Kokinov et al. (Eds.): CONTEXT 2007, LNAI 4635, pp. 482–492, 2007.

attention. To our knowledge, it is the first to examine if speakers actually change these devices across manipulations in mutual belief, more specifically manipulations in *visual common ground*.

Our experimental procedure, called *Eye Believe*, manipulates participants' beliefs about whether or not the other interlocutor can see what they can see. In each trial, participants watched four people give their opinions on a certain topic (e.g., the gulf war, vegetarianism). The 'talking heads' appeared in the four corners of a computer screen. The participants then discussed the topic between themselves. We varied two factors: whether participants could still see the four 'talking heads' onscreen, and whether they each believed the other could see the talking heads on screen. We predicted that interlocutors will alter their message depending on what they believe to be the type of *visual common ground* that they share, and that this will be reflected in differences in their linguistic data. Will speakers exploit their shared visual environment by using spatial or visual when referring to this information or will they refer to the non-situated aspects of four talking heads' viewpoint? Last, feedback is an essential part of coordinating joint attention, and so we examined interlocutors' use of backchannels across belief conditions.

1.1 Mutual Belief and Pitch Contours

The coordination of speakers' beliefs is an essential aspect of how they achieve their communicative goals and how speakers construct their utterance. Pierrehumbert & Hirschbirg (1990) introduced a similar term called *mutual belief space*, which roughly corresponds to what a speaker believes a listener believes. Depending on what is active in this space, a speaker might augment the type of *pitch contour* that she uses in changing the propositional meaning of her utterance. For example, words marked with the highest pitch point in intonational phrase (*accented* or H*) usually denotes "new" information in the discourse, whereas points in the lowest part of the pitch range (*deaccented* or L*) usually refer to "given" information in the discourse.

Dahan et al (2002) found that although new information is frequently accented, given information can either be accented or deaccented based on its salience in the discourse structure. Bauman & Grice (2006) argue that this distinction is better conceptualized in degrees of accessibility than the binary category of given vs. new information in discourse. These studies show that specific collateral signals, in this case intonation, vary according to speaker belief. Whether or not they are part of a "code' [19] is debatable, however we restrict our discussion to the functional aspects of these collateral signals. Moreover, these studies have not examined how the *situational accessibility* of referents effects speakers' production of pitch (see [4] for a discussion of *accessibility*].

Will shared visual information effect the type of *pitch contours* speakers use when generating references? Most, if not all, empirical studies examining *pitch contours* have had a textual bias and have conceptualized their studies with a stenographer-like permanent registry or discourse record that information theory suggests [10]. We argue that the use of pitch is not only contingent on speaker belief, however also depends on the situated nature of dialogue in interlocutors shared visual world.

As mentioned above, this does not represent the majority of linguistic interactions that we face day in and day out. Ito & Speer (2005) examined the use of H* and

L+H* accents on visual search in a Christmas tree decoration task and found that L+H* accents caused listeners to expect contrast. Whilst this study examined the effect of *pitch accents* on visual search in an unscripted collaboration task, it did not examine the coordination of beliefs during joint reference.

Another type of intonational contour whose function has been recently debated is the *high rise terminal contour*. These contours have also been associated with *uptalk*, which is thought to have originated in Valley Girl Talk [22], however also has origins in Australian English [21] and has recently spread to British English [23]. Pierrehumbert & Hirshberg (1990) originally proposed that final rising contours have a "forward-looking" function, i.e. direct a listener's attention to upcoming information. This function, however, is couched in terms of information structure and does not reflect what Allen (1984) referred to as their collaborative function. Fletcher et al (2002) attempted this hypotheses and found that final rises starting in the lower part of a speaker's pitch range (L*L-H%) consisted of more backward looking functions (agreements, understanding, etc.), whereas final rises starting higher up in a speaker's pitch range (L*H-H%) entail more "forward-looking functions" (action directives, statements, and information requests). Fletcher et al (2002) couldn't explain these differences and concluded that these differences may have emerged as a function of the map task itself. We propose that these differences are not distal, i.e. "backward-looking" or "forward-looking", rather are proximal to the intents and purposes of the conversation at hand. In other words, these contours are used to coordinate joint attention online and we predict that these contours are more likely to illicit back-channels across belief conditions.

Our study examined these contours in an unscripted fashion where interlocutors spontaneously discussed four opinions on a variety of topics as opposed to an action-based task, such as a map task. This will enable us to see how interlocutors employ different pitch contours during belief manipulation. More specifically, preliminary data analysis showed a pattern that speakers were using *rising boundary tones* (either H-H% or L-H%) similar to that of a question to seek affirmation in a proposition. These *confirmation contours* as we will refer to them may be a useful device in the coordination of attention. We will restrict our analysis to these specific pitch contours and will address other pitch contours (H* and L* accents) in future work.

In our paper we will provide an alternate account by examining intonation as a mechanism that interlocutors use to coordinate attention (see [13] for an account of *shared knowledge*). More specifically, we examine how speakers mark references to shared visual space when mutual belief has been manipulated.

1.2 Referring to a Shared World

Speakers and listeners jointly agree upon, and in some instances create, terms and labels in the course of a conversation (referred to as *conceptual pacts* in [5]). Schober (1993) examined if interlocutors egocentrically refer to their shared environment or if they take shared perspectives into consideration across different seating arrangements, which altered the perspective of their partner. He found that speakers don't always use egocentric descriptions of their shared environment, rather that interlocutors collaborate by taking into consideration the perspective of the other interlocutor. An important distinction made in this study is the separation of *spatial* and *conceptual*

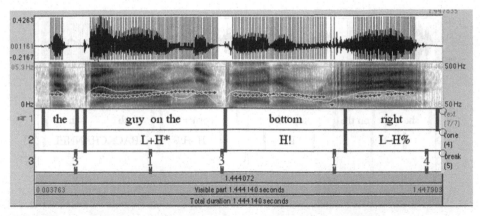

Fig. 1. *Rising contour* - high rise terminal contour on "right"

perspectives. Spatial perspectives are defined as the reference of physical locations corresponding to a particular point of view (usually that of the speakers. *Conceptual perspectives* refer to a point of view that is common in all perspectives. We will adopt a similar distinction in our study, however our participants will always share the same point of view, namely have identical images (depending on condition) in front of both of them. Therefore, we will distinguish reference types as *visual* or *content* references, however not in terms of perspective, rather in terms of situated or non-situated information in joint visual representations.

To test the notion that interlocutors will exploit their shared visual environment, we will examine if speakers change how they reference particular viewpoints of four talking heads in an unscripted spontaneous speech.   Will speakers use spatial information in generating their references if they believe that the listener can see what they can see? Likewise, will speakers compensate for the discrepancy between shared visual environments by referring to talking heads based on the content of their viewpoint?

1.3 Back-Channeling

When we speak, we coordinate whose turn it is to speak [15]. *Back-channels* amount to words such as *um, uh-huh, ok*, etc. that signal to the speaker that the listener has understood what the speaker has said [16]. Also, speakers can make pauses after certain propositions to illicit back-channels to seek the implicit discretion of the listener to continue [15]. Prosodic cues are thought to illicit back-channels, however the relationship between prosodic cues and back-channels is not one-to-one [24]. It follow then that the elicitation of back-channels is based more on situational variables, i.e. the need to ground utterances in conversation.

We are interested in examining under which belief conditions interlocutors use more back-channels in grounding references. If mutual belief is low, i.e. the mismatched belief conditions, then we expect interlocutors to use more back-channels to coordinate their attention.

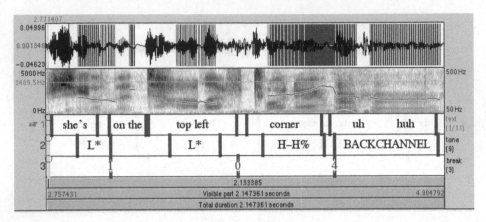

Fig. 2. Rising contour with back-channel from listener

2 Method

2.1 Participants

Participants were 24 UC Santa Cruz undergraduates (12 conversational dyads) who completed the study in partial fulfillment of course requirements.

2.2 Apparatus

Participants were ran, two at a time, in the Eye Think lab's speech and gaze tracking system. Each participant sat in a cubicle in reclining chair, looking up at an arm mounted 19" LCD screen approximately 60cm away. The participant wore a headset, through which they could hear the stimuli and speak to the experimenter and the other participant as the experimenter required.

Participants' speech was digitally recorded via a Yamaha MG16/GFX mixer onto a Mac G5. Audio files were originally recorded into a MPEG file and a stereo WAV file was extracted with PRAAT at 44100 Hz.

2.3 Stimuli

Participants watched a series of four 'talking heads' give their opinions on various topics. Each video clip subtended approximately 9° visual angle, and were shown on a 2x2 black grid with a white background. Each talking head appeared serially, i.e. one after the other, however in random order across conditions.

2.4 Procedure and Design

Stimuli were presented in random order across pairs one talking head a time. Prior to beginning the experiment, both participants were told that they would be referred to as "participant B". By default they believed the other participant to be participant A. Both participants watched a QuickTime movie of four talking heads introducing different viewpoints appearing one after the other in random order. After watching the talking heads, the participants were instructed to have a discussion about the four viewpoints presented by the talking heads. The critical experimental manipulation is as follows; participants were either told that 1) both participant A & B could see the talking heads on the screen (*present-present* condition) 2) participant B could see the screen, however participant A could not see the talking heads on the screen (*present-absent* condition) 3) participant A could see the screen, however participant B could not see the talking heads on the screen (*absent-present* condition) or 4) both participant A & B could not see the talking heads on the screen (*absent-absent* condition). In other words the visual information that both participants shared during their conversation was either present or absent to the speaker during their unscripted conversation and/or it was believe by the speaker that the listener either could or could not see the talking heads during the conversation.

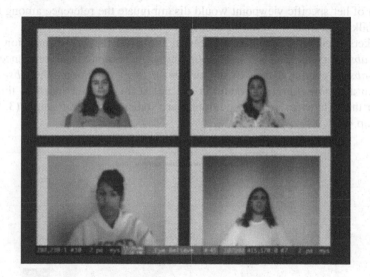

Fig. 3. Screen shot of talking heads

3   Results

3.1   Reference Type

All references by participants to the talking heads or the viewpoints they expressed were coded. The two main categories against which the references were coded were *visual* or *content*. A *visual* reference entailed information that was visually available such as position on the screen (which quadrant), gender, or order of appearance (1st, 2nd, 3rd. etc.). For example, a speaker might refer to a talking head by saying, "the guy on the top right", "the girl with the red shirt", "the first guy", etc. *Content* references specifically entailed information pertaining the particular viewpoint of the talking head or information not visually available when the talking heads were present. For example, "I agree with the idea of the Iraq war being all about oil" or " I don't have a MySpace page because of all of the perverts on the Internet". The first example demonstrates a speaker expressing her agreement with an explicit viewpoint of a talking head, whereas the second example includes the viewpoint of a talking head as a justification for a pre-existing disposition. Despite *content references* taking many forms, the speaker chose to reference the viewpoint of a talking head in this specific form.

In a few cases, both types of references were used. In these cases, the reference was coded in terms of the piece of information that disambiguated the reference. For example, a reference such as "the guy on the top left who said that you can't stop steroid abuse" would be coded as *visual*. On the other hand, a reference such as "the girl who was talking about UCSC's natural beauty" would be coded as a *content* reference if there was more than one female amongst the four talking heads. Only the mention of her specific viewpoint would disambiguate the reference among the other female talking heads.

Speakers used more visual references in the *present-present* condition than the *present-absent* condition, and correspondingly more non-visual references in the *present-absent* condition than in the *present-present* condition. The *absent-absent* condition and *absent-present* condition did not seem to differ much in this regard, however the differences across conditions were statistically significant, $\chi^2(3, N = 314) = 16.21, p < .01$.

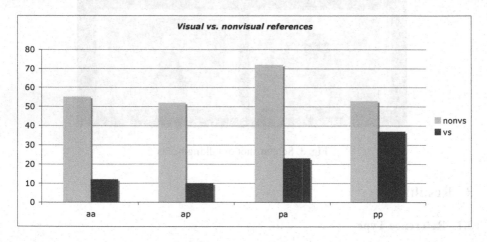

Fig. 4. Visual vs. non-visual references

Similarly, speakers used more content references than non-content references in the *present-absent* condition, whereas the opposite pattern emerged in the *present-present* condition. There were more content than non-content references in both the *absent-absent* and *absent-present* condition, however this pattern was more pronounced in the *absent-present* condition. The differences between conditions were statistically significant, $\chi^2(3, N = 314) = 9.62, p < .03$.

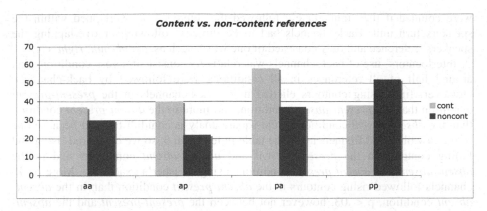

Fig. 5. Content vs. Non-content references

3.2 Pitch Contours

We were interested in examining the effect of rising boundary tones on the coordination of joint attention. In other words, do *conformation contours* direct attention the way that pointing or gestural information may? We compared phrase final rising intonation to final falling pitch contours across different belief conditions to see if speakers consciously are more likely to seek confirmation in matching or mismatching belief conditions. It should also be noted that many *confirmation contours* are followed by back-channels, but not always. The following section will present a breakdown of back-channels following pitch contours.

Speakers tended to use more rising *confirmation contours* in the *present-present* condition than in the *present-absent condition*, and more in the *absent-present* condition than in the *absent-absent* condition. These results were statistically significant, $\chi^2(3, N = 132) = 8.77$, $p < .05$.

Table 1. Confirmation contours across belief conditions

Rising vs. falling final contour	Rising contour	Falling contour	Total
absent-absent	10	16	26
absent-present	16	13	29
present-absent	20	18	38
present-present	29	10	39
Total	75	57	132

3.3 Back-Channeling

We hypothesized that listeners may be more likely to back-channel in certain belief conditions to compensate for the lack of gesture use and pointing. Back-channels were counted if they immediately followed the reference or overlapped within the speakers turn unit. Back-channels had to be directly following or overlapping the speakers' reference and only consisted of one word, such as, *ok, uh-huh, right,* etc.

Interlocutors' use of back-channels was relatively consistent across conditions, i.e. around half of all references in all conditions were followed by back-channels. However, final rising contours elicited more back-channels in the *present-present* condition than the *present-absent* condition, and more in the *absent-present* condition than the *absent-absent* condition. A chi-square analysis couldn't be used because one of the raw observed frequencies in the table in less than 5, so we compared rising and falling contours in the *present-present* and *present-absent* conditions and in the *absent-absent* and *absent present* conditions using a Fisher's exact test. More back-channels followed rising contours in the *absent-present* condition than in the *absent-absent* condition, p < .03, however not between the *present-present* and the *absent-absent* condition, p >.05.

Table 2. Back-channels illicited by contour across belief conditions

Back-channels after rising or falling contour	Rising contour	Falling contour	Total
absent-absent	7	8	15
absent-present	12	2	14
present-absent	10	11	21
present-present	12	6	18
Total	41	27	68

4 Conclusion

We examined interlocutors' use of *collateral signals* across manipulation of belief of shared visual common ground. Interlocutors altered their utterances in ways that exploited their mutual beliefs and compensated for their lack of visual common ground. Following previous findings [14], current work is examining participants' eye movements during their conversation, to see if certain types of references are indeed more efficient at coordinating attention.

Speakers used more visual references when they believed that both they and the listeners could see the 4 talking heads on the screens (*present-present* condition). In other words, interlocutors exploit their shared visual common ground. In contrast, when speakers believed that only they could see the screen (*present-absent* condition), they were more likely to use content references than when speakers thought that both they and the listeners saw the same images (*present-present* condition). This also happened when speakers thought that only the listener could see the talking heads, however to a lesser degree. This result makes sense because it suggests that speakers are taking into account their belief that the listener cannot see what they can, i.e. do not share visual common ground, and hence exploit their non-visual common ground, i.e. the talking head's verbal messages.

Participants use of *confirmation contours* was determined by what they believed their conversational partner could see. When they believed their partner could see items onscreen, *confirmation contours* increased. Moreover, these *confirmation contours* elicited more back-channels in both the the *absent-present* condition than in the *absent-present* condition, however this finding did not differ reliably between the *present-present* and the *present-absent condition*. Future research needs to examine not only the reliability of these findings, but also the temporal relationships between these pitch contours and back-channels.

By experimentally manipulating mutual belief, we were able to examine how interlocutors selectively use *collateral signals* to achieve common ground. Together, our findings suggest that speakers formulate their utterance based on what they believe to be in the common ground. To our knowledge, no other study has manipulated speaker belief about common ground, whilst keeping the common ground information itself constant. This paradigm seems promising especially as it relates to investigating how interlocutors manipulate prosodic features in spontaneous speech. These data also provide evidence against the claim [20] that interlocutors construct utterances egocentrically and show how speakers coordinate joint attention by exploiting situational variables, especially as they relate to speaker belief.

These findings shed light on the situational variables that interlocutors take into consideration when generating their messages. These data provide evidence for *embedded language* [25] in that they show how linguistic forms prepare interlocutors for situated action [3]. Also, this study shows that prosodic features such as intonation have an important functional role within conversation. Also, it appears that their functions are situationally variable and are inextricably related to what these prosodic features "mean". Therefore, any theory of intonational meaning must take into consideration these functional and situational properties.

Our study examined how situational variables such as shared visual environment can effect how speakers generate utterances. We take this as evidence that some functional aspects of linguistic communication are situated in communicative environments as opposed to being part of a *code* [19]. Further research needs to directly address the temporal effects of *collateral signals* on joint attention in shared visual environments. In other words, do linguistic changes across belief conditions directly affect joint attention and to what extent do interlocutors use these utterances to navigate their shared visual world?

References

[1] Arnold, J.E., Tanenhaus, M.K., Altman, R.J., Fanano, M.: The old and thee, uh, new; Disfluency and reference resolution. Psychological Science 15(9), 578–582 (2004)
[2] Bangerter, A., Clark, H.H.: Navigating joint projects with dialogue. Cognitive Science 27, 195–225 (2003)
[3] Barsolou, L.H.: Language comprehension: Archival memory or preparation for situation action? Discourse Processes 28, 61–80 (1999)
[4] Bauman, S., Grice, M.: The intonation of accessibility. Journal of Pragmatics 38(10), 1636–1657 (2006)

[5] Brennan, S.E., Clark, H.H.: Conceptual pacts and lexical choice in conversation. Journal of Experimental Psychology: Learning, Memory, and Cognition 22, 1482–1493 (1996)

[6] Brennan, S.E., Schober, M.F.: How listensers compensate for disfluencies in spontaneous speech. Journal of Memory and Language 44, 274–276 (2001)

[7] Clark, H.H.: Speaking in time. Speech Communication 36, 5–13 (2002)

[8] Clark, H.H., Fox Tree, J.E.: Using uh and um in spontaneous speech. Cognition 84, 73–111 (2002)

[9] Clark, H.H., Krych, M.A.: Speaking while monitoring addressees for understanding. Journal of Memory and Language 50(1), 62–81 (2004)

[10] Dahan, D., Tannenhaus, M.K., Chambers, C.G.: Accent and reference resolution in spoken-language comprehension. Journal of Memory and Language 47, 292–314 (2002)

[11] Ito, K., Speer, S.R.: The effect of intonation on visual search: An eye-tracking study. Paper presented at the Experimental Pragmatics: Exploring the Cognitive Basis of Conversation, Cambridge (2005)

[12] Pierrehumbert, J., Hirshberg, J.: The Meaning of Intonational Contours in the Interpretation of Discourse. In: Cohen, P.R., Morgen, J., Pollack, M.E. (eds.) Intentions in Communications, pp. 271–311. The MIT Press, Cambridge (1990)

[13] Prince, E.F.: Toward a taxonomy of given-new information. In: Cole, P. (ed.) Radical Pragmatics, pp. 223–256. Academic Press, New York (1981)

[14] Richardson, D.C., Dale, R., Kirkham, N.Z.: The art of coordination is in conversation: Common ground and the coupling of eye movements during dialogue. Psychological Science (in press)

[15] Schegloff, E.A., Jefferson, G., Sacks, H.: The preference for self-repair in the organization of repair in conversation. Language 53, 361–382 (1977)

[16] Stenström, A.B.: An Introduction to Spoken Interaction. Longman, London (1994)

[17] Swerts, M.: Filled Pauses as markers of discourse structure. Journal of Pragmatics 30, 485–496 (1998)

[18] Schober, M.: Spatial perspective-taking in conversation. Cognition 47(1), 1–24 (1993)

[19] Wilson, D., Wharton, T.: Relevance and prosody. Journal of Pragmatics 38(10), 1559–1579 (2006)

[20] Keysar, B., Barr, D.J., Balin, J.A., Brauner, J.S.: Taking perspective in conversation: The role of mutual knowledge in comprehension. Psychological Science 11, 32–38 (2000)

[21] Allen, K.: The high rise terminal contour. Australian Journal of Linguistics 4, 19–32 (1984)

[22] Lakoff, R.T.: Language and a women's place. Harper Colophon, New York (1975)

[23] Fletcher, J., Stirling, L., Mushin, I., Wales, R.: Intonational rises and dialog acts in the Australian English Map Task. Language and Speech 45(3), 229–252 (2002)

[24] Ward, N., Tsukahara, W.: Prosodic features which cue back-channel responses in English and Japanese. Journal of Pragmatics 32, 1207–1777 (2000)

[25] Spivey, M.J., Richardson, D.C.: Language embedded in the environment. in The Cambridge Handbook of Situated Cognition (to appear) (in press)

Investigating the Specifics of Contextual Elements Management: The CEManTIKA Approach

Vaninha Vieira[1,2], Patrícia Tedesco[1], Ana Carolina Salgado[1], and Patrick Brézillon[2]

[1] Center of Informatics, Federal University of Pernambuco, PO Box 7851, Recife, PE, Brasil
{vvs,acs,pcart}@cin.ufpe.br
[2] LIP6, University of Paris 6, 104 Avenue du Président Kennedy, 75016 Paris, France
{vieira,brezil}@poleia.lip6.fr

Abstract. In times where users need to process an ever increasing amount of information to perform more complex tasks in less time, the introduction of context in computer systems is becoming a necessity. However, building a context-sensitive system entails more work in comparison to traditional systems development: in the former, one must care for context-related tasks, such as the acquisition, processing, storage, manipulation and presentation of contextual elements. Context management proposes the separation of context related tasks from the application's business features. This paper presents a study on context management and discusses our proposal for a context manager, called CEManTIKA (*Contextual Elements Management Through Incremental Knowledge Acquisition*). A scenario is presented to illustrate its applicability.

Keywords: Context, Context Management, Context-Sensitive System.

1 Introduction

Users of computer systems often have problems to carry out their tasks effectively, since they have to process an ever increasing amount of information to perform more complex tasks in less time. Computing systems, in general, are not proactive, and usually act the same way and provide the same answers without considering the differences between their users. Hence, developers are seeking ways to build applications that are more adaptive, flexible and easy to use. The goal is to provide services that transparently ease the interface between humans and machines.

Context is what underlies the ability to differentiate one situation from another and to characterize entities and events. Differently from human to human interaction, where context is a well known and understood concept, to model and manipulate context in human to computer interactions is not a trivial task. Besides, context management generally is not the main feature but an optional, secondary functionality in a system. Also, most context-sensitive systems do not take into account requirements such as modularity, reusability or interoperability [1] and implement context manipulation tasks in a proprietary way, so as to fulfil the particular needs of each system.

B. Kokinov et al. (Eds.): CONTEXT 2007, LNAI 4635, pp. 493–506, 2007.

Context management aims at providing solutions to separate context manipulation tasks from applications' business. This enables systems to reuse solutions and to share contextual elements. Generally, a context manager is responsible for context-related tasks such as: the acquisition, representation, processing, storage and dissemination of contextual elements.

In this paper we discuss the topic of context management and present our proposal for a context management system, named CEManTIKA (*Contextual Elements Management Through Incremental Knowledge Acquisition*). What differentiates our approach from others proposed in the literature (e.g. [2-6]) is that the existing ones restrict the contextual elements to those that can be perceived by sensors, such as location, identity, devices and activities. Since context is complex and dynamic, we believe that it is impractical for a system analyst to define *a priori* all contextual elements that must be managed by the system. Moreover, not all contextual elements that should be considered in the system can be perceived by sensors.

In this light, CEManTIKA proposes the incremental acquisition of contextual elements according to the usage of the context-sensitive system and addresses two main issues: (1) the definition and management of as much contextual elements as possible in the application domain; (2) the identification of the best way of using how to use these contextual elements to assist a specific situation distinguishing the set of relevant contextual elements.

The rest of the paper is organized as follows: Section 2 discusses the definition of context that we use throughout the paper; Section 3 introduces the topic of context management; Section 4 introduces the CEManTIKA system, discussing how it intervenes in context dynamics, presenting its architecture and exemplifying its usability through an example of use; Section 5 discusses some related works comparing them to our approach; and, Section 6 points out some final considerations and further work.

2   Our Working Definition of Context

In this work we use the context definition proposed by Brézillon and Pomerol [8]. According to their model, context is always related to a focus (e.g. a task or a step in a problem solving or decision making). At a given focus the context is the aggregation of three types of knowledge: *Contextual Knowledge* (CK), *External Knowledge* (EK) and *Proceduralized Context* (PC). CK is the part of the context that is relevant for the current focus while EK is the part that is not relevant. EK includes the knowledge unknown by the user or system while in the focus. The CK is the knowledge known by the user that is relevant to the focus at hand, and that could be activated to support the user in that focus. CK acts as a filter that defines, at a given time, what knowledge pieces must be taken into account (explicit knowledge), separating them from those that are not necessary or that are already shared (implicit knowledge). The PC is the dynamic part of the context; the one that will be effectively used in the focus. The PC set is composed by a subset of the CK that is assembled, organized and instantiated to address the current focus and effectively support the task at hand.

From a conceptual point of view, it is important to consider the EK, CK and PC whenever thinking about context, since the transformation of the EK into the CK is related to the context dynamics. Not all contextual knowledge is instantly known in a focus, and to support the task it may be necessary to look for information that helps establish the context (acquired from the EK set).

Thinking in terms of implementation, we use the term *contextual element* (CE) to refer to pieces of data, information or knowledge that can be used to define the context. This separation is necessary because contextual knowledge, in fact, comprises what is in the user's mind and thus is too abstract. In order to treat context computationally, it is important to make this distinction between contextual data, contextual information and contextual knowledge.

Contextual data is the basic, atomic part of the context that can be acquired directly through virtual or physical sensors, such as location coordinates, people's identification or weather temperature. *Contextual information* is the CE that can be derived from several contextual data through association. For example, the contextual data set {[location=Paris], [month=01], [temperature=18°C]} implies the contextual information [weather=hot]. If we change the location to Recife (Brazil) the equivalent contextual information will be [weather=cold]. So, we may have the same set of data with different interpretations: While the information is something that once inferred can be easily instantiated and shared between human and software agents, the *contextual knowledge* is personal and is inside people's head as mental schemas that help them to interpret external events.

We identify and manipulate CEs in terms of CE Sets. A *CE Set* comprises one CE and its instances. Furthermore, a CE may have one or more instances, which are themselves CEs. For example, consider a CE [MissionOfficialReasons] that has as instances the set {[Presentation], [Experimentation], [Meeting]}, meaning that the official reasons of an academic mission may be for a presentation, an experimentation *in loco* or a meeting. In its turn, the instance [Presentation] is itself a CE and has as instances the subset {[Seminar], [ConferencePaper]}.

Another term we use in our work is Instantiated CE (*ICE*). An ICE means the chosen instance for a CE in a given focus by a specific user. For example, a user Luce in her mission identified that the reason for her mission was to present a paper in a conference. So the ICE for Luce related to the CE [MissionOfficialReasons] is the path {[Presentation]/[ConferencePaper]}. An ICE may also include a value for a CE (e.g. {[MissionLocation]="Paris"}. An *ICE Set* is used to define the PC in a focus, meaning the set of all relevant ICE in that focus.

Because a CE can itself have a context, we meet McCarthy's observations [9]: (1) a context is always relative to another context, (2) Contexts have an infinite dimension; (3) Contexts cannot be described completely; and (4) When several contexts occur in a discussion, there is a common context above all of them to which all terms and predicates can be lifted.

3 Context Management

Context-sensitive systems are those that understand and use contextual elements to provide relevant services and/or information to the users or to other applications during the execution of some task. The building of a context-sensitive system comprises tasks such as: to specify the CEs needed in the application domain; to build components to acquire and instantiate these CEs; to create aggregation and reasoning modules that enable it to process the instantiated CEs according to the application needs; and to effectively use the identified set of instantiated CEs in a focus to provide for the application adaptability.

Context management involves the definition of models and systems to assist the acquisition, manipulation and maintenance of a shared repository of CEs, thus enabling the usage of these elements by different context-sensitive systems. The main idea is to reduce the complexity of building context-sensitive systems, by transferring tasks related to CE manipulation to an intermediate layer. In this light, the task of managing context includes the definition of: (1) a representation model to describe and share CE sets; (2) an infrastructure to detect, update and query CE sets; (3) mechanisms to process, reason about, and infer new CE sets from existing ones; and (4) mechanisms to identify the ICE in a focus.

An overview of the context management process and its main functionalities is illustrated in Fig. 1. The first step is to *acquire* the CEs associated to a situation. Computer systems may use virtual and physical sensors, user interfaces (e.g. forms), persistent databases, and so on, to acquire these elements. After that, the system must use knowledge bases, and inference engines to *process* the acquired CEs through reasoning and associations. The interpreted context is used to infer information and to trigger services that must be provided and executed.

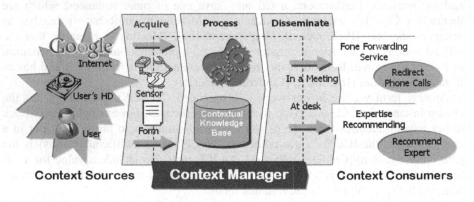

Fig. 1. Overview of a Generic Context Manager Main Functionalities

For example, the context manager may acquire information about a given user's presence, activities scheduled in her/his calendar and location from context sources such as web search engines, message exchanging programs (e.g. MSN and Yahoo), the user's hard disk, or the user her/himself. The acquired elements are then processed and the manager may infer that "the user is available at her/his desk". With this inferred CE, a Phone Forwarding Service can redirect phone calls to the user's desk. If the manager infers that the user is in a meeting, than the phone forwarding service may redirect the phone calls to the user's mobile phone or to her/his secretary. The example described before is about functionalities that may be provided by any context-sensitive system. However, a context management system brings the added advantages described below:

- *Reusability*: the solution for each context management task can be done in a generic way and be reused by several applications;
- *Sharing*: Applications can share CEs acquired from different and heterogeneous context sources;
- *Context source independence*: Applications are developed independently from the underlying contextual source;
- *Ease of use*: Application developers can focus on their business model and leave details of context management to the manager implementation.

In order to be effective, a context manager must take into account aspects such as: separation of the context model and the application domain model; maintenance of a sharable context model that enables communication between different components or systems; provision of descriptions and interfaces for the manager internal components and their formats to allow communication and interoperability among the manager's components and context consumers.

4 Managing Contextual Elements with CEManTIKA

This section presents our proposal for a context manager, named CEManTIKA. We discuss an overview of the system, its relation with context dynamics, and its architecture. A more complete description of the system can be found in the project site [10].

4.1 CEManTIKA and Context Dynamics

Since context is what enables the characterization of entities (e.g. people, devices, actions, events, software components and so on) and entities exist within a knowledge domain, context is also strongly influenced by the domain it is applied in. This means that when introducing and managing CEs for an application domain one must first identify the CE Sets that characterize the entities in that domain, and construct the Contextual Elements Base (CEB) for the domain. Different domains necessarily entail building different CEBs since the CE could have different meanings in different domains.

Context is a dynamic construction that evolves with the focus. As the focus changes, the set of CEs that must be considered changes accordingly. Context dynamics is represented by the transformation of External Knowledge into Contextual Knowledge and then into Proceduralized Context influenced by the focus as stated in Brézillon and Pomerol's model [8] and illustrated in Fig. 2. CEManTIKA manages the different focus in the domain and, for a given focus, it identifies which CE Sets must be considered and instantiated to support the task at hand (the ICE Set). A Proceduralized Context Base (PCB) maintains historical cases of the ICE Set built and their respective focus. The historical ICE Sets stored in the PCB aid the identification of the relevant CEs in other focus.

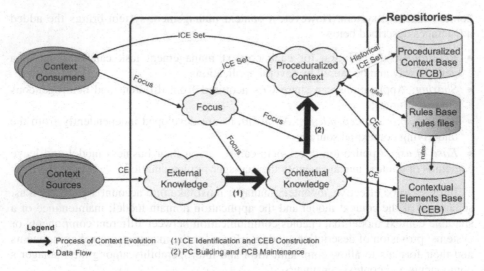

Fig. 2. The Role of CEManTIKA in Context Dynamics

The context management in CEManTIKA comprises two main processes (as illustrated in Fig. 2): (1) the CE Identification and CEB Construction; and (2) the PC Building and PCB Maintenance. These processes are detailed in the next sections.

4.1.1 CE Identification and CEB Construction

This process comprises the identification of the CEs in a domain and the acquisition of CEs from different context sources by CEManTIKA. Since context is a very subtle concept and has an infinite dimension, it is impossible to think about context management in a totally generic way without defining and limiting the scope of what will be characterized. So, it is important to identify and delimit the domain and the entities that the contextual elements are about.

To be effective, a context manager must know the domain entities very well. Thus, a well designed and filled in CEB is a key factor. It is necessary to look increasingly deeper and specifically in the domain , so that the manager can identify how a change in the context affects the state of the entities and consequently the system's actions and events.

To understand this requirement we can think about a GPS system, a very successful example of context-sensitive system, which aids drivers to identify the best itinerary from one place to another. As dynamic contextual element, GPS consider the user's location at a given moment. According to that location the system shows the path that the user must follow to arrive at the destination; as the user moves on, the GPS updates this path and indicates the next steps that the user must take until finally arriving at the destination. To provide the appropriate itineraries the system counts with as much knowledge as possible related to the region it will be used in. For instance, a base with information about France will be really useless in Brazil.

The difficulty of identifying the CE Sets in a domain is that the interpretation of the contextual elements changes widely, varying according to different systems' users. Hence, it is very difficult and not very reliable for a system designer to describe *a priori* all contextual elements related to a domain/task based exclusively on her/his own experience. We believe that the CE Sets must be identified and defined incrementally during the system usage with the users' participation. As stated by Brézillon in [7], the incremental acquisition of CEs may occur either by: the acquisition of new knowledge pieces; the learning of a new knowledge structure while building the PC; or learning by structuring the contextual knowledge through the user's feedback after using the proceduralized context. Thus, the manager will be able to learn and accumulate several views from different people acting as a kind of memory support system.

4.1.2 PC Building and PCB Maintenance

The PC building process is related to the identification of the CE and ICE Sets that must be considered to support the current focus and to the maintain the PCB. Here, CEManTIKA acts in four points:

(i) Given a focus, CEManTIKA identifies and extracts from the CEB the CE sets that should be considered;

(ii) After that, using rules defined in a rule base, CEManTIKA selects a CE subset that is instantiated and that will be used to build the PC in the focus (the ICE set) from the identified CE sets . To build the PC, the manager also considers the historical ICE sets maintained in the PCB;

(iii) The manager gives the user the opportunity to identify if the chosen CEs were really useful, allowing the user to validate the PC built in the ICE Set.;

(iv) The last point is the manager's ability to learn from the user's feedback, which entails the following activities: building a new ICE Set including and instantiating additional CEs necessary; or changing the current focus and rebuilding the ICE Set according to this new focus.

The ICE Set thus built affects the focus and may demand the instantiation of other CEs or the inclusion of new CEs (acquired from context sources) into the system. For example, consider a scenario of a system that support users in planning travels, where the user's focus is *booking a hotel*, and the current ICE Set is {[hotelType]=[comfortable]; [hotelLocation]=[near the conference]}. According to this ICE Set the system proposes a list of hotels that fits the user's current context. Later, when the user's focus is *verifying mission costs*, s/he observes that the nearest hotels are also the most expensive and so s/he cannot afford to pay for them thus, another CE {[maxPrice]<[availableHotelResource]} is inserted into the ICE Set. Thus, when the user is again in the focus *booking a hotel* this new ICE Set will be used; allowing the system to build a new list of hotels considering also this new CE.

4.2 CEManTIKA Architecture

An overview of the CEManTIKA architecture is presented in Fig. 3. CEManTIKA components are located in two different hosts: (1) *the context-aware system host*, where the context-sensitive system that uses the manager is running; (2) *the CEManTIKA server host* that maintains the core components and the repositories (CEB and PCB). The context sources and consumers (components in light gray in Fig. 3) are the interaction points between the context-sensitive system and CEManTIKA.

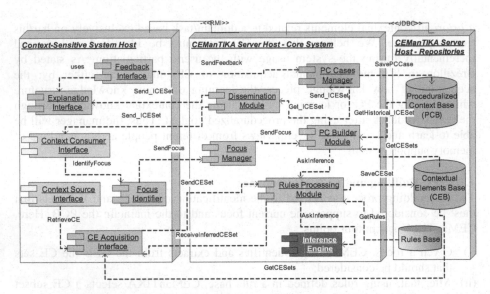

Fig. 3. Overview of CEManTIKA Architecture (using UML notation)

The process described in Section 4.1.1 is performed by an instantiation of the component *CE Acquisition Interface*, attached to a context source. Each context source is associated to one or more acquisition components. The acquired CE Sets are sent to the *Rule Processing Module* that uses the pre-defined rules and an inference engine to process the CE sets, verifying inconsistencies, and inferring new CE sets that are sent back to the acquisition module.

The process discussed in Section 4.1.2 in the items (i) and (ii) occurs as follows: inside the client host, the component *Focus Identifier* discovers what the user's current focus is and sends this information to the *Focus Manager*. The Focus Manager then informs the current focus to the module *PC Builder,* which triggers the generation of a new ICE Set. To do this the *PC Builder* identifies what are the CE Sets associated with the focus in the CEB and retrieves their instantiated values. Also, the PC Builder looks in the PCB for historical ICE Sets built before for the same focus. With these two inputs the PC Builder decides which CEs will be considered and builds the final ICE Set. After that, it sends the ICE Set to the *Dissemination Module* that will redistribute it to the *Context Consumer* and the *Explanation Interface*. The Explanation Interface provides the user with an explanation about how the ICE set was built, including what rules were activated or what decisions were made to restrict the set of CEs that was finally considered. Through the *Feedback Interface* the user (or a software agent) can indicate to CEManTIKA how useful was the ICE Set for her/him during his task development and how much the ICE Set has really expressed her/his current context. This feedback is sent to the *PC Cases Manager* that stores the new case in the PCB for later usage.

The current version of CEManTIKA is implemented in Java (the core components) and PhP (the users' web interfaces). As communication protocols we are using: RMI (*Remote Method Invocation*) to enable the communication between the client and

CEManTIKA Server, and JDBC (*Java Database Connectivity*) as interface with the repositories host. The repositories are currently described using the relational model in MySQL databases. And, as reasoning technique we are using first order logic through production rules that are processed by the inference engine JEOPS (Java Embedded Object Production System [11].

4.3   Example of CE Manipulation

To illustrate the functioning of CEManTIKA, let us consider the domain of academic missions. Researchers frequently have to plan their travels to accomplish missions in other organizations, generally located in different cities. These missions may have different purposes, such as to present a paper in a conference, to perform research experiments or to participate in a meeting. The mission planning demands that the researcher takes care of several tasks; some of which are illustrated in Fig. 4: (F1) provide the general description of the mission; (F2) book transport; (F3) book accommodation; and (F4) execute the procedures to effectuate the payment. Each task has a specific objective and represents a different focus for the user.

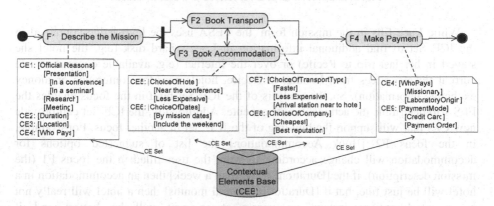

Fig. 4. Illustration of some foci and related CE sets in a mission planning

Each focus activates a different set of CEs. In the example, the focus F1 has the following CE Set {[Official Reasons]; [Duration]; [Location]; [Who pays?]}. Since, a CE may instantiate others CE Sets, the CE [Official Reasons] instantiates the CE Set {[Presentation]; [Research]; [Meeting]}, and so on.

In this domain we have specified a context-sensitive system called Form Filling Support Agent (FFSA). FFSA is an assistant that aids missionaries in their mission planning through a dynamic form that follows the user through the different phases (i.e. focus) related to the mission. FFSA interact with CEManTIKA to obtain the corresponding CE Sets given a new focus. Through the instantiated CE sets FFSA can, for example, emphasize the fields in the form the user must fill or suggest related information that could interest the user and support her/his decisions.

As an example we can consider a missionary named Luce, which is as a professor at the London United University. Luce must prepare a new mission to Recife (Brazil)

to present a paper in a conference and she uses the FFSA to assist her in this mission planning. The mission form is composed initially with the CE Sets stored in the CEB, associated to each focus (as illustrated in Fig. 4), and each focus activates a different CE Set. During the form filling Luce can instantiate the existing CE Sets with information about her mission. Fig. 5 illustrates the ICE Set related to Luce's mission in the focus F1: {[Official Reasons]/[Presentation]/[In a conference]; [Duration]=[less than a week]; [Location]=[Brazil/Recife]; [Who Pays]=[London United University]}.

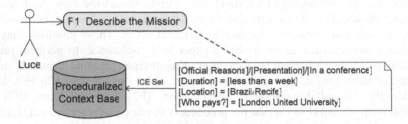

Fig. 5. Example of an ICE set related to a user in a focus

While Luce fills in the mission form, the FFSA uses the knowledge contained in the ICE Set to find additional information in Luce's hard disk (e.g. the hotel she stayed in her last trip to Recife) or over the internet (e.g. available companies and current tickets' prices from London to Recife, hotels near the conference or money exchange information). So, the analysis of the ICE Set built in the focus enables the FFSA to determine the actions it must execute. Additionally, the ICE Set can provide new CEs that will support the building of the ICE Set in another focus. For example, in the focus F2 [Book Accommodation] the list of suggested options for accommodation will change according to what the user filled in the focus F1 (the mission description): if the [Duration]=[less than a week] then an accommodation in a hotel will be just fine, but if [Duration]=[several months] then a hotel will really not be a good option, instead an apartment to rent will be better; and if [Duration]=[several years] the user could also consider to buy a property (apartment or house).

This is a small example of how a context-sensitive system may benefit from the management of CEs with CEManTIKA, through the manipulation of the user's current focus and the corresponding ICE Sets. Besides, integrating the context manipulation with the system functionality seems to be a good approach, since the manager may "learn" the contextual elements while the user executes her/his tasks.

5 Related Works

The proposals for context management that appear in the literature are associated to toolkits [2], frameworks [3], middlewares [6], engines [4] and specifications [5]. We selected one work representative of each category in different application areas to describe and compare them with our proposal.

5.1 Existing Approaches for Context Management

SOPHIE [4] is a reactive and integrated information environment that tracks the constant changes in an environment to adapt to them, for example, through the dissemination of the correct information to different receivers. As context model it uses an extension of ORM (*Object-Role Modeling*) [12] to define context concepts in high levels of abstraction. SOPHIE is integrated to a context engine that has four main layers: *context sensing*, to acquire contextual information; *context augmentation*, to store contextual information associating them to the related subject; *contextual adaptation*, to adapt the system behavior according to changes in the current context; and *contextual resource discovery*, to discover relevant context-dependent information resources. Contextual information is acquired from two sources: the application level (information stored in databases); and the environment level (dynamic information about the real, physical world).

SOCAM is a middleware for rapid prototyping of context-aware services in intelligent environments [6]. As a context model it uses an ontology named CONON (*Context Ontology*), which represents concepts related to locations, users, activities and computational entities. To assist context management, SOCAM provides support for context acquisition, sharing, reasoning, storage and dissemination. A knowledge base is used to store the acquired and inferred contextual knowledge. A service-locating service provides ways for context providers to publish the context information they can provide.

CXMS is a framework that offers a tool set to ease the development of context-sensitive systems [3]. They consider the context to be composed by elements such as identity, location, time and environment, represented by key-value pairs. A *context toolkit* implements the context management through four tasks: *context acquisition*, by the sensor layer; *context modeling*, through the semantic layer that provides context interpretation, semantic enrichment and context evolution management; *application adaptation behavior definition*, through the control layer, which decides the actions that must be executed in particular conditions; and *adequate information presentation*, through the actuation layer, which maps the decisions made by the control layer to actions.

CMA [5] is a standard specification for a Context Management Architecture applied to the domain of Clinical Applications. It is intended to manipulate patient contextual data, as part of the CCOW (*Clinical Context Object Workgroup*) [5]. CMA defines the interfaces and privacy policies between clinical applications known as context participants and a context manager. Context Participants query the context manager when they need to determine the current context and when they wish to update the patient's context. A CCOW-based context manager should be implemented according to the specifications in order to support different applications providing a unique sign-on portal, enabling patient's context to be propagated and interchanged between these applications. Examples of commercially available products implementing the CCOW specification are the Sentillion Vergence, Carefx Fusion and Orion Health's Concerto Context Management Suite [5].

5.2 Comparison with Our Proposal

In general, context managers take care of tasks such as: context acquisition, representation, processing, storage and dissemination. The main difference between our proposal and the approaches found in the literature is the way of reasoning about context and, consequently, the way of processing and managing it. Other approaches restrict the type of CE managed too much, limiting it, in general, to those that can be automatically acquired from physical and logical sensors (e.g. location, identity, devices and activities). Even activities are also limited to a small set of predefined options. Moreover, such managers do not provide much flexibility to change the types of CEs initially considered and managed. Another difference is that other managers do not consider the dynamics of context and generally reason in static terms.

The problem with managing context is that context is a very complex and dynamic concept, comprising much more knowledge than what sensors can perceive. We propose a context manager that can increase incrementally the types of managed CE according to the usage of the context-sensitive system, thus enabling context evolution. The manager defines the procedures and infrastructure to manipulate the CE independently from the domain or from the focus at hand. In this light, CEManTIKA is not limited to a static and pre-defined set of CE and can be reused in different domains by different applications.

6 Conclusions and Further Work

Context is becoming a necessity in computer systems. However, building a context-sensitive system entails high development cost because several context-related tasks (e.g. context identification, representation, acquisition, processing, storage, and usage) must be addressed by systems developers. Context management systems propose the separation of context manipulation tasks from the applications' business features, enabling modularity and reusability, to facilitate the building of context-sensitive systems.

This paper presented a study about context management and our proposal for a context management system, named CEManTIKA. CEManTIKA is centered around two main features: (1) to provide a domain-independent context manager that considers the dynamic nature of context, enabling the flexible and incremental building of a contextual elements base; (2) to promote the use of the current focus and case-based techniques to identify and instantiate the relevant contextual elements to support the task at hand (the Proceduralized Context).

What differentiates CEManTIKA from other approaches is that the latter restrict the contextual elements to those perceived by sensors, such as location, person identity, devices and activities. Since context is a complex concept we believe it is a better approach to enable the incremental construction of the contextual elements base according to the usage of the context-sensitive system. Also, we propose a generic, domain-independent manager that is based on a well known and accepted conceptual view of context, which guarantees that changes in the domain will not influence how the contextual elements are manipulated.

Although we understand the need to consider the interaction between the context manager and the user, this paper focused in describing the general ideas behind the manager, discussing in detail how the manager intends to support the dynamics of context evolution through the building of CEs and ICE Sets. Our studies assure us that a context manager leads to a flexible organization of the context in a changing focus, more powerful than the current fixed and rigid structures of database management systems.

Currently, we are working on the implementation of the example of use described in this paper, which includes the construction of a CEB in the academic mission domain and the prototype of the Form Filling Support Agent (FFSA). Also, we are implementing an External Information Retrieval Agent (EIRA), which makes contextualized searches in the internet for complementary information related to the mission that is being planned. The mission form will be a web page accessible by different researchers. The EIRA will provide search services in the web for transports and accommodation that match the mission values provided by the user. Changes in the focus and in mission context implies in different criteria of search by the EIRA.

We are also working on the validation of the generality of our approach by the instantiation of CEManTIKA components to the domain of expertise recommending with ICARE, a context-sensitive expert recommending system [13]. For the CE acquisition features, we are experimenting the usage of different acquisition agents attached to existing and popular working tools such as Microsoft Office (e.g. Word, Excel, PowerPoint and Outlook) and instant messenger systems (e.g. MSN). In the near future we plan to rewrite the CEB using ontologies instead of the current relational model. This is important because ontologies enable: the sharing and reuse of CE definitions between different domains; the explicit representation of the reasoning specification with its respective CE; and the usage of different existing inference engines to reason over the defined CE Sets [14].

Acknowledgments. First author wants to thank CNPq and CAPES for their financial support, and the UFBA for its support.

References

1. Riva, O.: A Context Infrastructure for the Support of Mobile Context-Aware Services (2005), Accessed in 03/2007, http://www.cs.helsinki.fi/u/kraatika/Courses/f4fMC/WS1/Riva.pdf
2. Dey, A.K., Salber, D., Abowd, G.D: A Conceptual Framework and a Toolkit for Supporting the Rapid Prototyping of Context-Aware Applications. Human Computer Interaction Journal 16, 97–166 (2001) Special Issue on Context-Aware Computing
3. Zimmermann, A., Lorenz, A., Specht, M.: Applications of a Context-Management System. In: Dey, A.K., Kokinov, B., Leake, D.B., Turner, R. (eds.) CONTEXT 2005. LNCS (LNAI), vol. 3554, pp. 556–569. Springer, Heidelberg (2005)
4. Belotti, R.: Sophie - Context Modelling and Control, Diploma thesis, Swiss Federal Institute of Technology Zurich (2004).
5. Seliger, R., Sentillion.: HL7 Context Management CCOW Standard: Technology and Subject-Independent Component Architecture (2003), Accessed in 03/2007, http://www.hl7.org.au/CCOW.htm

6. Gu, T., Pung, H.K., Zhang, D.Q.: A Service-Oriented Middleware for Building Context-Aware Services. Elsevier Journal of Network and Computer Applications (JNCA) 28(1), 1–18 (2005)

7. Brézillon, P.: Task Realization Models in Contextual Graphs. In: Dey, A.K., Kokinov, B., Leake, D.B., Turner, R. (eds.) CONTEXT 2005. LNCS (LNAI), vol. 3554, pp. 55–68. Springer, Heidelberg (2005)

8. Brézillon, P., Pomerol, J.-C.: Contextual Knowledge Sharing and Cooperation in Intelligent Assistant Systems. Le Travail Humain, PUF, Paris 62(3), 223–246 (1999)

9. McCarthy, J.: Notes on Formalizing Contexts. In: Proceedings of the Thirteenth International Joint Conference on Artificial Intelligence, San Mateo, California, pp. 555–560 (1993)

10. Vieira, V.: The CEManTIKA Project Homepage (2007), Accessed in 03/2007, http://www.cin.ufpe.br/~vvs/cemantika/

11. Figueira Filho, C.: JEOPS - The Java Embedded Object Production System (1999), Accessed in 04/2006, http://www.cin.ufpe.br/~jeops/

12. Henricksen, K., Indulska, J., Rakotonirainy, A.: Generating Context Management Infrastructure from High-Level Context Models. In: Chen, M.-S., Chrysanthis, P.K., Sloman, M., Zaslavsky, A. (eds.) MDM 2003. LNCS, vol. 2574, pp. 1–6. Springer, Heidelberg (2003)

13. Petry, H., Vieira, V., Tedesco, P., Salgado, A.C.: Um Sistema de Recomendação de Especialistas Sensível ao Contexto para Apoio à Colaboração Informal. In: Simpósio Brasileiro de Sistemas Colaborativos, Natal, RN, pp. 38–47 (2006)

14. Vieira, V., Tedesco, P., Salgado, A.C.: Towards an Ontology for Context Representation in Groupware. In: Fukś, H., Lukosch, S., Salgado, A.C. (eds.) CRIWG 2005. LNCS, vol. 3706, pp. 367–375. Springer, Heidelberg (2005)

Distributed Document Contexts in Cooperation Systems

Michael Vonrueden and Wolfgang Prinz

Fraunhofer Institute for Applied Information Technology FIT
Schloss Birlinghoven, 53754 Sankt Augustin, Germany
{michael.vonrueden, wolfgang.prinz}@fit.fraunhofer.de

Abstract. One of the foundations of cooperative work is the exchange of data and especially data that is bound to a file. The usage of tools like e-mail to exchange documents makes it difficult to keep the existing context and metadata linked to the document. A general light-weighted approach and system-architecture will be presented that prevents the loss of document-meta-information and organizes a distributed document-context as an abstract layer that summarizes and structures available metadata to a coherent unit.

Keywords: Metadata, Distributed Context, CSCW, System-Integration.

1 Introduction

One of the foundations of cooperative work is the exchange of documents and files between groups or cooperation-partners. Email, Instant-Messaging, Document Management Systems and Shared Workspaces are just a few of manifold methods and tools for file exchange between two or more persons. But every transfer of a document implies almost a complete loss of context- and meta-information, such as history-data that is bound to the document and which cannot be reconstructed automatically by the remote cooperation-partner. Regardless of the former metadata and context of a document, each time a document crosses a system-border (e.g. a cooperative document management system) it leads to the consequence that a new document-context has to be established by the receiving cooperation partner.

With focus on cooperative working environments (CWE), this paper introduces a concept of a general architecture for a persistent binding between distributed contexts, the related metadata and documents in cooperative working-scenarios. For a better understanding of the presented concept, it is essential to provide first some details about the enclosing ECOSPACE-Project.

1.1 ECOSPACE

The ECOSPACE Integrated Project [1] – which is partly funded by the European Commission in the framework of the Collaborative Work Environments Framework – aims to simplify the daily work of an eProfessional[1] by reducing the complexity of

---

[1] http://europa.eu.int/information_society/activities/atwork/work_paradigms/experts_group/index_en.htm

B. Kokinov et al. (Eds.): CONTEXT 2007, LNAI 4635, pp. 507–516, 2007.

everyday tasks. Tasks, like organizing an appointment about a discussion of a particular document, will no longer be an administrative task (like inviting people, searching for contact-details, etc.), but rather an activity-centric task like *"discuss this document with all contributors within the next hour"*. To enable such an activity-oriented approach, it is necessary to integrate different types of systems (like Instant Messaging, Document Management Systems or Video-Conferencing-Tools). Based on a service oriented approach, all systems in ECOSPACE will provide basic services that can be combined to so-called Composite Collaboration Services (CoCoS). These service-types are modeled activity centric and are able to solve tasks like the above mentioned example. The concept of distributed document contexts uses this service-oriented approach to process and offer information about available document-contexts of all integrated systems.

1.2 Context and Documents

Before introducing a general concept on how to bind metadata, contexts and documents in a persistent way, the following will give an overview about the corresponding definition of a document-context.

An interpretation of 150 different context-definitions [2] showed that it is difficult to give one valid global definition of context. The variety of context-definitions *"arises from the fact that there is no absolute context, context being relative to something"* [2] Even if the definition of context is narrowed to the field of computer-science, this conclusion is absolutely valid, since there are different definitions that relate context to a special entity in the field of computer-science. As a context in ubiquitous computing scenarios for instance focuses on a user-context (e.g. a user relative to an environment) or a system-context (e.g. a system relative to available hardware), the context discussed in this paper is a relation between a document and distributed metadata that describes a document-context.

Similar to the term context, the term metadata is also very variable in its meaning and requires, as an information-source of a document-context, a further definition. Since the focus of our proposed approach is related to cooperative-scenarios, a document-context needs to have a minimal set of metadata that describes the current situation or context of a document. This minimal set (below described as 1st level context) is categorized into four relations that especially focus a document-context in a cooperative environment (see Fig. 1).

The 1st level context enables a context-consumer (e.g. a user or a system) to reason about the current role of a document in a specific cooperative-situation. In cooperative environments the relations of document consist mainly of the categories Users, Concepts, Resources and States.

The document-context can be enriched by adding more metadata that it origin in the provided basic-context of a document. The enriched context (2nd level context) will extend the Relations: User, Concept, Resource and State by more detailed and real-time information. For instance a context can be extended by information about the availability of an author in an instant messenger-session or by providing a list of related resources (e.g. links to web-documents, other keywords) of third party services or repositories.

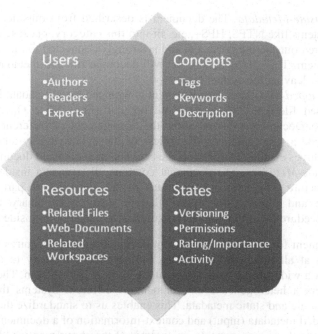

Fig. 1. Parts of Document-Context in Cooperative Settings

This paper outlines a new concept that permits a persistent binding of a document to several distributed contexts. It will be shown that a document context is not a static-setting of a fixed information source, but rather a highly dynamic setting that consists of different and variable systems that act as context-providers. The concept combines many context-providers to one single context-scope. The concept of context-scopes will be integrated, tested and evaluated in the ECOSPACE-Project as a standardized service for document-based context-information.

2   Concept of a Distributed Document Context

The conceptual design of our approach requires analyzing the main components of a distributed document context, which are documents on the one hand side and systems that provide information about these documents on the other. Questions like how a persistent binding of a document to a dynamic context can be achieved and how a dynamic context can be constructed and represented in an applicable way, have to be considered and discussed. The following section will introduce the concept of a distributed document-context with special focus to the ECOSPACE-Project [1]. Besides a general discussion how to bind metadata to a particular document, an extensible system for context-retrieval will be introduced.

2.1   Bind Metadata to Document

Analyzing the potential approaches that enable a persistent relation between context (metadata) and documents yield to three different and general methods that are summarized in the following list:

a) *Outside-Metadata*. The document is described from outside. Common file-systems like NTFS, HFS+, etc. fit into this category, because the metadata is stored outside the document and is strongly connected to the underlying file-system. This strong connection will decouple file and metadata immediately after leaving the system-boundary.

b) *Wrapped-Metadata*. The document is wrapped by a metadata-layer. Archive-based file-types becoming more popular (like Office Open XML [3] or OpenDocument [4]) and allow the arrangement of different data and files inside a single archive. Regardless of the underlying system, the usage of archives enables a strong linkage between metadata and document.

c) *Inside-Metadata*. The document contains all metadata inside the own file-structure. This approach integrates all metadata as own part of a particular file and requires for every file-type (especially binary ones) an own procedure for storing this information at a special point inside the file.

The requirement for a system-independent document-context requires the availability of metadata at all times and all places. Further it is necessary to standardize the metadata for a wide adoption and usage of the context information. The ECOSPACE-Project offers a heterogeneous environment of different systems that are able to provide dynamic and static metadata. This enables us to standardize the data-structure of the provided metadata (input) and context-information of a document (output).

In respect to those requirements, an analysis of the above mentioned methods yield to a mixed approach that uses *outside-* and *inside-metadata* in a special way[2]. Instead of providing all related metadata in the document itself, a document will just store a reference (inside-metadata) to a service that provides detailed context-information (outside-metadata). In relation to our concept, the inside-metadata is represented by a structure called ContextTag and the outside-metadata as a ContextScope.

2.2 ContextTag

To enable the document-context in a document, the file is marked with a ContextTag. A ContextTag is an XML-Structure that is integrated inside a file. This XML-Structure will give information about the following things:

1. A single document-id. This id represents a unique identifier to avoid ambiguous context in a single document.

2. One or more ContextScopes. A ContextScope points to a particular context of a document. The attribute *outdate* acts as a timestamp and informs about the last contact of a file or ContextTag with the ContextScope. The concept of ContextScope will be discussed in detail later.

The usage of the ContextTag outlines the mixed approach of inside- and outside metadata mentioned above. In contrast to the comparable XMP-Approach [5] where all metadata is written directly into the file, only a minimal set of information will be

---

[2] Although *wrapped-metadata* is comparable to the approach of *inside-metadata*, the overall-usage of archive-filetypes is (up to now) to little in respect to the usage of flat file-types and therefore considered as secondary issue.

integrated. This ContextTag (a set of references) points to different contexts and decouples the metadata from the document, without breaking the relation. Beside the avoidance of outdated-metadata, this reference-mechanism also ensures the privacy of a user or document owner, because all referenced scopes in this ContextTag are able to establish access-restrictions at every time.

```
<cx:context objectid="ec8030f7-c20a-464f-9b0e-13a3a9e97384">
    <cx:contextscope outdate="2006-11-02-16:02">http://my.files.org/cx.php</ cx:contextscope >
    <cx:contextscope outdate="2007-01-02-11:54">http://ws.extern.org/contextservice.do </ cx:contextscope >
</cx:context>
```

Fig. 2. ContextTag as XML

2.3 ContextScope

A ContextTag inside a document points to one or more ContextScopes. These scopes consist of different systems that are able to provide a valid context of a given document/object-id. These systems are divided into 1st and 2nd Level ContextProvider and provide different types of contexts. Document-Management-Systems, like the BSCW-System [6] provides a 1st level context (see green block, Fig. 3), because context information about Users, Concepts, Resources and States, are usually available in such systems. In the sense of BSCW the following information could be provided by a 1st Level Context Provider:

- Users
  - o   Name and affiliation of user
  - o   Contact-details like email, IM or telephone-number
  - o   Roles in a shared workspace
  - o   Workspace membership
- Concepts
  - o   Tags and keywords
  - o   Annotations and Document-Descriptions
- Resources
  - o   Files in the same container/folder
  - o   Files having the same tags
- States
  - o   Version of document
  - o   Permissions of user
  - o   Number of read-events

2nd level ContextProvider extend the base-context (see yellow block, Fig. 3), by enriching the information of the initial context. In the ECOSPACE-Project especially systems like the instant messenger Post-@[3] are able to extend the user-context by providing real-time information about availability and presence of other users in a

---

[3] http://www.jaytown.co.uk/_product_communicator.asp

cooperative-working- environment. A 2nd level context extends the 1st level context by very specific information (real-time and static):

- Presence and availability of related persons (e.g. status of co-author in Skype)
- Interests of co-author or reader, based on profile
- Documents that are related to the source-document (based on tags)
- Discussions about document and/or topic (e.g. in blogs, emails)
- Tracking of document, location of copies (e.g. different document-management systems, RFID)

A ContextTag inside a document can address multiple ContextScopes that are autonomous to each other. Thus a document can have two or more different contexts at once, without affecting each other.

The ContextBroker, as the key element in the context-system, is the link between a ContextScope and a consumer-application like an office-plug-in that queries for author-information. The broker manages the retrieval of single context-information and offers representations in form of webservices and user-interfaces of a special context. Both ContextBroker and ContextScope are aware of each other, so that on the one hand side, the broker is able to identify the systems that are part of the scope and on the other side each system is able to identify what context it belongs to.

Especially the last point is of particular importance, since a 1st level ContextProvider will initiate the integration of the ContextTag into the document. Fig. 4 discusses the scenario of uploading a document to a document-management-system such as BSCW. The formal procedure is to check, whether the document is already part of the ContextScope or not. This is achieved either by submitting the whole document to the ContextBroker or, based on the system-capabilities to examine a document, just by submitting the document-id. The ContextBroker will verify a ContextTag, returns available context-information and if provided the newly tagged document. Based on the information of the ContextBroker any ContextProvider can bind system- and metadata to the corresponding document and/or document-id. A ContextProvider like BSCW needs to make webservices available to enable the retrieval of metadata by submitting the unique document-id. The storage of the metadata is controlled by the service/provider itself and can be implemented freely. In the case of BSCW, the always available event-list of a document can act as repository for metadata.

In the ECOSPACE-Project the ContextBroker acts as a Composite Collaborative Service (CoCoS) that can be used by other services. A ContextBroker is a light-weighted server that provides web-services as well as a user-interface for the retrieval of a document-context. In relation to Fig. 3 the ContextBroker can be queried by a special client (1 in Fig. 3) that provides the id of a document. This initiates a broadcast-action, asking every 1st level-ContextProvider (2 and 3 in Fig. 3), that is part of the ContextScope, about specific metadata concerning a document-id. In a second step, this metadata will be extended by all 2nd level ContextProviders (4 in Fig. 3). The ContextBroker processes this data and provides this data for the client application or in a special and customizable user-interface (5 in Fig. 3).

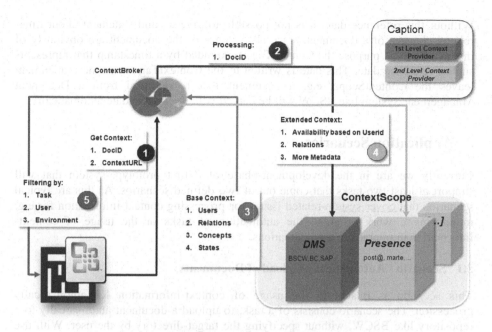

Fig. 3. Context Retrieval

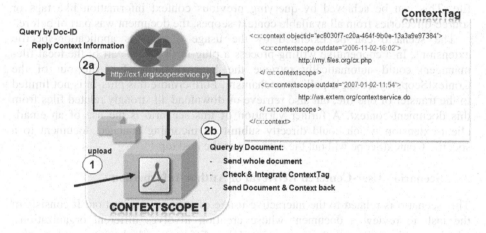

Fig. 4. ContextTag Integration and Validation

One of the problems in this concept is the difficulty to query time-related issues of a context, like a current version of a document or newly added tags since the last download of a document. As an important part of a document-context, it is mandatory to enable tracking of any changes starting from a particular date. To provide information about versions, the context-consumer (e.g. a desktop-application) needs to provide a reference date, which marks the last state of a local document-copy.

Without this reference date, it is not possible to give a valid statement about time-related changes of a document, since all changes of the document are obviously of interest. For this purpose the ContextTag is extended by a timestamp that represents such a reference date. This date is written to the ContextTag each time a document leaves the ContextScope, e.g. a document that is retrieved from a Document Management System like BSCW will be tagged with the current date automatically.

3 Application Scenarios

Currently we are in the development-phase of a first prototype-system that will support at least two tasks that come out of two defined scenarios. As this are typical scenarios that cover system-related issues for processing context-information for e.g. monitoring a work progress, the automation of tasks or the usage of context-information in interactive users-situations.

3.1 Scenario - Automatically Upload of Documents

This scenario is related to the usage of context-information for automatically procession. The scenario consists of a task, to upload a document automatically to a repository like BSCW, without specifying the target-directory by the user. With use of the ContextBroker the "upload-application" (e.g. a desktop-applet or server-component), is able to reason about an appropriate upload-directory for a particular file. This can be achieved by querying previous context information like tags or source-directories from all available context-scopes, the document was part of before.

The scenario can be extended by the usage of various application-specific extensions. In a cooperative writing-process a plug-in (e.g. as a part of the local file-manager) could automatically retrieve the latest version of a file out of the ContextScope by a simple polling mechanism. Furthermore this plug-in is not limited to the transfer of one file, but also retrieve or download all strongly related files from this document-context. A further variation of this scenario is the use of an email-client-extension which could directly submit an incoming attached document to a specific ContextScope without the detour over the desktop.

3.2 Scenario - User-Centered Retrieval of Author-Information

This scenario is related to the interactive usage of context-information. It consists of the task to review a document whose creation involves different organizations, whereas each organization is represented by different and changing authors that should contribute a section to a document. To finalize the document, each partner is asked to provide an executive summary of each section and to proof-read the document. Because there are a number of authors that have read or contributed to the document, it is necessary to inform all authors who have a high involvement in the document-context.

The difficulty to solve such a review-task is on the one hand, the identification of relevant authors and on the other hand the notification of these persons. Both tasks can be supported by analyzing the 1st and 2nd level context of a document as

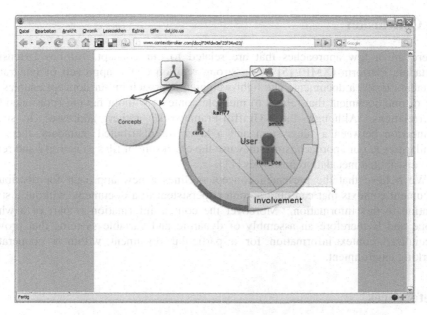

Fig. 5. Prototype-GUI for Document-Context Retrieval

successive steps. The ContextBroker will provide weighted information about the context of a document, so that authors that have a high relation to a document are displayed bigger than ones with a lower involvement. The prototype-visualization in Fig. 5 shows how to use the context-information dynamically. In Fig. 5 the involvement of different users in respect to a document is outlined. The GUI allows the direct selection of context-objects (e.g. user-objects), which can be processed in respect to the provided data, e.g. it is possible to send immediately an email to the selected user-objects in Fig. 5.

The realization of the proposed scenarios require the (at least partly) development of all building-blocks described in this document. In preposition of the prototype-development we will focus on how to formalize the exchange of context, since there are several issues to consider, like a categorization of context as hierarchies [7] in the proposed order: Users, Relations, Concepts and States.

The first prototypes will use and evaluate available formats like Dublincore [8] or FOAF [9] to represent a subset of context information. The prototype ContextBroker-Service will provide a visualization of the context-information, that enables the user to gain an overview of the context and the ability to browse the context in more detail (based on information that is provided by the context-levels).

Depending on the valuable usage of these formats (Dublincore, FOAF, etc) for context-representation issues, we will evaluate an integration of a simple descriptive naming system (introduced by Cohen, Castro and Misra) [10] to describe a generic context-type of a provider. In relation to the identified 1st and 2nd Level Context, a context-provider will inform a ContextBroker about the self-provided type or category of a context-information, e.g. service XY is able to provide user-related information.

4 Conclusion

There are a few approaches that are related to our concept. Adobes Extensible Metadata Platform (XMP) [5] has a strong relation to the approach of integrating metadata inside a document. The light-weighted approach in our concept enables the use of one document that relates to multiple contexts without having (non-intended) interrelations. Although the "Graffiti-Framework" rather addresses a strong connection between a file-system and a layer for distributed metadata, there are similarities to our approach, since they use the checksum of files to identify and relate it to distributed metadata-repositories [11].

We believe that the presented concept outlines a new approach for distributed document-contexts that can bind a context persistent to a document, without a static relation to this information. Moreover the context-information is part of a whole scope and is therefore an assembly of dynamic and variable systems that provide specialized context-information for a particular document within a cooperative working environment.

References

1. Prinz, W., et al.: ECOSPACE – Towards an Integrated Collaboration Space for eProfessionals. CollaborateCom2006, Atlanta, USA. pp. 1–7 (2006)
2. Bazire, M., Brézillon, P.: Understanding Context Before Using It. In: Dey, A.K., Kokinov, B., Leake, D.B., Turner, R. (eds.) CONTEXT 2005. LNCS (LNAI), vol. 3554, pp. 29–40. Springer, Heidelberg (2005)
3. Ngo, T.: Office Open XML Overview (March 13, 2007), http://www.ecma-international. org/news//TC45_current_work/OpenXML%20White%20Paper.pdf
4. OASIS: OASIS Open Office Specification (Feburary 1, 2007), http://docs.oasis-open.org/office/v1.1/OS/OpenDocument-v1.1-html/OpenDocument-v1.1.html
5. Adobe Inc.: Adding intelligence to media (March 13, 2007), http://www.adobe.com/products/ xmp/overview.html
6. Appelt, W.: WWW Based Collaboration with the BSCW System. In: Bartosek, M., Tel, G., Pavelka, J. (eds.) SOFSEM 1999. LNCS, vol. 1725, pp. 66–78. Springer, Heidelberg (1999)
7. Dorn, C., Dustdar, Sch.: Sharing hierarchical context for mobile web services. Distributed and Parallel Databases, vol. 21(1), pp. 85–111. Kluwer Academic Publishers, Hingham, MA, USA (2007)
8. DCMI Usage Board: DCMI Metadata Terms (December 18, 2006), http://dublincore. org/documents/ /2006/12/18/dcmi-terms/
9. Brickley, D., Miller, L.: FOAF Vocabulary Specification (January 29, 2006), http:// xmlns.com/foaf/0.1/
10. Castro, P., Misra, A., Cohen, N.: Descriptive Naming of Context Data Providers. In: Dey, A.K., Kokinov, B., Leake, D.B., Turner, R. (eds.) CONTEXT 2005. LNCS (LNAI), vol. 3554, pp. 112–125. Springer, Heidelberg (2005)
11. Bobb, N., Eads, D., Storer, M.W., et al.: Graffiti: A framework for testing collaborative distributed metadata (2006), http://www.ssrc.ucsc.edu/Papers/maltzahn-ddas07.pdf

Integrating Engineering, Cognitive and Social Approaches for a Comprehensive Modeling of Organizational Agents and Their Contexts

Marielba Zacarias[1,2], H. Sofia Pinto[3,4], and José Tribolet[1,3]

[1] Center for Organizational Engineering, INESC, Lisboa, Portugal
[2] Universidade do Algarve, ADEEC-FCT, Faro, Portugal
[3] Department of Information Systems and Computer Science, IST/UTL, Lisbon, Portugal
[4] ALGOS, INESC-ID, Lisboa, Portugal
mzacaria@ualg.pt, sofia@algos.inesc-id.pt, jose.tribolet@inov.pt

Abstract. Organizational models produced within computer science fields have proved to be effective communication tools in developing shared understandings of the design of organizations and systems. We argue that these models can also be valuable in capturing the actual implementation of organizations. However, this kind of usage requires the development of enterprise representations that (1) acknowledge the complexity of organizations and its agents and (2) are able of capturing the situated and dynamic behavior of organizational agents. This paper describes how engineering, cognitive and social approaches to context are integrated in a conceptual framework to model organizational agents and their contexts of interaction to address these issues. This integration is illustrated with examples from a case study.

Keywords: organizational modeling, context modeling, organizational agents.

1 Introduction and Motivation

Developing shared understandings of the characteristics and operation of organizations is an essential pre-requisite for effective action, decision-making and learning processes [8]. Models have proved to be effective artifacts in supporting human communication. Since they offer simplified views of reality, they are useful not only in helping to design and evaluate systems, but also in helping to understand the behavior of complex systems [20]. Organizations understand, communicate and design their structure and processes with models. Organizational modeling has a long tradition in organizational and management sciences. In this area, models aim at producing ways of thinking about the organization, as well as management theories and principles based on these ways of thinking. Contemporary models of organizational sciences regard organizations as complex, adaptive socio-technical systems that result from the interactions among its component parts, which can also be complex entities. Though founded on solid theoretical backgrounds, these models are described in natural language, restricting them to human use and leading to different interpretations.

B. Kokinov et al. (Eds.): CONTEXT 2007, LNAI 4635, pp. 517–530, 2007.

The fields of Information Systems (IS) and Artificial Intelligence (AI) have also addressed organizational modeling activities, seeking to support the design of applications aligned with the business. Within these fields, models are intended to facilitate the communication among human agents and the inter-operability between systems. Hence, they provide representation languages that seek to reduce ambiguities. Most enterprise representations are formal, semi-formal or graphical means to represent organization's structure and processes i.e., aspects of the organization's *design*.

We argue that enterprise models can also be valuable tools in facilitating shared understandings of the *actual implementation of organizations* i.e., of the *specific subjects* that fulfill tasks, the *specific ways* of performing these tasks, as well as *where*, *when* and *with whom* they perform them. In our research, we are developing a modeling approach to as means to *better understand, communicate and analyze work realities*. From our point of view, facilitating semi-formal, graphical depictions of actual execution allows (1) uncovering problems related to particular work practices rather than process design, (2) tracing the actual relationship of workers with organizational tasks, resources and other workers, (3) assessing the alignment with designed processes and (4) evaluating how work evolve in time. Therefore, a better knowledge of organization's implementation is useful not only for IS developers but also for organization analysts and managers. Even individual workers can benefit from a better understanding of how their work is related with business processes and resources. Due to their focus on organization's design, IS approaches provide process-centered, role-based models that do not capture actual execution. Moreover, organizations are typically regarded as static, mechanistic and deterministic systems that not reflect the nature of human behavior. We need a semi-formal modeling framework capable of capturing the *complexity*, *situated* and *dynamic* behavior of organizational agents.

In this paper we integrate engineering, social and cognitive approaches to context within a comprehensive modeling approach of organizational agents and their interactions contexts. We argue that the context notion is essential to enable a situated modeling of organizational agents. We also show that the different approaches to context complement each other to display different concerns of the interactions among organizational agents. This integrated context notion is illustrated with examples from a case study conducted in a real organizational setting. The remaining of this paper is structured as follows. Section 2 summarizes related work on context and enterprise modeling. Section 3 describes our modeling approach. Section 4 illustrates the integrated notion of context with examples from a case study. Section 5 gives our conclusions and future directions.

2   Related Work

Our approach integrates organizational and context modeling concepts. Thus, section 2.1 summarizes the notion and uses of context relevant for our research and section 2.2 describes related work on organizational modeling.

2.1 The Notions of Context

Although the notion of context plays an important role in disciplines such as pragmatics, natural language semantics, linguistics, artificial intelligence cognitive and social sciences, there is no standard concept, theory or model [1]. In an effort to enlarge a shared understanding of this notion, Bazire and Brézillon [9] identify the main components of context on the basis of 150 definitions. This work concludes that context acts as a set of *constraints* that *influence* the *behavior* of a system *embedded in a given task*. However, some questions relative to the nature of context (e.g. its dynamic/static or information/process nature) were pointed as non-consensual. Hence, the definition of context remains dependent on its application area. This section synthesizes context definitions from computer, cognitive and social sciences. Since research on context is very extensive, this review does not intend to be exhaustive. Rather, it is restricted to the approaches influencing our framework.

2.1.1 Classical Context Notions in Computer Sciences

A very early notion of context is used in the *Operating Systems* field, which refers to the context of processes [7]. Contexts are regarded as a *state* and are implemented with tables maintained by the operating system that have an entry for each process. This entry contains information about the state of processes (running, blocked or waiting), its program counter, stack pointer, memory allocation, the status of its open files and everything that must be saved when the process is switched back from running to ready or blocked state so it can be restarted later as if it had never been stopped.

The *Artificial Intelligence* field has developed an extensive research on context. In this field, context is viewed as a collection of things (sentences, propositions, assumptions, properties, procedures, rules, facts, concepts, constraints, sentences, etc) associated to some specific situation (environment, domain, task, agents, interactions, conversations, etc). This consensus is reflected in the "box metaphor" [2]. The intuition is that context can then be seen as a container where its content depends on some set of situational parameters or dimensions. Different sets of parameters have been defined according the application area [4,5,6]. Parameter set and values, as well as the box content vary according the three fundamental dimensions of context-dependent representations defined in [2]; *partiality*, *approximation* and *perspective*. A representation is partial when it describes only a subset of a more comprehensive state of affairs. Approximation is related to the granularity or level of detail of the representation. Perspective encodes a spatio–temporal, logical, or cognitive point of view on a given situation.

2.1.2 An Approach from Cognitive Sciences

B. Kokinov [11] developed a dynamic approach to context modeling to understand how human cognitive processes are influenced by context and how to model this influence in computer simulations. This work defines context as *the set of all entities that influence human (or system's) behavior on a particular occasion*. This context model assumes that mental representations involved in the current context are being formed by the interaction between at least three processes: *perception* that builds new representations of the current environment; *memory* that reactivates or builds representations of old experiences; and *reasoning* that constructs representations of generated goals, inferred facts, induced rules, etc. It is also assumed that context in turn influences perception, memory, and reasoning processes. The main principles of the dynamic theory of context are: (1) context is a state of the mind, (2) context has no clear-cut boundaries, (3) context consists of all associatively relevant elements and (4) context is dynamic.

2.1.3 Sociological Approaches

Sociological approaches typically regard context as networks of interacting entities (people, agents or actors and artifacts). These approaches focus on the structural properties of contexts, resulting from recurrent interactions among entities. Whereas some focus on the network elements, others focus on its emergent properties. In the latter case, the context itself is regarded as sets of rules and resources, which support and regulate interactions among its members [3]. Activity Theory [12] and Actor-Network Theory [10] have been widely used in modeling social contexts. Both theories approach contexts as networks.

2.2 The Notion of Agent in Organizational Modeling

Contemporary theories and models of organizational sciences regard organizations as complex, adaptive systems, where agents itself are complex and adaptive. Within this field, Axelrod and Cohen [19] have further refined this view and have taken the principles of complexity and evolution to put together a conceptual framework for organizational analysis ends, based on concepts such as *agents, populations, artifacts, strategies, selection processes* and *interaction and activation patterns* [8].

IS enterprise modeling approaches are commonly referred as Enterprise Architectures. One distinctive feature of IS approaches is enabling to model organizations from different perspectives or viewpoints and to provide means to assess the alignment between them. The most commonly depicted perspectives are the *process, information, application* and *technology* perspectives [14]. In most IS approaches, agents are regarded as simple resources of business process. Consequently, they are included within the process view.

In the AI field, enterprise models are better known as enterprise ontologies. Two well known AI enterprise ontologies are the Enterprise Ontology (EO) proposed by Uschold [18] and the ontologies developed within the TOVE project [22]. The paradigm shift in Multi-Agent Systems design from agent-centered to organization-centered approaches has also motivated the creation of meta-models comprising several social and organizational concepts, which include single-agent, two-agent, group and organizational level concepts [21]. AI Enterprise ontologies and meta-models provide an organizational perspective that offer richer sets of agent-related concepts, where agent autonomy is also acknowledged. The concepts of *goal, agent, interaction pattern, role, group or teams, divisions* and *organizational units* are common to these ontologies.

Questions not answered by current approaches

Capturing work practices requires answering how given subjects accomplish their work. It is also important to capture its evolution. More specifically, it is necessary to answer questions such as: *Which roles plays agent X? , How does Agent X perform activity Y?, In which context, How does Agent X interact with Agent Y?, Which event(s) trigger Agent X's role? , How Agent X coordinate activities or manage resources? How does Agent X coordinates itself?* Also, it entails the ability to answer time-related questions such as ***during a particular time interval t:*** *What role plays Agent X? Which activity(ies) performs? Which resource(s) uses? With which agents interacts, Which commitments is handling?* Current enterprise modeling approaches provide generic descriptions of activities and agent roles. Consequently, they are not able of tracing the relationships of given individuals with activities and resources and do not address these questions.

3   An Architecture of Organizational Agents and Their Contexts

We lay out the foundations of an ontology to address the aforementioned questions in [8]. In this section, we summarize the fundamental concepts of this ontology, and describe a layered definition of context that integrates engineering, cognitive and social notions. We depart from a position that regards organization as complex, adaptive systems, which result from successive actions of individual and social agents. We also acknowledge two essential considerations of organizational approaches: (1) the situated nature of agent behavior and (2) regarding the operation and evolution of individual and organizations as inter-dependent processes. The first consideration leads to an explicit modeling of agent contexts. The second leads to an approach integrating different concerns of individual agents and collective agents, including the whole organization.

Fundamental Concepts
Activities describe what organizations do and are identified with *verbs*. Activities are abstract entities that use and produce resources. **Resources** are the things relevant for the operation of the organization and are identified with *nouns* (in our model, entities are synonym of organizational resources). Resources can be *persons, machines, places, concepts* or *capabilities*. **Agents** are regarded as physical and animate *resources* with special capabilities that enable them to (1) perform, coordinate and change activities and (2) provide, consume, manage and change resources and (3) monitor, coordinate and change their own activity and the activity of other agents. Agents are identified with *nouns*. **Actions** define atomic acts performed by single agents that change the state of a resource. **Interactions** are adjacent pairs of communicative actions exchanged between two or more agents. **Roles** define the observable behavior of an entity in the scope of particular interaction contexts. Agents play several roles and interact with other agents through these roles. Roles are temporal. Thus, agents perform several activity or resource-related roles, at different times. Roles are also linked to particular contexts. **Contexts** define situations that emerge from successive interactions among resource and activity-related agents. Later in this section we describe how this notion integrates computer sciences, cognitive and social approaches to context. It is important to note that since activities are abstract entities that may overlap, depending on their definition. Hence, a single context may be related to one or more activities and vice-versa.

Integrating Agent and Enterprise Architectures

Enterprise models address organizational complexity defining several, inter-related architectural perspectives. However, these models do not acknowledge the complexity of individual agents. In cognitive modeling, agent complexity has been also addressed using architectures. According to Sloman [16], a typical cognitive architecture has the following components: (1) a perception box at the left, (2) a (motor) action box at the right, and (3) three internal layers connecting those two boxes. These internal layers are the *reactive layer, deliberative* and *reflective* layers. **Reactive** mechanisms define agent pre-defined behavior. **Deliberative** mechanisms correspond to planning, scheduling and decision-making. **Reflective** mechanisms reflect agent abilities to change the behavior of the previous layers. In our work, we address both agent and organization's complexity through an integration of agent and enterprise architectures. Current enterprise architectural perspectives can be classified according two main dimensions; *activity* and *resources*. Thus, the organization as a whole is modeled in terms of these two perspectives. In turn, each organizational agent is modeled on the basis of the three-layered architecture described in [16].

As a result, the organization is modeled as a network of situated interactions between autonomous resource and activity-related agents. Figure 1 depicts the model basic architecture and related concepts. Resource-related agents provide and/or consume resources at the action layer, manage resources (including themselves) at the decision-making layer and design (or redesign resources, including themselves) at the change/learn layer. Analogously, activity-related agents perform activities at the action layer, coordinate activities at the decision-making layer and design (or redesign activities) at the change layer. The **Action Layer** captures action and interaction patterns between activity performers and resource provider/consumer agents. Action and interaction patterns are recurrent sequences or flows of valid action, interaction and resource types and vary according to specific contexts. The **Decision-making Layer** captures the activation rules of resource managers and activity coordinators. This layer regards agents as non-deterministic state machines. Interactions are events that change the state of agents. Events trigger rules, which activate a particular context, along with its associated action-layer role (resource provider/consumer, activity performer) and patterns. The **Change/Learn Layer** addresses interactions between activity and resource designer agents. This layer aims at capturing (re)design of interaction and activation strategies of resource managers, producer and consumers, as well as activity coordinators and performers. This layer comprises mostly emergent behavior. Therefore, we do not model agent behavior at this layer. Rather, we focus on detecting changes of the previous layers.

Context definition at each layer

Several social theories acknowledge that human communication is mediated by physical, psychological or social artifacts [3,12,19]. We regard mediating artifacts are resources that support and constrain agent interactions and define contexts as the network of mediating artifacts used in agent interactions. The kind of mediating artifact used varies according the layer.

1. At the **action** layer, the mediating artifacts are (a) the expected interaction types and (b) resource types exchanged. Each interaction type is related to a specific set of resource types.

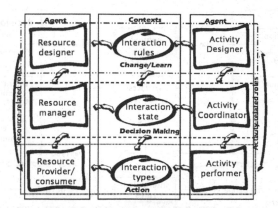

Fig. 1. Basic architecture and Ontology

2. In the **decision-making** layer, mediating artifacts are commitments between activity and resource-related agents. Commitments are related to the notions of pledge, promise, agreement or contract. According to Speech Act Theory [16], interactions produce, modify, re-schedule or cancel commitments. Commitments reflect the state of interactions. Each specific interaction type is related to a set of possible commitments.

3. At the **change/learn** mediating artifacts are interaction rules. Interaction rules of this layer refer to higher-order rules governing interaction patterns and activation rules. Resource and activity (re)design is on one side, both constrained and supported by current interaction rules of the corresponding activities and resources. On the other side, activity and resource (re)design may trigger changes on corresponding activity-resource interaction rules.

Figure 2 depicts the concepts used to define agents and contexts in each layer. In the action layer, context is regarded from the *classical engineering* perspective. Although defining context as the product of agent interactions draws on sociological approaches, restricting this definition to the interactions among resource and activity-related agents aims at establishing limits to this concept. This delimitation allows applying the box metaphor, where and the parameters refer to specific sets of *resources, activities* and *agents* and the box content, their associated *artifacts* (interaction types and patterns, commitments or rules). In terms of the *partiality* dimension, we focus on subsets of the states of affairs between agents, related to the execution of specific activities and associated resources. In the decision-making layer, contexts are regarded as a state. Therefore, we follow *operating systems* and *cognitive sciences* approaches. In this layer, context is a dynamic entity with several state variables. In the change/learning we are strictly drawing on *social theories* supporting a notion of context as s set of –mostly unobservable- rules governing observable agent patterns of behavior.

The architecture of agents and contexts can be applied at several levels of detail i.e. at personal, inter-personal, group and at even that level of whole organizations. This is related with another basic dimension of context dependence: *approximation*. Since

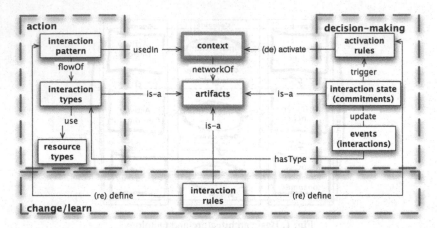

Fig. 2. The concept of context in the three layers

we aim at capturing actual work practices, we are applying the framework at individual and inter-personal layers. At these levels, we focus on persons and resources such as: *information items*, *applications* and *skills* provided by other persons. Whereas at the interpersonal-level we capture inter-personal interactions, at the individual level we do not see interactions. Rather, we see individual actions that may be communicative or not-communicative.

Agent and Context Representations: Model Acquisition Approach
Typical model acquisition techniques in enterprise modeling include interviews, surveys, questionnaires and field observations. We proposed build agent and context representations accordingly to our model of organizational agents i.e. *from actions and interactions*. In our approach, we build context-based agent representations from action repositories for organizational analysis ends. The specific purpose of our modeling approach is to help in understanding and communicating the web of relationships among organizational agents, activities and resources, as well as its dynamics.

4   Case Study: Agents and Contexts at Each Layer

In this section, we describe and illustrate with examples from a case study, how contexts and agents are modeled at each layer.

Case Study
The case study involved a software development team of 4 programmers (*Gonçalo, Carla, Catarina, Alexandre*) and the project leader (*Mariana*). The team develops web applications for a commercial bank. During the observation, the team performed tasks on the following applications; *Suppliers, Claims, Mail, Evictions web service* and *Marketing Campaigns*. Observation was performed by team members, and coordinated by the team leader. A set of computer and non-computer mediated actions

was manually collected through a three-week observation period, totaling over 650 sentences.

Action Repositories

Agent and context representations are acquired from action repositories. We defined the following structure for actions; *subject-**verb**-object, (Gonçalo **solve** problem in Suppliers Application).* Communicative actions were further structured using speech theory. Using speech act theory [15] in analyzing sentences allows finding the action implicated in some message. The structure of communicative actions took the form *Mariana **request** (Gonçalo **solve** problem in Suppliers Application).* Thus, communicative actions had an embedded action in it. When necessary, object descriptions included others resources used (tools, information or human competencies). During the observation, the following set of action types were identified: *accept, analyze, annotate, answer, ask assist, calculate, decide, detect, discuss, ellaborate, evaluate, find, help, inform, install, modify, obtain, perform, prepare, print, program, promise, propose, reject, , request, research, send, solve, supervise, test, update.*

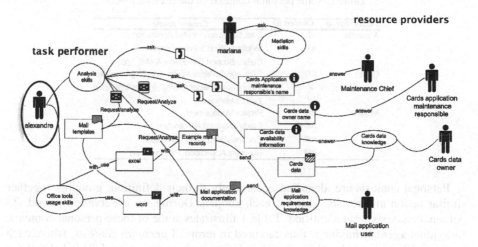

Fig. 3. An example personal context at the action layer (context **a1** in table 2)

Agent and Contexts at the Action Layer

When applying our framework at the level of individuals, contexts refer to **personal contexts** i.e groupings of individual actions and personal resources related to one or more tasks. Figure 3 depicts an example context of Alexandre, an individual of our case study. This personal action contexts depicts the interactions between *Alexandre* (acting as task performer) and *Mariana, Cards Application Responsible, Cards data Owner* and *Mail application user* (acting as resource providers).

At the **action layer**, this example context is regarded as a network composed of:

- **Action types:** ask, answer, request, analyze, send. These interactions use the following resources:

- **Information items:** example mail records, mail template, mail application documentation, cards application responsible name, cards availability, cards data
- **Applications:** Microsoft Word, Excel®
- **Skills/Knowledge:** analysis skills, office application skills belong to Alexandre. The cards application knowledge, programming skills, mail application requirements knowledge and mediation skills are provided by other subjects.

Regarding the fundamental contextual dimension of *perspective*, personal contexts reflect *personal views* of particular interaction contexts. Figure 4 depicts the personal Alexandre's view on the actions related to collecting data for the mail application. He regards himself as the task performer, while other individuals are resource providers or consumers. For example, the view that Mariana has on the actions related on the data collection context of Alexandre is different. In Mariana's view, these actions are grouped in a different context (Project Management m1). In table, we distinguished a sub-context *m011* to illustrate this situation. In context m1, Mariana is the *task performer* and Alexandre a *resource consumer*.

Table 1. Some personal contexts of the team members

Person Name	Context ID	Context Name
Alexandre	a1	Data Collection for Mail Application
	a3	Evictions Web Service Problem
	a5	Carla's Support (Web Serv & Mail App)
Carla	c1	Common Services Application Programming
	c2	Programming support (Mail & Suppliers App)
	c3	Team Meetings
Mariana	m1	Project Management
	m011	Cards Information Collection
	m6	Evictions Web Service Problem
	m8	Suppliers Application Programming

Personal contexts are identified accordingly to their definition; grouping together similar action and resource sets of each subject. During the observation period, 33 personal contexts were identified. Table 1 illustrates some of these personal contexts. Individual **agent behavior** is thus captured in terms of *personal contexts*, where each context reflects *typical actions*, *action patterns* and *resources* used. This behavior is also situated for particular time intervals.

Once personal contexts are identified and labeled by their owners, we identify inter-personal contexts by grouping together interaction threads between two given individuals *and* personal contexts. In the action layer, inter-personal contexts reveal inter-personal networks created by the interactions among them. However, since individuals always interact from specific personal contexts, these networks need to be situated on the personal contexts of the interacting individuals. Whereas any two individuals share a single inter-personal relationship, they may share several inter-personal contexts. This idea is depicted in figure 4.

Figure 5 depicts an example of the context-based inter-personal networks captured in our case study. Discovering resource or task flows from groups of single interactions is difficult because mapping these interactions with tasks or resources is

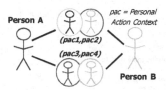

Fig. 4. Context-based (inter-personal)interaction contexts

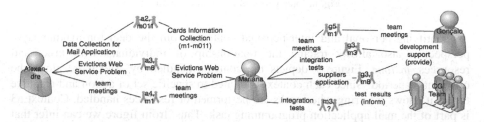

Fig. 5. A sample of inter-personal contexts depicted at the action layer

not always straightforward. Since personal action contexts are related to typical action and resource sets, they facilitate the construction of task and/or resource flows. **Inter-agent behavior** is thus modeled as multiplex networks.

Agents and Contexts at the Decision-Making layer

The **decision-making** layer captures agents as activity coordinators or resource managers. In this layer, context is regarded in terms of the state of its actions and resources. Individuals coordinate their actions and manage their own resources based on their actions to-do (and their priority). Table 2 reflects how a sample of the to-do list related to the personal context of fig. 4, and how it changes change in time.

Table 2. Personal Context at the Decision-Making Layer

Day	Order of Occurrence	Action to-do
6	15	**Assist** to Team Meeting
6	20	**Request** mail records and template
6	21	Request mail records and template
6	53	Assist to team meeting
9	120	**Analyze** mail records and template
9	123	Analyze mail records and template

At the inter-personal level, contexts reflect the commitments produced by interactions between specific personal action contexts of two individuals. Commitments have a date, type (determined by the type of the communicative action e.g. promises, requests, proposals, etc.), original and actual date of accomplishment and state (pending, done, cancelled or re-scheduled). Figure 6 illustrates an example of two inter-personal context entries of our case study (mariana-pac10, catarina–pac 5). Regarding agents their *to-do lists* and *commitments* allows discovering agent activation rules. We use this approach to model multitasking behavior [8,17]. Table 3 depicts some context activation rules discovered in our case study.

- *Date:* 06-12
  - *Commited-by:* Mariana (pac10)
  - *Commited-to:* Catarina (pac5)
  - *Type:* ACCEPT/REJECT PROPOSAL
  - *Description:* solution to the automatic table update problem
  - *Original date of accomplishment:* 06-12
  - *Actual date of accomplishment:* 09-12

- *Date:* 06-12
  - *Commited-by:* Catarina (pac5)
  - *Commited-to:* Mariana (pac10)
  - *Type:* PROPOSE
  - *Description:* solution to the automatic table update problem
  - *Original date of accomplishment:* 06-12
  - *Actual date of accomplishment:* 06-12

Fig. 6. Inter-personal commitment entries

Identifying personal and inter-personal contexts from the decision-making layer perspective also allows tracing the relationship of individuals with tasks and resources, *in time*. Figure 7 depicts the contexts handled by Alexandre along the observation period. Since each context is related to specific set of action and resource types, it allows inferring when tasks are performed or resources handled. Context a3 is part of the mail application programming task. Thus, from figure we can infer that this task was performed by Alexandre on days 9, 17, 20 and 22. The mapping between contexts and tasks is not always clear cut. We observed contexts related to several tasks, and tasks present in several contexts. Nonetheless, analyzing each context provided reasonable approximations of executed tasks and resources and allowed the elaboration of time-based graphs of individuals versus tasks, and individuals versus resources. These graphics are illustrated in [8].

Table 3. Agents at Decision-Making Layer: *Context Activation Rules*

Rule	Trigger (event)	Trigger (commitment)		Activate Context
1	meeting accepted	ellaborate project list	m1	project reports and meetings
2	Dept. Head's request	ellaborate project status report provide information of the	m1	project reports and meetings
3	Alexandre's request	cards application	m011	cards information collection
4	CG team informs test failure	resume tests	m3	Integration tests
5	Catarina's request	perform message maintenance	m9	message maintenance

Change/Learn level: Interaction Rules
At the designer level, context represents the higher-order rules governing the observable behavior of the individual i.e. in activating a particular context or using a particular interaction pattern. These rules are mostly tacit and unobservable [3]. Although we acknowledge their existence, we do not address its representation. However, it is possible to infer some of these rules from observable patterns of

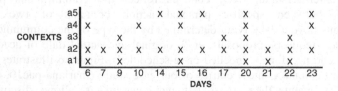

Fig. 7. Personal contexts handled by Alexandre each day

behavior We illustrate some personal and inter-personal rules governing multitasking behavior, inferred from context activation rules in [18].

5 Conclusions and Future Work

In this work we describe how engineering, cognitive and social approaches of the notion of context are integrated within a conceptual framework to model organizational agents. Our conceptual framework joins together agent and enterprise architectures to address different concerns of agent behavior and uses the notion of context to enable a situated modeling of organizational agents. In this paper, we illustrate how the different notions of context are captured and represented using examples from a case study. Due to their complexity, grasping work realities is not straightforward. We use our modeling approach as a means to *understand* and *communicate* the different concerns of the relationships of human agents with organizational activities and resources. Our purpose is to *facilitate the extraction of action and decision layer patterns from action repositories*, for organizational analysis ends. Currently, our approach has been applied in case studies conducted within limited time intervals and organizational settings. In these case studies we have gathered empirical evidence of how semi-formal, graphical depictions of work practices built from action repositories are useful in improving the degree of awareness of the actual execution of activities.

A wider implementation of the proposed approach requires first, further formalizing our model. Since this framework aims mainly at facilitating organizational analysis rather than systems specification, this formalization will be accomplished iteratively, from lessons learned from its application on case studies. We aim at achieving a formalization degree that allows embedding our model in applications for a semi-automated support in acquiring and updating agent and context representations from action and interaction logs. Second, creating and updating representations for the personal and inter-personal levels entails analyzing high volumes of fast-changing, frequently unstructured data. We are currently researching semantic technologies for capturing, structuring and analyzing logs from tools supporting individual and collaborative work. Preliminary results on the application of clustering techniques to discover personal contexts from action and interaction logs are reported in [14]. Finally, this framework has been applied in analyzing individual and inter-personal levels. Its usefulness in analyzing higher organizational levels remains to be validated.

References

1. Bouquet, P., Ghidini, C., Giunchiglia, F., Blanzieri, E.: Theories and Uses of Context in Knowledge Representation and Reasoning. Journal of pragmatics - Special issue on context 35(3), 455–484 (2002)
2. Benerecetti, M., Bouquet, P., Ghidini, C.: On the dimensions of context dependence: partiality, approximation, and perspective. In: Akman, V., Bouquet, P., Thomason, R.H., Young, R.A. (eds.) CONTEXT 2001. LNCS (LNAI), vol. 2116, pp. 59–72. Springer, Heidelberg (2001)
3. Giddens, A.: The Constitution of Society. University of California Press (1984)

4. Lenat, D.: The Dimensions of Context-Space, CycCorp. Retrieved August 2001, http://casbah.org/resources/cyccontextspace.shtml
5. Maus, H.: Workflow Context as a Means for Intelligent Information Support. In: Akman, V., Bouquet, P., Thomason, R.H., Young, R.A. (eds.) CONTEXT 2001. LNCS (LNAI), vol. 2116, pp. 261–274. Springer, Heidelberg (2001)
6. Dey, A., Abowd, G.: Towards a Better Understanding of Context and Context-Awareness, GVU Technical Report (1999), ftp://ftp.cc.gatech.edu/pub/gvu/tr/1999/99-22.pdf
7. Tannenbaum, A.S.: Modern Operating Systems, 2nd edn. Prentice-Hall, Englewood Cliffs (2001)
8. Zacarias, M., Magahães R., Caetano A., Tribolet J.: Towards Organizational Self-Awareness: An Initial Architecture and Ontology. In: Ritten, P. (ed) Ontologies for Business Interactions (in Press)
9. Brazire, M., Brezillon, P.: Understanding Context before Using It. In: Dey, A.K., Kokinov, B., Leake, D.B., Turner, R. (eds.) CONTEXT 2005. LNCS (LNAI), vol. 3554, Springer, Heidelberg (2005)
10. Latour, B.: Reassembling the Social: An Introduction to Actor-Network. Oxford University Press, Oxford (2005)
11. Kokinov, B.: A dynamic approach to context modeling. In: Proceedings of the IJCAI Workshop on Modeling Context in Knowledge Representation and Reasoning, London (1995)
12. Engeström, Y., Miettinen, R., Punamäki, R.L.: Perspectives on Activity Theory. Cambridge University Press, Cambridge (2005)
13. Zacarias, M., Gomes, R., Coimbra, J., Pinto, H.S., Tribolet, J.: Discovering Personal Action Contexts with SQL Server Analysis and Integration Services. In: proceedings of the International Conference on.NET Technologies IVNET '06 Conference, Brazil (2006)
14. Schekkerman, J.: How To Survive In The Jungle of Enterprise Architecture Frameworks. Trafford, Victoria, Canada (2004)
15. Searle, J.: Austin on locutionary and illocutionary acts. The Philosophical Review 77, 405–442 (1978)
16. Sloman, A.: Architecture-Based Conceptions of Mind. In: Gardenfors, P., Kijania-Placek, K., Wolenski, J. (eds.) Scope of Logic, Methodology, and Philosophy of Science (vol. II), Synthese Library, vol. 315, pp. 403–427. Kluwer Publishers, Dordrecht (2002)
17. Zacarias, M., Pinto, H.S., Tribolet, J.: Discovering Multitasking Behavior at Work: A Context-Based Ontology. In: Coninx, K., Luyten, K., Schneider, K.A. (eds.) TAMODIA 2006. LNCS, vol. 4385, pp. 292–307. Springer, Heidelberg (2007)
18. Uschold, M.: Building Ontologies: Towards a Unified Methodology. In: Paper presented at the16th Annual Conf. of the British Computer Society Specialist Group on Expert Systems, Cambridge UK (1996)
19. Axelrod, R., Cohen, M.: Harnessing Complexity: Organizational Implications of a Scientific Frontier. Basic Books, New York (2000)
20. Carroll, J.: HCI Models, Theories and Frameworks: Toward a Multi-Disciplinary Science. Morgan-Kauffman, San Francisco (2003)
21. Ferber, J., Gutknecht, O., Fabien, M.: From agents to organizations: An organizational view of multi–agent systems. In: Giorgini, P., Müller, J.P., Odell, J.J. (eds.) Agent-Oriented Software Engineering IV. LNCS, vol. 2935, pp. 214–230. Springer, Heidelberg (2004)
22. Fox, M.S., Barbuceanu, M., Gruninger, M., Lin, J.: An Organization Ontology for Enterprise Modelling. In: Prietula, M., Carley, K., Gasser, L. (eds.) Simulating Organizations: Computational Models of Institutions and Groups, Menlo Park CA, pp. 131–152. AAAI/MIT Press, Stanford, California, USA (1998)

Fields as Dimensions of Context: An Application of Bourdieu's Sociological Theory to Modelling of Context of Social Action

Tomasz Zarycki

Institute for Social Studies
Warsaw University
ul.Stawki 5/7, 00-183 Warszawa, Poland
t.zarycki@uw.edu.pl
http://www.iss.uw.edu.pl/zarycki

Abstract. The present paper is an attempt to construct a theoretical model of the context of social action based on a reinterpretation of the sociological theory of social fields as developed by Pierre Bourdieu. Using his notions of different types of capital and other tools, a multidimensional model of context is presented in which dimensions are defined as fields affected by (and affecting) a given social action. Focus in the paper is on discursive behaviour, but following the assumptions of linguistic pragmatics, discourse is considered here just as a specific form of broadly defined social action. Thus an attempt is made at linking studies on context from linguistics with those from sociology. Social action is theorized, as in Bourdieu's models, as a process of conversion of different types of capital. The strategic use of particular types of capital is considered as another dimension of contextualization of social action.

Keywords: sociology, discourse analysis, pragmatics, social field, social capital cultural capital, contextualization, social stratification, Bourdieu, Bakhtin.

1 Introduction

This paper presents a model of contextual analysis of social action based on the theory of types of capital(s) developed by the eminent French sociologist Pierre Bourdieu (1930-2002). In particular, the paper argues that any social action can be seen as taking place in a multidimensional (at least two dimensional) context. At the same time the paper will refer to classic theories of linguistic pragmatics and discourse analysis, relying on their perspective on language as a mode of social action rather than the means of thinking or conveying knowledge/information.

In this paper, context will be taken to refer to all the relevant features of a social situation in which a particular social behaviour occurs or in which a specific linguistic activity, which can be formalized as a speech act (Searle[1]), takes place. The relevance of these features will be defined by their ability to make the behaviour or linguistic activity under analysis understandable. Alternatively features can be defined by their usefulness for finding an interpretation of the overall social situation in which

B. Kokinov et al. (Eds.): CONTEXT 2007, LNAI 4635, pp. 531–544, 2007.

the given behaviour will appear as coherent. However, context will not be seen here as an "objectively" existing reality but rather as a negotiated social construct produced both by actors and the interpreters of actor's actions. In such a perspective, as for example Bauman and Briggs[2] point out, context both influences and is influenced by social action. Thus, the process of contextualization of social action may be seen as the negotiation of context between actors and interpreters.

I will argue that models of social contexts that are defined in this way, can considerably benefit from sociological theory, in particular the framework provided by the writings of Pierre Bourdieu. Moreover cooperation between disciplines will increase the power of analyses and interpretations of human and human-like behaviour. While the main area of reference of this paper is sociological theory, I hope that presentation below will convincingly show that many of the notions developed within the institutional setting of sociology have a high potential for application in such disciplines as linguistics or artificial intelligence. As it seems, the proposed application of the sociological theory could be considered as extension, or in fact, contextualization of the analysis of discursive behaviour, which will be treated here merely as one of the multiple forms of social action. Thus, this paper may be also seen as a response to those who call for a better integration of studies on discursive and non-discursive aspects of human behaviour, the need of which is being realized more and more (e.g. Akman [3], Blommaert [4], Chalaby [5] or Emirbayer [6]).

2 The Bourdieu's Field Theory

Bourdieu developed his theoretical approach to the analysis of social action over several decades and its elements are discussed in his numerous books and papers (see for example [7], [8] or [9] as well as in secondary sources e.g. [10] or [11]). A discussion of his theory in this paper will necessarily be selective and general therefore this account should not be read as a summary of Bourdieu's approach. Moreover, this paper presents a reinterpretation of the instruments he contributed to the study of context, and this may not be fully compatible with original Bourdieu's writings.

Thus, from the point of view of contextual analysis, the key notion introduced by Bourdieu is that of a social field. Field is understood by him as a social arena in which people manoeuvre and compete for desirable resources. Field could be also seen as a system of social positions, structured internally in terms of power relationships. One must note that the Bourdieu's field theory is only one type of what can be called a "general social field theory". John Levi Martin [12] recently summarized a number of theories of this kind distinguishing three main source domains: social psychology, sociology and institutional analysis. Martin considers social psychologist Kurt Lewin [13] to be the pioneer of field theory in the social sciences. The concept of social field according to Martin originates from physical sciences with classical electromagnetism as a standard point of reference. Lewin, for example claimed to find inspiration in the Einstein's approach to the notion of a field.

Let us return, however, to Bourdieu's perspective. Fields are characterized by the actors that inhabit these fields as well as by the relationships between these actors. However, first and foremost, fields are defined by the values assigned to different types of capital. Bourdieu distinguished three fundamental forms of capital. Firstly, there is the classic notion of **economic capital** defined as command over economic resources and possession of financial assets. In addition to this Bourdieu distinguished two other types of capital: social and cultural. **Social capital**, according to his definition, consists of relationships and the networks of influence and support that people can tap into by virtue of their social position. It can be also defined as membership of formal and informal groups that gives privileged access to different types of resources. Political capital (party membership or political connections) is seen by Bourdieu as a special form of social capital. **Cultural capital** refers to explicit and implicit, formal and informal cultural competences. These include the skills that parents provide their children with when they developing their attitudes and knowledge that makes the educational system a comfortable familiar place in which they can succeed easily. According to Bourdieu's definition, cultural capital appears as: the "embodied" state (personal character, life-style, ways of thinking, aesthetic taste, manners etc.), the "institutionalized" state (formal educational qualifications, competences confirmed by credentials) and the "objectified" state (objects of cultural value, mainly works of art). Bourdieu also mentioned a fourth type of capital: **symbolic capital**, which is defined differently than the three previous types. It can be identified by the institutionalized and/or universally (often subconsciously) recognized benefits from the three abovementioned main types of capital, the prestige and social status associated with them.

The division of human resources, and consequently types of fields, into economic, social and cultural can be perceived as arbitrary, but Bourdieu saw his system as a flexible model and assumed it was possible to distinguish other specific sub-types of capital, depending on particular circumstances and the nature of social structures being analyzed. Each of the types of capital can, in fact, have unlimited numbers of local variants (such as, for example, currencies in the financial markets) which are in constant competition. Bourdieu, as a general sociologist focused on wider social structures, which meant he was interested in universal and national fields of economics, politics or culture. However, the tools of his analysis can be applied to far lower-level social structures, even small temporary groups, with *ad hoc* simple structures, local social fields and the specific types of capital they define. In other words, analysis of social interaction in terms of Bourdieu's notions does not have to involve a full scale sociological study of a given society, although it may sometimes appear necessary, especially when the scope of references to general social context is considerable.

It is notable that Bourdieu's system with its three fundamental types of capital represents an attempt to widen the narrow, classic rational-choice-theory-based philosophy used in analyses of social processes. While not undermining the assumption of "rationality" of human behaviour, Bourdieu suggests that it should be defined in wider terms. He thus challenges the one-sided economic point of view which emphasises a striving for material profits as the main explanation for human action. Bourdieu argues that social and cultural capital can be seen as formal tools that model other dimensions of the social structures and desirable assets which drive social behaviour. Of particular importance here is that from a purely economic point of view many human actions may seem, and indeed often are, counterproductive but they may still be justified from the points of view of other fields than an economic one. In any case, the assumption in Bourdieu's theory is that all social actors in any situation strive to improve or at least defend their overall social status defined in terms of different the types of capital that are at the basis of their power and freedom to act.

According to Bourdieu's model, different types of capital occupy different social positions in specific fields. In the simplest configuration, a given type of capital will have the highest value in its own "pure" field. Such a field may just be a theoretical concept, but in other cases it is embedded in institutionalized forms. For example, economic capital will be most appreciated in the field of economics or business whereas it will seem far less useful in the fields of culture or politics. The elites of the culture or politics fields are defined by high levels of cultural and political capital respectively. This does not mean that financial resources have no impact within the realms of politics or culture. Financial resources are important in other areas, but not in terms of representing the main assets and values, rather as the currency to acquire the specific capital of the respective field: political and cultural. This mechanism has been labelled in Bourdieu's model as the 'conversion of capitals' (or types of capital). The rules of conversion between the different forms of capital differ for each field and these rules can also be considered a constitutive element of a field. By definition, the dominating type of capital: i.e. the most desirable asset in given realm, will possess the strongest "exchange rate" or value within that particular field relation to other types of capital. It should also be noted that besides their value being defined by the specific field, the types of capital also differ in terms of their fluidity or the time required for their accumulation. The most fluid form of capital is usually economic capital, which can be in most cases converted instantly in unlimited amounts. In contrast some of the sub-types of social and cultural capital are very stable which means their accumulation and/or loss often takes time. Classic examples of social and cultural capital are aristocratic or academic titles which may require life-time efforts and early socialization in specific social milieu. Many of them, in particular hereditary titles, may be possessed by families over several generations.

One should note that the greater the value of a given type (or sub-type) of capital in the general social system, the more dominant globally speaking the elites possessing such capital are. Another important notion used by Bourdieu is that of autonomy of field. Thus a given type of capital may not necessarily have universally dominant status but if its field is autonomous, its possession guarantees high social status within such a field irrespectively of possession of other types of capital. If autonomy of a field is low, in order to attain a key social position in a given social space possession of other types of capital, in particular of the globally dominating types, will be as important as possession of the field-specific type of capital. In extreme cases, autonomous field can be defined in contrast to the dominant field of the given social system. In such circumstances, value of the types of capital characteristic for a dominant field may be negative in a specific autonomous field. Bourdieu [8] gave the example of the intellectual field in France, which punished its actors for spectacular successes in the economic and political fields. However, even the elites of the highly autonomous intellectual field can not function without using some form of economic and social capital, although they may not emphasize this in their image of self. This is why in real-life situations actors usually use a whole portfolio of different types of capital and simultaneously act in different fields.

3 Field as Context

It is clear that a social field defined in this way can be considered as framework to formally describe the context of any social action. The notion of context has been already mentioned before in the writings of Bourdieu and his interpreters. Richard Jenkins [11:] wrote for example that, *"the field is the crucial mediating context wherein external factors – changing circumstances – are brought to bear upon individual practice and institutions. The logic, politics and structure of the field shape and channel the manner in which 'external determinations' affect what goes on within the field, making them appear a part of the ongoing history and operation of the field itself".*

However, it seems that so far nowhere has a systematic link been made between Bourdieu's field theory and context theory. Thus we could suggest that by using Bourdieu's theory, the context of social action can be characterized in the following way. If a given field is an established social structure with a considerable degree of autonomy it is best defined in terms of the nature of its specific, and therefore, dominant type of capital. Social position in a particular field is defined primarily by the type of assets specific to the capital of a given field. Thus, for appropriate interpretation of behaviour of someone acting in the economic field, knowledge about his material resources will be crucial. Following this logic, the elite of a field will be composed of those possessing the most assets of the dominant and defining type of capital. Another classic example from Bourdieu is the previously mentioned intellectual field with its particular dominant intellectual capital and intellectual elite. However, the autonomy of the intellectual field varies between different societies. Where it is high (as for example seems to be the case in France and Poland) intellectual capital will be "expensive" and have high "purchasing power" that is conversion rates will privilege its owners. Thus an exact characterization of a given field will require specification of its particular "table of exchange rates". This is because the intellectual fields (in a different countries, regions or cities) may be similar in the degree of their general autonomy that is overall status of the intellectual capital. But specific forms of intellectual capital may differ in their relations with particular types of capital. Thus one intellectual field may radically ignore, or undervalue economic capital, while relatively appreciating the value of say political capital. Another intellectual field, while equally autonomous may allow a better exchange rate for economic capital but disregard the value of some types of social capital as for instance the political capital or aristocratic titles.

Thus context in which social action takes place in a specific well-established and autonomous field may be described by specifying its dominant capital, which in turn is characterized by its rates and rules of conversion (e.g. time required for conversion) to other types of capital. Another example of such an analysis may be interpretation of social processes taking place in communist countries (e.g. Soviet Union). Since communist societies and countries may be defined in terms of hegemony of the political capital (and political field) [14], interpretation of any significant social actions located within their borders must take into account the nature of the political capital and its relations with other (usually subordinated) types of capital. This implies for example that any form of public action in such context must have formal backing of the communist government otherwise it can be considered as "subversive" by the authorities.

This dependence on "political field" seems to be a key dimension of interpretation for any observer and also for any social actor. In fact in many communist countries even passive observation (including listening or reading) of things considered illegal may be considered a crime. This seems to illustrate clearly how relative the distinction between an actor and observer can be.

Besides such well defined general fields of social interaction, which are usually adequate tools of analysis of social action at macro level, we can think of a whole spectrum of less formalized and dependent fields of social interaction down to *ad hoc* situations in which a given social action takes place. Such fields may also include instances of micro social analysis. In such contexts, because of their lack of a (socially recognized) identity and history, it is usually difficult to talk about specific types of capital characteristic for given fields. In such situations social positions will be defined by the overall value of the portfolios of capital possessed by the field actors. If a given social situation is not framed in the context of a specific autonomous field, the value of the portfolios will be measured according to the average conversion rules prevailing in a given society. In case an *ad hoc* group of people is defined within a framework of an established sub-field (e.g. participants at an academic conference) the "exchange rates" of such higher order social framework will be used (in our example those from academia or a specific discipline). However the *ad hoc* field will not necessary automatically reflect the logic of social hierarchy of its superior field. It may be altered by the strongest actors of an *ad hoc* (or rising) field, who may differ in terms of the composition of their capital portfolios from the elites of the superior field who define the basic rules of capital exchange. This may happen because the dominant actors of any field usually try to enhance the value of those types of capital assets over which they have most control. Because of the unpredictable nature of the elite formation process in a new social group, one could argue that conversion rules and in turn social hierarchy of any *ad hoc* (new) field are to some degree emergent phenomena. They result from the superior (or original) field and the assets, aspirations and strategies of the actors who have become active in this new (ad hoc) field.

It is important to emphasize the process of elite formation in a new field. Elite is by definition a social structure of highest concentration of the dominant (or most valuable) types of capital in a given field. It can be therefore seen as possessing a "magnetic force" proportional to its combined assets of capital. The composition of elite capital portfolios as well as conversion rates within a field, all define the vector of a field's "magnetic" direction and force.

4 Conversion of Capital as a Social Action

Thus any case social action in such perspective can be described as a process of conversion of capital. The effect of such a process is that an actor's portfolio of capitals changes and consequently his social position in all respective fields will alter.

One has to emphasize that in such a view no social actor can act in only one single field. In fact, the possession of any type of capital makes us actors in the respective fields of that particular type of capital. In other words possession of a portfolio of a number of types of capital makes a person an actor in several fields. Therefore, for example, by acquiring a small amount of financial capital one, at least theoretically, becomes an actor on the financial market. By acquiring citizenship in a democratic country we automatically obtain right to vote in elections and in effect become actors in the political field of that country. Thus any conversion between two or more types of capital will affect our standing in at least these two or more fields of social interaction. This implies that in order to understand (or find a coherent interpretation) of any social behaviour we have to identify these (at least) two fields in which a given action is taking place. Since, as suggested above, fields can be identified with contexts, any context of social action in such model will have to consist of at least two or more dimensions. Such an assumption seems to differ considerably form the classic models of context of communicative behaviour which often single out several of its aspects, but usually define it as one dimensional description of a more or less abstract social situation (for example van Dijk's models of context [15] of Hymes [16] "SPEKING" model). In some models of context an analysis in terms of "dimensions" is utilized, but these dimensions are in fact defined as incomparable aspects of the same social situation as for example by Goodwin and Duranti [17]. Referring to Ochs [18] they propose to distinguish the following: "dimensions of context" of linguistic behaviour: "setting", "behavioural component", "language as context" and "extra-situational context". Harris [19] distinguishes seven dimensions of context: world knowledge dimension, knowledge of language dimension, authorial dimension, generic dimension, collective dimension, specific dimension, textual dimension. As Bauman and Briggs point out, "all such definitions of context are overtly inclusive, there being no way to know when an adequate range of contextual factors has been encompassed. The seemingly simple task of describing >the context< of a performance can accordingly become an infinite regress". [2]

In contrast, the model proposed in this paper defines dimensions of context as parallel fields of respective types of capital which are involved in the conversion process constituted by a given social act. These dimensions can also be further analyzed in terms of their different aspects. But what is of importance here is that the dimensionality of the context will be defined not in a schematic and pre-defined way, as it seems to be the case in the above quoted examples, where different domains of context are distinguished without any clear criterion. Such an approach may, in particular, involve reification of context, as Bauman and Brigs warn. Therefore in our model dimensionality will be defined on the basis of the complexity of a specific conversion process and its interpretation. Complexity in this case would be defined by the number of types and subtypes of capital involved in the given conversion process. In a basic two-dimensional case a given social action would be seen as simultaneously taking place in two fields: first the field of the capital which is being converted that is "spend" or "used" and in the second field in which the other type of capital is "acquired" or "bought" (to which the former type of capital is converted into).

Importance of each of the dimensions of context can be measured/estimated assuming either equal importance of all fields or differentiated importance of fields, which may be in particular defined by:

- Actor's personal hierarchy of fields.
- Observer's personal hierarchy of fields
- Estimated general hierarchy of fields in a given sphere (e.g. in a given country, society, region or institutional domain).

The importance of each dimension may be also measured by the scale of change which occurred in a given field in effect of the social action under consideration. It me be defined either from the perspective of an actor or generalozed view on social system. Thus it would be defined as:

1. The scale of change in actors' assets of a given capital type and its share in his capital portflio. If a given type of capital represents a major part of actors' capital portfolio, changes in its assets will be proportionally important.
2. The scale of a given capital transfer in relation to its overall stock in the field (or in other words the scale of ownership structure change in a given field) implied by a given action.

5 Examples of Interpretation

A simple example of such process is selling an art object, for example a painting. Someone possessing a precious painting inherited from his/her ancestors may decide to sell it at an auction. Most of his/her assets of "objectified" cultural capital will be in this way converted into economic capital. To understand the sense of this transaction well we have to understand both the position of the given person in the cultural field as well as in the economic one. Another example, from the linguistic field could be (e.g. in form of recognition in closed social circles) that someone who can attend an expensive language course can make profitable use of knowing a foreign language. An even simpler example is that of using of a password. Passwords can be obtained in different fields (e.g. bought in the economic field or obtained from fields of the military or governmental agencies). Their use (in form of utterance in an appropriate situation or filling a web-site form) may bring also benefits in different fields (financial, social, or cultural e.g. in form of access to protected internet content).

As mentioned earlier, every speech act can be perceived as an instance of social behaviour and consequently analyzed in the similar contextual terms. A good example of complex speech acts are the texts of academic papers presented within the context of a conference. They can be analyzed in multidimensional terms of complex conversion of capitals. Thus for example preparation, submission and presentation of a paper at a conference may be imagined as a multidimensional investment process. The investment may be defined first in terms of use of cultural capital that is knowledge of the specific field, information about the described phenomena, competences including linguistic and stylistic as well as access to a particular language register (academic English in this case) [20] etc. The second investment can also be in the form of social capital, for example, connections used to acquire the relevant literature (which may be especially important in countries where access to foreign publications is difficult), proof-reading of the paper and correction of grammar and spelling. Third, investments may also include economic capital, since for instance the process of writing of a paper may consume considerable amount of time which could be otherwise spend on activities directly generating tangible economic resources. Subsequent presentation of a paper may also incur considerable financial costs related to travel, accommodation, registration fee etc. We can note that for each conference participant, the costs in terms of particular types of capital may be very different. The same refers to the dimension of profits generated by a given paper. It can of course first of all bring considerable gains in terms of cultural capital. Presentation and publication of a paper in a prestigious location may directly translate into scholarly recognition, increase of status and later enable access to formal academic titles which are the most tangible form of cultural capital. On the other hand, participation in a conference and attraction of attention by an interesting paper may lead to establishing new important contacts or even friendships, which constitute forms of social capital. In some cases, as for example of invited speakers, presentation at a conference may translate into direct gains in terms of economic capital. For others, the main benefits of conference participation may be related to the visit in a country or a city in which the event is taking place. Visiting an exotic country or a city rich in cultural objects may be also considered as a process of acquiring of cultural capital.

One could note that in the case of an interdisciplinary conference within the context: conference, papers can be also analyzed in terms of disciplines within which they are located. Thus, we have disciplines in the same framework as the authors and the literature to which their texts refer. At the same time we have the audience which can belong to the same circle as the author belongs, or they can be a mixed group of academics from diverse disciplines. This may be the case in the example of the Context conference. Such audience may be an instance of the above defined new "emergent" (or *ad hoc)* field in which capital exchange rates and the composition of the elite (centre of the gravity of the field) is not obvious at the outset.

Complete comprehension of any paper and a thorough understanding of its meaning and significance is not be possible without an awareness of the contexts of the investment and profit dimensions. Sometimes fields in which the relative change of capital resources of a given actor is minimal may seem irrelevant. For example for a wealthy scholar, the economic capital investment necessary for the preparation of his/her paper may be relatively unimportant. At the same time cultural capital gains may be equally irrelevant to a renowned. However, these dimensions of context may be meaningful from the point of view of an overall interpretation of social action. Of crucial importance in such an interpretation would be those dimensions of context where the most significant change (and/or investment) of capital assets has occurred.

Thus the relevant context of an academic paper, as any other social action will include a list of significant capital expenditures on one hand and a list of significant capital gains on the other. In particular it may be defined in the disciplinary terms, say as in the case of this paper where the primary investments may be located in the framework of sociology and the primary gains are supposed the appear in the emergent field of context studies.

Similar analysis of context understood as a capital conversion process may be also be applied to lower level social acts as simple statements or speech acts. In particular the so called performative speech acts may be considered as clear instances of capital conversion as they are supposed to change (or/and define) social situations. Thus for example by pronouncing the classic statement "I declare you a husband and a wife" a minister may engage his cultural capital (knowledge of the ritual) and social capital (official title and institutional prerogatives) in order to convert it into economic capital. Very clear capital conversion process may take place in case of pronouncing of even seemingly descriptive statements on controversial issues. Thus let say descriptions of people in terms of their ethnicity, competences or sexual preferences may involve significant costs (for example in terms of accusations of racisms, homophobia etc.) as well as gains (for example in terms of social support of those sharing a given point of view but afraid of its expression). The issue of symbolic costs of statements in social situation has been recently discussed by Strauss [21] who defines them in terms of "cultural standing".

Thus, in our perspective, a field would restrict social action by defining its social costs for a particular individual. If a move (upward) in a given field is defined by acquisition of the capital dominant in that particular field, an actor must always consider the costs of such move in terms of other types of capital they would have to spend in order to acquire the desired capital type. Therefore, their actions (and interpretation) are not only restricted by the field they are visibly moving in, but also by all other fields in which the capitals they use are defined. As soon as their resources in these other salient fields become depleted they will not be able to move any higher in the main field even if their position in it is relatively high. The only option they have in a such situation is to convert mono-dimensional capital into other forms of capital in other fields.

6 Similarities with Other Theoretical Approaches

The multidimensional model of context presented above can be linked to some of the earlier approaches to the analysis of social action. One of the most interesting models presented in the framework of "context studies" seem to be the definition of context by Edmonds [22]. While he is not so much interested in an analysis of any social behaviour but in the "pragmatics of learning and applying knowledge" Edmonds' definition of context seems to have an important resemblance to the model introduced in this paper. Thus according the Edmonds context is, *"the abstraction of those elements of the circumstances in which a model is learnt, that are not used explicitly in the production of an inference or prediction when the model is later applied, that allow the recognition of new circumstances where the model can be usefully applied"* [22].

What seems of importance here is the distinction Edmonds makes between the two parallel dimensions: circumstances of learning and circumstances of knowledge application. It seems these two dimensions could be related to the field of capital which is spent and the field of capital which is acquired. After all, the process of knowledge acquisition and use can also be theorized in the Bourdieuan terms. It could be defined in such perspective as investment in cultural capital and its subsequent conversion into other types of capital. As is correctly pointed out by Edmonds, this process should be analyzed in the framework of two separate dimensions and key differences between them.

A much earlier example of a view suggesting inherent multidimensionality of context is found in the work of the Russian literary theorist Mikhail Bakhtin [23]. Of particular interest here is his notion of the dialogic character of literature. As Bakhtin suggests, when analyzing any literary text we should differentiate between its object, its immediate addressee, and a *super-addressee*. This is what Bakhtin describes as the tertiary nature of dialogue. Of particular interest in this place is the notion of super-addressee which may be related to a hidden (or potential) "profit generating" dimension of context as it was defined in this paper. In other worlds, addressee and *super-addressee* may be seen as those rewarding an actor with the capital from the fields they are located in. A text (as well as any social action in general) with its "object" would be probably situated in field from which capital is used in a given situation. Verschuveren [24] has pointed to the possibility of characterizing context by the list of persons present in a given situation (whom he divided into interpreters and non-interpreters, participants and non-participants etc.) or Goffman [25] who emphasized the role of the "public" as the context of social behaviour, context may be also defined in terms of a particular audience and its members. Bakhtin seems to focus our attention on the multidimensional nature of context, in which he distinguishes the third dimension besides the two fundamental dimensions defined in this paper, namely the investment and profit dimension of conversion process. Bakhtin distinguishes a third dimension of "actual" context, or the formal audience which may sometimes appear simply irrelevant. Classic examples of such situations are statements by important politicians or most famous scholars. They chose relatively unimportant venues with low key audiences to make important political statements or to present crucial academic papers. An explanatory interpretation of their declarations sees these audiences and locations as being of marginal importance; what counts is the status of the speakers and their "real" audiences or *super-addresses* in Bakhtin's terms.

Some of the research on context signalling by social actors can also be explained using the above model of multidimensional context. In particular Gumperz's [26] works on "contextualization cues", which could be linked to the wider analysis of field identification in social interaction, may be of interest here. "Contextualization cues" may in particular be used to suggest the identity of a *super-addresse* of a message and thus be understood as ways of indication of the dimensions of context as they have been defined above. The linguistic notion of "code switching" [27] may also appear useful in this context. "Codes" used in communication, if understood on a high level of abstraction, may also refer to norms of communication, styles of behaviour and values in different fields in which action is taking place. Thus an actor may switch between codes of the field from which he is using capital and field in which he is investing. In this way he may emphasize (or negotiate) the nature of the conversion of capital he is attempting at. The classic examples of code switching are those of multilingual immigrants who use interchangeably languages of their countries (regions) of residence and origin.

7 Conclusions

The paper argued that on the basis of Pierre Bourdieu's view of social action as a process of conversion of different types of capital, we could define context as a multidimensional notion consisting of fields in which a given social process takes place. Two basic dimensions of context defined in this way are the field from which capital is spend and the field in which it is invested and converted into a new form (type of capital). Both of these two dimensions may consist of several sub-dimensions also defined as fields. There will be as many fields involved in an analysis of a context of particular social process as many types (and sub-types) of capital may be seen to be involved in the process of capital conversion. They can be further arranged according to their role in general social status definition.

Fields in such an analysis should be characterized in the ways which would reflect their specific nature. Thus established, well known general fields will be described in other ways than *ad hoc* or new fields with emerging elites. Characterization of fields should be of course performed in the pragmatic way: that is be restricted only to specification of those fields and those of their key traits which are not obvious and/or are possibly controversial for those interpreting a given social action and the actors.

Identification of relevant fields constituting the context in this model may of course involve reference to the categories used in other, traditional models of context. Thus, it may include such aspects of social action as genre, setting, norms, audience, behaviour etc. This approach however, will require first of all specification to which "side" of the conversion process fields characterized in one or another way belong to. Are they fields where capital is obtained from or fields in which it is spent? Thus for example, reference to a genre of a discursive activity should specify to which of the two categories the specific genre being used belongs? Is it a genre in which (and possibly in competence in) an actor "invested" in order to move upward in a field defined as the primary dimension of definition of his or her social status? Or is it a genre belonging to his "natural" repertoire, being an original "resource" used in the conversion process? Depending on the status of such genre, the interpretation of the very same discursive activity may be very different. Such questions can, for instance, be asked in the context of papers submitted for a conference Context. Are their specific genres the effects of authors' attempts to fit in with the standards of the conference or are they "traditional" genres particular to each author's own discipline? In other words are these attempts to introduce a "new" type of discourse or genre into the conference sphere or are they attempts to "translate" new knowledge into a discourse or "language" that is compatible with the genres already in use at the conference? Depending on the answer to these questions, merits of a paper would be assessed in completely different ways.

The above introduced distinction may seem artificial in many contexts as most aspects of social actions discussed in this paper are obvious to most social actors. However, the model discussed in this paper may be useful in attempts to formalize the mechanisms of social behaviour interpretation and in particular in models of discourse comprehension. Artificial agents may considerably benefit from ability to make a fundamental distinction between the two basic dimensions of model of context presented in this paper.

Acknowledgment. The author is grateful to the Netherlands Institute for Advanced Study (NIAS) for providing him with the opportunity, as a Fellow-in-Residence, to complete this paper.

References

1. Searle, J.R.: What is a speech act? In: Black, M. (ed.) Philosophy in America, pp. 221–239. Alien and Unwin, London (1965)
2. Bauman, R., Briggs, C.L.: Poetics and Performance as Critical Perspectives on Language and Social Life. Annual Review of Anthropology 19, 59–88 (1990)
3. Akman, V.: Rethinking context as a social construct. Journal of Pragmatics 32, 743–759 (2000)
4. Blommaert, J.: Context is/as Critique. Critique of Anthropology 21, 13–32 (2001)
5. Chalaby, J.K.: Beyond the Prison-House of Language: Discourse as a Sociological Concept. The British Journal of Sociology 47, 684–698 (1996)
6. Emirbayer, M.: Manifesto for a relational sociology. American Journal of Sociology 103, 281–317 (1997)
7. Bourdieu, P.: The Forms of Capital. In: Richardson, J.G. (ed.) Handbook of Theory and Research for Sociology of Education, pp. 241–258. Greenwood Press, New York, Westport, Connecticut, London (1986)
8. Bourdieu, P.: The rules of art. Genesis and structure of the literary field. Polity Press, Cambridge (1996)
9. Bourdieu, P., Wacquant, L.J.D.: An invitation to reflexive sociology. University of Chicago Press, Chicago (1992)
10. Anheier, H.H., Gerhards, J., Romo, F.P.: Forms of Capital and Social Structure in Cultural Fields: Examining Bourdieu's Social Topography. American Journal of Sociology 100, 859–903 (1995)
11. Jenkins, R.: Pierre Bourdieu. Routledge, London and New York (2002)
12. Martin, J.L.: What is Field Theory? American Journal of Sociology 109, 1–49 (2003)
13. Lewin, K.: Field theory in social science. Selected theoretical papers. Harper, New York (1951)
14. Eyal, G., Szelényi, I., Townsley, E.R.: Making capitalism without capitalists: class formation and elite struggles in post-communist Central Europe. Verso, London New York (1998)
15. van Dijk, T.A.: Context Models in Discourse Processing. In: Oostendorp, H.v, Goldman, S.R. (eds.) The construction of mental representations during reading, Lawrence Erlbaum, Mahwah, NJ (1998)
16. Hymes, D.: Models of the interaction of language and social life. In: Gumperz, J.J., Hymes, D. (eds.) Directions in Sociolinguistics: the Ethnography of Communication, pp. 35–71. Holt, Rinehart and Winston, New York (1972)
17. Goodwin, C., Durnati, A.: Rethinking context: an introduction. In: Goodwin, C., Duranti, A. (eds.) Rethinking context. Language as an interactive phenomenon, Cambridge University Press, Cambridge (1992)
18. Ochs, E.: Introduction: What Child Language Can Contribute to Pragmatics. In: Ochs, E., Schiefflin, B.B. (eds.) Developmental Pragmatics, Academic Press, New York (1979)
19. Harris, W.V.: Interpretive acts. In: search of meaning, Clarendon Press, Oxford (1988)
20. Swales, J.: Genre analysis. English in academic and research settings. Cambridge University Press, Cambridge (1990)
21. Strauss, C.: Cultural standing in expression of opinion. Language in Society 33, 161–194 (2004)
22. Edmonds, B.: The Pragmatic Roots of Context. In: Bouquet, P., Serafini, L., Brézillon, P., Benercetti, M., Castellani, F. (eds.) CONTEXT 1999. LNCS (LNAI), vol. 1688, pp. 119–132. Springer, Heidelberg (1999)

23. Bakhtin, M.M.: The dialogic imagination. Four essays. University of Texas Press, Austin (1981)
24. Verschueren, J.: Understanding pragmatics. Arnold, London (1999)
25. Goffman, E.: The presentation of self in everyday life. Allen Lane, London (1969)
26. Gumperz, J.J.: Discourse strategies. Cambridge University Press, Cambridge (1982)
27. Auer, P.: Code-switching in conversation. Language, interaction and identity. Routledge, London (1998)

Context Sensitivity: Indexicalism, Contextualism, Relativism

Dan Zeman

Central European University, Department of Philosophy, Nador u. 9, H-1051,
Budapest, Hungary

Abstract. The paper is primarily concerned with laying out the space
of positions that purport to account for semantic context sensitivity of
natural language expressions and with making a prima facie case for
relativism. I start with distinguishing between pre-semantic, semantic
and post-semantic context sensitivity. In the following section I briefly
present the classic picture of indexicals due to David Kaplan and assess some arguments for the introduction of certain parameters in the
circumstances of evaluation (specifically, time). In section III I envisage
two views that purport to expand semantic context sensitivity beyond expressions from "the basic set": indexicalism and contextualism. In section
IV, by means of an example taken from John Perry, I draw attention to a
specific form of semantic context sensitivity, namely that in which what
is affected by context are the circumstances of evaluation of utterances
rather than their content. The example leads to the necessity of distinguishing between two roles of context: a content-determinative one and
a circumstance-determinative one. In section V I introduce relativism
as the view incorporating the claim that context has a circumstance-
determinative role and contrast it with the two views presented before.
In the final section I analyze a certain type of argument usually adduced
in favor of contextualism (the so-called "context-shifting arguments")
and show that in order to work it has to rule out relativism. I conclude
by claiming that the battle must be fought by giving arguments to the
effect that a certain parameter should or should not be part of the circumstances of evaluation rather than the content of utterances.

1 Forms of Context Sensitivity

The phenomenon of context sensitivity of linguistic expressions is pervasive in
any language. For reasons of economy, we use the same expressions to refer to a
multitude of objects, with different intentions. For purposes of communication,
we have to rely on a variety of non-linguistic aids and clues to identify the
objects talked about or the intentions with which our peers go on to speak. The
sum of these aids and clues could be called, in an intuitive and non-technical
way, *context*. Context is what helps us to successfully communicate in various
situations by using a limited set of expressions.

There is more than one form of context sensitivity. Following Stanley
and Szabo (2000), we could distinguish between pre-semantic, semantic and

B. Kokinov et al. (Eds.): CONTEXT 2007, LNAI 4635, pp. 545–557, 2007.
© Springer-Verlag Berlin Heidelberg 2007

post-semantic context sensitivity.[1] In its pre-semantic form, context sensitivity has to do with phenomena like homonymy and ambiguity. If someone produces the sound "yes", it is important to know where it was produced in order to catch what has been expressed, since in different languages the same sound may form different words. Further, English words like "bank" exhibit what is called lexical ambiguity the fact that under the same vocable there are two different words with two different meanings. Ambiguity could appear not only at the level of words, but also at the level of whole sentences. This is the phenomenon of syntactic ambiguity.[2]

Semantic context sensitivity has to do not with homonymy or ambiguity, but with the use in different contexts of expressions whose meaning we have already deciphered. That is, even after we know the language to which a given expression belongs and have solved all the ambiguities, we still need context in order to identify the objects referred to by an expression. The paradigms of semantic context sensitivity are *indexicals*. Pronouns like "I", "you", "he" or "she", adverbs like "here", "now" or "actual", nouns like "today" or "yesterday", change their semantic values with the context in which they are used.

Third and finally, there is a form of context sensitivity that influences not the content of what is explicitly said, but what is conveyed by what is explicitly said. This form of context sensitivity is post-semantic, or pragmatic. Granted, here the notion of context at stake changes: it will include not only "external", non-linguistic factors like the place where an utterance was produced, but also "internal" ones, such as the topic of the previous conversation, the background knowledge of those participating in it, and so on. Thus, according to this kind of context sensitivity, in order to retrieve what is conveyed by a given utterance, not only we have to understand what is explicitly said, but we also need to know things from the larger context in which the utterance was made. If, for example, somebody witnesses a conversation in which a person is ironically said to be a good friend, she needs to know something about the person's misgivings in order to understand that what is explicitly said serves to convey something else (in this case, the opposite that the person spoken about is not a good friend at all).

Although all three forms of context sensitivity are equally important, I will be concerned in this essay only with the second one. Within it, there are a number of ways in which context might play a role in establishing the truth-value of utterances. The most obvious one is providing elements that go into the content of what is expressed. However, there is another way in which context influences the truth-value of an utterance: namely, by providing parameters that become part of the circumstances of evaluation with respect to which the utterance is evaluated. This role of context can rightfully be described as semantic, since one

---

[1] Perry (1998) makes a similar distinction, but his take on post-semantic context sensitivity is different from that of Stanley and Szabo. Although I'm following here Stanley and Szabo, I will talk a lot about what Perry calls "post-semantic context sensitivity" later in the paper.

[2] A nice example of syntactic ambiguity without involving any lexical ambiguity is the sentence "She begun to speak almost inaudibly".

of the aims of a semantic theory is to capture all what is relevant for the truth of linguistic expressions. This particular form of semantic context sensitivity will be my topic in what follows.

2 Indexicals: The Classic Picture

The classic definition of indexicals is that they are expressions whose semantic value changes with context.[3] In David Kaplan's (1989) framework, an indexical expresses different contents in different contexts of utterance. The notions of context and content are connected with the issue of the meaning of indexicals. For Kaplan, the meaning of an indexical is twofold. On one hand, we have that aspect of meaning which is constant across uses of the same expression in different contexts: this is what Kaplan calls *character*. Character is the meaning of indexical expressions in the sense of what is known by competent speakers of the language; it is not the meaning of an indexical in the sense that it is synonymous with it. For Kaplan, indexicals are means of direct reference; that is, they contribute to the compounds they appear in the very object they refer to. This leads us to the second component of an indexical's meaning: what Kaplan calls content. The relation between character and content is such that the character gives the rules by which a particular content gets expressed in a given context. Their connection is best explained by saying that the character is a function from contexts to contents.

For the evaluation of contents we need what Kaplan calls *circumstances of evaluation*. While the context of an utterance is the particular situation in which it is produced, circumstances of evaluation are "both actual and counterfactual situations with respect to which is appropriate to ask for the extensions of a given well-formed expression" (Kaplan, 1989: 502). Circumstances serve as arguments for the function that defines contents: these are simply functions from circumstances of evaluations to truth-values. A circumstance of evaluation "will usually include a possible state or history of the world, a time, and perhaps other features as well" (Kaplan, 1989: 502).

The issue of what features a circumstance of evaluation should comprise is not a trivial one. One well-known debate in last decades' semantics was about whether time should be part of the circumstances of evaluation of tensed sentences or not. According to *eternalists*, the content expressed by an utterance of a tensed sentence must contain the time when the sentence was produced in order for that content to be fully truth-evaluable. In contrast, *temporalists* claim that the content expressed by a tensed sentence should be time-neutral and that time should be instead a parameter in the circumstances. As a defender of temporalism, Kaplan has given the following argument to the effect that time must figure in the circumstances rather than made explicit in the content:

---

[3] There is an issue about exactly which expressions are indexicals. To set it aside, throughout this paper I will use the term "the basic set" (borrowed from Cappelen and Lepore (2005)) to refer to those expressions that turn out to be indexicals according to our final theory about them.

If we built the time of evaluation into the contents (thus removing time from the circumstances leaving only, say, a possible world history, and making contents specific as to time), it would make no sense to have temporal operators. To put the point another way, if what is said is thought of as incorporating reference to a specific time, or state of the world, or whatever, it is otiose to ask whether what is said would have been true at another time, in another state of the world, or whatever. Temporal operators applied to eternal sentences (those whose contents incorporate a specific time of evaluation) are redundant. Any intensional operators applied to perfect sentences (those whose contents incorporate specific values for all features of circumstances) are redundant. (Kaplan, 1989: 503.)

However, this argument is not decisive. As King (2003), among others, has noted, the mainstream in nowadays linguistics is to treat tenses and temporal expressions not as sentential operators (as Kaplan and Lewis thought), but as predicates of times. This has the consequence that circumstances of evaluation don't need to include time among their parameters. King rests his case against the introduction of temporal and location parameters in the circumstances of evaluation on this kind of considerations. His conclusion is that the only parameters we need to include in the circumstances are worlds (and maybe standards of precision). If this is the case and, indeed, temporal expressions like "sometimes" or "somewhere" are understood as quantifiers over times, then the argument that we need time, space and maybe other features in the circumstances of evaluation is rebutted.

Some authors have argued that King's argument can be resisted (Recanati, ms.), so the issue is not entirely settled. However, I think that what this unfinished debate suggests is that we need other arguments to the effect that certain features of the context must be included in the circumstances of evaluation.

Here is such an argument. It comes from the necessity of preserving what might be called "temporal innocence", and it is best presented by making a parallel with the modal case. Imagine that in the past our language didn't contain modal operators or any other devices for inquiring into what would have been the case if things would have been otherwise. There are two things to be said about such a language. First, a (contemporary) semanticist would still need possible worlds in his theory about the past language. Second, were we to enrich the language with modal expressions, we would still speak in ordinary talk like before; it is just that now we have the means to inquire into what would have been the case if things would have been otherwise. If we are told that for the enriched language we need to specify worlds whenever we talk about ordinary things, that would lead to a loss of our "modal innocence" and cancel the difference between sentences like "Snow is white" and "Actually, snow is white".

The same, the argument goes, happens with time. We can imagine a past language that didn't contain temporal operators or any other devices for inquiring into what would have been the case at other times than the present. By parallel reasoning, introducing time in the content of what is expressed would lead to a loss of our "temporal innocence" and would cancel the difference between sentences like "It is raining" and "It is raining now".[4]

I don't claim that this argument is decisive. What I rather want to show is one way to argue for the introduction of certain parameters in the circumstances of evaluation in this case time that could be taken as a model for arguing for the introduction of other parameters. What is important to note here is the fact that, whatever the outcome of the debate, there is a fairly well entrenched principle that all participants seem to agree upon. This principle, called "the distribution principle", will prove to be important in the discussion that follows. Here is one of its formulations:

> [*Distribution*] The determinants of truth-value distribute over the two basic components truth-evaluation involves: content and circumstance. That is, a determinant of truth-value, e.g. a time, is *either* given as an ingredient of content *or* as an aspect of the circumstance of evaluation. (Recanati, forthcoming.)

3   Indexicalism and Contextualism

Indexicality has been long seen as the paradigm of semantic context sensitivity. However, recent debates in philosophy of language have witnessed a flourishing of views holding that the phenomenon of semantic context sensitivity is by no means limited to expressions from the basic set. There are two ways in which such context sensitivity might be transferred to other expressions. The first is to treat more expressions as indexicals; the second is to account for them by means of pragmatic mechanisms that affect the content of sentences. These strategies have emerged from the recent debate between "traditionalists" and "contextualists" that occupies the front stage in nowadays philosophy of language.

The debate is basically over the limits of context in establishing the content of expressions as used in particular situations of communication. At the traditional end of the spectrum there is *minimalism*.[5] Minimalism holds that the meaning of a sentence is its literal meaning, and restricts the intervening of context to the fixing of reference of expressions from the basic set. Phenomena that seem to require explanations in terms of context intervening are given pragmatic explanations along the usual Gricean lines. However, the view is note spared with troublesome examples. This has lead philosophers keen to the claim that the meaning of a sentence is its literal meaning to an alternative explanation of the context sensitivity of other expressions than those from the basic set. According to this alternative explanation, sentences containing expressions suspected to be affected by context have a logical form that differs from their surface, grammatical form. The former is rendered as comprising an argument place for a hidden indexical, which takes semantics values that vary with context.[6] Thus it was

---

[4] In presenting the argument I drew heavily on Recanati (2004), chapter 9.

[5] The representative view is Cappelen and Lepore (2005).

[6] The representative view is Stanley (2000).

possible to hold that certain types of expressions are similar to indexicals therefore the label *indexicalism*. According to indexicalists, then, the set of context sensitive expressions must be expanded beyond the basic set such that to include a host of expressions that used to be considered non-indexical.

Contextualism could be contrasted with indexicalism on a couple of scores. Contextualists contend that the linguistic meaning of an expression is rarely enough to give the truth-conditions of our utterances. Their motivation lies in such remarks as Travis':

> What words mean plays a role in fixing when they would be true; but not an exhausting one. Meaning leaves room for variation in truth conditions from one speaking to another. (Travis, 1996: 451, quoted in Cappelen and Lepore, 2005)

This stance is reflected in how contextualists conceive the way in which context intervenes into what is expressed by utterances in particular situations of communication. The crucial difference between the two positions concerns the mechanisms by means of which context is doing its intervening job. The basic distinction is that between what Recanati (2004) called the phenomenon of saturation and that of *free enrichment*: while saturation takes as a starting point an expressed part of the utterance, free enrichment has no starting point in any expressed part of the utterance. (In this sense, indexicals are subject to saturation.) Here one notion that proves important for contextualists is that of "unarticulated constituents".[7] By free enrichment constituents that are unarticulated both at the linguistic and at the level of logical form get into the content expressed. It is important for contextualists that the mechanisms they hold to be functional in the work done by context should not be confused with the role context has been thought of having in pragmatics as making possible the transition from "what is said" to "what is meant", in the Gricean sense of these terms. This is why Recanati (2004) sharply distinguishes between primary pragmatic processes and secondary pragmatic processes. The main difference between them is that while secondary pragmatic processes intervene after a content has been expressed (the Gricean "what is said"), primary pragmatic processes intervene precisely in order to establish what content is expressed.

4   Context as Affecting the Evaluation of Utterances

As briefly mentioned in the previous section, the notion of "unarticulated constituent" is an important component in the contextualist's view, for it is the notion that allows her to explain how contexts affects content. But, *ab initio*,

---

[7] Though not only contextualists can appeal to the notion of "unarticulated constituents". Stanley (2000), for example, admits constituents that are unarticulated *linguistically*, but holds that they are articulated in the logical form of the sentences in which they don't appear: the logical form contains argument places for hidden indexicals. This is why the means by which context works is saturation, rather than enrichment.

in the works of John Perry, the notion has been used to highlight other roles of context besides that of supplying semantic values for the content of our utterances.

The idea first emerged in Perry's paper "Thought without Representation". Here Perry considers utterances such as "It is raining" made in different contexts. In one story we are told that Perry's son looks at the window from their house in Palo Alto and utters "It is raining". Perry understands that it is raining in Palo Alto, where they both are, and goes back to sleep. Now, we are asked to imagine another situation in which Perry's son speaks on the phone with his brother who resides in Murdock. Answering Perry's question "How are things there?" the son utters "It is raining", but this time Perry understands that it is raining in Murdock, where the brother is. What should be said about these cases? It would be fair to claim that in both cases the place where it rains is a constituent of the content of the son's utterance of "It is raining": in the first scenario the constituent is Palo Alto, whereas in the second it is Murdock. But if so, the place is an *unarticulated* constituent, since in neither case it figures in the uttered sentence. In Perry's terms, both utterances in the two cases are *about* the place where it rains: Palo Alto and Murdock, respectively.

Further Perry considers the Z-landers, a "small isolated group, living in a place called Z-land. Z-landers do not travel to, or communicate with, residents of other places, and they have no name for Z-land" (Perry, 1993: 212). When uttering "It is raining", the Z-landers simply say that it rains in Z-land. But Z-land is not part of the content (mental or linguistic) of their utterances. In this case, Perry claims, the place in which it rains (namely, Z-land) is a factor of the circumstance of evaluation of the Z-landers' utterances. In their mouths, utterances of "It is raining" are not about Z-land, but, as Perry says, they *concern* Z-land.

Perry's main claim in the paper is that "there is a little of the Z-lander in the most well-traveled of us" (Perry, 1993: 216). That is so because we utter sentences like "It is raining" in different "language games". One such language game might be talk about local weather; another, talk about weather in several locations. When talking about local weather, there is no need to articulate the place we are at. "When I look outside and see rain and grab an umbrella or go back to bed, a relatively true belief, *concerning* my present surroundings, will do as well as a more articulated one, *about* my present surroundings" (Perry, 1993: 216, my emphasis). The coordinating job done by the belief in this case is satisfactory, even if the belief does not contain the place as a constituent.

It is obvious from the discussion above that context has a double role: in some cases it supplies the content of utterances with unarticulated constituents; in others it just supplies a parameter for the circumstance of evaluation with respect to which utterances are evaluated. MacFarlane (ms), who also distinguishes between several kinds of context sensitivity, dubbed these two roles of context the *content-determinative role* and the *circumstance-determinative role*. Now, there is a crucial question that must be answered regarding these two roles context has namely, how are we to distinguish between cases in which context has a content-determinative role and when it has a circumstance-determinative one? Is there any criterion that could do the job? Without such a criterion, it seems, the distinction would lose not only its usefulness, but also its plausibility.

Following some hints in Perry's paper, Recanati has suggested that the required criterion is the

> *Externality Principle*
> For an unarticulated constituent to be an aspect of the situation rather than an implicit ingredient of the *lekton*, it must be contributed by the external environment rather than cognitively discriminated (Recanati, ms.: 181).[8]

Both in the case of the Z-landers and in that of Perry's son uttering "It is raining" when looking at the window in Palo Alto, there is an "external guarantee" that the respective utterances concern the relevant parameter (here, the place). In the first case the guarantee comes from the fact that the Z-landers (by definition) have no representation of the place they live in, while in the second it comes from the fact that the relevant parameter is fixed by the environment, such that the subject doesn't have to cognitively discriminate it himself. In contrast, in the case of Perry's son talking on the phone with his brother in Murdock, the subject has to discriminate (and, hence, to express) what the thought is about since there is no external fact that will provide the circumstance for evaluating it.

However, Recanati rejects this principle and neutralizes the arguments in its favor.[9] One of these arguments is "the mental articulation argument". Perry's diagnosis of the case in which his son talks on the phone with the brother in Murdock is that Murdock must be an articulated constituent of the mental representation underlying the speaker's intentions and beliefs. On the assumption that an utterance's content is the same with that of the belief it helps to express, it follows that Murdock must be an (unarticulated) constituent of the utterance itself. So, Murdock is part of the content expressed by the son's utterance of "It is raining". Recanati agrees that Murdock has to be articulated in *some* mental representation of the speaker, but denies that it has to be articulated in the very utterance expressing the content that the speaker intends to communicate. The mental representation in which Murdock is articulated serves as background for the utterance, but it doesn't have to be the very mental representation whose content the utterance expresses. Specifically, Murdock is articulated in the son's mental representation of Perry's question about Murdock ("How are things there?"), and not in that corresponding to the son's utterance of "It is raining". In Perry's own terms, the son's utterance *concerns* Murdock, but it not *about* it. This allows Recanati to treat scenarios like the Murdock case on the same par as

---

[8] Here "situation" and "lekton" reflect Recanati's choice of terminology, but also some underlying substantial views that this paper is not committed to. However, the principle could be easily reformulated in Kaplanian terms by replacing "situation" with "circumstance of evaluation" and "lekton" with "content".

[9] There are three such arguments: the mental articulation argument, the behavioral argument and the argument from invariance. I will present only Recanati's rejection of the first, since it has some consequences that I will take up later in the paper.

scenarios involving the Z-landers and to conclude that "in many cases (including the Murdock case), the situation which an utterance or thought concerns is determined by cognitive factors such as the topic of conversation or what the thinker is mentally focusing on, rather than by external factors like the location of the speaker" (Recanati, ms.: 184). The *Externality Principle* is thus rejected.

5 Relativism

Relativism, as I use the term in this paper, is the view that the same utterance of a sentence could be true relative to one set of parameters and false relative to another set. A set of parameters is simply a circumstance of evaluation. The semantic apparatus that allows the relativist to express her view (which incorporates the claim that context has a circumstance-determinative role) is a slight modification of the traditional, Kaplanian framework. We have already seen that besides worlds, Kaplan admitted time as a parameter of the circumstances of evaluation. Lewis (1981), who's view differs in important aspects from that of Kaplan's, but which for reasons that matter here is quite similar to it, admitted places, agents and maybe standards of precision as "coordinates" of "indices" his term for Kaplan's circumstances of evaluation. From here to various versions of relativism is just a small step. It simply consists in supplementing the circumstances of evaluation with more parameters, suited for each particular version. Thus, for example, a relativist about taste will claim that an utterance containing a taste predicate needs to be evaluated against a standard of taste parameter, along with the other parameters; a relativist about knowledge attribution will claim that an utterance containing the word "know" needs to be evaluated against a standard of knowledge parameter (again, along with the other parameters), and so on. Since the parameters used might yield different results in establishing an utterance's truth-value, the relativist can claim that the content expressed by the utterance could vary in truth-value with the new introduced parameter.[10]

---

[10] Lasersohn (2005) holds relativism for taste discourse, whereas Kölbel (2004) advocates relativism for the evaluative sphere in general. Both positions are particular applications of the framework I'm presenting here. Other applications include Mac-Farlane (2003) for future contingents, Egan, Hawthorne and Weatherson (2005) for epistemic modals, MacFarlane (2005) for knowledge attributions, etc. A few comments are in order with respect to MacFarlane's position. First thing to note is that MacFarlane's framework, although formally not very different, departs from the view presented in this paper by introducing one more relativization of truth: that to contexts of assessment. This introduces more flexibility in the evaluation of utterances: whereas ordinary relativists like Lasersohn and Kölbel will say that the truth of an utterance is relative to the circumstances in play at its context of utterance, Mac-Farlane will claim that the truth of an utterance is relative to the circumstances in play at the context of its assessor. This difference, although important in itself and ultimately leading to different results in the views' treatment of particular cases, could be safely ignored for the purposes of this paper. The main reason is that the phenomenon MacFarlane claims to have unveiled that of the assessment sensitivity

I think relativism gains considerable plausibility from the considerations put forward above about the circumstance-determinative role of context. If Perry and Recanati are right, then it follows that there are cases in which context has an evaluation-determinative role; consequently, in these cases there is no need to introduce any constituent (articulated or unarticulated) into the content, but instead treat it as a parameter of the circumstance of evaluation. Moreover, although this is not the main consequence of the failure of the *Externality Principle*, features that could be treated as parameters of the circumstance of evaluation are not limited to external factors; that is, "internal" factors might come into play. This in turn opens the possibility of relativism, at least for areas in which the evaluation of utterances is dependent upon some intrinsic features of the subject: the so-called subjective discourses (as opposed to objective ones). This is a welcome result for the relativist because it shows that relativism is not such an outlandish doctrine. Not only does relativism make sense as a purely semantic doctrine, but it also has a foot in the common practice of evaluating the utterances of others.

It is important to understand the difference between relativism on one side, and indexicalism and contextualism on the other. The last two views are views that take context to affect the content of utterances. In contrast, as already pointed out, relativism sees context as affecting the circumstances of evaluation with respect to which utterances have to be evaluated. That these views are at odds shouldn't come as a surprise: it is a straightforward consequence of the *Distribution principle* (section II). All three views claim to offer the best account of linguistic phenomena belonging to various discourses. To be sure, in a way all of them could be said to be theories that purport to offer accounts of the context sensitivity of linguistic expressions; but while indexicalism and contextualism locates the effect of such sensitivity in the content of utterances, relativism locates it in the circumstances needed for the evaluation of those utterances. This fact has been neglected in recent debates, leading to positions that where called relativist, but which actually are indexicalist or contextualist views.[11] The confusion is based on a claim that some authors think to be "one

---

of certain expressions could be incorporated into the more general phenomenon of semantic context sensitivity. Specifically, an expression being assessment sensitive is one particular way in which context plays a circumstance-determinative role, as opposed to it playing a content-determinative one. This claim is supported by the fact that for MacFarlane contexts of assessment are simply contexts in which given utterances are evaluated with respect to some salient circumstances of evaluation. The difference between the ordinary relativists and MacFarlane stems from what they take those salient circumstances to be.

[11] Dreier (1990) is a clear example of indexicalism about moral terms, despite the fact that he calls his view "speaker relativism". Although things are not totally clear, Harman's "moral relativism" also seems to be a form of indexicalism: his main claim, that "[f]or the purposes of assigning objective truth-conditions, a judgment of the form, it would be morally wrong of P to D, has to be understood as *elliptical* for a judgment of the form, in relation to moral framework M, it would be morally wrong of P to D" (Harman, 1996: 43, my emphasis) easily supports such a reading.

of the classical principles of semantics, viz. that a difference in truth-value of two claims implies a corresponding difference in the propositions expressed." (Marvan, 2006: 5, fn. 17). The next section is devoted to an illustration of the claim that this principle is false.

6   Context-Shifting Arguments

There is a certain type of argument that has been seen as lying at the heart of all contextualist positions. To argue for their view, contextualists use what Cappelen and Lepore called "context-shifting arguments" (CSA). Essentially, a CSA involves putting forward an experiment in which the same sentence is uttered in two different contexts. The experiment is supposed to trigger our intuitions that what is said in the two contexts differs in truth-value. The conclusion is then drawn that the two utterances express different contents. Therefore, if the truth-values of the two utterances differ, this means that there is a difference in the content expressed by the two utterances. This conclusion is then taken to show that some expressions in the sentences uttered are context sensitive i.e., they change their semantic value with the context in which the sentence containing them is uttered. Contextualism is vindicated.

Some authors (notoriously Cappelen and Lepore (2005)) have denied CSA their ability to provide tests for context sensitivity. In contrast, I don't want to claim that CSA cannot be seen as suitable tests for context sensitivity. That is, I agree with the contextualists that in the cases they present in CSA a real shift in context takes place. Where I disagree with them is how this shift should be interpreted. For, once one takes into account relativism, there is a simple explanation why context-shifting arguments fail to establish that a given expression is context sensitive in the sense contextualism wants it to be that is, that for a given expression context has a content-determinative role.

As MacFarlane (ms) aptly remarked, in order to be able to draw the conclusion that an expression is context sensitive in the way the contextualist wants it to be that is, that it contributes to the sentence in which appears different semantic values in different contexts we need another premise: that the circumstances of evaluation with respect to which the sentence is evaluated are the same in the two contexts. Only then we could safely conclude that the difference in truth-value leads to a difference in the content of the two utterances uttered in the two contexts. Otherwise, it is entirely possible what all we get is a difference in the circumstances of evaluation against which the two sentences are evaluated in their respective contexts. Let's make this clearer by an example.

Contextualists in epistemology maintain that the word "know" is context sensitive. Imagine a situation in which John, after parking his car in the driveway, goes up to his flat and utters "I know that my car is in the driveway". Few minutes later, after watching some news about the favorite area of a gang of car stealers, which happens to include the very street John lives on, he utters the same sentence again. John's first utterance is, as most of us agree, true. But his second utterance, with the possibility of the car being stolen brought into the picture, is false. Therefore, we are invited to believe, the two utterances must express different contents. But applying MacFarlane's point, in order to draw this conclusion, the contextualist has to secure that the epistemic standards with respect to which the two utterances are evaluated coincide. And the problem is that she cannot secure that. For saying that the standards are the same in the two contexts means to say that there is no variation, and therefore that "know" is not context sensitive. This is downright invariantism about knowledge attributions. On the other hand, saying that the standards should be employed in *evaluating* the utterances made rather than as being part of the contents expressed would be to concede to the relativist that context has a circumstance-determinative role and not a content-determinative one. Of course, the contextualist is free to deny that, but in doing so she cannot avail herself of arguments of the type we are analyzing. That would simply to beg the question.

Note that in making the above claim I didn't presuppose that relativism is right. Rather, the claim is a conditional one: if relativism is right, then CSA cannot provide support to contextualism.[12] However, in order to show that relativism is right one has to come up with suitable arguments that certain parameters (in the example above case, knowledge standards) must figure in the circumstances of evaluation rather than in the content of what is expressed by given utterances and that is something that I haven't done. Nevertheless, if Perry and Recanati's considerations are correct, then there is a prima facie case for relativism. Unless the contextualists tell us something that would preclude interpreting the shift in standards as a result of the circumstance-determinative role of the context, rather than as its content-determinative one, they cannot naively use CSA in support of their view. What I tried to provide in this paper is not an argument for a given position, but a sketch of the landscape where the confrontation should take place.

References

1. Cappelen, H., Lepore, E.: Insensitive Semantics. In: A Defense of Semantic Minimalism and Speech Act Pluralism, Blackwell Publishing, Oxford (2005)
2. Dreier, J.: Internalism and Speaker Relativism. Ethics 101, 6–26 (1990)
3. Egan, A., Hawthorne, J., Weatherson, B.: Epistemic Modals in Context. In: Preyer, G., Peter, G. (eds.) Contextualism in Philosophy. Knowledge, Meaning, and Truth, pp. 131–170. Clarendon Press, Oxford (2005)
4. Harman, G.: Moral Relativism. In: Harman, G., Thomson, J.J. (eds.) Moral Relativism and Moral Objectivity, pp. 1–64. Blackwell Publishers, Oxford (1996)
5. Kaplan, D.: Demonstratives. In: Almog, J., Perry, J., Wettstein, H. (eds.) Themes from Kaplan, pp. 481–563. Oxford University Press, Oxford (1989)

---

[12] One might be tempted to say that, if relativism is right, not only CSA fail to establish that context has a content-determinative role, but also that they directly show that context has a circumstance-determinative role. But this would be trivial. It would simply follow from the fact that relativism is right (that is, that context has a circumstance-determinative role and not a content-determinative one) together with *Distribution*.

6. King, J.: Time, Modality and Semantic Values. Philosophical Perspectives 17, 195–245 (2003)
7. Kölbel, M.: Indexical Relativism versus Genuine Relativism. International Journal of Philosophical Studies 12, 297–313 (2004)
8. Lasersohn, P.: Context Dependence, Disagreement and Predicates of Personal Taste. Linguistics and Philosophy 28, 643–686 (2005)
9. Lewis, D.: Index, Context, and Content. In: Lewis, D. (ed.) Papers in Philosophical Logic, pp. 21–44. Cambridge University Press, Cambridge (1998)
10. MacFarlane, J.: Future Contingents and Relative Truth. The Philosophical Quarterly 53, 321–336 (2003)
11. MacFarlane, J.: The Assessment Sensitivity of Knowledge Attributions. In: Gendler-Zsabo, T., Hawthorne, J. (eds.) Oxford Studies in Epistemology, pp. 197–223 (2005)
12. MacFarlane, J., (ms.): Non-indexical Contextualism, retrievable at http://sophos.berkeley.edu/macfarlane/nonindexical-contextualism.pdf
13. Marvan, T.: Obstacles to the Relativity of Truth. Organon F XIII(4), 439–450 (2006)
14. Perry, J.: Thought without Representation. In: Perry, J. (ed.) The Essential Indexical and Other Essays, pp. 205–219. Oxford University Press, New York, Oxford (1993)
15. Perry, J.: Indexicals, Contexts and Unarticulated Constituents. In: Proceedings of the 1995 CSLI-Amsterdam Logic, Language and Computation Conference, pp. 1–16. CSLI Publications, Stanford (1998)
16. Recanati, F.: Literal Meaning. Cambridge University Press, Cambridge (2004)
17. Recanati, F.: Moderate Relativism. In: Garcia-Carpintero, M., Kölbel, M. (eds.) Relativizing Utterance Truth (forthcoming)
18. Recanati, F., (ms.): Perspectival Thought. A Plea for Moderate Relativism, retrievable at http://jeannicod.ccsd.cnrs.fr/docs/00/09/48/48/PDF/RelativismBOOK69.pdf
19. Stanley, J.: Context and Logical Form. Linguistics and Philosophy 23, 391–434 (2000)
20. Stanley, J., Szabo, Z.: Quantifier Domain Restriction. Mind and Language 15, 219–261 (2000)

An Operational Definition of Context

Andreas Zimmermann, Andreas Lorenz, and Reinhard Oppermann

Fraunhofer Institute for Applied Information Technology
Schloss Birlinghoven
53754 Sankt Augustin, Germany
{Andreas.Zimmermann, Andreas.Lorenz,
Reinhard.Oppermann}@fit.fraunhofer.de

Abstract. The definition of context experienced an evolution in the research area of context-aware computing, but still suffers from either generality or incompleteness. Furthermore, many definitions are driven by the ease of implementation. This paper introduces two extensions to available context definitions that provide a natural understanding of this concept to users of context-aware applications and facilitates the engineering of this concept for software developers of such applications.

1 Introduction

Since the term *context-aware computing* was first introduced by Schilit et al. in 1994 [20], a large number of definitions of the terms *context* and *context-awareness* has been proposed in the area of computer science. In [7], Dey presents alternative views on context and its definition. Basically the majority of existing definitions of the term context can be categorized into definition by synonyms and definition by example. Context experienced various characterizations using synonyms such as an application's environment [13] or situation [2]. Many authors define context by example [3, 10, 19] and enumerate context elements like location, identity, time, temperature, noise, as well as the beliefs, desires, commitments, and intentions of the human [5].

For the operational use of context, such indirect definitions by synonym or example suffer from generality in the first and incompleteness in the latter case. Specifically if the term context, situation and environment are used with similar meaning, any definition including one of the terms is self-referencing in loops. The practical usefulness of such a definition is limited. The definitions fail to establish any fundamental basis for their construction, since they are basically driven by the ease of implementation. However, the active involvement of users in a user-centered design process for the creation of usable context-aware applications requires a formal and operational definition of context that can be communicated to the users. This paper introduces a context definition comprising three canonical parts: a definition per se in general terms, a formal definition describing the appearance of context and an operational definition characterizing the use of context and its dynamic behavior. In contrast to other context definitions, this structured approach to a definition aims at bridging the user-developer gap, since it provides both, a natural understanding of the concept for users and the ease of the engineering of the concept for software developers.

B. Kokinov et al. (Eds.): CONTEXT 2007, LNAI 4635, pp. 558–571, 2007.

2 Extending Available Context Definitions

Addressing the quite limited notions and early definitions of context, Dey provided the following general definition, which is probably the most widely accepted: *"Context is any information that can be used to characterise the situation of an entity. An entity is a person, place, or object that is considered relevant to the interaction between the user and the application, including the user and the applications themselves."* [7]

This application-centric definition clearly states that context is always bound to an entity and that information that describes the situation of an entity is context. However, in using indefinite expressions such as "any information" and "characterize the situation" the definition becomes general. Practically, the provided notion of context includes any kind of information that is relevant to the interaction between a user and an application, and thus, any application defined as adaptive in traditional terms, is actually a context-aware application.

Dey also introduces the user's task as an important concept in context-aware computing through his definition of context-aware systems. The task itself is also part of the context as it "characterizes" the situation of the user. This central role of the task is shared by [6] and [15] who assume that user's actions are generally goal driven. They introduce the term activity to accurately capture the observation that the user is concerned with several tasks simultaneously. In a more recent work, Chen documents his understanding of context that *"extends to modelling the activities and tasks that are taking place in a location"* [5]. Henricksen even puts the task in the centre in her specific definition of context: *"The context of a task is the set of circumstances surrounding it that are potentially of relevance to its completion."* [12]

Each of the provided definitions introduces a considerable amount of expert knowledge that needs to be incorporated in further research. However, many approaches fail provide a justification of their context definition. Dey's definition is intended to be adequately general to cover the work conducted by research in context-based interaction. In order to further constrain its universality, this general definitions need to be enclosed by a formal and an operational part:

Definition: Context
Context is any information that can be used to characterize the situation of an entity [7]. Elements for the description of this context information fall into five categories: *individuality*, *activity*, *location*, *time*, and *relations*. The activity predominantly determines the relevancy of context elements in specific situations, and the location and time primarily drive the creation of relations between entities and enable the exchange of context information among entities.

The following sections explicitly address the two extensions to Dey's definition comprising the formal and the operational part of the definition.

3 Formal Extension: Categories of Context Information

A context model rapidly becomes large and complex and can only marginally comply with demands on the comprehensibility and manageability [1]. This section introduces a formal structure of context information, which constricts and clusters this information into five fundamental categories. This structuring of context is vital for any pragmatic approach and facilitates the engineering of a context model for context-aware applications, since these fundamental context categories determine the design space of context models.

3.1 Available Structuring Approaches

As constituents of the context Schilit et al. (1994) enumerate *"the location of use, the collection of nearby people, hosts, and accessible devices, as well as to changes to such things over time"* [20]. On a conceptual level it is also argued that further issues, such as lighting, noise level, communication cost, and social situation are of interest and can be regarded as context. Dey et al. (2001) extend their definition of context with the statement *"Context is typically the location, identity and state of people, groups, and computational and physical objects"* [8]. A high amount of enumerations separates context into personal and environmental context [10, 18]. Most of the issues that are classified as personal context are often also referred to as user profiles and usually stay the same during the operation of the application. Environmental contexts are of a more general nature and include attributes like *"the time of day, the opening times of attractions and the current weather forecast"* [18].

In the field of modeling and reasoning within real world knowledge, Lenat suggests to concretely define context as a point in a twelve dimensional space in which context information is characterized [16]. These contextual dimensions organize the background knowledge for reasoning processes. Four of these dimensions refer to spatio-temporal issues and most of the remaining eight dimensions allocate human intent. In [21] Schmidt provides some structure for the characterization of context, as well, and qualifies context as a three-dimensional space with the dimensions *self*, *activity* and *environment*. The *self* dimension introduces a relation of the context to one specific entity (user, device, application, etc.). However, his description lacks an approach of how his model would capture a setting comprised of many interacting entities, each bound to a context by the self dimension. The dimensions time and location are consciously missing due to the fact that time is implicitly captured in the history and due to the observation that context is not necessarily related to location.

3.2 Fundamental Categories of Context

Any information describing an entity's context falls into one of five categories for context information as shown in Fig. 1: Individuality, activity, location, time, and relations. The individuality category contains properties and attributes describing the entity itself. The category activity covers all tasks this entity may be involved in. The context categories location and time provide the spatio-temporal coordinates of the respective entity. Finally, the relations category represents information about any possible relation the entity may establish with another entity. The following paragraphs describe these five categories of context information in more detail.

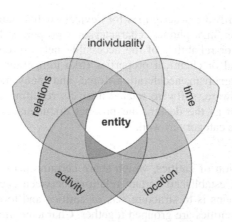

Fig. 1. Five Fundamental Categories for Context Information

3.2.1 Individuality Context

This category gives access to contextual information about the entity the context is bound to. This information comprises anything that can be observed about an entity, typically its state. An entity can either be an individual entity or groups of entities that share common aspects of the context. Entities can act differently within a context-aware system or obtain different roles. Basically they can be active, i.e. able to manipulate other entities, or passive. In addition, entities can be real, i.e. existing in the real world, or virtual, i.e. only existing in information space. Furthermore, there exist mobile, movable and fixed entities. The following sections cluster individuality context information into four entity types: natural, human, artificial and group entities.

Natural Entity Context

This category comprises the characteristics of all living and non-living things that occur naturally and are not the result of any human activity or intervention. The natural environment is usually different form to "the built environment" and includes for example plants, stones, and other things relating to nature without any artificial add-on. Furthermore, any product of the interaction between nature and humans is part of this category as well.

Human Entity Context

This category of context information covers the characteristics of human beings. In order to automatically perform adaptations that meet the user's necessities, adaptive system need to base their decisions on the evaluation of the user behavior and consider basic user properties such as preferences in language, color schemes, modality of interaction, menu options or security properties, and numberless other personal favorites. The General User Model Ontology (GUMO) by Heckmann provides a comprehensive view on the characteristics that potentially are taken into account [11].

Artificial Entity Context

The artificial entity denotes products or phenomena that result from human actions or technical processes. In a broad sense, this category covers descriptions for any human-built thing like buildings, computers, vehicles, books, and many more. It includes computing hardware descriptions for devices such as laptops, Personal Digital Assistants (PDAs) or Smartphones, characterizing properties like screen or display size, the bandwidth or reliability of the accessible network connection. All sensors that measure physical or chemical properties (like temperature, humidity, pressure, sound, lightness, magnetism, acceleration, force, and many more) are also artificial entities. Beside hardware, software related artifacts resulting from a software engineering process such as the design, the product documentation, an application, or service are part of the category as well.

Group Entity Context
A group is a collection of entities, which share certain characteristics, interact with one another or have established certain relations between each other. The primary purpose of using groups is to structure sets of entities and to capture characteristics that only emerge, if entities are grouped together. Characteristics that members of the group may share include interests, skills, cultural background, or kinship ties in a social sense, and computing power, network connections, or display size in a technological sense. As members of the group, these entities share a common identity. Groups may be large (e.g. "the Germans") or small (e.g. "the Smith family"), and in principle, entities may belong to none, one, or many groups. The membership to groups may emerge dynamically during system operation, e.g. based on observations, or in advance, e.g. to express a fixed relation (cf. Section 3.2.5).

3.2.2 Time Context

Time is a vital aspect for the human understanding and classification of context because most statements are related over the temporal dimension [10]. This category subsumes time information like the time zone of the client, the current time or any virtual time. A straightforward representation of time is the Central European Time (CET) format, which facilitates mathematical calculations and comparisons. Overlay models for the time dimension are often applied in context-aware computing and provide categorical scales like working hours or weekends. Other domains require a more process-oriented view of the time concept (e.g. work flows). The ability to represent intervals of time also constitutes a fundamental requirement on the context model. In combination with the ability to capture and express recurring events (e.g. always on Sundays), intervals are a significant feature for modeling user characteristics.

Persistently storing context or situations creates a data pool containing a history of obtained contextual information. This history forms the basis for accessing past context information, analyzing the interaction history, inferring usage habits of users and predicting future contexts. The evaluation of the interaction of users with the system includes the history of the usage process in order to establish a continuous context model for a short-term or a long-term perspective. Moreover, context management issues also benefit from the access to historical context information, since incomplete or imprecise context values can be extrapolated.

3.2.3 Location Context

With the development of portable computing devices the location became a parameter in context-aware systems. Physical objects and devices are spatially arranged and humans move in mobile and ubiquitous computing environments. Since tasks often include mobility, this category describes location models that classify the physical or virtual (e.g. the IP address as a position within a computer network) residence of an entity, as well as other related spatial information like speed and orientation [26]. Furthermore, a location may be described as an absolute location, meaning the exact location of something, or as a relative location, meaning the location of something relative to something else. Models for physical locations can be split into quantitative (geometric) location models, and qualitative (symbolic) location models [22].

Quantitative location models refer to coordinates with two, two and a half, or three dimensions. For example the two-dimensional geographic coordinate system expresses every location on Earth in the format degrees, minutes and seconds for the longitude and latitude. Tracking or positioning systems such as the satellite-based Global Positioning System (GPS) supply location information through measuring distances or angle to known reference points and translating these relative positions into absolute coordinates. Furthermore, such systems can be classified according their indoor or outdoor operating mode, their granularity of position determination and their underlying technology, e.g. radio or light signals [17].

Instances of qualitative spatial information are buildings, rooms, streets, countries, etc. that depict a mutually nested relationship. Such qualitative information increases the transparency for humans regarding their spatial cognition, since they introduce several spatial granularity levels. Overlay models allow for an interpretation of quantitative spatial information and transformation into appropriate qualitative information. Stahl and Heckmann undertook an investigation on spatial concepts and models, and propose a hybrid location modeling approach [22]. In general, an entity always possesses one physical qualitative location, which can be represented by different quantitative locations, but also several virtual locations at the same time.

3.2.4 Activity Context

An entity's activity determines to a great extend its current needs. The activity context covers the activities the entity is currently and in future involved in and answers the question "What does the entity want to achieve and how?" It can be described by means of explicit goals, tasks, and actions. In most situations when interacting with a context-aware system, an entity is engaged in a (potentially demanding) task that determines the goals of the performed activities [4].

A task is a goal-oriented activity expectation and represents a small, executable unit [14]. Tasks include operation sequences with a determined goal, to which a context-aware system can adapt the necessary functions and sequences of functions. In particular human entities change their goals very frequently depending on quickly appearing conditions or decisions, even without leaving the session with a computing system. Therefore a differentiation between low-level goals, which can change quite often, and high-level goals, which are more consistent, is reasonable. Accordingly, the activity context can be represented by (domain-specific) task models that structure tasks into subtask hierarchies, which is the most advanced representation of possible user goals [24]. The determination of the current goal is either specified by the entity or a choice from the set of goals, which depicts the highest probability.

3.2.5   Relations Context

This category of context information captures the relations an entity has established to other entities. Such surrounding entities can be persons, things, devices, services, or information (e.g. text, images, movies, sounds). The set of all relations of the entity builds a structure that is part of this entity's context. A relation expresses a semantic dependency between two entities that emerges from certain circumstances these two entities are involved in. The characteristics of the entity's environment (i.e. presence and the arrangement of other entities) are primarily determined by the spatial and temporal context of this entity. Secondarily, the individuality of the respective entity description impacts the relations (e.g. people of the same age). In general, each entity plays a specific role in a relation. Potentially, an entity can establish any number of different relations to the same entity. Additionally, relations are not necessarily static and may emerge and disappear dynamically. Section 4.2 describes the exploitation of relations between entities. Since the set of possible relation types between two entities is large, a clustering of relations regarding the types of the entities involved is helpful. Therefore, the relation category is subdivided into social, functional and compositional relations:

Social Relations

This sub-category describes the social aspects of the current entity context. Usually, interpersonal relations are social associations, connections, or affiliations between two or more people. For instance, social relations can contain information about friends, neutrals, enemies, neighbors, co-workers, and relatives. One important aspect in a social relations context is the role that the person plays in this relationship. Social relations differ in their levels of intimacy and sharing, which implies the discovery or establishment of common ground. Information about shared characteristics with other people, or in turn about individual differences, also contributes to the characteristics of a person. From this, patterns in behavior may be derived or groups of people with identical interests, goals, or levels of knowledge.

Functional Relations

A functional relation between two entities indicates that one entity makes use of the other entity for a certain purpose and with a certain effect, e.g. transferring a specific input into a specific output. For example, such relations exhibit physical properties like using a hammer, sitting on a chair or operating a desktop computer. Furthermore, functional relations show communicational and interactional properties like typing in a word or speaking into a microphone. Moreover, this relations subcategory indicates mental and cognitive properties like reading an article, giving a presentation or reasoning a concept.

Compositional Relations

A very important relation between entities is the relation between a whole and its parts. In the aggregation, the parts will not exist anymore if the containing object is destroyed. For example, the human body *owns* arms, legs, etc. The association is a weaker form of the composition, because it does not imply ownership and parts can have more then one whole they belong to. For example, a fax machine may belong to different secretariats or different departments.

4 Operational Extension: The Use of Context

Context obtains a specific role in communication, since it is an operational term: something is context because of the way it is used in interpretation, not due to its inherent properties [25]. When interacting and communicating in everyday life, the perception of situations, as well as the interpretation of the context is a major part [10]. Humans already have an informal sense of interpreting and using context information. The following paragraphs present the operational additive to the general definition that addresses dynamic properties of context and fosters a systematic foundation of the use of context in context-aware applications: the transitions between contexts of one entity and the sharing contexts among several entities.

4.1 Context Transitions

Entities, particularly human entities, change contexts and actually two consecutive contexts are never exactly the same. The knowledge necessary for context changing is basically contained in the context itself and thus, closely enlaced with the categories of context information and their characteristics. The following paragraphs describe the coherences of how context attributes change from one context entering another.

4.1.1 Variation of Approximation
While migrating from one context to another, the contextual knowledge represented by the current context experiences a specialization or an abstraction. The level of specialization or abstraction of the context is closely connected to the different levels of granularity exhibited by context information [23]. A representation of the real context of an entity is always an approximation. Fig. 2 shows the variation of approximation within the boundaries of the context model. The notion of approximation is relative: one representation is more approximate than the other, because details that the other takes into account are lost by abstraction. Through varying the degree of approximation a partial ordering over contexts emerges: if two contexts are compared with each other, one contains all the information of the other and probably more. An additional mechanism for varying the degree of approximation is the memorization of past situations in context histories. This accumulated knowledge leads to making experiences explicit in the context representation and to transferring knowledge from one category to another.

4.1.2 Change of Focus
The focus of a context refers to the reachability or accessibility of specific elements of the context description in a specific situation. Context information has a time and a point or region of origin, at which the focusing or relevancy of this context information is maximal [21]. For an entity, the spatial and temporal distance to the source of this context attribute determines, whether this attribute is in focus or not. As Fig. 3 shows, this relevancy, as well as the certainty on the correctness of the provided value, decreases with an increasing temporal or special distance from the origin of the context information. This fact can contribute to the disambiguation of multiple values for the same type of context information.

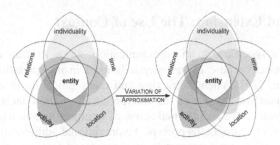

Fig. 2. Variation of Approximation

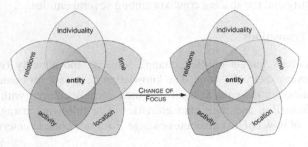

Fig. 3. Change of Focus

4.1.3 Shift of Attention

The current activity and the task of an entity have influence on the type and amount of knowledge required for their processing, including contextual knowledge. More precisely, the activity determines the focus of attention on specific aspects of the contextual knowledge. Features of the world become context through their use [25]. The focus of attention is switched when the activity of an entity changes, indicating that a new task is to be performed. A switch in the attention focus changes the need for contextual knowledge and therefore leads to different perspectives on the context information. Fig. 4 illustrates a shift of attention towards a more location-oriented perspective. Each aspect of the context plays a specific role during the performance of a task and this role might show considerable variance across the course of an activity. For example, the context attribute heart beat of a person is most likely irrelevant during the task of driving to the hospital, but it might become highly relevant during a task like being operated.

4.2 Shared Contexts

A shared context emerges, when the contexts of two entities overlap and parts of the context information become similar and shared. Besides the occupancy of its own context, an entity can belong to one or more different (parts of) contexts owned by other entities. Thus, through sharing contexts an entity can be viewed under different perspectives. Additionally, a group of entities sharing certain context parts share knowledge of how things are done and understood in this group. In the following, the emergence and exploitation of shared context is described: First, the correlation

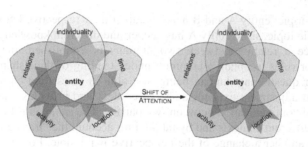

Fig. 4. Shift of Attention

concerning time and space enables the detection of a relation between two or more contexts. Second, the regression of time and space enables estimating which type of relation is detected. Third, the newly established relation is consolidated.

4.2.1 Establishing Relations

The human's attention, action and perception of context are strongly dependent on the current point in time and position of the user. This observation can be transferred to entities that converge in one or the other way: spatial and temporal proximity enable them to start responding to each other. Before two entities can establish shared contextual knowledge, time and space are the cardinal bridging mechanisms for detecting similarities between two contexts. Fig. 5 depicts the process of establishing a relation between two entities A and B: The two entities approach each other, time and location overlap and a new relation between A and B is established. Additionally, temporal and spatial proximity leads to reciprocity of two entities' contexts and thus, forms the basis for the creation of groups or communities. It is worth mentioning, that similar locations in particular appear in various forms: visitor in front of a painting, people on the same bus, or two persons accessing the same web page.

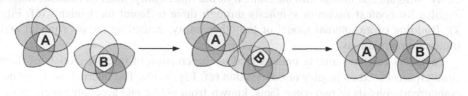

Fig. 5. Establishing a Relation

4.2.2 Adjusting Shared Contexts

Humans possess a different perception of contextual information, which mostly is due to the availability of context information on different levels of granularity or abstraction. The participants in an interaction need to share the same understanding or interpretation of the meaning "behind" a context description. For example, the granularity of the discussion between two doctors will be different compared to a doctor-patient conversation about the same disease, since more detailed and precise context information will be required. Fig. 6 exemplifies such an adjustment of the abstraction level regarding one topic: entity A and B need to adjust their respective knowledge regarding this specific topic, since entity A has deeper and different knowledge compared to entity B. Once a relation between two humans is established, they use specific mechanisms or rules to obtain a common understanding of their shared context. By observation or questioning, human beings are able to assess and clarify specific aspects. Such an adjustment expands a shared context and provides a common understanding in the communication between two parties. The same object can have different names in different contexts and by taking into account the "translation" of a representation into another a change of the perspective is possible. For example, a disambiguated reference to an article both parties read may result in an additional shared experience and thus, immediately lead to a better understanding of each other through uncovering a lot of background knowledge.

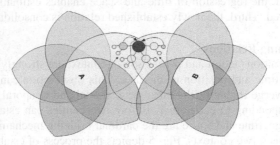

Fig. 6. Adjusting Shared Contexts

4.2.3 Exploiting Relations

The larger the shared context between two interacting parties, the more it facilitates communication, since they better understand what is expected without being explained in detail. After a relation is established and the shared context is adjusted, an entity gains special insight into the context of the other entity. Such an intense relation enables for context fusion or synthesis through three different mechanisms (cf. Fig. 7): Building of an internal model of the other entity, extending the own model and transcending relations.

Persistent relations among entities lead to the creation of internal models of their counterparts based on inquiry or observation (cf. Fig. 7 (a)). The internal model of the counterpart consists of two parts: facts, known from public and accessible parts of the partner's context, and assumptions, which are uncertain derivations and inferences about private and inaccessible parts. Since this internal model relies on interpretation and derivation, a mismatch may exist between this model and the real entity. An example is the system's model of the user's context, which will always be an approximation because of the limited capabilities of the computer system regarding inference mechanisms and representation. The "intellect" of a computer system comprises the rules and algorithms that it works with and that a developer implemented.

Furthermore, established relations can be exploited in a way that the own context is extended by attributes that lie in the intersection of the two shared contexts (cf. Fig. 7 (b)). For example, if a user establishes a "carries"-relation with a mobile device that

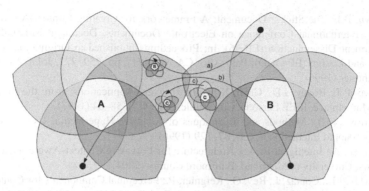

Fig. 7. Three Ways of Exploiting a Relation

obtains its position through GPS, this position implicitly can be transferred to the position of the user, since it is likely that both entities share the same location. Moreover, the exploitation of relations between entities includes the recognition and discovery of transitive relations that allow for reaching further unknown entities. From within a shared context, entities can "reach" any entity that belongs to the relations of an entity within that context and build an internal model of this entity (cf. Fig. 7 (c)). Potentially, this procedure can be repeated recursively with any entity that lies on the path. For example, if user A established a "trusts"-relation with user B, who in turn "trusts" user C, it is likely that user A can trust user C to a certain degree.

5 Conclusion

The core contribution of this paper lies in the introduction of a context definition that comprises three canonical parts: a definition per se in general terms, a formal definition describing the appearance of context and an operational definition characterizing the use of context and its dynamic behaviour. The resulting perception of context puts each entity in the centre of a surrounding individual context. This definition fosters a systematic foundation for the use of context in context-aware applications and emphasizes the dynamic properties of context emerging from context transitions and sharing contexts among entities. Furthermore, the paper contributed a formal structure of context information and presented five fundamental context categories that determine the design space of context models. This definition bridges the user-developer gap because it provides a natural understanding of the concept for users and eases the engineering of the concept for software developers. This understanding of the notion of context has been successfully applied in various context-aware applications [27].

References

1. Brézillon, P.: Using Context for Supporting Users Efficiently. In: Sprague, R.H. (ed.) 36th Hawaii International Conference on System Sciences (HICSS'03), pp. CD Rom IEEE Computer Society Press, Los Alamitos (2003)

2. Brown, P.J.: The Stick-e Document: A Framework for Creating Context-Aware Applications, International Conference on Electronic Documents, Document Manipulation, and Document Dissemination (EP 96). In: Proceedings published in Origination, Dissemination, and Design (EP-ODD), Palo Alto, CA, vol. 8(1), pp. 259–272. John Wiley & Sons, Chichester (1996)
3. Brown, P.J., Bovey, J.D., Chen, X.: Context-aware Applications: from the Laboratory to the Marketplace. IEEE Personal Communications 4(5), 58–64 (1997)
4. Brusilovsky, B.: Methods and Techniques of Adaptive Hypermedia. User Modeling and User-Adapted Interaction 6(2-3), 87–129 (1996)
5. Chen, H.: An Intelligent Broker Architecture for Pervasive Context-Aware Systems. Ph.D. Thesis, University of Maryland, Baltimore County (2004)
6. Crowley, J.L., Coutaz, J., Rey, G., Reignier, P.: Perceptual Components for Context Aware Computing. In: Borriello, G., Holmquist, L.E. (eds.) UbiComp 2002. LNCS, vol. 2498, Springer, Heidelberg (2002)
7. Dey, A.K.: Understanding and Using Context. Personal Ubiquitous Computing 5(1), 4–7 (2001)
8. Dey, A.K., Salber, D., Abowd, G.D.: A Conceptual Framework and a Toolkit for Supporting the Rapid Prototyping of Context-Aware Applications. Anchor article for Special Issue on Context-Awareness 16(2-4), 97–166 (2001)
9. Greenberg, S.: Context as a Dynamic Construct. Human-Computer Interaction 16(2-4), 257–268 (2001)
10. Gross, T., Specht, M.: Awareness in Context-Aware Information Systems. In: Oberquelle, Oppermann, Krause (eds.) Proceedings of the Mensch und Computer - 1. Fachübergreifende Konferenz, pp. 173–182. Teubner-Verlag, Bad Honnef, Germany (2001)
11. Heckmann, D.: Ubiquitous User Modeling. PhD Thesis, Saarland University, Saarbrücken, Germany (2005)
12. Henricksen, K.: A Framework for Context-Aware Pervasive Computing Applications. Ph.D. Thesis, University of Queensland, Queensland, Queensland (2003)
13. Hull, R., Neaves, P., Bedford-Roberts, J.: Towards Situated Computing. In: Krulwich, B. (ed.) The First International Symposium on Wearable Computers (ISWC '97), Cambridge, MA (1997)
14. Klemke, R.: Modelling Context in Information Brokering Processes. PhD Thesis, RWTH Aachen, Aachen (2002)
15. Kofod-Petersen, A., Cassens, J.: Using Activity Theory to Model Context Awareness. Modeling and Retrieval of Context (MRC2005), Edinburgh, UK, pp. 1–17 (2005)
16. Lenat, D.B.: The Dimensions of Context-Space, Cycorp, Austin (Texas), US (1998)
17. Lorenz, A., Schmitt, C., Oppermann, R., Eisenhauer, M., Zimmermann, A.: Location and Tracking in Mobile Guides. In: Proceedings of the 4th Workshop on HCI in Mobile Guides, Salzburg, Austria (2005)
18. Mitchell, K.: A Survey of Context-Awareness, University of Lancaster, Lancaster, UK (2002)
19. Ryan, N., Pascoe, J., Morse, D.: Enhanced Reality Fieldwork: the Context-Aware Archaeological Assistant. In: Gaffney, V., van Leusen, M., Exxon, S. (eds.) Computer Applications in Archaeology 1997, British Archaeological Reports, Oxford (1998)
20. Schilit, B.N., Adams, N.I., Want, R.: Context-Aware Computing Applications. In: Proceedings of the Workshop on Mobile Computing Systems and Applications, Santa Cruz, CA, pp. 85–90 (1994)
21. Schmidt, A.: Ubiquitous Computing Computing in Context. Ph.D. Thesis, Lancaster University, Lancaster, U.K (2002)

22. Stahl, C., Heckmann, D.: Using Semantic Web Technology for Ubiquitous Location and Situation Modeling. Journal of Geographic Information Sciences CPGIS 10(2), 157–165 (2004)
23. Strang, T., Linnhoff-Popien, C.: A Context Modelling Survey. In: Workshop on Advanced Context Modelling, Reasoning and Management as part of UbiComp 2004, Nottingham (2004)
24. Vassileva, J.I.: A Task-Centered Approach for User Modeling in a Hypermedia Office Documentation System. User Modeling and User-Adapted Interaction (UMUAI) 6, 185–223 (1996)
25. Winograd, T.: Architectures for Context. Human-Computer-Interaction, Special Issue on Context-Aware Computing, vol. 16(2-4) (2001)
26. Zimmermann, A., Lorenz, A., Specht, M.: User Modeling in Adaptive Audio-Augmented Museum Environments. In: Brusilovsky, P., Corbett, A.T., de Rosis, F. (eds.) UM 2003. LNCS, vol. 2702, pp. 403–407. Springer, Heidelberg (2003)
27. Zimmermann, A., Lorenz, A., Specht, M.: Applications of a Context-Management System. In: Dey, A.K., Kokinov, B., Leake, D.B., Turner, R. (eds.) CONTEXT 2005. LNCS (LNAI), vol. 3554, pp. 556–569. Springer, Heidelberg (2005)

Author Index

Lecture Notes in Artificial Intelligence (LNAI)

Vol. 4426: Z.-H. Zhou, H. Li, Q. Yang (Eds.), Advances in Knowledge Discovery and Data Mining. XXV, 1161 pages. 2007.

Vol. 4411: R.H. Bordini, M. Dastani, J. Dix, A.E.F. Seghrouchni (Eds.), Programming Multi-Agent Systems. XIV, 249 pages. 2007.

Vol. 4410: A. Branco (Ed.), Anaphora: Analysis, Algorithms and Applications. X, 191 pages. 2007.

Vol. 4399: T. Kovacs, X. Llorà, K. Takadama, P.L. Lanzi, W. Stolzmann, S.W. Wilson (Eds.), Learning Classifier Systems. XII, 345 pages. 2007.

Vol. 4390: S.O. Kuznetsov, S. Schmidt (Eds.), Formal Concept Analysis. X, 329 pages. 2007.

Vol. 4389: D. Weyns, H.V.D. Parunak, F. Michel (Eds.), Environments for Multi-Agent Systems III. X, 273 pages. 2007.

Vol. 4384: T. Washio, K. Satoh, H. Takeda, A. Inokuchi (Eds.), New Frontiers in Artificial Intelligence. IX, 401 pages. 2007.

Vol. 4371: K. Inoue, K. Satoh, F. Toni (Eds.), Computational Logic in Multi-Agent Systems. X, 315 pages. 2007.

Vol. 4369: M. Umeda, A. Wolf, O. Bartenstein, U. Geske, D. Seipel, O. Takata (Eds.), Declarative Programming for Knowledge Management. X, 229 pages. 2006.

Vol. 4343: C. Müller (Ed.), Speaker Classification. X, 355 pages. 2007.

Vol. 4342: H. de Swart, E. Orłowska, G. Schmidt, M. Roubens (Eds.), Theory and Applications of Relational Structures as Knowledge Instruments II. X, 373 pages. 2006.

Vol. 4335: S.A. Brueckner, S. Hassas, M. Jelasity, D. Yamins (Eds.), Engineering Self-Organising Systems. XII, 212 pages. 2007.

Vol. 4334: B. Beckert, R. Hähnle, P.H. Schmitt (Eds.), Verification of Object-Oriented Software. XXIX, 658 pages. 2007.

Vol. 4333: U. Reimer, D. Karagiannis (Eds.), Practical Aspects of Knowledge Management. XII, 338 pages. 2006.

Vol. 4327: M. Baldoni, U. Endriss (Eds.), Declarative Agent Languages and Technologies IV. VIII, 257 pages. 2006.

Vol. 4314: C. Freksa, M. Kohlhase, K. Schill (Eds.), KI 2006: Advances in Artificial Intelligence. XII, 458 pages. 2007.

Vol. 4304: A. Sattar, B.-h. Kang (Eds.), AI 2006: Advances in Artificial Intelligence. XXVII, 1303 pages. 2006.

Vol. 4303: A. Hoffmann, B.-h. Kang, D. Richards, S. Tsumoto (Eds.), Advances in Knowledge Acquisition and Management. XI, 259 pages. 2006.

Vol. 4293: A. Gelbukh, C.A. Reyes-Garcia (Eds.), MICAI 2006: Advances in Artificial Intelligence. XXVIII, 1232 pages. 2006.

Vol. 4289: M. Ackermann, B. Berendt, M. Grobelnik, A. Hotho, D. Mladenič, G. Semeraro, M. Spiliopoulou, G. Stumme, V. Svátek, M. van Someren (Eds.), Semantics, Web and Mining. X, 197 pages. 2006.

Vol. 4285: Y. Matsumoto, R.W. Sproat, K.-F. Wong, M. Zhang (Eds.), Computer Processing of Oriental Languages. XVII, 544 pages. 2006.

Vol. 4274: Q. Huo, B. Ma, E.-S. Chng, H. Li (Eds.), Chinese Spoken Language Processing. XXIV, 805 pages. 2006.

Vol. 4265: L. Todorovski, N. Lavrač, K.P. Jantke (Eds.), Discovery Science. XIV, 384 pages. 2006.

Vol. 4264: J.L. Balcázar, P.M. Long, F. Stephan (Eds.), Algorithmic Learning Theory. XIII, 393 pages. 2006.

Vol. 4259: S. Greco, Y. Hata, S. Hirano, M. Inuiguchi, S. Miyamoto, H.S. Nguyen, R. Słowiński (Eds.), Rough Sets and Current Trends in Computing. XXII, 951 pages. 2006.

Vol. 4253: B. Gabrys, R.J. Howlett, L.C. Jain (Eds.), Knowledge-Based Intelligent Information and Engineering Systems, Part III. XXXII, 1301 pages. 2006.

Vol. 4252: B. Gabrys, R.J. Howlett, L.C. Jain (Eds.), Knowledge-Based Intelligent Information and Engineering Systems, Part II. XXXIII, 1335 pages. 2006.

Vol. 4251: B. Gabrys, R.J. Howlett, L.C. Jain (Eds.), Knowledge-Based Intelligent Information and Engineering Systems, Part I. LXVI, 1297 pages. 2006.

Vol. 4248: S. Staab, V. Svátek (Eds.), Managing Knowledge in a World of Networks. XIV, 400 pages. 2006.

Vol. 4246: M. Hermann, A. Voronkov (Eds.), Logic for Programming, Artificial Intelligence, and Reasoning. XIII, 588 pages. 2006.

Vol. 4223: L. Wang, L. Jiao, G. Shi, X. Li, J. Liu (Eds.), Fuzzy Systems and Knowledge Discovery. XXVIII, 1335 pages. 2006.

Vol. 4213: J. Fürnkranz, T. Scheffer, M. Spiliopoulou (Eds.), Knowledge Discovery in Databases: PKDD 2006. XXII, 660 pages. 2006.

Vol. 4212: J. Fürnkranz, T. Scheffer, M. Spiliopoulou (Eds.), Machine Learning: ECML 2006. XXIII, 851 pages. 2006.

Vol. 4211: P. Vogt, Y. Sugita, E. Tuci, C.L. Nehaniv (Eds.), Symbol Grounding and Beyond. VIII, 237 pages. 2006.

Vol. 4203: F. Esposito, Z.W. Raś, D. Malerba, G. Semeraro (Eds.), Foundations of Intelligent Systems. XVIII, 767 pages. 2006.

Vol. 4201: Y. Sakakibara, S. Kobayashi, K. Sato, T. Nishino, E. Tomita (Eds.), Grammatical Inference: Algorithms and Applications. XII, 359 pages. 2006.

Vol. 4200: I.F.C. Smith (Ed.), Intelligent Computing in Engineering and Architecture. XIII, 692 pages. 2006.

Vol. 4198: O. Nasraoui, O. Zaïane, M. Spiliopoulou, B. Mobasher, B. Masand, P.S. Yu (Eds.), Advances in Web Mining and Web Usage Analysis. IX, 177 pages. 2006.

Vol. 4196: K. Fischer, I.J. Timm, E. André, N. Zhong (Eds.), Multiagent System Technologies. X, 185 pages. 2006.

Vol. 4188: P. Sojka, I. Kopeček, K. Pala (Eds.), Text, Speech and Dialogue. XV, 721 pages. 2006.

Vol. 4183: J. Euzenat, J. Domingue (Eds.), Artificial Intelligence: Methodology, Systems, and Applications. XIII, 291 pages. 2006.